American Metal Typefaces of the Twentieth Century

SECOND, REVISED EDITION

American Metal Typefaces of the Twentieth Century

By MAC McGREW

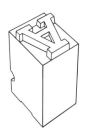

1993
Oak Knoll Books
New Castle, Delaware

Published by
OAK KNOLL BOOKS
414 Delaware Street, New Castle, Delaware 19720, U.S.A.

This work is based on a Preliminary Edition published by Myriade Press,
New Rochelle, New York, in 1986.

Copyright © 1986, 1993 by Mac McGrew

Library of Congress Cataloging-in-Publication Data

McGrew, Mac.
American metal typefaces of the twentieth century / by Mac McGrew.
p.   cm.
Includes biographical references and indexes.
ISBN: 0-938768-34-4 (hardback)—ISBN: 0-938768-39-5 (paperback)
1. Type and type-founding—United States—History—20th century—Dictionaries.
2. Printing—Specimens—Dictionaries. I. Title.
Z250.M137 1992 686.2'24—dc20
91-33384
CIP

Printed in the United States of America

Dedicated to the memory of my wife

Laura

whose faith and patience during the years
I spent in preparing this book
helped make it possible.

Preface

F OR FIVE CENTURIES after its invention by Johann Gutenberg in the middle of the fifteenth century, metal type was the essence of nearly all printing. Great printers were known for the quality of their type and typography. Until the recent development of offset printing and photo-typesetting, the composing room was a basic and essential part of virtually all printing establishments.

For four of those centuries there had been little change in the art of making type. Punches were meticulously cut by hand for every letter of every size of every face. These were stamped into blanks, usually copper, to make the matrices from which type was cast, letter by letter. This type was then set by hand for every book, every newspaper, every magazine. Both typefounding and typesetting were crafts requiring painstaking care and unending patience.

In the latter part of the nineteenth century, many details of the industrial revolution began to come together to produce a revolution in printing and typesetting. An automatic typecasting machine was completed in 1885, and in the same year a punch-cutting machine was perfected and later adapted for engraving matrices directly.

Meanwhile numerous schemes were being tried to set type mechanically. Most of them worked on the principle of assembling precast foundry type, some with moderate success, but in 1886 Ottmar Mergenthaler's revolutionary idea of casting a line of type in one piece from assembled matrices—his Linotype machine—was successfully demonstrated. About the same time Tolbert Lanston was working on another fantastic idea—a machine which cast single letters in sequence as required, in perfectly justified lines—the Monotype, which was demonstrated in 1891.

In 1892, twenty-three of the thirty-some typefounders in America merged to form American Type Founders Company. This brought together much of the best talent in the industry—including Henry Barth and his typecaster, and Linn Boyd Benton and his engraving machine and numerous other inventions—and by early in the twentieth century the company had become the world's leading producer of type.

Numerous other important changes were also taking place. The point system was generally adopted in 1886, after years of controversy. Its range of precise numerical sizes replaced the old system of sizes with such names as "brevier" and "long primer," which varied from one source to another. This, along with changes in taste away from the ornate types of the preceding years, made many types of the time obsolete. In the latter years of the nineteenth century, several private presses awakened interest in fine printing, developing a new awareness of legibility, grace, and beauty in types and typography.

These changes and influences didn't all occur at once, but their results all came together very close to the beginning of the twentieth century. Thus our story concentrates on this century, although a few earlier types are included, either for their historic importance or because their popularity extended well into the new century. We have focused primarily on typefaces designed *and* produced in the United States, but have also given considerable attention to those designed *or* produced here by primary typefounders or matrix-makers. (Incidentally, although the twentieth century actually began with 1901, the author has chosen to begin the book with 1900 to make "the 1900s" complete.)

Most important, type design in the twentieth century reached new heights in quality and variety, spurred on to a considerable extent by the growth of printed advertising and the development of advertising typography. An important element was the conception of the *family* of typefaces, first deliberately applied on a large scale to *Cheltenham*. With this idea, the

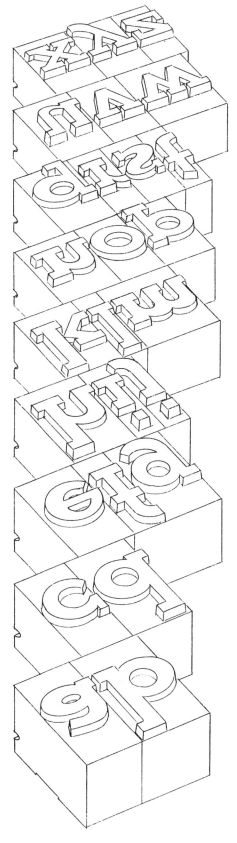

deliberately applied on a large scale to *Cheltenham*. With this idea, the typographer had a range of weights, widths, and italics from which to select harmonious types, instead of the older selection of unrelated designs.

This book covers in detail virtually every metal typeface designed or produced in America in the twentieth century, with designers' names, dates, production data, and many other facts. About 1600 specimens illustrate these faces in all their vast array—the winners and the losers—the stylish and the quaint—those that are most popular and those that are forgotten.

In the latter part of the twentieth century, many of the typefaces in this book have been reborn for photographic or electronic typesetting methods—sometimes considerably modified, but often without the subtle adjustments from one size to another that characterized most metal types. (See "Visual Reproportioning" on page 80.) In any case, these are the originals, as envisioned by their designers or as adapted by the original founders from those visions—the prototypes for the new generation of typefaces.

This book is the result of years of work by the author—mostly a labor of love—following a lifetime of involvement with various aspects of type and typesetting. It concentrates on metal type and the matrices used in its casting, as made for usual printing processes. It excludes types of wood, brass, steel, rubber, etc. made for special processes, as well as the signs, symbols, borders, and other decorative units that supplemented the alphabetic fonts. And the author makes no apology for the byways he might have explored further—for additional years—for the most obscure faces, or foreign imports and their copies, or earlier faces and their resurrections, although some of these are mentioned briefly in the appendix.

In 1986 a preliminary edition was published by The Myriade Press, Inc., of New Rochelle, New York, intended for distribution to a number of typographic experts and others who could supply any of the missing type specimens or furnish complete specimens for the imperfect ones shown, or add to the information provided. Sadly, the principal of the press, Dr. J. Ben Lieberman, did not live to see the completion of the project, but his family fulfilled the contract. The limited first edition was his idea, and it brought much valuable response, which has been incorporated into this volume.

Acknowledgments

T HIS BOOK could not have been as extensive, if possible at all, without the generous assistance and encouragement of many friends, from Emil Klumpp who encouraged me to expand office memos into full-fledged articles, to those who have set specimens to my format, or contributed important information, or helped in various other ways, large and small. Those who have personally set individual specimens, in whole or in part, are named with the specimen. Otherwise it is not possible to detail each contribution, but these friends include those listed below.

Thanks also to the Typophiles and to Myriade Press for permission to reprint specimens of certain rare Dwiggins and Goudy typefaces from their publications.

If I have omitted anyone who should be included, I'm sorry. Many others have helped through friendly encouragement, conversation, correspondence, and otherwise. But I especially wish to thank my son, Jon, for his gifts of word processing equipment which have eased the task of preparing this material; and most of all my late wife, Laura, who yielded much family time to the creation of this work. My sincere thanks to all.

MAC McGREW

August 1993

Dorothy Abbe
Victor Ables, Sr.
Phil Ambrosi
Frank J. Anderson
Mark Ardagna
Alfred P. Babcock
Ralph Babcock
Leonard Bahr
Lance J. Bauer
Harold Berliner
Steve Boerner
Guy Botterill
Jim Broadston
Walter H. Brovald
Charles L. Bush
Phillip J. Cade
Matthew Carter
David C. Churchman
William M. Danner
Gerda DaRif
Ed Davis, Jr.
Stephen H. Derring
Wilbur L. Doctor
Lucy Stovall Douglas
John Dreyfus
Phillip Driscoll
Robert M. DuBois
Clair Dunn
Paul Hayden Duensing
The Rev. William D. Eddy
Ed Fisher, Jr.
Roger C. Frith

Mac Gardner
George Gasparik
Lauren R. Geringer
Larry Girard
David F. Greer
William M. Greer
Robert Halbert
Gary Hantke
Herbert G. Harnish
Elizabeth Harris
Jack Hatcher
Clifford L. Helbert
Boyd Hill
Richard Hoffman
Richard L. Hopkins
John Horn
Yvonne Huntress
Richard E. Huss
Darrell Hyder
William M. Johnson
David L. Kent
Charles H. Klensch
Harry Kosel
Stan Kroeger
Ivend H. Krohn
Merle Langley
Alexander Lawson
Clifford S. Leonard, Jr.
Edward M. Lewis
Frederick J. Liddle
J. Ben Lieberman
Alan Ligda

Bob Long
Walter Long
Jack A. Massey
Carl Masson
Gary Metras
Robert H. Middleton
Lewis Mitchell
W. Gale Mueller
Stanley Nelson
Elizabeth Nevin
J. Ed Newman
Bruce Northrup
David M. Norton
Robert L. Orbach
David Pankow
Harvey Petty
Archie Provan
Lewis A. Pryor
Harvey Puckett
Larry J. Raid
Peyton Reavis
Hans Reichardt
Leonard Richardson
Jim Rimmer
Jane W. Roberts
Will Rueter
Stephen O. Saxe
John Schappler
Ward Schori
Duane C. Scott
Jack E. Scott
Herman Selvaggio
Edwin W. Shaar
Dr. John M. Shaw
Paul Shaw
Schuyler R. Shipley
Fred Sholty
Al Siegel
Charles R. Sikorski
Vernon Simpson
Ivan D. Snyder
Stanley Sollid
Dan X. Solo
Don Stewart
Gordon Sullivan
Michael Tarachow
George Thomas
Muriel Underwood
Rick von Holdt
Alan Waring
Henry Weiland
Sheldon Wesson
Fred C. Williams
William Wokoun

Contents

Introduction

METAL TYPE IN THE TWENTIETH CENTURY

This book is most concerned with the type*face,* or more particularly its impression on paper, which is essentially two-dimensional. But knowledge of the body of metal type and its production is helpful in understanding the possibilities and limitations of the face and its design.

At first printers designed and cast their own types, but by the early part of the sixteenth century typefounding became a separate business, and printers became dependent on typefounders for virtually all of their type. This dependence was lessened only by the invention of the Linotype and Monotype machines, especially in 1903 when Lanston Monotype Company developed a machine which could cast display type for hand composition. About the same time Compositype, Universal, Thompson, and other such machines appeared, with the promise of making every printer his own typefounder. While this was not literally practical, and while there were limitations to the quality of the results in some cases, it led to the establishment of many new "typefounders" who cast fonts on these machines for sale to other printers, and posed a new threat to traditional typefounders.

Monotype display matrix, composition matrix

This book cannot begin to cover all the concerns which produce fonts cast on the Monotype and similar machines, so it is limited to companies that manufacture matrices, to a substantial extent from original designs. This results in two categories, whose products are necessarily intermingled. First there are the basic type manufacturers—American Type Founders (ATF) and Barnhart Brothers & Spindler (BB&S), primarily, which are covered in great detail, along with lesser ones which are covered as completely as possible with finite time and resources. These foundries made matrices for their own use, and to some extent in earlier years for sale to each other. Then there are the companies whose end products are matrices and the machines on which they are used for casting type. These include Mergenthaler Linotype (Lino), Lanston Monotype (Mono), Intertype (Inter), and Ludlow, as described in more detail later. Other sources are mentioned in special cases.

ATF matrices

The stage was set for twentieth-century typography by the turn of the century, although important advances were made subsequently. *Linotype* extended its size range to 60-point in 1913, and introduced Duplex-Display, two-letter faces up to 24-point, in 1936, although the great majority of Linotype use is for the sizes up to 14-point. *Monotype* adapted the "qwerty" keyboard arrangement in 1907 and introduced a new style of matrix at the same time. It extended its size range to 72-point in 1925, took over production of the competitive Thompson display caster in 1929, and improved its composition casting machines at various times.

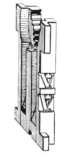

Linotype matrix

The *Ludlow Typograph,* which came to be called simply *Ludlow,* appeared in 1909. It became a popular and very successful machine for casting lines of type in slug form from manually-assembled matrices; newspapers in particular favored it for heads and advertising display. In 1913 the *Intertype* brought direct competition to the Linotype with a near-duplicate machine, combining expired Linotype patents with some advanced details of engineering. In 1934 the *All-Purpose Linotype* was perfected; it used manual assembly of mats for faces up to 144-point.

Further details on the mechanical side of typesetting are beyond the scope of this book, except for later comments on mechanical limitations imposed on type design.

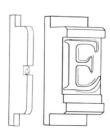

Ludlow matrices

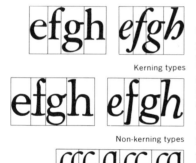

THE THIRD DIMENSION OF TYPE

The drawing shows a standard piece of foundry type, with its various parts. The *shoulder* and parts above are formed by the matrix in casting. They include the *face*, which receives ink and transfers it to paper in the printing process; the *counter*, any non-printing portion which is enclosed or mostly enclosed by printing areas; and the *beard* or *neck*, the nearly vertical part between face and shoulder. The shoulder is formed by a blank portion of the matrix.

The *body* or *shank* is formed by the mold, which is adjustable in width according to the requirement of each different character. Distinctive features of the body are the *nick*, *feet*, *groove*, and sometimes *pin mark*. The nick identifies the position of the face on the body, always being toward the bottom of the face (except in some foreign types), so the compositor can readily position the character properly when setting type. Foundry type sometimes has two or more nicks in varying positions, so different type designs are readily distinguishable. However, as type production has declined fewer different molds have been used, so recently cast type does not necessarily have the same set of nicks as the same face cast years ago. The feet form the precise height of the type, which in Anglo-American use is 0.918 inch, or approximately $^{11}/_{12}$ inch. The groove is the hollow between the feet where the jet, formed in casting, has been removed. Early casting machines had a pin which helped deliver the newly cast piece of type properly from the mold; this pin was commonly engraved with initials or a symbol identifying the founder. Later machines did not require the pin, but dummies were sometimes still used for identification. More recently, pin marks have often been omitted.

PRACTICAL DESIGN LIMITATIONS

The design of most characters in separate type can be contained within the rectangle formed by the type body, as indicated in the illustration. Where required, though, portions of the design may extend beyond the edges of the body. These projections are called *kerns,* and a specific typeface is called *kerning* or *non-kerning*, where this is significant, depending on whether it includes any kerned characters (see *Powell Italic*, a "non-kerning" face). Traditional roman faces often include a kerned *f;* to avoid conflict between the kern and an adjoining character, f-ligatures (ff fi fl ffi ffl) have become traditional, and are even included in many fonts which don't really need them.

The long *s* (see *Caslon Oldstyle* for specimens) had a similar kern but required many more ligatures. It was common in Colonial American times, but became obsolete around the end of the eighteenth century. Diphthongs (Æ, Œ, æ, œ) were commonly supplied until about the end of the nineteenth century, and for many faces well into the twentieth century.

Italic designs usually require many more kerns, and thus have been more of a challenge to typefounders, as well as requiring more careful handling by typesetters to avoid breaking the overhangs. Some non-kerning italics have been designed (*Cheltenham Medium Italic,* for instance), and some foundry italics are cast from matrices which are deeper than usual to produce stronger kerns. But several special styles of casting have been developed to eliminate or minimize the problem.

Many traditional script faces, with greater slant and longer flourishes, are cast on *wing body,* which produces a cantilevered support for the long, delicate lines; production is slower and more involved for these faces, thus they are more expensive. About 1902, BB&S devised *offset body,* with a full-depth projection for any character requiring it; a notch on the other side of all characters received it. About 1930, ATF developed *angle body,* with slanted sides to accommodate the characters but with short straight sections to assure proper alignment and fit.

All these systems are reasonably easy to set, but require special spaces.

xiv

Mortised body was sometimes used to reduce the apparent space between certain letter combinations, especially in large sizes. About 1927, ATF applied this idea to swash characters for *Caslon Italic* and a few other faces. Certain lowercase letters were cast on smaller bodies in those fonts for use with the mortised letters.

None of the special foundry bodies are available for Monotype casting. Otherwise the product of that machine is basically the same as foundry type, although with less depth of drive in nearly all cases. Foundry faces which have been copied by Monotype are invariably modified in composition sizes—the amount of modification varies from slight to substantial—and sometimes in display sizes.

Kerns are technically impossible on the slug machines—Linotype, Intertype, and Ludlow— because each character must be contained within the straight sides of its matrix for assembly into complete lines. All three machines have provided extensive sets of logotypes (such as *fa*), incorporating flowing *f*s with adjoining characters, for traditional faces that are enhanced by such letters. However, their use is more time-consuming, involving hand insertion or special equipment, and therefore few typesetters have used them.

Linotype and Intertype have another mechanical limitation. Each matrix in the common sizes (generally up to 14-point, or up to 24-point for some popular styles) has the corresponding character for two faces—normally roman and italic or roman and bold—for easy mixing of the two. This requires precisely the same lateral space for both characters, although in foundry type italics are usually narrower and boldfaces are often wider than their related romans. For their most discriminating clients, Linotype developed "Typographic Refinement" characters in 1935, under the direction of Kurt H. Volk, New York typographer. These included combinations such as *af* rather than *fa*, several other combinations such as *Wh*, and sometimes a special italic lowercase font with narrower letters than those normally supplied. (See Typographic Refinement characters on pages 74-75.)

Ludlow and the All-Purpose Linotype (APL) have the same restriction as the other slug machines in regard to roman faces on straight-sided matrices, but without the pairing of two faces. However, both provide more freedom for italics by the use of slanting matrices, which give a full-kerning effect without the need for *fa* style logotypes. Ludlow has one standard angle (17 degrees) developed in 1922, plus a greater slant of 40 degrees for a few faces, while APL has three standard angles (12, 15, and 22 degrees) to accommodate various designs.

Monotype had its own limitations for keyboard faces in its earlier days. A standard "C" arrangement was developed (see page 294), wherein each character in the roman and related italic font was assigned a standard unit value, the unit being a measure of width, 1/18 of an em. Although the em was not necessarily a square as in foundry type, but could be narrower or wider depending on the requirements of the specific face, individual characters could not vary from their prescribed proportions. "C-1" and "C-2" arrangements were developed to accommodate normal or wide boldface designs—see *Modern Antique* and *Modern Antique Condensed*. Thus all composition (keyboard-set) sizes of early Monotype faces were necessarily redrawn and reproportioned to fit the standard arrangements. In some cases the reproportioned patterns were used for display sizes of the same face; this has been noted in this book as far as possible.

Apparently at the insistence of Frederic W. Goudy, when he became art director for Monotype in 1920 and designed *Garamont,* the concept of special arrangements was developed, so that each letter generally had to be modified only to the nearest unit width rather than to a prescribed value. This greatly improved the quality of Monotype faces; a few which had originally been cut to standard arrangement were recut to a special arrangement. (See *Mid-Gothic* for example.)

Mortised bodies

abcdefghijklmnopqrstuvw
abcdefghijklmnopqrstuvw

Duplex roman and italic, Linotype

abcdefghijklmnopqrstuvwxyz

Narrower one-letter italic

abcdefghijklm

Ludlow italic

SOURCES: THE TYPEFOUNDERS

Primary: *American Type Founders (ATF),* Elizabeth, New Jersey, was formed in 1892 by the merger of twenty-three founders; others were acquired later. Some faces from predecessor companies survived into this century and are mentioned here; these foundries include *MacKellar, Smiths & Jordan (MS&J),* Philadelphia; *Marder, Luse & Co.,* Chicago; *Boston Type Foundry,* Boston; *Central Type Foundry,* St. Louis; and *Dickinson Type Foundry,* Boston. ATF later had other divisions for presses, etc., but our references are always to the Type Division. In 1970 a large number of ATF drawings, patterns and matrices were given to the Smithsonian Institution.

Barnhart Brothers & Spindler (BB&S), Chicago, was sold to ATF in 1911 but operated independently until 1929. During several years before 1929, though, BB&S and ATF exchanged some of their most popular faces.

Bruce's New York Type Foundry joined ATF in 1901, but a number of its faces survived, especially as Antique Revivals (see Appendix I).

Damon & Peets or *Damon Type Foundry,* New York, was principally a sales organization. Its foundry operations were small, but it issued specimen books from 1897 to 1929, after which the foundry closed.

H. C. Hansen Type Foundry, Boston, remained independent until about 1922. Matrices, including a number of original faces mentioned in this book, apparently were scrapped when the foundry closed.

Inland Type Foundry, St. Louis, produced many original faces before it was sold to ATF in 1912. At that time its matrices and other equipment were divided between BB&S and ATF's main plant.

Keystone Type Foundry, Philadelphia, created a number of lasting faces before its sale to ATF in 1919.

Western Type Foundry, Chicago, produced some original faces and copies of ATF and other faces until it was bought by BB&S in 1918.

A number of smaller foundries are mentioned in the text in special circumstances, and in recent years several private or hobby foundries have come into being.

* * *

Secondary: *Baltimore Type & Composition Co. (Balto* or *Baltotype),* Baltimore; *Los Angeles Type Founders,* Whittier, California; *Castcraft,* Skokie, Illinois; and others cast fonts primarily from American and/or English Monotype matrices, but also cut a few original faces or copies of antique or foreign faces which are listed in our main text or appendixes.

SOURCES: THE MATRIX MAKERS

These companies manufactured machines on which the printer could set and cast his own type. In their early years, their type designs were copies or adaptations of popular foundry faces, but by about 1920 they were cutting original designs and developing mechanical improvements to raise the quality of their products. The machines which produce single types have been used by some companies to cast fonts for sale, as mentioned above. Although these companies generally call themselves "typefounders," this book reserves that term for the companies listed above, who operate(d) heavy-duty machines built for that purpose. We refer to the others as "secondary suppliers."

Lanston Monotype Machine Co. (Mono), Philadelphia, manufactured the popular keyboard and caster for producing type in justified lines; also a standard caster for display sizes to 36-point, and a Giant caster for sizes to 72-point. In 1929 Lanston acquired the Thompson Type Machine Co. and manufactured its caster, which went to 48-point, until about 1964. Lanston matrices for all of these machines are called "Mono" in this book. Lanston was liquidated in 1969; matrix-making equipment went to ATF, where copies of Helvetica and Melior may have been the only new series of matrices produced. In 1975 the facilities for making cellular (composition) matrices went to Hartzell Machine Works in Chester, Pennsylvania, and in 1983 to Mackenzie-Harris

Corporation in San Francisco. More recently some of these resources have gone to Giampa Textware Corp. in Vancouver, British Columbia, for conversion to electronic typesetting methods.

Mergenthaler Linotype Co. (Lino), Brooklyn, had its popular slug-casting machine in wide use by the early 1890s. In recent years the company has converted entirely to electronic typesetting, but some matrices are still available from England.

Intertype Company (Inter), Brooklyn, began business in 1912 when basic Linotype patents expired. Its machine is essentially a duplicate of the Linotype, and matrices made by either company can be used with either machine. Both companies issued lists of "interchangeable" matrices, apparently casting identical faces; in our lists of data these are shown as "Lino = Inter" and the size range includes the smallest and largest from either source. Intertype, now a division of Harris Corporation, has moved to Florida and has also converted to electronic typesetting, with some matrices available from England.

Ludlow Typograph Co. (Ludlow), Chicago, produced matrices for manual assembly and casting as a complete line. Early faces were copied from foundry sources, but all later ones were original.

All-Purpose Linotype (APL) was a 1933 development of Mergenthaler Linotype. It combined manual assembly with an adaptation of the mechanism of the Linotype machine to produce slugs of faces up to 144-point.

Compositype, Universal or *Nuernberger-Rettig*, and *Thompson* were early competitors of the Monotype for casting type for hand composition. The manufacturers of each of these machines made many fonts of matrices, some of which may still be in existence; however, since I have found no evidence of any original designs being made, they are not included in this book. From 1929 until about 1964 Lanston Monotype made the Thompson machine and mats for it—these are included in "Mono" listings.

Linograph was a simplified machine similar to the Linotype. Originally it used its own unique style of matrices, but again I have found no evidence of original type designs so have not included it. Linograph machines were later redesigned to use standard Linotype or Intertype matrices.

National Matrix & Type, Baltimore; *Triangle Type Foundry*, Chicago; and a few others produced matrices for use on Monotype or other casting machines.

FOREIGN SOURCES

Foreign sources producing typefaces or matrices by American designers include the following. These are shown for faces which have not been produced by a domestic source, and only the primary foreign source is shown, but some of their popular faces are shown under Imports in the Appendix. Some of these founders are no longer in operation or have been acquired by others.

Amsterdam Typefoundry, Amsterdam, Netherlands.
Bauer Typefoundry, Frankfurt, Germany.
Linotype & Machinery, Ltd., London, England.
Matrotype Co., Maidenhead, Berkshire, England.
Monotype Corporation (Eng Mono), Redhill, Surrey, England.
Stempel Typefoundry, Frankfurt, Germany.
Stephenson Blake Co., Sheffield, England.

* * *

Universal Type Foundry (Univ), Hong Kong. This source is mentioned only because it still makes copies of a number of American types that are no longer available here. It is listed only for such cases.

THE SPECIMENS

Great care has been taken to authenticate the specimens. To the best of my knowledge, all are reproduced from impressions of metal type set essentially as shown, although in many cases it has been necessary to reassemble portions of proofs (making two lines out of four or five, for instance), and sometimes additional photographic copying steps have been necessary.

Specimens have been gathered from many sources, primarily the specimen books of manufacturers, printers, and typographers. Reassembling has been minimized, both to save time and to preserve the accurate spacing and alignment of actual type as far as possible; thus the format varies somewhat among specimens.

Some of the best specimens have been specially set to my format and contributed by a number of professional and hobby printers and typographers who have rare faces in their shops. These are acknowledged with each such specimen, although in some cases only a portion of the specimen was contributed.

Where a specimen in the desired size was not obtainable, a larger size has been shot down or a smaller size has been used as is—enlargements have generally been avoided because smaller sizes often are modified more than larger ones.

Wherever possible, the source of the type used in the specimen has been stated.

Facts and data regarding typefaces have been obtained from many sources, but primarily from the literature of the typefounders and other suppliers involved, from *The Inland Printer* and other trade publications, and from my personal experience with types and their sources. Often it has been necessary to decide which seems to be the most authentic of conflicting details, particularly of dates. Some sources state the date when a face was designed; others the date when it was put on the market. There can be an interval of a very few weeks to several years between these events, but it is not always known which event is noted. Credit has been given to the originating source of each face as far as possible.

Where alphabetic specimens have been unobtainable, words or phrases have been reproduced from old specimen books.

COPIES, DUPLICATES, "SIMILAR TO—"

Comparable faces from different sources are not necessarily exact duplicates. However, I have made extensive comparisons and have tried to make note of important or noticeable differences. Generally, typefaces of the same name from different sources—or corresponding faces under different names as noted—may be presumed to be reasonably alike, except for the Monotype and slug-machine modifications previously mentioned.

Some sources may include more swash or other alternate characters than others. Generally, foundry types tend to have more alternate characters, but the composing machines tend to include ligatures and diphthongs more often. Sources sometimes add, delete, or redesign characters during the life of a face, therefore it is impossible to be entirely comprehensive.

SIZE RANGES

The usual range of sizes for foundry types is 6-, 8-, 10-, 12-, 14-, 18-, 24-, 30-, 36-, 42-, 48-, 60-, and 72-point, although many faces are made only in the smaller, intermediate, or larger size ranges. A few are made in 84-, 96-, 120-point—even 144-point or larger. A very few are made smaller than 6-point. A few were made in 7-, 9-, 11-, 16-point or other intermediate sizes. The Anglo-American point is 0.01383 inch; the Didot or European point is slightly larger.

On Linotype and Intertype, the usual size range is 6- to 14-point, with some faces available in 4- or 5-point or fractional sizes; 7-, 9-, and 11-point are much more common than in foundry type. With special molds, larger sizes can be handled—up to 60-point in a few cases. A separate machine, the All-Purpose Linotype (APL), features manual assembly of matrices for casting slugs of faces up to 144-point; comparatively few of these machines were ever put in use.

The most common range of sizes for Monotype composition (keyboard) casting is 6- to 12-point, with a few faces going down to 4- and 5-point. With special equipment, composition casting can be done up to 18-point for some popular faces (24-point on English machines). Monotype display casting—type cast for hand assembly—goes up to 36-point on the standard machine, up to 48-point on the Thompson caster, and up to 72-point on the Giant caster. Some appropriate typefaces are made for casting oversize cap and figure fonts, as 42- on 36-point or 84 on 72. Monotype designates these as 36H4-, 72H4-point, etc.

The Ludlow size range is 6- to 48-point (down to 4-point in a very few faces) on standard matrices, and up to 96-point on oversize mats. A few faces are made up to 216-point for casting single letters the long way of the slug. Slugs are 12 points thick—less for small sizes—with faces overhanging as necessary.

The stated point size is always the body size, which has only a general relation to the height of capitals—the most apparent visual size. Generally the point size is the same as the distance from top of ascenders to bottom of descenders, but there are exceptions. Moreover, the relationship of cap height to point size varies greatly, even in variations of one design. For various reasons, two or more sizes are sometimes made on the same body size (e.g., *Copperplate Gothic*), but there is no uniform set of designations for such sizes. Where necessary, this book includes terminology such as "6s" or "6L," meaning the small(est) or large(st) face size on 6-point body.

ALIGNMENT

With the great variety of proportions in various type designs, attempts at standardization were not successful until late in the nineteenth century, when a system of standard alignment was instituted by the leading foundries, and existing designs were gradually modified over several years to conform. The benefits of being able to mix two or more styles of type in one line and have them align with each other were widely acclaimed, but just as important, when different sizes had to be used together, they could be aligned by the use of point-multiples of spacing material. Previously compositors often had to cut strips of paper or card to try to achieve alignment.

Art line, long descenders

Under standard alignment, the descending parts of letters were allotted about 20 to 25 percent of the body size, and virtually all types conformed to this for a number of years. An exception was title-line faces—all-cap fonts with no need for descenders, with a shoulder of only one or two points at the bottom. Formerly many cap-and-lowercase designs were also made in Title versions without the lowercase; such faces are listed in this book under the regular version, and cross-indexed if the name is significantly different. A few novelty faces, such as *Advertisers Gothic* and *Broadway,* were designed with nondescending lowercase, and cast on title line.

Standard line, short descenders

The successful revival of *Caslon Oldstyle* encouraged ATF to design *Bodoni* with longer descenders than standard alignment permitted. To accommodate them, Art Line was developed, with an allotment for descenders of about 30 to 33 percent of body size. Some foundry faces are made to special alignments. But in all cases, foundry types maintain a point-multiple scale of alignments, which are precisely adhered to.

Title line, no descenders

The first three examples shown are 42-point *Caslon Oldstyle No. 471,* a typical long-descender face; 36-point *Caslon No. 540,* a short-descender version of the same design; and 30-point *Old Style No. 43,* an obsolete title version of Caslon without lowercase. See Comparison of Caslons on page 62.

Combination body

Large sizes of some ATF types are cast on combination bodies, designated 72/60-point, for instance; descenders are on the full body size, and all other characters on the smaller body, as shown here for *Bodoni Bold.*

On Monotype, Linotype, and Intertype, the nominal point size is stated, but long or short descenders are available for many faces, for casting on larger or smaller bodies as required.

Other standards, seldom to point multiples, exist for Monotype casters. The precision of alignment on these machines depends on the skill of the operator. Moreover, alignment can be deliberately changed to some extent; thus the same face from different Monotype sources may not have the same alignment, and in many cases will not align perfectly with foundry type.

In addition to the typefaces which are the subject of this book, typefounders and matrix makers made a vast array of accented characters, borders, ornaments, symbols, and other typographic material, cast in the same manner as the fonts shown here. But they are beyond the scope of this book. In the same category are decorative initials; only some most closely related to the fonts are shown here.

Abbreviations

APL—All-Purpose Linotype.
ATF—American Type Founders Company.
BB&S—Barnhart Brothers & Spindler.
Bruce—Bruce's New York Type Foundry.
EMono or Eng Mono—The Monotype Corporation, England
    (English Monotype).
Inter—Intertype Corporation.
LATF—Los Angeles Type Foundry.
Lino—Mergenthaler Linotype Company.
Ludlow—Ludlow Typograph Company.
Mono—Lanston Monotype Machine Company.
MS&J—MacKellar, Smiths & Jordan.
TFP—Typefounders of Phoenix.
Univ—Universal Type Foundry.
Companies referred to above are identified more completely in the foregoing
    Introduction.

* * *

c (*circa*): about, approximately.
e.g. (*exempli gratia*): for example.
fl.: flourished.
i.e. (*id est*): that is.
q.v. (*quod vide*): which see.

* * *

L: larger or largest of two or more sizes of type on one body size.
s: smaller or smallest of two or more sizes of type on one body size.

American Metal Typefaces of the Twentieth Century

ABCDEFGHIJKLMNOPQRSTUVWXYZCRSW
abcdefghijklmnopqrstuvwxyzr& 1234567890
£$.,=;:!?'TT©.ingOO~

ABCDEFGHIJKLMNOPQRSTUVWXYZ&
abcdefghijklmnopqrstuvwxyz $1234567890 .,-:;'!?
æ ch ct œ sh st th ft Æ Œ £

Standard BIND RIB Conflict

ABCDEFGHIJKLMNOPQRSTUV
WXYZ&$1234567890.,:;'!?-
abcdefghijklmnopqrstuvwxyz
R a h m n u ♂ ↣ ⚶ ⚜ ✀ of The

ABCDEEFGHIJKLMNNOOPQRRSSTTUVWXYZ&THTh.,:;!?'"''"-–*()
aabccdeeffgghijkllmmnoopqrrssttuvwxyzff 12345678900$¢%

ABCDEFGHIJKLMNOPQRSTUVW
abcdefghijklmnopqrstuvwxyz.:,;- ''!?()[]–& $1234567890 XYZ
⊤ ♂ % ¼ ⅓ ½ ⅔ ¾

Name in parentheses after some specimens
indicates person who has set that specimen,
in whole or in part, to our format.

ABBEY TEXT—see *Bradley.*

ABBOTT OLDSTYLE is an eccentric novelty typeface designed in 1901 by Joseph W. Phinney for ATF. Upright stems taper inward slightly near the ends, while most other strokes are curved. Like many other typefaces of the day, each font contains several alternate characters, logotypes, and ornaments as shown.

Some early specimens call it *Abbot Oldstyle,* without the doubled *t.* It bears ATF's serial number 1 because it headed the alphabetical list when the numbering system was introduced about 1930, rather than being their oldest face.

Walter Long, who supplied the specimen, writes: "All the fonts (sizes) are the same as to content and every item is shown on the specimen proof." So this may be the first complete font proof published, as the face was obsolete before founders and printers began showing all characters, and advertising typographers were still far in the future. However, a few characters in the specimen are worn or broken. Compare *Bizarre Bold.*

Abbott Oldstyle, ATF No. 1 (6-72pt)

ACME—see *Menu Shaded.*

ADCRAFT. The three weights shown by BB&S in 1927 under this name were assembled from three different sources. While they are acceptable as family members, their resemblance to each other is merely co-incidental and not as pronounced as in most families. The unifying feature is their rugged or irregular shape, a popular style of the time.

Adcraft Black, the oldest member, was introduced by BB&S under the name of *Plymouth Bold* in 1900 or earlier. It is very heavy, and the most rugged of the group. Fonts contained all the Special characters shown, except for certain ones in the largest sizes. The regular weight of *Plymouth* (q.v.) was called *Adcraft Bold* by some users, but that name does not seem to be in any of the founders' literature.

Adcraft Medium was formerly known as *Rugged Medium* or *Alfred [Medium];* it was originated by Inland Type Foundry and patented by William A. Schraubstädter in 1910. *Adcraft Lightface* originated with Western Type Foundry in 1911 as *Carlton* and was taken over by BB&S as *Rugged Lightface;* it was also made under the name *Puritan* by Hansen, which is the source of this specimen. *Adcraft Lightface* fonts contained all the Special characters shown plus capital *AE* and *OE* diphthongs, but *Adcraft Medium* fonts had *ct* and *st* ligatures only. Compare *Avil, Drew.*

Adcraft Lightface, BB&S-ATF 1501 (8-48pt); Puritan, Hansen (8-48pt)
Adcraft Medium, BB&S-ATF 1502 (6-72pt)
Adcraft Bold or Plymouth, BB&S (6-120pt)
Adcraft Black or Plymouth Bold, BB&S-ATF 1500 (6-72pt)

AD LIB is an irregular, novel gothic letter, designed by Freeman Craw in 1961 for American Type Founders, probably in response to the new-found freedom of photolettering techniques. The effect, suggestive of a woodcut technique, was reportedly achieved by cutting the letters out of a black sheet material with scissors. The complete font as shown features alternate designs for a number of characters; in addition, it is aligned so that several characters can be inverted to form additional alternates, such as *u* for *n* and vice versa. It is made only in three sizes. The alternate characters were later discontinued. *Samoa,* a nineteenth-century typeface, had somewhat similar invertible characters.

Ad Lib, ATF 718 (18,36,60pt)

ADMIRAL SCRIPT is a spirited, unconnected script designed by Robert H. Middleton for Ludlow in 1953. Lowercase is small and the effect is precise, with the appearance of careful pen lettering. Compare *Raleigh Cursive.*

Admiral Script, Ludlow 49-BIC (12-48pt)

ADONIS, ATF 24-pt.

ABCDEFGHIJKLMNOPQRSTUVWXYZ& AABGℰVW
abcdefghijklmnopqrstuvwxyz $1234567890£ ,;:.-'!?`

ADSCRIPT, ATF (48-pt. at 50%) (Sheldon Wesson)

ABCDEFGHIJKLMNOPQRSTUVWXYZ &1234567890$
abcdefghijklmnopqrstuvwxyz & .,-:;!?',

ADSTYLE, BB&S (96-pt. at 25%) (John Horn)

ABCDEFGHIJKLMNOPQRSTUVWXYZ&?!:;'.-
abcdefghijklmnopqrstuvwxyz $123467890 äöü

ADSTYLE ITALIC, BB&S 18-pt.

ABCDEFGHIJKLMNOPQRSTUVWXYZ&Th?-!
abcdefghijklmnopqrstuvwxyz ff$1234567890

ADSTYLE CONDENSED, BB&S 24-pt.

RENOWNED CHARACTER Exhibited Advertisement

ADSTYLE EXTRA CONDENSED, BB&S 24-pt. (part reduced) (Gary Hantke)

ABCDEFGHIJKLMNOPQRSTUVWXZ& $1234567890.,-:;!?
Greatest Utility Represented Delightful

ADSTYLE WIDE, BB&S 24-pt. (Gary Hantke)

ABCDEFGHIJKLMNOPQRS
TUVWXYZ&.,-;:"?!1234567890
abcdefghijklmnopqrstuvwxyz$

ADSTYLE BLACK, BB&S 24-pt. (part reduced) (Duane Scott, Herb Harnish)

ABCDEFGHIJKLM'NOPQRSTUVWXYZ1234567890
abcdefghijklmnopqrstuvwxyz &.,-:;'!?$

ADSTYLE BLACK OUTLINE, BB&S 24-pt. (part reduced) (Duane Scott, Herb Harnish)

ABCDEFGHIJKLM,NOPQRSTUVWXYZ1234567890
abcdefghijklmnopqrstuvwxyz &.,-:;!?$

4

ADONIS is a novel creation by Willard T. Sniffin for ATF in 1930, popular for stationery and announcements but with little use otherwise. Lines are monotone throughout, and lowercase letters are linked, although it is not really a script. There are alternate versions of several of the capitals. The 30-point size was cut, but seldom if ever shown.

Adonis, ATF 543 (8-30pt); Inter (10-18pt)

ADSCRIPT was designed by Morris F. Benton in 1914. It has only a slight inclination, and the finishing stroke of each lowercase letter and some capitals in most instances meets a heavy stroke of the next letter. This gives the connected effect of continuous script, with only a slight, almost unnoticeable break in some combinations, but avoids the joining of two delicate hairlines which causes problems in most traditional script designs. ATF says of it: "Here is a series that appears to be a script, yet it is not exactly a script, for the letters are cast in regular straight body and there are no kerns or overhanging characters; the letters do not join as in script type, and there are no hairlines. Capitals and lowercase of various sizes can be used together, something not practicable when using the regular script faces." Compare *Typo Upright.*

Adscript, ATF 2 (12-48pt)

ADSTYLE was a popular BB&S series designed by Sidney C. Gaunt. It is a square-serif design but shows strong traits of its Clarendon ancestry; although most serifs on major strokes are squared, elsewhere they are bracketed or rounded, and there is moderate contrast between thick and thin strokes. The first member, identified in specimens as *Adstyle Series,* was designed about 1906; its proportions would ordinarily be called condensed, and it is rather heavy. Several variations appeared in the period 1907 to about 1911, including: *Adstyle Condensed,* just a little narrower than the original; *Adstyle Extra Condensed,* still narrower and also lighter in weight; *Adstyle Headletter,* a title version of the Extra Condensed; *Adstyle Wide,* a greatly extended version; *Adstyle Italic,* about the same weight as *Adstyle* but a normal width; *Adstyle Lightface; Adstyle Black,* only a little heavier than the original but not as narrow; and *Adstyle Black Outline,* cut to register with *Adstyle Black* for two-color work. Another version, *Adstyle Shaded,* was also designed by Gaunt and introduced in 1914. Compare *John Hancock, Bold Antique, Contact Bold Condensed.*

Adstyle, BB&S-ATF 1503 (6-120pt)
Adstyle Italic, BB&S-ATF 1509 (6-72pt)
Adstyle Condensed, BB&S-ATF 1506 (10-120pt)
Adstyle Extra Condensed, BB&S-ATF 1507 (10-108pt); also Adstyle Headletter (title), BB&S-ATF 1508 (18-120pt)
Adstyle Wide, BB&S-ATF 1511 (6-60pt)
Adstyle Lightface, BB&S (no data available)
Adstyle Black, BB&S-ATF 1504 (6-96pt)
Adstyle [Black] Outline, BB&S-ATF 1505 (12-96pt)
Adstyle Shaded, BB&S-ATF 1510 (10-72pt)

ADSTYLE SHADED, BB&S 24-pt.

CHOICE EXHIBITS Compounded Metal

A B C D E F G H I J K L M N O P Q R S
'S T U V W X Y Z & 1 2 3 4 5 6 7 8 9 0

BIG SALE BISCUITS CONVERTS
$10 SUIT DIAMONDS TRAINS

ADTYPE, Mono (36-pt. at 67%) (Ward Schori, Len Richardson)

ABCDEFGHIJKLMNOPQRSTUVWXYZ&.,-:;'!?
abcdefghijklmnopqrstuvwxyz$1234567890

ADTYPE ITALIC, ATF 24-pt. (part reduced)

PUMPKIN PIE BAKE NEW ENGLAND
Remarks Other Household Bean Hostelry

ADVER CONDENSED, ATF (36-pt. at 67%) (Herb Harnish)

ABCDEFGHIJKLMNOPQRSTUVWXYZ&$1234567890
abcdefghijklmnopqrstuvwxyz.,-:;'!?

ADVERTISERS GOTHIC, BB&S-ATF 18-pt.

ABCDEFGHIJKLMNOPQRSTUVWXYZ&
abcdefghijklmnopqrstuvwxyz $1234567890 .,-:;'!?

ADVERTISERS GOTHIC CONDENSED (30-pt. at 80%) (Dave Churchman)

AABCDEFGHIJKLMNOoPQRS/TUVWXYZ '?!,.;:-
abcdefghijklmnooopqrstuvwxyz (&$1234567890

ADVERTISERS GOTHIC OUTLINE, BB&S-ATF 24-pt. (Guy Botterill, John Horn)

AABCDEFGHIJKLMNOoPQRS/TUV
WXYZ&1234567890$.,-::;!?'
abcdefghijklmnopqrstuvwxyz

ADVERTISERS GOTHIC CONDENSED OUTLINE, BB&S-ATF 24-pt.

RENOUNCED METHODS Actions Prove Unbelief

6

ADSTYLE BORDERS. Although these are primarily decorative border units rather than type fonts, they had considerable popularity for expressing names and slogans in the borders of ads and otherwise. Designed by T. C. Robinson in 1908, the letters are a plain gothic style, somewhat thick and thin, similar to nineteenth-century designs. There are seven series:

No. 1: negative characters in rimmed circle.
No. 2: positive characters in circle.
No. 3: negative characters in plain circle.
No. 4: positive characters in square.
No. 5: negative characters in square.
No. 6: positive characters in diamond.
No. 7: negative characters in diamond.

Monotype Special Reversed Figures No. 132S are very similar to *Adstyle Border No. 5,* and in the 12-point size they include *X,* period, and comma, and single and double figures to *20.*

Adstyle Borders, BB&S-ATF (12-24pt)
Special Reversed Figures, Mono 132S (12,18pt)

ADTYPE is a square-serif face patented in 1903 by W. F. Capitaine and introduced by ATF. An early example of this sort of square-serif letter, it is distinguished by its high-waisted *R* and unusual *g.* Compare *Adstyle, John Hancock, Bold Antique, Contact Bold Condensed.* Figures and some other characters are narrower in the Monotype cutting shown, which was produced about 1912. The italic is inclined an extreme 24 degrees.

Adtype, ATF 3 (6-72pt); Mono 163 (6-36pt)
Adtype Italic, ATF (6-72pt)

ADVER CONDENSED was introduced by ATF in 1902, and is essentially a condensed version of *Schoeffer Oldstyle* (q.v.), an 1897 product of the same foundry, featuring the same sort of small, blunt serifs. Although undistinguished by later fashions, it avoids the eccentricities of many of the types of the period.

Adver Condensed, ATF 5 (8-72pt)

ADVERTISERS GOTHIC was a popular novel gothic, designed by Robert Wiebking in 1917 for Western Type Foundry and taken over by BB&S in 1919. It features nondescending lowercase letters; therefore it can be cast on title line, with caps occupying almost the entire body size. It has many distinctive characters, some of which have breaks giving a stencil-like effect. The outline faces are cut to register with the solid faces for two-color work. Compare *Publicity Gothic.*

Advertisers Gothic, BB&S-ATF 1512 (6-72pt)
Advertisers Gothic Condensed, BB&S-ATF 1513 (6-72pt)
Advertisers Gothic Outline, BB&S-ATF 1515 (10-72pt)
Advertisers Gothic Condensed Outline, BB&S-ATF 1514 (10-72pt)

ADVERTISERS UPRIGHT SCRIPT is one of many old faces shown in the 1925 BB&S specimen book under new names. This one was originally *Oliphant,* introduced in 1895, and retains a nineteenth-century character.

Advertisers Upright Script, BB&S-ATF 1516 (14-72pt)

ADVERTISERS UPRIGHT SCRIPT, BB&S (36-pt. at 67%) (Dave Churchman)

ABCDEFGHIJKLMNOPQRSTUVWXYZ
abcdefghijklmnopqrstuvwxyz &:;.,-'?! $1234567890

AGENCY GOTHIC, ATF (36-pt. at 67%)

ABCDEFGHIJKLMNOPQRSTUVWXYZ& $1234567890 .,-:;'!?¢ A M

AGENCY GOTHIC OPEN, ATF (48-pt. at 50%)

ABCDEFGHIJKLMNOPQRSTUVWXYZ A $1234567890 ¢.,-:;'!?&

AIRPORT BLACK, Baltimore 24-pt.

ABCDEFGHIJKLMNOPQRSTUVWXYZ
abcdefghijklmnopqrstuvwxyz ff fi fl
‘‘$1234567890 (),.-;':'!?&

AIRPORT BLACK CONDENSED TITLE, Baltimore 24s

ABCDEFGHIJKLMNOPQRSTUVWXYZ& 1234567890$?!.,:;'-

AIRPORT BROAD, Baltimore 18-pt. (William Wokoun)

ABCDEFGHIJKLMNOPQRSTUVWXYZ
abcdefghijklmnopqrstuvwxyz
&1234567890$.,-:;!?'"

Nomenclature of Parts of Letters

The "lines"—waist, base, etc.—provide limits for characters and define their position in relation to other characters. Straight horizontal strokes coincide with these lines, while points and curves go slightly beyond for best visual effect. The cap line and ascender line are often the same, but either may be higher than the other.

8

AGENCY GOTHIC is a squarish, narrow, monotone gothic without lower-case, designed by Morris F. Benton in 1932. It has an alternate *A* and *M* which further emphasize the vertical lines. Sizes under 36-point were added in 1935.

Agency Gothic Open was drawn by Benton in 1932 and introduced in 1934; it follows the same style in outline with shadow, and probably has been more popular than its solid companion. Triangle Type Foundry, a Chicago concern that manufactured matrices, copied this face as *Slim Open,* adding some smaller sizes.

ATF's working titles for these faces, before release, were *Tempo,* later *Utility Gothic* and *Utility Open.* Compare *Raleigh Gothic Condensed, Poster Gothic, Bank Gothic.*

AIGRETTE—see *Bernhard Tango.*

AIRPORT GOTHIC. Most of this series is the first American copy of *Futura,* which originated in Germany in 1927, designed by Paul Renner for Bauer. One source says it was cut from original Futura drawings, smuggled out of that country, but it seems more likely that matrices were made by electrotyping the imported type. An extrabold weight, *Airport Black,* was cut by Baltimore about 1943; information on this cutting is scarce and contradictory—one account says it was designed by Bill Stremic or Bill Blakefield, another that it was designed by Carl Hupie (or Hooper), and cut by Herman Schnoor.

There is also *Airport Black Condensed Title* and *Airport Broad.* The latter is a modification of *Airport Black,* cut 50 percent wider on the pantagraph by Herman Schnoor.

Baltimore later cast some of its Airport series from Monotype *Twentieth Century* matrices, and in a few cases listed both series.

Airport Relief, Baltimore 299, is English Monotype *Gill Sans Cameo Ruled,* while *Airport Tourist,* Baltimore 602, is *Futura Display,* cast from electrotype mats of the German foundry type. See Imports in Appendix.

ALBERTUS—see Imports in Appendix.
ALDERBRINK—see *Seymour.*
ALDINE—see *Modern Roman.*
ALFRED—see *Adcraft Medium.*
ALLEGRO—see Imports in Appendix.

ALTERNATE GOTHIC NO. 1, Mono 24-pt., and CONDENSED GOTHIC, Ludlow (see text)

ABCDEFGHIJKLMNOPQRSTUVWXYZ   AACEFGKMNRSWY
abcdefghijklmnopqrstuvwxyzfiflffiffl .,-:;   '!?&$1234567890
A C E F G K M N R S U W X Y u w x y

ALTERNATE GOTHIC NO. 2, Mono, 24-pt.

ABCDEFGHIJKLMNOPQRSTUVWXYZ$1234567890
abcdefghijklmnopqrstuvwxyz.,-:;   '!?&fiflff

ALTERNATE GOTHIC ITALIC, Mono 24-pt.

ABCDEFGHIJKLMNOPQRSTUVWXYZ .,-:;"()!?&%
abcdefghijklmnopqrstuvwxyzfiflff $1234567890

ALTERNATE GOTHIC NO. 3, ATF 24-pt.

ABCDEFGHIJKLMNOPQRSTUVWXYZ .,-:; '!?&
abcdefghijklmnopqrstuvwxyz $1234567890

CONDENSED GOTHIC OUTLINE, Ludlow 24-pt.

ABCDEFGHIJKLMNOPQRSTUVWXYZ&
abcdefghijklmnopqrstuvwxyz 1234567890

AMERICAN BACKSLANT, ATF (36-pt. at 67%)

ABCDEFGHIJKLMNOPQRSTUVWXYZ& $1234567890
abcdefghijklmnopqrstuvwxyz , - ' ` : ; ! ?

AMERICAN EXTRA CONDENSED, ATF 18-pt.

ABCDEFGHIJKLMNOPQRSTUVWXYZ&   abcdefghijklmnopqrstuvwxyz $1234567890

AMERICAN ITALIC, ATF 24-pt. (Dave Churchman)

ABCDEFGHIJKLMNOPQRSTUVWXYZ&
abcdefghijklmnopqrstuvwxyz$1234567890.,-:;'!

AMERICAN SCRIPT, ATF (48-pt. at 50%) (Dave Churchman)

ABCDEFGHIJKLMNOPQRSTUVWXYZ
abcdefghijklmnopqrstuvwxyz £$1234567890 ';:-?! ,,¿¡ ć ' &Co.

10

ALTERNATE GOTHIC was designed in 1903 by Morris F. Benton for ATF, with the thought of providing several alternate widths of one design to fit various layout problems. Otherwise it is a plain, basic American gothic with no unusual features, but represents a more careful drawing of its nineteenth-century predecessors. The Monotype copies in display sizes are essentially the same as the foundry originals, with the addition of f-ligatures. The thirteen alternate round capitals shown in the first line of Alternate Gothic No. 1 were designed by Sol Hess in 1927 for Monotype, hence the "Modernized" name; with these letters the design is sometimes referred to as *Excelsior Gothic.*

Monotype keyboard sizes, as adapted by Hess about 1911, are considerably modified to fit a standard arrangement; caps are not as condensed as in the original foundry design. In 6-point, series 51 and 77 are both the same width, character for character, but some letters differ a bit in design. Note that these two narrower widths are simply called *Alternate Gothic* on Monotype, while the wider version is *Alternate Gothic Condensed!*

Alternate Gothic Italic, drawn about 1946 by Sol Hess for Monotype, matches No. 2, but may be used with other widths as well. *Condensed Gothic,* on Ludlow, is essentially a match for *Alternate Gothic No. 1,* but has a somewhat different set of variant characters, as shown in the third line. There is also *Condensed Gothic Outline* on Ludlow, introduced about 1953, essentially an outline version of *Alternate Gothic No. 2.* On Linotype and Intertype there is *Gothic Condensed No. 2* which is very similar to *Alternate Gothic No. 1* in the largest sizes only, but with even narrower lowercase and figures. Also compare *Trade Gothic Bold* and *Trade Gothic Bold Condensed.*

AMERICAN BACKSLANT was designed by Morris F. Benton for ATF in 1933, but not introduced until 1935 except for an "in preparation" line in the 1934 specimen book. It is a gothic with the appearance of being drawn with a round pen, with distinction gained mostly by its reverse slant. The working title was *Backhand Gothic.*

AMERICAN BASKERVILLE—see *Baskerville.*
AMERICAN CASLON—see under Caslon.

AMERICAN EXTRA CONDENSED is a medium weight gothic, popular for newspaper headlines, and was designed about 1905 but adapted from a late nineteenth-century style. It features 45-degree angles where curves would normally appear. Without the lowercase, similar designs were better known as *Chamfer Condensed* (q.v.) or *Herald Extra Condensed,* the latter introduced by Inland in 1909.

AMERICAN GARAMOND—see under Garamond.

AMERICAN ITALIC is a heavy, novel design by Herman Ihlenburg introduced by ATF in 1902, as a companion to *Columbus,* which had been designed for ATF's MacKellar Smiths & Jordan branch in 1892. The italic survived its roman mate, being shown by itself in 1906, but was gone by 1912. It is essentially a nineteenth-century design.

AMERICAN SCRIPT was introduced by ATF in 1898, and shown in 1906 as *American Script No. 2.* It is similar to *Typo Script,* except for an extra flourish on many of the capitals.

Alternate Gothic No. 1, ATF 6 (6-72pt); Inter (8-42pt); Alternate Gothic, Modernized, Mono 51 (6-72H4); Gothic No. 19 or Trade Gothic Extra Condensed Bold, Lino (6-24pt); Gothic Condensed No. 2, Lino = Inter (see text); Condensed Gothic, Ludlow 6-C (6-96pt)
Alternate Gothic No. 2, ATF 7 (6-72pt); Alternate Gothic, Mono 77 (6-36pt); Gothic No. 20 or Trade Gothic Condensed Bold, Lino (6-24pt); Condensed Gothic No. 2, Ludlow 6-C2 (12-72pt)
Alternate Gothic Italic (No. 2), Mono 771 (14-36pt)
Alternate Gothic No. 3, ATF 8 (6-72pt); Alternate Gothic Condensed, Mono 177 (14-36pt); Gothic Condensed No. 2, BB&S-ATF 1650 (6-72pt)
Condensed Gothic Outline, Ludlow 6-CO (18-48pt)

American Backslant, ATF 586 (12-48pt)

American Extra Condensed, ATF 9 (12-72pt); Gothic No. 14, Lino = Inter (18pt); also Herald Extra Condensed (title), ATF 192 (10-60pt)

American Italic, ATF (6-60pt)

American Script No. 2, ATF (12-60pt)

𝕬𝕭𝕮𝕯𝕰𝕱𝕲𝕳𝕴𝕵𝕶𝕷𝕸𝕹𝕺𝕻𝕼𝕽𝕾𝕿𝖀𝖁𝖂𝖃𝖄𝖅&
abcdefghijklmnopqrstuvwxyz $1234567890 .,:;-ˇ!?

ABCDEFGHIJKLMNOPQRSTUVWXYZ & .,-:;!?'/
abcdefghijklmnopqrstuvwxyz ff $1234567890

ABCDEFGHIJKLMNOPQRSTUVWXYZ&
abcdefghijklmnopqrstuvwxyz
$1234567890 .,-:;'!?()[] - - * % " " " " ¢ $ £ ·· ?

ABCDEFGHIJKLMNOPQRSTUVWXYZ
abcdefghijklmnopqrstuvwxyz fifffflffiffl
1234567890 $ $¢ £%,,.:--·-··.*()[]?!?!"""&

ABCDEFGHIJKLMNOPQRSTUVWXYZ
abcdefghijklmnopqrstuvwxyz
1234567890 $ $¢ £%,,.:--·-··.*()[]?!?!"""&

ABCDEFGHIJKLMNOPQRSTUVWXYZ
abcdefghijklmnopqrstuvwxyz
1234567890 $ $¢ £%.;.:--·-··*()[]?!?!"""

The thirsty Earth soaks up the Rain,
And drinks, and gapes for drink again.
The Plants suck in the Earth, and are
with constant drinking fresh and fair.

The Sea it self, which one would think
should have but little need of Drink,
Drinks ten thousand Rivers up,
so fill'd that they or'eflow the Cup.

ABCDEFGHIJKLMNOPRSTUVWXYZ&MRW$1234567890£
abcdefghijklmnopqrstuvwxyz.,-:;'!?

AMERICAN TEXT was designed by Morris F. Benton for ATF in 1932, as a modernized adaptation of the sort of face commonly called Old English. It seems to be constructed entirely of straight lines, with a very angular appearance. It has had some popularity in advertising, as well as for stationery.

American Text, ATF 567 (18-72pt)

AMERICAN UNCIAL was designed and cut by hand by Victor Hammer in 1943. This artist, who was born in Austria, had built a reputation for craftsmanship as a type designer, punch cutter, and printer in Italy. In 1939 he became professor of fine arts at Wells College in Aurora, New York, where he cut punches for this face. Matrices were made and type was cast by the Dearborn Typefoundry in Chicago, last of the small independent founders. Later the design was recut and cast by Klingspor in Germany.

American Uncial, Dearborn; Klingspor (12,16pt; Initials 30pt)

Uncial letters date to times before the common use of separate capital and lowercase alphabets. They are the basis for the lowercase of this font, to which Hammer has added a set of capitals. There is also a set of Initials, which follow mostly the lowercase design but with some modifications. Compare *Hammer Samson Uncial, Worrell Uncial*.

AMERICANA was introduced by ATF in 1966, the foundry calling it later "the most successful face ATF has introduced in many years; it is the result of an assignment to 'return to elegance,' being designer Richard Isbell's interpretation of that trend." It features short, slightly concave serifs, short ascenders, and capitals not quite as tall as ascenders, while being quite wide. Fonts include several characters not usually available, such as center dot, hyphen, and short dash positioned to center on cap height as well as versions in the usual lowercase position.

Americana, ATF 725 (10-72pt)
Americana Italic, ATF 728 (10-48pt)
Americana Bold, ATF 727 (8-72pt)
Americana Extra Bold, ATF 729 (8-72pt)

The interrobang, the first new punctuation mark to have been introduced in three hundred years and the only one invented by an American, is also featured in Americana. The interrobang, combining exclamation and question marks, was originated in 1962 by Martin K. Speckter, New York advertising executive and printing hobbyist. It was incorporated into all versions of Americana (ATF calling it "interabang"), but although it got considerable response at the time, it was not included in other type families.

Emil Klumpp directed the basic version while Whedon Davis directed the others, which were added in the following two or three years. *Americana Extra Bold* was the last new typeface created by ATF.

ANACREON was a whimsical pseudo-Greek typeface made or assembled for the Golden Eagle Press of Mt. Vernon, New York, for a translation from Greek of "Anacreon." (Actually, the author has assigned this name, no mention of a name for the typeface having been found otherwise.) Many of the lowercase characters are Linotype *Greek Elzevir,* selected for their visual resemblance to Latin characters rather than for their value in Greek. Thus, *p* is represented by *rho* (ρ) which is the Greek *r*. A few characters are inverted for better visual effect. Where there are no satisfactory characters in Greek, *Estienne* letters are used. Capitals are *Garamond No. 3* small caps. Presumably Linotype matrices were specially cut to respond to normal keyboard operation. The specimen is from a poor photocopy.

Anacreon, Lino (11pt) private

ANCIENT GOTHIC—see *Gothic Novelty Title*.

ANCIENT ROMAN was Keystone Type Foundry's adaptation in 1904 of the *Golden* type of William Morris, comparable to *Jenson Oldstyle* (q.v.), but distinguished by the unusual alternate versions of *MRW*; other differences were minor.

Ancient Roman, Keystone (6-72pt)

αBBcδEfGhijklmΝοpqrςτuvwxγz 1234567890 :;''/(-!?

ABBCGDDEFGGHIJKLMMNNOPPQRRSTTUVVWWXYZ
abcdefghijklmnopqrstuvwxyz 1234567890$.,',;.!?
& fiffflffiflfffifafefofrfutyng

ABCDEFGHIJKLMNOPQRSTUVWXYZ&
abcdefghijklmnopqrstuvwxyz $1234567890 .,-:;'!?'
f fi ff fl ffi ffl fa fe fo fr fu ng ry ty BGDMNPRVW

ABCDEFGHIJKLMNOPQRSTUVWXYZ @℔&£ æœÆŒ $1234567890
ABCDEFGHIJKLMNOPQRSTUVWXYZ @℔&£ æœÆŒ $1234567890
abcdefghijklmnopqrstuvwxyz fiflffffifffl ,.-;':'!?()[]*†|‡‖§¶--—⅛¼⅜½⅝¾⅞
abcdefghijklmnopqrstuvwxyz fiflffffifffl ,.-;':'!?()

ABCDEFGHIJKLMNOPQRSTUVWXYZ&
abcdefghijklmnopqrstuvwxyz .,-:;'!?
£$1234567890 ÆæŒœ

Superannuated STOREHOUSE MOUSETRAP Girls Finger Caught

Highschool ENDS

ABCDEFGHIJKLMNOPQRSTUVWXYZ$1234567890Æ
abcdefghijklmnopqrstuvwxyzfffiflffiffl.,-'!?

SPHINX OF ANCIENT EGYPT
Famous pyramid built by Cheops

14

ANDROMAQUE is a cursive form of uncial letter, mixing Greek forms of *aeklmnstz* with Roman forms of the other letters, yet retaining legibility and harmony. The original size was cut by Victor Hammer and cast in France. The 14-point size was begun by Hammer, but left unfinished at his death. The font was completed by his long-time friend, R. Hunter Middleton, in the early 1980s, and cast by Paul H. Duensing.

Andromaque, Middleton (14pt), private

ANGLO—see Antiques in Appendix.

ANNOUNCEMENT ROMAN and *Announcement Italic* were designed by Morris F. Benton in 1916, adapted from steel or copperplate engravings, but not completed and released until 1918. These delicate faces have had some popularity for announcements, social stationery, and a limited amount of advertising work, but are a little too fancy for extensive use. Oddly, some of the plain caps shown in the specimens, both roman and italic, do not seem to appear in any ATF specimens. Foundry records show that a 48-point size of the roman was cut in 1927, but no other listing or showing of it has been found. In fact, sizes over 24-point were discontinued after a few years, and all sizes were discontinued in 1954.

Announcement Roman, ATF 456 (6-48pt)
Announcement Italic, ATF 452 (6-36pt)

ANTIQUE in general is a generic nineteenth-century term applied to a variety of old type styles. A few that were given a new lease on life by Monotype and the slug machines are listed here; others were similar to the older *Clarendons, Dorics, Ionics,* etc. Also see *Bold Antique* and *Bold Condensed Antique, Modern Antique* and *Modern Antique Condensed,* and *Old Style Antique;* also *Cushing Antique, Latin Antique,* etc.

Antique No. 1 is similar to *Bookman. Antique No. 2* (Lino) is equivalent to *Antique No. 6* (Mono) and comes from BB&S, where it was later known as *Antique Bold. Antique No. 3* is equivalent to *Modern Antique. Antique No. 525* (ATF) is very similar to *Antique [No. 53]* (BB&S) and *Antique No. 1* (Inland); also to *Consort Light,* the 1950s English revival (see Clarendon). Hansen's *Antique No. 1* was slightly lighter than the others. *Antique Condensed* comes from BB&S.

Antique Extra Condensed was shown as *Skeleton Antique* by Marder, Luse in 1886 or earlier and by BB&S somewhat later, with many sources producing the same or very similar designs.

Antique Shaded was designed by Morris F. Benton in 1910 but not introduced until 1913, when it was described as "the first of a series of shaded typefaces." It was later promoted as part of "the new gray typography." This face was the first one cut on a new shading machine invented by the designer's father, Linn B. Benton. When Monotype copied it, the face was named *Rockwell Antique Shaded,* to tie it in with that company's Rockwell series (q.v.), but since Rockwell is often confused with Stymie, it is perhaps natural that *Antique Shaded* is sometimes though incorrectly called *Stymie Shaded.*

Antique No. 1, Lino = Inter (6-24pt)
Antique No. 1 Italic, Lino = Inter (6-18pt)
Antique No. 3, Lino = Inter (6-14pt);
  Modern Antique Condensed, Mono 76 (5-12pt)
Antique No. 525, ATF 227 (5½-42pt);
  Antique [No. 53], BB&S-ATF 1517 (5½-42pt); Antique No. 5, Keystone (5½-42pt)
Antique Condensed, BB&S-ATF 1519 (8-20pt); Lino (10-18pt)
Antique Extra Condensed [No. 150], Keystone (8-48pt); Lino (20pt); Skeleton Antique No. 55, BB&S (10-54pt)
Antique Bold, BB&S-ATF 1518 (6-36pt); Antique No. 2, Lino (5-8pt); Antique No. 6, Mono 233 (6pt)
Antique Shaded, ATF 12 (8-72pt); Rockwell Antique Shaded, Mono 193 (12-36pt)

ANTIQUE SHADED, Mono 24-pt.

ABCDEFGHIJKLMNOPQRSTUVWXYZ&
abcdefghijklmnopqrstuvwxyz
$1234567890 .,-:;'!?

ARCADIA, Lino 12-pt.

ABCDEFGHIJKLMNOPQRSTUVWXYZ& 1234567890
abcdefghijklmnopqrstuvwxyz [(,.:;?"!)]

ARIES, Goudy 16-pt., private

T SCOWRETH all scurfe and scalds from the head, being
therewith dailie washt before meales. Being moderatlie taken
[saith he] it sloweth age, it strengtheth youth, it helpeth diges-
tion, it cutteth flegme, it lighteneth the mind, it quickeneth the

ARRIGHI, Eng Mono 24-pt.

ABCDEFGHIJKLMNOPQRSTUVWXYZ&
abcdefghijklmnopqrstuvwxyz $1234567890 .,-:;'!?

ARTCRAFT, Ludlow 24-pt. (part foundry, reduced) (Duane Scott, Cliff Helbert, Herb Harnish)

ABCDEFGHIJKLMNOPQRSTUVWXYZ&
abcdefghijklmnopqrstuvwxyz 1234567890
ABDMNOOPRThry ctstthooff fiflffiffl.,-:;'?

ARTCRAFT ITALIC, BB&S-ATF 24-pt. (swash, Ludlow) (Duane Scott, Cliff Helbert)

ABCDEFGHIJKLMNOPQRSTUVWXYZ&
abcdefghijklmnopqrstuvwxyz fiflffiffl.,-:;'!? $123456789
ABDMNPRTChthctgstry ty of ⊙⊙⊙

ARTCRAFT BOLD, Ludlow 24-pt.

ABCDEFGHIJKLMNOPQRSTUVWXYZ&
abcdefghijklmnopqrstuvwxyz 1234567890

16

ANTIQUE OPEN—see *Beton Open* under Imports in Appendix.
ANZEIGEN GROTESQUE—see *Aurora* under Imports in Appendix.
ARBORET—see Antiques in Appendix.

ARCADIA was an experimental face designed by William A. Dwiggins for Mergenthaler in 1943-47, used in *Some Random Recollections,* by Alfred A. Knopf for the Typophiles as Chapbook XXII in 1949.

Arcadia and Italic, Lino (12pt) experimental

ARCHER—see *Gothic Novelty Condensed.*
ARGENT, ARGENTINE—see Antiques in Appendix.

ARIES was designed by Frederic W. Goudy in 1925 as a private type for the Aries Press of Spencer Kellogg, at Eden, New York, and became Goudy's first experience in cutting his own matrices. Only one lot, some 500 pounds, was cast for private use. In 1932 it was recut and renamed *Franciscan* (q.v.).

Aries, Goudy (16pt), private

ARISTON—see Imports in Appendix.
ARMSTRONG—see *Della Robbia.*

ARRIGHI is the italic companion to *Centaur.* It is calligraphic in style, and was derived from a 1524 typeface of Ludovico degli Arrighi. Although designed by Frederic Warde, New York calligrapher and typographer, it was cut first by Plumet in Paris in 1925, and then by English Monotype in 1929.

Arrighi, Eng Mono (6-48pt)

ARTCRAFT was designed in 1912 by Robert Wiebking and featured under the name of *Craftsman* in the first ad for his short-lived Advance Type Foundry, operated by Wiebking, Hardinge & Company, in Chicago. A short time later, the face was advertised as *Art-Craft,* and later as one word— *Artcraft.* Advance was soon taken over by Western Type Foundry, for whom Wiebking designed *Artcraft Italic* and *Artcraft Bold* a year or two later. Western in turn was taken over by Barnhart Brothers & Spindler in 1918. BB&S was already owned by ATF but operated separately until 1929; in the meantime, though, *Artcraft* and a number of other faces were shown in ATF specimens as well as those of BB&S.

Artcraft, BB&S-ATF 1527 (6-72pt); Mono 334 (14-36pt); Ludlow 10-L (10-48pt); Graphic Arts, Hansen (6-72pt)
Artcraft Italic, BB&S-ATF 1529 (6-48pt); Ludlow 10-LI (10-48pt); Graphic Arts Italic, Hansen (6-72pt)
Artcraft Bold, BB&S-ATF 1528 (6-72pt); Ludlow 10-B (6-48pt)

Artcraft has an unusual roundness in some of its serifs and line endings, and a line of it produces a rolling feeling; some characters have curlicues, such as the long curl at the top of the *a* and *f* and the exaggerated ear on the *g*. A number of auxiliary characters were made for roman and italic fonts; as these were sold separately, they were overlooked by many printers and typographers. The boldface has fewer eccentricities.

Artcraft was a popular face for a number of years; the roman was copied by Monotype in 1929 without the fancy characters, and all three faces were copied by Ludlow. Adaptation in 1924 of *Artcraft Italic* to the standard 17-degree slant of Ludlow italic matrices was the second assignment of Robert H. Middleton (after *Eusebius,* q.v.) at that company. Hansen called it *Graphic Arts.*

One source attributes the Artcraft family to Edmund C. Fischer, otherwise unidentified, but the details stated here are more generally accepted and seem to fit known facts better.

ARTLINE, Keystone 18-pt. (Stanley Sollid)

ABCDEFGHIJKLMNOPQRSTUVWXYZ &!?$1234567890
Around your hat ought to be a good musician.,- ;'

ARTSCRIPT, Mono 24-pt. (alternates 36-pt. at 67%) (Fred Sholty)

ABCDEFGHI JKLMNOPQRSTUVWXYZ&

abcdefghijklmnopqrstuvwxyz!?,.:;="ffflffifl1234567890$ aevmnt:~gg gy

ATHENA, Baltimore 24-pt. (part spaced)

ABCDEFGHIJKLMNOPQRSTUVWXYZ& 1234567890$ abcdefghijklmnopqrstuvwxyz .,-:;''?!¢$))

ATLANTIC & ITALIC, Mono 12-pt.

ABCDEFGHIJKLMNOPQRSTUVWXYZ&ÆŒ   ABCDEFGHIJKLMNOPQRSTUVWXYZ&ÆŒ
abcdefghijklmnopqrstuvwxyzæœ   fiflffffiffl   abcdefghijklmnopqrstuvwxyzæœ   fiflffffiffl
$1234567890   .,-'':;!? $1234567890   :;!?
ABCDEFGHIJKLMNOPQRSTUVWXYZ&ÆŒ

AURIOL, ATF 18-pt. (Steve Saxe)

ABCDEFGHIJKLMNOPQRSTUVWXYZÆŒ   F M P T

abcdefghijklmnoprstuvwxyzæœd'etc. &1234567890$.,-:;!?"«»

AURORA & ITALIC, Lino 8½-pt.

ABCDEFGHIJKLMNOPQRSTUVWXYZ&   ABCDEFGHIJKLMNOPQRSTUVWXYZ&
abcdefghijklmnopqrstuvwxyz   abcdefghijklmnopqrstuvwxyz
1234567890[£,.:;?!'-'*]   /†‡%⅛¼⅜½⅝¾⅞   1234567890[£,.:;?!'-'*]   /†‡%⅛¼⅜½⅝¾⅞

ARTLINE was introduced by Keystone in 1912. It is a mannered font of capitals and figures, with very small serifs and slight thick-and-thin contrast, for use on stationery and announcements and general advertising of the time. Apparently it did not survive when Keystone was absorbed by ATF in 1919. Compare *Della Robbia, Camelot.*

Artline, Keystone (6-48pt)

ARTSCRIPT is a delicate calligraphic letter designed by Sol Hess for Monotype, which calls it "an attempt to convert into rigid metal the graceful penmanship of the ancient scribe . . . based on the writing of Servidori of Madrid (1798)." It was designed in 1939 but not released until 1948, because of wartime restrictions. It is a pleasing design for limited use, but its delicacy requires special care in handling. Compare *Heritage, Lydian Cursive,* and *Thompson Quillscript.*

Artscript, Mono 225 (18-72pt)

ASTORIA—see *Comstock.*

ASTREE was announced by Linotype in 1926 as a copy of the face cast by Peignot in France, but no further evidence of it has been found.

ATHENA is a very narrow, light roman typeface with unusually tapered vertical strokes, designed and cut by George Battee of Baltimore Type about 1955. It is a distinctive novelty, useful for a limited amount of delicate display.

Athena, Balto 111 (24-72pt)

ATLANTIC (or *Atlantic Monthly*) was cut by Monotype in 1909 for *Atlantic Monthly* magazine, which used it as a body type for many years. The design is an adaptation of *Scotch Roman,* more regularized and with less emphasis on the capital letters than the original *Scotch Roman,* but hardly distinguishable from Monotype's keyboard sizes of that face, which were necessarily modified to fit mechanical limitations of the time. It can be classified as a modern face because of the sharp serifs and the contrast between thick and thin strokes. The face was recut and new sizes added in 1936. It is simply called *Modern* in some Monotype lists.

Atlantic [Monthly] and Italic, Mono 35ABC (6-12pt)

AUGUSTEA—see Imports in Appendix.

AURIOL was issued by ATF early in the century, by arrangement with the Peignot foundry in France. It is an unusual but dainty and artistic face—for the period—based on the distinctive lettering of Georges Auriol, French designer. Compare *Peignot.*

Auriol, ATF 13 (10-36pt)

AURORA is a newspaper face designed by Jackson Burke for Linotype in 1960, and is made only in 8½-point, combined with its own italic or a choice of standard bold faces, as far as we can determine.

Aurora and Italic, Lino (8½pt)

AURORA (other)—see Imports in Appendix.

AUTHORS OLDSTYLE, BB&S 24-pt. (Herb Harnish)

ABCDEFGHIJKLMNOPQRSTUVWXYZ
abcdefghijklmnopqrstuvwxyz .,-'?!ctst&$1234567890
CGJNORS& Qu Mc Co

AUTHORS OLDSTYLE ITALIC, BB&S 24-pt. (part reduced)

ENGLISH NUMBER Imported 38 Models Thanquet
Kimbirley MONSTER DOG Bought 69 Hearn

AUTHORS ROMAN, BB&S 18-pt.

ABCDEFGHIJKLMNOPQRSTUVWXYZ&?!
abcdefghijklmnopqrstuvwxyzfiflffffiffl$1234567890

AUTHORS ITALIC, BB&S 24-pt. (Dave Churchman)

ABCDEFGHIJKLMNOPQRSTUVWXYZ&.,-:;'!?
abcdefghijklmnopqrstuvwxyzfffiflffiffl $1234567890
Æ M St W ng rt & Ch Co The

AUTHORS ROMAN CONDENSED, BB&S 24-pt.

PROSCRIBED INVENTION Moving Pictures Released

AUTHORS ROMAN WIDE, BB&S 18-pt.

WESTERN RAILROAD SEARCHING the Far West
abcdefghijklmnopqrstuvwxyz

AUTHORS ROMAN BOLD, BB&S 24-pt.

ENTRANCING BOYS Northeast Workmen

AUTHORS ROMAN BOLD CONDENSED, BB&S 24-pt.

PROMOTERS REMARKS Groceries Establishment

AVIL, Inland (60-pt. at 40%) (Dave Churchman)

ABCDEFGHIJKLMNOPQRSTUVWXYZ -;.,!?
abcdefghijklmnopqrstuvwxyz&$1234567890 fifflfltth

AUTHORS ROMAN, *Authors Roman Italic,* and *Authors Roman Wide* were designed by Sidney Gaunt for BB&S in 1902, with other versions added in 1909 to 1915. It is a legible but generally undistinguished face, perhaps best in the Wide version. The italic includes a number of quaint swash characters, and was one of the first BB&S italics to be cast on its offset body, described elsewhere (see "The Third Dimension of Type" in the Introduction); the bold faces provide restrained complementary display for headlines. *Authors Oldstyle,* shown by BB&S in 1912, bears little resemblance to *Authors Roman.*

AVIL was advertised by Inland Type Foundry in 1904 as "a new typeface, most excellent for fine booklet and catalog work." It follows a popular style of the day, with tall ascenders, small x-height, and irregular edges. It is very similar to *Pabst Oldstyle* (q.v.), but narrower.

AYER was introduced by Keystone Type Foundry in 1909, which said it was "named for F. Wayland Ayer, founder of Keystone Type Foundry and the great advertising agency which bears his name." The non-kerning italic was added in 1910.

BACKSLOPE RAY SHADED—see *Delraye* under Antiques in Appendix.
BAILEY SHADED—see Antiques in Appendix.

BALLOON is a family of italic capitals in three weights, designed in 1939 for ATF by Max R. Kaufmann. They feature a plain, unadorned, hand lettered appearance, as though carefully drawn with a brush or a round lettering pen; in fact the working name of the series in the foundry was *Speedball Light, Bold,* and *Extra Heavy,* for a popular brand of lettering pens. Although featuring capital alphabets only, they are cast on Art line, which gives them an unnecessarily large shoulder. But this allows them to be used with the lowercase of the same designer's *Kaufmann Script,* which matches the two lighter weights. The name apparently comes from the "balloons" used to enclose conversation in comic strips. Compare *Cartoon.*

Authors Oldstyle, BB&S-ATF 1531 (5-72pt)
Authors Oldstyle Italic, BB&S-ATF 1533 (5-72pt)
Authors Oldstyle Bold, BB&S-ATF 1532 (5-72pt)
Authors Roman, BB&S-ATF 1534 (5-72pt)
Authors Roman Italic, BB&S-ATF 1530 (5-72pt)
Authors Roman Condensed, BB&S-ATF 1537 (6-72pt)
Authors Roman Wide, BB&S-ATF 1538 (5-48pt)
Authors Roman Bold, BB&S-ATF 1535 (5-72pt)
Authors Roman Bold Condensed, BB&S-ATF 1536 (6-72pt)

Avil, Inland (6-72pt)

Ayer, Keystone
Ayer Italic, Keystone

Balloon Light, ATF 675 (10-96pt)
Balloon Bold, ATF 676 (10-96pt)
Balloon Extrabold, ATF 677 (10-96pt)

AYER, Keystone 18-pt.

ABCDEFGHIJKLMNOPQRSTUVWXYZ
abcdefghijklmnopqrstuvwxyz 1234567890

AYER ITALIC, Keystone 18-pt.

LATEST FASHIONS
Newest Designs in Parisian Dresses and Blouses. $123

BALLOON LIGHT, ATF (36-pt. at 67%)

ABCDEFGHIJKLMNOPQRSTUVWXYZ& $1234567890 .,-:;'!?" "

BALLOON BOLD, ATF 24-pt.

ABCDEFGHIJKLMNOPQRSTUVWXYZ $1234567890&.,-:;'"\"''!?

BALLOON EXTRA BOLD, ATF 24-pt.

ABCDEFGHIJKLMNOPQRSTUVWXYZ $1234567890&.,-:;'"\"''!?

BALTIMORE SCRIPT, Balto 24-pt. (spaced)

A B C D E F G H I J K L M N O P Q R S T U V W X Y Z U W

a b c d e f g h i j k l m n o p q r s t u v w x y z f s y & $1234567890 .,-':;!?""○—((☞ ☜*

BAMBOO, BB&S 18-pt. (Schuyler Shipley)

ABCDEFGHIJKLMNOPQRSTUVWXYZ

abcdefghijklmnopqrstuvwxyz 1234567890 ..,::-'!?&$₵₭

BAM-STENCIL, RS&W 18-pt.

ABCDEFGHIJKLMNOPQRSTUVWXYZ$123456789

BANK GOTHIC LIGHT, ATF 18L

ABCDEFGHIJKLMNOPQRSTUVWXYZ
$1234567890.,-:;'''"()!?&

BANK GOTHIC MEDIUM, ATF 18L

ABCDEFGHIJKLMNOPQRSTUVWXYZ
$1234567890,.-;':'!?&

BANK GOTHIC BOLD, ATF 18L

ABCDEFGHIJKLMNOPQRSTUVWXYZ
$1234567890 .,-:;'!?'

BANK GOTHIC CONDENSED LIGHT, ATF 18L

ABCDEFGHIJKLMNOPQRSTUVWXYZ.,:;-"!?&$1234567890

BANK GOTHIC CONDENSED MEDIUM, ATF 18L

ABCDEFGHIJKLMNOPQRSTUVWXYZ.,:;-"!?&$1234567890

BANK GOTHIC CONDENSED BOLD, ATF 18L

ABCDEFGHIJKLMNOPQRSTUVWXYZ
.,:;-"!?&$1234567890

BALTIMORE SCRIPT is a fancy style designed by Tommy Thompson and cut by George Battee for Baltimore Type in 1955. The lowercase follows the general style of a script letter hand-written with a broad pen, although the inclination is slight and the letters don't quite connect. Capitals are flourished. It is suitable for stationery, announcements, and greeting cards, but its range of small sizes is hardly enough for advertising use.

BALTO GOTHIC—see *News Gothic.*

BAMBOO was originally known as *Freak,* patented 1889, at Great Western Type Foundry. It was shown by BB&S as late as 1925, in five sizes, of which the 18-point size was later copied by Typefounders of Phoenix as an antique revival.

BAM-STENCIL was designed by F. L. Amberger and reportedly cut by Ruttle, Shaw & Wetherill, a Philadelphia typographic firm, about 1937. It follows the general style of *Corvinus (Glamour) Bold,* but is heavier and has stencil-like breaks in the strokes. No lowercase was made.

BANK GOTHIC, in three weights and two widths, was designed in 1930-33 by Morris F. Benton for ATF, which introduced the normal widths in 1930. It is a more squarish, contemporary adaptation of letters on the order of *Copperplate Gothic,* useful primarily for the same sort of forms and stationery work. Linotype has the same face in regular widths; it is called *Commerce Gothic* on Ludlow and *DeLuxe Gothic* on Intertype, while Monotype *Stationers Gothic* is similar. From these sources it follows the usual custom of small lining types, with several sizes being made for each of several body sizes so that they can readily be used in a variety of cap-and-small-cap combinations. But Linotype cut condensed versions in 1936 as *Card Gothic,* in only one size each of 6- and 12-point.

Poster Gothic (q.v.) is the same design as *Bank Gothic Condensed Medium,* but made in larger sizes and fitted more tightly.

BANK SCRIPT is a formal, traditional Spencerian script, designed in 1895 for BB&S by James West. It is of medium weight, and seems to have served as a model for the heavier *Commercial Script* and the lighter *Typo Script,* which came along later. Like many scripts of the day, it was designed with several lowercase alphabets to be used with the same capitals; of these only the original (No. 1) set has endured, some sizes still being shown in the most recent ATF catalog. No. 2 lowercase had a larger x-height than No. 1, while No. 3 was both higher and wider.

BANNER—see *Gill Sans Cameo Ruled* under Imports in Appendix.

Baltimore Script, Baltimore 333 (12-24pt)

Bamboo, BB&S (10-30pt); TFP-LATF (18pt)

Bam-Stencil, RS&W (18-48pt)

Bank Gothic Light, ATF 532 (6s-18L); Lino (6s-12L); DeLuxe Gothic Light, Inter (6s-12L); Commerce Gothic Light, Ludlow 44-L (6s-18L)
Bank Gothic Medium, ATF 533 (6s-18L); Lino (6s-12L); DeLuxe Gothic Medium, Inter (6s-18L); Commerce Gothic Medium, Ludlow 44-M (6s-18L)
Bank Gothic Bold, ATF 534 (6s-18L)
Bank Gothic Condensed Light, ATF 574 (6s-18L); DeLuxe Gothic Light Condensed, Inter (4s-12L); Commerce Gothic Light Condensed, Ludlow 44-LC (6s-18pt)
Bank Gothic Condensed Medium, ATF 575 (6s-18L); (Univ 6s-18L); Card Gothic Medium, Lino (6,12pt); DeLuxe Gothic Medium Condensed, Inter (4s-12L); Commerce Gothic Medium Condensed, Ludlow 44-MC (6s-18L)
Bank Gothic Condensed Bold, ATF 576 (6s-18L); Card Gothic Bold, Lino (6,12pt)

Bank Script, BB&S-ATF 1540 (14-48pt)
Bank Script No. 2, BB&S-ATF 1712 (14-48pt)
Bank Script No. 3, BB&S-ATF 1713 (18-48pt)

BANK SCRIPT, ATF 24-pt.; 3rd line BANK SCRIPT NO. 2 and 3, BB&S (3, Cliff Helbert)

SQUARED FORMS Printers Being Pleased
Definite Result SECURED

ENORMOUS STRUCTURE
Builders Wrought with 62 Great Care

KINGS MENDING Butterflies Cultivated
Record Best METHODS

BARNHART Superior Copper-Mixed Type
QUALITY All Barnhart Productions

ABCDEFGHIJKLMNOPQRSTUVWXYZ
abcdefghijklmnopqrstuvwxyzfiflfffiffi.,-:; '!?&$1234567890

Ligatures

ff fi fl ffi ffl

Early typefaces had many combined letters or ligatures, in imitation of the work of the scribes. Gradually these disappeared, with only the f-ligatures generally surviving because otherwise f's with long, overhanging hooks would interfere with following tall letters. Typesetting machines provided keys for these f-ligatures, and they became a standard part of almost all fonts of serif styles and some serifless styles, even where not really needed. Where lacking in foundry fonts, Monotype and Linotype have almost always added them to their corresponding fonts.

BARNHART OLDSTYLE was designed in 1906 by Sidney Gaunt for BB&S, followed by the italic and *Barnhart Oldstyle No. 2* the next year. The latter appears to have the same caps as the first face but larger lowercase with shorter ascenders. There is also *Barnhart Lightface,* advertised in 1914 but perhaps designed earlier. This series seems undistinguished, but the original roman and italic were popular enough to be shown as much as twenty years later. Ascenders are long, and some characters have a bit of the irregularity that was popular at that time. The italic apparently was one of the first faces cast by BB&S on its offset body, which provided mortises to avoid overhanging kerns in italic designs.

Barnhart Oldstyle, BB&S-ATF 1544 (6-72pt)
Barnhart Oldstyle No. 2, BB&S-ATF 1545 (6-72pt)
Barnhart Oldstyle Italic, BB&S-ATF 1546 (6-72pt)
Barnhart Lightface, BB&S

P. T. BARNUM is the re-release, in 1933 and again in 1949, of *French Clarendon,* inherited by ATF from one of its predecessors, Marder, Luse & Company. It is a nineteenth-century design which several foundries offered in the same or similar cuttings, under the same name or various other names, including *Italian Condensed.* It is an unusual display letter, featuring greatly emphasized horizontal strokes at the top and bottom of the characters, and is named for Phineas Taylor Barnum, the flamboyant showman, probably because similar styles were commonly used for circus posters. Some intermediate sizes are more condensed than other sizes, and appear to be the same as Bruce's *Italian Condensed No. 341.*

P. T. Barnum, Keystone-ATF 944 (6-48pt); French Clarendon, BB&S-ATF 1729 (6-48pt); also TFP (10-36pt), LATF (14-30pt)

BARNUM HEAVY—see Antiques in Appendix; also *Hidalgo* under Imports in Appendix.
BARRISTER ITALIC—see *Law Italic.*
BARTLETT—see *Bodoni.*
BARTLETT OLDSTYLE—see *Bookman.*

BASKERVILLE ROMAN, ATF 24-pt.

ABCDEFGHIJKLMNOPQRSTUVWXYZ
abcdefghijklmnopqrstuvwxyzfiflffffiffl.,-:;'!?&$1234567890&

BASKERVILLE ITALIC, ATF 18L

ABCDEFGHIJKLMNOPQRSTUVWXYZ ABDEGMNPRY

abcdefghijklmnopqrstuvwxyz &fffiffififlffl ,.-;:'!?& $1234567890

BASKERVILLE, Mono 24-pt.

ABCDEFGHIJKLMNOPQRSTUVWXYZÆŒ 1234567890
abcdefghijklmnopqrstuvwxyzæœffflffiffl1234567890[(&$.,-":;!?)

BASKERVILLE ITALIC, Mono 24-pt.

ABCDEFGHIJKLMNOPQRSTUVWXYZ
abcdefghijklmnopqrstuvwxyzfifffflffi 1234567890&$.,-:;!? 1234567890

BASKERVILLE BOLD, Mono 24-pt.

ABCDEFGHIJKLMNOPQRSTUVWXYZ&
abcdefghijklmnopqrstuvwxyz $1234567890 .,-:;'!?

BASKERVILLE & ITALIC, Lino 14-pt.

ABCDEFGHIJKLMNOPQRSTUVWXYZ&ÆŒ ABCDEFGHIJKLMNOPQRSTUVWXYZ&ÆŒ
ABCDEFGHIJKLMNOPQRSTUVWXYZ&ÆŒ   * † ‡ § ¶ £ | ℔ @ % ℔
abcdefghijklmnopqrstuvwxyzæœfifffflffiffl 1234567890 [($.,-":;!?- —)] 1234567890
abcdefghijklmnopqrstuvwxyzæœfifffflffiffl 1234567890 [($.,-":;!?- —)] 1234567890

BASKERVILLE BOLD & ITALIC, Lino 14-pt.

ABCDEFGHIJKLMNOPQRSTUVWXYZ&
ABCDEFGHIJKLMNOPQRSTUVWXYZ&
abcdefghijklmnopqrstuvwxyzæœfifffflffiffl 1234567890 [($.,-":;!?- —)] * %
abcdefghijklmnopqrstuvwxyzæœfifffflffiffl 1234567890 [($.,-":;!?- —)]

BEACON, Hansen 24-pt.

BEST METHODS HIGHEST IDEAL

26

BASKERVILLE. There are two distinct varieties of Baskerville in America, both based on the types of John Baskerville, distinguished eighteenth-century English printer and typefounder, who was noted for his quest for perfection. His types are based on Caslon and other popular faces of the day, but are more precise and have a little more contrast, with stress more nearly vertical, making them the first transitional designs between oldstyles typified by *Caslon* and moderns typified by *Bodoni.* A consistently noticeable characteristic is the lowercase *g,* with its lower loop not completely closed. All versions have rather long ascenders, and present an appearance of dignity and refinement.

The ATF version, which is called *Baskerville Roman* in foundry specimens but which most typesetters call *American Baskerville,* is produced from strikes (unfinished matrices) brought from Stephenson Blake, English typefounders, in 1915. In England it is known as the Fry Foundry version, and is said to have been cast from original matrices cut about 1795 by Isaac Moore as a close copy of Baskerville's own types. Small sizes to 14-point tend to be rather light and narrow, while sizes from 30-point up have more weight and vigor. Production was discontinued about 1950, perhaps because most specimens didn't show the handsome larger sizes in sufficient detail; it was reinstated in 1957 without the sizes below 18-point.

ATF *Baskerville Italic* was designed in 1915 by Morris F. Benton. It is a handsome face in itself, but has little in common with its roman mate other than adjustment to the narrowness of small sizes. It is not made above 18-point, nor—since it was reinstated—below small 18-point. Compare *Century Catalogue Italic.*

Linotype *Baskerville,* said to be based on original punches which are still in existence, is much like the ATF face, but differs in details of capitals *C, Q, W,* and lowercase *w, y,* and *&.* It was cut in 1926 under the direction of George W. Jones, British typographer. The italic was recut in 1936 under Linotype's program of typographic refinements.

Lanston Monotype *Baskerville* is virtually a duplicate of the English Monotype face, which is based on original letters but is more regularized and has somewhat less contrast between thick and thin strokes than the Fry and Linotype versions. It was cut in 1923 under the direction of Stanley Morison, being derived from the great primer (18-point) size of Baskerville's type, and copied by Lanston in 1931. The Intertype roman face is substantially the same as Monotype except for adaptation to mechanical requirements. But while the Monotype italic is considerably narrower than the roman, on Intertype the two faces are necessarily the same width.

Monotype *Baskerville Italic* has only the swash-like capitals *JKNTYZ* of the original, while both Linotype and Intertype have replaced these letters with regular characters in standard fonts, but offer a variety of swashes as alternates.

Linotype, Monotype, and Intertype each provide their own versions of *Baskerville Bold.* All are similar, but the Monotype version is slightly heavier over all; this version was designed by Sol Hess, and is claimed to have been adapted from an original heavy face created by John Baskerville about 1757 and not generally known. Linotype and Intertype also have bold italics, the former designed by C. H. Griffith in 1939. (*Latin Condensed* was called "Baskerville" in ATF's 1898 book.)

Baskerville Roman, ATF 15 (6-72pt)
Baskerville Italic, ATF 16 (6-18L)
Baskerville, Mono 353 (6-36pt); Lino (6-16pt); Inter (6-24pt)
Baskerville Italic, Mono 3531 (6-36pt); Lino (6-14pt); Inter (6-24pt)
Baskerville Bold, Mono 453 (8-72pt)
Baskerville Bold with Italic, Lino (7-14pt); Inter (6-14,8-12pt)

BAUER BODONI, BAUER CLASSIC—see Imports in Appendix.

BEACON was cast by Hansen in the mid-1910s. Many characters seem to duplicate *Forum,* but a number of others are distinctly different.

Beacon, Hansen (10-36pt)

BELAIR—see *Park Avenue.*

BELL, Mono 24-pt.

ABCDEFGHIJKLMNOPQRSTUVWXYZ 1234567890$
abcdefghijklmnopqrstuvwxyz fiffflffiffl .,-:;!?'' ÆŒæœ()[]

BELL ITALIC, Mono 24-pt.

ABCDEFGHIJKLMNOPQRSTUVWXYZ 1234567890$
abcdefghijklmnopqrstuvwxyz fiffflffiffl .,-:;?!''()&ŒÆæœ
AKNTV æœh ct ft st

BELL GOTHIC & BOLD, Lino 8-pt.

ABCDEFGHIJKLMNOPQRSTUVWXYZ&ÆŒ abcdefghijklmnopqrstuvwxyzææfiflffffiffl 1234567890$£,.:;-'?!-|— ...()*†‡¶§[]% 1/8 1/4 3/8 1/2 5/8 3/4 7/8
ABCDEFGHIJKLMNOPQRSTUVWXYZ&ÆŒ abcdefghijklmnopqrstuvwxyzææfiflffffiffl 1234567890$£,.:;-'?!-|—... ()*†‡¶§[]% 1/8 1/4 3/8 1/2 5/8 3/4 7/8

BEMBO, Mono 24-pt.

ABCDEFGHIJKLMNOPQRSTUVWXYZ 1234567890
abcdefghijklmnopqrstuvwxyz&$1234567890.,-:;''"!?fiflffffiffl ★†§

BEMBO ITALIC, Mono 24-pt.

ABCDEFGHIJKLMNOPQRSTUVWXYZ ÆŒ $1234567890
abcdefghijklmnopqrstuvwxyz æœ fffiffiflffl [ ]( ),.-;':'!?& 1234567890

BEN FRANKLIN, Keystone 24-pt. (Dave Norton)

ABCDEFGHIJKLMNOPQRSTUVWXYZ&
aabccdefghijklmnopqrsſtuvwxyz.,-:;'!?""
$12345678901234567890£Dr.ThetheandofToC

BEN FRANKLIN CONDENSED, Keystone 24-pt. (Dave Norton)

ABCDEFGHIJKLMNOPQRSTUVWXYZ&.,-:;'!?""()[]¶$1234567890£
aabcdefghijklmnopqrstuvwxyz

BEN FRANKLIN OPEN, Mono (36-pt. at 67%) (Dave Greer)

ABCDEFGHIJKLMNOPQRSTUVWXYZ&
aabccdefghijklmnopqrstuvwxyz.,-:;'!?""
$1234567890ThetheandofTo

BELL as cut by Lanston Monotype in 1940 is a copy of the face of the same name cut in 1930 by English Monotype at the instigation of Stanley Morison, and was originally cut by Richard Austin for the English printer John Bell in 1788. Lanston describes it as a delicate and refined rendering of *Scotch Roman,* but without the unduly heavy capitals and some other objectionable characteristics of that face. English Monotype says the letters are open and inclined to roundness; they possess a certain crispness reflecting a French copperplate engraved inspiration. The face has been referred to as the first English modern face, with its sharply contrasted shading, vertical stress, and the earliest consistently horizontal top serifs on the lowercase.

Bruce Rogers found an unidentified face at Riverside Press in 1900; he called it *Brimmer* and used it to good effect in book work. The same face was called *Mountjoye* by D. B. Updike at the Merrymount Press. It was later identified as *Bell,* and this may have led to its resurrection by English Monotype.

Bell, Mono 402 (8-36pt)
Bell Italic, Mono 4021 (8-30pt)

BELL GOTHIC was developed in 1937 by C. H. Griffith of Mergenthaler Linotype, primarily for use in the New York City telephone directory, but quickly became standard for telephone books nationwide. The aim was to eliminate roman types with objectionably thin serifs and hairlines. *Furlong* and *Market Gothic* were specialized adaptations of this face for newspaper work, the former with special figures and other characters for setting racetrack results, the latter in 1941 with other special characters for stock market details. The basic *Bell Gothic* was also cut by Intertype in 1939.

Compare *No. 11* and *No. 12,* shown under *Numbered Faces,* previously used for directory work.

Bell Gothic with Bold, Lino = Inter (6-8pt)
Furlong Light with Bold, Lino (7pt)
Market Gothic, Lino (6pt)

BEMBO was cut in 1929 by the English Monotype corporation under the direction of Stanley Morison, and shortly thereafter by Lanston Monotype in America. It derives from the first roman type used by Aldus Manutius in the dialogue *De Aetna,* by Pietro Bembo, printed in Venice in 1495. Punches were cut by Francesco Griffo of Bologna, the designer responsible four years later for the first italic types. This face is probably the most popular and successful of the numerous faces revived by Morison as typographic adviser to the English company. Morison attributed its success to the fact that "it was inspired not by writing but by engraving; not script but sculpture." The italic is adapted from a 1524 face of Giovanni Taglienti, and has a natural grace of its own. English Monotype also made *Bembo Bold* and *Bembo Bold Italic.*

Bembo, Mono 405 (8-36pt)
Bembo Italic, Mono 4051 (8-36pt)

BEN FRANKLIN types were originated by Keystone Type Foundry in 1899 (regular and *Open*), with *Condensed* added in 1904, as display faces in the popular irregular style of the time. The *Condensed* is very narrow, little more than half the width of the regular. The Auxiliaries (*Dr. To The the and of* and ornaments) were sold separately, as were the hanging figures, but were typical of many faces of the day. Compare *Blanchard, Buffalo, Post Oldstyle, Roycroft.*

Ben Franklin, Keystone-ATF 807 (6-72pt)
Ben Franklin Condensed, Keystone-ATF 808 (6-120pt)
Ben Franklin Open, Keystone-ATF 809 (12-72pt); Ben Franklin Outline, Mono 44 (14-36pt)
Ben Franklin Initials, Keystone (36-84pt)

BENEDICTINE & ITALIC, Lino 14-pt. (18-pt. swash)

ABCDEFGHIJKLMNOPQRSTUVWXYZ& 1234 1234 ABCDEFGHIJKLMNOPQRSTUVWXYZ&
ABCDEFGHIJKLMNOPQRSTUVWXYZ& 1234 1234

abcdefghijklmnopqrstuvwxyzfiflffffiffl ($$ £,.:;'-'?!*†‡§¶)
abcdefghijklmnopqrstuvwxyzfiflffffiffl ($$ £,.:;'-'?! †‡§¶)

ABCDEGJMNPRTUY

BENEDICTINE BOOK & ITALIC, Lino 14-pt. (18-pt. swash)

ABCDEFGHIJKLMNOPQRSTUVWXYZ&1234 1234 ABCDEFGHIJKLMNOPQRSTUVWXYZ&
ABCDEFGHIJKLMNOPQRSTUVWXYZ& 1234 1234

abcdefghijklmnopqrstuvwxyzfiflffffiffl ($$ £,.:;'-'?!*†‡§¶)
abcdefghijklmnopqrstuvwxyzfiflffffiffl ($$ £,.:;'-'?! †‡§¶)

ABCDEGJMNPRTUY

BENEDICTINE BOLD & ITALIC, Lino 14-pt.

ABCDEFGHIJKLMNOPQRSTUVWXYZ&123 123
ABCDEFGHIJKLMNOPQRSTUVWXYZ& 123 123

abcdefghijklmnopqrstuvwxyzfiflffffiffl ($$ £,.:;'-'?!*†‡§¶)
abcdefghijklmnopqrstuvwxyzfiflffffiffl ($$ £,.:;'-'?!*†‡§¶)

BENTON, ATF 24-pt.

ABCDEFGHIJKLMNOPQRSTUVWXYZ&
abcdefghijklmnopqrstuvwxyz(.,-:;"!?)$1234567890

BERLIN ANTIQUE & ITALIC, Lino 14-pt.

ABCDEFGHIJKLMNOPQRSTUVWXYZ& ,.:;?!(|)*''-—ÆŒtb
ABCDEFGHIJKLMNOPQRSTUVWXYZ& ,.:;?!( )*''-—ÆŒtb
abcdefghijklmnopqrstuvwxyz fi fl ff ffi ffl æ œ £ $1234567890
abcdefghijklmnopqrstuvwxyz fi fl ff ffi ffl œ œ £ $1234567890

BERNHARD BOOKLET, ATF 24- & 18-pt. (Gary Metras)

ABCDEFGHIJKLMNOPQRSTUVWXYZ&
abcdefghijklmnopqrstuvwxyz   .,-"""";!?§ $1234567890¢

BERNHARD BOOKLET ITALIC, ATF 24-pt.

ABCDEFGHIJKLMNOPQRSTUVWXYZ& Th
abcdefghijklmnopqrstuvwxyz $1234567890£ ,,::-'''!?''

30

BENEDICTINE was designed for Mergenthaler Linotype in 1915. It was adapted by Joseph E. Hill, under the direction of Edward E. Bartlett, from the types of Plato de Benedictis, an Italian master printer of the fifteenth century, who produced some thirty-three books between 1487 and 1495. Thus it represents the period of the Italian Renaissance, when artists and master craftsmen were creating beautiful things under the inspiration of classic architecture, fine manuscripts and paintings. Compare *Medieval*.

Benedictine with Italic, Lino (6-36 and 6-30pt)
Benedictine Book with Italic, Lino (6-36 and 6-30pt)
Benedictine Bold with Italic, Lino (6-36 and 6-30pt)

BENTON was designed by Morris F. Benton in 1930, under the name *Cambridge,* but was not released until 1934, when the name became *Benton*. It is similar to *Baskerville* and other faces; but has a number of distinctive little details of its own, such as the almost calligraphic foot on the *d* and *u*. The font has no f-ligatures—only the minimum number of characters shown in the specimen.

Benton, ATF 566 (6-72pt) or Whitehall (8-48pt)

This face was the only one of more than two hundred designs by Morris Benton to bear his name. It was discontinued some years after its introduction, then reintroduced in 1953 under the name *Whitehall;* the new name was taken from a New York telephone exchange, before the days of all-numerical dialing. According to a foundry spokesman, it was renamed because too many type names start with A, B, and C, and too many tons of type would have to be moved on stockroom shelves to put it in proper alphabetical order. The ban on *ABC* names was later forgotten, before *Americana, Brush, Craw Clarendon,* and others came along.

An italic was designed for *Benton,* and carried as far as pattern plates and trial castings, but was never completed.

BERLIN ANTIQUE was cut by Linotype in 1910 or earlier. The name suggests that it was derived from a German source, and it is similar to a face known there as *Romana* but also common elsewhere under other names. It is a bold face compatible with mid-nineteenth-century romans known generally as *French Old Style* or *Elzevir,* which were also the inspiration for *DeVinne* (q.v.). Intertype has *Remson Bold,* a similar face.

Berlin Antique with Italic, Lino (10-14)

BERNHARD BOOKLET and *Italic* were designed by Lucian Bernhard in 1932; he had previously drawn the *Bernhard Gothic* series for ATF after coming to this country from Germany where he had designed a number of successful typefaces. These new faces are somewhat similar to his *Bernhard Roman* and *Lucian* series done there (see Imports in Appendix), featuring small lowercase and tall ascenders. In 1937 several characters were redesigned, and it was reissued as *Bernhard Modern Roman* and *Italic* (q.v.).

Bernhard Booklet, ATF 559 (8-72pt)
Bernhard Booklet Italic, ATF 563 (8-72pt)

BERNHARD CURSIVE—see Imports in Appendix.

BERNHARD FASHION, ATF 24-pt.

ABCDEFGHIJKLMNOPQRSTUVWXYZ A A

abcdefghijklmnopqrstuvwxyz$$1234567890.,-:;` !?&«» E E N S W

BERNHARD GOTHIC LIGHT, ATF 24-pt.

ABCDEFGHIJKLMNOPQRSTUVWXYZ& $1234567890

abcdefghijklmnopqrstuvwxyz.,-:;'!?1234567890 ❖ EKSaekrsuz

BERNHARD GOTHIC LIGHT ITALIC, ATF 24-pt. (Frank Anderson)

ABBCDDEEEFFGHHIJKKLMNOPPQRRSSTUVWXYZ&

aabcdeefghijkklmnopqrrsstuuvwxyz 1234567890 ,;:.-'!?'

BERNHARD GOTHIC MEDIUM, ATF 24-pt. (Rick von Holdt)

ABCDEEFGHIJKKLMNOPQRSSTUVWXYZ&

aabcdeefghijkklmnopqrrsstuuvwxyz th Th

$$1234567890$1234567890·'.,:;-'!?❖

BERNHARD GOTHIC MEDIUM ITALIC, ATF 24-pt.

ABCDEFGHIJKLMNOPQRSTUVWXYZ&

abcdefghijklmnopqrstuvwxyz!?$ "":;.,- 1234567890

The HOPEFUL Doke's Sauerkraut

BERNHARD GOTHIC MEDIUM CONDENSED, ATF (96-pt. at 25%, with 18-pt. Alternates and Oldstyle Figures) (Rick von Holdt)

ABCDEFGHIJKLMNOPQRSTUVWXYZ AEFKMNW

abcdefghijklmnopqrstuvwxyz .,;:-?!"¢$$& 1234567890 $1234567890

BERNHARD GOTHIC HEAVY, ATF 24-pt. (part reduced)

ABCDEFGHIJKLMNOPQRSTUVWXYZ EK a k r s u

abcdefghijklmnopqrstuvwxyz.,-:;'""!?&$❖·$1234567890

BERNHARD GOTHIC EXTRA HEAVY, ATF 24-pt.

ABCDEEFGHIJKKLMNOPQRSTUVWXYZ& · ❖

abcdefghijklmnopqrsstuvwxyz.,:;-'!? $1234567890

BERNHARD FASHION was designed by Lucian Bernhard for ATF in 1929. It is a very delicate sans-serif, useful for fashion advertising and social printing. It has the unusual feature of different alignments for caps and lowercase, with the latter positioned normally on the type body, but with the oversize caps positioned lower and occupying almost the entire body. A bold weight was tried but never completed. The Intertype copy was made in 1938.

BERNHARD GOTHIC was one of the first contemporary American sans-serifs, designed in 1929-30 by Lucian Bernhard for ATF to counter the impor-tation of the new European designs such as *Futura* and *Kabel*. It features long ascenders and a number of unusual design details, which perhaps prevented it from achieving the popularity of other such faces. Capitals are low-waisted, with the crossbars or arms of *E, F,* and *H* being below center. *M* is widely splayed in some weights. Lowercase *a* is roman in design, and the cross-stroke of *t* is wide and below the mean line. All but the *Title* versions have a number of alternate characters, later discontinued. The comma, semicolon and apos-trophe, usually comparable, have three different forms.

Bernhard Gothic was made only by ATF, but some weights could be simulated with special characters of Monotype *Sans-Serif* and Ludlow *Tempo*. The Title versions, several sizes of caps on each body in the manner of Copperplate Gothics, were added in 1936, and copied by Intertype as *Greeting Gothic*. Around 1938 *Bernhard Gothic Medium Condensed* was added.

BERNHARD MODERN ROMAN. In 1937 several characters of *Bernhard Booklet* and *Italic* (q.v.) were redrawn by Lucian Bernhard, the original designer, at the request of ATF, and it was reissued as *Bernhard Modern Roman* and *Italic*. In 1938 *Bernhard Modern Bold* and *Bold Italic* were added, also drawn by Bernhard. They are lively and sparkling faces, precise but not mechanical. Since *H* and *m,* the characters with the series number stamped on the shoulder, were not redesigned, some fonts of *Bernhard Modern Roman* appear to have been produced with the series number (559) of the earlier *Bernhard Booklet*. Compare *Cochin;* also *Drew*.

Bernhard Fashion, ATF 527 (12-72pt); Inter (12-18pt); (Univ 12-48pt)

Bernhard Gothic Light, ATF 528 (6-120pt); also Bernhard Gothic Light Title, ATF 655 (6s-12L); Greeting Gothic Light, Inter (6s-6L); (Novelty Gothic Light, Univ 6-72pt)
Bernhard Gothic Light Italic, ATF 545 (6-72pt); (Novelty Gothic Light Italic, Univ 6-48pt)
Bernhard Gothic Medium, ATF 525 (6-144pt); also Bernhard Gothic Medium Title, ATF 656 (6s-12L); Greeting Gothic Medium, Inter (6s-6L); (Novelty Gothic Medium, Univ 6-72pt)
Bernhard Gothic Medium Italic, ATF 537 (6-72pt); (Novelty Gothic Medium Italic, Univ 6-48pt)
Bernhard Gothic Medium Condensed, ATF 672 (12-96pt)
Bernhard Gothic Heavy, ATF 530 (8-120pt); (Novelty Gothic Bold, Univ 8-72pt)
Bernhard Gothic Extra Heavy, ATF 546 (12-72pt); (Novelty Gothic Extra Bold, Univ 12-72pt)

Bernhard Modern Roman, ATF 668 (8-72pt)
Bernhard Modern Italic, ATF 669 (8-72pt)
Bernhard Modern Bold, ATF 670 (8-72pt)
Bernhard Modern Bold Italic, ATF 671 (8-72pt)

BERNHARD MODERN ROMAN, ATF 24-pt.

ABCDEFGHIJKLMNOPQRSTUVWXYZ
abcdefghijklmnopqrstuvwxyz.,-:;""""!?§$1234567890¢&

BERNHARD MODERN ITALIC, ATF 24-pt.

ABCDEFGHIJKLMNOPQRSTUVWXYZ
abcdefghijklmnopqrstuvwxyz.,-:;""""!?&Th£$1234567890

BERNHARD MODERN BOLD, ATF 24-pt.

ABCDEFGHIJKLMNOPQRSTUVWXYZ
abcdefghijklmnopqrstuvwxyz.,-:;""""!?§$1234567890¢&

BERNHARD MODERN BOLD ITALIC, ATF 24-pt.

ABCDEFGHIJKLMNOPQRSTUVWXYZ
abcdefghijklmnopqrstuvwxyz.,-:;""""!?&ff$1234567890¢

BERNHARD TANGO, ATF 24-pt.

ABCDEFGHIJKLMNOPQRSTUVWXYZ
abcdefghijklmnopqrstuvwxyz$1234567890.,-:;""''!?&

BERNHARD TANGO SWASH, ATF 30-pt.

ABCDEFGHIJKLMNOPQ
RSTUVWXYZ D

Original D

BERTHAM, Goudy 16-pt.

A B C D E F G H I J K L M N O P Q R S T U V W X Y Z & . , ' ; : ! ? ·
a b c d e f g h i j k l m n o p q r s t u v w x y z fi ff fl ct st 1 2 3 4 5 6 7 8 9 0

BETON MEDIUM & BOLD, Inter 14-pt.

ABCDEFGHIJKLMNOPQRSTUVWXYZ æœÆŒ $1234567890
ABCDEFGHIJKLMNOPQRSTUVWXYZ æœÆŒ $1234567890
abcdefghijklmnopqrstuvwxyz fi fl ff ffi ffl ,.-;':'!?() @℔&£ % []*†|‡|| §¶——⅛¼⅜½⅝¾⅞
abcdefghijklmnopqrstuvwxyz fi fl ff ffi ffl ,.-;':'!?() @℔&£% []*†‡ §¶-——⅛¼⅜½⅝¾⅞

BETON WIDE & EXTRA BOLD, Inter 14-pt.

ABCDEFGHIJKLMNOPQRSTUVWXYZ !?() @℔&£ æœÆŒ $1234567890
ABCDEFGHIJKLMNOPQRSTUVWXYZ !?() @℔&£ æœÆŒ $1234567890
abcdefghijklmnopqrstuvwxyz ,.-;':' fi fl ff ffi ffl % [] *†|‡|| §¶-⅛¼⅜½⅝
abcdefghijklmnopqrstuvwxyz ,.-;':' fi fl ff ffi ffl % [] *† ‡ §¶-⅛¼⅜½⅝
$1234567890ijtyAKQ **$1234567890ijtyAKQ**

BETON EXTRA BOLD & OBLIQUE, Inter 12-pt.

ABCDEFGHIJKLMNOPQRSTUVWXYZ $1234567890 @ ℔ & % £ [] * † | ‡ || § ¶ -- — æ œ Æ
ABCDEFGHIJKLMNOPQRSTUVWXYZ $1234567890 @ ℔ & % £ [] * † ‡ || § ¶ -- — æ œ Æ
abcdefghijklmnopqrstuvwxyz fi fl ff ffi ffl ,.-;'-'!?() / ¢'"° ⅛¼⅜½⅝¾⅞⅓⅔
abcdefghijklmnopqrstuvwxyz fi fl ff ffi ffl ,.-;'-'!?() / ¢'"° ⅛¼⅜½⅝¾⅞⅓⅔

BEWICK ROMAN, ATF 24-pt. (Jane Roberts)

ABCDEFGHIJKLMNOPQRSTUVWXYZ ACGOO
abcdefghijklmnopqrstuvwxyzffttctqustℬ1234567890§!?.,:;'-¶

BERNHARD TANGO, designed by Lucian Bernhard about 1931 but not cut until 1934, is a formalized italic with a number of unusual cursive features, such as the way upstrokes of *BPR* start from the bottom serif and are separate from the main stroke. A companion series of swash letters is made considerably oversize for each size of *Tango,* which is known in Europe as *Aigrette.*

Bernhard Tango, ATF 582 (18-72pt)
Bernhard Tango Swash Capitals, ATF 593 (30-120pt)

BERT BLACK was designed by Gilbert P. Farrar of Intertype in 1928, and privately cast for use as display heads in *Collier's Weekly* magazine. No specimen is available. See *Collier Heading.*

BERTHAM was Frederic W. Goudy's one-hundredth type design, done in 1936. He relates that the design was completed, matrices cut, and type cast within sixteen working days of receipt of a request to write an article for *The American Printer* on his hundredth type. It is based on a fifteenth-century type used to print Ptolemy's *Geographica,* and is named for and dedicated to Goudy's wife, Bertha M. Goudy—combining her first name and middle initial.

Bertham, Goudy (12-24pt)

BETON is a square-serif face designed by Heinrich Jost for Bauer Typefoundry in Germany, copied by Intertype in 1934-36. *Beton Wide* was added by Intertype in 1937 to fit two-letter matrices with the *Extra Bold.* Like the other members, it features several unusual design details, but several alternate characters and a set of redesigned figures are furnished to more nearly approximate American square-serif designs. Unlike other such faces, serifs are bracketed on strokes which would be thin in contrasting romans.

Bauer also made *Beton Light, Medium Condensed, Bold Condensed,* and *Open* versions, some of which have been copied here by secondary suppliers. *Beton Open* has sometimes though incorrectly been called *Stymie Open.* (See Imports in Appendix.)

Beton Wide, Inter (8-24pt)
Beton Medium and Italic, Inter (8-24pt; italic 8-14pt)
Beton Bold, Inter (8-36pt)
Beton Extra Bold and Oblique, Inter (8-36pt, oblique 8-24pt)
Beton Bold Condensed, Inter (not confirmed)
Other Betons—see Imports in Appendix.

BEWICK ROMAN was designed by Will Bradley in 1904 and issued by ATF the following year. It is a quaint display type with a number of unusual characteristics. Several capitals have both wide and narrow versions, although generally the face is rather narrow; there are also several tied characters and ornaments in the font, as was common with nineteenth-century designs. Compare *Rogers, Vanden Houten.*

Bewick Roman, ATF 18 (6-72pt)

BINNY OLD STYLE, Mono 24-pt.

ABCDEFGHIJKLMNOPQRSTUVWXYZ&
abcdefghijklmnopqrstuvwxyzfifflflffiffl
$1234567890 $1234567890 .,-:;'!?

BINNY ITALIC, Mono 24-pt.

ABCDEFGHIJKLMNOPQRSTUVWXYZÆŒ
abcdefghijklmnopqrstuvwxyzæœfifflflffiffl&$.,-' :;!?

BIXLER ROMAN, Bixler

ABCDEFGHIJKLMNOPQRSTUVWXYZ& 1234567890
abcdefghijklmnopqrstuvwxyz.,;:-◦◦()fifl$ꝗ·[]!?¹²³⁴⁵⁶⁷⁸⁹⁰

BIZARRE BOLD, BB&S 24-pt.

Dedicated MINES

BLAIR, ATF 18L

ABCDEFGHIJKLMNOPQRSTUVWXYZ&
$1234567890 .,-:;'!?

CONDENSED BLAIR, ATF 18L

ABCDEFGHIJKLMNOPQRSTUVWXYZ &$1234567890.,-:;'!?

BLANCHARD, Inland 18-pt.

ABCDEFGHJKLIMNOPQRSTUVWXYZ&⌀
abcdefghijklmnopqrstuvzwxy$?1234567890

BLANCHARD ITALIC, Inland 24-pt. (Dan X. Solo)

AABBCDDEFGHIJKLMNOPPQ
RRRSSTGUVWXYZ&1234567890
abcdefghijklmnopqrſstuvwxyz

LIGHT FACE BLANCHARD, Inland 24-pt. (Dan X. Solo)

ABCDEEFGHIJKLMNOPQRRSTUV
WXYZ& 1234567890
aabcdefghhijklmmnnopqrsstuvwxyz

BINNY OLD STYLE has been a popular Monotype face since it was cut for that machine in 1908. McMurtrie calls it "one of the best faces available for everyday 'bread and butter' use in sizes 14-point and below; in larger sizes it is most unsatisfactory." Monotype adapted it from a face of the same name (originally known as *Old Style No. 77*) produced by MS&J about 1886. This in turn was based on a face cut in Scotland about 1863 as a modernization of Caslon. It was named for Archibald Binny, who with James Ronaldson established the first permanent typefoundry in America—a firm which eventually became MS&J and then ATF. In 1900 ATF advertised the face as "an original and beautiful series of old style letter adapted to the printing of fine books and magazines." Monotype also cut a modified version for Curtis Publishing Company; and another version, slightly larger and wider and derived from another foundry source, as *Overgrown No. 80,* which was used for text in *Ladies' Home Journal* beginning in 1935.

Binny Old Style No. 77 and Italic, ATF; Binny Old Style and Italic, Mono 21 and 2111 (4½-36pt)
Binny Old Style Modified and Italic, Mono 321EFG (5½pt)
Overgrown No. 80 and Italic, ATF (5½-12pt); Mono 221EFG (9pt)

BIXLER ROMAN was designed in 1968 by Mike Bixler, then a student at Rochester Institute of Technology. Matrices were cut in Japan and the face was cast privately.

Bixler Roman, Bixler, private

BIZARRE BOLD was originally known as *Edwards,* designed in 1895 by Nicholas J. Werner for Inland Type Foundry. It was renamed, most appropriately, by BB&S in 1925 after that foundry took over Inland. A companion face called *Inland,* by the same designer, was produced at the same time using some of the same characters but with even more unusual twists to others. Compare *Francis.*

Bizarre Bold, BB&S-ATF 1548 (6-60pt)
Inland, Inland (8-60pt)

BLAIR was advertised in 1900 by Inland Type Foundry as new and original, calling it "an exact imitation of the small gothic letter now so popular with engravers for stylish stationery." Its production was continued by ATF until the 1950s. It is similar to *Copperplate Gothic Light,* but without the tiny serifs of that face. *Litho Gothic* is the same design but with lowercase; *Mitchell* is the same design but slightly heavier.

The condensed version was produced in 1903 or earlier. Hansen copied Blair as *Card Gothic No. 2.* Compare *Lightline Gothic.*

Blair, Inland-ATF 19 (6s-24L); Card Gothic No. 2, Hansen (6s-12L)
Condensed Blair, Inland-ATF 111 (6s-24L)

BLANCHARD is one of the many display letters with irregular edges produced around the turn of the century for use where strength, boldness, and an effect of solidity were wanted. The roman and italic were issued by Inland Type Foundry in 1900, with other versions added the following year. Curiously, only the italic and condensed forms seem to have survived long enough to be included in ATF's inventory of matrices when numbers were assigned. Compare *Ben Franklin, Buffalo, Roycroft.*

Blanchard, Inland (6-72pt)
Blanchard Italic, Inland-ATF 21 (6-72pt)
Condensed Blanchard, Inland-ATF 112 (6-72pt)
Light Face Blanchard, Inland (6s-60pt)
Blanchard Bold Italic, Inland
Blanchard Condensed Bold, Inland

CONDENSED BLANCHARD, Inland (48-pt. at 50%) (John Horn)

ABCDEFGHIJKLMNOPQRSTUVWXYZ&!?',.;-.
abcdefghijklmnopqrstuvwxyz $1234567890

ABCDEFGHIJKLMNOPQRSTUVWXYZ
abcdefghijklmnopqrstuvwxyzfiflffffiffl.,-:;'!?&$1234567890 ""'""
ATF

ABCDEFGHIJKLMNOPQRSTUVWXYZ& ''""''
abcdefghijklmnopqrstuvvwwxyz 1234567890$.,-:;'!?&fiflffffiffl

ABCDEFGHIJKLMNOPQRSTUVWXYZ&
abcdefghijklmnopqrstuvwxyz $1234567890 .,-:;'!? fiflffffiffl " "

ABCDEFGHIJKLMNOPQRSTUVWXYZ& ., ;:-'' ' "" ''"" ?!
abcdefghijklmnopqrstuvvwwxyz 1234567890$ fi fl ff ffi ffl

ABCDEFGHIJKLMNOPQRSTUVWXYZ abcdefghijklmnopqrstuvwxyz $1234567890

ABCDEFGHIJKLMNOPQRSTUVWXYZ $1234567890&
abcdefghijklmnopqrstuvwxyzffffiflffiffl.,-:;''''""''!? **gjpqy,;Q**
Newspaper Bodoni Bold

ABCDEFGHIJKLMNOPQRSTUVWXYZ $1234567890
abcdefghijklmnopqrstuvwxyz.,-:;'!?&fiflffffiffl fgjpqy''''""***vw***
ABCDMNPRSW
ATF
Ludlow

ABCDEFGHIJKLMNOPQRSTUVWXYZ&
abcdefghijklmnopqrstuvwxyz .,-:;'!? fiflffffiffl æœ
$1234567890 1234567890

BODONI. All versions of this popular type family are based on the work of Giambattista Bodoni, eighteenth-century Italian master printer generally credited with originating the style of letter known as "modern," featuring mechanical perfection of form and more severe contrast between thick and thin strokes than traditional faces.

There have been numerous interpretations of Bodoni's typefaces, but the most popular in America are those drawn by Morris F. Benton for ATF or adapted from his work by other manufacturers. His *Bodoni, Bodoni Italic, Bodoni Book* and *Italic,* and *Bodoni Bold* and *Italic,* introduced by ATF in 1910-11, have been duplicated by several sources, as detailed below. The ATF Bodoni series, with its long descenders, was the first new creation to successfully counter the popularity of standard alignment, introduced around the turn of the century. However, it was inspired by the successful revival of the original version of *Caslon Oldstyle.* Henry L. Bullen encouraged the resurrection of the Bodoni design, first of a series of such recreations, while his Typographic Library at ATF provided the resources for research into the works of the historic master designers.

Monotype brought out its own interpretation of *Bodoni* and *Italic* in 1911. This is its No. 175 series, also based on historic Bodoni types but differing in many details from Benton's design. Notice especially the alternate French oldstyle figures, which depart from the usual style of oldstyle figures; ATF *Bodoni* also has similar alternate figures in small sizes, although they are rarely seen. In 1930 Monotype adapted Benton's Bodoni design as its No. 375 series. Neither 175 nor 375 suffers from the mechanical restrictions of Monotype's standard arrangement, but because *Bodoni Bold* and *Italic* required considerable reproportioning as first cut for that machine, Monotype later brought out *Recut Bodoni Bold* and *Italic,* which by means of a special arrangement are very close to ATF's original design. *Bodoni Book* and *Italic* were adapted to Monotype after special arrangements became more common. Notice the alternate *v* and *w* shown in the specimen of *Bodoni Italic*; these letters were made by ATF in all three weights of italic but not copied by any other source except Monotype *Bodoni Book Italic.* Perhaps because of the lighter *Bodoni Book,* some users apply the name "Bodoni Medium" to the regular weight.

ATF's *Newspaper Bodoni Bold* is the same as *Bodoni Bold,* but with descenders (*gjpqy,;Q* as shown after the *Bodoni Bold* specimen) substantially shortened to permit casting each size on a smaller body, from 36/30 (36-point face on 30-point body) to 144/120. Ludlow *Bodoni Bold* offers similarly shortened descenders in large sizes. ATF *Bodoni Bold Italic* was cast for a while in the 1960s with greatly shortened descenders though not on smaller bodies. Apparently the intention was to reduce the size of kerns and the chance of breakage.

(Bodoni continues)

Bodoni, ATF 22 (6-72pt); Mono 375 (6-72H4); Lino = Inter (6-36pt); APL (14-72pt); Bodoni Trueface, Ludlow 3-T (6-72pt)
Bodoni Italic, ATF 23 (6-72pt); Mono 3751 (6-36pt); Lino = Inter (6-30pt); APL (18-72pt); Bodoni Trueface Italic, Ludlow 3-TI (6-72pt); also Bodoni Italic Cancelled, Lino (12,14)
Bodoni Book, ATF 27 (6-48pt); Mono 875 (6-36pt); Lino = Inter (6-30pt)
Bodoni Book Italic, ATF 28 (6-36pt); Mono 8751 (6-36pt); Lino = Inter (6-30pt)
Bodoni Book Extra Condensed, Lino (18pt)
Bodoni Bold, ATF 24 (6-144pt); Mono 275 (6-72pt); Lino = Inter (6-42pt); APL (14-144pt); Ludlow 3-B (6-96pt); Recut Bodoni Bold, Mono 975 (6-12pt); Bodoni Trueface Bold, Ludlow 3-BT or 3-TB (6-72pt); also Newspaper Bodoni Bold, ATF 24N (36/30-144/120pt)
Bodoni Bold Italic, ATF 25 (6-72pt); Mono 2751 (6-72pt); Lino = Inter (6-36pt); APL (18-72pt); Ludlow 3-BI (6-72pt); Recut Bodoni Bold Italic, Mono 975K (6-12pt); Bodoni Trueface Bold Italic, Ludlow 3-BTI or 3-TBI (6-72pt)
Bodoni and Italic, Mono 175-1751 (5-36pt)

BODONI 175 ITALIC, Mono 24-pt.

ABCDEFGHIJKLMNOPQRSTUVWXYZ&
abcdefghijklmnopqrstuvwxyz fiflffffiffl-.,:;!?'$1234567890

BODONI LIGHT, Ludlow 24-pt.

ABCDEFGHIJKLMNOPQRSTUVWXYZ& . : , ; – ' ' ! ? ( )
abcdefghijklmnopqrstuvwxyz $1234567890 ı 2 3 4 5 6 7 8 9

BODONI LIGHT ITALIC, Ludlow 24-pt.

ABCDEFGHIJKLMNOPQRSTUVWXYZ&
abcdefghijklmnopqrstuvwxyz 1234567890

BODONI MODERN, Ludlow 24-pt. (3rd line—see text)

ABCDEFGHIJKLMNOPQRSTUVWXYZ $1234567890
abcdefghijklmnopqrstuvwxyz ff fi ffi fl ffl ( ) , . - ; ' : ' ! ? — &
RWt4 ı2345789

True-Cut Bodoni

BODONI MODERN ITALIC, Ludlow 24-pt. (3rd line—see text)

ABCDEFGHIJKLMNOPQRSTUVWXYZ $1234567890
abcdefghijklmnopqrstuvwxyz ff fi ffi fl ffl ( ) , . - ; ' : ' ! ? — &
R tfi 7ı 2 3 4 5 6 7 8 9 o

True-Cut Bodoni Italic

BODONI CONDENSED, Lino 24-pt.

ABCDEFGHIJKLMNOPQRSTUVWXYZ&
abcdefghijklmnopqrstuvwxyz 1234567890($,.:;'-'?!)

BODONI BOLD CONDENSED, Mono 24-pt.

ABCDEFGHIJKLMNOPQRSTUVWXYZ&
abcdefghijklmnopqrstuvwxyz ' ; : - ! ? ' 1234567890$ ff fi ffi fl ffl

BODONI BOLD EXTRA CONDENSED, Inter — SLIM BODONI, Inter (60-pt. at 50%)

INTERTYPE MATRIC 12   INTERTYPE MATRICES EXCEL 12

CARD BODONI, ATF 24s (Stan Kroeger)

ABCDEFGHIJKLMNOPQRSTUVWXYZ
1234567890&$.,-'':;!?

Ludlow's first offering in this family was *Bodoni Light* and *Italic,* designed by Robert Wiebking and introduced in 1923; it was similar to Monotype *Bodoni No. 175* but lighter. Five years later Ludlow brought out *True-Cut Bodoni* and *Italic,* designed by Wiebking from original Bodoni works in Chicago's Newberry Library. The serifs and hairlines of this face turned out to be too delicate for practical use, so in 1936 Robert H. Middleton modified the design and it was reissued as *Bodoni Modern* and *Italic.* The basic design is the same except for a few redrawn letters, but it is recut a little narrower and with slightly more strength to the hairlines. This is probably the most faithful recreation of Giambattista Bodoni's original types. The third lines of specimens of the latter face, both roman and italic, show some of the original *True-Cut Bodoni* characters before they were redesigned.

Ludlow *Bodoni Bold* and *Italic,* cut by Wiebking before 1930, were replaced by *Bodoni Trueface Bold* and *Italic,* close copies of the Benton face. *Bodoni Trueface* and *Italic* in the regular weight were also added.

Bodoni Bold Condensed was drawn by Sol Hess for Monotype in 1934, and other versions were designed independently by some other sources; such a face was drawn by the ATF staff in 1933 but not produced. The basic Bodoni designs were narrowed by Linotype and Intertype in the larger sizes to fit early mechanical restrictions; when later machines permitted full width faces in these sizes, the narrow versions were renamed *Bodoni Condensed* and *Bodoni Book Extra Condensed.* Intertype also cut *Bodoni Bold Extra Condensed* and *Slim Bodoni.*

ATF's *Card Bodoni* and *Card Bodoni Bold,* drawn by Benton in 1912-16, are adaptations of the regular faces to all-cap fonts, with several sizes cast on 6- and 12-point and larger bodies for use on stationery and forms; notice the redrawn *J, Q,* comma, and semicolon. *Engravers Bodoni* is a wide version of *Bodoni Bold* made the same way; it was drawn by Benton in 1926 but apparently not introduced until 1933.

Bodoni Bold Shaded was designed by Benton in 1912 for ATF. *Bodoni Open,* also by Benton in 1918, was discontinued after a time and reintroduced in 1930. *Bodoni Bold Panelled* was designed by Sol Hess for Monotype in 1928; it has no lowercase, points or figures, only the basic characters shown. All three faces are adaptations of *Bodoni Bold.*

(Bodoni continues)

Bodoni Light, Ludlow 3-L (12-42pt)
Bodoni Light Italic, Ludlow 3-LI (12-48pt)
Bodoni Modern, Ludlow 3-M (6-72pt)
Bodoni Modern Italic, Ludlow 3-MI (6-72pt)
True-Cut Bodoni, Ludlow 3-TC (8-48pt)
True-Cut Bodoni Italic, Ludlow 3-TCI (8-48pt)
Bodoni Condensed, Lino = Inter (24,30pt)
Slim Bodoni or Bodoni Thin, Inter (18-60pt)
Bodoni Bold Condensed, Mono 775 (14-72H4); Lino = Inter (18-36pt); APL (24,30pt); Ludlow 3-BC (14-72pt)
Bodoni Bold Extra Condensed, Inter (60pt)
Card Bodoni, ATF 43 (6s-24L)
Card Bodoni Bold, ATF 443 (6s-24L)
Engravers Bodoni, ATF 501 (6s-24L)
Bodoni Bold Shaded, ATF 26 (8-48pt); Mono 194 (12-36pt)
Bodoni Open, ATF 544 (10-48pt)
Bodoni Bold Panelled, Mono 575 (18-60pt)

ENGRAVERS BODONI, ATF 18L (Leonard Bahr)

ABCDEFGHIJKLMNOPQRSTUVWXYZ
&.,:;""!? 1234567890

BODONI BOLD SHADED, ATF 18-pt. (Al Siegel)

ABCDEFGHIJKLMNOPQRSTUVWXYZ
abcdefghijklmnopqrstuvwxyz ?!&$1234567890

BODONI OPEN, ATF 24-pt. (slightly spaced)

ABCDEFGHIJKLMNOPQRSTUVWXYZ&.,-:;!?""
abcdefghijklmnopqrstuvwxyzff fi fl ffi ffl$1234567890

BODONI BOLD PANELLED, Mono 18-pt.

ABCDEFGHIJKLMNOPQRSTUVWXYZ&OII

ULTRA BODONI, Mono 24-pt.

ABCDEFGHIJKLMNOPQRSTUVWXYZ&
abcdefghijklmnopqrstuvwxyz.,-:;'"!?
$1234567890

ULTRA BODONI ITALIC, Mono 24-pt.

ABCDEFGHIJKLMNOPQRSTUVWXYZ
abcdefghijklmnopqrstuvwxyz.-,:;'' !?$&
1234567890

ULTRA BODONI CONDENSED, ATF 18-pt.

ABCDEFGHIJKLMNOPQRSTUVWXYZ&
abcdefghijklmnopqrstuvwxyz $123456789

ULTRA BODONI EXTRA CONDENSED, ATF 24-pt.

ABCDEFGHIJKLMNOPQRSTUVWXYZ&
abcdefghijklmnopqrstuvwxyz $1234567890 .,-:;'!? '

BODONI MODERN & ITALIC, Inter 14-pt.

ABCDEFGHIJKLMNOPQRSTUVWXYZ $1234567890 æœÆŒ
ABCDEFGHIJKLMNOPQRSTUVWXYZ $1234567890 æœÆŒ
abcdefghijklmnopqrstuvwxyz fiflffffiffl ,.-;':'!?()@ ℔ & £-—
abcdefghijklmnopqrstuvwxyz fiflffffiffl ,.-;':'!?() ℔ & £-—
[ ] * † | ❖ ‖ § ℭ % ⅛ ¼ ⅜ ½ ⅝ ¾ ⅞

POSTER BODONI & ITALIC, Lino 14-pt.

ABCDEFGHIJKLMNOPQRSTUVWXYZ&
ABCDEFGHIJKLMNOPQRSTUVWXYZ&
abcdefghijklmnopqrstuvwxyz 1234567890 ($£,.:;'-'?!*)
abcdefghijklmnopqrstuvwxyz 1234567890

BODONI CAMPANILE, Ludlow 24-pt.

ABCDEFGHIJKLMNOPQRSTUVWXYZ & $1234567890
abcdefghijklmnopqrstuvwxyz [] () ,.-;':'!? — ¾ ⅔ ½ ¼ ⅓ %

Ultra Bodoni and its variations are now well established under the Bodoni name, but historically they hardly belong here, being more closely related to the nineteenth-century English "fat" faces. One reviewer called *Ultra Bodoni* "an old Bruce face with a few redrawn characters." Actually it was entirely redrawn, but the resemblance is there. The Ultra Bodonis do not have the long ascenders and descenders of other Bodonis, and the transition from thick to thin is more abrupt. *Ultra Bodoni* and *Italic,* designed by Morris Benton in 1928 for ATF, were also made by Monotype; Intertype made them as *Bodoni Modern* and *Italic.*

Linotype has *Poster Bodoni* and *Italic,* similar to *Ultra Bodoni* but with somewhat heavier hairlines, designed by C. H. Griffith. Ludlow's *Bodoni Black* and *Italic,* designed by Robert H. Middleton in 1930, are distinctly different but generally comparable; a later *Condensed* version was also designed by Middleton. ATF's *Ultra Bodoni Condensed,* drawn by Benton in 1930, is rarely seen but his *Ultra Bodoni Extra Condensed* of 1933 has enjoyed some limited use. *Onyx* (q.v.), called *Poster Bodoni Compressed* by Linotype, is comparable. Ludlow's *Bodoni Campanile* (called *Palisade* on Intertype) and *Italic* are somewhat similar to *Onyx,* but less formal; they were designed by Middleton in 1936 and 1942 respectively.

Bartlett was Damon Type Foundry's name for its copy of the Bodoni series. Compare *Louvaine, French Round Face, Suburban French.* Also see *Bauer Bodoni* under Imports in Appendix.

Ultra Bodoni, ATF 518 (6-120pt); Mono 675 (6-72pt); Bodoni Modern, Inter (8-36pt)
Ultra Bodoni Italic, ATF 516 (6-72pt); Mono 6751 (6-72pt); Bodoni Modern Italic, Inter (8-30pt)
Ultra Bodoni Condensed, ATF 562 (18-72pt)
Ultra Bodoni Extra Condensed, ATF 573 (12-72pt)
Poster Bodoni, Lino (8-36pt); APL (18-144pt)
Poster Bodoni Italic, Lino (8-24pt); APL (18-60pt)
Poster Bodoni Compressed, Lino (18-36pt = Onyx)
Bodoni Campanile, Ludlow 3-BEC (14-96pt); Palisade, Inter (18-48pt)
Bodoni Campanile Italic, Ludlow 3-BECI (18-48pt)
Bodoni Black, Ludlow 3-H (6-72pt)
Bodoni Black Italic, Ludlow 3-HI (12-72pt)
Bodoni Black Condensed, Ludlow 3-HC (18-48pt)

BODONI CAMPANILE ITALIC, Ludlow 24-pt.

ABCDEFGHIJKLMNOPQRSTUVWXYZ&
abcdefghijklmnopqrstuvwxyz 1234567890

BODONI BLACK, Ludlow 24-pt.

ABCDEFGHIJKLMNOPQRSTUVWXYZ
abcdefghijklmnopqrstuvwxyz&.,-:;‘’!?✦—()[]%
1234567890ᶜ½¼⅓¾⅔

BODONI BLACK ITALIC, Ludlow 24-pt.

ABCDEFGHIJKLMNOPQRSTUVWXYZ
abcdefghijklmnopqrstuvwxyz.,-:;‘’!?•—()[]
$1234567890&% ABDMNPWY

BODONI BLACK CONDENSED, Ludlow 24-pt.

ABCDEFGHIJKLMNOPQRSTUVWXYZ& . : , ; - ‘ ’ ! ? ( ) [ ] — ✦
abcdefghijklmnopqrstuvwxyz 1234567890$ % ¼ ⅓ ½ ⅔ ¾

43

BOLD ANTIQUE, ATF 24-pt.

ABCDEFGHIJKLMNOPQRSTUVWXYZ&
abcdefghijklmnopqrstuvwxyzfffiflffiffl
1234567890$.,-:;!?'

BOLD ANTIQUE CONDENSED, Mono 24-pt.

ABCDEFGHIJKLMNOPQRSTUVWXYZ&
abcdefghijklmnopqrstuvwxyz $1234567890 .,-:;'!?

BOLD FACE NO. 1, Lino 7-pt. (Al Siegel)

ABCDEFGHIJKLMNOPQRSTUVWXYZ Œ Æ Ib
abcdefghijklmnopqrstuvwxyz fi fl ff æ æ 1234567890 $ & ! ?

BOLD FACE NO. 2, Lino 10-pt.

ABCDEFGHIJKLMNOPQRSTUVWXYZ& 1234567890
abcdefghijklmnopqrstuvwxyz fiflffffiffl [($£,.:;'-'?!*†‡§¶)]

BOLD FACE NO. 9, Lino 12L

ABCDEFGHIJKLMNOPQRSTUVWXYZ1234567890$.,-:;''!? ( ) &

BOLD FACE NO. 520 & ITALIC, ATF 12-pt.

PROMINENT PHOTO ARTIST   *SIXTEENTH CENTURY*
Received Honorable Mention National S *Architecture Edifice Builder Replaced*
Given It $1234567890 First Prize *Costing $1234567890 Dollars*

BOLD SCRIPT, ATF (36-pt. at 67%) (Dave Norton)

ABCDEFGHIJKLMNOPQRSTUVWXYZ&&Co.$1234567890
abcdefghijklmnopqrstuvwxyz.,-:;'!?

BOOKLET OLDSTYLE, ATF 18-pt.

SHE SEES HOMES SHE COMMON SENSE HAS
lasting lesson for graft pers the seventh regiment rollin

44

BOLD ANTIQUE was designed by Morris F. Benton in 1904 and issued by ATF in 1905. *Bold Antique Condensed* was drawn by Benton in 1906 and issued in 1908 or 1909. As plain, thick-and-thin, square-serif faces of considerable weight, they enjoyed many years of popularity. The unusual lowercase *f* with the crossbar bracketed at upper left was later replaced by one more like the condensed version, but the original style remained in f-ligature combinations and in most sizes of the Monotype copy.

About 1963 these faces were reissued as *Whitin Black* and *Whitin Black Condensed,* but were discontinued in 1968. The name came from Whitin Machine Works, of which ATF had become a subsidiary in 1960, as a play on words which it was hoped would more firmly establish the proper pronunciation of the company name. Compare *John Hancock, Contact Bold Condensed.*

Bold Antique or Whitin Black, ATF 29 (6-72pt); Bold Antique, Mono 144 (14-36pt)
Bold Antique Condensed or Whitin Black Condensed, ATF 30 (6-72pt); Bold Antique Condensed, Mono 145 (6-36pt)

BOLD FACE is a generally descriptive name for many nineteenth-century and earlier typefaces, before type families were developed and more distinctive names became common. Most foundries had several such faces, further identified by numbers, but comparable faces from different sources often had different numbers. After the turn of the century, many were copied by Linotype and Monotype, sometimes under other names. Many of these faces were made only in one or a few sizes, within the size range of 5- to 18-point; some had matching italics. It is not practical to list more than a few of the more important survivors here.

Bold Face No. 1, Linotype (cut 1904) and Intertype, is the same as *Bold Face No. 2,* Mono 328J, and similar to *Modern Roman Medium,* BB&S (q.v.). *Boldface No. 2,* Lino and Inter, is a general-purpose face, adjusted in proportions to match the widths of various newspaper faces and a few older romans; as paired with *Textype* it is almost indistinguishable from *Textype Bold* (q.v.) which is furnished with *Textype Bold Italic. Bold Face No. 6,* Lino, is essentially the same as *John Hancock,* ATF. *Bold Face No. 9,* Lino and Inter, is very similar to *Brandon. [Lining] Boldface No. 520,* ATF, was originally *Bold Face No. 120,* but it was renumbered to indicate adjustment to American standard alignment. Compare *Modern Romans.*

Bold Face No. 1, Lino = Inter (5½-12pt); Bold Face No. 2, Mono 328J (6-8pt)
Bold Face No. 2, Lino = Inter (5-14pt)
Bold Face No. 2 Condensed, Lino (5½pt)
Bold Face No. 9, Lino = Inter (6s-18L)
[Lining] Boldface No. 520, ATF 230 (5-12pt); Modern Roman Medium, BB&S-ATF 1786 (5-48pt); Bold Face No. 150, Hansen (5½-12pt)
[Lining] Boldface Italic No. 520, ATF (6-12pt); Modern Roman Italic, BB&S-ATF 1784 (6-12pt)

BON AIRE—see *Flamme* under Imports in Appendix.

BOND SCRIPT is a typical Spencerian style of connected script from the early part of the century. It was introduced by ATF in 1905, and advertised as "equal to copperplate printing." It is similar to the older and more popular *Bank Script,* but with fewer flourishes on the caps; it was discontinued by the early 1930s.

Bond Script, ATF 32 (12-48pt)

BOOKFACE—see *Bookman.*

BOOKLET OLD STYLE was designed by Frederic W. Goudy for ATF in 1916, as one of the types called for by an arrangement to design exclusively for that company. Goudy speaks of it as a letter simple in construction, plain and unobtrusive, and not terribly distinctive. It is named for the first press established by Goudy in Chicago in 1895. It does not seem to appear in any ATF specimens or literature, nor in the list of ATF matrices inventoried in 1930.

Booklet Old Style, ATF

BOOKMAN OLDSTYLE, Mono 24-pt. (swash ATF 36-pt. at 67%; 4th line Ludlow 24-pt.)

ABCDEFGHIJKLMNOPQRSTUVWXYZ&
abcdefghijklmnopqrstuvwxyz fi fl ff ffi fl ffl æ œ
$.,;:-'?!£1234567890 *A MR r y of & The*
A MR y of r The &

ATF

Ludlow

BOOKMAN ITALIC, Mono 24-pt. (swash ATF 36-pt. at 67%; last group Ludlow 24-pt.)

ABCDEFGHIJKLMNOPQRSTUVWXYZ&
abcdefghijklmnopqrstuvwxyz fi ff ffi fl ffl.,;:-,'?!
$1234567890 A MR S s y   A H MR S s y

ATF

Ludlow

BOOKMAN OLDSTYLE CONDENSED, Mono 24-pt.

GREATEST PROFIT MAKING SYSTEM $1234567890

NEW BOOKMAN, Mono 24-pt.

ABCDEFGHIJKLMNOPQRSTUVWXYZ.,-:;"!?&
abcdefghijklmnopqrstuvwxyzfiflffffiffl $1234567890

BOOKMAN LIGHTFACE (CUSTER, Western 18-pt.)

ABCDEFGHIJKLMNOPQRSTUV 1234567890
readers of the printed page and a mini-

BOOKMAN BOLD, BB&S 24-pt.

POOR EVIDENCES Brought Out Result

BOOKMAN BOLD CONDENSED, BB&S (48-pt. at 50%) (Gary Hantke)

ABCDEFGHIJKLMNOPQRSTUVWXYZ
abcdefghijklmnopqrstuvwxyz &$1234567890.,-:;'!?

BOSTON BRETON, ATF 18-pt. (Alan Ligda, Dave Churchman)

ABCDEFGHIJKLMNOPQRSTUVWXYZ
&1234567890$.,-:;!?' Useful Letters Modern Faces

BOSTON BRETON CONDENSED, ATF 24-pt.

ABCDEFGHIJKLMNOPQRSTUVWXYZ&
abcdefghijklmnopqrstuvwxyz $1234567890

46

BOOKMAN OLDSTYLE has become a lastingly popular "workhorse" design for plain, easy-to-read text, and to some extent for display as well. It is derived from an oldstyle antique face designed by A. C. Phemister about 1860 for the Scottish foundry of Miller & Richard, by thickening the strokes of an oldstyle series. This face was copied by Bruce Type Foundry in this country as *Antique No. 310,* by MacKellar, Keystone and others as *Oldstyle Antique* (q.v.), and by Hansen as *Stratford Old Style* (q.v.). In 1901 Bruce brought out *Bartlett Oldstyle,* based on the small sizes of their older face, refitted and otherwise improved. In that year Bruce was taken over by ATF, which thought well of *Bartlett* but changed the name to *Bookman Oldstyle;* it was cast at the Bruce foundry under both names until the plants were actually combined in 1906.

Few roman faces have swash letters. In our specimen, the first group of swash letters for both roman and italic was drawn by Wadsworth A. Parker for ATF, the second group, somewhat different, is by Ludlow. For printers who preferred type without the swash characters, *Oldstyle Antique No. 560* was introduced; it is identical to *Bookman* and *Bartlett* except for those characters. In fact, some of the original matrices for *Bruce Antique No. 310* were used for many years for casting *Bookman* after the other names had vanished.

Bookman was adapted to the Monotype in 1909. Composition sizes are only slightly modified to fit mechanical requirements, but display sizes are virtually exact copies of the ATF face, including roman swash letters other than *M* and *The,* which are too wide for Monotype molds in the larger sizes. Intertype issued its *Bookface,* a close copy of *Bookman* including all swash letters and with alternate oldstyle figures, about 1920. Ludlow *Bookman* and *Italic* are close copies of the ATF faces, but with redesigned swash characters, as shown.

C. H. Griffith redesigned Bookman in 1936 for Linotype, staying close to the feeling of Bookman but omitting swash and alternates. A further modification is *New Bookman,* designed by Sol Hess for Monotype in 1927; it departs more than the others in such details as serifs, but maintains the general feeling of the original face. *Bookman Old Style Condensed* was designed for Monotype by Sol Hess in 1916—figures are the same as Bookman and there is no lowercase. *Antique No. 1* (q.v.) is quite similar to Bookman, and in fact is often but erroneously called *Bookman* by Linotype and Intertype users.

BB&S *Bookman Oldstyle* appears to be an exact copy of the ATF face but lacks swash letters other than *The* and *of;* matrices undoubtedly came from Western Type Foundry when BB&S acquired it in 1918. Other BB&S Bookmans were renamed in 1925 from Western faces originally issued under other names. *Bookman Lightface* was Western's *Custer,* in turn a copy of ATF's *Cushing No. 2; Bookman Bold* was Western's *Custer Bold,* similar to *Cushing Oldstyle. Bookman Bold Condensed* was formerly BB&S's *Monitor No. 5,* first shown in 1895. Inland's *Faust* is the equivalent of Bookman.

Bookman Oldstyle, ATF 34, BB&S-ATF 1552 (6-72pt); Mono 98 (6-36pt); Bookman, Lino (6-14pt); Ludlow 14-L (12-48pt); Bookface, Inter (6-30pt)
Bookman Italic, ATF 33 (6-72pt); Lino (6-14pt); Ludlow 14-LI (12-48pt); Bookman Old Style Italic, Mono 981 (6-36pt); Bookface Italic, Inter (6-24pt)
Bookman Old Style Condensed, Mono 298 (12-36pt)
New Bookman, Mono 398 (14-72pt)
Bookman Lightface, BB&S-ATF 1551 (6-24pt)
Bookman Bold, BB&S-ATF 1549 (6-72pt)
Bookman Bold Condensed, BB&S-ATF 1550 (6-72pt)

BOSTON BRETON was introduced by ATF about 1900. It was redrawn from the earlier *Breton,* originated by one of ATF's predecessors, the Boston Type Foundry, in the early or mid-1890s. It is a bold, rather wide square-serif face, suggestive of *Stymie Bold* which came thirty-some years later. But its large lowercase and short ascenders are suggestive also of the modifications designers have given such faces in phototype adaptations, seventy years or more later. *Boston Breton Condensed* and *Extra Condensed* came from the same source in 1909 or earlier. All have the same unusual sort of *Q.*

Boston Breton, ATF 35 (6-72pt)
Boston Breton Condensed, ATF 36 (6-144pt)
Boston Breton Extra Condensed, ATF 37 (6-72pt)

BOSTON BRETON EXTRA CONDENSED, ATF (72-pt. at 33%)

ABCDEFGHIJKLMNOPQRSTUVWXYZ abcdefghijklmnopqrstuvwxyz 1234567890

BOSTON GOTHIC (42-pt. at 57%) (Jane Roberts)

ABCDEFGHIJKLMNOPQRSTUVWXYZÆŒ.,-';:;!?£$
abcdefghijklmnopqrstuvwxyzæœ&1234567890

BOSTON ITALIC, Hansen 24-pt.

REAPS HARVEST Treasure of Gold

BOUL MICH, BB&S 18-pt. (Dave Churchman)

ABCDEFGHIJKLMNOPQRSTUVWXYZ&.,-:;"!?
$1234567890

BOXHEAD GOTHIC NO. 103, ATF 5-pt. (see text)

ABCDEFGHIJKLMNOPQRSTUVWXYZ& abcdefghijklmnopqrstuvwxyz $1234567890 .,-:;'!?

BRADLEY, ATF 24-pt. (Dave Norton)

ABCDEFGHIJKLMNOPQRSTUVWXYZ& $1234567890£
abcdefghijklmnopqrstuvwxyz .,-:;'!? ÆŒæœrg~

BRADLEY ITALIC, ATF 24-pt. (Dave Norton)

*ABCDEFGHIJKLMNOPQRSTUVWXYZ&.,-:;'!?
abcdefghijklmnopqrstuvwxyz$1234567890£ ÆŒæœCo.*

BRADLEY EXTENDED, ATF 24-pt.

ABCDEFGHIJKLMNOPQRSTUVWXYZÆŒdæ
abcdefghijklmnopqrstuvwxy₃.,-:;"!?§œrgöäüß~
$1234567890

BRADLEY OUTLINE (36-pt. at 67%)

ABCDEFGHIJKLMNOPQRSTUVWXYZ& $1234567890
abcdefghijklmnopqrstuvwxyz .,-:;'!? Æ Œ æ œ rg £ ~

BOSTON GOTHIC is an inline version of *Medium Gothic No. 7,* which was produced by Hansen in 1903 or earlier as a copy of *Mid-Gothic* (q.v.). The solid form is reasonably good in a commonplace sort of way but the inline is awkward in places.

Boston Gothic, Hansen (18-72pt)

BOSTON ITALIC is an inline version, produced by Hansen in 1909, of *Gothic Italic,* which Hansen copied earlier from *Doric Italic* (q.v.).

Boston Italic, Hansen (18-60pt)

BOSTON OLDSTYLE—see Cheltenham.

BOUL MICH. During the period of "modernistic" typography of the 1920s, BB&S, the large Chicago typefoundry, brought out *Boul Mich* in 1927, the name being an advertising man's idea for a tie-in with the fashion advertising of the smart shops on Chicago's Michigan Boulevard [Avenue], according to Richard N. McArthur, then advertising manager of BB&S. An unidentified clipping with a bit of hand-lettering had been sent to the foundry; Oswald Cooper of *Cooper Black* fame was asked to sketch the missing letters to guide the foundry's pattern makers in cutting a new face, but he disclaimed any credit for the design. Apparently there is no truth in the persistent myth that *Boul Mich* was named for Boulevard Saint-Michel in Paris. Compare *Broadway.*

Boul Mich, BB&S-ATF 1553 (12-72pt)

BOULEVARD—see Imports in Appendix.

BOXHEAD GOTHICS are identical to the smallest sizes of several popular gothics, except for being cast on minimum bodies to save space and permit setting more copy in small box headings on forms. The 4-, 4½-, and 5-point sizes are equivalent to the three smallest 6-point sizes respectively of:
   01-02-03: *Light Copperplate Gothic*
   11-12-13: *Heavy Copperplate Gothic Condensed*
   21-22-23: *Heavy Copperplate Gothic*
   31-32-33: *Light Copperplate Gothic Condensed*
   101-102-103: *Lightline Title Gothic*

Boxhead Gothics, ATF 38 (4-5pt)

BRACELET—see *Tuscan Ornate* under Antiques in Appendix.
BRADFORD—see *MacFarland.*

BRADLEY (or *Bradley Text*) was designed by Herman Ihlenburg—some sources credit it to Joseph W. Phinney—from lettering by Will H. Bradley for the Christmas cover of an *Inland Printer* magazine. It was produced by ATF in 1895, with *Italic, Extended,* and *Outline* versions appearing about three years later. It is a very heavy form of black-letter, based on ancient manuscripts, but with novel forms of many letters. *Bradley* and *Bradley Outline,* which were cut to register for two-color work, have the peculiarity of lower alignment for the caps than for the lowercase and figures, as may be seen in the specimens; *Italic* and *Extended* align normally. The same face with the addition of German characters (some of which are shown in the specimen of Bradley Extended) was sold as *Ihlenburg,* regular and *Extended.*

Bradley [Text], ATF (6-48pt); Mono 75 (18pt)
Bradley Italic, ATF (8-60pt)
Bradley Extended, ATF (6-60pt)
Bradley Outline, ATF (18-60pt)
Bradley Outline Italic, ATF (18-60pt)

Similar types, based on the same source and issued about the same time, were *St. John* by Inland Type Foundry, and *Abbey Text* by A. D. Farmer & Son. They were not as enduring as *Bradley,* which was resurrected for a while in 1954 by ATF. Also compare *Washington Text.*

BRANDON, ATF 12L

ABCDEFGHIJKLMNOPQRSTUVWXYZ& $1234567890

BROAD-STROKE CURSIVE, Mono 24-pt.

ABCDEFGHIJKLMNOPQRSTUVWXYZ&
abcdefghijklmnopqrstuvwxyz $1234567890 -.,:;!?" fiflff

BROADWAY, Mono 18-pt.

ABCDEFGHIJKLMNOPQRSTUVWXYZ.,-:;'!?&
abcdefghijklmnopqrstuvwxyz $1234567890

BROADWAY CONDENSED, ATF 18-pt. (Dave Churchman)

ABCDEFGHIJKLMNOPQRSTUVWXYZ ſſſ &
abcdefghijklmnopqrstuvwxyz $1234567890.,:;'!?

BROADWAY ENGRAVED, Mono 18-pt.

ABCDEFGHIJKLMNOPQRSTUVWXYZſſſ
.,-:; '!?&$1234567890

BRODY, ATF 24-pt.

ABCDEFGHIJKLMNOPQRSTUVWXYZ&
abcdefghijklmnopqrstuvwxyz $1234567890 .,-:;'!? 'ó¢%"""

50

BRAGGADOCIO—see Imports in Appendix.

BRANDON is a thick-and-thin title face, similar to *Engravers Roman,* designed by Nicholas J. Werner and introduced by Inland Type Foundry in 1898. It was named for a printer in Nashville, Tennessee. Like a number of other such faces, it has no lowercase but was cast in several sizes on each of several bodies so numerous cap-and-small-cap combinations could easily be made. This style was popular for stationery and business forms. Hansen called the face *Plate Roman.* On Linotype and Intertype *Bold Face No. 9* is essentially the same face but a little narrower; typesetters not infrequently call it *Engravers Roman.* There was also a *Brandon Gothic,* cut only in two small 6-point sizes, which was similar to *Combination Gothic,* but with a letterspaced effect.

Brandon, Inland-ATF 39 (6s-24pt); Plate Roman, Hansen (6s-24pt); Bold Face No. 9, Lino = Inter (6s-18L)
Brandon Gothic, Inland-ATF 40 (6s-6pt)

BRETON—see *Boston Breton.*
BRIMMER—see *Bell.*

BRITANNIC is the casting by Baltimore and others of English Monotype *Monoline Script.* See Imports in Appendix.

BROAD-STROKE CURSIVE is Lanston Monotype's name for *Script Bold* of English Monotype, one of the few connecting scripts on those machines. The thick-and-thin lines seldom have a thin-to-thin connection, which would be more difficult to produce properly. Characters are designed so that none of them appear to be kerned, which adds to the durability of the type. Having the same series number (322) from both sources raises doubt as to whether Lanston made matrices or only sold English mats, but their name appeared on specimen sheets, and there appears to be no other Lanston use of that number.

Broad-Stroke Cursive, Mono 322 (14-36pt)

BROADWAY was designed by Morris F. Benton in 1927 for ATF, and introduced in 1928. It is a serifless face of extreme thicks and thins, designed with no lowercase and therefore very large on the body. The following year it was duplicated by Monotype, where Sol Hess added a lowercase alphabet with virtually no descenders. There is also *Broadway Condensed,* designed by Benton for ATF in 1929, with lowercase and more normally proportioned descenders. *Broadway Engraved,* drawn by Sol Hess for Monotype in 1928, is like the original Broadway caps but with a narrow white line engraved on the left side of the heavy strokes. ATF discontinued its versions in 1954. Compare *Boul Mich.*

Broadway, ATF 506 (6-72pt; no l.c.); Mono 306 (12-36pt; with l.c.)
Broadway Condensed, ATF 529 (6-72pt)
Broadway Engraved, Mono 307 (14-36pt)

BRODY was designed by Harold Broderson for ATF about 1953, as part of that company's effort to replace its delicate old connecting scripts with contemporary lettering styles. This rather heavy, vertical design has the appearance of being rapidly lettered with a brush. It is the most informal of several faces produced in that program, but makes a very attractive appearance where informality is desired. Compare *Kaufmann, Brush,* and *Repro Script.*

Brody, ATF 704 (18-72pt)

BRUCE ANTIQUE—see *Bookman.*
BRUCE MIKITA—see Antiques in Appendix.

BRUCE OLD STYLE & ITALIC, Mono 12-pt.

ABCDEFGHIJKLMNOPQRSTUVWXYZ&ÆŒ   ABCDEFGHIJKLMNOPQRSTUVWXYZ&ÆŒ
ABCDEFGHIJKLMNOPQRSTUVWXYZ&ÆŒ

abcdefghijklmnopqrstuvwxyzæœfifffflffiffl   1234567890 .,-'':;!?   1234567890
abcdefghijklmnopqrstuvwxyzæœfifffflffiffl 1234567890 $:;!?¡¿ 1234567890

BRUSH, ATF 24-pt. (Dave Norton)

ABCDEFGHIJKLMNOP2RSTUVWXYZ&%'cᴌᴌᵒᵉTh
abcdefghijklmnopqrstuvwxyz$$1234567890¢.,-:;'""'!?() t thtt

BUFFALO, 18-pt. (see text) (Gale Mueller)

ABCDEFGHIJKLMNOPQRSTUVWXYZ&ÆŒæœ
aabcdefghijklmnopqrstuvwxyz.,:;'!?1234567890Theof

BUFFALO ITALIC, Hansen 18- & 8-pt. (Jane Roberts)

MEMOIR OF JANE M   *ABCDEFGHIJKLMNOP2RSTUVWXYZabcdefghij*
A thrilling tale of '52   *klmnopqrsftuvwxyz.'-,:!;?&1234567890$ ₰ ɟₛ°*

BUFFALO CONDENSED, Hansen 24-pt.

BIG DINNER SERVED PICNIC GROUNDS
The Hotel Vere $1.00 Annual Outing 89

BUFFALO OUTLINE, Hansen (30-pt. at 80%) (Dave Greer)

ABCDEFGHIJKLMNOPQRSTUVWXYZ&
abcdefghijklmnopqrstuvwxyz .,₌°°₀'!?
$1234567890 ofThes₯

BULFINCH OLDSTYLE, ATF (36-pt. at 67%) (Dave Norton)

ABCDEFGHIJKLMNOPQRSTUVWXYZ$1234567890
abcdefgghijklmnopqrstuvwxyz.,-:;'!?

BULLETIN TYPEWRITER, ATF 24-pt.

ABCDEFGHIJKLMNOPQRSTUVWXYZ&
abcdefghijklmnopqrstuvwxyz
.,:;-'"!?()‾@¢*%# $1234567890

BRUCE OLD STYLE and *Bruce Old Style Italic* were the first of scores of faces adapted by Sol Hess to fit the mechanical requirements of Monotype casting, shortly after he joined Monotype in 1902. In 1909 Hess redesigned *Bruce* to fit a new development in the machine, and *Bruce Italic* became the first kerned italic for Monotype casting. It is derived from a face produced by George Bruce's Son & Company in 1869 or earlier, and is a plain, very legible, but quietly attractive face, which has been popular for magazines and other extensive reading requirements.

Bruce Old Style and Italic, Mono 31EFG (6-12pt); Old Style No. 3 and Italic, Lino (6-12pt)

BRUCE TITLE—see *Menu Title.*

BRUSH was designed in 1942 by Robert E. Smith as one of ATF's group of contemporary scripts, intended to replace designs from the early part of the century. This one has a handlettered, freely-drawn appearance, with the letters joined skillfully so the connections are not obvious. The availability of the face on Monotype mats has given it a much greater range of popularity and usefulness. A heavier weight was projected but not completed. Compare *Brody, Hauser Script, Kaufmann, Repro Script.*

Brush, ATF 689 (12-84pt); Mono 302 (14-36pt)

BUDDY—see *Roycroft.*

BUFFALO was the Hansen Type Foundry's answer to such popular boldface types with irregular edges as *Blanchard, Post,* and *Roycroft,* introduced in 1902 or earlier, including an *Outline* version. *Buffalo Italic* was shown in 1903; it is quite similar to *Blanchard Italic,* especially in the lowercase. The specimen shows an apparent duplicate cast by Kelsey when that supplier had its own typefoundry.

Buffalo, Hansen (6-72pt)
Buffalo Italic, Hansen (6-48pt)
Buffalo Condensed, Hansen (6-72pt)
Buffalo Outline, Hansen (12-48pt)

BULFINCH OLDSTYLE was designed in 1903 by William Martin Johnson on behalf of the Curtis Publishing Company, owner of *The Ladies' Home Journal.* Curtis specified a design devoid of oddity or freakishness, yet graceful and legible. Adjustments for practical foundry production were made by Morris F. Benton. Although it was used extensively as heads in their magazine, it was advertised to printers in general in 1905. Compare *Meriontype.*

Bulfinch Oldstyle, ATF 41 (6-72pt)

BULLETIN or *Bulletin Script* was introduced in 1899 by the Keystone Type Foundry. It is a heavy, informal script, with most letter combinations joining, but not all. Compare *Charcoal.*

Bulletin [Script], Keystone-ATF 811 (14-36pt)

BULLETIN TYPEWRITER. Although this book doesn't generally include typewriter faces, *Bulletin Typewriter* is shown because it is one of the few made in display sizes, and the only one made as large as 36-point. Otherwise it is representative of the scores of such faces made in small sizes. It was cut in 1925, with the largest size added in 1933. Monotype makes a very similar but lighter *Remington Typewriter,* in 24-point as well as 10- and 12-point sizes.

Bulletin Typewriter, ATF 491 (18-36pt)

BULLETIN, Keystone 24-pt.

ABCDEFGHIJKLMNOPQRSTUVWXYZ&
abcdefghijklmnopqrrstuvwxyz   1234567890 $?!.,:;'=

BULMER ROMAN, ATF 24-pt.

ABCDEFGHIJKLMNOPQRSTUVWXYZ
abcdefghijklmnopqrstuvwxyzfiflfffffiffl$1234567890.,-:;''!?&%
1234567890   1234567890

Original

BULMER ITALIC, ATF 24-pt. (Dave Norton)

ABCDEFGHIJ JKLMNOPQRSTUVWXYZ&$1234567890
abcdefghijklmnopqrstuvwxyz.,-:;''!?ffffifffffiffl 1234567890 1234567890

Original

CAIRO & ITALIC, Inter 14-pt.

ABCDEFGHIJKLMNOPQRSTUVWXYZ $1234567890 ABCDEFGHIJ KLMNOPQRSTUVWXYZ
ABCDEFGHIJKLMNOPQRSTUVWXYZ $1234567890 Æ Œ & % [ ] * † | ‡ ‖ § ¶
abcdefghijklmnopqrstuvwxyz fi fl ff ffi ffl ,.-;':'!?() @℔&£· œœÆŒ ⅛ ¼ ⅜ ½ ⅝ ¾ ⅞
abcdefghijklmnopqrstuvwxyz fi fl ff ffi ffl ,.-;':'!?() @℔&£ œœÆŒ ⅛ ¼ ⅜ ½ ⅝ ¾ ⅞
Ak afy 1234567890 a E J K m n w 2 3

CAIRO MEDIUM & ITALIC, Inter 14-pt.

ABCDEFGHIJKLMNOPQRSTUVWXYZ $1234567890 ABCDEFGHIJ KLMNOPQRSTUVWXYZ
ABCDEFGHIJKLMNOPQRSTUVWXYZ $1234567890 Æ Œ & % [ ] * † | ‡ ‖ § ¶
abcdefghijklmnopqrstuvwxyz fi fl ff ffi ffl ,.;':'!?()@℔&£ œ œ Æ Œ ⅛ ¼ ⅜ ½ ⅝ ¾ ⅞
abcdefghijklmnopqrstuvwxyz fi fl ff ffi ffl ,.;':'!?()@℔&£ œ œ Æ Œ ⅛ ¼ ⅜ ½ ⅝ ¾ ⅞

CAIRO BOLD & ITALIC, Inter 12-pt. (and 14-pt. Alternates)

ABCDEFGHIJKLMNOPQRSTUVWXYZ $1234567890 ABCDEFGHIJKLMNOPQRSTUVWXYZ œ œ Æ Œ Æ Œ &
ABCDEFGHIJKLMNOPQRSTUVWXYZ $1234567890 œ œ Æ Œ Æ Œ &
abcdefghijklmnopqrstuvwxyz fi fl ff ffi ffl ,.-;':'!?()@ ℔ & £ % [ ] * † | ‡ ‖ § ¶ – — ⅛ ¼ ⅜ ½ ⅝ ¾ ⅞
abcdefghijklmnopqrstuvwxyz fi fl ff ffi ffl ,.-;':'!?()@ ℔ & £ % [ ] * † | ‡ ‖ § ¶ – — ⅛ ¼ ⅜ ½ ⅝ ¾ ⅞
A K a f y ABCDEFGHIJKLMNOPQRSTUVWXYZ&ÆŒ   1234567890 a E K m n w 2
A K a f y ABCDEFGHIJKLMNOPQRSTUVWXYZ&ÆŒ

CAIRO HEAVY, Inter 12-pt.

ABCDEFGHIJKLMNOPQRSTUVWXYZ œœÆŒ $1234567890 ⅛ ¼ ⅜ ½ ⅝ ¾ ⅞ ⅓ ⅔
abcdefghijklmnopqrstuvwxyz fi fl ff ffi ffl ,.-;':'!?()@ ℔ & £   % [ ] * † | ‡ ‖ § ¶ – — ° ' " ¢ /

CAIRO CONDENSED, Inter (30-pt. at 80%)

INTERTYPE matrices excel in type des 12345

CAIRO MEDIUM CONDENSED, Inter 18-pt.

ABCDEFGHIJKLMNOPQRSTUVWXYZ $1234567890 a A E K m n w
abcdefghijklmnopqrstuvwxyz fi fl ff ffi ffl ,.-;':'!?() @ ℔ & £ æœÆŒ

54

BULMER ROMAN and *Bulmer Italic* were adapted by Morris Benton from a face cut about 1790 by William Martin for William Bulmer and the Shakspeare Press in London. This Press was established for the purpose of producing a magnificent national edition of the works of William Shakespeare, "in which splendour of production was to go hand in hand with correctness of text." George Nicol, one of the publishers of the work, writes that "with regard to the Typographical part of the work, the state of printing in England, when it was first undertaken [1786], was such that it was found necessary to establish a printing-house on purpose to print the work; a foundry to cast the types; and even a manufactory to make the ink."

William Bulmer was credited with greatly advancing the art of book printing in England, and these types were hailed as illustrious designs, derived from Baskerville but modified by their designer's admiration of Bodoni.

Various sources disagree on dates for the present recutting, with Benton's work said to be as early as 1923. But foundry records show that trial cuttings of the roman were made in 1925 and of the italic in 1926, with all sizes of each cut a year later. However, ATF's "advance proof" of the faces is dated May 1928.

As first issued by ATF, *Bulmer* and *Bulmer Italic* had intermediate size figures, as shown in the specimens; these were replaced by a choice of lining or oldstyle figures in 1940, as also shown.

The Monotype cutting of *Bulmer,* about 1954, is unusually faithful to the ATF original for a machine-set face; the Intertype cutting, first shown in 1958, is less satisfactory, due to shortened descenders and mechanical restrictions applied to the italic.

Bulmer Roman, ATF 497 (6-48pt); Bulmer, Mono 462 (6-36pt); Inter (6-14pt)
Bulmer Italic, ATF 498 (6-48pt); Mono 4621 (6-36pt); Inter (6-14pt)

CABLE—see *Sans Serif.*
CADMUS—see *Elzevir.*

CAIRO is Intertype's adaptation of *Memphis,* originally designed by Rudolf Weiss for Stempel in Germany about 1929, and first imported into the United States as *Girder.* Except for *Litho Antique,* this was the first of the modern square-serif faces, which are revivals of older faces known as Egyptians. The Intertype faces appeared in 1933 to 1940. *Lining Cairo* features several sizes of caps on 6- and 12-point bodies in the manner of *Copperplate Gothic.* Compare *Memphis, Stymie, Karnak.*

Cairo with Italic, Inter (6-60pt, 6-24 Italic)
Cairo Medium with Italic, Inter (6-30pt)
Cairo Bold with Italic, Inter (6-60pt, 6-30 Italic)
Cairo Heavy with Italic, Inter (6-18pt, 6,18 Italic)
Lining Cairo with Bold, Inter (6s-12L)
Cairo Condensed, Inter (30,36pt)
Cairo Medium Condensed, Inter (18-36pt)
Cairo Bold Condensed, Inter (8-36pt)
Cairo Extra Bold Condensed, Inter (8-48pt)
Cairo Open, Inter (60pt)

CAIRO BOLD CONDENSED, Inter 18-pt.

ABCDEFGHIJKLMNOPQRSTUVWXYZ $1234567890   ACEFGHMNSWY
abcdefghijklmnopqrstuvwxyz fi fl ff ffi ffl ,.-;`:'!?( ) œ œ Æ Œ £ &

CAIRO EXTRA BOLD CONDENSED, Inter 18-pt.

ABCDEFGHIJKLMNOPQRSTUVWXYZ $1234567890   a A E K M N W
abcdefghijklmnopqrstuvwxyz fi fl ff ffi ffl ,.-;`:'!?( ) @ ℔ & £ æ œ Æ Œ

CAIRO OPEN, Inter (60-pt. at 50%)

FINE PRINTING PR 1234

CALEDONIA & ITALIC, Lino 14-pt.

ABCDEFGHIJKLMNOPQRSTUVWXYZ& ABCDEFGHIJKLMNOPQRSTUVWXYZ

ABCDEFGHIJKLMNOPQRSTUVWXYZ&

abcdefghijklmnopqrstuvwxyzæœfifffflffiffl 1234567890 [($.,-°:;!?——)] 1234567890 gjpqy

abcdefghijklmnopqrstuvwxyzæœfifffflffiffl 1234567890 [($.,-°:;!?——)] 1234567890

CALEDONIA BOLD & ITALIC, Lino 14-pt.

ABCDEFGHIJKLMNOPQRSTUVWXYZ&ÆŒ **ABCDEFGHIJKLMNOPQRSTUVWXYZ&ÆŒ**

ABCDEFGHIJKLMNOPQRSTUVWXYZ&ÆŒ

abcdefghijklmnopqrstuvwxyzæœfifffflffiffl [(.,-°:;!?——)] 1234567890 gjpqy

abcdefghijklmnopqrstuvwxyzæœfifffflffiffl [(.,-°:;!?——)] 1234567890

CALEDONIA BOLD CONDENSED, Lino (36-pt. at 67%)

LINOTYPE faces are standard throug 123

CALIFORNIAN, Mono 24-pt. (Guy Botterill, Rich Hopkins)

ABCDEFGHIJKLMNOPQRSTUVWXYZ ÆŒæœ&ctst1234567890

abcdefghijklmnopqrstuvwxyzfffflffiffl &1234567890$.,-:;!?"()[]

ABCDEFGHIJKLMNOPQRSTUVWXYZ &ÆŒ

CALIFORNIAN ITALIC, Mono 24-pt. (Guy Botterill)

ABCDEFGHIJKLMNOPQRSTUVWXYZ ÆŒ

abcdefghijklmnopqrstuvwxyzæœfifffflffiffl&st1234567890[(&$.,-':;!?)]

CAMBRIDGE, Hansen 18-pt. (Peyton Reavis)

ABCDEFGHIJKLMNOPQRSTUVWXYZ&Æ

abcdefghijklmnopqrstuvwxyz.,-:;'?$123456780 æœ

NEW CAMBRIDGE, Hansen 24-pt. (part reduced)

THE NEW CAMBRIDGE SERIES DESIGN

An Attractive Typographic 5 Series

CAMELOT OLDSTYLE, ATF 24-pt. (Rick von Holdt)

ABCDEFGHIJKLMNOPQRSTUVWXYZMRſ&.,-:;!?'

abcdefghijklmnopqrstuvwxyzfffflffiffl&ahm$1234567890

56

CALEDONIA and *Caledonia Italic* were designed by William A. Dwiggins for Linotype in 1938, with *Caledonia Bold* and *Bold Italic* added two years later. A *Bold Condensed* version was produced by Lino for newspaper headline use. *Caledonia* has been described as a modernization of *Scotch Roman* (and Caledonia is the ancient name for Scotland), but it is more than that. It also shows the influence of the *Bulmer* typeface, with a large portion of Dwiggins' individuality. He describes the face as having a "liveliness of action . . . that quality is in the curves—the way they get away from the straight stems with a calligraphic flick, and in the nervous angle on the under side of the arches as they descend to the right." Being designed specifically for the Linotype and its mechanical limitations, rather than being adapted from a foundry face, *Caledonia Italic* is particularly successful, and the whole family has become very popular. In text sizes, short descenders may be cast on nominal body sizes, while the more handsome long descenders (not made for italics) require one point larger body size. Compare *Baskerville, Bulmer, Scotch.*

Caledonia with Italic, Lino (6-24pt)
Caledonia Bold with Italic, Lino (6-24pt, 36 roman)
Caledonia Bold Condensed, Lino (36pt)
Caledonia is known as Cornelia in Germany.

CALEDONIAN—see *Clarendon.*
CALEDONIAN ITALIC—see *Law Italic.*

CALIFORNIAN and *Californian Italic* were cut by Monotype in 1958 as a reissue of *University of California Old Style* and *Italic,* which had been designed by Frederic W. Goudy in 1938 as a private type for the Press of that school. Goudy notes that "I elected to make a type for general use the desideratum, rather than a type for more sumptuous work." He further states that he "endeavored to give it the utmost distinction compatible with its purpose and especially strived for the greatest legibility possible. . . . For my italic I wanted to draw a refined letter that could not be called prudish. Some of the characters may be a bit exuberant, but not more so than due regard for its purpose permits." It is a distinguished face. An unusual detail is the inclusion of small capitals in large sizes; they are designed separately rather than being reductions of the regular capitals. Compare *Deepdene.*

Californian, Mono 300 (8-36pt); University of California Old Style, Goudy
Californian Italic, Mono 3001 (8-36pt); University of California Italic, Goudy

CAMBRIDGE was Hansen Type Foundry's copy of *Windsor Condensed,* drawn early in the century by Elisha Pechey for the Stephenson, Blake foundry in England. *New Cambridge,* cut in 1909, was an inline version of the same face, apparently originated by Hansen. Some other versions of Windsor are shown under Popular Imports in the Appendix.

Cambridge, Hansen (6-72pt)
New Cambridge, Hansen (18-60pt)

CAMBRIDGE (other)—see *Benton.*

CAMELOT or *Camelot Oldstyle* was the first typeface designed by Frederic W. Goudy. He offered it to Dickinson Type Foundry (part of ATF) in Boston, which accepted it and sent him $10, twice what he had modestly asked for it. This was in 1896; it was apparently cut and released the following year as drawn, without lowercase. In February 1900 a design patent was issued in the names of Goudy and Joseph W. Phinney, and assigned to ATF. Phinney was a well-known designer for Dickinson-ATF, and apparently it was he who added the lowercase alphabet. Its success encouraged Goudy to make a distinguished career of type designing, and this face was included in ATF specimen books as late as 1941. Compare *Canterbury.*

Camelot Oldstyle, ATF 42 (6-36pt)

CAMEO, Ludlow 24-pt.

ABCDEFGHIJKLMNOPQRSTUVWXYZ& .,:;!?
abcdefghijklmnopqrstuvwxyz 1234567890 flfffffi

CAMEO ITALIC, Ludlow 24-pt.

ABCDEFGHIJKLMNOPQRSTUVWXYZ!?&
abcdefghijklmnopqrstuvwxyz 1234567890$

CAMERA, Inter 12-pt.

ABCDEFGHIJKLMNOPQRSTUVWXYZ   1234567890
abcdefghijklmnopqrstuvwxyz   %₀†§‡¶ ( )$,.=;':'!?&⅛ ¼ ⅜ ½ ⅝ ¾

CANTERBURY, ATF 24-pt. (John Shaw, Herb Harnish)

ABCDEFGHIJKLMNOPQRSTUVWXYZ&   ABCEHLMNTUW

abcdefghijklmnopqrstuvwxyz ffffffffflffl $1234567890 .,-:;'!?'

CARD ITALIC, Lino 18-pt.

ABCDEFGHIJKLMNOPQRSTUVWXYZ&
abcdefghijklmnopqrstuvwxyz ($,.:;'-'?!) 12345678

CARD MERCANTILE, ATF 18-pt. (Leonard Bahr)

ABCDEFGHIJKLMNOPQRST
UVWXYZ $1234567890 .,:;'-&!?

CAMEO was designed by R. Hunter Middleton for Ludlow in 1926. It is derived from a heavy version of Caslon, with a thin white line within the left side of each heavy stroke, giving a very pleasing appearance. A 1926 Ludlow ad says of it, "Designed and punches produced in our own plant"—apparently it was the first, or one of the first, so produced. Compare *Caslon Shaded, Caslon Openface, Caslon Shadow Title, Gravure, Narciss.*

Cameo, Ludlow 19 (12-72pt)
Cameo Italic, Ludlow 19-I (12-48pt)

CAMEO (other)—see *Gill Sans Cameo* under Imports in Appendix.

CAMERA is a novel cursive letter with light, monotone strokes suitable for use on personal stationery and announcements. The design originated with Stempel in Germany in 1913, after a design by F. Schweimanns, the Intertype face appearing in 1936. Compare *Card Italic.*

Camera, Inter (12,14pt)

CAMPANILE—see *Bodoni Campanile.*

CANTERBURY is a novelty face designed by Morris F. Benton for ATF in 1920, when trials were cut, but not completed for production until 1926. It features a very small x-height, with long ascenders and descenders; monotone weight with minute serifs; and a number of swash capitals. It is primarily suitable for personal stationery and announcements. Compare *Camelot Oldstyle.*

Canterbury, ATF 508 (12-48pt)

CANTERBURY [CAPITALS]—see *Floriated Capitals* under Imports in Appendix.
CAPRICE—see Imports in Appendix.
CAPTION—see *Compact.*
CARD BODONI—see under *Bodoni.*
CARD GOTHIC—see *Bank Gothic, Blair, Wedding Gothic.*

CARD ITALIC is a Linotype copy of *Ella Italic,* designed by S. H. DeRoos in 1915 for Amsterdam Type Foundry. It is a novelty cursive letter, with a more frivolous appearance than the somewhat similar Intertype face, *Camera* (q.v.). Like the latter, it is most suitable for stationery, announcements, and greeting cards.

Card Italic, Lino (10-18pt)

CARD LIGHT LITHO, CARD LITHO—see *Litho Roman.*

CARD MERCANTILE was produced by Dickinson Type Foundry in the 1890s or earlier. Except for a few letters, it appears to be a duplicate of *Extended No. 3* of Stevens, Shanks in England. In 1901 Morris Benton redesigned the two smallest sizes for ATF, successor to Dickinson, for better compatibility with the other sizes. It is a very delicate, wide, thick-and-thin style without lowercase (but the English face has lowercase), somewhat similar to *Engravers Roman,* which supplanted it in popular use. An 1899 ad said, "For imitating the work of steel engravers there can be nothing more beautiful picked from a case, and it is difficult if not impossible to imagine how anything finer ever can." Compare *Engravers Roman, Brandon, Litho series.*

Card Mercantile, ATF 46 (6s-30pt)

CARD ROMAN, ATF 24-pt. (George Gasparik)

ABCDEFGHIJKLMNOPQRSTUVWXYZ& ,;:.-'!?
abcdefghijklmnopqrstuvwxyz fifflffiffl $1234567890£

CARDINAL, Keystone 18-pt.

ABCDEFGHIJKLMNOPQ 1234567890
Few general readers know by name the different sizes or styles

CARDINAL ITALIC, Keystone 12-pt.

THE COPYISTS OF THE MIDDLE AGES
May be properly divided into two classes: the class
that considered copying an irksome duty and that did

CARDSTYLE, BB&S 18L (Jim Broadston)

AABCDEFGHIJKLMNOPQRSTUVWXYZ&1234567890$.,-:;!?'©.LY Mᶜ ᵀᴴ Wᵐ

CARTOON LIGHT, Bauer 18-pt.

ABCDEFGHIJKLMNOPQRSTUVWXYZ&
1234567890 $¢?!.,:;'—

CARTOON BOLD, Bauer 18-pt.

**ABCDEFGHIJKLMNOPQRSTUVWXYZ&
1234567890 $¢?!.,:;-*()**

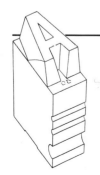

Depth of Drive

This term refers to the depth to which punches were driven into the matrix blank, which is equivalent to the distance from printing face to the shoulder of the piece of type or slug.

The depth of drive varies from 0.043 inches—about ¹⁄₂₄ inch, for Linotype and Intertype slugs and small handset types—to about ⅛ inch. For a short time in the 1950s or thereabouts, ATF produced a series of "deepa-cast" type, with a 0.187- or ³⁄₁₆-inch depth of drive, for specialty work. Alternate Gothic No. 3 (D8), Franklin Gothic (D162), and News Gothic Condensed (D339) were cut in 14- to 48-point sizes, using the original patterns for each face.

CARD ROMAN was designed by Morris Benton for ATF in 1921, when a trial size was cut, although it was not completed for marketing until 1925. But it was gone before publication of the next ATF specimen book in 1934, so specimens are very rare; the ones shown here come from ATF files. It is a very light roman, with mostly oldstyle characteristics, but with unusual twists to several characters, including *J, Q,* and *g.* Cap *U* has the lowercase form.

Card Roman, ATF 488 (6-36pt)

CARD ROMAN (other)—see *Engravers Roman.*
CARD TEXT—see *Typo Text.*

CARDINAL was Keystone Type Foundry's version of *Cushing Monotone* (q.v.). The italic is very similar to *Cushing No. 2 Italic.*

Cardinal, KTF (6-48pt)
Cardinal Italic, KTF (6-12pt)

CARDSTYLE is an unusual face designed in 1914 by Sidney Gaunt for BB&S. It is a medium weight monotone, rather narrow, with tiny serifs, and was intended for use on announcements. There is no lowercase, but caps are cast in several sizes on each of three bodies, for cap-and-small-cap combinations. Notice the logotypes, which were more common around the turn of the century.

Cardstyle, BB&S-ATF 1558 (6s-18L)

CARLTON—see *Adcraft Lightface.*
CARNET DE BAL—see *Tuscan Outline* under Antiques in Appendix.
CARNIVAL—see *Tuscan Ombree* under Antiques in Appendix.

CARTOON is an informal letter, preserving the freedom of handlettering, with its name apparently suggested by the lettering in comic strips. Its two weights were drawn by Howard Allen Trafton, New York designer, in 1936. It is one of the few faces by American designers that was not cut and cast in this country; this was hand-cut (probably in one size, with other sizes derived from it) and cast by Bauer Type Foundry in Germany. Compare *Balloon.*

Cartoon, Bauer (8-36pt)
Cartoon Bold, Bauer (8-48pt)
Cartoon Bold is called Comique by some sources.

CASCADE—see *News with Clarendon.*

ABCDEFGHIJKLMNOPQRSTUVWXYZ& .,-:;'!?()[]
abcdefghijklmnopqrstuvwxyz 1234567890$ fffiffiflffl
ABCDEFGHIJKLMNOPQRSTUVWXYZ& ſ ſi ſl ſſ ſſi ſſl ſb ſh ſk ſt ct st

ABCDEFGHIJJKLMNOPQQRSTTUVWXYZ& .,-:;'!?
abcdeεfghhijkklmnopqrstuvvvwwxyzz 1234567890$ fffiffiflffl
ſ ſi ſl ſſ ſſi ſſl ſb ſh ſk ſt ct st

ABCDEFGHIJKLMNOPQRSTUVWXYZ
abcdefghijklmnopqrstuvwxyz $1234567890&
fffiflffiffictct.,:;!?()[]'-

ABCDEFGHIJJKLMNOPQQRSTTUVWXYZ
abcdefghhijklmnopqrstuvwxyz 1234567890$&
fffiflffiffil.,:;!?( )'-

Caslon Oldstyle No. 471 vs. Caslon No. 540

42-pt. 471   36-pt. 540

abcdefghijklm   abcdefghijklm

36-pt. 471   30-pt. 540

abcdefghijklmnop   abcdefghijklmnop

30-pt. 471   24-pt. 540

abcdefghijklmnopqrstu   abcdefghijklmnopqrstu

24-pt. 471   20-pt. 540

abcdefghijklmnopqrstuvwxy   abcdefghijklmnopqrstuvwxy

22-pt. 471   18-pt. 540

abcdefghijklmnopqrstuvwxyz   abcdefghijklmnopqrstuvwxyz

18-pt. 471   14-pt. 540

abcdefghijklmnopqrstuvwxyz   abcdefghijklmnopqrstuvwxyz

14-pt. 471   12-pt. 540

abcdefghijklmnopqrstuvwxyz   abcdefghijklmnopqrstuvwxyz

CASLON is "the oldest living typeface," having survived in almost exactly its original form since every character was hand-cut by William Caslon more than 250 years ago. Virtually the same design is still available, along with a myriad of imitations, derivatives, and attempts at improvement. Altogether, they form a number of families, for there is little or no compatibility between many faces which now bear the name Caslon. In fact, Caslon is perhaps the hardest set of types to group into reasonable categories; therefore some of the following classifications are arbitrary.

* * *

The original Caslon. Prior to 1722 English typefounding was at a low ebb, and most printers in that country used Dutch types. But in that year William Caslon completed the first sizes of his new style, which quickly gained dominance over the Dutch types. This new English style was also extensively exported to other countries, including the American Colonies, where it was popular before the Revolution. In fact, the Declaration of Independence of the new United States was first printed in Caslon's types. Benjamin Franklin met Caslon in London, admired and recommended his types, and used them extensively in his printshop.

Caslon's types have gone through several periods of decline and revival. In America they died out by about 1800, and had little or no further use for nearly sixty years. In 1858, Laurence Johnson, a prominent Philadelphia typefounder, visited London and arranged with the successors to William Caslon to duplicate the Caslon types. There are several accounts of how this was done; some say Johnson had fonts specially cast, from which he made electrotype matrices. Another account says he had strikes—unfinished matrices—made from the original punches, while a third account says he obtained the original matrices. The latter account is most unlikely, but the other two possibilities are interestingly credible.

Many of the mats still available at ATF, successors to Johnson, are electrotypes—but then, mats wear out anyway, and are commonly replaced by electrotyping existing virgin cast type when patterns or punches are not available. If strikes were finished in this country—the usual process of accurately fitting them for width and position on the type body—this would allow for the fact that some sizes, especially in the 14- to 24-point range, are more loosely fitted here than in England. Otherwise there is virtually no difference between the American and English versions, except for later additions such as dollar mark and various swash letters—the latter are discussed later.

Johnson simply called the face *Old Style,* as family names were a later development. When Johnson's foundry merged with MacKellar Smiths & Jordan foundry, the face was designated *Original Old Style,* to distinguish it from other faces in the same category. MS&J was part of the great merger that formed ATF in 1892, and the face became *Old Style No. 71.* When ATF's first specimen book was being prepared in 1897, the advertising manager, Henry Lewis Bullen, renamed the series *Caslon Old Style.* Later *"No. 471"* was added, the "4" designating faces obtained from MS&J.

Meanwhile, a prominent New York printer, Walter Gilliss, had promoted the adoption of *Caslon* for setting *Vogue* magazine, a fashion and art journal which was started in 1892, and the face quickly returned to popularity. A. D. Farmer & Son copied the face under the name *Knickerbocker Old Style.*

But this was the time when standard alignment was being heavily promoted, necessitating the shortening of descenders. Inland Type Foundry, St. Louis, advertised its own version of *Caslon Old Style* in 1901, with the claim, "We have obtained the sole right from the originating house to manufacture this series in the United States. Inland is the only type foundry which casts this face on standard line...." This meant that they had considerably shortened the descending letters; they had also redesigned the italic extensively. ATF countered with *Caslon No. 540,* with similarly shortened descenders but essentially the original roman and italic designs otherwise. Several other

(Caslon continues)

Caslon Oldstyle No. 471, ATF 50 (6-72pt); [MacKellar] Caslon Old Style, Mono 337 (7-36pt); Hansen (6-16pt); True-Cut Caslon, Ludlow 1-TC (8-72pt)

Caslon Oldstyle Italic No. 471, ATF 51 (6-48pt); [MacKellar] Caslon Old Style Italic, Mono 3371 (7-36pt); Hansen (6-16pt); True-Cut Caslon Italic, Ludlow 1-TCI (8-72pt); also Caslon Oldstyle Italic No. 471 Swash, ATF 663 (6-48pt)

Caslon No. 540, ATF 233 (6-120pt)

Caslon Italic No. 540, ATF 234 (6-96pt); also Caslon Italic No. 540 Swash, ATF 664 (36-96pt)

Caslon Oldstyle, BB&S-ATF 1569 (6-72pt); Caslon Oldstyle No. 2, Hansen (6-72pt)

Caslon Oldstyle Italic, BB&S-ATF 1570 (6-42pt); Caslon Oldstyle Italic No. 2, Hansen (6-42pt)

CASLON OLDFACE & ITALIC, Lino 14-pt. (Fred Williams)

ABCDEFGHIJKLMNOPQRSTUVWXYZ& ($£,.:;'-?!*†) ABCDEFGHIJKLMNOPQRSTUVWXYZ&

ABCDEFGHIJKLMNOPQRSTUVWXYZ& ($£,.:;'-?! †)

1234567890 abcdefghijklmnopqrstuvwxyzfiflffffiffl 1234567890

1234567890 abcdefghijklmnopqrstuvwxyzfiflffffiffl 1234567890 *ABCDEGJMNPQuQuRTY*

CASLON OLDSTYLE NO. 472, ATF 18-pt. (second line) compared with Caslon Oldstyle No. 471, ATF (first line)

ABCDEFGHIJKLMNOPQRSTUVWXYZ abcdefghijklmnopqrstuvwxyz

ABCDEFGHIJKLMNOPQRSTUVWXYZ abcdefghijklmnopqrstuvwxyz

CASLON OLDSTYLE ITALIC NO. 471 SWASH, ATF 24-pt. (etc.—see text)

ABCDEFJGHHKKLLMNOPR SUWE gy W JU ABCDEGJKLMNPQRTUY ctkvwz

3371   540   4371

CASLON ITALIC SPECIALS, BB&S (36-pt. at 50%, spaced)

ABCDEFGHIJKLMNOPQRSTUV WY — & ε-з ꝏ ꝏ

ENGLISH CASLON OLDSTYLE 37, Mono 24-pt.

ABCDEFGHIJKLMNOPQRSTUVWXYZ.,-';:;!?

abcdefghijklmnopqrstuvwxyzfiffflffiffl1234567890&$

ENGLISH CASLON OLDSTYLE ITALIC, Mono 24-pt.

ABCDEFGHIJKLMNOPQRSTUVWXYZ.,':;!?

abcdefghijklmnopqrstuvwxyzfiffflffifflh1234567890&$

BDJPRTYW

CASLON NO. 4, Inter 18-pt.

ABCDEFGHIJKLMNOPQRSTUVWXYZ

abcdefghijklmnopqrstuvwxyz , . - ; ' : ' ! ? ( ) – & $1234567890

INLAND CASLON OLDSTYLE 137 & ITALIC, Mono 12-pt.

ABCDEFGHIJKLMNOPQRSTUVWXYZ&ÆŒ ABCDEFGHIJKLMNOPQRSTUVWXYZ&ÆŒ

ABCDEFGHIJKLMNOPQRSTUVWXYZ&ÆŒ

abcdefghijklmnopqrstuvwxyzæœfiffflffiffl 1234567890 $.,-":;!?¡¿

abcdefghijklmnopqrstuvwxyzæœfiffflffiffl 1234567890 $:;!?¡¿   *Q JQTY h*

64

foundries, including BB&S, Hansen, and Keystone, produced similar Caslons.

One of the most noticeable features of Caslon is its lack of uniformity from one size to another. This is due to the fact that all the original characters were cut by hand, before the invention of precise mechanical systems for enlarging and reducing drawings. In *Caslon 540,* each size is the equivalent of the next larger size of 471, including some obsolete odd sizes. Thus 14-point 540 is equivalent to 18-point 471, 18 to 22, 20 to 24, etc. The difference is primarily in the descenders, very unattractively shortened in some sizes of 540; lining figures replace the hanging style, and a few other slight changes have been made. The additional large sizes are an attractive generalized design.

To overcome objections to the wide fitting of some sizes of *Caslon Oldstyle No. 471,* ATF brought out *Caslon Oldstyle No. 472* in 1932; the design is identical but it is fitted more closely. It is made only in 18-, 22- and 24-point sizes.

In the specimens shown here, notice the small caps shown with *Caslon Oldstyle No. 471,* for which they are made up to 36-point—one of the very few faces to include such letters above 14- or 18-point. Most of these appear to be cut separately, rather than being regular caps of a smaller size. Long-*s* characters and combinations have also been made for *Caslon Oldstyle* roman and italic by ATF and Monotype, and for *Caslon No. 540* roman by ATF; they are called *Quaint Characters.*

* * *

Swash versions of the *Caslon Oldstyle Italic* capitals *J, Q, T,* and *Y,* also lowercase *h* with the final stroke turned inward, were the only forms shown in Caslon's original specimen sheet, although other similar swash letters were made for Dutch types at least a century earlier. Later, plain versions of these letters were added, and both forms are included in some fonts. About 1920, Thomas M. Cleland designed a dozen swash letters to be used with *Caslon Oldstyle Italic No. 471,* and a dozen more were designed in 1923 for Curtis Publishing Company, perhaps by another designer. These were cast in regular molds, with some letters having long, delicate kerns. By 1927 most of these letters, plus a few others, were being made for *Caslon Italic No. 540.* These were cast with mortises where necessary, greatly reducing the problem of breakage. Thereafter the larger sizes of *Caslon No. 471 Italic* were also adapted to mortise molds. Lowercase swash letters *e, k, v, w,* and *z* are part of the swash font for both 471 and 540 italics. Vowels are also cast on smaller bodies to fit within the mortises. Compare *Scotch Open Shaded Italic.*

About 1927 an ATF specimen said, "The five largest sizes of *Caslon Italic No. 540* are the equivalent of 60-, 72-, 84-, 96-, and 120-point *Caslon Oldstyle Italic No. 471.* Some of the Swash Capitals are cast on these bodies and long descenders cast on these larger bodies will be ready shortly, which will give the full effect of the popular No. 471 Italic." No evidence has been found that this was ever completed.

In the specimen of *Caslon Oldstyle Italic No. 471 Swash* shown here, these characters are shown on the first line; these are made in all sizes of the face. *Caslon Italic No. 540* includes—only in sizes from 36-point up—many of these letters plus the *I* and *U* shown separately; fullface letters in this series are cast on the next larger body and thus are identical to 471. Incidentally, the swash *J* in these fonts is identical when inverted to the pound sterling mark furnished with English fonts. Ludlow *True-Cut Caslon Italic* also includes many of the 471 swash letters. Monotype *Caslon Old Style Italic No. 3371* includes some of the same, plus the *W* shown separately.

Monotype *Caslon Old Style Italic No. 4371,* which was copied from Stephenson Blake's *Caslon Old Face* in the 42- to 72-point sizes, has a different set of swash letters as shown on the latter part of the second line. Linotype *Caslon Old Face Italic* has a similar set of swash letters, only some of which are shown in the specimen. Linotype *Caslon Italic* (not Old Face) has no swash letters but the otherwise identical Intertype face does, as shown,

(Caslon continues)

Caslon Oldstyle No. 472, ATF 558 (18-24pt); Caslon Old Style, Mono 437 (42-72pt); Caslon Old Face, Lino (6-36pt); Inter (18-30pt); APL (18-120pt)

Caslon Old Style Italic, Mono 4371 (42-72pt); Caslon Old Face Italic, Lino (6-24pt); APL (18-72pt)

Caslon Italic Specials, BB&S (12-72pt)

English Caslon Old Style, Mono 37 (6-36pt); Caslon No. 2, Lino (6-12pt); Caslon No. 4, Lino = Inter (18pt)

English Caslon Old Style Italic, Mono 371 (6-36pt); Caslon No. 2 Italic, Lino (6-12pt)

Inland Caslon Oldstyle No. 584, ATF 196 (6-72pt); Inland Caslon Old Style, Mono 137EF (6-12pt); Caslon No. 137, Lino (7-12pt)

Inland Caslon Oldstyle Italic No. 584, ATF 197 (6-42pt); Inland Caslon Old Style Italic, Mono 137G (6-12pt); Caslon Italic No. 137, Lino (7-12pt)

CASLON & ITALIC, Inter 12-pt.

ABCDEFGHIJKLMNOPQRSTUVWXYZ $1234567890 ABCDEFGHIJ KLMNOPQRSTUVWXYZ $1234567890

ABCDEFGHIJKLMNOPQRSTUVWXYZ $1234567890 *$1234567890*

abcdefghijklmnopqrstuvwxyz fiflffffffiffl ,.-;':'!?() @℔&£ æœÆŒ Æ Œ & [ ] * † | ‡ ‖ § ¶ - — ⅛ ¼ ⅜ ½ ⅝ ¾

abcdefghijklmnopqrstuvwxyz fiflff ffifl ,.-;':'!?() @℔&£ æœÆŒ

ABCDEFGILMNPTY g j p q y J Qu g j p q y Qu

Long descenders

CASLON ITALIC, Lino 18-pt.

ABCDEFGHIJKLMNOPQRSTUVWXYZ&

abcdefghijklmnopqrstuvwxyz 1234567890$,.:;-"?!–()

CASLON NO. 2 & ITALIC, Lino 12-pt.

ABCDEFGHIJKLMNOPQRSTUVWXYZ&ÆŒ ABCDEFGHIJKLMNOPQRSTUVWXYZ&ÆŒ

ABCDEFGHIJKLMNOPQRSTUVWXYZ&ÆŒ

abcdefghijklmnopqrstuvwxyzæœfiffflffiffl 1234567890 [($.,-":;!?-—)] 1234567890 gjpqy

abcdefghijklmnopqrstuvwxyzæœfiffflffiffl 1234567890 ($.,-":;!? —)

CASLON LIGHTFACE, ATF (42-pt. at 57%) (Fred Liddle)

ABCDEFGHIJKLMNOPQRSTUVWXYZ$.,-:;!?'

abcdefghijklmnopqrstuvwxyzst&1234567890

CASLON LIGHTFACE ITALIC, Keystone 18-pt.

ABCDEFGHIJKLMONPQRSTUVWXYZ?

&abcdefghijklmnopqrstuvwwxyz!$1234567

CASLON LIGHTFACE CONDENSED, ATF 24-pt. (Dave Greer)

ABCDEFGHIJKLMNOPQRSTUVWXYZ&

abcdefghijklmnopqrstuvwxyz 1234567890$.,-:;'!?

RECUT CASLON, ATF 24-pt. (William Greer)

ABCDEFGHIJKLMNOPQRSTUVWXYZ

abcdefghijklmnopqrstuvwxyz 1234567890$& f.,-:;'!?

RECUT CASLON ITALIC, ATF 24-pt. (William Greer)

ABCDEFGHIJKLMNOPQRSTUVWXYZ

abcdefghijklmnopqrstuvwxyz 1234567890$& .,-:;'!?

Name in parentheses after some specimens
indicates person who has set that specimen,
in whole or in part, to our format.

including the peculiarly reversed *T,* which was later corrected. Also note the swash letters shown with some following Caslon italics.

Caslon Italic Specials are swash letters of a completely different sort, designed by Carl S. Junge in 1924 for BB&S, for use with that foundry's *Caslon Italic* and various similar faces.

* * *

Monotype produced an adaptation of Caslon to its mechanical restrictions as early as 1903, when Sol Hess drew *English Caslon Old Style No. 37* at the request of the Gilliss Press in Boston. (Two years later Monotype adopted a new set of matrix and other mechanical improvements which required redesigning nearly all its faces.) Display sizes of this face were also drawn by Hess, presumably adapted from the original English face, as the italic has several swash letters similar to the English version. Otherwise display sizes of this roman and italic are very similar to Inland Type Foundry's short-descender adaptation of the original Caslon. On Linotype and Intertype, *Caslon No. 4* is essentially the same.

Monotype also has *Inland Caslon Old Style No. 137,* presumably adapted from the Inland face mentioned above, but the italic seems identical to that of No. 37. Linotype has a copy of *Caslon No. 137* under that name.

About 1915 Monotype cut yet another version of *Caslon Old Style—No. 337,* designated "MacKellar Caslon" in some early literature because it is closer to the original face associated with that foundry. Display sizes are virtually an exact copy of No. 471. Composition sizes are well adapted, though necessarily modified to fit the standard arrangement; they are made with short descenders on standard alignment, but were the first Monotype face with alternate long descenders. Oddly, all three Monotype Caslons—37, 137, and 337—are the same set width—letter for letter—in all keyboard sizes made, which means that any given character is precisely the same width from one face to another in any composition size. In addition, 12-point No. 337, which with long descenders must be cast on 13- or 14-point body, is essentially the same size and width as 14-point of the same face. Sizes of this face above 36-point were later copied from Stephenson Blake's *Caslon Old Face* and called *Caslon Old Style No. 437,* as previously noted.

Linotype and Intertype have *Caslon* and *Italic,* similar to *Caslon No. 540* and cut about 1903; long descenders are available in place of the regular short descenders, making a fair approximation of *Caslon Oldstyle No. 471;* this *Caslon Italic* in 18- to 30-point sizes is more regularized as shown, similar to *Caslon Light Italic.* Linotype also has *Caslon No. 2,* a copy of Monotype *Caslon No. 37,* also with alternate long descenders; and the previously-mentioned *Caslon No. 137,* cut in 1936. For greatest authenticity, Linotype went back to the English original in 1923 for its *Caslon Old Face;* the roman is almost indistinguishable, but the italic is necessarily modified considerably. Most smaller sizes have both long and short alternate descenders available. Intertype offers the same face, roman only, in 18- to 30-point. Ludlow's *True-Cut Caslon* and *Italic,* cut in 1922 and 1928 respectively, are close copies of *Caslon Oldstyle No. 471* and *Italic.*

* * *

Several attempts have been made to regularize Caslon and improve its so-called faults, but these have generally lost much of the character of the face, and have seldom achieved widespread use. They include *Recut Caslon* (Inland 1907), *Caslon Lightface* (Keystone 1910-12), *Clearface Caslon* (Robert Wiebking for Western 1913), etc., all with italics and some with condensed versions; *Caslon Lightface Italic* is non-kerning.

New Caslon, introduced in 1905 by Inland, was the most successful of these attempts. In addition to eliminating irregularities, the aim of this face was to strengthen the design so that under modern printing conditions it would more closely resemble the effect of the original Caslon when printed heavily on dampened rough paper, as was commonly done in the eighteenth century. The italic followed in 1906. In 1919 ATF (successor to Inland) re-

(Caslon continues)

Caslon, Lino = Inter (6-14, 36pt)
Caslon Italic, Lino = Inter (6-30pt)
Caslon Lightface, Keystone-ATF 821 (5-72pt)
Caslon Lightface Italic, Keystone-ATF 823 (6-48pt)
Caslon Lightface Condensed, Keystone-ATF 822 (6-72pt)
Recut Caslon, ATF 365 (6-84pt)
Recut Caslon Italic, ATF 366 (6-48pt)

CASLON CLEARFACE (CASLON LIGHT, Ludlow) 24-pt.

ABCDEFGHIJKLMNOPQRSTUVWXYZ&
abcdefghijklmnopqrstuvwxyz 1234567890 $.,-:;'!?

CASLON CLEARFACE ITALIC, BB&S 24-pt.

ABCDEFGHIJKLMNOPQRSTUVWXYZ&
abcdefghijklmnopqrstuvwxyz $1234567890 .,-:;'!?

NEW CASLON, Mono 24-pt.

ABCDEFGHIJKLMNOPQRSTUVWXYZ$&
abcdeffghijklmnopqrstuvwxyz.,:;'!?1234567890

NEW CASLON ITALIC, ATF 24-pt.

ABCDEFGHIJKLMNOPQRSTUVWXYZ&
abcdefghijklmnopqrstuvwxyz fiffflffifl.,:;'!?$1234567890

AMERICAN CASLON, Mono 24-pt.

ABCDEFGHIJKLMNOPQRSTUVWXYZ&
abcdefghijklmnopqrstuvwxyz $1234567890 .,-:;'!?

AMERICAN CASLON ITALIC, ATF 24-pt.

ABCDEFGHIJKLMNOPQRSTUVWXYZ& ff fi fl ffi ffl
abcdefghijklmnopqrstuvvwwxyz 1234567890 $1234567890 .,:;-'!?
ABCDEFGHIJLMNPRSTVWY Qu ct st

CONDENSED CASLON, Mono 24-pt.

ABCDEFGHIJKLMNOPQRSTUVWXYZ
abcdefghijklmnopqrstuvwxyz.,:;-'!?&$1234567890

CASLON EXTRA CONDENSED, ATF 24-pt.

ABCDEFGHIJKLMNOPQRSTUVWXYZ&
abcdefghijklmnopqrstuvwxyz 1234567890$

versed the descender-shortening trend with the design by Morris Benton of long descenders, oldstyle figures, and italic swash characters as *American Caslon;* otherwise this face and *New Caslon* are identical. *New Caslon* was adapted to Linotype and Intertype as *Caslon No. 3,* which some users call *Caslon Bold,* although it was not intended to be a bold face. However, in 18-point and larger, *Caslon No. 3* and *Italic* are copies of *Caslon Bold* rather than *New Caslon.*

Condensed Caslon is a modification of *New Caslon,* by Inland in 1907; it was inherited by ATF and copied by Monotype, both of which gave it the same series number (the only such incidence); printers often but incorrectly call it *Caslon Bold Condensed. Caslon Extra Condensed* is also derived from *New Caslon,* sometime between 1912 and 1917. *Caslon Catalog,* with heavied hairlines, was designed by Robert Wiebking for his Advance Type Foundry in 1913 under the name of *Caslon Antique* (not to be confused with a later use of this name); it was also shown by Laclede, and was renamed when BB&S acquired it.

Caslon Medium and *Italic,* as the name implies, are somewhat heavier versions, offered by BB&S as *Modern Caslon* and *Italic* about 1924—the roman at least was shown by Western Type Foundry in the mid-teens. However, the italic appears to be identical to Ludlow's *Caslon Light Italic,* also credited to Wiebking but advertised as early as 1922; it was the first face cut for Ludlow's development of italic matrices which permitted kerning designs without the fragility of the kerns on single types. Strangely, though, Ludlow *Caslon Light* (roman) matches *Caslon Clearface.*

The newest Caslon was designed in 1965, when ATF commissioned a "beefed up" version of *Caslon No. 540,* by Frank Bartuska. The result was *Caslon No. 641,* an arbitrary number. It is a handsome face, reflecting the best of 540, but without the latter's variations from one size to another. It also includes all the ancillary characters of ATF's later creations as shown, including percent and pound marks, a variety of quotation marks, and center

(Caslon continues)

Caslon Clearface, BB&S-ATF 1565 (6-72pt); Caslon Light, Ludlow 1-L (4-72pt)
Caslon Clearface Italic, BB&S-ATF 1566 (6-48pt)
New Caslon, ATF 331 (5-84pt); Mono 537 (6-72H4); Caslon No. 3, Lino = Inter = APL (6-14pt, see text)
New Caslon Italic, ATF 332 (5-48pt); Mono 5371 (6-60pt); Caslon No. 3 Italic, Lino = Inter = APL (6-14pt); Caslon Fullface Italic, Hansen (6-36pt)
American Caslon, ATF 458 (6-48pt); Mono 637 (8-72pt)
American Caslon Italic, ATF 471 (6-72pt); Mono 6371 (8-72pt)
Condensed Caslon, ATF 113 (6-96pt); Mono 113 (5-72pt)
Caslon Extra Condensed, ATF 153 (6-72pt)
Caslon Catalog, BB&S-ATF 1564 (6-72pt)
Caslon Medium, BB&S-ATF 1567 (6-72pt)
Caslon Medium Italic, BB&S-ATF 1568 (6-48pt); Caslon Light Italic, Ludlow 1-LI (6-72pt)
Caslon No. 641, ATF 723 (10-72pt)
Condensed Caslon is called Caslon Old Face Heavy Compressed by Stephenson Blake.

CASLON CATALOG, BB&S 24-pt.

DEMAND GOODS Lifting Higher Hand

CASLON MEDIUM, BB&S 24-pt. (John Horn)

ABCDEFGHIJKLMNOPQRSTUVWXYZ&
abcdefghijklmnopqrstuvwxyz$1234567890.,''?!-;:

CASLON MEDIUM ITALIC (CASLON LIGHT ITALIC, Ludlow) 24-pt.

ABCDEFGHIJKLMNOPQRSTUVWXYZ&
abcdefghijklmnopqrstuvwxyz 1234567890

CASLON NO. 641, ATF (36-pt. at 67%) (Bob Long)

ABCDEFGHIJKLMNOPQRSTUVWXYZ&
abcdefghijklmnopqrstuvwxyzctfffiflffiffl
$$1234567890¢£.,-:;""""""!?----—·()*%

ABCDEFGHIJKLMNOPQRSTUVWXYZ.,-:;'!?&
abcdefghijklmnopqrstuvwxyz $1234567890
ÆŒfiflffffiffl œ ct st Tg AGas

Mono   Hansen

ABCDEFGHIJKLMNOPQRSTUVWXYZ
abcdefghijklmnopqrstuvwxyz ff fi ffi fl ffl ,.-;:'!?&
$1234567890

ABCDEFGHIJKLMNOPQRSTUVWXYZ
abcdefghijklmnopqrstuvwxyz,.-;:'!?&$1234567890 ct st AG

Hansen

A B C D E F G H I J K L M N O P Q R S T U
V W X Y Z & $ 1 2 3 4 5 6 7 8 9 0 . , - ' : ; ! ?
a b c d e f g h i j k l m n o p q r s t u v w x y z ct st

ABCDEFGHIJKLMNOPQRSTUVWXYZ&
abcdefghijklmnopqrstuvwxyz 1234567890

ABCDEFGHIJKLMNOPQRSTUVWXY
abcdefghijklmnopqrstuvwxyz 123456789

ABCDEFGHIJKLMNOPQRSTUVWXYZ& .,:;!?
abcdefghijklmnopqrstuvwxyz 1234567890

ABCDEFGHIJKLMNOPQRSTUVWXYZ&
abcdefghijklmnopqrstuvwxyz 1234567890

dot, hyphen, and dash in two positions to center on caps or lowercase. An italic was started but never completed. This face has considerable similarity to *Caslon Medium,* for which ATF still had mats when the new face was commissioned.

* * *

Boldface Caslons have been made by several sources. The most popular *Caslon Bold* was introduced by Keystone Type Foundry in 1905, followed by *Italic* in 1906 and *Condensed* and *Extended* versions about 1911; this is the version made by ATF and in regular widths by Monotype. Monotype keyboard sizes (including large composition to 18-point) are modified considerably to fit standard arrangements, but the only apparent difference in display sizes is the redrawn *T* and *g* shown separately in the specimen alphabet—and the addition of ligatures and diphthongs. On Linotype and Intertype, *Caslon No. 3* matches ATF *Caslon Bold* from 18-point up, although smaller sizes match *New Caslon.*

Hansen's *Caslon Fullface* and *Caslon Fullface Condensed* were close copies of *Caslon Bold* and *Caslon Bold Condensed,* differing most apparently in the characters shown (*AGas,* condensed *AG*), but Hansen's *Caslon Fullface Italic* matches *New Caslon Italic.*

A somewhat different *Caslon Bold* series is made by Ludlow, and a *Caslon Black* series by BB&S, from Western Type Foundry in the mid-teens.

Caslon Adbold, originating with Keystone in 1913, is characterized by heavier strokes throughout; *Extended* and *Extra Condensed* versions fol-

(Caslon continues)

Caslon Bold, Keystone-ATF 817 (5-96pt); Mono 79 (5-72pt); Lino (5,6pt); Caslon No. 3, Lino = Inter (18-30pt, see text); APL (18-72pt); Caslon Fullface, Hansen (6-72pt)

Caslon Bold Italic, Keystone-ATF 820 (5-60pt); Mono 791 (6-72pt); Lino (5,6pt); Caslon No. 3 Italic, Lino = Inter (18-30pt); APL (18-72pt)

Caslon Bold Condensed, Keystone-ATF 818 (6-120pt); Lino (14-36pt); APL (18-72pt); Caslon Fullface Condensed, Hansen (6-72pt)

Caslon Bold Extended, Keystone-ATF 819 (6-72pt); also Caslon Title Extended, Keystone-ATF 826 (6-24pt)

Caslon Bold, Ludlow 1-B (6-72pt)

Caslon Bold Italic, Ludlow 1-BI (6-48pt)

Caslon Bold Condensed, Ludlow 1-BC (6-72pt)

Caslon Bold Extra Condensed, Ludlow 1-BEC (12-72pt); Lino (24,30pt)

Caslon Black, BB&S-ATF 1561 (6-72pt)

Caslon Black Italic, BB&S-ATF 1563 (6-72pt)

Caslon Black Condensed, BB&S-ATF 1562 (6-72pt)

Caslon Bold is known as Old Style Bold in England.

CASLON BLACK, BB&S 24-pt.

MINES DEMAND QRSTUVWXYZ 6789012345
Enormous Output of successive steps. Man in

CASLON BLACK ITALIC, BB&S 24-pt.

RIDE SECURED XYZABCDEFG1234567890
Foremen Demand of successive steps. Man in

CASLON BLACK CONDENSED, BB&S 24-pt. (part reduced)

BOLD DESIGN STRO SECURED
Suitable For Narrow H Printing Job Contract

CASLON ADBOLD, ATF 24-pt.

ABCDEFGHIJKLMNOPQRSTUVWXYZ&
abcdefghijklmnopqrstuvwxyz 1234567890$

CASLON ADBOLD EXTRA CONDENSED, ATF (36-pt. at 67%)

ABCDEFGIJKLMNOPQRSTUVWX& abcdefghijklmnopqrstuvwxyz $1234

CASLON ADBOLD EXTENDED, ATF 14-pt.

**A B C D E F G H I J K L M N O P Q R
S T U V W X Y Z & $ 1 2 3 4 5 6 7 8 9 0
a b c d e f g h i j k l m n o p q r s t u
v w x y z ct st . , - ' : ; ! ?**

HEAVY CASLON, ATF 24-pt.

ABCDEFGHIJKLMNOPQRSTUVWX&
abcdefghijklmnopqrstuvwxyz 1234567890 $?!.,:;'-

CASLON OLD FACE HEAVY ITALIC, Ludlow 24-pt., Inter 10-pt.

ABCDEFGHIJKLMNOPQRSTUVWXYZ
abcdefghijklmnopqrstuvwxyz 12345678

*ABCDEFGHIJKLMNOPQRSTUVWXYZ 1234567890
abcdefghijklmnopqrstuvwxyz [ ] %†§‡¶*( )$,.-;':'!?&⅛¼⅜½⅝¾⅞*

CASLON OPENFACE (30-pt. at 80%) (Dave Norton)

ABCDEFGHIJKLMNOPQRSTUVWXYZ&
abcdefghijklmnopqrstuvwxyzfffiflffl.,--:;'!?$1234567890

CASLON SHADED, ATF 24-pt.

ABCDEFGHIJKLMNOPQRSTUVWXYZ
abcdefghijklmnopqrstuvwxyz,.-;:'!?&$1234567890

CASLON SHADOW TITLE, Mono (36H4 at 50%, spaced)

A B C D E F G H I J K L M N O P Q R S
T U V W X Y Z & . ,

lowed in 1915 to 1917; all were patented and presumably designed by R. F. Burfeind.

Heavy Caslon was issued by Inland in 1906 or earlier; Ludlow copied it as *Caslon Old Face Heavy* in 1925 and Intertype in 1937. Ludlow has a companion italic, while Intertype's italic is a sloped roman design. See *Caslon Shaded*.

* * *

Caslon Openface was originated by BB&S in 1915, where it was first called *College Oldstyle*. It started out as a reproduction of a delicate 18th-century French face known as *Le Moreau le Jeune,* by the foundry of G. Peignot & Son, but in the American version some strokes are heavier. In a later ad, BB&S said, "Placing it in the Caslon group of types is taking a liberty, but it assuredly 'belongs.' " Actually it has somewhat more affinity for the Cochin types.

Caslon Shaded was adapted by ATF from *Heavy Caslon* in 1917, by W. F. Capitaine. *Caslon Shadow Title* was adapted from *Caslon Bold* by Monotype about 1928. Compare *Cameo, Cochin Open, Gravure, Narciss.*

* * *

Caslons in name only. *Caslon Antique* and *Italic* were designed by Berne Nadall and brought out by BB&S in 1896-98 as *Fifteenth Century* (*XIV Century* in one early announcement) and *Italic*. Although they aren't really representative of types of that time, being a poor copy of a crude early face cut about 1475 in Venice, they have become popular for the simulation of supposedly quaint American types of the eighteenth and nineteenth centuries. Disregarding the usual practice of increasing the proportionate width of a face as the size decreases, *Caslon Antique* maintains uniform proportions in all sizes, and thus appears narrow and cramped in small sizes.

Caslon Antique is also the original (1913) name of Advance Type Foundry's *Caslon Catalog,* mentioned earlier, while in the early 1920s Laclede Type Foundry applied that name to "a brand-new, entirely machine-cut face of Old Style Antique," a duplicate of the Advance face.

Caslon Old Roman is discussed later under its original name, *Old Roman.*

Caslon Text originated with William Caslon in 1734. Inland Type brought out a reproduction of it in 1899 as part of their agreement with the Caslon Type Foundry in England. It later became the property of ATF, and was copied by Linotype. Being handcut originally, it shows the expected variations from one size to another, but some characters show decidedly different forms in some sizes. See *Cloister Black* and *Engravers Old English,* which are derived from this face.

Caslon Adbold, Keystone-ATF 814 (6-72pt)
Caslon Adbold Extra Condensed, Keystone-ATF 816 (6-72pt)
Caslon Adbold Extended, Keystone-ATF 815 (6-72pt)
Heavy Caslon, ATF 817 (6-84pt); Caslon Old Face Heavy, Inter (8,10pt); Ludlow 1-OFH (6-48pt)
Caslon Heavy Italic, Ludlow 1-HI (14-48pt); Inter (8,10pt)

* * *

Caslon Openface, BB&S-ATF 1571 (8-48pt); (Univ 8-48pt); also Caslon Open Title, BB&S-ATF 1572 (6-42pt)
Caslon Shaded, ATF 52 (10-84pt)
Caslon Shadow Title, Mono 379 (36H4)

* * *

Caslon Antique, BB&S-ATF 1559 (8-48pt)
Caslon Antique Italic, BB&S-ATF 1560 (8-48pt)
Caslon Old Roman, Mono 78 (6-36pt); [Caslon] Old Roman, BB&S-ATF 1804 (6-72pt); Old Roman, Lino (8-14pt)
Caslon Old Roman Italic, Mono 781 (6-36pt); [Caslon] Old Roman Italic, BB&S-ATF 1810 (6-48pt); Old Roman Italic, Lino (8-14pt)
Caslon Text, ATF (8-36pt); Lino (10,12pt)

CASLON ANTIQUE, ATF 24-pt.

ABCDEFGHIJKLMNOPQRSTUVWXYZ 1234567890
abcdefghijklmnopqrstuvwxyz $1234567890.,-:;'!?&

CASLON ANTIQUE ITALIC, ATF 24-pt.

ABCDEFGHIJKLMNOPQRSTUVWXYZ 1234567890
abcdefghijklmnopqrstuvwxyz $1234567890.,-:;'!?&

CASLON TEXT, ATF 24-pt.

ABCDEFGHIJKLMNOPQRSTUVWXYZ
abcdefghijklmnopqrstuvwxyz 1234567890&$.,-'::;!?

CATALOG OLDSTYLE, ATF 24-pt. (part reduced)

ABCDEFGOMPOSI-
abcdefghijk tion, an imp1234567890
A M T & oo The of ſ ſ th f st ly

CATHEDRAL TEXT, ATF 18-pt. (part reduced) (Dave Greer)

ABCDEFGHIJKLMNOPQRSTUVWXYZ & ffffi
abcdefghijklmnopqrstuvwxyz ffffi £$1234567890.,-:;'!?

CAXTON INITIALS, ATF 18-pt.

ABCDEFGHIJKLMNOPQRSTUVWXYZ

CENTAUR, Eng Mono 24-pt.

ABCDEFGHIJKLMNOPQRSTUVWXYZ&
abcdefghijklmnopqrstuvwxyz $1234567890 .,-:;'!?

What's In a Font

ABCDEFGHIJKLMNOPQRSTUVWXYZ
ABCDEFGHIJKLMNOPQRSTUVWXYZ
ABCDEFGHIJKLMNOPQRSTUVWXYZ

12345	abcdefghijklmnopqrstuvwxyz	67890
VBCDE	*abcdefghijklmnopqrstuvwxyz*	FGRTJ

,.:;?!(|)*'' - — Æ Œ ℔ & £ $ . . .   fi fl ff ffi ffl æ œ
,.s;?!AIQO'' - — Æ Œ ℔ N £ P L   . . . *fi y ff* w m k h

12345	Z & : ( ) fl ffi ffl $ æ œ QU Qu	67890	} ?
12345	u *&* : ( ) *fl ffi ffl* $ *æ œ QU Qu*	*67890*	} ?

⅛ ¼ ⅜ ½ ⅝ ¾ ⅞   x z & Æ Œ   @   % † ‡ § ¶ – [ ]

SWASH CHARACTERS   OLD STYLE FIGURES
A B C D E G J K L M N P Q R T U Y &   1234567890 *1234567890*

TWO-LETTER LOGOTYPES
F. P. Ta Te To Tr Tu Tw Ty T. Va Ve Vo V. Wa We Wi Wo Wr W. Ya Ye Yo Y.
F. P. Ta Te To Tr Tu Tw Ty T. Va Ve Vo V. Wa We Wi Wo Wr W. Ya Ye Yo Y.

fa fe fo fr fs ft fu fy ffa ffe ffo ffr ffs ffu ffy f, f. f- ff, ff. ff- f ff
fa fe fo fr fs ft fu fy ffa ffe ffo ffr ffs ffu ffy f, f. f- ff, ff. ff- f ff

LONG DESCENDERS   SHORT DESCENDERS
g j p q y   *g j p q y*   J g j p q y 3 4 5 7 9 ( )   *g j p q y 3 4 5 7 9*

ONE-LETTER ITALIC LOGOTYPES
FA PA TA VA WA YA Th Wh

f af aff ef eff hf if iff kf lf mf nf of off pf rf sf tf uf uff yf If Of Off

ONE-LETTER ITALIC   SPECIAL TWO-LETTER SMALL CAPS
SPECIAL NO. 5   ABCDEFGHIJKLMNOPQRSTUVWXYZ&
abcdefghijklmnopqrstuvwxyz   *ABCDEFGHIJKLMNOPQRSTUVWXYZ&*

74

CASTELLAR—see Imports in Appendix.

CATALOG OLD STYLE is a BB&S face, formerly known as *Old Style Antique,* which probably dates from the 1890s. It is similar to *Bookman* but heavier and less refined; in fact it is much like the face from which Bookman was derived. A condensed version, known as *Monitor No. 5,* was later re-named *Bookman Bold Condensed* (q.v.).

Catalog Old Style, BB&S-ATF 1574 (6-72pt)

CATHEDRAL TEXT is an extremely heavy form of Blackletter or Old English, introduced by ATF around the turn of the century, but duplicating Bruce Type Foundry's *Black No. 400.* The extraordinary contrast between thick and thin elements results in awkward design and proportions for many characters.

Cathedral Text, ATF 54 (6-60pt)

CAXTON INITIALS were designed by Frederic W. Goudy in 1905. He says of them, "These are a rather clumsy form of Lombardic capitals. At this time I had not given text letters much study and while the forms of these capitals are correct enough, they lack the delicate hairlines which I learned later are an important feature of letters of this kind." The font includes only the 26 letters shown and a small leaf ornament. Compare *Lombardic Capitals.*

Caxton Initials, ATF (12-72pt)

CELTIC—see *Latin Expanded.*
CELTIC ORNATE—see Antiques in Appendix.

CENTAUR was designed by Bruce Rogers in 1914, based on the beautiful roman type first used by Nicolas Jenson in 1470, and a refinement of *Montaigne* (q.v.), designed a decade earlier by Rogers. *Centaur* was first cut by Robert Wiebking of BB&S as a private type for the Museum Press of the Metropolitan Museum of New York. In 1929 it was recut under the joint sponsorship of Lanston Monotype and Monotype Corporation, England, but issued only by the latter. Some critics have called it the best recutting of the Jenson letter. *Arrighi* (q.v.) was cut as an italic companion to *Centaur.* Compare *Cloister, Eusebius, Italian Old Style;* also *Jenson.*

Centaur, ATF (14pt, private); also English Monotype (6-72pt)

What's In a Font

In fact, what *is* a font? For our purposes, it is the complete set of letters and related characters in one style. To the user of handset type, it is the assortment of one size and style of type as made by the typefounder, including multiple units of each letter in proportion to its average use. To the machine typesetter, it is the assortment of matrices needed for one face.

These are the components of a most complete font:

CAPS or CAPITALS or UPPER CASE or MAJUSCULES (the ampersand is usually included).
SMALL CAPS, in smaller sizes of some faces.
LOWER CASE or MINUSCULES, except in a few specialized designs.
LIGATURES, in many fonts. (See page 24.)
FIGURES, lining and/or hanging or old style, including dollar mark and sometimes pound Sterling mark.
POINTS or PUNCTUATION MARKS.
REFERENCE MARKS, in most Linotype and Intertype fonts; available as generic extras in Monotype and foundry fonts.

SWASH LETTERS, in some fonts, mostly italic.
DIPHTHONGS (Æ etc.), in most machine-set faces and a few foundry faces, although obsolescent in American usage.
FRACTIONS, in most Linotype and Intertype fonts; available as extras in most Ludlow fonts and some Monotype and foundry fonts.
ALTERNATE or SPECIAL CHARACTERS, such as long or short descenders, certain reproportioned or redrawn characters, etc., in a few fonts.
TYPOGRAPHIC REFINEMENTS, narrower italic lower case with special logotypes, and "true-cut" small caps, available for some Linotype faces. Some similar characters are also made for Intertype and Ludlow, to overcome limitations of slug machine matrices.
In addition, a great many accented characters have been made for other languages, especially for the machine-set faces. Also, a great many signs and symbols are available, but almost always as generic designs rather than matching specific faces.
The opposite page shows the characters, other than accents, available for Linotype Caslon Old Face.

THE CENTURY FACE was designed to make for the Century Magazine a blacker and more readable type than the thin and gray-printing old-style letter in which it had been printed for many years. The hair-compact composition in a narrow measure, this style of face is properly adapted. THESE ARE THE SMALL CAPITALS and *these the italic characters of this font.*

THE CENTURY BROAD-FACE was made by the De Vinne Press for service on books to be set in a broad measure, which do not require a compression of letters for the saving of space. relief of white is diminished. THESE ARE THE SMALL CAPITALS and *these the italic characters of this font.* The lower-case alphabet of this

CENTURY EXPANDED, Mono 24-pt.

ABCDEFGHIJKLMNOPQRSTUVWXYZ,.-;:'!?&
abcdefghijklmnopqrstuvwxyz ff fi ffi fl ffl $1234567890

CENTURY EXPANDED ITALIC, ATF 24-pt.

ABCDEFGHIJKLMNOPQRSTUVWXYZ&.,:;!?'-
abcdefghijklmnopqrstuvwxyzff fi fl ffi ffl 1234567890$

CENTURY BOLD, Mono 24-pt.

ABCDEFGHIJKLMNOPQRSTUVWXYZ.,-:;'!?&
abcdefghijklmnopqrstuvwxyz fi ff fl ffi ffl $1234567890

CENTURY BOLD ITALIC, ATF 24-pt.

ABCDEFGHIJKLMNOPQRSTUVWXYZ.,-';:!?&
abcdefghijklmnopqrstuvwxyz fi ffi ff fl ffl $1234567890

CENTURY BOLD CONDENSED, ATF 24-pt.

ABCDEFGHIJKLMNOPQRSTUVWXYZ
abcdefghijklmnopqrstuvwxyz ff fi ffi fl ffl .,:;'- !?& $1234567890

CENTURY BOLD CONDENSED ITALIC, Mono 24-pt.

ABCDEFGHIJKLMNOPQRSTUVWXYZ&
abcdefghijklmnopqrstuvwxyz ff fi ffi fl ffl $1234567890 .,-:;'!?

CENTURY BOLD EXTRA CONDENSED, Lino (30-pt. at 80%)

ABCDEFGHIJKLMNOPQRSTUVWXYZ $1234567890

CENTURY BOLD EXTENDED, Mono (30-pt. at 80%)

ABCDEFGHIJKLMNOPQRSTUVWXYZ.,:;-'!?
abcdefghijklmnopqrstuvwxyz &$12345678

CENTURY ROMAN was designed in 1894 by Linn Boyd Benton at the request of Theodore L. DeVinne, publisher of *Century* Magazine at his De-Vinne Press in New York City. Benton was the mechanical genius of the young American Type Founders Company; DeVinne was regarded as an outstanding printing craftsman, who was dissatisfied with the types then available for magazine and book work. As he wrote later, "Readers of failing eyesight rightfully ask for types that are plain and unequivocal, that reveal the entire character at a glance, and are not discerned with difficulty by body marks joined to hairlines and serifs that are but half seen or not seen at all."

Century Roman was planned to get as many characters per line as the face previously used for the magazine, but because the x-height was increased, it appeared to be condensed. Hairlines were thickened for greater clearness. It was made only as foundry type, handset for several years for *Century Magazine* and for numerous books. Although shown in ATF specimen books, it was not used to any great extent by other printers because it was considered a little too narrow. A wider version, called *Century Broad-Face* or *Century Roman No. 2,* was thereafter designed by Benton, but little used except by DeVinne.

* * *

L. B. Benton's principal interest was the mechanical end of the typecasting industry, and he turned his attention back to this. About this time his son, Morris Fuller Benton, joined ATF after graduation from Cornell, and was assigned the task of unifying and updating the numerous styles of type the company had inherited from its many predecessors.

One of the younger Benton's early assignments was redesigning *Century Roman,* extending it slightly to meet the Typographical Union standards of the day, on which rates for typesetting were based. The result was named *Century Expanded,* issued in 1900. DeVinne, showing it in his company specimen book, said, "The expansion is upward, enabling one to get much matter in small space"—essentially what he had said of the earlier face. But it is obviously expanded in width also, compared with the original face.

(Note: Some sources, including a publication by ATF itself and DeVinne's own specimen book, credit the elder Benton with designing *Century Expanded.* But study reveals that the face shown by DeVinne is not quite as wide as that later shown by ATF. Apparently the elder Benton designed an early version, cut it in one trial size, then turned the task over to his son. Undoubtedly, though, he collaborated in the redesign.)

Century Expanded and *Italic* were made in an unusual number of sizes, including 4-, 4½-, 5-, 5½-, 6-, 7-, 8-, 9-, 10-, 11-point, and all the usual sizes to 72-point. The two smallest sizes were identical as to face except for length of descenders, likewise 5½- and 6-point.

Century Bold and *Italic* were designed by Morris Benton in 1904 and released by ATF the following year. Although the name doesn't include "Expanded," they are obviously the companion boldfaces. *Century Bold Condensed* and *Extended* were both designed in 1906 but not released until 1909 and 1910 respectively; both were also by Benton. *Century Bold Condensed Italic* was designed by Sol Hess for Monotype in 1938. Linotype cut *Century Bold Extra Condensed* as a newspaper headline face to fit the limits of its standard magazines.

(Century continues)

Century Roman and Italic, ATF (8-10pt)
Century Broad-Face or Century Roman No. 2 and Italic, ATF (10pt)
Century Expanded, ATF 59 (4-72pt); Mono 20 (6-72pt); Lino = Inter (4-36pt); Ludlow 5-E (12-42pt); Century Roman, BB&S-ATF 1576 (6-24pt); also Modified No. 20, Mono 120
Century Expanded Italic, ATF 60 (4-72pt); Mono 201 (6-36pt); Lino = Inter (4-24pt); Century Italic, BB&S-ATF 1575 (6-24pt)
Century Bold, ATF 55 (6-120pt); Mono 118 (5½-72pt); Lino = Inter (6-48pt); APL (18-72pt); Ludlow 5-B (12-96pt); also Century Bold Cancelled, Lino (12,14pt)
Century Bold Italic, ATF 58 (6-72pt); Mono 1181 (6-72pt); Lino = Inter (6-36pt); APL (18-48pt); Ludlow 5-BI (12-72pt)
Century Bold Condensed, ATF 56 (6-72pt); Mono 418 (14-72H4); Lino = Inter (12-30pt); Ludlow 5-BC (18-72pt)
Century Bold Condensed Italic, Mono 4181 (14-72pt); Inter (18pt)
Century Bold Extra Condensed, Lino (30pt caps)
Century Bold Extended, ATF 57 (6-72pt); Mono 518 (14-48pt); Ludlow 5-BE (12-96pt)

CENTURY OLDSTYLE, Lino 24-pt.

ABCDEFGHIJKLMNOPQRSTUVWXYZ&,.:;?!'-—ÆŒ
abcdefghijklmnopqrstuvwxyz fi fl ff ffi ffl æ œ $1234567890

CENTURY OLDSTYLE ITALIC, ATF (30-pt. at 80%)

ABCDEFGHIJKLMNOPQRSTUVWXYZ 1234567890
abcdefghijklmnopqrstuvwxyz

CENTURY OLDSTYLE BOLD, ATF 24-pt.

ABCDEFGHIJKLMNOPQRSTUVWXYZ ,.-;:'!?&
abcdefghijklmnopqrstuvwxyz $1234567890

CENTURY OLDSTYLE BOLD ITALIC, ATF 24-pt.

ABCDEFGHIJKLMNOPQRSTUVWXYZ
abcdefghijklmnopqrstuvwxyz 1234567890$

CENTURY OLDSTYLE BOLD CONDENSED, ATF 14-pt.

A B C D E F G H I J K L M N O P Q R S T U V W
X Y Z & $ 1 2 3 4 5 6 7 8 9 0 . , - ' : ; ! ?
a b c d e f g h i j k l m n o p q r s t u v w x y z ff fi fl ffi ffl

CENTURY OLDSTYLE, Mono 24-pt.

ABCDEFGHIJKLMNOPQRSTUVWXYZ& .,:;-'!?
abcdefghijklmnopqrstuvwxyz $1234567890

CENTURY OLDSTYLE & ITALIC, Mono 12-pt. (5th line, with long ascenders and descenders)

ABCDEFGHIJKLMNOPQRSTUVWXYZ&ÆŒ   ABCDEFGHIJKLMNOPQRSTUVWXYZ&ÆŒ
ABCDEFGHIJKLMNOPQRSTUVWXYZ&ÆŒ
abcdefghijklmnopqrstuvwxyzæœfifffflffiffl 1234567890 $.,-":;!?-—
abcdefghijklmnopqrstuvwxyzæœfifffflffiffl 1234567890 $:;!?
abcdefghijklmnopqrstuvwxyzæœfifffflffiffl

CENTURY CATALOGUE, ATF 24-pt. (Dave Churchman)

ABCDEFGHIJKLMNOPQRSTUVWXYZ.,-:;""''!?
abcdefghijklmnopqrstuvwxyzfffiflfflffi$1234567890

Meanwhile, the development of the Century family took a different turn when Benton designed *Century Oldstyle* in 1906. Released in 1908-09, this face is much like *Century Expanded* in weight and height, but with old-style serifs. An ATF ad in 1909 called it "the newest and by far the best old-style ever designed." *Century Oldstyle Bold* was designed and cut in 1909 and *Bold Italic* in 1910, while *Bold Condensed* was designed in 1911 but not released until 1915. Although closely related, the *Century Oldstyle* family is not really a part of the *Century Expanded* family. Another related face is *Schoolbook Oldstyle* (q.v.). Also see *University Old Style.*

Retreating, perhaps, from the large x-height of *Century Oldstyle,* a modified oldstyle named *Century Catalogue* was brought out by Benton in 1917 with longer ascenders but essentially the same general design. Curiously, *Century Catalogue Italic* was cut from the patterns for *Baskerville Italic.* Except for the caps *A, V,* and *W* and the omission of swash letters, the faces are almost identical in the 18-point size; in smaller sizes the Century face is wider, as modified by pantagraph during the cutting of mats.

A third family of Century followed when Ginn & Company, publishers of schoolbooks, asked ATF to develop a typeface for maximum legibility. After many studies of eyesight and reading factors dating from 1912, *Century Schoolbook* and *Italic* were designed by Morris Benton in 1917-19 and released in 1918-21. *Century Schoolbook Bold* was designed in 1919 and cut in 1923.

(Century continues)

Century Oldstyle, ATF 61 (6-72pt); Mono 157 (6-36pt); Inter (36pt); same or Old Style No. 7, Lino (24pt); Old Style No. 9, Inter (8-10pt)
Century Oldstyle Italic, ATF 62 (6-72pt); Mono 157G (6-12pt); Old Style No. 9 Italic, Inter (8-10pt)
Century Oldstyle Bold, ATF 63 (5-120pt)
Century Oldstyle Bold Italic, ATF 64 (5-72pt)
Century Oldstyle Bold Condensed, ATF 65 (6-120pt)
Century Catalogue, ATF 444 (6-36pt); (Century Roman, Univ 6-18pt)
Century Catalogue Italic, ATF 468 (6-18pt); (Century Roman Italic, Univ 6-18pt)
Century Schoolbook, ATF 454 (6-48pt); Mono 420 (6-36pt); Inter (6-18pt); Century Modern, Ludlow 5-M (12-72pt)
Century Schoolbook Italic, ATF 465 (6-48pt); Mono 4201 (6-36pt); Inter (6-18pt); Century Modern Italic, Ludlow 5-MI (12-72pt)
Century Schoolbook Bold, ATF 479 (6-48pt); Mono 620J (6-16pt); Inter (6-14pt); Century Modern Bold, Ludlow 5-MB (12-96pt)
Century Schoolbook Bold Italic, Inter (10pt)*
*Included in lists of sources named, but not confirmed otherwise.

CENTURY CATALOGUE ITALIC, ATF 18- & 14-pt.

PROPER METHOD *QUESTION INVENTOR*
Expect Unbiased Judge *Inform Enterprising Student*

CENTURY SCHOOLBOOK, Mono 24-pt.

ABCDEFGHIJKLMNOPQRSTUVWXYZ ,.-;':'!?&
abcdefghijklmnopqrstuvwxyz ff fi ffi fl ffl $1234567890

CENTURY SCHOOLBOOK ITALIC, Mono 24-pt.

ABCDEFGHIJKLMNOPQRSTUVWXYZ ,.-;':'!?&
abcdefghijklmnopqrstuvwxyz ff fi ffi fl ffl $1234567890

CENTURY SCHOOLBOOK BOLD, ATF 24-pt.

ABCDEFGHIJKLMNOPQRSTUVWXYZ ,.-;:'!?&
abcdefghijklmnopqrstuvwxyz ff fi ffi fl ffl $1234567890

CENTURY SCHOOLBOOK & BOLD, Inter 14-pt.

ABCDEFGHIJKLMNOPQRSTUVWXYZ ÆŒæœ$1234567890
ABCDEFGHIJKLMNOPQRSTUVWXYZ ÆŒæœ$1234567890
abcdefghijklmnopqrstuvwxyz fi fl ff ffi ffl ,.-;':'!?()[]*†‡||§¶&@℔£%¢/——
abcdefghijklmnopqrstuvwxyz fi fl ff ffi ffl ,.-;':'!?()[]*†‡||§¶&@℔£%¢/——

CENTURY NOVA, ATF 24-pt. (complete 4-part font shown)

ABCDEFGHIJKLMNOPQRSTUVWXYZ 1234567890
abcdefghijklmnopqrstuvwxyzffffffiffflfl $$¢£%.:,;--–-·()?![]""""*&

CENTURY NOVA ITALIC, ATF 24-pt. (complete 4-part font shown)

ABCDEFGHIJKLMNOPQRSTUVWXYZ 1234567890
abcdefghijklmnopqrstuvwxyzfffffffflfl $$¢£%.:,;--–-·()?![]""""*&

Visual Reproportioning

Metal typefaces commonly vary in proportions from one size to another, especially in small sizes.

One reason is that fine lines would tend to disappear in small sizes or look too coarse in large sizes. Another is to maintain legibility in very small sizes and a greater sense of relationship between sizes.

Two leading designers, though, had opposite views of this principle. Morris Benton's designs for ATF carry this reproportioning further than usual, while Frederic Goudy's designs—where he was directly involved in their production—show little or no modification.

In each of these groups, the first line is set in 8-point and enlarged fifty percent; the second line is 12-point actual size; the third line is 24-point reduced to half size.

Bookman, Monotype
abcdefghijklmnopqrstuvwxyz
abcdefghijklmnopqrstuvwxyz
abcdefghijklmnopqrstuvwxyz

Caledonia Bold, Linotype
abcdefghijklmnopqrstuvwxyz
abcdefghijklmnopqrstuvwxyz
abcdefghijklmnopqrstuvwxyz

Century Bold Italic, ATF
abcdefghijklmnopqrstuvwxyz
abcdefghijklmnopqrstuvwxyz
abcdefghijklmnopqrstuvwxyz

Cheltenham Wide, Monotype
abcdefghijklmnopqrstuvwxyz
abcdefghijklmnopqrstuvwxyz
abcdefghijklmnopqrrstuvwxyz

Garamond, ATF
abcdefghijklmnopqrstuvwxyz
abcdefghijklmnopqrstuvwxyz
abcdefghijklmnopqrstuvwxyz

Garamont, Monotype
abcdefghijklmnopqrstuvwxyz
abcdefghijklmnopqrstuvwxyz
abcdefghijklmnopqrstuvwxyz

Lightline Gothic, ATF
abcdefghijklmnopqrstuvwxyz
abcdefghijklmnopqrstuvwxyz
abcdefghijklmnopqrstuvwxyz

Ultra Bodoni, ATF
abcdefghijklmnopqrstuvwxyz
abcdefghijklmnopqrstuvwxyz
abcdefghijklmnopqrstuvwxyz

The only Century design by an "outsider" during Benton's life, other than modifications for the composing machines, was *Century Bold Condensed Italic* by Sol Hess. But long after the end of Morris Benton's distinguished career, the immortal family was enriched with another member—*Century Nova* and *Italic*—designed in 1964 by Charles E. Hughes, who had been commissioned by ATF for the project. This is a condensed face, following the spirit of *Century Expanded.* Unknowingly, Hughes brought Century back to just about the same proportions it had started with some 70 years earlier.

* * *

Century Expanded and its variations have been copied extensively by Monotype, Linotype, Intertype, and Ludlow, under the same names. *Century Schoolbook* is also offered by Monotype and Intertype, while Ludlow calls its version *Century Modern,* offered in 1964. Some of these faces suffer a bit from adaptation to the mechanical restrictions of the various machines, but they are essentially the same. Intertype's *Century Schoolbook Bold,* though, while necessarily much narrower than the original, is a handsome face in its own right.

Century Oldstyle is also made by Monotype, but its version differs substantially from the original; capitals are wider and fitting is looser throughout. This modification was required for keyboard sizes but was carried into display sizes as well. Linotype offered a faithful copy of *Century Oldstyle* in 24-point only—originally under the same name; later it was renamed *Old Style No. 7,* although it is not at all the same face as smaller sizes shown under that name. Intertype offered *Century Oldstyle* only in 36-point, but copied the Monotype version in some small sizes under the name *Old Style No. 9.*

Monotype *Century Oldstyle* has another distinction. Quite a number of faces have alternate long descenders, but this face also has alternate long *ascenders* in the 12-point size. With these, it is suggestive of *Century Catalogue.*

Western Type Foundry and its successor, BB&S, offered *Century Roman;* however, this was a copy of *Century Expanded* rather than the original *Century Roman* of ATF.

Three mystery names turned up in the preparation of this section of the book. An Intertype list includes "Cent. Schoolbook Bd. with Italic," but if this means *Bold Italic,* no other trace of it has been found. A Monotype list includes "Century Mono-Photo, No. 520," and "Century Text, No. 618," both indicated as being made as matrices for metal typesetting, but it has been impossible to identify them otherwise.

Century Nova, ATF 719 (10-72pt)
Century Nova Italic, ATF 721 (10-48pt)
Century Mono-Photo, Mono 520*
Century Text, Mono 618*
*Included in lists of sources named, but not confirmed otherwise.

CHAMFER GOTHIC, Ludlow 30-pt.

ABCDEFGHIJKLMNOPQRSTUVWXYZ& 1234567890 $.:,;-!?''

CHANCERY ITALIC, Duensing 11/14-pt.

ABCCDEFGHIJKLMNOPQRSTUVWXYZ&AYQu. ,=:;'"?ftflßſaædçeè:ẹln_g₃uÿy of fr:m s⟶

CHARCOAL, Keystone 24-pt. (Fred Sholty, Rick von Holdt)

ABCDEFGHIJKLMNOPQRSTUVWXYZ&.,=:;'""!?⁓
abcdefghijklmnopqrstuvwxyz $1234567890 ᴄʟ⟶ro The

CHARTER, Lino 14-pt.

abcdefghijklmnopqrstuvwxyz ℳ 𝔗 𝔙 ℘

CHARTER OAK, 24-pt.

ABCDEFGHIJKLMNOPQRSTUVWXYZ&
abcdefghijklmnopqrstuvwxyz
$1234567890 .,-:;'!?

CHAUCER TEXT, ATF (48-pt. at 50%) (Rick von Holdt)

ABCDEFGHIJKLMNOPQRSTUVWXYZ
abcdefghijklmnopqrstuvwxyz 1234567890$&

CHAMFER GOTHIC is a nineteenth-century style which was popular for newspaper headlines. Predecessors of ATF had *Chamfer Condensed* in 1871 or earlier, and *Herald Extra Condensed,* a very similar face, a little later. A plain, extra-condensed design, it features straight diagonal lines in place of the usual curves, being named for a term meaning to bevel or cut off a corner decoratively. Similar designs were made by most founders, under several names; some included lowercase although the all-cap versions were longer lasting. *Gothic No. 14* on Linotype and Intertype is essentially the same face, but includes lowercase in 18-point only. Compare *American Extra Condensed,* with lowercase; also *Octic Gothic; Slim Outline* under *Oldtyme Outline.*

Chamfer Gothic, Ludlow 6-HP (30-48pt); Chamfer Condensed, Keystone-ATF (18-96pt); Mono 121; Gothic Chamfer, BB&S-ATF 1643 (12-54pt); Herald Extra Condensed, ATF 192 (10-60pt); Gothic No. 14, Lino=Inter=APL (18-60pt)

CHAMPLEVÉ—see *Sylvan* under Imports in Appendix.

CHANCERY ITALIC was modeled on an italic font of the sixteenth century or thereabouts, perhaps by Castiglione. It was designed by Paul Duensing and matrices were cut by him in 1966 at The Private Press and Typefoundry of Paul Hayden Duensing, one of very few such operations in this country. The original font included the oversize *C.* There is only one size.

Chancery Italic, Duensing (11/14pt)

CHARCOAL is a heavy novelty script introduced by Keystone Type Foundery in 1899. It is the same as *Bulletin* (q.v.), except for a spotty texture as though written with a stick of charcoal. It was later recut by Charles Broad of Typefounders of Phoenix, the mats eventually going to Los Angeles Type Founders.

Charcoal, Keystone-ATF 828 (14-48pt); TFP-LATF (18,24pt)

CHARTER was an experimental, special-purpose face designed by William A. Dwiggins for Mergenthaler between 1937 and 1942. An upright script, only the lowercase and the few other characters shown were completed. For tests, these were combined with *Electra* caps. It was used in a limited edition book, *The Song Story of Aucassin and Nicolete,* designed and printed in 1946 by S. A. Jacobs at the Golden Eagle Press, Mt. Vernon, New York, with Electra small caps in place of regular caps.

Charter, Lino (14pt) experimental

CHARTER OAK is a heavy, inclined gothic introduced by Keystone in 1899. There is a fair amount of contrast, and round letters are flat sided or nearly so. *London Gothic* (q.v.) was a comparable upright face, and *Royal Gothic* of the 1880s from another foundry is quite similar. Compare *Doric Italic.*

Charter Oak, Keystone-ATF 829 (6-60pt)

CHAUCER—see *Morris Romanized Black.*

CHAUCER TEXT (or *Chaucer Old English*) is a heavy, condensed form of Blackletter or Old English, cut by ATF in 1904. Capitals and a few lowercase letters have unusual, rather crude forms that make the whole face hard to read, and unattractive to more modern tastes. Compare *Cloister Black, Engravers Old English, Goudy Text,* etc.

Chaucer Text, ATF 66 (6-96pt)

CHELTENHAM OLDSTYLE, ATF 24-pt.

ABCCDEFGHIJKLMNOPQRSTUVWXYZ&ÆŒQu

abcdefghijklmnopqrrstuvwxyzæœfifffffffifflctst

1234567890[&$.,-'ʼ":;!?]¶ Ga CGg
Ludlow Hansen

CHELTENHAM ITALIC, ATF 24-pt.

ABCDEFGHIJKLMNOPQRSTUVWXYZ& ?!.,:;'-

abcdefghhijjklmnopqrrstuvvwwxyyz 1234567890$ fiflffffifffl

ABDEGMNPRTU&Qu

CHELTENHAM CURSIVE, Ludlow 24-pt.

ABCDEFGHIJKLMNOPQRSTUVWXYZ

CHELTENHAM OLDSTYLE CONDENSED, Mono 24-pt.

ABCDEFGHIJKLMNOPQRSTUVWXYZ&

abcdefghijklmnopqrstuvwxyz $1234567890 .,-:;'!? fi fl ff ffi ffl Qu r ct st

CHELTENHAM EXTRA CONDENSED ITALIC, Lino 18-pt.

ABCDEFGHIJKLMNOPQRSTUVWXYZ& 1234567890

abcdefghijklmnopqrstuvwxyz ($,.:;'-'?!fiflffffiffl)

CHELTENHAM WIDE, Mono 24-pt.

ABCDEFGHIJKLMNOPQRSTUVWXYZ&

abcdefghijklmnopqrrstuvwxyz 1234567890$.,-:;'!?

CHELTENHAM WIDE ITALIC, Mono 24-pt.

ABCDEFGHIJKLMNOPQRSTUVWXYZ&

abcdefghijklmnopqrstuvwxyz $1234567890 .,-:;'!?

CHELTENHAM MEDIUM, ATF 24-pt.

ABCDEFGHIJKLMNOPQRSTUVWXYZ&

abcdefghijklmnopqrstuvwxyz $1234567890 .,-:;'!?

CHELTENHAM MEDIUM ITALIC, ATF 18-pt.

ABCDEFGHIJKLMNOPQRSTUVWXYZ&

abcdefghijklmnopqrstuvwxyz $1234567890

CHELTENHAM. The design of *Cheltenham Oldstyle* and *Italic* is credited to Bertram Grosvenor Goodhue, an architect who had previously designed *Merrymount,* a private press type. For *Cheltenham* he had the assistance of Ingalls Kimball, director of the Cheltenham Press in New York City, who suggested and supervised the face. Original drawings were made about 14 inches high, and were subjected to much experimentation and revision. Further modification of the design was done by the manufacturers. Some historians credit this modification or refinement to Morris F. Benton; another source says it was done at the Boston branch of ATF, which suggests that the work may have been done by Joseph W. Phinney. In fact, Steve Watts says the face was first known as *Boston Oldstyle.*

Mergenthaler Linotype also claims credit for developing the face, but it was first marketed by ATF. Trial cuttings were made as early as 1899, but it was not completed until about 1902, and patented in 1904 by Kimball. It was one of the first scientifically designed faces. The thin lines were strengthened to avoid the emaciated look of many types of the period. It is almost a monotone, but with just enough difference between light and heavy lines to avoid monotony. The small serifs and short, compact lowercase make a high character count.

Ascenders are unusually long, while descenders are quite short. This was done as a result of studies that showed the greater importance of the upper half of a line of type in creating readily recognizable word shapes and resulting readability.

The face has had much adverse criticism, especially because of its short descenders and the unusual design of several characters—notably *A* with the extension of its thick stroke at the top, *G* with the curve extended at the bottom, and *g* with its angular, unclosed tail. The alternate form of *r,* with its arm raised above x-height, has also been criticized, but this is mostly the result of misuse. It is disturbing within a word, but adds a bit of grace at the end of a word. Oddly, original fonts had only this form, with the more regular *r* added later; most fonts for handsetting include both forms of *r,* but those for machine setting include only the normal form or in a few cases only the more exotic form.

Morris Benton, ATF's chief designer, produced *Cheltenham Bold* in 1904 and a score of variations up to 1913, methodically exploring the possibilities of various combinations of weight and width, and making this the first true large type family. Benton's variations include *Cheltenham Bold Condensed,* 1904; *Cheltenham Bold Italic, Cheltenham Bold Condensed Italic, Cheltenham Wide* and *Cheltenham Bold Outline,* 1905; *Cheltenham Bold Extra Condensed* and *Cheltenham Bold Extended,* 1906; *Cheltenham Inline, Inline Extra Condensed* and *Inline Extended,* 1907; *Cheltenham Oldstyle Condensed,*

(Cheltenham continues)

Cheltenham Oldstyle, ATF 87 (6-72pt); Mono 64 (6-72pt); Ludlow 2-L (12-48pt); BB&S (6-72pt); Cheltenham, Lino = Inter* (7-36pt); Craftsman Old Style, Hansen (6-72pt)
Cheltenham Italic, ATF 82 (6-72pt); Lino = Inter* (7-30pt); BB&S (6-72pt); Cheltenham Oldstyle Italic, Mono 641 (6-36pt); Ludlow 2-LI (12-48pt); Craftsman Old Style Italic, Hansen (6-24pt)
Cheltenham Cursive, Ludlow 2-LIC (12-48pt)
Cheltenham Oldstyle Condensed, ATF 88 (6-72pt); Mono 264 (8-36pt); Ludlow 2-LC (12-48pt); Cheltenham Condensed, Lino = Inter* (8-30pt)
Cheltenham Extra Condensed Italic, Lino (18-30pt)
Cheltenham Wide, ATF 89 (6-72pt); Mono 164 (6-36pt); Lino = Inter* (6-36pt); Ludlow 2-LW (6-36pt); BB&S (6-72pt)
Cheltenham Wide Italic, Mono 1641 (6-36pt)
Cheltenham Medium, ATF 83 (6-72pt); Mono 186 (5-72pt); Inter* (8-36pt); Ludlow 2-M (48-72pt); BB&S (6-72pt)
Cheltenham Medium Italic, ATF 84 (6-72pt); Mono 186K (9-12pt); Inter* (8-30pt); BB&S (6-72pt)
Cheltenham Medium Condensed, ATF 85 (6-48pt); Lino (18-30pt); Inter* (18-30pt)
Cheltonian Medium Condensed Italic, Inter (18,24pt)
Cheltenham Medium Expanded, ATF 86 (6-48pt)
*In all cases, the Intertype face is Cheltonian.

CHELTENHAM MEDIUM CONDENSED, Lino 24-pt.

ABCDEFGHIJKLMNOPQRSTUVWXYZ&ÆŒ 1234567890$
abcdefghijklmnopqrstuvwxyzæœfiflffffiffl ,.:;-''?!– .()⅛¼⅜½⅝¾⅞

CHELTONIAN MEDIUM CONDENSED ITALIC, Inter 24-pt.

INTERTYPE faces are made on modern wide too 12345

CHELTENHAM MEDIUM EXPANDED, ATF 18-pt.

ABCDEFGHIJKLMNOPQRSTUVWXYZ&
abcdefghijklmnopqrstuvwxyz $1234567890

ABCDEFGHIJKLMNOPQRSTUVWXYZ Gg

Hansen

abcdefghijklmnopqrstuvwxyz $1234567890.,-:;'!?&

fiflffffiffl æ œ Æ Œ Ga ¼ ½ ¾ ⅓ ⅔ ⅛ ⅜ ⅝ ⅞ % ¢

Ludlow

ABCDEFGHIJKLMNOPQRSTUVWXYZ& G

Hansen

abcdefghijklmnopqrstuvwxyz $1234567890 .,-:;'!?

ABCDEFGHIJKLMNOPQRSTUVWXYZ.,-;:'!?&

abcdefghijklmnopqrstuvwxyz $1234567890

ABCDEFGHIJKLMNOPQRSTUVWXYZ&

abcdefghijklmnopqrstuvwxyz $1234567890 .,-:;'!? fiflffffiffl

ABCDEFGHIJKLMNOPQRSTUVWXYZ.,-:;'!?&

abcdefghijklmnopqrstuvwxyzfiflffffiffl$1234567890 AG

Hansen

ABCDEFGHIJKLMNOPQRSTUVWXYZ& 1234567890

abcdefghijklmnopqrstuvwxyz ($,.:;'-'?!fiflffffiffl)

ABCDEFGHIJKLMNOPQRSTUVWXYZ&

abcdefghijklmnopqrrstuvwxyz .,-:;'!?

1234567890

ABCDEFGHIJKLMNOPQRSTUVWXYZ&12345

abcdefghijklmnopqrrstuvwxyzffffififlffffiffl67890$;!?

1909; *Cheltenham Medium,* 1909; *Medium Italic,* 1910; *Cheltenham Extra-bold,* 1910; *Cheltenham Bold Shaded, Bold Italic Shaded* and *Extrabold Shaded,* 1912; and *Cheltenham Medium Condensed* and *Expanded,* 1913.

Linotype, Monotype, and Ludlow each have duplicates of a dozen or more Cheltenhams, while Intertype has the same under the name *Cheltonian.* Nearly all of these are essentially the same, except for the addition of f-ligatures and diphthongs in some display fonts (as shown for *Cheltenham Bold*), and the modification of keyboard sizes to fit mechanical requirements, but this is substantial in some cases. A curious exception is *Cheltenham Bold Outline;* in the original foundry version it is cut from the same patterns as Bold so they will register for two-color work, while Monotype display sizes have several characters rather crudely redesigned—note *H, P, R, e, h, u* shown separately.

Some of these other sources have also added versions of their own, notably *Cheltenham Cursive,* designed by Robert H. Middleton for Ludlow, and *Cheltenham Wide Italic* on Monotype, probably designed by Sol Hess. The latter carries the modifications required for machine-set sizes into display sizes as well.

There are several oddities in the Cheltenham family. *Cheltenham Wide* is identical with *Cheltenham Oldstyle* except for the lowercase, in handset fonts. The same figures and punctuation marks from these two faces are also shared by *Cheltenham Oldstyle Condensed,* again in handset fonts. In the specimens shown here, compare *Oldstyle* and *Wide.* The former, set in ATF type, has two forms of cap *C,* which that foundry supplied with both faces, while the latter, set in Monotype, has two forms of cap *W,* which that company made only for that face. The unusual paragraph, prime and double prime marks, as well as parentheses and brackets, were made by ATF in some sizes of all three faces, but by Monotype only in *Cheltenham Oldstyle.* There is no *Cheltenham Condensed Italic,* but Linotype has a *Cheltenham Extra Con-*
(Cheltenham continues)

Cheltenham Bold, ATF 67 (6-120pt); Mono 86 (5-72H4); Lino = Inter* (5-36pt); Ludlow 2-B (6-72pt); BB&S (6-120pt); APL (8-144pt); Craftsman Bold, Hansen (6-72pt)

Cheltenham Bold Italic, ATF 73 (6-72pt); Mono 861 (5-72pt); Lino = Inter* (5-30pt); Ludlow 2-BI (6-72pt); BB&S (6-72pt); APL (8-48pt); Craftsman Bold Italic, Hansen (6-48pt)

Cheltenham Bold Condensed, ATF 68 (6-72pt); Mono 88 (5-72H4); Lino = Inter* (6-60pt); Ludlow 2-BC (6-72pt); BB&S (6-72pt); APL (18-144pt); Craftsman Bold Condensed, Hansen (6-48pt)

Cheltenham Bold Condensed Italic, ATF 69 (6-72pt); Mono 881 (6-72pt); Lino = Inter* (6-36pt); Ludlow 2-BCI (12-72pt); BB&S (6-72pt); APL (18-48pt)

Cheltenham Bold Extra Condensed, ATF 70 (6-120pt); Mono 141 (6-72H4); Lino = Inter* (14-60pt); Ludlow 2-BEC (12-72pt); BB&S (6-120pt); APL (84-120pt); Craftsman Bold Extra Condensed, Hansen (6-72pt); also Cheltenham Bold Extra Condensed Title, ATF 71 (6-96pt)

Cheltenham Bold Extra Condensed Italic, Lino = Inter* (18,24pt)

Cheltenham Bold Extended, ATF 72 (6-72pt); Mono 287 (6-36pt); Inter* (6-14pt); Ludlow 2-BE (12-48pt); BB&S (6-72pt)

Cheltenham Extrabold, ATF 77 (6-72pt)

Cheltenham Extrabold Shaded, ATF 78 (8-48pt)

Cheltenham Inline, ATF 79 (24-72pt); Mono 286 (24-36pt)

Cheltenham Inline Extra Condensed, ATF 81 (36-120pt); Mono 288 (36pt)

*In all cases, the Intertype face is Cheltonian.

CHELTENHAM EXTRABOLD SHADED, ATF 18-pt. (Cliff Helbert)

ABCDEFGHIJKLMNOPQRSTUVWXYZ&&$1234567890
abcdefghijklmnopqrstuvwxyz.,-:;"'!?ffffifflffifl

CHELTENHAM INLINE, ATF 24-pt.

ABCDEFGHIJKLMNOPQRSTUVWXYZ&
abcdefghijklmnopqrstuvwxyz 1234567890$.,-':;!?

CHELTENHAM INLINE EXTRA CONDENSED, ATF (42-pt. at 57%)

ABCDEFGHIJKLMNOPQRSTUVWXYZ abcdefghijklmnopqrstuvwxyz $1234567890

CHELTENHAM INLINE EXTENDED, ATF (42-pt. at 57%)

ABCDEFGHIJKLMNOPQRSTUVWXYZ 90
abcdefghijklmnopqrstuvwxyz $12345678

CHELTENHAM BOLD OUTLINE, ATF 24-pt. (and Mono—see text)

ABCDEFGHIJKLMNOPQRSTUVWXYZ& .,-:;"'!?
abcdefghijklmnopqrrstuvwxyz 1234567890$ HPRehu

Mono

87

CHELTENHAM BOLD SHADED, Mono 24-pt. (Dave Greer)

ABCDEFGHIJKLMNOPQRSTUVWXYZ& .,-:;'!?
abcdefghijklmnopqrrstuvwxyz $1234567890 fffiffflffiffl

CHELTENHAM BOLD ITALIC SHADED, ATF 24-pt.

ABCDEFGHIJKLMNOPQRSTUVWXYZ&
abcdefghijklmnopqrstuvwxyz 1234567890$

CHESTER TEXT, BB&S 14-pt.

Artist Designs Superb Commercial Type Face

CHIC, ATF 18-pt. (part reduced) (Dave Greer)

ABCDEFGHIJKLMNOPQRSTUVWXYZ&
$1234567890 .,-:;'!?'"" R

CHURCH TEXT, ATF 18-pt. (Carl Masson)

ABCDEFGHIJKLMNOPQRSTUVWXYZ
abcdefghijklmnopqrstuvwxyz 1234567890 $ &.,-:;'!?

CIVILITÉ, ATF 24-pt. (Guy Botterill, Wilbur Doctor)

ABCDEFGHIJKLMNOPQRSTUVWXYZ&
abcdefghijklmnopqrstuvwxyza dee_g hl mnyps t b wp ndve1234567890&$.,-':;!?

Name in parentheses after some specimens
indicates person who has set that specimen,
in whole or in part, to our format.

densed Italic (so-called), which is actually a little wider than *Cheltenham Condensed* (roman)—why it is called extra condensed is not known. It suffers from adaptation to straight matrices, with annoying gaps between some letter combinations. But *Cheltenham Medium Italic* was designed more successfully by Benton to fit straight type bodies without kerns. Figures in the medium, bold, and extrabold weights differ from those of the Oldstyle; also notice how the x-height increases with weight.

Ludlow Cheltenham is distinguished by the greater slant of some of its italics, and by the rounder top on the roman lowercase *a* and the rounder lower spur on capital *G,* as shown in some of the specimens.

Western Type Foundry copied several members of this family as *Chesterfield;* Hansen had the *Craftsman* series, differing most noticeably in the few characters shown; and other foundries around the world copied it under a variety of names. Also see *Kenilworth, Lowell, Venetian.*

Cheltenham Inline Extended, ATF 80 (18-72pt); Mono 285 (18-36pt)
Cheltenham Bold Outline, ATF 75 (8-72pt); Mono 12 (8-36pt); Ludlow 2-BO (18-36pt)
Cheltenham Bold Shaded, ATF 76 (8-72pt); Mono 218 (12-36pt)
Cheltenham Bold Italic Shaded, ATF 74 (8-72pt)
*In all cases, the Intertype face is Cheltonian.
Cheltenham is called Gloucester by English Monotype, Bodonia in Italy.

CHESTER TEXT is a fancy shaded letter designed by Sidney Gaunt in 1914 for BB&S. It features caps and small caps, and is intended for stationery and social work, but is hard to read and not suited to anything but a few simple names or words.

Chester Text, BB&S-ATF 1577 (8-14pt)

CHESTER TITLE—see *Engravers Roman Shaded.*

CHIC is a novelty face designed by Morris Benton in 1927 and released by ATF the following year. It has no lowercase; its thin lines are very delicate and its normally thick lines are opened with two parallel white lines. The result is airy but very mechanical. The 48-point size was cut but no showing has been found; in fact the series was not shown at all in specimens appearing as early as 1931. Compare *Boul Mich, Broadway, Gallia.*

Chic, ATF 514 (12-48pt)

CHINESE—see *Mandarin* under Antiques in Appendix.
CHISEL—see Imports in Appendix.

CHURCH TEXT is a plain, narrow Blackletter or Old English style, introduced by ATF early in the century. It is somewhat similar to *Chaucer Text,* but being a little plainer and lighter it is more pleasing and not as hard to read. Compare *Cloister Text, Goudy Text.*

Church Text, ATF 90 (6-72pt)

CICERO, CIRCULAR SCRIPT, CIRCUS—see Antiques in Appendix.
CITY [COMPACT]—see Imports in Appendix.

CIVILITÉ in its modern adaptation was designed by Morris Benton in 1922 and cut by ATF in 1923-24. The original version was cut by Robert Granjon in 1557 to imitate the semi-formal writing then in vogue, and is believed to be the first cursive design cut in type. It became popular for the printing of poetry and for books of instruction for children, where the type itself could serve as a perfect model of handwriting. The first of these books was titled *La Civilité puérile,* printed at Antwerp in 1559. The books were so popular that the design came to be known as "civility" type. Other interpretations of the letter have been made, including *Cursive Script,* cut in the nineteenth century in 18-point only from French sources by ATF predecessors and by Hansen, but Benton's seems more attractive and legible to modern eyes.

The French pronunciation of *ci-vil'i-tay* is indicated by the accented *e,* which was used only in ATF's earliest showings. The many alternate characters were included in fonts as originally sold; later they were sold separately and finally discontinued, although the basic font was still listed in recent ATF literature. Also see *Zapf Civilité;* compare *Freehand, Motto, Verona.*

Civilité, ATF 482 (10-48pt)

CLARENDON (CONSORT BOLD CONDENSED—see text) 24-pt.

ABCDEFGHIJKLMNOPQRSTUVWXYZ
abcdefghijklmnopqrstuvwxyz 1234567890

CLARENDON, Mono 81 (CONSORT CONDENSED—see text) 24-pt.

ABCDEFGHIJKLMNOPQRSTUVWXYZ& 1234567890
abcdefghijklmnopqrstuvw fiflffffiffl ?!.,:;'-

CLARENDON MEDIUM or CALEDONIAN, BB&S 24-pt.

ABCDEFGHIJKLMNOPQRSTUVWXYZ fiflffffi
abcdefghijklmnopqrstuvwxyz$1234567890.,-:;'!?&

CLARENDON BOLD, BB&S (30-pt. at 80%)

Intellect BOUND

CLARENDON BOLD EXTENDED, Mono 24-pt.

ABCDEFGHIJKLMNOPQRW123456
abcdefghijklmnopqrstuvwxyz7890

CLARENDON & BOLD, Lino 10-pt.

$&
(*/-)
abcdefghijklmnopqrstuvwxyz
1234567890
ABCDEFGHIJKLMNOPQRSTUVWXYZ
';,?—!..'

,;?'—'!:.
ABCDEFGHIJKLMNOPQRSTUVWXYZ
1234567890
abcdefghijklmnopqrstuvwxyz
(*/-)
&$

CLARENDON MEDIUM, Ludlow 24-pt.

ABCDEFGHIJKLMNOPQRSTUVWXYZ
abcdefghijklmnopqrstuvwxyz 12345678

CLARENDON BOLD, Ludlow 24-pt.

ABCDEFGHIJKLMNOPQRSTUVWXYZ
abcdefghijklmnopqrstuvwxyz.,-:;"!?()[]·
&$1234567890 ¼½¾⅓⅔%

90

CLARENDON is a traditional English style of typeface, dating from the 1840s, the name coming from the Clarendon Press at Oxford, or, according to some sources, from Britain's Earl of Clarendon and his interest in that country's Egyptian policies. (Such faces were classified as Egyptians, and inspired such later designs as *Cairo, Karnak, Memphis,* and *Stymie.*)

Early Clarendons were used primarily as titles and display faces, for which their strong and sturdy nature was well suited. They have the general structure of romans, but lack the hairlines typical of those faces. Being heavier, the traditional Clarendons were often used as boldfaces with romans, before the family idea provided matching boldface designs.

Similar faces were known as *Doric* or *Ionic,* before more individualized type names became common; in fact, all three names were sometimes used interchangeably. Most foundries had versions of Clarendon, and sometimes Doric and Ionic, in the nineteenth century, but most of these faces were obsolescent by the turn of the century. However, a few were copied by Linotype, Intertype and Monotype, and thus given a renewed lease on life.

Clarendon Medium of BB&S was formerly known as *Caledonian;* ATF had a similar face known as *Ionic No. 522.* Keystone showed *Clarendon Condensed* in 1890. *Clarendon [No. 5]* of BB&S was called *Winchendon* by Hansen, and extended to 48-point. Like many pre-point-system faces, some foundries adapted them to point-system standards by casting them on oversize bodies, others on undersize bodies with overhanging descenders.

In the later 1950s Stephenson Blake in England revived several of these early Clarendons under the new name of *Consort,* which became a popular import (and the source of some of our specimens). *Consort Bold Condensed* is said to be the first Clarendon, of 1845. (Some added members of the Consort family are noted under Popular Imports in the Appendix.)

In 1953 a new version of Clarendon was developed by Hermann Eidenbenz for the Haas Typefoundry in Switzerland and later acquired by Stempel in Germany. The *Haas Clarendon* was copied by Linotype in 1966, in light and bold weights, and about the same time Ludlow brought out three weights of essentially the same face. This was created primarily to set the newspaper ads of a large department store, but it was a good addition to the resources of Ludlow. ATF commissioned a modernized rendition of Clarendon from Freeman Craw, and this was brought out in 1955 as *Craw Clarendon* (q.v.).

About 1961 Monotype brought out *Clarendon Bold Extended,* similar to *Craw Clarendon* but heavier. Also see *Ionic, News with Clarendon, Manila.*

CLARION is an interesting but elusive text face, made by Intertype only in the 8-point size, as far as we can discover. Roman, italic, and bold are shown in the 1955 book; italic is listed but not shown in the 1958 book. All are listed as obsolete and not shown in later books we have checked. *Clarion* is similar to *Waverley* (q.v.), but is a little heavier, having shorter ascenders and greater x-height, resulting in a larger face for the body size.

CLASSIC—see *Dickens, MacFarland.*

Clarendon [No. 5], BB&S-ATF 1578 (5-24pt); Winchendon, Hansen (6-48pt)
Clarendon, Mono 81 (6-24pt); Clarendon Condensed, Inter (10-24pt)
Clarendon Extra Condensed No. 5, BB&S-ATF 1580 (6-36pt)
Clarendon Medium [Caledonian No. 5], BB&S-ATF 1581 (5-36pt); Ionic No. 522, ATF 272 (5-18pt); Ionic, Mono 62 (18-36pt)
Clarendon Bold or Lining Doric, BB&S-ATF 1579 (6-48pt); Doric No. 520, ATF 255 (6-42pt)
[Haas] Clarendon, Lino (6-12pt); Clarendon Medium, Ludlow 58-M (14-72pt)
[Haas] Clarendon Bold, Lino (6-12pt); Clarendon Bold, Ludlow 58-B (14-72pt)
Clarendon Heavy, Ludlow 58-H (14-72pt)
Clarendon Bold Extended, Mono 665 (14-36pt)

Clarion with Italic or Bold, Inter (8pt)

CLARENDON HEAVY, Ludlow 24-pt. (Herb Harnish)

ABCDEFGHIJKLMNOPQRSTUVWXYZ
abcdefghijklmnopqrstuvwxyz .,-:;"'!?()[]·—
&$1234567890

CLARION & ITALIC & BOLD, Inter 8-pt.

INTERTYPE wide tooth matrices give long s 12345
INTERTYPE wide tooth matrices give long s VBCDE

INTERTYPE wide tooth matrices give long 12345
INTERTYPE wide tooth matrices give long 12345

ABCDEFGHIJKLMNOPQRSTUVWXYZ&
ABCDEFGHIJKLMNOPQRSTUVWXYZ&

abcdefghijklmnopqrstuvwxyz fiflffffifl 1234567890
abcdefghijklmnopqrstuvwxyz fiflffffifl 1234567890

[($ £ ,.:;'-'?!*†‡§¶)] ⅛ ¼ ⅜ ½ ⅝ ¾ ⅞ ⅓ ⅔ ⅕ ⅖ ⅗ ⅘ ⅙ ⅚
[($ £ ,.:;'-'?!*†‡§¶)] ⅛ ¼ ⅜ ½ ⅝ ¾ ⅞ ⅓ ⅔ ⅕ ⅖ ⅗ ⅘ ⅙ ⅚

ABCDEFGHIJKLMNOPQRSTUVWXYZ&
abcdefghijklmnopqrstuvwxyz
1234567890 ($,.:;'-'?!*)
¼ ½ ¾ ⅓ ⅔

CLEARCUT OLDSTYLE & ITALIC, BB&S 24- and 10-pt.

REQUIRE MORE Moderate Selection
CHARGE MADE Bring Retrenchment

ABCDEFGHIJKLMNOPQRSTUVWXYZ& .,'-:;!?()[]— ffflffiflffl $1234567890£
ABCDEFGHIJKLMNOPQRSTUVWXYZ& abcdefghijklmnopqrstuvwxyz

ABCDEFGHIJKLMNOPQRSTUVWXYZ& .,'-:;!? ff fi ffi fl ffl $1234567890
abcdefghijklmnopqrstuvwxyz

CLEARCUT SHADED CAPS, 24-pt. (spaced)

CLEARFACE, ATF 24-pt. (Ed Davis, Jr.)

ABCDEFGHIJKLMNOPQRSTUVWXYZ&
abcdefghijklmnopqrstuvwxyz .,-:;'!? ffffifl 1234567890$

CLEARFACE ITALIC, ATF 24-pt.

ABCDEFGHIJKLMNOPQRSTUVWXYZ&
abcdefghijklmnopqrstuvwxyz $1234567890 .,-:;'!?

CLEARFACE BOLD, ATF 24-pt.

ABCDEFGHIJKLMNOPQRSTUVWXYZ&
abcdefghijklmnopqrstuvwxyz $1234567890 .,-:;'!?

CLEARFACE BOLD ITALIC, ATF 24-pt.

ABCDEFGHIJKLMNOPQRSTUVWXYZ&
abcdefghijklmnopqrstuvwxyz $1234567890 .,-:;'!?

CLEARFACE HEAVY, ATF 24-pt. (Frank Anderson)

ABCDEFGHIJKLMNOPQRSTUVWXYZ 12345
abcdefghijklmnopqrstuvwxyz

CLASSIFIED is a hybrid Linotype face intended for use in newspaper classified ads as an alternative to sans serif or the older romans. Its lowercase appears to be a duplicate of *Times Roman,* while the rest of the font appears to be *Paragon,* one of the Legibility Group faces. It is made with its own boldface. *Classified Display,* offered in 1955, is essentially *Futura Light,* being narrower and more compact than Linotype *Spartan Light.* It is made in multiples of the usual 5½-point classified ad line, and is obviously intended for headlines in such ads.

Classified and Bold, Lino (5½pt)
Classified Display, Lino (11-38pt)

CLAYTONIAN—see Antiques in Appendix.

CLEARCUT OLDSTYLE is a conventional nineteenth-century oldstyle letter of the sort that started out as an attempt to "refine" Caslon. The result is legible but not particularly attractive or distinguished. Although more regular than Caslon, there is some variation from one size to another, especially in the italic, where the 24-point size in particular has less slope than the rather extreme inclination of other sizes. The faces were formerly known as *Oldstyle No. 5* or *No. 59,* with italic. There was also a *Clearcut Oldstyle Condensed.* Compare *Binny, Franklin Oldstyle.*

Clearcut Oldstyle, BB&S-ATF 1582 (5-72pt)
Clearcut Oldstyle Italic, BB&S-ATF 1584 (5-72pt)
Clearcut Oldstyle Condensed No. 52, BB&S-ATF 1583 (10-72pt)

CLEARCUT SHADED CAPS [*Capitals*] were designed by Will Ransom in 1924 for BB&S, to work with the regular Clearcut series or similar faces. They are an interesting set of flourished, decorative letters. They are rather reminiscent of French copperplate lettering, although it is said the designer had no particular model at hand. They are sometimes called *Ransom Shaded Initials.* There is no *X* or *Z,* but fonts include decorative dashes and brackets.

Clearcut Shaded Caps or Ransom Shaded Initials, BB&S-ATF 1585 (12-48pt); (Univ 12-48pt)

CLEARFACE was designed by Morris Benton with his father, Linn B. Benton, as advisor. The bold was designed first, in 1905, and cut the following year. The other weights and italics were produced through 1911. As the name implies, the series was intended to show unusual legibility, which it certainly achieved. The precision of cutting and casting for which ATF is noted produced a very neat and handsome series, which had considerable popularity. *Clearface Heavy Italic* has less inclination than the lighter weights, and is non-kerning, a detail which helped make it popular for newspaper use; the specimen shown here is from a very worn font.

Some of the faces have been copied by the matrix makers. But the face Monotype calls *Clearface* and *Italic* is the weight called *Bold* by other sources. Monotype also includes *Clearface Italic No. 289,* a copy of the lighter weight.

Clearface, ATF 91 (5-72pt)
Clearface Italic, ATF 97 (5-72pt); Mono 289 (6-12pt)
Clearface Bold, ATF 92 (5-72pt); Lino (14-30pt); Inter (8-12pt); Ludlow 8-B (18-48pt); Clearface, Mono 89 (6-36pt)
Clearface Bold Italic, ATF 93 (5-72pt); Lino (14-30pt); Inter (8-12pt); Ludlow 8-BI (14-48pt); Clearface Italic, Mono 891 (6-36pt)
Clearface Heavy, ATF 95 (6-72pt)
Clearface Heavy Italic, ATF 96 (6-72pt)

CLEARFACE GOTHIC was designed by Morris Benton for ATF in 1908, and cut in 1910. It is a neat, clean gothic, somewhat thick and thin, which incorporates some of the mannerisms of the *Clearface* (roman) series. However, it can hardly be considered a part of that family. There is only one weight, and fonts contain only the minimum number of characters, as shown.

Clearface Gothic, ATF 94 (6-72pt)

CLEARFACE HEAVY ITALIC, ATF 18-pt. (see text) (Cliff Helbert)

ABCDEFGHIJKLM OPQRSTUVWXYZ&
abcdefghijklmnopqrstuvwxyzfffiflffiffl1234567890$.,-:;!?'

CLEARFACE GOTHIC, ATF 24-pt.

ABCDEFGHIJKLMNOPQRSTUVWXYZ&
abcdefghijklmnopqrstuvwxyz $1234567890 .,-:;'!?

CLOISTER BLACK, Mono 24-pt.

𝕬𝕭𝕮𝕯𝕰𝕱𝕲𝕳𝕴𝕵𝕶𝕷𝕸𝕹𝕺𝕻𝕼𝕽𝕾𝕿𝖀𝖁𝖂𝖃𝖄𝖅
abcdefghijklmnopqrstuvwxyz3.,-:;' !?&$1234567890 a V W

CLOISTER OLDSTYLE, ATF 24-pt. (Lewis Pryor, Alan Waring)

ABCDEFGHIJKLMNOPQRRSTTUVWXYZ& 1234567890 ijf.,;:"!?
abcdefghijklmnopqrstuvwxyz 1234567890$ ffffifflffiffl Qu & .,-:;'"''""!? () []

Cloister No. 2

CLOISTER ITALIC, ATF 24-pt.

ABCDEFGHIJKLMNOPQRSTUVWXYZ& 1234567890$ ff fi fl ffi ffl & st
abcdefghijkklmnopqrstuvvwwxyz .,-:;'!?() ABCDEGFMNPRTUY Qu

CLOISTER CURSIVE, ATF 24-pt. (lowercase spaced)

ABCDEFGHIJKLMNOPQRSTUVWXYZ&
abcdefghijklmnopqrstuvvwwxyzff fi fl ffi ffl][() & st .,-""''':;!? 1234567890

CLOISTER WIDE & CLOISTER BOLD, Lino 14-pt.

ABCDEFGHIJKLMNOPQRSTUVWXYZ&
ABCDEFGHIJKLMNOPQRSTUVWXYZ&

abcdefghijklmnopqrstuvwxyzfifflffffifl ($£,.:;'-'?!*†) 1234567890
abcdefghijklmnopqrstuvwxyzfifflffffifl ($£,.:;'-'?!*†) 1234567890

CLOISTER TITLE, ATF 18-pt.

ABCDEFGHIJKLMNOPQRS 1234567890

CLOISTER LIGHTFACE, ATF 24-pt. (spaced)

ABCDEFGHIJKLMNOPQRSTUVWXYZ&1234567890
abcdefghijklmnopqrstuvwxyzffffifflffiffl&Qu()[].,-"""'':;!?

CLOISTER LIGHTFACE ITALIC, ATF 24-pt. (spaced)

AABCCDEEFGGHIJJKLMMNOPQRRSTTUVUW
XYZ&1234567890"""'.!;.,
abcdefghijkklmnopqrstuvvwwxyzffffiflffiffl st Qu()[]

CLOISTER BOLD, Mono 24-pt.

ABCDEFGHIJKLMNOPQRRSTUVWXYZ& Qu &
abcdefghijklmnopqrstuvwxyz 1234567890$.,-:;'!?"""fiffflffiffl

94

CLOISTER BLACK (or *Cloister Text*) was introduced by ATF in 1904. Its design is generally credited to Joseph W. Phinney, of ATF's Boston foundry, but some authorities give some or all of the credit to Morris Benton. It is an adaptation of *Priory Text*, an 1870s version of *Caslon Text* (q.v.), modernizing and eliminating the irregularities of that historic face, and making it one of the most popular versions of Old English. *Flemish Black* (q.v.), introduced at the same time, has the same lowercase and figures but a different set of capitals. Note the alternate *V* and *W*, and tied *ct*. ATF also makes a double lowercase *l*, while Monotype makes f-ligatures and diphthongs. Compare *Goudy Text, Engravers Old English*.

Cloister Black, ATF 98 (6-72pt); Mono 95 (6-36pt)

CLOISTER OLDSTYLE was designed by Morris Benton in 1913 and released by ATF early the next year. It follows quite closely the noted roman face used by Nicolas Jenson in 1470, but is slightly heavier to compensate for the improved printing conditions and smoother papers of the present time. *Cloister Italic*, released later in 1914, is based on an italic cast by Aldus Manutius in 1501, but does not follow this as closely as the roman does its source. *Cloister Bold* was designed in 1913; it and *Cloister Bold Italic* were cut in 1915. *Cloister Title* and *Bold Title* were cut in 1914-15; they are essentially the same as the regular Cloisters, but without lowercase, and cast full on the body. Cap *J* and *Q* were redesigned and the comma and semicolon shortened.

In the specimens shown here, the complete font of *Cloister Oldstyle* is shown, including two styles of figures, alternate *R* and *T,* and the array of quotation marks. *Cloister Title* shows the essential *J* and *Q* revisions; *Cloister Bold Title* is comparable.

Cloister Lightface was designed in 1919 but not cut until 1924, with *Italic* the following year. It is considered the most faithful reproduction of Jenson's original type; substantially the same as *Cloister Oldstyle* but cut lighter to allow for the heavying which results from printing on rough or dampened papers with a strong impression, as was done in the fifteenth century.

Cloister Cursive was cut in 1922. It has the same lowercase and figures as *Cloister Italic*, but a more freely designed set of capitals. *Cloister Bold Condensed* was designed in 1915 and cut in 1917.

All these versions of Cloister were designed by Morris F. Benton, who considered this the ideal typeface. For this assignment he thoroughly studied the life and times of Nicolas Jenson of Venice, the first great designer of a roman typeface. Jenson's type was the inspiration for numerous faces in this century, including the comparatively crude *Jenson Oldstyle*. Benton's design was probably the first to accurately recapture the spirit of the fifteenth-century type.

In 1992, ten characters of Cloister Oldstyle were redesigned with diamond-shaped dots for greater authenticity, and a long *s* added, in the 16-point

(Cloister continues)

Cloister Oldstyle, ATF 102 (6-72pt); Mono 395 (14-36pt); Inter (6-24pt); Cloister, Lino (6-36pt); APL (18-72pt)
Cloister Oldstyle No. 2, Rehak (16pt)
Cloister Italic, ATF 103 (6-72pt); Lino (6-30pt); APL (18-48pt); Cloister Old Style Italic, Mono 3951 (14-36pt); Inter (6-24pt)
Cloister Cursive, ATF 478 (6-72pt)
Cloister Wide, Lino (6-14pt)
Cloister Title, ATF 104 (6s-48pt)
Cloister Lightface, ATF 486 (6-48pt)
Cloister Lightface Italic, ATF 490 (6-48pt)
Cloister Bold, ATF 99 (6-72pt); Mono 295 (6-72pt); Lino, Inter (6-36pt); APL (18-72pt)
Cloister Bold Italic, ATF 100 (6-72pt); Mono 2951 (6-72pt); Lino, Inter (6-36pt); APL (18-60pt)
Cloister Bold Condensed, ATF 451 (6-72pt)
Cloister Bold Title, ATF 101 (6-48pt)

CLOISTER BOLD ITALIC, Mono 24-pt.

ABCDEFGHIJKLMNOPQRSTUVWXYZ& 1234567890$
abcdefghijklmnopqrstuvvwwxyz .,-:;'!?'" " ff fi fl ffi ffl ct st Qu
ABCDEGJMNPRTVY

CLOISTER BOLD CONDENSED, ATF 24-pt.

ABCDEFGHIJKLMNOPQRSTUVWXYZ 1234567890$&
abcdefghijklmnopqrstuvwxyz ff fi fl ffi ffl ct Qu .,;:"!?-""

CLOISTER BOLD TOOLED, Inter 14-pt.

ABCDEFGHIJKLMNOPQRSTUVWXYZ   1234567890
abcdefghijklmnopqrstuvwxyz   []%†§‡¶*()$,.-;':'!?&⅛¼⅜½⅝¾

CLOISTER CURSIVE HANDTOOLED, ATF 24-pt. (Wilbur Doctor)

ABCDEFGHIJKLMNOPQRSTUVWXYZ&
abcdefghijklmnopqrstuvwwxyz st&1234567890$.,-:;!?""'''' fiflffffiffl

COCHIN, Mono 24-pt.

ABCDEFGHIJKLMNOPQRSTUVWXYZ& .,-:;'!?
abcdefghijklmnopqrstuvwxyz $1234567890æœfifffflffiff

COCHIN ITALIC, Mono 24-pt.

ABCDEFGHIJKLMNOPQRSTUVWXYZ& .,-:;'!?
abcdefghijklmnopqrstuvwxyz $1234567890 æœfifffflffiffl

COCHIN BOLD, Mono 24-pt.

ABCDEFGHIJKLMNOPQRSTUVWXYZ&
abcdefghijklmnopqrstuvwxyz $1234567890.,-:;'!?

COCHIN BOLD ITALIC, Mono 24-pt.

ABCDEFGHIJKLMNOPQRSTUVWXYZ&
abcdefghijklmnopqrstuvwxyz $1234567890 .,-:;'!?

COCHIN OPEN, Mono 24-pt.

ABCDEFGHIJKLMNOPQRSTUVWXYZ
abcdefghijklmnopqrstuvwxyz.,;:-"'!?&$1234567890

COCHIN BOLD TOOLED, Mono 24-pt.

ABCDEFGHIJKLMNOPQRSTUVWXYZ&
$1234567890 .,-:;'!?

COLLIER, 24-pt.

ABCDEFGHIJKLMNOPQRSTUVWXYZ
abcdefghijklmnopqrstuvwxyz.,-"'?!

size for private use. These new characters were contrived from existing patterns by Theo Rehak, New Jersey typefounder, and the result designated *Cloister Oldstyle No. 2.*

Cloister Cursive Handtooled was designed by Benton and Charles H. Becker in 1923, but not completed until 1926; it is derived from *Cloister Bold Italic.* Curiously, what might be called a companion face was not made by ATF but by Intertype, as *Cloister Bold Tooled,* which had been issued by that company in 1920. *Cloister Wide* was introduced by Linotype in 1926; it was designed to match the width of *Cloister Bold* for duplexing on the same matrices. Compare *Centaur, Eusebius, Italian Old Style;* also *Cromwell.*

Cloister Bold Tooled, Inter (14-36pt)
Cloister Cursive Handtooled, ATF 493 (12-72pt)

COCHIN or *Cochin Old Style* originated with the Peignot Foundry in Paris, about 1915. It was based on the lettering of eighteenth-century French copperplate engravers. Sol Hess adapted it to the Monotype in 1917, while ATF copied the French face in 1925. Both Monotype and ATF replaced the French figures with the more usual lining figures. The roman is rather distinctive but the italic is much more so, being closer to formal handwriting or engraving than most italics. There are several unusual lowercase swash or terminal letters in the italic, where principal strokes have no serifs at the top.

Cochin Bold and *Italic* were designed exclusively for Monotype by Sol Hess in 1921. They follow the style of the lighter faces, but bold italic lacks the swash letters of the light italic. Hess also designed *Cochin Open,* an outline version of the regular face, in 1927. Quite possibly he was also responsible for *Cochin Bold Tooled,* similarly developed from *Cochin Bold* but lacking lowercase. Compare *Caslon Openface, Bernhard Modern, Drew.* Also see *Nicolas Cochin.*

Cochin Old Style, Mono 61 (6-36pt);
   Cochin, ATF 492 (6-14pt)
Cochin Old Style Italic, Mono 611 (6-36pt);
   Cochin Italic, ATF 495 (8s-14pt)
Cochin Bold, Mono 616 (6-72pt)
Cochin Bold Italic, Mono 6161 (6-36pt)
Cochin Open, Mono 262 (18-36pt)
Cochin Bold Tooled, Mono 253 (24pt)

COLLEGE OLDSTYLE—see *Caslon Openface.*

COLLIER HEADING was designed by Tommy Thompson in 1946 for *Collier's* magazine. It is an adaptation of an eighteenth-century style known generally as *Grecian,* and was cut by Monotype in a considerable range of sizes.

Other *Collier* or *Collier Heading* types have turned up; one was designed by Tommy Thompson for *Collier's* magazine, but not identified otherwise. It was probably also cut by Monotype. One of these could possibly be the *Bert Black* mentioned previously.

Collier Heading, Mono 630, private
Collier Heading (other)

COLLIER HEADING, Mono (reduced)

ABCDEFGHIJKLMNOPQRSTUVWXYZ .,-":;!? 12345678

COLLIER HEADING (other, see text) (Henry Weiland)

ABCDEFGHIJKLMNOPQRSTUVWXYZ.,:;""-!?.()[]

COLLIER OLD STYLE, Goudy 18-pt.

ABCDEFGHIJKLMNOPQRSTUVWXYZ
abcdefghijklmnopqrstuvwxyz&$,,;:.-'!?1234567890

COLONIAL, ATF 14-pt. (George Gasparik)

ABCDEFGHIJKLMNOPQRSTUVWXYZ& 123467890 °?!-.:,;°

COLONIAL, 24-pt. (see text) (Robert Halbert)

ABCDEFGHIJKLMNOPQRSTUVWXYZ

COLUMBIA, Amsterdam 24-pt.

ABCDEFGHIJKLMNOPQRSTUVWXYZ $1234567890
abcdefghijklmnopqrstuvwxyz.,-:;''''""!?&fiflffffiffl()[]–«»/*

COLUMBIA ITALIC, Amsterdam 24-pt.

ABCDEFGHIJKLMNOPQRSTUVWXYZ $1234567890
abcdefghijklmnopqrstuvwxyz.,-:;''''""!?&flffffiffl()[]–«»/*
ABDGIJKMNPQuRTVW

COLUMBIA BOLD, Amsterdam 24-pt.

ABCDEFGHIJKLMNOPQRSTUVWXYZ $1234567890
abcdefghijklmnopqrstuvwxyz.,-:;''''""!?&fiflffffiffl()[]–«»/*

COLUMBIA BOLD ITALIC, Amsterdam 24-pt.

ABCDEFGHIJKLMNOPQRSTUVWXYZ $1234567890
abcdefghijklmnopqrstuvwxyz.,-:;''''""!?&fiflffffiffl()[]–«»/*

COLWELL HANDLETTER, ATF 24-pt. (Dave Greer)

ABCDEFGHIJKLMNOPQRSTUVWXYZ&$1234567890
abcdefghijklmnopqrstuvwxyz .,-:;'!? fffiflffifflctst

COLWELL HANDLETTER ITALIC, ATF (36-pt. at 67%) (Harvey Puckett, Larry Girard)

ABCDEFGHIJKLMNOPQRSTUVWXYZ AGHMNY
abcdefghijklmnopqrstuvwxyzffffiflffiifflstct &1234567890$.,-:;!?"

98

COLLIER OLD STYLE was designed by Frederic W. Goudy in 1919 as a private type for Proctor & Collier, a Cincinnati advertising agency, which had its own printing plant. Matrices were engraved by Robert Wiebking. Goudy has remarked that this face "seemed to me to give a quality akin to that given by William Morris's *Golden* type without, however, imitating that famous letter."

Fonts were apparently cast for Goudy by ATF, for these matrices were among those given by ATF to the Graphic Arts Division of the Smithsonian Institution in 1970, and used for a special revival casting in 1982 by the Out of Sorts Letter Foundery.

Collier Old Style, Goudy-ATF (10-18pt), private

COLONIAL appears to be a recutting by ATF in 1933 of *Fry's Ornamented* (see Imports in Appendix), a revival by the Stephenson Blake foundry in England of a type cut by Richard Austin in 1796 for an eighteenth-century ancestor of that company. It has much the character of *Baskerville Roman,* which descends from the same source, but shaded and with an outline ellipse set into the middle of each main stroke. A similar face was shown by the Caslon foundry about the same time.

The second *Colonial* specimen shows a font of mats acquired by Bob Halbert in Texas from a Detroit typographer. It appears to be a duplicate of the English face, with a few characters redrawn. It is not identified otherwise.

Compare *Old Dutch, Dresden.*

Colonial, ATF 565 (12-36pt)

COLUMBIA series was drawn by Walter H. McKay, a New York designer, but cast by Typefoundry Amsterdam. There are two weights, with italics; a bold condensed was added by a staff designer. Work was started on it in 1947 but it was not released until 1956, following much testing and refining. It is a contemporary roman, evenly and expertly drawn, and neutral in feeling. There are small capitals and italic swash letters for the light weight.

Columbia, Typefoundry Amsterdam (6-60pt)
Columbia Italic, TA (6-36pt)
Columbia Bold, TA (6-72pt)
Columbia Bold Italic, TA (6-60pt)

COLUMBINE—see Antiques in Appendix.
COLUMBUS—see *American Italic.*
COLUMNA—see Imports in Appendix.

COLWELL HANDLETTER and *Italic* were designed in 1917 for ATF. Some accounts say they were designed by Elizabeth Colwell, a Chicago artist noted for her display work and hand-lettered pages, but it seems more likely that they were designed by another but based on her work. Although carefully drawn and legible, they have a number of eccentricities that precluded a long life.

Colwell Handletter, ATF 462 (6-48pt)
Colwell Handletter Italic, ATF 463 (6-48pt)

COMBINATION GOTHIC (Nos. 501 to 510)—see *Gothic No. 545.*
COMMERCE GOTHIC—see *Bank Gothic.*

COMMERCIAL SCRIPT, ATF 24-pt.

ABCDEFGHIJKLMNOPQRSTUVWXYZ
abcdefghijklmnopqrstuvwxyz.,=:;'!?'&$1234567890

COMPACT, ATF (48-pt. at 50%) (Herb Harnish)

ABCDEFGHIJKLMNOPQRSTUVWXYZ .,-:;'!?& abcdefghijklmnopqrstuvwxyz $1234567890

COMPANION OLDSTYLE, Mono 24-pt. (Ivend H. Krohn)

ABCDEFGHIJKLMNOPQRSTUVWXYZ& ffifffiflffl
abcdefghijklmnopqrstuvwxyz 1234567890 .,-:;'!?

COMPANION OLDSTYLE ITALIC, Mono 24-pt. (part reduced) (Ivend H. Krohn)

ABCDEFGHIJKLMNOPQR STUVWXYZ fffiflffifl &1234567890
abcdefghijklmnopqrstuvwxyz .,-:;'!? ABCDEMPR &g

COMPRESSED NO. 30, Mono 18-pt.

TWO-LINE OR THREE-LINE BOLDFACE FIGURES $1234567890
Combined with any size Roman for Newspaper Ad. and Catalogue

COMSTOCK, Mono 24-pt.

ABCDEFGHIJKLMNOPQRSTUVWXYZ&-:;'!?
abcdefghijklmnopqrstuvwxyz$1234567890

CONDENSED COMSTOCK, 18-pt.

ABCDEFGHIJKLMNOPQRSTUVWXYZ& $1234567890 .,-:;'!?

The Ampersand

& & & & & & & & & &

The short "and" is a utilitarian part of most fonts (packed
with the caps in fonts for handsetting). Style books usually
restrict its use to corporate names, but designers delight in
using the more decorative forms as a display element.

COMMERCIAL SCRIPT is a typical Spencerian script, designed by Morris Benton in 1906 and cut by ATF in 1908. It is a connecting face, similar to *Bank Script* but heavier and with fewer flourishes. It has continued in popularity, and is still shown in recent ATF specimens. Compare *Bank Script, Typo Script.*

Commercial Script, ATF 107 (12-60pt)

COMPACT is a medium weight, extra condensed roman type with some distinctive features, intended primarily for newspaper headlines and advertising. It was issued by ATF early in the century. Its large lowercase and short ascenders and descenders make it well suited for its purpose. *Caption* is the same face on Linotype and Intertype, but only the 36-point size has lowercase. ATF's *Heading Condensed* is an all-cap version of the same design. Compare *Headletter No. 2, Lafayette Extra Condensed, Miehle Extra Condensed.*

Compact, ATF 108 (8-72pt); Caption, Lino = Inter (24-42pt); also Heading Condensed (title), ATF (10-48pt)

COMPANION OLD STYLE and *Italic* were designed by Frederic W. Goudy in 1927 as a private face for headings in *Woman's Home Companion* magazine. After *Aries,* cut only in one size, this was Goudy's first experience in cutting an extensive series of sizes, as well as roman and italic. As he says, he learned the business of typefounding while working on this face. And of the face itself, Goudy says, "I believe that *Companion Old Style* and its italics show greater consistent original features than any other face I have ever made." From types cast in his matrices, Monotype made electro matrices for the typesetters of the magazine. And when that plant was liquidated several years ago, the matrices were acquired by Lester Feller, a private typecaster in Illinois, and a few fonts were cast for other private printers. There are no italic figures, and no plain versions of *v* or *w,* which would be necessary for good appearance within words.

Companion Old Style, Goudy; Mono 359 (10-48pt), private
Companion Old Style Italic, Goudy; Mono 3591 (10-48pt), private

COMPRESSED NO. 30 is a Monotype copy of an unidentified nineteenth-century foundry face, closely related to *Modern Roman Condensed* (q.v.).

Compressed No. 30, Mono 108 (14,18pt)

COMSTOCK was advertised by Inland Type Foundry in 1902 as "a striking novelty, our brand new face." It was revived by ATF in 1957. It is a medium weight conventional gothic, distinguished by a hairline surrounding each letter. The *G* lacks a crossbar, typical of many nineteenth-century gothics. The design was sponsored by A. H. Comstock of Omaha, according to a review at the time of its introduction. *Condensed Comstock* was introduced by Inland in 1905, but patented in the name of William A. Schraubstädter in 1908. It has no lowercase, but the design is more contemporary. Monotype has copied both faces, but Monotype *Comstock Condensed* is in 18-point only, without figures.

Comstock, Inland-ATF 110 (12s-36pt); Mono 202 (12-24pt)
Condensed Comstock, Inland-ATF 114 (12s-48pt); Comstock Condensed, Mono 203 (18pt); (Univ 12-30pt)

In both foundry faces, there are several sizes on 12-point body; No. 1 is the largest in regular, but No. 1 is the smallest in *Condensed.* In 1911, a copy of *Comstock* was issued by Bauer in Germany under the name *Astoria,* revived in 1957.

CONGRESS, Hansen 24-pt. (part reduced)

G. A. R. Encampment met at Washington 1234567890 B C D
FG H I J K L M N O P Q R S T U V W X Y Z

CONGRESSIONAL & ITALIC, Lino 14-pt.

ABCDEFGHIJKLMNOPQRSTUVWXYZ& Z & æ œ fl ffi ffl : ( ) 1234567890$ x z & Æ Œ
*ABCDEFGHIJKLMNOPQRSTUVWXY*un *Z & œ œ fl ffi ffl : ( ) 1234567890$*
abcdefghijklmnopqrstuvwxyz fi fl ff ffi ffl æ œ £ $1234567890 , . : ; ? ! (|) * ' ' - — Æ Œ ℔
abcdefghijklmnopqrstuvwxyz fi Y *ff* W M K H *£* P vBCDEFGRTJ , . s ; ? ! A I Q O '' - — *Æ Œ ℔*

CONTACT BOLD CONDENSED, ATF 24-pt.

ABCDEFGHIJKLMNOPQRSTUVWXYZ $$1234567890¢ᶜ&
abcdefghijklmnopqrstuvwxyz.,-:;''""''!?

CONTACT BOLD CONDENSED ITALIC, ATF 24-pt.

ABCDEFGHIJKLMNOPQRSTUVWXYZ $$1234567890&ᶜ£
abcdefghijklmnopqrstuvwxyz.,-:;!?''""   *AKMNS*

CONTOUR NO. 1, Mono 24-pt.

ABCDEFGHIJKLMNOPQRSTUVWXYZ&
abcdefghijklmnopqrstuvwxyz .,-:;'!?
$1234567890

CONTOUR NO. 4 (36-pt. at 67%)

ABCDEFGHIJKLMNOPQ 1234567890
abcdefghijklmnopqrstuvwxyz !?&$

CONTOUR NO. 5, ATF 24-pt. (Dave Churchman)

FOREIGN RACES 65 HORSE

CONTOUR NO. 6, Mono 24-pt.

ABCDEFGHIJKLMNOPQRSTUVWXYZ.,:;-'!?&$1234567890

CONDENSED CASLON, CONDENSED FOSTER, CONDENSED GOTHIC, etc.—see under primary name of *Caslon, Foster, Gothic,* etc.

CONDENSED GOTHIC (other), **CONDENSED GOTHIC OUTLINE—** see *Alternate Gothic.*

CONDENSED GOTHIC NO. 3—see *Headline Gothic.*

CONDENSED NO. 54—see *Modern Roman Condensed.*

CONDENSED OUTLINE—see *Howland Open.*

CONDENSED SANS SERIFS—see Imports in Appendix.

CONDENSED TITLE—see *Modern Roman.*

CONGRESS is a fancy face shown by Hansen in 1909 or earlier. It was sold as fonts of initials, caps only, for which it seems more suited, or as complete fonts with lowercase, figures and points.

Congress, Hansen (18-48pt)

CONGRESSIONAL is an adaptation of *No. 36* (see "Numbered Faces") for the U.S. Government Printing Office. It is a conventional modern roman, but rather compact and with long ascenders. The special feature is a canceled version in the auxiliary position on each matrix, the cancellation being a continuous horizontal line through each word when assembled. It has been used primarily for legal work.

Congressional and Italic, plain and Cancelled, Lino (14pt)

CONSORT—see *Antique, Clarendon;* also see Imports in Appendix.

CONTACT BOLD CONDENSED and *Italic* were designed by Frank H. Riley for ATF about 1942, but not released until 1948 because of war-time conditions. They are narrow and vigorous, with a large x-height and short ascenders and descenders, intended for newspaper and general advertising display. Other widths and weights were projected, but there is no evidence that they were completed. Compare *John Hancock Condensed, Bold Antique Condensed.*

Contact Bold Condensed, ATF 690 (8-84pt)
Contact Bold Condensed Italic, ATF 691 (8-72pt)

CONTOUR is a group of outline faces issued by Marder, Luse & Co., Chicago type foundry, in 1888-89. Several were copied by Monotype, and some of these are still being produced by the secondary typefounders who cast from those mats, although not always under the original names. *Contour No. 1* is an outline of the obsolete *Royal Gothic; No. 4* of *Latin Bold Condensed; No. 5* of *Interchangeable Gothic; No. 6* of *Condensed Gothic;* the others up to *No. 7* are obsolete. Marder, Luse joined the merger in 1892 that formed American Type Founders Company, where these faces continued to be cast for some time, but apparently the matrices did not survive until ATF assigned serial numbers. Also see *Modern Gothic Condensed Outline, Gothic Outline Title, Whedons Gothic Outline,* and other Outlines throughout this book.

Contour No. 1, Marder, Luse-ATF (12-48pt); Mono 40 (18-36pt); Outline, Keystone-ATF 898 (12-48pt)
Contour No. 4, Marder, Luse-ATF (28-72pt); Mono 59 (30,36pt)
Contour No. 5, Marder, Luse-ATF (24-48pt); Mono 73 (24pt)
Contour No. 6, Marder, Luse-ATF (12-72pt); Mono 123 (18-36pt); Outline Condensed, Keystone-ATF 899 (12-48pt); Gothic Condensed Outline, Lino (12,18pt)

COOPER, ATF 24-pt. (Dave Churchman)

ABCDEFGHIJKLMNOPQRSTUVWXYZ&.,-:;'!?—[
abcdefghijklmnopqrstuvwxyz $1234567890 ꝗ·❀↝ ꝗ

COOPER ITALIC, ATF 24-pt.

ABCDEFGHIJKLMNOPQRSTUVWXYZ&
abcdefghijklmnopqrstuvwxyz $1234567890 .,-:;'!?—( )

COOPER BLACK, Mono 24-pt.

ABCDEFGHIJKLMNOPQRSTUVWXYZ&
abcdefghijklmnopqrstuvwxyz.,-:;"!?[]·—ꝗ
$1234567890

COOPER BLACK ITALIC, ATF 24-pt.

ABCDEFGHIJKLMNOPQRSTUVWXYZ
abcdefghijklmnopqrstuvwxyz .,:;-'!? · ()
ABDEFGMNPRTY $&1234567890

COOPER BLACK CONDENSED, ATF 24-pt.

ABCDEFGHIJKLMNOPQRSTUVWXYZ&.,-:;"!?[ ]—
abcdefghijklmnopqrstuvwxyz $1234567890ꝗ

COOPER HILITE, BB&S 24-pt.

ABCDEFGHIJKLMNOPQRSTUVWXYZ&
abcdefghijklmnopqrstuvwxyz.,-:;"!?[]—
$1234567890

COOPER FULLFACE, BB&S (24-pt. at 67%)

ABCDEFGHIJKLMNOPQRSTUV
abcdefghijklmnopqrstuvwxyz
1234567890$·—.,'::!?   WXYZ&

COOPER TOOLED ITALIC, BB&S 24-pt.

ABCDEFGHIJKLMNOPQRSTUVWXYZ&   []
abcdefghijklmnopqrstuvwxyz $1234567890 .,-:;'!? ( )

104

COOPER BLACK is the best known of a number of typefaces designed by Oswald Bruce Cooper, Chicago lettering artist, but it is not the first or most unusual. They resulted from a policy of Barnhart Brothers & Spindler, the large Chicago type foundry, of seeking original designs and encouraging modern artists to add their talented contributions to typographic resources.

Cooper, an oldstyle letter with innovative rounded serifs, long ascenders and a close fit, was designed in 1918. Originally called *Cooper Oldstyle,* the shorter name was adopted before it was released. *Cooper Italic* was designed in 1924; it harmonizes well with the roman, but retains more of the quaintness and irregularity of hand-lettering through the unusual swing of such letters as *h, k, m,* and *n.* Roman and italic fonts include f-ligatures up to 18-point only. Note the unusual extras in roman—brackets, paragraph mark, "classic point," four-leaf clover, etc. Small caps were also made up to 18-point, but these were the same as the next smaller size of caps, including 16-point, with very little difference between them and regular caps in some sizes.

Cooper Black was issued in 1922, a super-black design which fully represented Cooper's unique style and started a new trend in advertising typography. Cooper called it, "for far-sighted printers with near-sighted customers." This became the foundry's best selling type before its merger with ATF seven years later, and ATF's all-time second-best-selling type (after *Copperplate Gothic*). *Cooper Black Italic* was completed in 1926, and quickly joined the ranks of best selling types. The dozen swash capitals were unusual for such a heavy face. Both italics are non-kerning, that is, none of the letters overhang the body, eliminating the major cause of breakage, for Cooper was as practical as he was talented. *Cooper Hilite* was created in 1925 by cutting a white line in *Cooper Black. Cooper Black Condensed* appeared in 1926; Cooper described it as "condensed but not squeezed."

Cooper Fullface, probably the most innovative of Cooper's creations, was issued by BB&S shortly before the foundry was closed in 1929; production was taken over by ATF, where it was renamed *Cooper Modern.* Of this face, Cooper said that it "differs from Bodoni in that its serifs are rounded, and its main stems drawn freely, with a suggestion of curve in almost every line." He added, "It is unusual in that it combines the sharp contrast of main and minor lines (as in Bodoni) with the free rendering (as in Caslon) of pen drawn characters." An italic was undertaken but never completed. We have the word of Richard N. McArthur, former BB&S advertising manager, that *Fullface* and *Modern* are the same face, but there is no explanation of the ATF listing of both names with different serial numbers for matrices in its vaults.

Cooper Tooled Italic was copied by BB&S in 1928 from an adaptation by a German foundry of *Cooper Italic,* the result of an agreement to exchange designs between the two foundries; BB&S later admitted it was the loser in this deal. This letter is basically heavier than the original, and very displeasing to Cooper. But *Cooper Tooled* is Monotype's adaptation by Sol Hess of *Cooper Black,* with a white line on the opposite side from *Cooper Hilite;* it was done in 1928.

Monotype also copied *Cooper* (both roman and italic) and *Cooper Black,* under the same names. Intertype's *Rugged Black* and *Italic,* issued 1929, are essentially like *Cooper Black* and *Italic* through 14-point; in larger sizes the roman is closer to *Cooper Black Condensed.* Compare *Ludlow Black, Pabst Extra Bold, Goudy Heavyface.*

Cooper, BB&S-ATF 1589 (6-72pt); Mono 482 (8-36pt)
Cooper Italic, BB&S-ATF 1595 (6-72pt); Mono 4821 (8-36pt)
Cooper Black, BB&S-ATF 1590 (6-120pt); Mono 282 (6-72pt); Rugged Black, Inter (10-60pt)
Cooper Black Italic, BB&S-ATF 1592 (6-120pt); Rugged Black Italic, Inter (10-14pt)
Cooper Black Condensed, BB&S-ATF 1591 (6-120pt)
Cooper Hilite, BB&S-ATF 1594 (18-120pt)
Cooper Fullface, BB&S-ATF 1593 or Cooper Modern, ATF 1942 (6-72pt)
Cooper Tooled, Mono 582 (18-72pt)
Cooper Tooled Italic, BB&S-ATF 1596 (10-72pt)

COOPER TOOLED, Mono 24-pt.

ABCDEFGHIJKLMNOPQRSTUVWXYZ&
abcdefghijklmnopqrstuvwxyz.,-:;'!?[]—¶·
$1234567890

COPPERPLATE GOTHIC LIGHT, ATF 18L

ABCDEFGHIJKLMNOPQRSTUVWXYZ&
$1234567890.,-:;'!?   R
Hansen

COPPERPLATE GOTHIC LIGHT CONDENSED, Mono 18L

ABCDEFGHIJKLMNOPQRSTUVWXYZ& $1234567890.,-:;'!?

COPPERPLATE GOTHIC LIGHT EXTENDED, ATF 18L

ABCDEFGHIJKLMNOPQRSTUVWXYZ&
1234567890$.,-:;'!?   PRINTING
BB&S

COPPERPLATE GOTHIC HEAVY, ATF 18L

ABCDEFGHIJKLMNOPQRSTUVWXYZ&
1234567890$,.-;:'!?   R
Hansen

COPPERPLATE GOTHIC ITALIC, ATF 18L

ABCDEFGHIJKLMNOPQRSTUVWXYZ&
$1234567890 .,-:;'!?   *G*
BB&S

COPPERPLATE GOTHIC HEAVY CONDENSED, ATF 18L

ABCDEFGHIJKLMNOPQRSTUVWXYZ&1234567890$-:;'!?R
Han
sen

COPPERPLATE GOTHIC HEAVY EXTENDED, ATF 18L

ABCDEFGHIJKLMNOPQRSTUVWXYZ
1234567890$.,-:;'!?&   PRINTING
BB&S

COPPERPLATE GOTHIC BOLD, ATF 18L

ABCDEFGHIJKLMNOPQRSTUVWXYZ&
1234567890 .,:;-!?$ R
Hansen

COPPERPLATE GOTHIC SHADED, ATF 12L (Gary Hantke)

ABCDEFGHIJKLMNOPQRSTUVWXYZ& 1234567890$.,-:;'!?

COPPERPLATE ROMAN, 10-pt. (David Greer)

ABCDEFGHIJKLMNOPQRSTUVWXYZ& $1234567890 .,-:;'!? ᴼᴿˢᵀ

COPPERPLATE ROMAN, Hansen 12-pt.

COPPERPLATE ROMAN LINCOLN MANUFACTURING CO.

106

COPPERPLATE—see *Inland Copperplate.*

COPPERPLATE GOTHIC HEAVY was designed in 1903 by Frederic W. Goudy, who is much better known for his classic roman faces. Other weights and widths were drawn shortly thereafter by Clarence C. Marder of ATF, except the *Shaded,* designed by Morris F. Benton in 1912. A rather wide, monotone, conventional gothic with the added feature of minute serifs, *Copperplate Gothic* is imitative of the work of engravers, as suggested by the name. It became ATF's all-time best seller, being used extensively for stationery and form work, especially in the small neighborhood printshops of the letterpress era. It is the typical lining gothic face, featuring four sizes each on 6- and 12-point bodies, and two sizes each of 18- and 24-point in foundry (composing-machine sizes differ somewhat), so that a wide variety of cap-and-small-cap combinations can readily be set.

Before Monotype developed its "Plate Gothic arrangement" (see under "Design Limitations" in Introduction) in 1919, permitting the keyboarding of all four sizes of 6- or 12-point at once, that company had made the Copperplate Gothics simply as cap-and-small-cap combinations, typically in 5-, 6-, 8-, 10-, and 12-point plus display sizes. Hence most of these gothics have two different series numbers on Monotype, the lower number for display sizes and the obsolete cap-and-small-cap combinations, the other for the four-size combination.

Several versions of *Steelplate Gothic* (q.v.) from BB&S were near duplicates of *Copperplate Gothic,* although a few characters differed slightly and the extended versions were not quite as wide. Hansen had *Engravers Gothic* in several versions, differing apparently only in the *R* as shown in the specimen. Compare *Plate Gothic, Whittier;* also see *Bank Gothic, Blair, Boxhead Gothics.*

Copperplate Gothic Light, ATF 128 (6s-24L); Light Copperplate Gothic, Mono 187 (5s-24L), 340 (6s-12L); Gothic No. 32, Lino = Inter (4s-12L); Lining Plate Gothic Light, Ludlow 6-LPL (6s-24L); Steelplate Gothic Light, BB&S-ATF 1867 (6s-24L); Engravers Gothic Light, Hansen (6s-24L)

Copperplate Gothic Light Condensed, ATF 131 (6s-24L); Light Copperplate Gothic Condensed, Mono 197 (5-24L), 341 (6s-12L); Gothic No. 29, Lino = Inter (6s-12L); Lining Plate Gothic Light Condensed, Ludlow 6-LPLC (6s-18L); Steelplate Gothic Light Condensed, BB&S-ATF 1869 (6s-24L)

Copperplate Gothic Light Extended, ATF 134 (6s-24L); Gothic No. 34, Inter (6s-12L); Lining Plate Gothic Light Extended, Ludlow 6-LPLE (6s-12L); Steelplate Gothic Light Extended, BB&S-ATF 1865 (6s-24L)

Copperplate Gothic Heavy, ATF 130 (6s-24L); Heavy Copperplate Gothic, Mono 168 (5s-24L), 342 (6s-12L); Gothic No. 31, Lino = Inter (4-18L); Lining Plate Gothic Heavy, Ludlow 6-LPH (6s-24L); Engravers Lining Gothic No. 35, Inter (7pt); Steelplate Gothic Heavy, BB&S-ATF 1868 (6s-24L); Engravers Gothic, Hansen (6s-24L)

Copperplate Gothic Italic, ATF 133 (6s-24L); Copperplate Gothic Bold Italic, Mono 346 (6s-24L); Steelplate Gothic Italic, BB&S-ATF 1871 (6s-24L)

Copperplate Gothic Heavy Condensed, ATF 129 (6s-24L); Heavy Copperplate Gothic Condensed, Mono 169 (5s-24L), 343 (6s-12L); Gothic No. 30, Lino = Inter (6s-18L); Lining Plate Gothic Heavy Condensed, Ludlow 6-LPHC (6s-18L); Steelplate Gothic Heavy Condensed, BB&S-ATF 1870 (6s-24L); Engravers Gothic Heavy Condensed, Hansen (6s-24L)

Copperplate Gothic Heavy Extended, ATF 135 (6s-24L); Heavy Copperplate Gothic Extended, Mono 166 (5s-18L), 266 (5,6pt), 344 (6s-6L); Gothic No. 35, Inter (6s-12L); Lining Plate Gothic Heavy Extended, Ludlow 6-LPHE (6s-12L); Steelplate Gothic Heavy Extended, BB&S-ATF 1866 (6s-24L)

Copperplate Gothic Bold, ATF 132 (6s-24L); Mono 345 (6s-24L); Gothic No. 33, Lino (6s-12L); Lining Plate Gothic Bold, Ludlow 6-LPB (6s-24L); Engravers Gothic Bold, Hansen (6s-24L)

Copperplate Gothic Shaded, ATF 136 (6s-36pt); (Univ 6s-24L)

Copperplate Gothic is known as Spartan in England, as Mimosa in Germany.

COPPERPLATE ROMAN was a delicate title roman face, similar to *Light Litho,* introduced by ATF in 1897 or earlier, but shown through 1923. Hansen had a different *Copperplate Roman,* copied from *Cesare de Sesto,* of the Nebiolo foundry in Italy.

Copperplate Roman, ATF 242 (6s-12L)
Copperplate Roman, Hansen (8s-12pt)

CORBITT, ATF (48-pt. at 50%) (Rick von Holdt)

ABCDEFGHIJKLMNOPQRSTUVWXYZ R
abcdefghijklmnopqrstuvwxyz&.,-;:'!?
$1234567890

CONDENSED CORBITT, ATF 24-pt. (part reduced) (Rick von Holdt)

ABCDEFGHIJKLMNOPQRSTUVWXYZ.,:;'?&
Experienced Employer   14567890

CORNELL & ITALIC & BOLD, Inter 14-pt.

ABCDEFGHIJKLMNOPQRSTUVWXYZ $1234567890 ABCDEFGHIJKLMNOPQRSTUVWXYZ
ABCDEFGHIJKLMNOPQRSTUVWXYZ $1234567890
abcdefghijklmnopqrstuvwxyz fi fl ff ffi ffl ,.-;':'!? ( ) @ ℔ & £ Æ Œ Æœ æœ &%[ ] * † ‖ ‡ §¶ ⅛¼⅜½⅝¾⅞
*abcdefghijklmnopqrstuvwxyz fi fl ff ffi ffl ,.-;'s'!? ( ) @ ℔ & £ Æ Œ Æœ æœ &%[ ] * † ‡§¶ ⅛¼⅜½⅝¾⅞*

ABCDEFGHIJKLMNOPQRSTUVWXYZ $1234567890 Æ Œ æ œ
abcdefghijklmnopqrstuvwxyz fi fl ff ffi ffl ,.-;':'!?()@ ℔ & £ % [ ] * † ‖ ‡ § ¶ — ⅛ ¼ ⅜ ½ ⅝ ¾ ⅞ ⅓ ⅔

CORONA & ITALIC, Lino 12-pt.

ABCDEFGHIJKLMNOPQRSTUVWXYZ&ÆŒ 1234567890$£ ABCDEFGHIJKLMNOPQRSTUVWXYZ&ÆŒ
ABCDEFGHIJKLMNOPQRSTUVWXYZ&ÆŒ 1234567890$£
abcdefghijklmnopqrstuvwxyzæœfiflffffiffl ,.:;'-'?!-|—   ...()*†‡¶§[]% ⅛¼⅜½⅝¾⅞⅓⅔⅕⅖⅗⅘⅕⅙⅚
abcdefghijklmnopqrstuvwxyzæœfiflffffiffl ,.:;'-'?!-|—...   ()†‡¶§[]% ⅛¼⅜½⅝¾⅞⅓⅔⅕⅖⅗⅘⅕⅙⅚*

CORONET, Ludlow 24-pt.

ABCDEFGHIJKLMNOPQRSTUVWXYZ& F J T

abcdefghijklmnopqrstuvwxyz 1234567890 $?!.,;'- % ¼ ⅓ ½ ⅔ ¾

CORONET BOLD, Ludlow 24-pt.

ABCDEFGHIJKLMNOPQRSTUVWXYZ F J T

abcdefghijklmnopqrstuvwxyz$1234567890.,-;'"—[]()!?& % ¼ ⅓ ½ ⅔ ¾

COSMOPOLITAN & ITALIC, Mono 12-pt.

ABCDEFGHIJKLMNOPQRSTUVWXYZ&ÆŒ   *ABCDEFGHIJKLMNOPQRSTUVWXYZ&ÆŒ*
abcdefghijklmnopqrstuvwxyzæœ   fiflffffiffl   *abcdefghijklmnopqrstuvwxyzæœ   fiflffffiffl*
$1234567890 .,-'":;!?   *$1234567890 :;!?*
ABCDEFGHIJKLMNOPQRSTUVWXYZ&ÆŒ

CORBITT is a heavy, thick-and-thin face with tiny serifs, designed by Nicholas J. Werner and issued by Inland in 1900. Although still showing many of the quaint design details of nineteenth-century types, it is somewhat more mature. *Condensed Corbitt* was advertised by Inland in 1902 as their "latest addition." Both versions were cast by ATF after Inland merged with that foundry in 1911, but only the *Condensed* seems to have survived until matrices were inventoried in 1930.

Corbitt, Inland-ATF (6-72pt)
Condensed Corbitt, Inland-ATF 115 (6-72pt)

CORDON, CORINTHIAN—see Antiques in Appendix.

CORNELL is an original, contemporary roman face of distinctive character, designed for Intertype by George Trenholm, who was typeface design counselor for that company. The roman and italic were introduced in 1948, with *Cornell Bold* in 1955.

Cornell with Italic, Inter (6-18pt)
Cornell Bold, Inter (6-14pt)

CORONA was drawn and cut by Linotype under the direction of C. H. Griffith in 1941. It is a member of the "Legibility Group" of faces designed for easy reading under newspaper conditions of stereotyping and high-speed printing with inks that could be trapped in close quarters. *Royal* on Intertype is a 1960 copy of *Corona*.

Corona and Italic, Lino (5-14, 5-12pt); Royal and Italic and Bold, Inter (5½-11pt)

CORONET and *Coronet Bold* are popular script types designed by R. Hunter Middleton for Ludlow in 1937, taking full advantage of the 17-degree mats of that system. Not quite connecting, the letters have a charming grace and swing, and are one of the comparatively few script families with two weights. The bold in particular has been popular with newspapers and most other installations of Ludlow equipment around the world, and fonts of separate type have been cast by secondary suppliers. Compare *Trafton Script, Stylescript*.

Coronet, Ludlow 42-MIC (14-72pt)
Coronet Bold, Ludlow 42-BIC (14-72pt)

CORVINUS—see *Glamour;* also see Imports in Appendix.

COSMOPOLITAN was cut by Monotype in 1902 for Mitchell Kennerley, publisher of *Cosmopolitan* magazine, who also used it in other publications. It is a rather narrow, compact face, with lowercase taller than most such faces; a matter-of-fact face, more unassuming than *Bodoni* and a little lighter than *Century Expanded*. Kennerley considered it one of the most legible roman faces ever cut. In 1936 it was modified and more sizes added. Compare *Century Expanded, Post Text*.

Cosmopolitan and Italic, Mono 4ABC (6-12pt)

COURTS—see *DeVinne Recut Italic*.
CRAFTSMAN—see *Artcraft*, also *Cheltenham*.

CRAW CLARENDON, ATF 24-pt.

ABCDEFGHIJKLMNOPQRSTUVWXYZ
abcdefghijklmnopqrstuvwxyz.,:;-''""!?&-()%
$1234567890

CRAW CLARENDON BOOK, ATF 24-pt.

ABCDEFGHIJKLMNOPQRSTUVWXYZ
abcdefghijklmnopqrstuvwxyz.,:;-''""!?&-
¢$1234567890

CRAW CLARENDON CONDENSED, ATF 24-pt.

ABCDEFGHIJKLMNOPQRSTUVWXYZ
abcdefghijklmnopqrstuvwxyz.,:;--''""!?&$¢1234567890

CRAW MODERN, ATF 24-pt.

ABCDEFGHIJKLMNOPQRSTUVW
abcdefghijklmnopqrstuvwxyz XYZ
$1234567890.,:;-''""!?&%¢-

CRAW MODERN ITALIC, ATF 24-pt.

ABCDEFGHIJKLMNOPQRSTUVWXY
abcdefghijklmnopqrstuvwxyz   Z&
$1234567890 .,-:;'!?-% " " ¢

CRAW MODERN BOLD, ATF 24-pt.

ABCDEFGHIJKLMNOPQRSTUVW
abcdefghijklmnopqrstuvwxyz
$1234567890.,-:;''""!?&%¢-   XYZ

CROMWELL, ATF 24-pt. (Larry J. Raid)

ABCDEFGHIJKLMNOPQRRSTTUVWXYZ$1234567890&
abcdefghijklmnopqrstuvwxyyzfffffiflfflffi.,-:;''""!? fafefofrfutyf

110

CRAW CLARENDON. In 1955, ATF commissioned Freeman Craw to develop an American version of the Clarendon letter, resulting in *Craw Clarendon.* The following year *Craw Clarendon Book,* a lighter weight, was released, and *Craw Clarendon Condensed* in 1960. Craw has commented that as a designer *of* type he faced different problems than as a designer *with* type. Perhaps this and the alleged rush production resulted in unfortunate compromise, as some sizes are small for the body, with excess shoulder. Otherwise they are excellent and deservedly popular faces. The normal widths are also made by Monotype. Also see *Clarendon.*

Craw Clarendon, ATF 710 (8-72pt); Mono 65 (7-36pt)
Craw Clarendon Book, ATF 712 (8-72pt); Mono 650 (7-36pt)
Craw Clarendon Condensed, ATF 717 (14-96pt)

CRAW MODERN is a contemporary interpretation of the modern roman style, designed by Freeman Craw for ATF in 1958. It is a very wide face, with large x-height and short ascenders and descenders, otherwise somewhat the character of Bodoni but a little less formal. *Craw Modern Bold* followed, and in 1964 *Craw Modern Italic* was introduced. These faces have the same general proportions and some of the general design characteristics as the same artist's *Craw Clarendon,* but the similarity ends there and the faces should not be considered part of the same family. Compare *Modern Roman, Litho series.*

Craw Modern, ATF 714 (6-72pt)
Craw Modern Italic, ATF 720 (10-48pt)
Craw Modern Bold, ATF 716 (6-72pt)

CRAWFORD—see *MacFarland.*
CRAYONETTE—see Antiques in Appendix.

CROMWELL is a rather playful typeface, designed by Morris Benton in 1913 but not released by ATF until three years later. It uses the same capitals as *Cloister* (q.v.) and has the same small x-height with long ascenders and descenders, but otherwise is quite different, with much less formality. Notice the alternate characters and the double letters including overhanging *f*'s.

Cromwell, ATF 138 (6-48pt)

CUBIST BOLD—the name tells it all. Designed by John W. Zimmerman, head of the matrix engraving department at BB&S, probably just before BB&S merged with ATF in 1929, this font of unusual capitals and figures is very large for the body and has no lowercase. Compare *Dynamic Medium, Modernique.*

Cubist Bold, BB&S-ATF 1599 (10-36pt)

CUBIST BOLD, BB&S 20-pt.

ABCDEFGHIJKLMNOPQRSTUVW
$1234567890 .,-:;'!? XYZ&

CURTIS POST, ATF 24-pt. (Dave Churchman, Gary Hantke)

ABCDEFGHIJKLMNOPQRSTUVXYZ&

abcdefghijklmnopqrstuvwxyzffffffffffffffl

$1234567890Theofoct&EORS.,-:;'!?

CUSHING NO. 2, ATF 24-pt.

ABCDEFGHIJKLMNOPQRSTUVWXYZ &

abcdefghijklmnopqrstuvwxyz.,-':;!?1234567890

CUSHING NO. 2 ITALIC, ATF 18-pt. (Herb Harnish)

ABCDEFGHIJKLMNOPQRSTUVWXYZ&$1234567890

abcdefghijklmnopqrstuvwxyz.,-:;'!?

CUSHING OLDSTYLE, Mono 24-pt. (Len Richardson)

ABCDEFGHIJKLMNOPQRSTUVWXYZ .,-:;'!?

abcdefghijklmnopqrstuvwxyz 1234567890&$

CUSHING OLDSTYLE ITALIC, Mono 24-pt.

ABCDEFGHIJKLMNOPQRSTUVWXYZ&

abcdefghijklmnopqrstuvwxyz $1234567890 .,-:;'!?

CUSHING MONOTONE, ATF 24-pt.

STUDIOUS YOUTH ENTHUSES

American Fashions Please Craftsmen

CUSHING ANTIQUE, Ludlow 24-pt.

ABCDEFGHIJKLMNOPQRSTUVWXYZ&

abcdefghijklmnopqrstuvwxyz 1234567890

Name in parentheses after some specimens
indicates person who has set that specimen,
in whole or in part, to our format.

112

CURTIS POST was produced by ATF in 1902 for the *Saturday Evening Post* magazine of Curtis Publishing Company, but soon released to printers in general. It is based on *Post Oldstyle Roman No. 2,* a style which previously had been handlettered for headings in the magazine. Like many fonts of the day, it contained several alternate characters and logotypes. Some specimens hyphenate the name as *Curtis-Post. Curtis Shaded Italic* was cut in 1910; it is uncertain whether this is the same as *Post Shaded Italic.* Compare the various *Post* faces.

Curtis Post, ATF 139 (12-72pt)
Curtis Shaded Italic, ATF

CUSHING is a group of typefaces rather than a family, for some members have little in common with each other, and were not intended to work together. Some accounts credit the design of these faces to Josiah Stearns Cushing, who in the late nineteenth century was president of the Norwood Press Company in Norwood, Massachusetts. Cushing was one of the most prominent printers of the day, but it seems more likely that he merely spelled out what he wanted in typefaces for his particular purposes, and that they were executed by others.

[Lining] Cushing No. 2, ATF 243 (6-24pt); Custer or Bookman Lightface, BB&S (6-24pt)
[Lining] Cushing No. 2 Italic, ATF 244 (6-24pt)
Cushing Oldstyle No. 2, ATF (6-72pt); Cushing Old Style, Mono 25 (5-36pt); Title No. 1, Lino (6-18pt); Richelieu, Keystone (6-84pt); Custer Bold or Bookman Bold, BB&S (6-72pt)
Cushing Oldstyle Italic, ATF (6-72pt); Mono 251 (6-36pt)
Cushing Monotone [No. 553, Lining], ATF (6-36pt); Mono 134EF (6-12pt)
Cushing Antique, ATF 140 (6-72pt); Ludlow 4 (12-42pt)

Cushing and *Cushing Italic* were cut about 1897 by ATF. They are conventional roman and italic in basic design, but are almost completely uniform in weight of stroke throughout, with small oldstyle serifs. They were intended to provide a letter particularly adapted for book work, to print clearly and readably, and to reproduce well by electrotyping. A few years later they were shown as *Lining Cushing No. 2* and *Italic,* the added words probably indicating that some adjustment had necessarily been made to adapt them to the new standard alignment. BB&S had a copy of this roman under the name of *Custer;* in 1925 it was reissued as *Bookman Lightface,* in the same sizes. Compare *Cardinal, Hunnewell.*

Frederic W. Goudy, the eminent type designer, includes *Cushing Italic* in his list of faces. In the book of his type designs, he says, "While in Hingham, Clarence Marder had me draw for him an italic to accompany the *Cushing Roman* already produced. . . . Whether the italic shown in the specimen of today is the one I drew I cannot be sure. . . ." It isn't; he went to Hingham in 1904; this *Cushing Italic* had been shown in 1898 or earlier.

Cushing Oldstyle (later known as *[Lining] Cushing Oldstyle No. 2)* was cut in the mid-1890s by ATF, and copied by Monotype in 1901. It is a sturdy, compact face, with a large x-height. In small sizes it is medium weight; from 18-point up it is a little heavier. The large, bracketed serifs and general style are similar to the early Ionics, Dorics, and Clarendons. A copy of this face was made by Keystone under the name of *Richelieu* (named for Cardinal Richelieu), Linotype had it as *Title No. 1,* and BB&S had a very similar face, *Custer Bold,* which in 1925 was renamed *Bookman Bold.*

[Lining] Cushing Oldstyle Italic was cut about 1906 by ATF. It was cut for Monotype in 1910; the Monotype roman follows the original, being a little heavier in larger sizes, but the italic is wider than the original and uniform throughout, as patterns for the modified composition sizes were apparently used for display sizes as well.

Cushing Monotone was cut about 1899, a refinement of an earlier face of the same name. It is generally a lighter version of *Cushing Oldstyle,* but not as light as *Cushing [No. 2].* It is neat but undistinguished for either text or display, somewhat similar to *Bookman* but lighter. *Uniline* was a similar face shown later by Linotype. Also compare *Cardinal.*

Cushing Antique was designed by Morris Benton for ATF in 1902, but not cut until 1905. An ATF announcement said of it, "Entirely redrawn and cut from new patterns. Conforms to approved outlines for antique face but modified to meet present-day requirements. Unquestionably the most complete and accurate series of antique made." It was copied by Ludlow in 1927. An italic was planned by ATF but not completed.

CUSTER—see *Bookman, Cushing.*

CZARIN, Baltimore 24-pt.

ABCDEFGHIJKLMNOPQRSTUVWXYZ
abcdefghijklmnopqrstuvwxyzfifffffffiffl $1234567890¢.,-:;'"'"'!?&()«».·+

DARTMOUTH, Duensing 22-pt.

A B C D E F G H I J K L M N O P
Q R S T U V W X Y Z $1234567890

DEEPDENE, Mono 24-pt.

ABCDEFGHIJKLMNOPQRSTUVWXYZ1234567890
abcdefghijklmnopqrstuvwxyzfifffflffiffl 1234567890(&$.,-';;!?)

DEEPDENE ITALIC, Mono 24-pt.

ABCDEFGHIJKLMNOPQRSTUVWXYZ ABCDEGMPRT
abcdefg ghijkklmnopqrstuvwxyzz fiffflffiffl 1234567890&$.,-';;!? gy gg

DEEPDENE MEDIUM, Goudy 24-pt.

ABCDEFGHIJKLMNOPQRSTUVWXYZ&
abcdefghijklmnopqrstuvwxyzfiflffffffiffl

DEEPDENE BOLD, Mono 18-pt. (Guy Botterill)

ABCDEFGHIJKLMNOPQRSTUVWXYZ&$1234567890
abcdefghijklmnopqrstuvwxyz.,-:;'!?fffiflffiffl

DEEPDENE BOLD ITALIC, Mono 24-pt. (Guy Botterill)

ABCDEFGHIJKLMNOPQRSTUVWXYZ
abcdefghijklmnopqrstuvwxyzfffifflffiffl &1234567890$.,-:;!?'

CZARIN and *Czarin Title* were produced by Baltimore Type & Composition Corporation about 1948, the name being derived from the Czarnowski family which owned the foundry. *Czarin Title,* issued first, is a copy of *Offenbach Medium,* a set of pen-drawn capitals designed by Rudolf Koch about 1935 for the Klingspor foundry in Germany. *Czarin* has minor changes in a few characters, but adds a lowercase, designed by Edwin W. Shaar, that is substantially different from that of *Steel,* the cap-and-lowercase version of *Offenbach.* The new lowercase harmonizes well with the capitals, and makes a handsome appearance. Compare *Lydian.*

Czarin, Balto 210 (12-72pt); also Czarin Title, Balto 110 (14-48pt)

DAILY NEWS GOTHIC was designed by Gerry Powell and cut by ATF in 1938 for that newspaper. No specimen has been found.

Daily News Gothic, ATF (120,144pt)

DANDY—see *Romantiques* under Antiques in Appendix.

DARTMOUTH may be the last new typeface cut in metal. Paul Duensing says it was designed by Will Carter as a titling letter for the college of that name for signage and other display uses. It was based on *Octavian Roman* which Carter and David Kindersley had co-designed in 1960-61 for English Monotype. New figures for this cutting were drawn by Will Rueter of Toronto. *Dartmouth* was cut and cast in 22-point in 1991 at Duensing's Private Press and Typefoundry.

Dartmouth, Duensing (22pt)

DEEPDENE. The roman of this series was designed and cut by Frederic W. Goudy in 1927 for his own Village Letter Foundery, and named for his estate at Marlboro-on-Hudson, which in turn was named for the street in Forest Hills, New York, where Goudy worked before moving to Marlboro in 1923. The accompanying italic was designed the following year, with matrices for the first trial size being cut by the designer's wife, Bertha M. Goudy. Of this italic, Goudy says, "I chose more or less to disregard tradition in an attempt to follow a line of my own, and drew each character without reference to any other craftsman's work. I think this italic shows a disciplined freedom which retains the essential quality of legibility." It has been described as having "an acid, typey quality," with interest, color, movement, and quaintness. Like many of Goudy's italics, the inclination is slight.

Deepdene, Goudy (12-36pt); Mono 315 (6-60pt)
Deepdene Italic, Goudy; Mono 3151 (6-60pt)
Deepdene Medium, Goudy (24pt); Mono 316
Deepdene Bold, Mono 317 (6-72pt)
Deepdene Bold Italic, Mono 3171 (6-72pt)

When Monotype obtained rights to reproduce *Deepdene,* slight adjustments were necessary to adapt it to mechanical requirements in keyboard sizes. Goudy resented not being asked to make these adjustments, as some of them displeased him although they are not apparent to others.

Deepdene Medium was designed by Goudy in 1931, and he cut one size. Monotype assigned a number to this face, but no evidence has been found that it was ever cut for that machine. *Deepdene Bold* and *Italic* were designed by Goudy in 1932-33 for Monotype, and released in 1934. Goudy says, "The Deepdene Bold Italic drawings gave me more trouble than any italic I had hitherto attempted. I finally scrapped all of my preliminary sketches and began a design that would not be merely a heavier facsimile of the italic Deepdene, since I had come to believe that a bold letter can do little more than approximate in form the roman it is to complement." Compare *Californian.*

Deepdene was recut with the addition of swash letters and redesign of several other characters by Richard Ellis, with Goudy's approval, for a Knopf edition of Arthur Waley's *Translations From the Chinese.*

DEEPDENE TEXT, Goudy, private 18-pt. (Dave Norton)

ABCDEFGHIJKLMNOPQRSTUVWXYZ.,-:;'!?1234567890

DELLA ROBBIA, ATF 24-pt. (Dave Greer)

ABCDEFGHIJJKLMNOPQRRSTUVWXYYZ&.,-:;'!?
abcdefghijklmnopqrstuvwxyz fffiflffifft ·.,-:;'!? £$1234567890
QUQuctÆæŒœ

DELLA ROBBIA LIGHT, ATF 18-pt.

ABCDEFGHIJKLMNOPQRSTUVWXY
abcdefghijklmnopqrstuvwxyz $1234567890 fi fl ffi ffl

DELLA ROBBIA INITIALS, Inter (30-pt. at 80%)

ABCDEFGHIJKLMNOPQRSTUVWXYZ

DELPHIAN OPEN TITLE, Ludlow 24-pt.

ABCDEFGHIJKLMNOPQRSTUVWXYZ&
1234567890$.,:;-="''?! ( )

DEMETER, BB&S 24-pt. (Rick von Holdt)

ABCDEFGHIJKLMNOPQRSTUV
WXYZ 1234567890 &

DENNISON SCRIPT (36-pt. at 67%) (Dave Churchman)

ABCDEFGHIJKLMNOPQRSTUVWXYZ
abcdefghijklmnopqrstuvwxyz .,=;:?!& $1234567890

DeROOS ROMAN & ITALIC, Inter 14-pt.

ABCDEFGHIJKLMNOPQRSTUVWXYZ $1234567890 ABCDEFGHIJKLMNOPQRSTUVWXYZ ÆŒ&
ABCDEFGHIJKLMNOPQRSTUVWXYZ $1234567890
abcdefghijklmnopqrstuvwxyzfifflffffiffl,.-;':'!?( )@℔&£ ÆŒæœ%[ ]*†‡§¶‖–—⅛¼⅜½⅝¾⅞⅓⅔⅙⅚⅕
abcdefghijklmnopqrstuvwxyzfiflffffiffl,.-;':'!?( )@℔&£ ÆŒæœ%[ ]*†‡§¶‖–—⅛¼⅜½⅝¾⅞⅓⅔⅙⅚⅕

116

DEEPDENE OPEN TEXT was designed by Frederic W. Goudy in 1931 as a heading type for Edmund G. Gress's book, *Fashions in American Typography,* for which Goudy had been asked to write an introduction. His *Deepdene* type was being used for text. Finding that nearly all letters were required for the many headings, Goudy completed the font. All letters are highlighted with a white line in the heavy strokes. The capitals are somewhat similar to *Lombardic Caps,* while the lowercase is somewhat like *Goudy Text Shaded* (q.v.), but much less rigid. Later Goudy cut the same face with the white line of the lowercase letters filled in, and called it *Deepdene Text.* Also see *Tory Text.*

Deepdene Open Text, Goudy
Deepdene Text, Goudy (18,24pt)

DEGREE GOTHIC—see *Gothic Italic.*

DELLA ROBBIA was designed by Thomas M. Cleland from his rubbings of a few stonecut caps, made during a visit to Rome. It was cut by ATF and first shown about 1902. The capitals have a good inscriptional quality, with almost no variation in thickness of line. The lowercase, with long ascenders and short descenders, has slight thick-and-thin contrast. The series is named for Luca Della Robbia, fifteenth-century Italian sculptor. The Monotype copy, issued in 1917, is virtually exact in display sizes and not seriously modified in composition sizes, but lacks the alternate characters of the foundry version, which also includes a long-tailed *Q* in *QU* and *Qu* combinations, a tied *ct,* and a distinctive paragraph mark.

Della Robbia Light was designed by Morris Benton and cast by ATF about 1913—some sources say 1918. Damon & Peat's *Armstrong* is equivalent. *Della Robbia Initials,* which have no apparent relationship to the family except in name, were issued by Intertype.

Della Robbia, ATF 141 (6-72pt); Mono 231 (6-36pt); Inter (24,30pt)
Della Robbia Light, ATF 445 (6-36pt); (Univ 6-36pt)
Della Robbia Initials, Inter (30pt)
Della Robbia is called Westminster Old Style by Stephenson Blake.

DELPHIAN OPEN TITLE was designed by R. Hunter Middleton and released by Ludlow in 1928. The delicate, classic capitals have heavy strokes divided by a white line into two lines which are the same weight as the thin strokes; serifs are very small. It is a chaste, dignified design based on inscriptional lettering, and is popular for titles and initials.

Delphian Open Title, Ludlow 21-OPT (18-60pt)

DELPHIN—see Imports in Appendix.
DELRAYE—see Antiques in Appendix.
DELUXE GOTHIC—see *Bank Gothic.*

DEMETER is a decorative, shaded letter produced by BB&S in 1925, by arrangement with Schriftguss A.-G. of Dresden, where it was designed by Peter A. Demeter. Serifs are leaf-like in form. This is one of a few German faces BB&S received in exchange for rights to the Cooper types.

Demeter, BB&S-ATF 1601 (12-30pt)

DENNISON SCRIPT was produced by BB&S; it is a thick-and-thin connected script, probably originating in the nineteenth century; at least it has that character. Strokes vary from hairline to heavy in lowercase letters, and to very heavy in the capitals.

Dennison Script, BB&S-ATF 1602 (14-48pt)

DeROOS is a handsome contemporary roman type designed by S. H. DeRoos in Amsterdam, Holland. Originally imported from a Dutch typefoundry, with additional weights and inline initials, this roman and italic were also cut by ATF about 1952, and by Intertype in 1954. A 1953 piece of ATF literature notes, "Cast at Elizabeth on Amsterdam line."

DeRoos Roman, ATF 697 (6-48pt); DeRoos, Inter (8-14pt)
DeRoos Italic, ATF 698 (6-36pt); Inter (8-14pt)
Also see Imports in Appendix.

DeVINNE & ITALIC, Lino 14-pt.

ABCDEFGHIJKLMNOPQRSTUVWXYZ& ABCDEFGHIJKLMNOPQRSTUVWXYZ&
ABCDEFGHIJKLMNOPQRSTUVWXYZ&
abcdefghijklmnopqrstuvwxyzfiflffffiffl12345($£,.:;'-'?!*†)67890
abcdefghijklmnopqrstuvwxyzfiflffffiffl12345($£,.:;'-'?! †)67890

DeVINNE, 24-pt. (Leonard Richardson, Rick von Holdt)

ABCDEFGHIJKLMNOPQRSTUVWXYZ .,=':;!?
abcdefghijklmnopqrstuvwxyz 1234567890&$
¼ ½ ¾ ⅓ ⅔ ⅛ ⅜ ⅝ ⅞ % 1234567890 ΓSs

DeVINNE ITALIC, 24-pt.

ABCDEFGHIJKLMNOPQRSTUVWXYZ
abcdefghijklmnopqrstuvwxyz $1234567890

DeVINNE CONDENSED, 24-pt. (Leonard Richardson)

ABCDEFGHIJKLMNOPQRSTUVWXYZ .,:;-?!' R ÆŒ
abcdefghijklmnopqrstuvwxyz 1234567890&$ æœ

DeVINNE EXTRA CONDENSED, ATF (36-pt. at 67%) (Guy Botterill)

ABCDEFGHIJKLMNOPQRSTUVWXYZ RÆŒ£=
abcdefghijklmnopqrstuvwxyzæœ&1234567890$.,-:;!?'

DeVINNE COMPRESSED, BB&S 24-pt. (part reduced)

Rebuilding BRIDGES Constructed HOUSES

DeVINNE EXTRA COMPRESSED, 24-pt. (Dave Norton)

ABCDEFGHIJKLMNOPQRSTUVWXYZ&R$1234567890£
abcdefghijklmnopqrstuvwxyz.,-:;'!?

DeVINNE EXTENDED (36-pt. at 50%) (Gary Hantke)

ABCDEFGHIJKLMNOPQRSTUVWXYZ&.,=!?
abcdefghijklmnopqrstuvwxyz $1234567890

DeVINNE BOLD, BB&S 24-pt. (part reduced)

Sought RIB RUB Medal

DeVINNE types were designed and named for Theodore L. DeVinne, one of the most prominent American printers of the late nineteenth and early twentieth centuries. His DeVinne Press pioneered in various methods of producing high-quality books and magazines, and DeVinne himself had considerable influence on typeface design as well as printing methods and other aspects of the business, and was the author of several books on the subject; however, he was not the actual designer of these faces.

DeVinne, as produced by Linotype in 1902, is a legible but plain version of modern roman, with long, thin serifs and considerable contrast. It does not appear in the 1907 book, *Types of the DeVinne Press,* although there are other very similar types. Other faces bearing the DeVinne name, described below, are more distinctive and much better known. They might be considered the first large type family, although they developed helter-skelter from several sources rather than being created as a unified family.

DeVinne, the display face, is credited with bringing an end to the period of overly ornate and fanciful display faces of the nineteenth century, and with restoring the dignity of plain roman types. It is derived from faces generally known as *Elzevir* or *French Oldstyle* (q.v.). DeVinne says of it, "This face is the outcome of correspondence (1888-90) between the senior of the DeVinne Press (meaning himself) and Mr. J. A. St. John of the Central Type Foundry of St. Louis, concerning the need of plainer types of display, to replace the profusely ornamented types in fashion, of which the printers of that time had a surfeit. The DeVinne Press suggested a return to the simplicity of the true old-style character, but with the added features of thicker lines and adjusted proportion in shapes of letters. Mr. St. John approved, but insisted on grotesques to some capital letters in the belief that they would meet a general desire for more quaintness. Mr. Werner of the Central Type Foundry was instructed to draw and cut the proposed face in all sizes from 6- to 72-point, which task he executed with great ability.

"The name given to this face by Mr. St. John is purely complimentary, for no member of the DeVinne Press has any claim on the style as inventor or designer. Its merits are largely due to Mr. Werner; its few faults of uncouth capitals . . . show a desire to please eccentric tastes and to conform to old usage. The new face found welcome here and abroad; no advertising face of recent production had a greater sale."

Thus DeVinne himself credits the face to Central Type Foundry and its design to Nicholas J. Werner, but Werner says, "To correct the general impression that Theodore L. DeVinne was the designer of the face named after him, I would state that it was the creation of my partner, Mr. (Gustav) Schroeder." The design was patented under Schroeder's name in 1893.

Central was part of the merger that formed American Type Founders Company in 1892, but continued to operate somewhat independently for a few more years. Meanwhile, *DeVinne* was copied by Dickinson, BB&S, Hansen, and Keystone foundries, and perhaps others—in fact, Keystone advertised that it patented the design in 1893, Connecticut Type Foundry copied it as *Saunders,* and Linotype as *Title No. 2.* Dickinson called it "a companion series to *Howland*" (q.v.). When Monotype developed an attachment in 1903 to cast display sizes, *DeVinne* was the first type shown in their first announcement.

Later ATF specimens showed this face and several derivatives as *DeVinne No. 2,* probably because of adjustments to conform with standard alignment.

DeVinne Italic and *DeVinne Condensed* were drawn by Werner and produced by Central in 1892 and copied by some other sources. *Howland,* shown by Dickinson in 1892, is essentially the same as *DeVinne Condensed No. 3,* later shown by Keystone. ATF introduced *DeVinne Extended* in 1896, while BB&S showed *DeVinne Compressed, Extra Compressed,* and *Bold* in 1898-99. Keystone's *DeVinne Title* is another version of bold, not as wide as that of BB&S.

(DeVinne continues)

DeVinne and Italic, Lino = Inter (6-14pt); also DeVinne and Italic Cancelled, Lino (10,11pt)
DeVinne [No. 2], ATF 248 (5½-72pt); BB&S 1604 (6-72pt); Mono 11 (5-36pt) and 211J (5½pt); [No. 3], Hansen (6-60pt); Dickinson (6-48pt); Keystone (5½-72pt); etc.; Title No. 2, Lino (6-24pt)
DeVinne Italic [No. 2], ATF 252 (6-72pt); Mono 1111 (8-36pt); DeVinne Slope, Keystone (6-48pt); Title Italic, Lino (8-12pt); [No. 3], Hansen (6-48pt)
DeVinne Condensed [No. 2], ATF 249 (6-72pt); Keystone (6-72pt); Mono 111 (6-36pt); Lino (8-30pt); [No. 3], Hansen (6-48pt)
DeVinne Extra Condensed [No. 2], ATF 251 (12-72pt); Keystone (12-72pt); Mono 210 (10-36pt); Lino (12-24pt); Inter (18pt); [No. 3], Hansen (12-72pt)
DeVinne Compressed, BB&S-ATF 1606 (6-72pt)
DeVinne Extra Compressed, BB&S-ATF 1607 (10-72pt)
DeVinne Extended [No. 2], ATF 250 (6-72pt); Hansen (6-48pt)
DeVinne Title, Keystone (6-48pt)
DeVinne Bold, BB&S-ATF 1605 (6-60pt)

THE TIMES WHEN ADVERTISERS
INSISTED UPON A HEAVY BLACKFACE OR
Gothic in displaying advertisements are
past. The educational forc $1234567890

PRESENT ELEGANT SLOPE FACE
Considers This Beautiful Type Perfect
Grand Entertainments Pleased Critics
Famous Aeroplane King $1234567890

ABCDEFGHIJKLMNOPQRSTUVWXYZ&.,=;:'!?
abcdefghijklmnopqrstuvwxyz $1234567890

ABCDEFGHIJKLMNOPQRSTUVWXYZ .,'!?
abcdefghijklmnopqrstuvwxyz $1234567890

SERVICEABLE CONDITIONS
Artists Appreciate 78 Latest Production

ABCDEFGHIJKLMNOPQRSTUVWXYZ
abcdefghijklmnopqrstuvwxyz $1234567890

STANDARD LINE Commands Attention 6

ABCDEFGHIJKLMNOPQRRSTUVWXYZ& .,=;:
abcdefghijklmnopqrstuvwxyz $1234567890 '!?

SPECIMENS OF THE EARLY BOOKS
The specimens of book-making during the period
of transition from writing to printing, give us some
notions of the estimation in which the process was

In 1898 Frederic W. Goudy was asked to take the famous display type and make a book face of it. The resulting *DeVinne Roman,* Goudy's second type design, was cut the following year by the Central branch of ATF. *DeVinne Slope,* essentially the same design but sloped rather than a true italic, was cut by the foundry about the same time, perhaps from the same patterns as the roman.

DeVinne Open or *Outline* and *Italic* also originated with Central. In the roman and smaller sizes of italic only the heavy strokes are outlined; in larger sizes of italic, certain thin strokes are also outlined. Monotype cut the open faces in 1913. *DeVinne Shaded* is another form of the outline, created by Dickinson in 1893; parts of the outline are much thicker than others.

DeVinne Recut and *Recut Outline,* shown by BB&S, are not true members of this family, but are a revival of *Woodward* and *Woodward Outline,* designed by William A. Schraubstädter for Inland Type Foundry in 1894; there were also condensed, extra condensed, and extended versions, all "original" by Inland.

DeVinne Recut Italic was a rename of *Courts,* by Werner about 1900, also from Inland. Compare *McNally.*

DeVinne Roman, ATF (6-12pt)
DeVinne [Roman] Slope, ATF (6-12pt)
DeVinne Open [No. 2], ATF 254 (12-72pt);
 DeVinne Outline, Mono 42 (8-36pt); Lino
 (10-36pt); Keystone (12-72pt)
DeVinne Italic Outline [No. 2], ATF 253
 (12-72pt); DeVinne Outline Italic, Mono
 41 (12-36pt); Lino (12,14pt)
DeVinne Shaded, Dickinson-ATF (12-48pt)
DeVinne Recut or Woodward, BB&S-ATF
 1608 (6-60pt); Title No. 4, Lino (8-14pt)
DeVinne Recut Outline or Woodward
 Outline, BB&S-ATF 1609 (12-60pt)

DIAMOND INLAID—see Antiques in Appendix.

DICKENS was cut by Keystone in 1906 or earlier, and named for Charles Dickens. It is known as *Classic* on Linotype. Also see *MacFarland.*

Dickens, Keystone (6-12pt); Classic, Lino
 (6-14pt)
Dickens Italic, Keystone (6-12pt); Classic
 Italic, Lino (6-14pt)

DIETZ TEXT was designed by August Dietz, Sr., of Richmond, Virginia, about 1927, for BB&S. It is an unusual adaptation of Old English, as though lettered with a broad pen divided into three parts, thus producing three parallel lines in all heavy strokes. The drawings were not suitable for making patterns, so Oswald Cooper was asked to redraw it. He did this grudgingly, as it was an arduous task on which he spent two months. Although it was an interesting novelty, used occasionally to good effect, not enough of it was ever sold to repay a fraction of the cost of production. Matrices apparently were destroyed when the foundry was taken over by ATF. Compare *Waldorf Text.*

Dietz Text, BB&S (14-48pt)

DIMENSION—see Antiques in Appendix.

DODGE was cut by Monotype about 1920 or earlier, for the private use of Dodge Brothers, to harmonize with the distinctive lettering in the advertising of that auto manufacturer. The specimen shown here is from a very poor photocopy.

Dodge, Mono private (6-12pt)

DIETZ TEXT, BB&S (36-pt. at 67%) (Alan Waring)

DODGE, Mono private 12-pt.

ABCDEFGHIJKLMNOPQRSTUVWXYZ$1234567890¢&?%
abcdefghijklmnopqrstuvwxyz.,-:;! _ThTTttssflff''""

ABCDEFGHIJKLMNOPQRSTUVWXYZ$1234567890¢&!?%
abcdefghijklmnopqrstuvwxyz.,-:; _ThTTttflff''""

ABCDEFGHIJKLMNOPQRSTUVWXYZ&
abcdefghijklmnopqrstuvwxyz fffl $1234567890 .,-:;'!?_¢"

ABCDEFGHIJKLMNOPQRSTUVWXYZ(.,-:;'!?)
abcdefghijklmnopqrstuvwxyz &$12345678.

EXCURSION BEARING WEST
Every Question Being Arbitrated

ABCDEFGHIJKLMNOPQRSTUVWXYZ& $1234567890 .,-:;'!?
Light Dorsey is a Peculiarly Adaptable Type Face

PURCHASING BEAUTIFUL LIGHT DORSEY ITALIC
Kind Magistrate Sentenced Rough Prisoner to Lockup

ABCDEFGHIJKLMNOPQRSTUVWXYZ&$?!
abcdefghijklmnopqrstuvwxyz.,;:'-

NUMBERING FOR IDENTIFICATION PURPOSE
Victorious Olympic Athletes Returning Homeward

DOM CASUAL is a very informal, contemporary design with a brush-lettered effect, produced by Pete Dom (Peter Dombrezian) for photolettering, and cut by ATF about 1952 at the instigation of Steve Watts. Its popularity prompted the design of *Dom Diagonal,* an italicized version, soon after, and *Dom Bold* in 1953. There are several unusual ligatures, but no f-ligatures except as shown. Compare *Flash, Trend, Balloon.*

Dom Casual, ATF 696 (18-72pt)
Dom Diagonal, ATF 699 (18-72pt)
Dom Bold, ATF 703 (18-72pt)

DORCHESTER SCRIPT—see Imports in Appendix.

DORIC ITALIC was cast by ATF in the 1890s or earlier, and copied by Hansen as *Gothic Italic* and by others. In comparatively recent years it again became popular under the name *Old Gothic Bold Italic,* cast by Amsterdam Typefoundry in Holland, the source of the specimen shown here. Hansen also cut an inline version, which they called *Boston Italic* (q.v.), in 1909. Compare *Charter Oak.*

A traditional but entirely different Doric is mentioned under Clarendon.

Doric Italic, ATF (6-60pt); Gothic Italic, Hansen (6-60pt)
Boston Italic, Hansen (18-60pt)
Doric Italic is called Etrusco in Italy.

DORMER—see *Pekin.*

DORSEY was designed by Inland Type Foundry in 1904, and named for a printer in Dallas, Texas. It is an oldstyle antique series, much like *Bookman* but with slightly more contrast. *Light Dorsey,* introduced in 1910, is somewhat similar to *Cushing Monotone,* but with smaller x-height and longer ascenders. There were also condensed and extra condensed versions; note that the *Dorsey Condensed* shown here is badly battered and worn.

Dorsey, Inland-ATF 144 (6-72pt)
Light Dorsey, Inland-ATF 220 (5-60pt)
Light Dorsey Italic, Inland-ATF 221 (6-18pt)
Dorsey Condensed, ATF 116 (5-72pt)
Dorsey Extra Condensed, ATF 154 (6-60pt)

DRAFTSMAN GOTHIC (or *Draftsman Italic*) is a light gothic with an extreme slope of about 30 degrees, intended for map work. It was produced by Monotype for the U.S. Geodetic Survey in Washington, D.C., and was released in 1948.

Draftsman Gothic, Mono 124 (5-14pt)

DRESDEN is a very decorative face designed by Peter A. Demeter for Schriftguss A.G. in Dresden and cut by BB&S in 1925 by arrangement with that firm, part of the deal by which the German company got rights to copy *Cooper.* In this face, the main strokes as well as the serifs are leaf-like. Compare *Columbine* in Antiques.

Dresden, BB&S-ATF 1611 (12-30pt)

DRAFTSMAN GOTHIC, Mono 14-pt.

ABCDEFGHIJKLMNOPQRSTUVWXYZ
abcdefghijklmnopqrstuvwxyz 1234567890 .,-:'( )— " "

DRESDEN, BB&S 24-pt.

ABCDEFGHIJKLMNOPQRSTUVWXYZ
&$1234567890.,~°°'!?()

DREW, 24-pt.

ABCDEFGHIJKLMNOPQRSTUVWXYZ
abcdefghijklmnopqrstuvwxyz 1234567890$&

DYNAMIC MEDIUM, ATF (30-pt. at 80%)

ABCDEFGHIJKLMNOPQRSTUVWXYZ
abcdefghijklmnopqrstuvwxyz
$ $ 1 2 3 4 5 6 7 8 9 0 & . , : ; - ' ' ! ?

E-13-B, ATF

0 1 2 3 4 5 6 7 8 9⑆⑇⑈⑉

EAGLE BOLD, ATF 18-pt.

ABCDEFGHIJKLMNOPQRSTUVWXYZ
1234567890&$.,-'':;!?

EDEN LIGHT, Ludlow 24-pt. (Herb Harnish)

ABCDEFGHIJKLMNOPQRSTUVWXYZ& .,-:;'!?()[]
abcdefghijklmnopqrstuvwxyz 1234567890 $·—

EDEN BOLD, Ludlow 24-pt.

ABCDEFGHIJKLMNOPQRSTUVWXYZ& [](),-;'!?—&
abcdefghijklmnopqrstuvwxyz $1234567890

Variant Characters: a g versus ɑ g

The basic shape of most letters is the same from one design to another, with variations of serifs, proportions, weights of lines, contrast, etc., providing the character of the face.

Two exceptions are lower-case *a* and *g,* which can take on the shapes shown here by News Gothic on the left or by Futura on the right. There are no generally accepted names for these variations, but the News Gothic shape, which is common to most roman serif types, has been called

"roman," or "two-storied" for the a or "two-bowled" or "two-looped" for the *g,* while the Futura version, more often seen in italics, has been called "round," "script," or "one-storied" for the *a* or "one-looped" or "one-bowled" for the *g.*

Monotype *Sans Serif,* Linotype *Spartan,* Ludlow *Record Gothic* and several other faces offer both forms of one or both of these letters, while certain other faces offer lesser variants of a few other characters, also.

DREW is a delicate, compact roman type with a pen-lettered effect. It has long ascenders and comparatively small x-height. The long serifs are mostly unbracketed, but the general feeling is informal and closer to oldstyle in details. It originated with Inland Type Foundry and was shown in 1910. Compare *Adcraft, Avil;* also *Bernhard Modern, Cochin.*

Drew, Inland-ATF 145 (6-48pt)

DYNAMIC MEDIUM was designed by Morris Benton for ATF in 1928 but introduced in 1930. It is a high contrast face without serifs, but with large triangles at the end of thin strokes. Compare *Broadway, Cubist Bold.*

Dynamic Medium, ATF 535 (6-120pt)

DYNAMIC (other)—see Imports in Appendix.

E-13-B magnetic ink bank figures were cut in 1959 by ATF, Linotype, and Intertype in cooperation with the American Banking Association and electronics manufacturers, for electronic processing of checks and other financial documents.

E-13-B, ATF; Lino=Inter

EAGLE BOLD is a by-product of the depression of the 1930s. The National Recovery Administration of 1933 had as its emblem a blue eagle with the prominent initials NRA, lettered in a distinctive gothic style. Morris Benton took these letters as the basis for a font of type, released later that year by ATF, to tie in with the emblem, which businesses throughout the country displayed prominently in advertising, stationery, and signs; naturally it was named for the eagle. Compare *Novel Gothic.*

Eagle Bold, ATF 581 (18-96pt)

EASTMAN OLDSTYLE—see *Latin Oldstyle Bold.*
EASYREAD—see *Post Text.*
EATONIAN GOTHIC—see *Gothic No. 545.*
ECCLESIASTIC—see Antiques in Appendix.

EDEN is a modern thick-and-thin letter, severely squared and compact, designed by Robert H. Middleton for Ludlow in 1934. It is a smart, distinctive display face, but a little too hard to read for extensive text. Compare *Glamour (Corvinus).*

Eden Light, Ludlow 37-L (8-72pt)
Eden Bold, Ludlow 37-B (10-72pt)

EDWARDS—see *Bizarre Bold.*
EGIZIO—see Imports in Appendix.

ABCDEFGHIJKLMNOPQRSTUVWXYZ $1234567890 ABCDEFGHIJKLMNOPQRSTUVWXYZ&ÆŒ $1234567890
ABCDEFGHIJKLMNOPQRSTUVWXYZ

abcdefghijklmnopqrstuvwxyz fi fl ff ffi ffl .,-;':'!?()@ ℔ & £ æœÆŒ % [ ] * † | ‡ ‖ § Ⅎ – — ⅛ ¼ ⅜ ½ ⅝ ¾ ⅞
*abcdefghijklmnopqrstuvwxyz fi fl ff ffi ffl .,-;':'!?()@ ℔ & £ æœÆŒ % [ ] * † | ‡ ‖ § Ⅎ – — ⅛ ¼ ⅜ ½ ⅝ ¾ ⅞*

A B D E G H M N P T Y

ABCDEFGHIJKLMNOPQRSTUVWXYZ $1234567890 ABCDEFGHIJKLMNOPQRSTUVWXYZ&ÆŒ $1234567890
ABCDEFGHIJKLMNOPQRSTUVWXYZ

abcdefghijklmnopqrstuvwxyz fi fl ff ffi ffl .,-;':'!?()@℔&£ æœÆŒ % [] * † | ‡ ‖ § Ⅎ – — ⅛ ¼ ⅜ ½ ⅝ ¾ ⅞
*abcdefghijklmnopqrstuvwxyz fi fl ff ffi ffl .,-;':'!?()@℔&£ æœÆŒ % [] * † | ‡ ‖ § Ⅎ – — ⅛ ¼ ⅜ ½ ⅝ ¾ ⅞*

A B D E G H M N P T Y

ABCDEFGHIJKLMNOPQRSTUVWXYZ **$1234567890** **ABCDEFGHIJKLMNOPQRSTUVWXYZ** **$1234567890**
ABCDEFGHIJKLMNOPQRSTUVWXYZ *1234567890 1234567890* 1234567890 *1234567890*

abcdefghijklmnopqrstuvwxyz fi fl ff ffi ffl .,-;':'!?()@℔&£ æ œ Æ Œ % [ ] * † | ‡ ‖ § ¶ – — ⅛ ¼ ⅜ ½ ⅝ ¾ ⅞
abcdefghijklmnopqrstuvwxyz fi fl ff ffi ffl .,-;':'!?()@℔&£ æ œ Æ Œ % [ ] * † | ‡ ‖ § ¶ – — ⅛ ¼ ⅜ ½ ⅝ ¾ ⅞

ABCDEFGHIJKLMNOPQRSTUVWXYZÆŒ& ***ABCDEFGHIJKLMNOPQRSTUVWXYZÆŒ&***

A B C D E F G H I J K L M N
O P Q R S T U V W X Y Z

ABCDEFGHIJKLMNOPQRSTUVWXYZ&ÆŒ ABCDEFGHIJKLMNOPQRSTUVWXYZ&ÆŒ
ABCDEFGHIJKLMNOPQRSTUVWXYZ&ÆŒ
abcdefghijklmnopqrstuvwxyzæœfiflffffiffl 1234567890 [($.,-":;!?-—)] 1234567890
abcdefghijklmnopqrstuvwxyzæœfiflffffiffl 1234567890 [($.,-":;!?-—)] 1234567890

ABCDEFGHIJKLMNOPQRSTUVWXYZ& 1234567890 ABCDEFGHIJJKLMMNOPQRSTUVWXYZ&
ABCDEFGHIJKLMNOPQRSTUVWXYZ& 1234567890
abcdefghijklmnopqrstuvwxyzfiflffffiffl ($£,.:;'-'?!*§†‡(⸙⸙⸙))
abcdefghijklmnopqrstuvwxyzfiflffffiffl ($£,.:;'-'?! §†‡(⸙⸙⸙))
abcdefghijklmnopqrstuvwxyz æ œ fi fl ff ffi ffl

ABCDEFGHIJKLMNOPQRSTUVWXYZ&ÆŒ ABCDEFGHIJKLMNOPQRSTUVWXYZ&ÆŒ
ABCDEFGHIJKLMNOPQRSTUVWXYZ&ÆŒ
abcdefghijklmnopqrstuvwxyzæœfiflffffiffl 1234567890 $£,.:;'-'?!-|——() *†‡(§[])% 1234567890
abcdefghijklmnopqrstuvwxyzæœfiflffffiffl 1234567890 $£,.:;'-'?!-|——()&*†‡(§[])% 1234567890
abcdefghijklmnopqrstuvwxyzæœfiflffffiffl& ⅛¼⅜½⅝¾⅞⅓⅔⅕⅖⅗⅘⅙⅚ ⅛¼⅜½⅝¾⅞⅓⅔⅕⅖⅗⅘⅙⅚

EGMONT is a modern interpretation of classic letter forms, designed by S. H. DeRoos for Amsterdam Typefoundry in the 1930s, and subsequently cut by Intertype. It is an elegant face, with long ascenders which have double serifs. There are three weights in roman and italic, all with three styles of figures as shown in the bold specimen. Italic swash letters are made for all three weights. *Egmont Decorative Initials* were added by George F. Trenholm in 1936; they are sometimes called *Egmont Medium Italic,* from which they are derived. Compare *Bernhard Modern.*

Egmont Light and Italic, Inter (8-42pt)
Egmont Medium and Italic, Inter (6-42pt)
Egmont Bold and Italic, Inter (8-30, 8-24pt)
Egmont Decorative Initials, Inter (36pt)

EGYPTIAN—see Imports in Appendix.
EGYPTIAN SHADED—see Antiques in Appendix.

ELDORADO is a contemporary roman designed by W. A. Dwiggins for Linotype about 1950, based on early Spanish models. The lowercase is compact, with a small x-height and long ascenders. Several italic letters have cursive or decorative forms; also notice the cap *Y,* with curved, serifless arms.

Eldorado and Italic, Lino (6-12pt)

ELECTRA is a contemporary modern face designed by W. A. Dwiggins for Linotype. The light weight was drawn in 1935, the bold a few years later. Aside from its readability and distinctive character, *Electra* is distinguished by a choice of italic forms. *Electra Italic* is really a sloped roman, while *Electra Cursive,* released in 1944, is more nearly a conventional italic form; only the lowercase is different. Like a number of the better Linotype faces, *Electra* also has a choice of short descenders, which will cast on the nominal body, or long descenders, which must be cast one point larger. Compare *Fairfield.*

Electra and Italic, Lino (7-14pt)
Electra and Cursive, Lino (8-14pt)
Electra Bold and Italic and Cursive, Lino (8-14pt)

ELEGANTE is a decorative, nearly monotone face cut by George Battee for Baltimore Type, after the German face *Sensation* of 1913, from Foundry Heinrich Hoffmeister. It is upright, with flourished caps and loops on some of the ascenders and descenders, and is suitable particularly for announcements and personal stationery. Compare *Greeting Monotone.*

Elegante, Baltimore 106 (10-42pt)

ELIZABETH—see Imports in Appendix.
ELLA ITALIC—see *Card Italic.*
ELONGATED ROMAN SHADED—see Imports in Appendix.

ELEGANTE, Balto (30-pt. at 80%) (Rick von Holdt, Al Siegel)

ABCDEFGHIJKLMNOPQRSTUVWXYZ&
abcdefghijklmnopqrstuvwxyz.,-:;?!$1234567890Etc Qu es t

ELZEVIR NO. 3 & ITALIC, Lino 14-pt.

ABCDEFGHIJKLMNOPQRSTUVWXYZ& ABCDEFGHIJKLMNOPQRSTUVWXYZ&
ABCDEFGHIJKLMNOPQRSTUVWXYZ&

abcdefghijklmnopqrstuvwxyzfiflffffiffl1234($£,.:;'-'?!*†)123
abcdefghijklmnopqrstuvwxyzfiflffffiffl1234($£,.:;'-'?! †)123

ELZEVIR NO. 5, BB&S 24-pt. (Dave Norton)

ABCDEFGHIJKLMNOPQRSTUVWXYZ&
abcdefghijklmnopqrstuvwxyz$1234567890 .,-:;'!?

EMERSON, Eng Mono 24-pt.

ABCDEFGHIJKLMNOPQRSTUVWXYZ&1234567890
abcdefghijklmnopqrstuvwxyz

EMERSON ITALIC, Eng Mono 24-pt.

ABCDEFGHIJKLMNOPQRSTUVWXYZ&1234567890
abcdefghijklmnopqrstuvwxyz

EMPEROR, Balto 14-pt.

**A B C D E F G H I J K L M N O P Q R S T U V
W X Y Z & a b c d e f g h i j k l m n o p q r s t u
v w x y z $ 1 2 3 4 5 6 7 8 9 0 . , - ' : ; ! ? ' " " ¢ % ( ) '**

EMPIRE, ATF 36-pt.

ABCDEFGHIJKLMNOPQRSTUVWXYZ.,-:;" !?&$1234567890

EMPIRE GOTHIC, Keystone 24-pt.

TENTING IN TROPIC CLIMES $123
Gigantic insects hold council outside

ENCORE, Keystone 24-pt.

FINE NEWSPAPER AND JOB LETTER $1234
Handsome display faces draw constant business

ENCORE CONDENSED 18-pt. (Dave Norton)

ABCDEFGHIJKLMNOPQRSTUVWXYZ&abcdefghijklmnopqrstuvwxyz$1234567890£.,-:;'!?""

128

ELZEVIR types are named for the most prominent family of seventeenth-century Dutch printers, who developed slender types for use in a series of small books which they popularized. The present-day Elzevir types are based on revivals of types brought out in the 1870s by Gustave Mayeur of Paris, and are commonly known also as *French Oldstyle* (q.v.) or *French Cadmus*. They were popular in the late nineteenth century and have had some popularity in this century, especially for text use when *Elzevir No. 3* was revised under the direction of E. E. Bartlett in 1919 for Linotype. The style is weak for display, though. Linotype *Elzevir No. 2* is entirely different, being a copy of *Schoeffer Oldstyle* (q.v.), an 1898 ATF design.

Elzevir, Lino = Inter (8-14pt)
Elzevir No. 3 and Italic, Lino (6-24, 6-14pt); French Cadmus and Italic, Mono 22EFG (6-12pt)
Elzevir is known as Romano Antico in Italy.

EMERSON, a wide, medium weight roman, somewhat similar to *Ronaldson,* was cut by Keystone and shown in 1909. Apparently matrices did not survive when Keystone merged with ATF a decade later.

Emerson, Keystone (6-48pt); also Emerson Title, Keystone (6-24pt)

EMERSON and *Emerson Italic*—a completely different style, unrelated to the one above—were designed by Joseph Blumenthal, New York printer and book designer. The original version was hand-cut by Louis Hoell in Germany, and the face was cast by the Bauer Foundry in 1930. It was called *Spiral* for the press at which this distinguished typographer produced many notable books, and was renamed *Emerson* when the Monotype Corporation of London recut it in 1935. It is a modernized oldstyle letter, adapted for photogravure reproduction, but retaining a reasonably light face, fairly condensed.

Emerson and Italic, Eng Mono (8-24pt)

EMPEROR is a 1957 adaptation by Baltimore Type of *Wide Latin* which was cut by Stephenson Blake in England and related to nineteenth-century faces under other names. However, this Baltimore Type version has been modified and resized, and is less successful due to excess space between letters (although not as much as in the specimen shown here, which is letterspaced). *Emperor* was originally shown as *Imperial.*

Emperor, Baltimore 112 (14-36pt)

EMPIRE was designed by Morris F. Benton and issued by ATF in 1937. It is a thick-and-thin, serifless face, extra condensed, with unusual emphasis on vertical strokes, although it is not a bold face. There is no lowercase. For a time it was used as a headletter in *Vogue* magazine for a smart, sophisticated look.

Empire, ATF 597 (36-96pt)

EMPIRE GOTHIC was offered by Keystone Type Foundry in 1912. Although the name does not identify it as an italic, it is somewhat similar to *Medium Gothic Italic.*

Empire Gothic, Keystone (6-96pt)

ENCORE is a quaint series of roman types issued by Keystone in 1901-02, but the novel features are less pronounced than in a number of other types of the period. The lowercase is narrow and quite tall; *Encore Condensed* is more the proportion of most extra condensed faces, while the *Encore Extended* is only a little wider than usual.

Encore, Keystone (6-72pt)
Encore Condensed, Keystone (6-72pt); Lino (18,24pt)
Encore Extended, Keystone (6-72pt)

ENCORE EXTENDED 18-pt. (Dave Norton)

ABCDEFGHIJKLMNOPQRSTUVWXYZ&.,-:;'!?""''
abcdefghijklmnopqrstuvwxyz$1234567890£

ENGRAVERS OLD ENGLISH, ATF 24-pt. (Herb Harnish, Rick von Holdt)

ABCDEFGHIJKLMNOPQRSTUVWXYZ&$
abcdefghijklmnopqrstuvwxyzffifflffiffl.,-:;'!?,,æctckœŒÆ£
1234567890 I$ yz

Ludlow

ENGRAVERS OLD BLACK, BB&S (48-pt. at 50%) (Herb Harnish)

ABCDEFGHIJKLMNOPQRSTUVWXYZ& H The Ch of Co
abcdefghijklmnopqrstuvwxyz.,';:-!? fifflflffiffla $1234567890 ∾

ENGRAVERS OLD ENGLISH BOLD, Mono 24-pt. (Bob Halbert)

ABCDEFGHIJKLMNOPQRSTUVWXYZ&
$1234567890 H J
abcdefghijklmnopqrstuvwxyz.,-:;'!?

ENGRAVERS OLD ENGLISH OPEN, ATF 14-pt. (Herb Harnish)

ABCDEFGHIJKLMNOPQRSTUVWXYZ&$1234567890
abcdefghijklmnopqrstuvwxyz ffifflfiffiffl .,-:;'!?" ÆŒæœ

ENGRAVERS ROMAN, BB&S 18L

ABCDEFGHIJKLMNOPQRSTUVWXYZ
&$1234567890 .,-:;'!?

ENGRAVERS ROMAN CONDENSED, BB&S 24- & 18-pt.

DELIGHTING PERFORMERS CORPORATION

ENGRAVERS BOLD, 18L

ABCDEFGHIJKLMNOPQRSTUV
WXYZ& .,:;-!? 1234567890$

ENGRAVERS LITHO BOLD, BB&S 24-pt. (Rick von Holdt)

ABCDEFGHIJKLMNOPQRSTUVWXYZ
abcdefghijklmnopqrstuvwxyzny&.,:;'-?!
$1234567890

Name in parentheses after some specimens
indicates person who has set that specimen,
in whole or in part, to our format.

130

ENGRAVERS BODONI—see under Bodoni.
ENGRAVERS BOLD—see *Engravers Roman.*
ENGRAVERS GOTHIC—see *Typo Gothic;* also *Copperplate Gothic.*
ENGRAVERS LINING GOTHIC—see *Copperplate Gothic.*
ENGRAVERS LITHO—see *Engravers Roman.*

ENGRAVERS OLD ENGLISH is a plain, sturdy rendition of the Blackletter style, commonly known as Old English. It was designed in 1901 by Morris Benton and another person identified by ATF only as Cowan, but has also been ascribed to Joseph W. Phinney. It is a modernization of *Caslon Text,* and has been widely used. *Engravers Old English Open* was produced by ATF in 1902. Sidney Gaunt designed *Engravers Old Black,* very similar to *Engravers Old English,* for BB&S in 1910, but BB&S later produced *Engravers English,* a copy of *Engravers Old English.* It has also been copied by Intertype, and by Ludlow as *Old English.* Hansen's *Lafayette Text* (q.v.) was very similar. *Engravers Old English Bold* was designed by Morris Benton for ATF in 1910.

The unfamiliar characters of Old English types are often misused, and the alternate forms of some letters add to the confusion. *I* and *J* are particularly subject to mix-up, because they were originally the same letter, and never developed as definite a distinction in these styles as in roman letters. In Ludlow *Old English,* cap *I* is comparable to the one in the Bold weight, but this style has not been found elsewhere in the regular weight. Curiously, in the *Engravers Old English Bold* specimen shown, the letters appear as the Monotype copy presents them; however, Monotype's *I* and *J* are respectively the second and first forms of *I* as originally designed, while the specimen here shows separately the original foundry *J,* which Monotype does not make, along with the alternate *H.*

Compare *Wedding Text,* a similar design in lighter weight; also *Cloister Black; Shaw Text; Lafayette Text.*

Engravers Old English, ATF 148 (6-72pt); Inter (12-36pt); (Univ 6-48pt); Engravers English, BB&S-ATF 1621 (6-72pt); Old English, Ludlow 20 (8-48pt)
Engravers Old English Bold, ATF 149 (6-72pt); Mono 188 (6-24pt)
Engravers Old English Open, ATF 150 (8-18pt)
Engravers Old Black, BB&S (6-96pt)

ENGRAVERS ROMAN was designed by Robert Wiebking and advertised by BB&S in 1899 as the "latest design"—"the only genuine." Other founders had introduced some similar faces a short time before, all imitating favorite designs of copperplate and steelplate engravers for fine stationery and announcements; Hansen called its version *Card Roman. Engravers Roman* was shortly supplemented by *Engravers Roman Condensed* and *Engravers Title*—the latter was a companion bold face which was displaced by *Engravers Bold,* designed by Morris Benton for ATF in 1902, and later cast also by BB&S. Western Type Foundry and later BB&S also had *Engravers Bold Condensed,* and a companion cap-and-lowercase face known as *Engravers Litho Bold Condensed,* designed by Robert Wiebking in 1914. However, *Engravers Litho Bold,* designed by Wiebking in 1915 for Western as *Rogers Roman,* was a substantially different face. Compare *Card Mercantile, Brandon, Litho series.*

(Engravers continues)

Engravers Roman, BB&S-ATF 1627 (6s-24pt); Mono 223 (4½-24pt) and 347J (6s-6L); Inter (6-12pt); also Offset Engravers Roman, BB&S-ATF 1798 (6s-18pt); Card Roman, Hansen (6s-24pt)
Engravers Roman Condensed, BB&S-ATF 1628 (6s-24pt)
Engravers Bold, ATF 147 and BB&S-ATF 1619 (6s-36pt); Mono 323 (4H-24pt) and 348J (6s-6L); Inter (6s-6L); Ludlow 17 (6s-24pt); also Engravers Title, BB&S-ATF 1630 (6s-24pt); also Offset Engravers Title, BB&S-ATF 1799 (6-18pt)
Engravers Litho Bold, BB&S-ATF 1623 (6-48pt)
Engravers Litho Bold Condensed, BB&S-ATF 1624 (5-48pt); also Engravers Bold Condensed (title), BB&S-ATF 1620 (6s-48pt)

ENGRAVERS LITHO BOLD CONDENSED, BB&S 24-pt. (Herb Harnish)

ABCDEFGHIJKLMNOPQRSTUVWXYZ&$
abcdefghijklmnopqrstuvwxyzfffifflffiffl.,-:;'!?
1234567890 Ccġ

ENGRAVERS SHADED, ATF 18s

ABCDEFGHIJKLMNOPQRSTUVWXYZ
$1234567890 ,.-;:"!?&

ENGRAVERS ROMAN SHADED, BB&S-ATF 18L

ABCDEFGHIJKLMNOPQRSTUVWXYZ&
$1234567890 .,-:;'!?

ENGRAVERS TEXT, ATF 18L (Gary Hantke)

ABCDEFGHIJKLMNOPQRSTUVWXYZ abcdefghijklmnopqrstuvwxyz .,-;:'!?&$1234567890

ENGRAVERS UPRIGHT SCRIPT (PEN TEXT), BB&S (28/30-pt. at 80%) (Dave Greer)

AABBCCDDEEFFGHHJIJJKLLMNMNOOPPQQ
RRSSTTUUUVWWXXYYZZ& œœäöü
abcdefghijklmnopqrstuvwxyz .,-;:'!?($1234567890ffffiffl

ERBAR BOLD, Lino 14-pt.

ABCDEFGHIJKLMNOPQRSTUVWXYZ&ÆŒ
abcdefghijklmnopqrstuvwxyzæœfifIflfffffiffl 1234567890$ £,.:;'-'?!–|—...   ()*†‡¶§[]%

ERBAR LIGHT CONDENSED, Lino 18-pt.

ABCDEFGHIJKLMNOPQRSTUVWXYZ& A E F G K M N S W Y
abcdefghijklmnopqrstuvwxyz 1234567890 ($,.:;-'?!)

ERBAR MEDIUM CONDENSED, Lino 18-pt.

ABCDEFGHIJKLMNOPQRSTUVWXYZ& AEFGKMNSWY
abcdefghijklmnopqrstuvwxyz 1234567890($,.:;-'?!)

ERBAR BOLD CONDENSED, Lino 18-pt.

ABCDEFGHIJKLMNOPQRSTUVWXYZ& A E F G K M N S W Y
abcdefghijklmnopqrstuvwxyz 1234567890($,.:;-'?!)

ESTIENNE & ITALIC, Lino 14-pt.

ABCDEFGHIJKLMNOPQRSTUVWXYZ& ABCDEFGHIJKLMNOPQ
RSTUVWXYZ& abcdefghijklmnopqrstuvwxyzfifIflfffffiffIctst 1234567890
($£,.:;'-'?!) *†‡¶§[]
ABCDEFGHIJKLMNOPQRSTUVWXYZ& abcdefghijklmnopqrs
tuvwxyzfiflffffifflctst 1234567890 ($£,.:;'-'?!) *†‡¶§[]

ATF issued *Engravers Shaded,* designed by Morris Benton about 1906, while BB&S had *Engravers Roman Shaded,* formerly *Chester Title,* designed by Sidney Gaunt in 1914. Compare *Lithograph Shaded.*

Offset Engravers Roman and *Offset Engravers Title* were cut in reverse for a process of transferring proofs of type to lithographic stones.

Engravers Shaded, ATF 151 (6s-18L); (Univ 6s-18L)
Engravers Roman Shaded, BB&S-ATF 1629 (6s-36pt); (Univ 6s-24L)
Engravers Roman is known as Orlando in Italy.

ENGRAVERS TEXT is a greatly modified form of Old English, designed by Morris Benton for ATF in 1930. Heavy strokes are opened with a white line, and most of the letters are straight across at the base. Compare *American Text.*

Engravers Text, ATF 541 (10-24L); Inter (10-16pt); (Univ 10-24pt)

ENGRAVERS UPRIGHT SCRIPT was formerly *Pen Text No. 5,* originating about 1879 with Cincinnati Type Foundry, and renamed by BB&S in 1925, when the fancy capitals were dropped.

Engravers Upright Script, BB&S-ATF 1631 (8-30pt); Pen Text No. 5, BB&S-ATF 1835 (8-30pt)

ERA—see *Pastel.*

ERBAR originated in Germany in the 1920s as part of the new wave of sans-serifs; it was designed by Jakob Erbar for Ludwig & Mayer. Three weights of *Erbar Condensed* have been copied by Linotype—*Bold* in 1933, *Light* in 1934, and *Medium* in 1937—and have been used especially for newspaper headlines. Unique Caps were added for all three weights in 1938, designed by Linotype. The regular width of *Erbar Bold* has been substantially modified by Linotype to match the letter widths of various roman newspaper faces, in order to be duplexed on the same matrices. Except for this width modification, the face looks more like *Futura Demibold* than the original *Erbar Bold.* Compare *Futura, Spartan, Tempo,* etc.

Erbar Bold, Lino (5-14pt)
Erbar Light Condensed, Lino (8-60pt); APL (18-144pt)
Erbar Medium Condensed, Lino (18-42pt)
Erbar Bold Condensed, Lino (8-60pt); APL (18-144pt)

ERIC GILL SHADOW—see *Gill Sans Shadow* under Imports in Appendix.

ESTIENNE is a distinguished book face designed by George W. Jones, the eminent English printer, and released by Linotype in 1930. It is related to Garamond but more delicate, with longer ascenders and descenders. The roman makes a distinctive and very attractive appearance in text, but the italic is rather loosely fitted, necessitated by fitting the long ascenders and descenders to straight matrices. It is named for a distinguished sixteenth-century French printing family. Compare *Granjon, Garamond.*

Estienne and Italic, Lino (8-18, 8-14pt)

EUROSTILE—see Imports in Appendix.

EUSEBIUS, Ludlow 24-pt. (see text) (Richard Huss)

ABCDEFGHIJKLMNOPQRSTUVWXYZ& .,-:;"'!?()—
abcdefghijklmnopqrstuvwxyz 1234567890 $ fi ffi ff fl ffl Jf

Original

EUSEBIUS ITALIC, Ludlow 24-pt. (Richard Huss)

ABCDEFGHIJKLMNOPQRSTUVWXYZ&
abcdefghijklmnopqrstuvwxyz 1234567890$ fi fl ff ffi ffl .,-:;"'!?()— QU Qu Th
A B C D E G L M N P R Y e g k n t z

EUSEBIUS BOLD, Ludlow 24-pt.

ABCDEFGHIJKLMNOPQRSTUVWXYZ& QU Qu ct st [ ]
abcdefghijklmnopqrstuvwxyz 1234567890 .,-:;"'!?()—fifffflffiffl f

EUSEBIUS BOLD ITALIC, Ludlow 24-pt. with 18-pt. Swash

ABCDEFGHIJKLMNOPQRSTUVWXYZ&
abcdefghijklmnopqrstuvwxyz 1234567890 .,-:;"'!?()
ABCDEGLMNPR Y QUQu

EUSEBIUS OPEN, Ludlow 24-pt.

ABCDEFGHIJKLMNOPQRSTUVWXYZ&
abcdefghijklmnopqrstuvwxyz 1234567890 $.,-:;"'!?
fi fl ff ffi ffl ct st QU Qu 1234567890

EXCELSIOR & ITALIC, Lino 14-pt.

ABCDEFGHIJKLMNOPQRSTUVWXYZ&ÆŒ ABCDEFGHIJKLMNOPQRSTUVWXYZ&ÆŒ
ABCDEFGHIJKLMNOPQRSTUVWXYZ&ÆŒ
abcdefghijklmnopqrstuvwxyzæœfiflffffiffl 1234567890 $£ ,.:;-"?! ()@℔*†‡¶§[]% ⅛ ¼ ⅜ ½ ⅝ ¾ ⅞
abcdefghijklmnopqrstuvwxyzæœfiflffffiffl 1234567890 $£ ,.:;-"?!()@℔ †‡¶§[]% ⅛ ¼ ⅜ ½ ⅝ ¾ ⅞

FAIRFIELD & ITALIC, Lino 14-pt.

ABCDEFGHIJKLMNOPQRSTUVWXYZ& ABCDEFGHIJKLMNOPQRSTUVWXYZ&
ABCDEFGHIJKLMNOPQRSTUVWXYZ&
abcdefghijklmnopqrstuvwxyzfiflffffiffl 123456 [($£,.:;-'?!*†‡§¶)] 123456
abcdefghijklmnopqrstuvwxyzfiflffffiffl 123456 [($£,.:;-'?!*†‡§¶)] 123456

EUSEBIUS is Ludlow's distinctive adaptation of the types of Nicolas Jenson, which were first used about 1470 and have served as inspiration for many of the best roman typefaces ever since. This face was designed by Ernst Detterer in 1923, and issued as the *Nicolas Jenson* series. Robert H. Middleton, who had been an art school student of Detterer's, was first hired by Ludlow for the temporary assignment of seeing this face through production. By 1929 he had designed matching bold, italics, and open.

Slight modifications were later made to the Nicolas Jenson series by Middleton (who remained at Ludlow for a distinguished career, designing scores of faces over forty-seven years), and it was reintroduced in 1941 under the series name of *Eusebius.* This name comes from the 1470 book in which Jenson's original type was first used. In the specimen of *Eusebius,* the *J* and *f* shown separately at the end are the original Detterer design of the letters most obviously redesigned; other changes were minor.

In addition to the characters shown in the specimens here, with the usual *f*-ligatures for all fonts, oldstyle figures were available for *Eusebius* and *Italic* and *Open,* while *QU* and *Qu* combinations with long tails and *f* combinations with overhangs were made for regular, *Bold,* and *Open.* Compare *Centaur, Cloister, Italian Old Style.*

Eusebius, Ludlow 40-L (6-72pt)
Eusebius Italic, Ludlow 40-LI (8-72pt)
Eusebius Bold, Ludlow 40-B (6-72pt)
Eusebius Bold Italic, Ludlow 40-BI (8-72pt)
Eusebius Open, Ludlow 40-OP (14-48pt)

EVE—see *Rivoli;* also Imports in Appendix.

EXCELSIOR was cut for Linotype in 1931 under the direction of C. H. Griffith. It is a plain type, but designed for the utmost readability, with only slight variation from thick to thin, and careful fitting that makes the characters flow into easily recognizable words. Long or short descenders are available in certain sizes. Like a number of Linotype face intended primarily for newspaper work, *Excelsior* is available in closely graded sizes, including odd and some half-point multiples.

Excelsior and Italic, Lino (5-14pt)

EXCELSIOR (other)—see Imports in Appendix.
EXCELSIOR GOTHIC—see *Alternate Gothic.*
EXTENDED LINING GOTHIC—see *Philadelphia Gothic.*
EXTRA CONDENSED—see *Modern Roman Extra Condensed;* also Gothic, etc.

FAIRFIELD is a contemporary, modernized style of type which retains oldstyle characteristics, moderately compact, with long ascenders. It was designed for Linotype by Rudolph Ruzicka and released in 1940, with *Fairfield Medium* following in 1949. Italics are especially well designed to conform to the slug machine's mechanical limitations. Compare *Electra.*

The *Fairfield Medium* swash characters, shown here in 12-point, have not been found in any Mergenthaler literature, but the mats are marked like the rest of the font.

Fairfield and Italic, Lino (6-14pt)
Fairfield Medium and Italic, Lino (6-14pt)

FAIRFIELD MEDIUM & ITALIC, Lino 11-pt.

ABCDEFGHIJKLMNOPQRSTUVWXYZ ff fi ffi fl ffl
abcdefghijklmnopqrstuvwxyz   –[]% *(),.-;':'!?—&&
ABCDEFGHIJKLMNOPQRSTUVWXYZ $1234567890
⅛ ¼ ⅜ ½ ⅝ ¾ ⅞

ABCDEFGHIJKLMNOPQRSTUVWXYZ ff fi ffi fl ffl
*abcdefghijklmnopqrstuvwxyz   –% *(),.-;':'!?—&*
⅛ ¼ ⅜ ½ ⅝ ¾ ⅞   *$1234567890*

FALCON & ITALIC, Lino 12-pt.

ABCDEFGHIJKLMNOPQRSTUVWXYZ 1234567890
abcdefghijklmnopqrstuvwxyz 1234567890
ABCDEFGHIJKLMNOPQRSTUVWXYZ
abcdefghijklmnopqrstuvwxyz 1234567890
ABCDEFGHIJKLMNOPQRSTUVWXYZ 1234567890

FARMERS OLDSTYLE, Mono 12-pt. & ITALIC, 10-pt.

ABCDEFGHIJKLMNOPQRSTUVWXYZ& .,-:;'!? ABCDEFGHIJKLMNOPQRSTUVWXYZ&ÆŒ
abcdefghijklmnopqrstuvwxyz fffiffiflffl $1234567890   abcdefghijklmnopqrstuvwxyzæœ fiflffffiffl
$1234567890   :;!? $1234567890

FAUST TEXT, BB&S 18-pt.

ABCDEFGHIJKLMNOPQRSTUVWXYZ&abcdefghijklmnopqrstuvwxyz?$12

FELLOWSHIP, Rimmer 24-pt.

ABCDEFGHIJKLMNOPQRSTUVWXYZ&
abcdefghijklmnopqrstuvwxyzfffififlffiffl&.,-'::!?1234567890

FLAIR, Ludlow (36-pt. at 67%)

ABCDEFGHIJKLMNOPQRSTUV
WXYZ$1234567890.,,-"!?()[]— dghijklptty
abcdefghijklmnopqrstuvwxyz &-´ŧ'on of or oo ÆŒæœ£'ßij%

FLASH, Mono 24-pt.

ABCDEFGHIJKLMNOPQRSTUVWXYZ $$1234567890¢
abcdefghijklmnopqrstuvwxyz.,-:;'""!?&

FLASH BOLD, Mono 24-pt.

ABCDEFGHIJKLMNOPQRSTUVWXYZ$$1234567890¢
abcdefghijklmnopqrstuvwxyzfififfffiffffi.,-:;'""()!?&%

136

FALCON was designed during World War II for Linotype by William A. Dwiggins and released in 1961. It seemed to him, he said, "to hit the middle ground between mechanical exactitude and the flow and variety of a written hand—suggesting some of that flow and variety but controlling it, so the letter can be repeated."

Falcon and Italic, Lino (6-12pt)

FARGO—see Antiques in Appendix.
FARLEY—see *Steelplate Gothic*.

FARMERS OLD STYLE was one of the very first book types made available for machine typesetting. The first sizes were cut in 1899, adapted from *Old Style Series No. 5* of the A. D. Farmer & Son Foundry in New York City. It is light and rather wide, and has some modern characteristics in spite of the name.

Farmers Old Style and Italic, Mono 15EFG (6-12pt)

FAUST—see *Bookman*.

FAUST TEXT was a quaint design introduced by BB&S in 1898, and based on uncial lettering. For the 1925 specimen book it was renamed *Missal Text*.

Faust Text or Missal Text, BB&S (8-36pt)

FELLOWSHIP was designed and cut by Jim Rimmer in Vancouver in 1986, and cast by him for private use. He says, "The design is the result of the feeling of joviality and 'fellowship' I experienced at the meeting (American Typecasting Fellowship in Washington, D.C.). The design was not so much drawn as it was written. The letters were written quickly in a calligraphic manner with an edged pencil and then enlarged and inked to make a dry transfer sheet. As in my two previous designs (see *Juliana Oldstyle* and *Nephi Mediaeval*), *Fellowship* was cut not in steel, but in type metal, and then electroplated to make castable matrices."

Fellowship, Rimmer, private (24pt)

FIFTEENTH CENTURY—see *Caslon Antique*.
FIGARO—see Imports in Appendix.
FILLIGREE—see Antiques in Appendix.

FLAIR is a unique and very informal script, designed by R. Hunter Middleton and issued by Ludlow in 1961. Lowercase is practically monotone, with very small x-height and long, looped ascenders, while caps, figures, and several alternate lowercase letters are emphasized by heavy strokes. Matrices angled at 40 degrees, much more than usual Ludlow italics, permit lowercase letters to join without hampering an unusually free flow.

Flair, Ludlow 48-MIC (36,48pt)

FLAMME is called *Bon Aire* or *Torch* by some sources; see Imports in Appendix.

FLASH is an informal brush-drawn script letter, cut by Monotype in 1939. It was the first face designed by Edwin W. Shaar, who designed *Flash Bold* the following year. The lighter weight is somewhat similar to *Dom Diagonal,* cut later by ATF. Also compare *Balloon.*

Flash, Mono 373 (14-72pt)
Flash Bold, Mono 473 (14-72pt)

FLEMISH BLACK, ATF (30-pt. at 80%) (Herb Harnish)

ABCEFGHIJKLMNOPQRSTUVWXYZ
abcdefghijklmnopqrstuvwxyz ,.=;:'!?& $1234567890

FLEX, Amsterdam 24-pt.

ABCDEFGHIJKLMNOP&
abcdefghijklmnopqrstuvwxy $12

FLORENTINE OLD STYLE, ATF 24-pt. (Dave Greer)

AABBCDEEFFGHIJKLMMNNOOPPQRRSSTUVWYYZ&£
aabcdeefghijklmnoopqrstuvwxyz $1234567890 .,-:;'!?

FLORENTINE BOLD, ATF 24-pt. (Herb Harnish)

AABCDEFGHIJKLMNOPQRSTUVWXYZ& .,:;'!?£
abcdefghijklmnopqrstuvwxyz $1234567890

FLORENTINE BOLD CONDENSED, ATF 24-pt.

ARTISTIC MURAL DESIGNER
Characteristic Foreign Residence

FLORENTINE CURSIVE, Ludlow 24-pt.

ABCDEFGHIJKLMNOPQRSTUVWXYZ& :,;-'''!?(
abcdefghijklmnopqrstuvwxyz $1234567890 % ¼ ⅓ ½ ⅔ ¾ I V X & & 1 2 3 4 5 6 7 8 9 0

FORMAL SCRIPT, Ludlow 24-pt.

ABCDEFGHIJKLMNOP2RSTUVWXYZ&.:,:- '''!?()
abcdefghijklmnopqrstuvwxyz $1234567890 % ¼ ⅓ ½ ⅔ ¾ I V X S a c r s.

FORUM, Mono 24-pt. (Guy Botterill)

ABCDEFGHIJKLMNOPQRSTUVWXYZ&
1234567890 .,'

FLEMISH BLACK was designed by Joseph W. Phinney about 1902. It has the same lowercase as *Cloister Black,* which was introduced at the same time, but a distinctly different set of capitals. *Cloister Black* attained much greater popularity and longer life.

Flemish Black, ATF 157 (6-72pt)

FLEX is a ribbon-like face designed by George Salter in 1937, while he was living in New York, but was cast only by Amsterdam Typefoundry.

Flex, Amsterdam

FLORENTINE or *Florentine Oldstyle* was advertised by ATF in 1896 as a cap-and-small-cap design, but quickly replaced by *Florentine Oldstyle No. 2,* with lowercase instead of small caps. *Florentine Heavyface* followed in 1898. The latter was renamed *Florentine Bold,* and condensed and extra condensed widths were added in 1903, and became popular advertising faces. Some of these were patented in the name of Ludvig S. Ipsen, and presumably he was the designer. ATF said of the Oldstyle: "Many of the characters are transcripts of the lettering of a famous Italian monument of the sixth century," although it is a rather bizarre novelty series.

Florentine Oldstyle, ATF (6-48pt)
Florentine Oldstyle No. 2, ATF (6-72pt)
Florentine Heavyface or Bold, ATF (5-72pt)
Florentine Bold Condensed, ATF (6-120pt)
Florentine Bold Extra Condensed, ATF (8-120pt)

FLORENTINE CURSIVE is a delicate, formal cursive design drawn by R. Hunter Middleton for Ludlow in 1956, in which letters don't quite join. It is lighter and much more sedate than the same designer's *Coronet* series, but has also been popular for announcements, title pages, and the like.

Florentine Cursive, Ludlow 52-LIC (12-36pt)

FLORIATED CAPITALS, FOLIO, FONTANESI—see Imports in Appendix.

FORMAL SCRIPT is derived from *Typo Script,* one of the most used Spencerian styles of script letter. The adaptation to Ludlow matrices was done by Robert H. Middleton in 1956. It has the appearance of joining, but doesn't quite do so. Matrices were cut at a much greater angle than usual for Ludlow italics.

Formal Script, Ludlow 51-MIC (14-36pt)

FORTUNE or FORTUNA—see Imports in Appendix.

FORUM or *Forum Title* was designed by Frederic W. Goudy in 1911, originally intended for headings in a book to be set in *Kennerley.* The letters are based on rubbings Goudy had made during a visit to Rome the previous year; some of these were on the Arch of Titus in the Roman Forum, hence the name. This is a font of capitals only, as lowercase letters were not in existence for several hundred years after Roman times, but they reflect inscriptional lettering at its classic best. Also see *Kennerley, Beacon.*

Forum Title, Goudy; Forum, Mono 274 (10-48pt)

FORUM I & II—see Imports in Appendix.

FOSTER, ATF 24-pt. (Dave Greer)

ABCDEFGHIJKLMNOPQRSTUVWXYZ&$
abcdefghijklmnopqrstuvwxyz 1234567890 .,-:;'!?

CONDENSED FOSTER, ATF 24-pt.

GERMAN DESTROYS FORTIFICATION
Souvenir Hunters Purchase Finest Picture

FOSTER ABSTRACT, Goudy 24-pt.

FOSTEL ABSTLACT
THE ESSENTIAL LETTEL FOLM

FOURNIER, Eng Mono 24-pt.

ABCDEFGHIJKLMNOPQRSTUVWXYZ&1234567890
abcdefghijklnopqrstuvwxyzæœfiflffffiffl.,:;-!?"()ÆŒ£

FOURNIER ITALIC, Mono 14-pt.

ABCDEFGHIJJKLMNOPQRSTUVWXYZ& $1234567890
abcdefghijklmnopqrstuvwxyz fifffffiffl .,-'':;!? $1234567890

FOURNIER [LE JEUNE], ATF 24-pt.

ABCDEFGHIJKLMNOPQRSTUVWXYZ
1234567890&$.,-';:;!?

FOURTEENTH CENTURY, Hansen 12-pt. (Wilbur Doctor)

ABCDEFGHIJKLMNOPQRSTUVWXYZⱯ abcdefghijklmnopqrstuvwxyz & fffifl ſſhſiſl ſt ᵈᵉʰʳˢᵗ $1234567890 .,-:;'!

FRANCIS, Inland 24-pt.

STANDARD LINING
The Unexcelled Method 32

FRANCISCAN, Goudy 16-pt.

ÆB C D E G F G H I J K L M N O O P Q R S T U V W X Y Z ↄ & & .:; /?!'
a b c d e f g h i j k l m n o p q r s t u v w x y z ff fi fl ffi ffl & 1 2 3 4 5 6 7 8 9 0

FOSTER is a heavy square-serif letter, patented and probably designed by William Schraubstädter and introduced by Inland in 1905. It seems rather crude by later *Stymie* standards—even compared with the earlier *Boston Breton*—particularly for the narrow *G,* the wide *J,* the high-waisted *B, P,* and *R,* and several other unusual letters. *Condensed Foster,* introduced by the same foundry in 1908, is comparable. See *Webb* for the outline version of the same design.

Foster, Inland-ATF 161 (6-84pt)
Condensed Foster, Inland-ATF 117 (6-84pt)

FOSTER ABSTRACT is a very heavy, serifless type of futuristic design, in which parts of some letters are suggested rather than actually presented. It was designed by Robert Foster in 1931, and matrices were cut by Frederic W. Goudy for private casting. Some letters are much like *Sans Serif Extrabold.* The specimen shown here is from a very poor print. Compare *Pericles.*

Foster Abstract, Goudy (casting, private)

FOURNIER is an aristocratic roman face which had its inception in letters engraved and cast by Pierre Simon Fournier, a famous mid-eighteenth-century French typefounder. It is transitional, almost modern, in character, with a distinct French flavor, but with more grace and style than traditional French oldstyle designs. This modern character influenced the later work of Bodoni. This adaptation was made by English Monotype in 1925, and copied by Lanston Mono in 1940. The specimen of the roman shown here is from English Monotype, in the absence of a good American specimen, but the italic is from Lanston.

Fournier, Mono 403 (8-36pt)
Fournier Italic, Mono 4031 (8-18pt)

FOURNIER or *Fournier le Jeune,* with the exception of the figures, is a reproduction of *Le Fournier le Jeune* originally cut in France in 1768 by the Peignot foundry, and revived in 1913. ATF secured the American rights in 1926. It is a decorative face, also based on the work of Pierre Simon Fournier. The figures were added by ATF to meet the needs of the American printer. ATF has always used only the single name, while Monotype used both the short and long names in various references.

Fournier, ATF 485 (18-30pt); Mono 305 (18-30pt)

FOURTEENTH CENTURY is a novelty face with a rough, antique feeling, produced by Hansen in one size only, and shown about 1909.

Fourteenth Century, Hansen (12pt)

FRANCIS is a novelty face introduced by Inland in 1904. Compare *Bizarre Bold.*

Francis, Inland

FRANCISCAN is the redesigned and recut *Aries* face of Frederic W. Goudy, renamed in 1932 by Edwin Grabhorn, an eminent San Francisco printer, who used it for several distinctive and award-winning books. Monotype made mats from the types cast by Goudy for private use of the California printer, calling the design *Goudy Franciscan.*

Franciscan, Goudy; Goudy Franciscan, Mono 432

FRANKLIN GOTHIC, Mono 24- & 12-pt.

ABCDEFGHIJKLMNOPQRSTUVWXYZ ,.-;:'!?&
abcdefghijklmnopqrstuvwxyz $1234567890
ff fi ffi fl ffl Æ Œ æ œ Rt t ABCDEFGHIJKLMNOPQRSTUVWXYZ& .,-:;'!?
abcdefghijklmnopqrstuvwxyz fffiffifIffl $1234567890

Ludlow

FRANKLIN GOTHIC ITALIC, ATF (3rd line Ludlow) 24-pt.

ABCDEFGHIJKLMNOPQRSTUVWXYZ,.-;:'!?&
abcdefghijklmnopqrstuvwxyz ff fi $1234567890
abcdefghijklmnop ABCDEFGHIJK 1234567890

FRANKLIN GOTHIC CONDENSED, Mono 24-pt.

ABCDEFGHIJKLMNOPQRSTUVWXYZ.,-:;"!?&
abcdefghijklmnopqrstuvwxyz $1234567890

FRANKLIN GOTHIC CONDENSED ITALIC, ATF (30-pt. at 80%)

ABCDEFGHIJKLMNOPQRSTUVWXYZ 1234567890
abcdefghijklmnopqrstuvwxyz $£.:,;-?!"&

FRANKLIN GOTHIC EXTRA CONDENSED, ATF 24-pt.

ABCDEFGHIJKLMNOPQRSTUVWXYZ
abcdefghijklmnopqrstuvwxyz $1234567890.,-:; '!?&

FRANKLIN GOTHIC WIDE, ATF 24-pt.

ABCDEFGHIJKLMNOPQRSTUVWXYZ
abcdefghijklmnopqrstuvwxyz
$1234567890.,-:;''""!?&

FRANKLIN GOTHIC CONDENSED SHADED, ATF 36-pt.

ABCDEFGHIJKLMNOPQRSTUVWXYZ $12
abcdefghijklmnopqrstuvwxyz 34567890

[FRANKLIN] GOTHIC CONDENSED OUTLINE, Balto 24-pt.

ABCDEFGHIJKLMNOPQRSTUVWXYZ&.,.:;-!?1234567890$

FRANKLIN GOTHIC might well be called the patriarch of modern American gothics. Designed in 1902 by Morris Fuller Benton, it was one of the first important modernizations of traditional nineteenth-century faces by that designer, after he was assigned the task of unifying and improving the varied assortment of designs inherited by ATF from its twenty-three predecessor companies. *Franklin Gothic* (named for Benjamin Franklin) not only became a family in its own right, but also lent its characteristics to *Lightline Gothic, Monotone Gothic,* and *News Gothic* (q.v.). All of these faces bear more resemblance to each other than do the faces within some other single families.

Franklin Gothic is characterized by a slight degree of thick-and-thin contrast; by the double-loop *g* which has become a typically American design in gothic faces; by the diagonal ends of curved strokes (except in *Extra Condensed*); and by the oddity of the upper end of *C* and *c* being heavier than the lower end.

The principal specimen here is Monotype, but the basic font is virtually an exact copy of the ATF face in display sizes, except that Monotype has added f-ligatures and diphthongs.

Franklin Gothic Condensed and *Extra Condensed* were also designed by Benton, in 1906; *Italic* by the same designer in 1910; and *Condensed Shaded* in 1912 as part of the "gray typography" series. Although Benton started a wide version along with the others, it was abandoned; the present *Franklin Gothic Wide* was drawn by Bud (John L.) Renshaw about 1952. *Franklin Gothic Condensed Italic* was added by Whedon Davis in 1967.

Monotype composition sizes of *Franklin Gothic* have been greatly modified to fit a standard arrangement; 12-point is shown in the specimen—notice the narrow figures and certain other poorly reproportioned characters. The 4- and 5-point sizes have a single-loop *g*. *Gothic No. 16* on Linotype and Intertype is essentially the same as *Franklin Gothic* up to 14-point; in larger sizes it is modified and more nearly like *Franklin Gothic Condensed*. However, some fonts of this face on Lino have *Gagtu* redrawn similar to *Spartan Black*, with the usual characters available as alternates; 14-point is shown. Western Type Foundry and later BB&S used the name *Gothic No. 1* for their copy of *Franklin Gothic,* while Laclede had another similar *Gothic No. 1* (q.v.).

On Ludlow, this design was originally known as *Square Gothic Heavy,* with a distinctive *R* and *t* as shown separately after the Monotype diphthongs; when the name was changed to *Franklin Gothic* in 1928, *t* was redrawn (third letter in *Rtt* shown), closer to *Franklin Gothic* but still a bit top-heavy; the unique *R* was retained in standard fonts but an alternate version like that of ATF was made available separately; also a *U* with equal arms, a single-loop *g*, and a figure *1* without foot serifs. Ludlow *Franklin Gothic Italic,* partially shown on the third line of the specimen, is slanted much more than other versions, to fit the standard 17-degree italic matrices of that machine.

Modern Gothic Condensed and *Italic* (q.v.) are often though not properly called *Franklin Gothic Condensed* and *Italic,* especially by Monotype users. Also see *Streamline Block*.

Franklin Gothic, ATF 162 (4-96pt); Mono 107 (4-72H4pt); Ludlow 6-F (6-84pt); Lino, Inter (6-36pt); APL (18-144pt); Gothic No. 1, BB&S-ATF 1674 (4-72pt); Gothic No. 16, Lino = Inter (4-36pt, see text)

Franklin Gothic Italic, ATF 166 (5-72pt); Ludlow 6-FI (18-72pt); Inter (6-14pt); APL (18-60pt)

Franklin Gothic Condensed, ATF 163 (6-72pt); Mono 707 (12-72pt); APL (96,144pt)

Franklin Gothic Condensed Italic, ATF 726 (10-48pt)

Franklin Gothic Extra Condensed, ATF 165 (6-120pt); Mono 507 (14-72pt); Ludlow 6-FEC (12-96pt); APL (18-144pt); Gothic No. 1 Condensed, BB&S-ATF 1675 (6-72pt); also Franklin Gothic Extra Condensed Title, Ludlow 6-FECT (96 pt); Gothic Condensed Title, APL (96pt)

Franklin Gothic Wide, ATF 701 (6-72pt)

Franklin Gothic Condensed Shaded, ATF 164 (8-48pt)

FRANKLIN OLD STYLE was intended to be a modernization of Caslon, cut in 1863 by Alexander Phemister, once of Edinburgh, later of Boston, for Phelps, Dalton & Company. Being more regularized, it has lost the individ-
(Franklin Old Style continues)

Franklin Old Style and Italic, Lino (6-18pt)

FRANKLIN OLDSTYLE & ITALIC, Lino 14-pt.

ABCDEFGHIJKLMNOPQRSTUVWXYZ ABCDEFGHIJKLMNOPQRSTUVWXYZ
ABCDEFGHIJKLMNOPQRSTUVWXYZ

$1234567890   abcdefghijklmnopqrstuvwxyz $1234567890
$1234567890   abcdefghijklmnopqrstuvwxyz $1234567890

143

ABCDEFGHIJKLMNOPQRSTUVWXYZ&

abcdefghijklmnopqrstuvwxyz 1234567890$ fffiflffifffi.,-:;'!?

ABCDEFGHIJKLMNOPQRSTUVWXYZ&

abcdefghijklmnopqrstuvwxyz $1234567890 .,-:;!?

DIRECTORS FOR THE PETER AND
Matthew Church Have Officially Quizzed

Each Member About the Actual Number of
Meetings Attended in Month $1234567890

ABCDEFGHIJKLMNOPQRSTUVWXYZ&ÆŒ
abcdefghijklmnopqrstuvwxyzæœfiffflffiffl 1234567890 $.,-'':;!?– —
ABCDEFGHIJKLMNOPQRSTUVWXYZ&ÆŒ
ABCDEFGHIJKLMNOPQRSTUVWXYZ&ÆŒ
abcdefghijklmnopqrstuvwxyzæœfiffffifffl 1234567890 $:;!?

DESCRIBE HORSE Honest Investments

ABCDEFGHIJKLMNOPQRSTUVWXYZ&$1234567890

abcdefghijklmnopqrstuvwxyz.,-:;'!? DTbbr for oc to ~()

ABCDEFGHIJKLMNOPQRSTUVWXYZ&

abcdefghijklmnopqrstuvwxyz $1234567890 .,-:;'!? oc r r. rs. ó

ABCDEFGHIJKLMNOPQRSTUVWXYZ&

abcdefghijklmnopqrstuvwxyz.,-:;'!? $1234567890

A B C D E F G H I J K L M N O P Q R S T U V W X Y Z & Æ Œ . , - ' : ; ! ?
a b c d e f g h i j k l m n o p q r s t u v w x y z æ œ fi fl ff ffi ffl $ 1 2 3 4 5 6 7 8 9 0

A A B C D E E F G H Ħ I J K L M N O P Q R S T T U V W X Y Z & ct ff fl ffl
a a ʙ b b c d ꝺ e e f g ᵹ h i j k l m n o p q r ꞃ s t u v w x y z . , ' ; : ! ! / · ⁊ ⚹ ✱ 1 2 3 4 5 6 7 8 9 0

uality and most of the charm of Caslon, but is a clear, legible face that has had considerable popularity. It was one of the early faces cut by Linotype for book work; the italic has an extreme slant for a slug-machine face, but composes remarkably well. Compare *Binny, Clearcut Oldstyle.*

FREEHAND, a face based on pen-lettering, was designed for ATF by Morris Benton in 1917. The working title before release was *Quill.* Derived from Old English, it is an interesting novelty, and has had quite a bit of use. Compare *Civilité, Motto, Verona.*

Freehand, ATF 469 (6-48pt)

FRENCH CADMUS—see *Elzevir No. 3.*
FRENCH CLARENDON—see *P. T. Barnum.*
FRENCH CLARENDON SHADED—see Antiques in Appendix.

FRENCH ELZEVIR or *French Oldstyle* was derived from types popularized in France in the eighteenth to early nineteenth centuries, and again became popular in the late nineteenth and early twentieth centuries, with several variations identified only by a supplemental number. They are modernized oldstyle faces, rather narrow but not tightly set, with moderate contrast and very small serifs. Foundry italics have a number of swash capitals. They have been made by a number of foundries; those listed here are the last survivors, but are typical of the general style. The BB&S romans listed are similar but not identical to the ATF face, but the italics appear to be the same.

French Oldstyle faces were the inspiration for *MacFarland* and *DeVinne* (q.v.). Also see *Elzevir.*

French Oldstyle No. 552, ATF 258 (6-72pt); French Old Style, Mono 71 (6-36pt); Hansen (6-48pt); Lino (10pt); French Oldstyle No. 2, Lino (18,22pt); also French Oldstyle No. 3, BB&S-ATF 1639 (6-18pt); Hansen (6-48pt); French Elzevir, BB&S-ATF 1633 (6-48pt); also French Oldstyle No. 56 (title), BB&S-ATF 1640 (6-48pt)
French Oldstyle Italic No. 552, ATF 259 (6-12pt); French Old Style Italic, Mono 71G (6-12pt); Hansen (6-12pt); Lino (10pt); French Elzevir Italic No. 5, BB&S-ATF 1637 (6-12pt)

FRENCH PLATE SCRIPT (or *French Plate*) was designed by Sidney Gaunt for BB&S in 1904. It is an upright script, otherwise similar to the same founder's *Wedding Plate Script,* both derived from types cut by Mayeur of Paris which were based on eighteenth-century engraving. Both are connecting scripts, the former being similar to *Typo Upright* (q.v.).

Inland Type Foundry showed a similar *French Script* in 1905, patented by William Schraubstädter, and later listed by ATF. Douglas C. McMurtrie, in his book *Type Designs,* calls this "one of the finest script types ever produced."

French Plate Script, BB&S-ATF 1641 (14-36pt)
French Script, Inland-ATF 503 (12-54pt)

FRENCH ROUND FACE, originally called *Didot Roman* or simply *Modern,* was one of the first revivals of the faces cut by Firmin Didot in France about 1784. This was cut for Monotype in 1910, under the direction of J. Horace MacFarland and William Dana Orcutt. The italic is unusual in that some lowercase letters have serifs like the roman. *No. 16* on Linotype and Intertype is similar but heavier. Compare *Suburban French.*

French Round Face and Italic, Mono 150-1501 (6-36pt); also French Round Face Cancelled, Mono 195A (10,11pt)

FRIAR. Frederic W. Goudy says, "Friar type was designed for my own amusement. . . . For the lowercase, I drew on the half-uncial forms of the fourth, fifth, and sixth centuries, on eighth-century uncials. . . . For my capitals, I combined letters based on the square capitals of the fourth century, the Rustic hands of the mediaeval scribes—and to all of these suggestions I added my own conceits." Designed in 1937, only a few fonts were ever cast.

Friar, Goudy (12pt), private

FRY'S ORNAMENTED—see *Colonial;* also see Imports in Appendix.
FURLONG—see *Bell Gothic.*

FUTURA LIGHT & OBLIQUE, Inter 14-pt.

ABCDEFGHIJKLMNOPQRSTUVWXYZ ff fi ffi fl ffl
abcdefghijklmnopqrstuvwxyz % * ( ),.-;':'!?—&
⅛ ¼ ⅜ ½ ⅝ ¾ ⅞ ⅓ ⅔ $1234567890

ABCDEFGHIJKLMNOPQRSTUVWXYZ ff fi ffi fl ffl
abcdefghijklmnopqrstuvwxyz % * ( ),.-;':'!?—&
⅛ ¼ ⅜ ½ ⅝ ¾ ⅞ ⅓ ⅔ $1234567890

FUTURA BOOK & OBLIQUE, Inter 14-pt.

ABCDEFGHIJKLMNOPQRSTUVWXYZ&
abcdefghijklmnopqrstuvwxyz fffiffififlffl $1234567890 .,-:;'!?()—*%
ABCDEFGHIJKLMNOPQRSTUVWXYZ&
abcdefghijklmnopqrstuvwxyz fffiffififlffl $1234567890 .,-:;'!?()—*%

FUTURA MEDIUM & OBLIQUE, Inter 14-pt.

ABCDEFGHIJKLMNOPQRSTUVWXYZ ff fi ffi fl ffl
abcdefghijklmnopqrstuvwxyz % *(),.-;':'!?—&
⅛ ¼ ⅜ ½ ⅝ ¾ ⅞ ⅓ ⅔ $1234567890

ABCDEFGHIJKLMNOPQRSTUVWXYZ ff fi ffi fl ffl
abcdefghijklmnopqrstuvwxyz % *(),.-;':'!?—&
⅛ ¼ ⅜ ½ ⅝ ¾ ⅞ ⅓ ⅔ $1234567890

FUTURA MEDIUM CONDENSED, Inter 14-pt.

ABCDEFGHIJKLMNOPQRSTUVWXYZ %*(),.-;':'!?—& ff fi ffi fl ffl
abcdefghijklmnopqrstuvwxyz ¼ ½ ¾ $1234567890

FUTURA DEMIBOLD & OBLIQUE, Inter 14-pt.

ABCDEFGHIJKLMNOPQRSTUVWXYZ ff fi ffi fl ffl
abcdefghijklmnopqrstuvwxyz % *(),.-;':'!?—&
⅛ ¼ ⅜ ½ ⅝ ¾ ⅞ ⅓ ⅔ $1234567890

ABCDEFGHIJKLMNOPQRSTUVWXYZ ff fi ffi fl ffl
abcdefghijklmnopqrstuvwxyz % *(),.-;':'!?—&
⅛ ¼ ⅜ ½ ⅝ ¾ ⅞ ⅓ ⅔ $1234567890

FUTURA BOLD & OBLIQUE, Inter 14-pt.

ABCDEFGHIJKLMNOPQRSTUVWXYZ ff fi ffi fl ffl
abcdefghijklmnopqrstuvwxyz % *(),.-;':'!?—&
⅛ ¼ ⅜ ½ ⅝ ¾ ⅞ $1234567890

ABCDEFGHIJKLMNOPQRSTUVWXYZ ff
abcdefghijklmnopqrstuvwxyz % *(),.-;
⅛ ¼ ⅜ ½ ⅝ ¾ ⅞ $1234

FUTURA BOLD CONDENSED, Inter 18-pt.

ABCDEFGHIJKLMNOPQRSTUVWXYZ& $1234567890
abcdefghijklmnopqrstuvwxyz ½¼¾⅛⅜⅝⅞⅓⅔

FUTURA EXTRA BOLD & OBLIQUE, Inter 14-pt.

ABCDEFGHIJKLMNOPQRSTUVWXYZ 1234567890$ 1234567890$ æœÆŒ%£¢
ABCDEFGHIJKLMNOPQRSTUVWXYZ 1234567890$ 1234567890$ æœÆŒ%£¢
abcdefghijklmnopqrstuvwxyz ¼½¾⅓⅔ fiflffffiffl,.-':';!?()*@℔&—[]†‡§₢
abcdefghijklmnopqrstuvwxyz ¼½¾⅓⅔ fiflffffiffl,.-':';!?()*@℔&—[]†‡§₢

FUTURA EXTRA BOLD CONDENSED & OBLIQUE, Inter (24-pt. at 57%)

ABCDEFGHIJKLMNOPQRSTUVWXYZ ABCDEFGHIJKLMNOPQRSTUVWXYZ
abcdefghijklmnopqrstuvwxyz 1234567890 abcdefghijklmnopqrstuvwxyz 1234567890

146

FUTURA is a geometric, serifless type designed by Paul Renner for Bauer Typefoundry in Germany in 1927, and features reproportioning which at first seemed radical in relation to the traditional gothics. It first gained popularity in America as imported foundry type. The first copies in this country were made by Baltimore Type under the name *Airport* (q.v.). One source says it was cut from original Futura drawings, but most likely it was electrotyped from imported fonts. Three extrabold versions were added by Baltimore Type, apparently being introduced before their counterparts from other sources. *Airport Black* and *Airport Black Condensed Title* were cut about 1943. *Airport Broad* is essentially a modification by pantagraph of *Airport Black*, being cut 50 percent wider. These faces are heavier than most of their counterparts, none of which copy them exactly, although *Spartan Extra Black* is about the same weight.

Intertype copied a number of Futura faces under the original names in 1939, with additional weights designed by Edwin W. Shaar and Tommy Thompson up to 1956. Monotype copied the series under the name *Twentieth Century,* with additional versions by Sol Hess.

Spartan is claimed to have been redrawn from various European sources, but is almost indistinguishable from *Futura;* it was cut cooperatively by American Type and Linotype, with smaller sizes matching from both sources. Linotype introduced its *Sanserif 52,* later renamed *Spartan Black,* in 1939, while other weights appeared as late as 1955. Some of the additional weights were drawn for ATF by Bud Renshaw and Gerry Powell.

On Ludlow, *Tempo Alternate* is a near copy of *Futura,* but not quite as close as the other faces listed; in addition, this face has several alternate letters and figures which change the character of the design when substituted.

Distinguishing between Futura and its various counterparts is difficult, and can't be explained in complete detail here. The careful researcher, though, should observe the quotation and question marks, which vary in form between certain sources. Imported fonts and some Baltimore fonts have *ff, fi, fl,* and *ft* ligatures; Monotype has the first three of these. Other sources generally have the usual five ligatures including *ffi* and *ffl.* Linotype and Intertype offer an alternate roman form of *a* in some fonts. Bauer *Futura, Airport,* and *Twentieth Century* have cap-height ascenders up to 12-point, taller ascenders in larger sizes. Other faces in this category have ascenders taller than caps in all sizes.

In Futura and its counterparts, the names of weights vary greatly from one series to another. In the following data, the Futura names are the original or "generic" titles, with asterisks indicating the versions which originated in Germany. All faces in each group are substantially the same, but vary more in Extrabold than in the other weights. *Airport Tourist* was Bauer's *Futura Display.* Bauer's *Futura Inline* and *Futura Black* are shown under Imports in Appendix.

See *Airport, Spartan, Tempo Alternate, Twentieth Century;* also *Bernhard Gothic, Metro, Tempo, Vogue,* etc.; also *Classified Display.*

Futura Light, Inter* (6-14pt); Spartan Light, Lino (6-24pt); Twentieth Century Light, Mono 606 (6-72pt)

Futura Light Oblique, Inter* (6-14pt); Twentieth Century Light Italic, Mono 6061 (6-72pt)

Futura Book, Inter* (6-24pt); Spartan Book, ATF 707 (6-36pt), Lino (5½-24pt); Twentieth Century Semi-Medium, Mono 613 (6-12pt)

Futura Book Oblique, Inter* (6-14pt); Spartan Book Italic, Lino (6-24pt); Twentieth Century Semi-Medium Italic 613K (6-12pt)

Futura Book Condensed, Inter (8-24pt); Spartan Book Condensed, Lino (5½-36pt)

Futura Medium, Inter* (6-36pt); Spartan Medium, ATF 680 (6-120pt), Lino (6-36pt); Twentieth Century Medium, Mono 605 (6-72pt); Tempo Alternate Medium, Ludlow 28-AM (6-72pt); Airport Gothic, Balto 102 (6-48pt)

Futura Medium Oblique, Inter* (6-30pt); Spartan Medium Italic, ATF 681 (6-72pt), Lino (6-36pt); Twentieth Century Medium Italic, Mono 6051 (6-72pt); Airport Gothic Italic, Balto 202 (6-48pt)

Futura Medium Condensed, Inter* (8-30pt); Spartan Medium Condensed, ATF 706 (6-48pt), Lino (5½-24pt); Twentieth Century Medium Condensed, Mono 608 (10-72pt); Airport Medium Condensed, Balto 608 (10-72pt)

Twentieth Century Medium Condensed Italic, Mono 6081 (10-36pt); Airport Medium Condensed Italic, Balto 6081 (10,12pt)

Spartan Bold, Lino (14-36pt)

Spartan Bold Italic, Lino (14-36pt)

Spartan Bold Condensed, Lino (18-36pt)

Spartan Bold Condensed Italic, Lino (18-24pt)

Futura Demibold, Inter* (6-36pt); Spartan Heavy, ATF 685 (6-120pt), Lino (5½-36pt); Twentieth Century Bold, Mono 604 (6-72pt); Tempo Alternate Bold, Ludlow 28-AB (6-96pt); Airport Semibold, Balto 302 (6-72pt)

Futura Demibold Oblique, Inter* (6-36pt); Spartan Heavy Italic, ATF 686 (6-72pt), Lino (6-36pt); Twentieth Century Bold Italic, Mono 6041 (6-72pt); Tempo Alternate Bold Italic, Ludlow 28-ABI (18-48pt); Airport Semibold Italic, Balto 3021 (6-48pt)

Futura Demibold Condensed, Inter (8-24pt); Spartan Heavy Condensed, Lino (5½-36pt); Twentieth Century Bold Condensed, Mono 612 (14-36pt)

Futura Bold, Inter* (6-36pt); Spartan Black, ATF 683 (6-120pt), Lino (6-36pt); Twentieth Century Extrabold, Mono 603 (6-72pt); Tempo Alternate Heavy, Ludlow 28-AH (6-72pt); Airport Bold, Balto 402 (6-72pt)

Futura Bold Oblique, Inter* (6-30pt); Spartan Black Italic, ATF 684 (6-72pt), Lino (6-36pt); Twentieth Century Extrabold Italic, Mono 6031 (6-72pt); Airport Bold Italic, Balto 4021 (6-48pt)

Futura Bold Condensed, Inter* (6-36pt); Spartan Black Condensed, ATF 687 (10-120pt), Lino (8-36pt); Twentieth Century Extrabold Condensed, Mono 607 (8-72H4); Airport Bold Condensed, Balto 502 (8-72pt)

Spartan Black Condensed Italic, ATF 688 (10-72pt), Lino (8-36pt); Twentieth Century Extrabold Condensed Italic, Mono 6071 (8-72H4); Airport Bold Condensed Italic, Balto 5021 (8-72pt)

Futura Extrabold, Inter (10-30pt); Spartan Extra Black, ATF 694 (10-72pt), Lino (14-24pt); Twentieth Century Ultrabold, Mono 609 (8-72pt); Airport Black, Balto 702 (12-72pt)

Futura Extrabold Oblique, Inter (6-30pt); Spartan Extra Black Italic, Lino (14-24pt); Twentieth Century Ultrabold Italic, Mono 6091 (8-72pt)

Futura Extrabold Condensed, Inter (12-36pt); Twentieth Century Ultrabold Condensed, Mono 610 (8-72pt); Airport Extrabold Condensed, Balto 610 (14-72pt)

Futura Extrabold Condensed Oblique, Inter (12-24pt); Twentieth Century Ultrabold Condensed Italic, Mono 6101 (14-72pt); Airport Extrabold Condensed Italic, Balto 6101 (14-72pt)

Twentieth Century Ultrabold Extended, Mono 614 (14-48pt); Airport Broad, Balto 712 (14-48pt)

Airport Black Condensed Title, Balto 802 (18-48pt)

Airport Tourist, Balto 602 (14-72pt)

*Faces originally imported from Bauer in Germany, but sizes are those made by Intertype.

GALLIA, Mono 18-pt.

A A B C D E F G H I J K L M N O P Q R S T T U V W
$1234567890 .,.~::""!?&S XYZ

GARAMOND, ATF 24-pt. & Auxiliaries 18-pt. (part reduced—see text)

ABCDEFGHIJKLMNOPQRSTUVWXYZ&$1234567890
abcdefghijklmnopqrstuvwxyzffffifflffifflctst.,.:;-"!? EFJLU&

Original

a e m n t 𝕾 1 2 3 4 5 6 7 8 9 0

¶ @ % ‰ ℔ ℞ * § † ( ) [ ] ‖ [ ] † - – — ¢ « » ︵ ︵

GARAMOND ITALIC, ATF 24-pt. (see text)

Original Angle-body

ABCDEFGHIJKLMNOPQRSTUVWXYZ&$1234567890 *J& Jfj £*

abcdefghijklmnopqrstuvvwxyz .,-:;"!? fffifflffifflctst as is us frll sp tt

A B C D E G L M N P R T Y & The a e m n t

1 2 3 4 5 6 7 8 9 0 ſ ſſ ſſi ſſl ſh ſi ſl ſp ß ſl gy

GARAMOND BOLD, Mono 24-pt.

ABCDEFGHIJKLMNOPQRSTUVWXYZ$1234567890

abcdefghijklmnopqrstuvwxyz.,-:;"!?&ffffifflffiffl

GARAMOND BOLD ITALIC, Mono 24-pt.

ABCDEFGHIJKLMNOPQRSTUVWXYZ&.,-:;'!?$1234567890

abcdefghijklmnopqrstuvvvwwxyz ABCDEGLMNPRTY&

a e k m n t ctst as is us ll sp tt fr gy ke The (): fi ff fl ffl ffi 1234567890

GARAMOND OPEN, ATF 24-pt.

ABCDEFGHIJKLMNOPQRSTUVWXYZ &

abcdefghijklmnopqrstuvwxyz .,-:;''!? $1234567890

GARAMOND & ITALIC, Lino 14-pt. (Swash 30-pt. at 50%)

ABCDEFGHIJKLMNOPQRSTUVWXYZ& ($£,.:;'-'?!*†) ABCDEFGHIJKLMNOPQRSTUVWXYZ&
ABCDEFGHIJKLMNOPQRSTUVWXYZ& ($£,.:;'-'?! †)
1234567890 abcdefghijklmnopqrstuvwxyz 1234567890
1234567890 abcdefghijklmnopqrstuvwxyz 1234567890 ABCDELGMNPRTY&stct

GALLIA is a unique decorative letter designed by Wadsworth A. Parker for ATF in 1927, and copied by Monotype the following year. It is a severe thick-and-thin style, with main strokes divided by two white lines into a thick and two thin lines. There are flourished alternate forms of several letters, for use as initials or terminals. Compare *Modernistic*.

GARAMOND. Claude Garamond was a distinguished sixteenth-century type designer and founder, the first person to establish typefounding as a business separate from printing. Fonts known as *caractères de l'Université* and ascribed to Garamond are preserved in the Imprimerie Nationale in Paris. These were the inspiration for the *Garamond* face designed by Morris Benton for ATF and *Garamont* designed by Frederic W. Goudy for Monotype. Several years after they were released, Beatrice Warde, writing under the pseudonym of Paul Beaujon, established that the source types were actually the work of Jean Jannon, a master printer in Paris in the early seventeenth century. But this disclosure did nothing to diminish the popularity of the elegant types named for Garamond.

Benton started work on his design in 1917, and it was released two years later, with *Italic. Garamond Bold* was added in 1920 and *Bold Italic* in 1923; they have achieved great popularity and wide use, and for many years were a basic choice for advertising display.

In 1922 Thomas M. Cleland designed a set of swash letters and other auxiliary characters for the *Garamond* series. He also redesigned several characters in the fonts. In the specimen here, redesigned characters are shown in the alphabets, while *EFJLU&* and italic *J&,* shown separately, are Benton's original designs. *Garamond Bold* had similar characters. About 1930 *Garamond Italic* and *Bold Italic* were modified slightly for casting on angle body, and for a time were offered both ways. The separate *J* and *f* in the *Italic* specimen show the most obvious modifications for angle body, which had no ligatures, swash, or other extra characters.

Garamond Open was designed by Benton for ATF in 1931. Aside from a short *J* and non-kerning *f,* it follows the revised style of *Garamond*.

Intertype introduced a copy of *Garamond* in 1926, shown first under the name *Garatonian;* a short time later the *Garamond* name was applied and has remained. Edward E. Bartlett of Linotype went back to original Garamond specimens for a different and more authentic version of the face, introduced in 1929 with bold and italics; although these were handsome faces they never achieved the popularity of the ATF design. Later Linotype adapted the Benton design as its *Garamond No. 3* series. ("Garamond No. 2" is said to have been applied to a few fonts of German Linotype *Garamond* brought to the United States.)

Monotype issued Goudy's *Garamont* in 1921, although Monotype had an agreement that permitted reproduction of ATF faces. No boldface was designed for *Garamont,* so Mono copied ATF's *Garamond Bold* and *Italic,* which were mechanically incompatible with Goudy's design for keyboard typesetting. But popularity of the Benton design was such that Monotype copied it in

(Garamond continues)

Gallia, ATF 502 (12-72pt); Mono 313 (14-72pt)

Garamond, ATF 459 (6-72pt); Inter (6-48pt); Garamond No. 3, Lino (6-24pt); APL (18-42pt); American Garamond, Mono 648 (6-12pt)
Garamond Italic, ATF 460 (6-48pt); Inter (6-36pt); Garamond No. 3 Italic, Lino (6-24pt); American Garamond Italic, Mono 648G (6-12pt)
Garamond Bold, ATF 474 (6-120pt); Mono 548 (6-72pt); Inter (6-36pt); Garamond Bold No. 3, Lino (6-30pt); APL (18-144pt)
Garamond Bold Italic, ATF 489 (6-72pt); Mono 5481 (6-72pt); Inter (6-30pt); Garamond Bold No. 3 Italic, Lino (6-18pt); APL (18-60pt)
Garamond Open, ATF 557 (18-72pt)
Garamond, Lino (6-36pt)
Garamond Italic, Lino (6-30pt)
Garamond Bold, Lino (6-36pt)
Garamond Bold Italic, Lino (6-30pt)

GARAMOND BOLD & ITALIC, Lino 14-pt.

ABCDEFGHIJKLMNOPQRSTUVWXYZ&($£,.:;'-'?!*†)
ABCDEFGHIJKLMNOPQRSTUVWXYZ&($£,.:;'-'?!†)*

1234567890 abcdefghijklmnopqrstuvwxyz 1234567890
1234567890 abcdefghijklmnopqrstuvwxyz 1234567890 fiflffffiffl ABCDEGLMNPRTY&ctst

149

ABCDEFGHIJKLMNOPQRSTUVWXYZ $1234567890
abcdefghijklmnopqrstuvwxyz ff fi ffi fl ffl ½ % (),.-;':'!?—&

ABCDEFGHIJKLMNOPQRSTUVWXYZ $1234567890
abcdefghijklmnopqrstuvwxyz ff fi ffi fl ffl ½ % (),.-;':'!?—&
ABCDEFGLMN PR YQUQu a e k m n t v w as is ct st us

ABCDEFGHIJKLMNOPQRSTUVWXYZ $1234567890
abcdefghijklmnopqrstuvwxyz ff fi ffi fl ffl ½ (),.-;':'!?—&

ABCDEFGHIJKLMNOPQRSTUVWXYZ $1234567890
abcdefghijklmnopqrstuvwxyz ff fi ffi fl ffl ½ % (),.-;':'!?—&
ABCDEFGLMN PR Y a e k m n t vw as is ct st us

ABCDEFGHIJKLMNOPQRSTUVWXYZ& 1234567890$
abcdefghijklmnopqrstuvwxyz fi fl ff ffi ffl .,;:-''?!1234567890
ÆŒ æœ ct st () [] ℂ QU Qu

ABCDEFGHIJKLMNOPQRSTUVWXYZ& 1234567890
abcdefghhijkklmnopqrstuvvwxyz 1234567890$.,-:;'!? fi fl ff ffi ffl
ABCDEGMNPRTUQu llæægyctst gg ÆŒ a e m n

ABCDEFGHIJKLMNOPQRSTUVWX
abcdefghijklmnopqrstuvwxyz$1234567890 Y Z .,:;!-?

ABCDEFGHIJKLMNOPQRSTUVWXYZ& $1234567890.,-

1938 under the name *American Garamond,* in composition sizes. This left *Garamond* and *Garamond Italic* almost the only important later ATF faces not copied by Monotype in display sizes.

One of the most delicate and distinctive versions of *Garamond,* with bold and italics, was designed by R. Hunter Middleton for Ludlow in 1929, based on authentic original sources. It also has a number of swash and terminal characters. In the specimens here, both light and bold italic swash letters are out of sequence—in each case, the letter preceding *G* is *J,* not *F.*

Also see *Garamont; Granjon.*

Garamond, Ludlow 24-L (6-72pt)
Garamond Italic, Ludlow 24-LI (6-72pt)
Garamond Bold, Ludlow 24-B (6-72pt)
Garamond Bold Italic, Ludlow 24-BI (6-72pt)
England, Germany and other countries have other versions of Garamond.

GARAMONT. When Frederic W. Goudy joined Monotype as art advisor in 1920, he persuaded the company to cut its own version of the types attributed to Claude Garamond, rather than copying the foundry face. The result was named *Garamont,* also at Goudy's suggestion, to preserve the distinction between the different renderings. Both spellings of the name had been used in Garamond's lifetime.

Garamont, Mono 248 (6-72pt)
Garamont Italic, Mono 2481 (6-72pt)

A comparison of ATF *Garamond* and Monotype *Garamont,* especially in the small sizes, demonstrates opposing views of two outstanding type designers, although the two faces are very similar in many ways. In most faces, the proportionate width increases as the size decreases, to overcome optical illusions and maintain legibility. (See "Visual Reproportioning" on page 80.) Benton carried this idea beyond usual practice; his 6-point *Garamond* is a little more than one third the width of 24-point. But Goudy believed in strict proportions; his 6-point *Garamont* is only very slightly more than one fourth (26 percent) the width of 24-point; thus in 6- and 8-point sizes *Garamont* seems smaller than *Garamond.* This, incidentally, is what makes it impossible to combine *Garamont* with *Garamond Bold* for typesetting in one operation.

Note also the characters *EFJL* in *Garamont,* which are closer to Benton's original *Garamond* designs than to Cleland's revision. *Garamont* has the short *J* in display sizes, but a long one in keyboard sizes. In the *Garamont* specimens, the last group of characters, both roman and italic, was obtained from a different source and is proofed much more heavily; actually the weight is uniform with the rest of the font.

GEORGIAN CURSIVE is a script face designed by George F. Trenholm in 1934; it was cast by Machine Composition Company in Boston in one size. It has some resemblance to *Coronet* and to *Trafton Script,* but is a little less formal; letters do not connect.

Georgian Cursive, Machine Comp (24pt)

GIANT TYPEWRITER is one of the very few such faces made in display sizes. Compare *Jumbo Typewriter.* Also see *Typewriter Faces.*

Giant Typewriter (18pt)

GILL FLORIATED—see *Floriated Capitals* under Imports in Appendix.
GILL SANS—see Imports in Appendix.
GILL SANS CAMEO RULED—see Imports in Appendix, also see *Airport Relief.*

GILLIES GOTHIC LIGHT, Bauer 24-pt.

ABCDEFGHIJKLMNOPQRSTUVWXYZ&

abcdefghijklmnopqrstuvwxyz $1234567890 .,-:;'!?( ) " " Th

GILLIES GOTHIC BOLD, Bauer 24-pt.

ABCDEFGHIJKLMNOPQRSTUVWXYZ&

abcdefghijklmnopqrstuvwxyz.,:;-!?1234567890$ ' " " (Th

GLAMOUR LIGHT, Mono 24-pt.

ABCDEFGHIJKLMNOPQRSTUVWXYZ

abcdefghijklmnopqrstuvwxyzfiflfffffiffl $1234567890.,-:;""""*†!?%&()

GLAMOUR MEDIUM, Mono 24-pt.

ABCDEFGHIJKLMNOPQRSTUVWXYZ&

abcdefghijklmnopqrstuvwxyz $1234567890 .,-:;'!?( )—*""†℄

GLAMOUR BOLD, Mono 24-pt.

ABCDEFGHIJKLMNOPQRSTUVWXYZ& fffifflfffflffi|%

abcdefghijklmnopqrstuvwxyz$1234567890.,-:;'!?( )""*†℄

GLOBE GOTHIC, Mono 24-pt.

ABCDEFGHIJKLMNOPQRSTUVWXYZ&

abcdefghijklmnopqrstuvwxyz $1234567890 .,-:;'!?

GLOBE GOTHIC CONDENSED, ATF 24-pt. (Dave Norton)

ABCDEFGHIJKLMNOPQRSTUVWXYZ&

abcdefghijklmnopqrstuvwxyz.,-:;'!?$1234567890

GLOBE GOTHIC EXTRA CONDENSED, Mono 24-pt.

ABCDEFGHIJKLMNOPQRSTUVWXYZ& abcdefghijklmnopqrstuvwxyz $1234567890 .,-:;'!?

GLOBE GOTHIC EXTENDED, 24-pt.

ABCDEFGHIJKLMNOPQRSTUVWXY

abcdefghijklmnopqrstuvwxyz Z&

$1234567890 .,-:;'!?

GILLIES GOTHIC is an unusual monotone cursive style, rather than a gothic in either meaning of that term. It was designed by William S. Gillies of New York City in 1935, in two weights, but cast only by Bauer in Germany. Aside from the fact that it is not a connected script, it is somewhat similar to *Kaufmann* (q.v.), although many letters have unusual forms. Medium and hairline weights are said to have been designed, but not cut.

Gillies Gothic Light, Bauer (18-84pt)
Gillies Gothic Bold, Bauer (18-84pt)

GIRARD was a rather clumsy face introduced by Keystone about 1910. It was of medium weight, with square serifs and moderate contrast between thick and thin strokes, with some similarity to *John Hancock.*

Girard, Keystone (6-84pt)

GIRDER—see Imports in Appendix.

GLAMOUR is the Monotype copy, released in 1948, of *Corvinus,* designed by Imre Reiner for Bauer Type Foundry in Germany about 1930. Its dazzling thick-and-thin contrast and stylized features were quite popular for a time. A note in Monotype literature hints at its delicacy: "When casting this series use extreme care." Italic and condensed versions of foundry *Corvinus* (see Imports in Appendix) have been grouped under the *Glamour* name by some typographers, but were not made by Monotype. Compare *Eden.*

Glamour Light, Mono 235 (14-36pt)
Glamour Medium, Mono 236 (14-36pt)
Glamour Bold, Mono 237 (14-36pt)
Also see Corvinus series under Imports in
  Appendix.

GLOBE GOTHIC is a refinement of *Taylor Gothic,* designed about 1897 by ATF at the suggestion of Charles H. Taylor of the Boston *Globe,* and used extensively by that paper. But *Taylor Gothic* has mostly the same lowercase as *Quentell,* though with hairlines heavied a bit. ATF's Central Type Foundry branch in St. Louis claims to have originated *Quentell* (q.v.) in 1895 or earlier. The conversion to *Taylor Gothic* was designed by Joseph W. Phinney, while the redesign as *Globe Gothic* in about 1900 is credited to Morris Benton. It is a serifless, thick-and-thin face, distinguished by the high crossbar on *E, F,* and *H;* the angular end on the stems of *V, W,* and most lowercase letters.

Globe Gothic, ATF 172 (6-120pt); Mono 240
  (6-36pt)
Globe Gothic Condensed, ATF 175 (6-
  120pt); Mono 239 (6-36pt)
Globe Gothic Extra Condensed, ATF 177
  (6-120pt); Mono 230 (6-36pt)
Globe Gothic Extended, ATF 176 (6-72pt)
Globe Gothic Bold, ATF 173 (6-72pt)
Globe Gothic Bold Italic, ATF 174 (6-72pt)

   Globe Gothic Condensed, Extra Condensed, and *Extended* were designed by Benton about 1900. *Globe Gothic Bold* and its italic are also credited to Benton, in 1907 and 1908 respectively. But Frederic W. Goudy, in the book on his typefaces, says, "This type (*Globe Gothic Bold*), drawn at the suggestion of Joseph Phinney, followed in the main certain points which he wished brought out. It never had much vogue and is the least satisfactory (to me) of all my types." This is puzzling, as the bold departs somewhat from the style of the lighter weights, but is not at all characteristic of Goudy's work—nor of Benton's, for that matter. *Studley* of Inland Type Foundry was similar. Compare *Ryerson Condensed, Radiant, Matthews, Pontiac, World Gothic.*

GLORIA—see Imports in Appendix.

GLOBE GOTHIC BOLD (48-pt. at 50%)

ABCDEFGHIJKLMNOPQRSTUVWXYZ&
abcdefghijklmnopqrsuw $1234567890.,-:;"!?

GLOBE GOTHIC BOLD ITALIC, 24-pt.

ABCDEFGHIJKLMNOPQRSTUVWXYZ1234
abcdefghijklmnopqrstuvwxyz.,:;!?

GOETHE, Goudy 16-pt.

A B C D E F G H I J K L M N O P Q R S T U V W X Y Z & . , ' : ; ! ? -
a b c d e f g h i j k l m n o p q r s t u v w x y z fi ff · fl ffi ffl æ 1 2 3 4 5 6 7 8 9 0

GOETHE ITALIC, Goudy 14-pt.

A B C D E F G H I J K L M N O P Q R S T U V W X Y Z & . , ' ; : ! ? -
a b c d e f g h i j k l m n o p q r s t u v w x y z fi fl ff ffi Th ä ô 1 2 3 4 5 6 7 8 9 0

GOLD RUSH, 24-pt.

ABCDEFGHIJKLMNOPQRSTUV
$1234567890 .,:;-'!?& WXYZ

INLAND GOTHIC NO. 6, Mono 149 12-pt.

ABCDEFGHIJKLMNOPQRSTUVW abcdefghijklmnopqrstuvwxyz $1234567890

GOTHIC NO. 16, Lino 14-pt.

ABCDEFGHIJKLMNOPQRSTUVWXYZ& 1234567890 ($£,.:;'-'?! *†)
abcdefghijklmnopqrstuvwxyzfiflffffiffl   1234567890

GOTHIC NO. 25 & NO. 26, Lino 12-pt.

ABCDEFGHIJKLMNOPQRSTUVWXYZ1234567890,.:;?!''""-()&$ÆŒ
ABCDEFGHIJKLMNOPQRSTUVWXYZ1234567890,.:;?!''""-()&$ÆŒ

GOTHIC NO. 18 (old), Lino 14-pt.

ABCDEFGHIJKLMNOPQRSTUVWXYZ& abcdefghijklmnopqrstuvwxyzfiflffffiffl 1234567890 ($£,.:;'-'?!*†)

The Most Prolific Type Designers

Numbers alone are not the measure of greatness of type designers, of course, but the following figures show this aspect. They include only completed designs, done in this century, and designed or cut in this country. Published accounts of Goudy's work, for instance, indicate a larger number of faces, but some of them were unfinished. Some other designers undoubtedly also drew typefaces which were not completed. Designers indicated by an asterisk also designed other typefaces abroad, or prior to the twentieth century, or for processes other than metal type.

Designer	Count
Morris F. Benton:	221
Robert H. Middleton:	99
Frederic W. Goudy:	90
Sol Hess:	85
Sidney Gaunt:	46
William A. Dwiggins:	36
Chauncey H. Griffith:	34
Robert Wiebking:	31
Edwin W. Shaar:	18*
Lucian Bernhard:	16*
Joseph W. Phinney:	15*
Nicholas J. Werner:	15*
Jackson Burke:	12
Willard T. Sniffin:	12
Oswald Cooper:	11
S. H. DeRoos:	11
George F. Trenholm:	11
Hermann Zapf:	11*
Warren Chappell:	10
Wadsworth A. Parker:	10

GOETHE is essentially a lighter version of *Goudy Modern,* with slight changes and refinements. Frederic W. Goudy, the designer, says, "It was drawn and cut specially to print a specimen I contributed to the Goethe Centenary Exhibition held in Leipzic in 1932." The italic was cut the following year "for use in the Limited Editions Club edition of *Frankenstein,* for which I had cut the 12- and 14-point sizes of the roman especially." *Goethe* has been called "a blending of modern and old style characteristics which produces a distinctively new result."

Goethe and Goethe Italic, Goudy

GOLD RUSH is ATF's revival in 1933 and again in 1949 of *Antique Shaded,* also known as *Ornamented No. 1514,* cut about 1865 with lowercase by Bruce foundry. The basic design is Egyptian, with a third-dimensional form provided by a hairline at the bottom and right of each stroke. It is sometimes also called *Klondike.* It was plated by Carroll in the 1950s, with his mats later going to Typefounders of Phoenix and then to Los Angeles Type Foundry.

Gold Rush, ATF 588 (24pt); Carroll, TFP, LATF (24pt)

GOLDEN TYPE—see *Jenson Oldstyle.*
GOTHAM—see *Gothic Novelty Title.*

GOTHIC, the purists say, is Blackletter or what we more often call Old English. But the name is so firmly established in American usage as meaning a plain block letter without serifs or hairlines, that we must accept that meaning. Also, it is part of many type names. But we prefer to go further, and reserve the term *gothic* for the traditional forms, and *sans serif* for the modified forms originating in Germany with the Bauhaus movement of the 1920s. Our preferred general term is *serifless.*

In this book, gothics having distinctive family names are listed alphabetically throughout—see *Alternate Gothic, Franklin Gothic, Modern Gothic, News Gothic,* etc. Those with merely descriptive names are included in this section under the following headings: Numbered Gothics, Condensed Gothics, Inclined or Italic Gothics, and Miscellaneous Gothics.

The term "Lining," added to many names when they were realigned to new standards around the turn of the century, has generally been ignored in this book, as it was later dropped in nearly all cases. Nineteenth-century gothics are not included except for a few representative ones or those that have been substantially used subsequently. "Title" gothics—all-cap versions usually occupying almost the entire body—are shown as secondary listings to the cap-and-lowercase versions where both exist.

Offset Gothics were cut in reverse for a process of transferring proofs of type to lithographic stones, or more recently to electronic parts. Also see *Record Gothic Offset.*

* * *

Numbered Gothics. Most such faces, except as cross-referenced below, are nineteenth-century designs; a few are shown because they were copied by Monotype or Linotype or otherwise survived for extensive use in this century. For ATF faces numbered in the 500s, the initial 5 generally indicates that the face has been adjusted to standard alignment from an older face with the same number otherwise; that is, *Gothic No. 544* was formerly *Gothic No. 44* to old standards.

Gothic No. 6, an 1895 Inland face, is important only because Monotype adapted it as a practical and widely used utility face before the advent of sans serifs. *Gothic No. 13* is included under Condensed Gothics.

Gothic No. 1 and *3*—see *Franklin Gothic* (also see below); *Gothic No. 14*—see *Chamfer Gothic; Gothic No. 16*—see *Franklin Gothic; Gothic Nos. 17 to 20*— see *Trade Gothic; Gothic No. 25, 38,* and *520 to 526*—see *Gothic No. 545; Gothic Nos. 29 to 35*—see *Copperplate Gothic; Gothic,* Mono 481, 496, 508—see *Helvetica; Gothic Nos. 39 to 45*—see *Metrolite.*

Gothic No. 6, Inland-ATF 207 (5-24pt); Inland Gothic, Mono 149 (5½-24pt); also Title Gothic No. 7, ATF (6s-20pt)
Gothic No. 16, Lino (4-36pt, see Franklin Gothic)
Gothic No. 25 and No. 26, Lino (6s-12pt, see Gothic No. 545)
Gothic No. 18 (old), Lino (12-24pt, see News Gothic Condensed)

(Gothic continues)

GOTHIC NO. 544, ATF 24-pt.

ABCDEFGHIJKLMNOPQRSTUVWXYZ&
abcdefghijklmnopqrstuvwxyz 1234567890$

GOTHIC NO. 545, Mono 66 24-pt.

ABCDEFGHIJKLMNOPQRSTUVWXYZ&.,-:;'!?
abcdefghijklmnopqrstuvwxyz $1234567890

GOTHIC NO. 578, ATF 24-pt.

Keystone

ABCDEFGHIJKLMNOPQRSTUVWXYZ& G
abcdefghijklmnopqrstuvwxyz 1234567890$

GOTHIC NO. 1, Laclede 24-pt.

HARVESTER USING MACHINES
County Fair Encouraging Winners

GOTHIC NO. 3, Laclede 24-pt.

DESIRES BOUNTIFUL SEASON
Expecting Most Generous Yields

GOTHIC NO. 3, Mono 249 12-pt.

ABCDEFGHIJKLMNOPQRSTUVWXYZ&
abcdefghijklmnopqrstuvwxyz fffiffififlffl $1234567890 .,-:;'!?

INLAND GOTHIC NO. 10, ATF 24-pt.

ABCDEFGHIJKLMNOPQRSTUVWXYZ&
abcdefghijklmnopqrstuvwxyz 1234567890$

NEW GOTHIC CONDENSED, Mono 543 (48-pt. at 50%)

ABCDEFGHIJKLMNOPQRSTUVWXYZ& abcdefghijklmnopqrstuvwxyz $1234567890

EXTRA CONDENSED TITLE GOTHIC NO. 12, ATF 24-pt. & EXTRA CONDENSED GOTHIC, 30-pt.

ABCDEFGHIJKLMNOPQRSTUVWXYZ 1234567890& .,-:;'!?
Guests Remained Quiet During Stay

GOTHIC NO. 13, Lino 18-pt.

ABCDEFGHIJKLMNOPQRSTUVWXYZ& ACEFGKMNSWY
abcdefghijklmnopqrstuvwxyz 1234567890($,.:;'-'?!)

156

Gothic Nos. 544 and *545* are typical plain nineteenth-century gothics, both shown by MacKellar in 1889 or earlier, but both have been copied extensively by other sources, and shown by ATF as late as 1979. Hansen's *New York Gothic* was equivalent to *Gothic No. 545.* There was also a comparable but lighter *Gothic No. 543,* which was not as long lasting. *Combination Gothic* and *Interchangeable Gothic* were similar to *Gothic No. 545,* but as title versions, with several sizes of caps on each of several bodies. Also see *Octic Gothic.*

Gothic No. 578 was shown as *Gothic No. 8* by Inland in 1898 as "the latest candidate for the printer's favor; a popular old face entirely recut." It was shown until 1941. It is a bold weight, and is quite similar to *Standard Bold* which as an import from Germany was very popular in this country in the 1950s. It is also similar to *Comstock,* but without the added outline. Keystone called it *Standard Gothic,* although it is not identical to the German face. As a nineteenth-century gothic, the cap *G* had no crossbar. *Paragon Gothic* is the same design, without lowercase, cast as a title face.

The small Laclede Type Foundry in St. Louis originated a pair of attractive gothics which apparently were scrapped when the foundry was taken over by BB&S. *Gothic No. 1* was similar to *Franklin Gothic,* and *Gothic No. 3* was similar to *Square Gothic,* but both had many small differences, the most noticeable being round dots on *i, j,* and punctuation marks. Another *Gothic No. 3* is made by Monotype, Linotype, and Intertype, probably from a nineteenth-century foundry source. It is similar to *Gothic No. 544.* Some other numbered gothics appear under Numbered Faces.

* * *

Condensed Gothics. Inland Type Foundry introduced its *Gothic Condensed No. 10* in 1904 as "an entirely new face, from which has been eliminated all of the inconsistencies and objectionable features so noticeable in similar series." Its companion *Gothic Condensed Title No. 11,* introduced in 1905, was shown by ATF as late as 1969; Monotype's *New Gothic Condensed* and *Gothic Condensed Title* are very similar; all are still handsome faces. Another Inland face of about the same age, *Extra Condensed Gothic No. 1,* survived almost as long in its all-cap version of *Extra Condensed Title Gothic No. 12.* BB&S had a very similar face, *Gothic Extra Condensed No. 6* and *Title No. 6.*

Gothic No. 13 is a traditional heavy condensed gothic in small sizes; from 24-point up it is basically the same as *Modern Gothic Condensed;* Unique Caps were added in 1937. *Gothic Condensed No. 523* was Keystone's *Universal Gothic,* introduced about 1906. *Gothic No. 47* of BB&S is somewhat similar. *Gothic Condensed No. 529* is a nineteenth-century design, and is similar to the later and more refined *Alternate Gothic,* but it remained in the ATF specimen books at least to 1979; most sources had comparable faces. Also see *Vertical Gothic.*

(Gothic continues)

Gothic No. 544, ATF 263 (6-60pt); Medium Gothic, Mono 129 (12-36pt)
Gothic No. 545, ATF 264 (6-72pt); Gothic No. 3, BB&S-ATF 1667 (6-72pt); Gothic [No. 545], Mono 66 (5-36pt) or 466 (6pt); Gothic No. 38, Lino (10-24pt); Eatonian Gothic, Inter (10-24pt); New York Gothic, Hansen (6-72pt); also Gothic No. 520 to 526 (title), ATF 261 (6s-60pt); Combination Gothic, ATF (6s-24pt); Gothic No. 525 (title), Mono 56; Lining Gothic (title), Mono 349 (6s-12L); Gothic No. 25 (title), Lino (6s-12pt)
Gothic No. 578, ATF 208 (5-72pt); Standard Gothic, Keystone (5-72pt); also Title Gothic No. 9, ATF (6s-72pt); Paragon Gothic (title), Keystone (6s-60pt)
Gothic No. 1, Laclede (6-72pt)
Gothic No. 3, Laclede (6-72pt)
Gothic No. 3, Mono 249 (6-12pt); Lino = Inter (6-12pt)
Gothic Condensed No. 10, Inland-ATF 200 (5-84pt); New Gothic Condensed, Mono 543 (48-72pt); also Gothic Condensed Title No. 11, Inland-ATF 123 (6s-72pt); Gothic Condensed Title, Mono 43 (42-72pt); APL (72,120pt)
Inland Extra Condensed Gothic No. 1, Inland-ATF 206 (12-84pt); Gothic Extra Condensed No. 6, BB&S-ATF 1654 (6-72pt); also Extra Condensed Title Gothic No. 12, Inland-ATF 156 (10-72pt); Gothic Extra Condensed Title No. 6, BB&S-ATF 1655 (6-60pt); Compressed Gothic, Keystone-ATF 1830 (6-72pt); Narrow Gothic (title), Keystone (6-60pt); Headline Gothic (title), Ludlow 6-H (30-60pt)
Gothic No. 13, Lino = Inter (7-60pt); APL (8-144pt)
Gothic Condensed No. 523, ATF 266 (6-72pt); Gothic No. 47, BB&S; Universal Gothic, Keystone (6-72pt); also Medium Title Gothic, Keystone
Gothic Condensed No. 529, ATF 268 (6-72pt); Condensed Gothic, Mono 515 (18pt); Gothic Condensed No. 2, Lino = Inter (6-36pt); APL (6-14pt); Inland Condensed Gothic No. 1, ATF 198 (6-72pt); Gothic Condensed No. 400, Hansen (6-72pt); also Gothic Condensed No. 521 (title), ATF 265 (6-72pt); Gothic Condensed Title No. 117, BB&S-ATF 1651 (5-120pt); Gothic Condensed No. 4, Hansen (6-48pt); Gothic Condensed No. 5 (title), Hansen (6-48pt)

GOTHIC CONDENSED NO. 523, ATF 24-pt. (Rick von Holdt)

ABCDEFGHIJKLMNOPQRSTUVW abcdefghijklmnopqrstuvw 123456

GOTHIC CONDENSED NO. 529, ATF 24-pt.

ABCDEFGHIJKLMNOPQRSTUVWXYZ& abcdefghijklmnopqrstuvwxyz $1234567890 .,-:;'!?

GOTHIC CAPS CONDENSED, Mono 48 12-pt.

ABCDEFGHIJKLMNOPQRSTUVWXYZ $1234567890

GOTHIC CONDENSED, Mono 49 12-pt.

ABCDEFGHIJKLMNOPQRSTUVWXYZ& abcdefghijklmnopqrstuvwxyz fiflffffiffl 1234567890 $?!.,:;'-

MEDIUM CONDENSED GOTHIC, Ludlow 24-pt. (Herb Harnish)

ABCDEFGHIJKLMNOPQRSTUVWXYZ& ACEFGKLMNRSTUWYXvwxy
abcdefghijklmnopqrstuvwxyz 1234567890$.,-:;'!?—

GOTHIC EXTRA CONDENSED, Ludlow 24-pt.

ABCDEFGHIJKLMNOPQRSTUVWXYZ abcdefghijklmnopqrstuvwxyz $1234567890
.:.,:-''!?()[]–·&%AKMNRVWXYkvwxy4

GOTHIC ITALIC NO. 512, ATF 24-pt.

ABCDEFGHIJKLMNOPQRSTUVWXYZ&.,-:;'!?
abcdefghijklmnopqrstu 1234567890$

GOTHIC ITALIC LIGHT (DEGREE GOTHIC NO. 2), BB&S 12-pt.

ABCDEFGHIJKLMNOPQRSTUVWXYZ& abcdefghijklmnopqrstuvwxyz $1234567890 .,-:;'!?

GOTHIC INCLINED, Mono 24-pt.

ABCDEFGHIJKLMNOPQRSTUVWXYZ&
$1234567890 .,-:;'!?

GOTHIC INCLINED LIGHT, BB&S 24- & 18-pt.

HUNDREDS SHOE FINISHED

LINING GOTHIC, Mono 106 12-pt.

ABCDEFGHIJKLMNOPQRSTUVWXYZ&
$1234567890.,:;-''!?
abcdefghijklmnopqrstuvwxyz

LINING GOTHIC, Mono 112 10-pt.

ABCDEFGHIJKLMNOPQRSTUVWXYZ&ÆŒ
ABCDEFGHIJKLMNOPQRSTUVWXYZ&ÆŒ
$1234567890 .,-'':;!? $1234567890 .,-'':;!?

GOTHIC NOVELTY, BB&S 10-pt. (Dave Norton)

ABCDEFGHIJKLMNOPQRSTUVWXYZ&abcdefghijklmnopqrstuvwxyz$1234567890£.,-:;'!?

GOTHIC NOVELTY CONDENSED, BB&S 12-pt. (Dave Norton)

ABCDEFGHIJKLMNOPQRSTUVWXYZ& abcdefghijklmnopqrstuvwxyz $1234567890 .,-;'!?

GOTHIC OUTLINE TITLE NO. 61, BB&S 24-pt.

ABCDEFGHIJKLMNOPQRSTUVWXYZ.,-:;'!?&$1234567890

158

Monotype has several utility gothics, including *Gothic Caps Condensed, No. 48,* designed to occupy roman small cap positions in the standard arrangement; and *Gothic Condensed, No. 49,* a medium weight conventional sort of gothic. A Monotype specimen sheet, issued in 1917, says of *Condensed Gothic, No. 515,* "This was formerly our 18-point No. 51. We found that it did not match the balance of the series, so we have given it a new number." See *Gothic Condensed No. 529.*

Gothic No. 1 Condensed—see *Franklin Gothic Extra Condensed. Gothic Condensed No. 2*—see *Gothic Condensed No. 529,* also *Alternate Gothic No. 3. Gothic Condensed No. 3*—see *Headline Gothic,* Ludlow. *Gothic Condensed No. 521*—also see *Vertical Gothic. Gothic Condensed Outline*—see *Contour No. 6. Condensed Gothic Outline*—see under *Alternate Gothic. Gothic Bold Condensed Title*—see *Railroad Gothic. Medium Gothic No. 7*—see *Mid-Gothic,* also *Boston Gothic.*

Medium Condensed Gothic, Ludlow, is a refinement of typical nineteenth-century, straight-sided gothics. It has been popular in newspaper work. Deluxe Variants are an additional feature of about 1939, when similar characters were designed for a number of gothics. Compare *Mid-Gothic; Modern Gothic Condensed.*

Ludlow also has two faces named *Gothic Extra Condensed,* 6-EC. The newer one, in 24- to 84-point sizes, is very similar to *Aurora Condensed* (q.v. under Imports in Appendix) from Germany, also known as *Inserat Grotesk* or *Enge Wotan,* with extremely short ascenders and descenders and lengthened white areas in the angular letters. The older Ludlow face, made only in 144-point, is similar to *Extra Condensed Title Gothic No. 12,* and has no lowercase. In this size, letters are cast individually on Ludlow, the long way of the slug, and used primarily for newspaper headlines.

* * *

Inclined or Italic Gothics. *Gothic Italic No. 512,* ATF, was advertised by Marder, Luse in 1893 or earlier as *Gothic Italic No. 3;* BB&S had matching *Gothic Italic,* formerly *Degree Gothic No. 1.* The BB&S *Gothic Italic Light* was formerly *Degree Gothic No. 2.* Several foundries had comparable faces; Inland called its comparable *Gothic Italic* "original."

Gothic Inclined, BB&S, was shown at least as early as 1889 as *Inclined Lining Gothic,* later known as *Inclined Gothic No. 120.* Inland advertised the same face as *Title Slope Gothic,* "improved." ATF and Monotype had a similar *Inclined Gothic,* and other founders had comparable faces. *Gothic Inclined Light* of BB&S was formerly *Slope Gothic No. 50* from 1879. *Bold Inclined Gothic*—see *Modern Gothic Italic.* Also see *Doric Italic, Draftsman Gothic, Boston Gothic.*

* * *

Miscellaneous Gothics. Monotype has several faces designated simply "*Lining Gothic.*" Those not cross-referenced were undoubtedly copied or adapted from undetermined foundry faces. *Lining Gothic No. 106* is very light, similar to *Lightline Gothic* but less refined; it has caps and lowercase. *No. 112* is a little heavier, with caps and small caps only in each size. *No. 176*—see *Mid-Gothic. No. 66* and *349*—see *Gothic No. 545. No. 350* is similar to No. 112 but has four sizes of caps in each of 6- and 12-point, in the manner of *Copperplate Gothic.*

Gothic Modern—see *Modern Gothic* series. BB&S's *Gothic Novelty Title* was formerly *Tasso,* 1890 or earlier. Other founders had the same design as *Gothic,* ATF; *Gotham,* Farmer Little; *Gothic No. 205,* Bruce; *Ancient Gothic,* Dickinson. *Gothic Novelty,* the same face with lowercase, was formerly *Tasso No. 2. Gothic Novelty Condensed* was formerly *Archer,* about the same age but unlike the other faces in this group. Hansen's *Extended Lining Gothic* was a copy of a *Philadelphia Lining Gothic. Gothic Shade* became *Jim Crow; Gothic Double Shade* became *Marble Heart* (q.v.).

Gothic Outline Title No. 61, formerly *Outline Gothic No. 61,* dates to 1890 or earlier, but was still shown by ATF in 1979. Compare *Contour Nos. 1* and *6; Franklin Gothic Condensed Outline, Whedons Gothic Outline.*

Gothic Caps Condensed, Mono 48 (5-12pt)
Gothic Condensed, Mono 49 (5-12pt)
Medium Condensed Gothic, Ludlow 6-B (6-72pt)
Gothic Extra Condensed, Ludlow 6-EC (24-84,144pt)
Gothic Italic No. 512, ATF 269 (8-24pt); Gothic Italic or Degree Gothic No. 1, BB&S-ATF 1600 or 1658 (6-24pt); Gothic Italic, Inland (6-24pt); Gothic Italic No. 4, Lino (6,8pt); also Title Gothic Italic No. 2, Inland
Gothic Italic No. 524, ATF (5-12pt); Gothic Italic Light or Degree Gothic No. 2, BB&S-ATF 1659 (5-12pt)
Inclined Gothic, ATF (6s-24pt); Gothic Inclined, BB&S-ATF 1656 (6s-24pt); Mono 2541 (6s-30pt); Keystone (6s-24pt); Hansen (6s-24pt)
Gothic Inclined Light, BB&S-ATF 1657 (6-24pt)
Lining Gothic [Light], Mono 106 (6-12pt)
Lining Gothic, Mono 112 (6-12pt)
Lining Gothic, Mono 350 (6s-12L)
Gothic Novelty, BB&S-ATF 1671 (8-14pt); also Gothic Novelty Title, BB&S-ATF 1673 (6-24pt)
Gothic Novelty Condensed, BB&S-ATF 1672 (12-60pt)
Gothic Outline Title No. 61, BB&S-ATF 1676 (12-72pt)

159

ABCDEFGHIJKLMNOPQRSTUVWXYZ& ¶ ❦ ct
abcdefghijklmnopqrstuvwxyz $1234567890 .,-:;'!? fiflffffffifl
ΓΔΘΛΞΠΣΥΦΨΩ

ABCDEFGGHIJJKLMNOPQRSTTUVWXYYZ .,-:;'!?&Qu
abcdefghijklmnopqrstuvwxyz 1234567890$1234567890 fiflffffffiffl ct

Mono figures

ABCDEFGHIJKLMNOPQRSTUVWXYZ
abcdefghijklmnopqrstuvwxyzfifffifflffifl1234567890&$.,-'";;!? ~
AJKNNRQUQuThe km n r vwx quct fs st

ABCDEFGHIJKLMNOPQRSTUV 1234567890&$.,-';;!?

ABCDEFGHIJKLMNOPQRSTUVWXYZ
abcdefghijklmnopqrstuvwxyz.,-:;!?ffffifflffiffl$1234567890

ABCDEFGHIJKLMNOPQRSTUVWXYZ
abcdefghijklmnopqrstuvwxyzffffifflffiffl ct&1234567890$.,-:;!?'

ABCDEFGHIJKLMNOPQRSTUVWXYZ& .,-:;'!?Qfff
abcdefghijklmnopqrstuvwxyz fiflffffffifl $1234567890

ABCDEFGGHIJKLMNOPQRSTUVWXYZ& .,-:;''!?
abcdefghijklmnopqrstuvwxyz 1234567890$ fiflffffffifl ct
ABCDEFGHIJKLMNOPQRST
UVWYZa e km n t v w

GOUDY is a famous and prolific type designer, a family of types, and a group of typefaces with little or no relationship. Frederic W. Goudy, the renowned designer, was responsible for most but not all of the types bearing his name, as well as a great many others.

The next entry will consider the family of types, which is perhaps best known; other faces with the Goudy name follow alphabetically. See list of designers in Appendix for other faces designed by him.

GOUDY OLDSTYLE was Goudy's 25th design, but his first for ATF, drawn in 1915. He based it on a few letters of classic form which he had copied from a portrait painting, although later he was never able to identify the exact source. He says, "The face, as finally produced, was, I felt, almost as great an innovation in type as my *Kennerley*. . . . I am almost satisfied that the design is a good one, marred only by the short descenders which I allowed the American Type Founders to inveigle me into giving *p, q, g, j,* and *y*—though only under protest." Monotype offers alternate long descenders for small sizes of its 1930 adaptation of this face, but these were probably not designed by Goudy himself. The face is distinguished by its slightly concave serifs, longer on one side than the other, and its diamond-shaped dots on *i, j,* and punctuation marks. ATF also provides a set of Greek caps, perhaps not designed by Goudy. (Those in the specimen here are from another source than the regular font, and are proofed more heavily.)

Goudy Oldstyle Italic, issued in 1918, was a problem for the designer, who had previously attempted only two italic designs. In studying classic faces, he found that some of the best italics had little or no slope, but were distinguished in other qualities. A slight inclination became standard in most of Goudy's italics. He says, "Taking the Aldine italic [developed by Aldus Manutius in 1500 from Italian cursive handwriting] as a starting point for my new font I began my work, and succeeded in producing an original letter which, I believe, constituted the first distinctive italic in modern times."

Goudy Cursive was designed by Goudy in 1916, on the suggestion that his *Goudy Italic* might have more utility if he added some characters to give it a still greater appearance of freedom and informality and something of the quality of hand lettering.

Goudy Title was made by ATF by enlarging Goudy's small capitals to a height almost that of the type body, thereby increasing the weight of the letters. Goudy says, "To permit a larger face without kern, the 'Q' was redesigned at the foundry to a form which irritates me mightily." ATF credits this adaptation to Morris Benton, in 1918.

Goudy Bold and its italic were designed by Benton in 1916 and 1919 respectively, as heavier companions to *Goudy Oldstyle.* They are probably the most popular and widely used members of the family. When these bold faces were put on Monotype in 1928, Sol Hess added a series of cursive capitals and terminals to the italic, comparable to *Goudy Cursive.* About 1940, *Goudy*

(Goudy continues)

Goudy Oldstyle, ATF 178 (6-72pt); Mono 394 (6-36pt); Goudy, Inter (6-14pt); No. 11 Light, Ludlow 11-L (6-48pt)

Goudy Italic, ATF 179 (6-72pt); Goudy Old Style Italic, Mono 3941 (6-36pt); Goudy Italic, Inter (6-14pt); No. 11 Light Italic, Ludlow 11-LI (6-48pt)

Goudy Cursive, ATF 477 (6-72pt); Mono 324 (14-36pt)

Goudy Title, ATF 180 (6s-48pt)

Goudy Catalogue, ATF 467 (6-72pt)

Goudy Catalogue Italic, ATF 470 (6-72pt)

Goudy Bold, ATF 446 (6-120pt); Mono 294 (6-72pt); Inter (6-36pt); No. 11 Bold, Ludlow 11-B (6-72pt)

Goudy Bold Italic, ATF 464 (6-72pt); Mono 2941 (6-72pt); Inter (6-36pt); No. 11 Bold Italic, Ludlow 11-BI (6-72pt)

Goudy Extrabold, ATF 494 (6-120pt)

Goudy Extrabold Italic, ATF 496 (6-72pt)

GOUDY EXTRABOLD, ATF 24-pt.

ABCDEFGHIJKLMNOPQRSTUVWXYZ&.,-:;'!?'
abcdefghijklmnopqrstuvwxyzfffifffiflffl $1234567890

GOUDY EXTRABOLD ITALIC, ATF 24-pt.

ABCDEFGGHIJKLMNOPQRSTUVWXYZ&'':;!?
abcdefghijklmnopqrstuvwxyz 1234567890$ff fi fl ffi ffl

GOUDY HANDTOOLED, 24-pt.

ABCDEFGHIJKLMNOPQRSTUVWXYZ& .,-:;'!?
abcdefghijklmnopqrstuvwxyz fi fl ff ffi ffl $1234567890

GOUDY HANDTOOLED ITALIC, 24-pt. (part reduced)

ABCDEFGHIJKLMNOPQRSTUVWXYZ& .,-:;'!?
abcdefghijklmnopqrstuvwxyz $1234567890 fifl ff ffiffl
A B C D E F G H I J K L M N O P Q R
S T U V W X Y Z a e k m n t v w

GOUDY ANTIQUE, Goudy 12-pt.

ABCDEFGHIJKLMNOPQURSTVWXYZ&
abcdefghijklmnopqrstuvwxyzstctfifflflffffi.,';;?! 1 2 3 4 5 6 7 8 9 o

GOUDY BIBLE, Mono 18-pt. (Cliff Helbert)

ABCDEFGHIJKLMNOPQRSTUVWXYZ
abcdefghijklmnopqrstuvwxyzfffiflffiffl æ 1234567890.,-:;!?' ○

GOUDY HEAVYFACE, Mono 24-pt. (Rich Hopkins)

ABCDEFGHIJKLMNOPQRSTUVWXYZ&Co.©Qu
abcdefghijklmnopqrstuvwxyz ff fi fl ffi ffl ch ct st
$1234567890 .,-:;'!? 1234567890 ~~~~&*¶[❖-

GOUDY HEAVYFACE ITALIC, Mono 24-pt. (Rich Hopkins)

ABCCDEFGHIJKLMMNOPPQRSTUVWXY
abcdefgghijklmnopqrstuvwxyz Z&
1234567890 .,-:;'!? & The and the of

GOUDY HEAVYFACE CONDENSED, Mono 24-pt.

ABCDEFGHIJKLMNOPQRSTUVWXYZ&
abcdefghijklmnopqrstuvwxyz $1234567890 .,-:;'!?

GOUDY HEAVYFACE OPEN, Mono (36-pt. at 67%)

GOOD NEWS A Heavyface open $1234

162

Bold was modified by ATF to eliminate its few kerns; *Q, f,* and *ff*—as shown at the right of the specimen—were redesigned, while j was repositioned on the body. These are similar to the characters required by the matrices of Intertype and Ludlow.

Goudy Catalogue and its italic were added by Benton in 1919 and 1921 as a medium weight of the same design. They are 15 percent heavier than the Oldstyle, just about the same as *Goudy Title.* In 1922, *Goudy Handtooled* and its italic were designed. This pair of faces, like *Goudy Bold* and *Italic* except for a white line in the heavy strokes, has been credited to Charles H. Becker by some authorities, and to Morris Benton and Wadsworth A. Parker by others. Again, Sol Hess added a set of cursive capitals and terminals to the Monotype version. In 1927 Benton further expanded the family with the addition of *Goudy Extrabold* and *Italic.*

Ludlow simply calls its copies of *Goudy Oldstyle* and *Goudy Bold* its *Number 11* series, cut in 1924.

Goudy Handtooled, ATF 475 (10-120pt); Mono 383 (10-72pt)
Goudy Handtooled Italic, ATF 476 (10-72pt); Mono 3831 (10-72pt)

GOUDY ANTIQUE was designed by Goudy in 1919, but except for a few characters it was not cut until 1930, when three sizes were completed. Goudy says, "My intention was to design a letter which would displace the monotonous *Bookman;* of the same color or weight, the individual letters of my *Antique* show a greater variety in their forms." Also see *Goudy Lanston.*

Goudy Antique, Goudy (12-18pt) private

GOUDY BIBLE is a modification of *Goudy Newstyle* (q.v.), adapted by Bruce Rogers with the assistance of Sol Hess for use in the Lectern Bible Rogers designed for World Publishing Company in 1948.

Goudy Bible, Mono 301 (18pt)

GOUDY FRANCISCAN—see *Franciscan.*
GOUDY FRIAR—see *Friar.*
GOUDY GIMBEL—see *Goudy Light Old Style.*

GOUDY HEAVYFACE and *Italic* were designed by Goudy in 1925 in response to a strong request by Monotype for a distinctive face on the order of the very popular foundry *Cooper Black.* Such faces had little appeal for Goudy, and he always felt that Monotype was disappointed in his efforts, but the result is more informal than other similar types, and has had considerable popularity. Note the extra set of figures and the unusual number of tied characters and ornaments in the font.

Goudy Heavyface Open is a variation produced by Monotype in 1926, probably designed by Sol Hess, who designed *Goudy Heavyface Condensed* in 1927.

Compare *Cooper Black, Ludlow Black, Pabst Extra Bold.*

Goudy Heavyface, Mono 380 (12-72pt)
Goudy Heavyface Italic, Mono 3801 (14-72pt)
Goudy Heavyface Condensed, Mono 382 (12-72pt)
Goudy Heavyface Open, Mono 391 (36pt)

GOUDY LANSTON, Mono 24-pt. (Rich Hopkins)

ABCDEFGHIJKLMNOPQRSTUVWXYZ& .,´;:!?
abcdefghijklmnopqrstuvwxyz $1234567890 æœct fiflffffffiffl

FOSTER/RATDOLT, BB&S 24-pt. (Rick von Holdt)

ABCDEFGHIJKLMNOPQRSTUVWXYZ
abcdefghijklmnopqrstuvwxyz 1234567890$&

FOSTER/RATDOLT ITALIC, BB&S 24-pt. (Rick von Holdt)

ABCDEFGHIJKLMNOPQRSTUVWXYZ
abcdefghijklmnopqrstuvwxyz 1234567890$

GOUDY LIGHT OLD STYLE, Mono 38E 24-pt.

ABCDEFGHIJKLMNOPQRSTUVWXYZ&.,-:;'!?
abcdefghijklmnopqrstuvwxyz $12345678901234567890

GOUDY LIGHT OLD STYLE ITALIC, Mono 24-pt.

ABCDEFGHIJKLMNOPQRSTUVWXYZ&.,-:;'!?
abcdefghijklmnopqrstuvwxyz $1234567890 1234567890

Decorative Initials

 GREAT VARIETY of decorative initials was once available from the typefounders, and a smaller selection from Monotype. Even Linotype, at one time, offered an assortment of electrotyped initials to complement some of its leading type families. The styles are too numerous for this book, except for a few most closely related to regular typefaces.

The *Cloister Initial* shown here was one of the most popular styles. It was designed by Frederic W. Goudy, and cast by ATF in 36- to 144-point sizes. Certain other styles were made as small as 10-point.

Most sets contained twenty-six characters, but some omitted the X and Z. Some sets were made for two-color work, or with color blanks to print under the initial.

GOUDY LANSTON is the ultimate and best-known name for a typeface with a confusing set of earlier names. When Frederic Goudy designed it in 1912 for a private book project, he called it *Goudy Old Style,* and cut it in 16-point only. When the book project fell through, he offered the type for sale through his own Village Letter Foundery. Three years later, when he drew a new face for ATF, that company requested permission to use the name for this new face, so Goudy renamed his older face *Goudy Antique.* A dozen years later, Lanston Monotype arranged to put this face on their machine, but asked permission to call it *Goudy Lanston,* in honor of Tolbert Lanston, inventor of the machine.

In announcing this typeface in 1912, Goudy said, "It is a sturdy letter free from affectation or caprice. . . . Mr. Goudy believes that in this new letter he has rediscovered a principle in spacing individual letters used by letter founders before the 16th century, but not since, a principle to which the harmonious quality of a page of Jenson is largely due. Each letter stands on solid serifs of unusual shape which are so planned as to make each letter form conterminous with the type body, while permitting sufficient white space to set each letter off from its neighbor without destroying the unity of the word formed by its separate characters, thus permitting close spacing and avoiding looseness of composition."

Caslon and Company of London acquired English rights to the face, but, in Goudy's words, "ruined the face (in my estimation) by putting it on standard line, and shortening the descenders to fit; also adding insult to injury by calling it 'Ratdolt.' It does not resemble Ratdolt's famous letter in any particular. The Caslons cut matrices and sent them to this country—an act contrary to customary ethics, since they owned English rights only—giving Hart, Schaffner & Marx the 'exclusive' right to the face. To this I protested, but took no other action. . . ."

In the widespread search for specimens for this book, a face which is surely this "exclusive" casting turned up in the cases of an Iowa private press operator, Rick von Holdt. He had acquired the type from a San Francisco typographer who knew nothing of its background. The typographer had shown it in his specimen book as *Foster,* although the cases were labeled *Moore.* It has the pin-mark of BB&S, but appears to match specimens of *Ratdolt* as shown by Stephenson Blake, successors to Caslon and Company. It has the shortened descenders which Goudy disliked, and a number of other little departures from his design. But surprisingly there is also a matching italic, likewise pinmarked BB&S. A line in a 1948 magazine refers to such a face—undoubtedly this one—as having been designed by Richard N. McArthur, advertising manager of that foundry at the time of that design.

GOUDY LIGHT OLD STYLE was designed by Goudy in 1908 for the original *Life* magazine, which was set by Monotype. At the time Goudy knew nothing of the mechanical restrictions of the Monotype, so many adjustments had to be made to his design to adapt it to that system. This seems to have delayed production of the face until long after the magazine wanted it. But just as it was released a big department store was opened in New York by Gimbel Brothers, and for a long time the face was used more or less exclusively for their advertising. In fact, it was often called *Goudy Gimbel.* Now it is sometimes called *Goudy Old Style,* which is incorrect, or *Thirty-Eight-E,* for the Monotype series number. Actually, "E" is the Monotype designation for oldstyle romans in keyboard sizes, while "G" designates oldstyle italics. So *Thirty-Eight-E* is a misnomer for display sizes, while *Thirty-Eight-E Italic* is more so. Although it is a delicate face with a certain amount of attractiveness, larger sizes are loosely fitted, and it has little of the distinction of later Goudy designs. Monotype includes *Goudy Cursive* swash characters with display sizes of this italic, although they are not a good match, having less slant and a different character. See *Hess Bold;* also *Process.*

Goudy Lanston, Mono 279 (14-36pt); Goudy Oldstyle or Goudy Antique, Goudy (16pt); also Ratdolt/Foster/Moore and Italic, BB&S (12-72pt) private

Goudy Light Old Style, Mono 38 (6-36pt) Goudy Light Old Style Italic, Mono 381 (6-36pt)

GOUDY MODERN, Mono 24-pt. (Harold Berliner, Rich Hopkins)

ABCDEFGHIJKLMNOPQRSTUVWXYZ&
abcdefghijklmnopqrstuvwxyz 1234567890$.,·':;!? fffiflffiffl

GOUDY MODERN ITALIC, Mono 24-pt. (Harold Berliner, Rich Hopkins)

ABCDEFGHIJKLMNOPQRSTUVW&
abcdefghijklmnopqrstuvwxyz $1234567890·,;:? fffiflffiffl ꟼ ƥ r

GOUDY OPEN, Mono 24-pt. (see text)

ABCDEFGHIJKLMNOPQRSTUVWXYZ& 1234567890
abcdefghijklmnopqrstuvwxyz $?!.,:;'- fiflffffiffl J Ω

60-pt. reduced

GOUDY OPEN ITALIC, Mono 24-pt.

ABCDEFGHIJKLMNOPQRSTUVWXYZ& 1234567890$
abcdefghijklmnopqrstuvwxyz fffiffiflffl .,-:;'!? ꟼ ƥ r

GOUDY NEWSTYLE, Goudy 18-pt.

ABCDEFGHIJKLMNOPQRSTUVWXYZ& 1234567890$ ⸿
abcdefghijklmnopqrstuvwxyz fi ffi ff fl ffl Qu .,-:;!?'' ᴀᴀʙʙᴅᴇᴇɢɪɪʟɴʀᴛ

GOUDY ORNATE, Mono 24-pt.

ABCDEFGHIJKLMNOPQRSTUVWXYZ&.,·

GOUDY REMINGTON ITALIC TYPEWRITER, Mono 10-pt.

ABCDEFGHIJKLMNOPQRSTUVWXYZ& abcdefghijklmnopqrstuvwxyz
.,-:; ?()'" $1234567890 ¼½¾ %@/¢#_

166

GOUDY MEDIAEVAL—see *Mediaeval.*

GOUDY MODERN and **GOUDY OPEN**. The first of these types was *Goudy Open,* which Goudy says was suggested by the caption of a French engraving. The letter forms have a modern feeling, something the designer had not attempted before, but without the formal rigidity of modern types such as Bodoni. Serifs are slightly bracketed and curves are more generous, suggestive of more traditional forms.

After the Open roman was produced, Goudy experimented with filling in the white line; the effect pleased him, so he ordered the cutting of a solid face from the same patterns. The result is *Goudy Modern.* Both of these faces were designed in 1918, matrices were cut by Robert Wiebking, and type was cast by Goudy's Village Letter Foundery. Both faces were copied by Monotype in 1924.

Goudy Modern Italic was designed the following year to accompany the roman face; in this case the solid face was made first. *Goudy Open Italic* was also made in 1919; it is identical to the *Modern Italic* except for the white line. In these italics, cap *C* and *S* have the lowercase form, with ball shapes instead of serifs.

In the specimens, only the *Modern Italic* is not quite complete. Note the redesigned *J* and *Q* of 60-point *Goudy Open;* the 60- and 72-point sizes have caps only, practically full body size—no lowercase or figures. Also see *Goethe.*

Goudy Modern, Mono 293 (12-36pt); Goudy
Goudy Modern Italic, Mono 2931 (12-36pt); Goudy
Goudy Open, Mono 291 (14-36; 60,72 title); Goudy
Goudy Open Italic, Mono 2911 (14-36pt); Goudy

GOUDY NEWSTYLE was designed by Frederic Goudy in 1921, and cut in 18-point only for his Village Letter Foundery. At the time Goudy was interested in using different forms of letters to represent different pronunciations, and added twenty-some alternate characters to this font. However, he never made any general use of the added characters. The basic font, though, was used for several books, notably by the Grabhorn Press in San Francisco. In 1935 Goudy recut the face without the special characters, and added other sizes. In 1942 he sold the design to Monotype, which later issued it with revisions as *Goudy Bible* (q.v.).

Goudy Newstyle, Goudy (12-18pt)

GOUDY OLDSTYLE—see first Goudy entry.

GOUDY ORNATE or *Ornate Title* is a simple, decorative face designed by Goudy in 1931, in capitals only. He says it has been used by some good presses for title pages where size of type was more important than blackness of line.

Ornate Title or Goudy Ornate, Goudy (18-36pt)

GOUDY REMINGTON ITALIC TYPEWRITER. This is one of the more unusual typefaces designed by Frederic W. Goudy, which he undertook at the request of the president of the Remington company, about 1929. As standard typewriters allot the same horizontal space for each character, letters which are normally wide or narrow must be squeezed or stretched to minimize the appearance of uneven spacing. Goudy did this by giving the letters a slight italic effect, which allowed him to lengthen the serifs of narrow letters and shorten those of wide characters. In his thorough way, Goudy made patterns, cut matrices, and cast enough type to set a trial paragraph.

Monotype later copied the design as produced by Remington.

Goudy Remington Italic Typewriter, Mono 701L (10pt)

GOUDY SANS SERIF LIGHT, Mono 18-pt. (Rich Hopkins)

AABCDEFGHIJKLMNOPQRRSSTTUVWXYZ&
aabcdeefghijklmnopqrstuvwxyz .„-:;'!?& fffif]flfffiffl$ 1234567890

GOUDY SANS SERIF LIGHT ITALIC, Mono 18-pt.

AABCDEFGHIJKLMNNOPQRSTUVWXYZ .,';:!?-
abcdefghijklmnopqrstuvwxyz& fi ff ffi fl ffl $1234567890

GOUDY SANS SERIF BOLD, Mono 18-pt.

AABCDEFGHIJKLMNNOPQRRSSTTUVWXYZ&
aabcdeefghijklmnopqrstuvwxyz $1234567890

GOUDY STOUT, Goudy 24-pt.

ABCDEFGHIJKLMNO
PQRSTUVWXYZ G & .,-

GOUDY TEXT, Mono 24-pt.

ABCDEFGHIJKLMNOPQRSTUVWXYZ&
abcdefghijklmnopqrstuvwxyz fffiffifflffl $1234567890 .,-:;'!? æœ

GOUDY TEXT SHADED, Mono (36-pt. at 67%, partly spaced)

ABCDEFGHIJKLMNOPQRSTUVWXYZ.,-:;'!?&
a b c d e f g h i j k l m n o p q r s t u v w x y z fi fl ff ffi ffl æ œ $1234567890

GOUDY THIRTY, Mono 18-pt. (Cliff Helbert, Wilbur Doctor)

ABCDEFGHIJKLMNOPQRSTUVWXYZBJGPSTTWZ.,-:;"!?&e&
abcdefghijklmnopqrstuvwxyzfffififlffiffifflctststæœasw1234567890

GOUDYTYPE, ATF 14-pt.

A A B B C C D D E F G H H I J K L M M
N N O P P Q R R S T T U V W X Y Y Z &
a b c d e f g h i j k l m n o p q r s t u v w x y z
ff fi fl ffi ffl ct . , - ' ' : ; ! ? $ 1 2 3 4 5 6 7 8 9 0

GOUDY SANS SERIF. In 1922, Frederic W. Goudy experimented with a letter he called *Goudy Gothic,* a less formal rendering of the traditional gothic that was intended to be more pleasing. In 1929 Lanston Monotype induced him to complete the design, which was issued the following year as *Goudy Sans Serif Bold* or *Sans Serif Heavy.* In 1930 a lighter weight was introduced, and the following year a light italic was added. Of the latter, Goudy says, "I have always felt that a sans-serif needed no italic and that to provide one could only be an incongruous addition." Compare *Metro.*

Goudy Sans Serif Light, Mono 384 (14-36pt)
Goudy Sans Light Italic, Mono 3841 (14-36pt)
Goudy Sans Serif Bold or Sans Serif Heavy, Mono 386 (14-36pt)

GOUDY STOUT was designed and cut by Goudy in 1930. He says, "In a moment of typographic weakness I attempted to produce a 'black' letter that would interest those advertisers who like the bizarre in their print. It was not the sort of letter I cared for, but requests from some advertisers who saw the first drawings induced me to cut one size and try out the effect. I never cut any but the one size, although I threatened to cut other sizes if any were demanded. None were!" Compare *Cooper Modern.*

Goudy Stout, Goudy (24pt)

GOUDY TEXT or *Goudy Black* was designed and cut by Goudy in 1928. Its design began with the style of letter in Gutenberg's 42-line Bible, the first printed book, but evolved into a freely rendered Gothic letter (in the old sense), composite in form from various sources. Monotype sought permission to copy the face, and to change the name to *Goudy Text,* as it is now generally known.

Goudy Black, Goudy; Goudy Text, Mono 327 (10-72pt)
Goudy Text Shaded, Mono 427 (36pt)

Goudy's *Lombardic Capitals* (q.v.) are designed and cast for use as alternates with this face. The shaded version was added by Monotype. Compare *Cloister Black, Engravers Old English.*

GOUDY THIRTY. When Monotype suggested that Goudy design a type that that company might bring out after his death, to be called *Goudy Thirty* (from the newspaper term for the end of a story), he thought of a design he had started for a western college. That commission had fallen through, so the design was unfinished. Then, as Goudy relates, "This design struck me as particularly adapted to the purpose. As I worked on it I had determined to make it, as far as I was able, my last word in type design, a type in which I would give my imagination full rein, and a type by which as a designer I would be willing to stand or fall."

Goudy Thirty, Mono 392 (18pt)

Completed in 1942, it was kept under cover by Monotype and not released until 1953—long after his death in 1947. But he designed several types after this one, so it was not the last one from his hands.

Goudy Thirty is a fine recreation of a fifteenth-century round gothic, excellent for period pieces.

GOUDY VILLAGE—see *Village.*

GOUDYTYPE was drawn for ATF in 1916 by Frederic W. Goudy, but not released by ATF until 1928. It is an original, lively design, slightly suggestive of his *Hadriano,* designed a little later. The swash capitals are unusual in a roman face. Although cut and marketed in a full range of sizes, it never achieved great use.

Goudytype, ATF 500 (6-72pt)

ABCDEFGHIJKLMNOPQRSTUVWXYZ&ÆŒ ABCDEFGHIJKLMNOPQRSTUVWXYZ&ÆŒ
ABCDEFGHIJKLMNOPQRSTUVWXYZ&ÆŒ

abcdefghijklmnopqrstuvwxyzæœfifffflffiffl 1234567890 [($.,-":;!?-—)] 1234567890 QU Qu
abcdefghijklmnopqrstuvwxyzæœfifffflffiffl 1234567890 [($.,-":;!?-—)] 1234567890 QU Qu &
A B C D E G J K L M N P R T U V gjpqy

ABCDEFGHIJKLMNOPQRSTUVWXYZ&
abcdefghijklmnopqrstuvwxyz fffiffifflffl $1234567890 1234567890 .,-:;'!?()

ABCDEFGHIJKLMNOPQRSTUVWXYZ&
abcdefghijklmnopqrstuvwxyz.,-;:!?' $1234567890

ABCDEFGHIJKLMNOPQRSTUVWX *abcdefghijklmnopqrstuvwxyz* *$1234567890*

ABCDEFGHIJKLMNOPQRSTUVWXYZ&
abcdefghijklmnopqrstuvwxyz .,-:;'"!? $1234567890 fifffflffiffi

ABCDEFGHIJKLMNOPQRSTUVWXYZ 1 2 3 4 5 6 7
abcdefghijklmnopqrstuvwxyz1234567890$&.,;:-'?!fifffflffiffi

ABCDEFGHIJKLMNOPQRSTUVWXYZ&
ABCDEFGHIJKLMNOPQRSTUVWXYZ&
abcdefghijklmnopqrstuvwxyz $1234567890 .,-:;'"!?¢ ""£%

ABCDEFGHIJKLMNOPQRSTUVWXYZ&
abcdefghijklmnopqrstuvwxyz.,-:;'!?()
$1234567890

ABCDEFGHIJKLMNOPQRSTUVWXYZ&
abcdefghijklmnopqrstuvwxyz ?!.,:;'-() $1234567890

GRANJON was designed for Linotype in 1928 by George W. Jones, distinguished English printer, to meet his own exacting requirements for fine book and publication work. It is derived from classic Garamond sources, but with refinements made possible by modern methods of punch cutting. In fact, one critic has called it "the purest form of Garamond." It is named for Robert Granjon, mid-sixteenth-century punch cutter noted in particular for his italics, from which the present *Granjon Italic* was derived. *Granjon Bold,* by C. H. Griffith, was added in 1931. Lanston Monotype acquired reproduction rights to the face from Mergenthaler.

Granjon, Lino (6-21pt), APL (18-72pt); Mono 400E (6-12pt)
Granjon Italic, Lino (6-18pt), APL (18-48pt); Mono 400G (6-12pt)
Granjon Bold, Lino (6-14pt); Mono 500J (8-12pt)

GRAPHIC—see *Lucian* under Imports in Appendix.
GRAPHIC ARTS—see *Artcraft.*
GRAPHIQUE—see Imports in Appendix.

GRASSET was designed by Eugene Grasset, French decorative artist, in 1898 for Deberny & Peignot, French typefounders, and cut by ATF in 1904. It was advertised as a chic, up-to-date face of the day, but has mannerisms that later became quite dated. The Monotype cutting in 1912 was modified and reproportioned to fit the early restrictions of that machine, but retains the quaintness of the foundry originals. However, the Monotype roman font shown here is cast quite a bit tighter than first planned.

Grasset, ATF (6-60pt); Mono 117 (6-36pt)
Grasset Italic, ATF (6-60pt); Mono 117K (6-12pt)

GRAVURE was designed by Morris F. Benton in 1927 for ATF. It is a freely drawn roman with a fine white line in the heavy strokes. The long descenders include a calligraphic style of *g* and *y,* while several other characters have a similar quality. Compare *Cameo, Narciss.*

Gravure, ATF 505 (12-72pt)

GRAYBAR BOOK is a delicate and unique typeface designed by Wadsworth A. Parker for ATF in 1930, intended for stationery and announcement purposes, as well as sophisticated fashion advertising of the day. Lining figures were originally furnished with the fonts, but were replaced about 1934 by the oldstyle figures shown. It did not survive long enough to appear in the next general specimen book of the foundry four years later.

Graybar Book, ATF 540 (6-48pt)

GRAYDA is an unusual and striking script designed by Frank H. Riley and introduced in 1939 by ATF. Lowercase letters are weighted at top and bottom, giving a strong horizontal emphasis; they are close fitting but not connected. Two sets of capital letters are available, designated Narrow and Swash. The 18-point size is cast on a 24-point body, the smallest size for which angle-body molds are used.

Grayda with Narrow Caps, ATF 678; Grayda Swash Caps, ATF 679 (18/24-96pt)

GRECO BOLD and *Italic* are Spanish faces of the mid-1920s. They are very heavy, with long ascenders and small x-height, and have a hand-lettered appearance. Linotype *Vulcan* (q.v.) is equivalent. National Matrix & Type Co. in Baltimore, one of several independent companies which made matrices for the popular casting machines, offered *Greco Bold* in 1929 as its series 100; this was the source of Baltimore Type's mats, but Baltimore and some other sources cast *Greco Bold* and *Italic* as series 326-3261. These numbers have not been found in Monotype literature; perhaps another independent source also made mats.

Greco Bold, (Mono) 100 or 326 (12-36pt)
Greco Bold Italic, (Mono) 3261 (12-36pt)
Also see Greco Adornado under Imports in Appendix.

Notice the figures, which are termed hanging or old style, although they do not follow the usual form. However, taller *1, 2,* and *0* are also available to convert the set to lining figures. Compare *Hess Monoblack.*

Greco Adornado, an ornamented version, has also been imported. See Appendix.

GREENWICH, Ludlow 36-pt.

ABCDEFGHIJKLMNOPQRSTUVWXYZ& abcdefghijklmnopqrstuvwxyz 1234567890

GREETING CARD, BB&S 18-pt. (Ivan Snyder)

ABCDEFGHIJKLMNOPQRSTUVWXYZ&$1234567890
abcdefghijklmnopqrstuvwxyz.,-:;'!? ✠ ⚹ ❧

GREETING CARD LIGHT, BB&S 24- & 18-pt.

Honorable MEMBER BANKING Rule Announced   .,:;-'!?
ABCDEFGHIJKLMNOPQRSTUVWXYZ&$✦❧ abcdefghijklmnopqrstuvwxyz1234567890

GREETING MONOTONE, ATF 24-pt. (Victor Ables)

ABCDEFGHIJKLMNOPQRSTUVWXYZ& Ch Th M
abcdefghijklmnopqrstuvwxyz $1234567890 .,-:;'!? n d e g

HADRIANO, Mono 24-pt.

ABCDEFGHIJKLMNOPQRSTUVWXYZ&
abcdefghijklmnopqrstuvwxyz fffiffifflffl QQU
$1234567890 .,´:;'!? ❀
Goudy

HADRIANO STONE-CUT, Mono 24-pt.

ABCDEFGHIJKLMNOPQRSTUVWXYZ
1234567890.,´&

HAIGHT, Inland 24-pt. (part reduced)

EXCEEDINGLY Interesting for 4 PERFECT Models in 6

GREENWICH is a modernized, extra condensed roman with a stylized lowercase, designed by William E. Fink in 1940 for Ludlow. Compare *Spire, Eden.*

Greenwich, Ludlow 46-MEC (36-72pt)

GREETING CARD and *Greeting Card Light* are two of the many faces renamed for the 1925 BB&S type book. These two were originally known as *Lyric* and *Lightface Lyric,* designed by Charles E. Heyer in 1882. They are novelty faces, with the newer names being more descriptive of their intended use.

Greeting Card, BB&S-ATF 1683 (10-24pt)
Greeting Card Light, BB&S-ATF 1684 (10-24pt)

GREETING GOTHIC—see *Bernhard Gothic Title.*

GREETING MONOTONE is a novelty face designed by Morris F. Benton in 1927 for ATF, and later copied by Intertype. Lowercase is very small, and many characters have a peculiar triangular shape. The name tells the intended use. In the specimen here, the alternate characters are from a different printer than the regular font, and are proofed more heavily.

Greeting Monotone, ATF 504 (10-24pt); Inter (10-18pt)

GRIMALDI—see Antiques in Appendix.
GROTESQUE—see Imports in Appendix.
GUARD—see *Latin Expanded.*

HADRIANO. While visiting the Louvre in Paris, Frederic W. Goudy was impressed by an inscription in marble from the first or second century A.D., and made a rubbing of the letters *P, E,* and *R.* Several years later, in 1918, he drew a set of capitals to harmonize with those three letters. The name "Hadriano" was part of the original inscription, and this became the name of Goudy's type, for which matrices were cut by Robert Wiebking.

Hadriano, Goudy (12-36pt); Mono 309 (12-36pt)
Hadriano Stone Cut, Mono 409 (24-36pt)

In 1930 Monotype asked him to add a lowercase. Goudy says, "I did not want to attempt a lowercase for a purely inscriptional letter, but the foundries say printers ask for lowercase regardless of the esthetics, and I allowed myself to be persuaded. I made what I thought was a good companion for the capitals, but . . . the type looked entirely too much like *Kennerley Bold.* I cut one size only and turned the type over to the Monotype. I do not think anything was ever done with it—praise be!" Apparently nothing was done with *that* lowercase, but in 1932 Monotype issued *Hadriano* with the actual *Kennerley Bold* lowercase, which is not quite the same; this is the one in the specimen shown here.

The capitals alone are quite distinctive; with lowercase the face is much less impressive.

About 1932 Sol Hess at Monotype tried the experiment of cutting a white line through each of the caps of the design, making *Hadriano Stone Cut.* Goudy says, "A proof of the changed letters pleased me so much that I immediately gave permission to issue matrices of the characters." Only the characters shown in the specimen here were made.

HAIGHT was introduced by Inland Type Foundry in 1902 as "one of our two most recent novelties." It was designed by A. V. Haight of Poughkeepsie, New York, and has a number of bizarre features similar to some other faces of the day.

Haight, Inland (6-72pt)

aBcᴅef[ʄ]ghiJɔklmnopqrstuvwxyz
1234567890

HAMPTON, Hansen 24-pt.

PROMPTNESS and reliability pays

HANDCRAFT, BB&S 24-pt. (part reduced)

CLEVER Effects Noted Artistic TOUCH

HANDCRAFT WIDE TITLE, BB&S 24- & 18-pt.

IMPORTED COMMENDED

HANSEN OLD STYLE NO. 30, Hansen 24-pt.

MODERN POSTER in large fonts suitable ❧ 1234567

HANSEN OLD STYLE ITALIC NO. 30, Hansen 24-pt.

NEW ITALIC FACE IN SIGHT OF LAND
Lining Hansen Old Style Italic No. 30

HARRIS ROMAN, Keystone 24-pt. (William Danner)

ABCDEEGHIJKLMNOPQRSTUVWXYZŒÆ
abcdefghijklmnopqrstuvwxyz&1234567890.,-:;!?'

HARRIS ITALIC, ATF 18-pt.

BRIGHTENS HOME Exquisitely Decorated

HAUSER SCRIPT, Ludlow 24-pt.

ABCDEFGHIJKLMNOPQRSTUVWXYZ & F T
abcdefghijklmnopqrstuvwxyz .,- ':;'!?[]()~% $1234567890 ¼ ½ ¾ ⅓ ⅔

HAVENS, Inland 24-pt. (Dave Norton)

AABBCDDEFGHHIJKLMNOPPQRRSSTTUVWXYZ
&abcddefghijklmnopqrstuvwxyz$1234567890.,-:;'!?

HEADING & HEADING OUTLINE, Hansen 24-pt.

THE FULL ADVANTAGE THAT THE FULL ADVANTAGE THAT 12345
Will be realized from using time slips is not secured if 67890

174

HAMMER SAMSON UNCIAL. This face was designed by Victor Hammer in Florence, Italy, about 1930, with punches cut by Paul Koch, and type cast by them and their private press associates. Their first book was Milton's *Samson Agonistes,* for which the type was named *Samson.* During World War II the type was lost or destroyed, but the punches survived. About 1970 R. Hunter Middleton made new matrices and directed a casting of new fonts as *Hammer Samson Uncial.* Compare *American Uncial.*

Hammer Samson Uncial, private

HAMPTON was introduced by Hansen about 1908. The general effect is similar to *John Hancock,* but the serifs are pointed instead of square.

Hampton, Hansen (6-48pt)

HANDCRAFT is a nineteenth-century series, renamed by BB&S for its 1925 specimen book. *Handcraft Title* was designed by Ernst Lauschke in 1887 as *Spenser;* this was followed by *Wide Spenser* which became *Handcraft Wide Title.* With lowercase added a few years later, *Spenser* became *Southey,* and later *Handcraft.*

Handcraft, BB&S-ATF 1686 (6-72pt)
Handcraft Title, BB&S-ATF 1687 (6-60pt)
Handcraft Wide Title, BB&S-ATF 1688 (6-30pt)

HANSEN OLD STYLE NO. 30 was basically the same as *Jenson,* but had pointed serifs instead of square ones. The roman appeared early in the century, the italic about 1909. *Hansen Old Style No. 40* is a duplicate of *Jenson.*

Hansen Old Style No. 30, Hansen (6-48pt)
Hansen Old Style Italic No. 30, Hansen (6-48pt)
Hansen Old Style No. 40, Hansen (6-36pt)

HARLEQUIN—see Antiques in Appendix.
HARMONY—see *Romantiques* under Antiques in Appendix.

HARRIS ROMAN was announced by Keystone Type Foundry in 1909. It was "named in honor of the late Joel Chandler Harris, author of *Uncle Remus."* It is a plain modernized roman, somewhat similar to *Century Expanded.* In 1910 *Harris Italic* was added; it was designed to be cast without kerns. Advertising claimed, "Non-kerning italics will save endless annoyances and losses resulting from broken letters, and the purchase price is the same as any other type of our make."

Harris Roman, Keystone-ATF 854 (5-72pt)
Harris Italic, Keystone-ATF 855 (5-20pt)

HAUSER SCRIPT is a freely drawn brush script, designed by George Hauser in 1936 for Ludlow, taking advantage of the slanting matrices of that machine. It is probably the most informal of American brush scripts, and characters are not joined. Compare *Brush, Brody.*

Hauser Script, Ludlow 38-HIC (18-72pt)

HAVENS was introduced by Inland Type Foundry in 1902 with the questionable claim, "as elegant an italic face as you may ever hope to see." Like many faces of the day it has a number of alternate characters, and a particularly odd lowercase *g.* Apparently matrices did not survive when Inland was absorbed into ATF in 1912.

Havens, Inland

HEADING and *Heading Outline* were shown by Hansen in 1908 or earlier. They are a medium weight, narrow gothic design with some unusual characters suggestive of the later *Othello* (q.v.).

Heading, Hansen (18-42pt)
Heading Outline, Hansen (18-42pt)

HEADING CONDENSED—see *Compact.*

175

PRINTERS LETTER HELD SOAP MADE IN CASTILE

ABCDEFGHIJKLMNOPQRSTUVWXYZ&$1234567890 abcdefghijklmnopqrstuvwxyz.,-:;'!? ÆŒæœ

ABCDEFGHIJKLMNOPQRSTUVWXYZ& 1234567890 $.:,;-''!?—

ABCDEFGHIJKLMNOPQRSTUVWXYZ&$1234567890 - '':;!'

ABCDEFGHIJKMN
abcdefghijklmnopqz

ABCDEFGHIJKLMONPQRSTUVWXYZ&
abcdefghijklmnopqrstuvwxyz?123456789

ABCDEFGHIJKLMNOPQRSTUVWXYZ $1234567890
ABCDEFGHIJKLMNOPQRSTUVWXYZ $1234567890
abcdefghijklmnopqrstuvwxyz ff fi ffi fl ffl []%(),.-;':'!?—&
abcdefghijklmnopqrstuvwxyz ff fi ffi fl ffl []%(),.-;':'!?—&

ABCDEFGHIJKLMNOPQRSTUVWXYZ&ÆŒ 1234567890$£,.:;'-'?!-|— ()@℔¢*†‡¶§[]%/
ABCDEFGHIJKLMNOPQRSTUVWXYZ&ÆŒ 1234567890$£,.:;'-'?!-|— ()@℔¢†‡¶§[]%/*
abcdefghijklmnopqrstuvwxyzæœfiflffffiffl ⅛¼⅜½⅝¾⅞⅓⅔
abcdefghijklmnopqrstuvwxyzæœfiflffffiffl ⅛¼⅜½⅝¾⅞⅓⅔

ABCDEFGHIJKLMNOPQRSTUVWXYZ&ÆŒ 1234567890$£,.:;'-'?!-|— ()@℔¢*†‡¶§[]%/
ABCDEFGHIJKLMNOPQRSTUVWXYZ&ÆŒ 1234567890$£,.:;'-'?!-|— ()@℔¢*†‡¶§[]%/
abcdefghijklmnopqrstuvwxyzæœfiflffffiffl ⅛¼⅜½⅝¾⅞⅓⅔⅕⅖⅗⅘⅙⅚
abcdefghijklmnopqrstuvwxyzæœfiflffffiffl ⅛¼⅜½⅝¾⅞⅓⅔⅕⅖⅗⅘⅙⅚

ABCDEFGHIJKLMNOPQRSTUVWXYZ&ÆŒ 1234567890$£,.:;'-'?-!—()@℔¢*†‡¶§[]%/
ABCDEFGHIJKLMNOPQRSTUVWXYZ&ÆŒ 1234567890$£,.:;'-'?-!—()@℔¢*†‡¶§[]%/
abcdefghijklmnopqrstuvwxyzæœfiflffffiffl ⅛¼⅜½⅝¾⅞⅓⅔⅕⅖⅗⅘⅙⅚
abcdefghijklmnopqrstuvwxyzæœfiflffffiffl ⅛¼⅜½⅝¾⅞⅓⅔⅕⅖⅗⅘⅙⅚

HEADLETTER CONDENSED ia a very narrow font of thick-and-thin capitals with rudimentary serifs, produced by BB&S around the turn of the century. Keystone had *Head Letter No. 2,* similar to the Barnhart face. Compare *Lafayette Extra Condensed.*

Headletter Condensed, BB&S-ATF 1689 (10-60pt)
Head Letter No. 2, Keystone (10-48pt)

HEADLINE—see Imports in Appendix.

HEADLINE GOTHIC on Ludlow is an all-cap face intended primarily for newspaper headlines. It is nearly the same as *Gothic Extra Condensed [Title] No. 6,* BB&S from Western Type Foundry, and some sizes of *Gothic Condensed No. 3* on Linotype and Intertype, and very similar to *News Gothic Extra Condensed.* But *Gothic Condensed No. 3* (which has lowercase only in 36-point, Linotype) is a hybrid face; most sizes are like *Headline Gothic,* but the odd sizes of 28- and 34-point are more like cruder nineteenth-century gothics such as BB&S's *Gothic Compressed No. 8* or *Light Condensed Gothic,* Monotype, or *Gothic Condensed No. 3* (title), Monotype.

A substantially different *Headline Gothic* was designed by Morris Benton for ATF in 1936, and was popular for major newspaper headlines, up to very large sizes. A sturdy, plain face, it was similar to nineteenth-century gothics but more refined, especially when compared with the wood types often used in large sizes. The cap *M* with its short vertex is particularly recognizable. Compare *Railroad Gothic, Tourist Gothic.*

Headline Gothic, Ludlow 6-H (30-60pt); Gothic Condensed No. 3, Lino = Inter (24-48pt); Gothic Extra Condensed No. 6, BB&S-ATF 1654 (6-72pt); Gothic Extra Condensed Title No. 6, BB&S-ATF 1655 (6-60pt); also Light Condensed Gothic, Mono 50 (30-60pt); Condensed Gothic No. 3 (title), Mono 222; Gothic Compressed No. 8, BB&S-ATF 1653 (10-72pt); Gothic Compressed Title No. 8, BB&S-ATF 1649 (8-60pt)
Headline Gothic, ATF 650 (24-120pt)

HEARST was produced by Inland in 1902, named for William R. Hearst, the newspaper publisher, and introduced as "the latest face, original and attractive character." Goudy claimed it was copied from lettering he had done for a booklet of verses for children; it has somewhat the character of *Pabst* and *Powell,* designed by him about that time, but has larger lowercase, with short ascenders and descenders. Generally it is a wide face, although some letters are disproportionate, ranging from cramped to very wide. *Hearst Italic* was produced in 1903. Compare *Avil, Pabst, Plymouth, Post Oldstyle, Powell.*

Hearst, Inland-ATF 185 (6-72pt)
Hearst Italic, Inland-ATF 186 (6-72pt)

HELLENIC WIDE—see Imports in Appendix.

HELVETICA originated as *Neue Haas Grotesk* at the Haas Typefoundry in Switzerland, where Max Miedinger, in cooperation with Edward Hoffman, drew the first version in 1957; this was acquired by Stempel in Germany and developed into an extensive series, which has become what is probably the most widely used typeface of the 1980s and 1990s. The name is derived from an ancient name for Switzerland.

Along with the foundry type, many fonts of German Linotype matrices were imported into the United States. In 1965 Mergenthaler Linotype copied several versions and later added more of its own. Since alignment standards are different, American typographers who had bought imported matrices had to replace them with domestic mats so the older versions would align with the added ones. Linotype's *Helvetica Bold* is the same weight as what is commonly known as *Helvetica Medium* in foundry type; this has caused much confusion. A spokesman says, "At Mergenthaler we use Medium to designate a weight that is in the text category. We have no Mediums that are designed for bold face emphasis. . . . We intend to stick with this system for all the future faces we produce."

Lanston Monotype, after it was taken over by ATF in the late 1960s, produced several weights of *Helvetica,* but listed them only as *Gothic* with their identifying numbers. Reportedly they were copied directly from Linotype cuttings, without the delicate adjustments normally made to fit the Monotype unit system; thus these faces have a somewhat spotty appearance when assembled. Compare *Record Gothic Medium-Extended.*

Helvetica Light and Italic, Lino (6-14pt); Gothic 481 and Italic, Mono 481JK (6-12pt)
Helvetica and Italic, Lino (6-24, 6-14pt); Gothic 496 and Italic, Mono 496JK (6-12pt)
Helvetica Bold and Italic, Lino (6-24, 6-14pt); Gothic 508 and Italic, Mono 508JK (6-12pt)
Helvetica Condensed and Bold Condensed, Lino (6-14pt)
Other weights and widths of Helvetica were made by Stempel in Germany; several versions were imported by ATF and several were copied by other U.S. sources.

ABCDEFGHIJKLMNOPQRSTUVWXYZ&
abcdefghijklmnopqrstuvwxyz fiflffffffifflft 12345678 $?!.,:;'""-() Qut.ttQ⸙

HESS BOLD, Mono 24-pt.

ABCDEFGHIJKLMNOPQRSTUVWXYZ&
abcdefghijklmnopqrstuvwxyz
$1234567890 .,-:;'!?()—

HESS BOLD ITALIC, Mono 14-pt.

A B C D E F G H I J K L M N O P Q R S T U V W X Y Z & $ 1 2 3 4 5 6 7 8 9 0
a b c d e f g h i j k l m n o p q r s t u v w x y z fi fl ff ffi ffl . , - ' : ; ! ?

HESS MONOBLACK, Mono (36-pt. at 67%)

KEEP TYPE fonts $12345

HESS NEOBOLD, Mono (36-pt. at 67%)

ABCDEFGHIJKLMNOPQRSTUVWXYZ.,-::'!? $1234567890&

HESS NEW BOOKBOLD & ITALIC, Mono 10-pt.

ABCDEFGHIJKLMNOPQRSTUVWXYZ&   *ABCDEFGHIJKLMNOPQRSTUVWXYZ&*
abcdefghijklmnopqrstuvwxyz fiflffffffiffl   *abcdefghijklmnopqrstuvwxyz fiflffffffiffl*
$1234567890 .,-'"'::;!?()   *$1234567890 .,-'"'::;!?*

HESS OLD STYLE, Mono 14-pt. & ITALIC, 12-pt.

ABCDEFGHIJKLMNOPQRSTUVWXYZ&
abcdefghijklmnopqrstuvwxyz ffffiffiflffl $1234567890 .,-:;'!?
ABCDEFGHIJKLMNOPQRSTUVWXYZ&
abcdefghijklmnopqrstuvwxyz ffffiffiflffl $1234567890 .,-:;'!?

HESS TITLE, Mono 14-pt. & ITALIC, 10-pt.

A B C D E F G H I J K L M N O P Q R S T U V W X Y Z & Æ Œ . , - ' : ; ! ?
a b c d e f g h i j k l m n o p q r s t u v w x y z æ œ fi fl ff ffi ffl $ 1 2 3 4 5 6 7 8 9 0 £

ABCDEFGHIJKLMNOPQRSTUVWXYZ&ÆŒ abcdefghijklmnopqrstuvwxyzæœ fiflffffiffl $1234567890 .,-'"::;!?

HERALD EXTRA CONDENSED—see *American Extra Condensed.*

HERITAGE is a carefully crafted contemporary script, designed for ATF by Walter H. McKay about 1952. It is very close fitting but not connected, with a slight slope, and resembles fine hand-lettering with a broad pen. Compare *Thompson Quillscript, Verona, Freehand.*

Heritage, ATF 702 (14-30pt)

HESS BOLD was designed by Sol Hess for Monotype about 1910, as a companion face for *Goudy Light,* drawn earlier by Frederic W. Goudy. Of medium weight, it accurately reflects the characteristics of the lighter face with a high degree of legibility, but neither face is distinguished. There is also an italic by Hess.

Hess Bold and Italic, Mono 159-1591 (6-36pt)

HESS MONOBLACK is a Monotype face that no doubt was drawn by Sol Hess, but it has not been found in any accounts of his work nor in the regular specimen books. The showing here is reproduced from Monotype's "specimen on request" sheet; no other information has been found except that there are only two sizes with seventy-seven characters each, a practical minimum for cap-and-lowercase fonts. Compare *Greco Bold.*

Hess Monoblack, Mono 325 (36,72pt)

HESS NEOBOLD was designed by Sol Hess for Monotype in 1934. It is a narrow, bold, and very squarish gothic with small serifs, designed for attention-getting display in a style of the day, but never made in more than one size. Compare *Airport Tourist (Futura Display), Othello.*

Hess Neobold, Mono 363 (36pt)

HESS NEW BOOKBOLD was designed for Monotype in 1946 by Sol Hess, with italic the following year; both were released in 1948. An adaptation of *Garamond Bold,* the face was reproportioned to fit a new standard arrangement which was intended to make it readily available for use with several standard oldstyle faces still in common use at the time, but little use seems to have been made of it. Ascenders and descenders are shorter than in Garamond, anticipating later phototype trends, weight is slightly greater, and letters are more tightly fitted.

Hess New Bookbold and Italic, Mono 600JK (6-12pt)

HESS OLD STYLE was designed about 1920 (one source says 1912) by Sol Hess for Monotype, which says it was modeled after a face shown by Nicolas Jenson about 1479. It is neat, but does not have much in common with *Centaur, Cloister,* and other faces based on Jenson's work. However, it is a little heavier than most of them and so works to good advantage on smooth papers. The italic followed in 1922.

Hess Old Style and Italic, Mono 242-2421 (6-36pt)

HESS POSTER—see *Poster.*

HESS TITLE and *Italic* were the first type designs drawn by Sol Hess. Produced in 1910 as advertising types, they were designed for and first used by a prominent New York department store. Only the roman was made in display sizes.

Hess Title and Italic, Mono 161-161K (6-36, 6-12pt)

HIDALGO—see Imports in Appendix; also see *Barnum Heavy* under Antiques in Appendix.

ABCDEFGHIJKLMNOPQRSTUVWXYZ abcdefghijklmnopqrstuvwxyz 1234567890 ff ffi ffl (,:?!°¶
ABCDEFGHIJKLMNOPQRSTUVWXYZ abcdefghijklmnopqrstuvwxyz

HOBO, ATF 24-pt. (Jim Broadston)

ABCDEFGHIJKLMNOPQRSTUVWXYZ.,-::;!?'
abcdefghijklmnopqrstuvwxyz1234567890$&

LIGHT HOBO, ATF 18-pt.

ABCDEFGHIJKLMNOPQRSTUVWXYZ&
abcdefghijklmnopqrstuvwxyz $1234567890

HOLLYWOOD, ATF 24-pt. (Elizabeth Nevin)

ABCDEFGHIJKLMNOPQRSTUVWXYZ 1234567890$&.,:;-!?'
abcdefghijklmnopqrstuvwxyz

HOMEWOOD, Balto 24-pt.

ABCDEFGHIJKLMNOPQRSTUVWXYZ
$1234567890.,-:"!?&»«()£

HOWLAND (30-pt. at 80%) (Dave Norton)

ABCDEFGHIJKLMNOPQRSTUVWXYZ&MR .,-:;'!?
abcdefghijklmnopqrstuvwxyz$1234567890£

HOWLAND OPEN (CONDENSED GOTHIC OUTLINE, Lino) 18-pt.

ABCDEFGHIJKLMNOPQRSTUVWXYZ ,.:;?!(|)"'-=—&$
12345 abcdefghijklmnopqrstuvwxyz 67890 ⅛ ¼ ⅜ ½ ⅝ ¾ ⅞

HUMANISTIC (LAURENTIAN, Mono) 21-pt.

ABCDEFGHIJKLMNOPQRSTUVWXYZ&

abcdefghijklmnopqrstuvwxyz .,-:;!?()[] 1234567890 aemn

HINGHAM was an experimental newspaper face, originally called *Newsface,* designed between 1937 and 1943 by William A. Dwiggins, for improved readability. Only the 7-point size was cut by Mergenthaler, and it was used only for tests.

Hingham and Italic, Lino (7pt)
experimental

HOBO is unusual in two respects—it is drawn with virtually no straight lines, and it has no descenders and thus is very large for the point size. It was designed by Morris F. Benton and issued by ATF in 1910. One story says that it was drawn in the early 1900s and sent to the foundry without a name, which was not unusual, but that further work on it was continually pushed aside, until it became known as "that old hobo" because it hung around so long without results. More time elapsed before it was patented in 1915. The working name was *Adface. Hobo* was also cut by Intertype in three sizes.

Light Hobo was also drawn by Benton, and released by ATF in 1915. It is included in one list of Monotype faces, but the same series number is shown elsewhere for another Monotype face, and no other evidence has been found that Monotype actually issued it.

Hobo, ATF 193 (6-48pt); Inter (10-14pt)
Light Hobo, ATF 448 (6-48pt); Mono 432
(see text)

HOLLYWOOD is a novelty gothic face designed by Willard T. Sniffin in 1932 for ATF. It was intended for smart, contemporary advertising, announcements, and stationery, but some of the characters have quaint shapes, suggestive of nineteenth-century styles. Compare *Gothic Novelty.*

Hollywood, ATF 568 (6-72pt)

HOMEWOOD is a recutting by Baltimore Type of *Metropolis Lined,* a German face of the 1930s. It was made from a large size of *Metropolis Bold* (see Imports in Appendix), with the fine white lines cut in, and differs from the original in minor details of the curves. Other sizes were cut by pantagraph and do not necessarily match original sizes.

Homewood, Balto 103 (18-48pt)

HORIZON—see Imports in Appendix.

HOWLAND was introduced by Dickinson in 1892 as a "companion series to DeVinne." The same design was called *DeVinne Condensed (No. 3)* by Keystone Type Foundry, but differs from the *DeVinne Condensed* issued by other sources. *Howland Open* followed in 1894; it was copied by Linotype as *Condensed Outline* and suggested through the 1940s as a display face for classified advertising pages which banned bold types. Compare *DeVinne Condensed, MacFarland Condensed.*

Howland, ATF (6-60pt); Mono 139 (6-36pt);
Hansen (6-48pt); DeVinne Condensed
(No. 3), Keystone (6-72pt)
Howland Open, ATF (10-60pt); Mono 96
(10-36pt); Condensed Outline, Lino (10-
30pt)

HUMANISTIC was designed by William Dana Orcutt and privately cast by ATF in 1904 for the University Press, Cambridge, Massachusetts. It is a careful rendering into type of the round humanistic writing of the Renaissance period, based in particular on the 1485 manuscript of Antonio Sinibaldi's *Virgil* in the Laurentian Library at Florence, Italy. This is considered by some to be hand-lettering in its most beautiful form, and occurred after the development of roman types as we know them.

In 1940 this type was adapted to Monotype keyboard composition, under the direction of Orcutt and Sol Hess, the 21-point size being used for a large edition of *Science and Health.* The Monotype cutting, known as *Laurentian,* shown here, closely follows the foundry version, including some but not all of the original alternate characters.

A few years later the design was modified by Stephenson Blake in England, and issued as *Bologna;* this in turn was adapted by ATF as *Verona* (q.v.).

Humanistic, ATF, private; Laurentian,
Mono, private (14,21pt)

ABCDEFGHIKLMNOPQRSTUVXY
abcdefghijklmnopqrstuvwxyz&567890$.,-:;!?Œ

TOUGH METALS
Best Quality of Type

ADMIRABLE FACES
Are Shown in This Book

ABCDEFGHIJKLMNOPQRSTUVWXYZ ÆŒÇ&Th
ʒ abcdefghijklmnopqrstuvwxyz fiflff âóèñüï
$1234567890 çæœ.,:;!?·-«»

ABCDEFGHIJKLMNOPQRSTUVWXYZ& $1234567890 .,-:;!? `+ A K M N W Y

ABCDEFGHIJKLMNOPQRSTUVWXYZ *ABCDEFGHIJKLMNOPQRSTUVWXYZ* **ABCDEFGHIJKLMNOPQRSTUV**
ABCDEFGHIJKLMNOPQRSTUVWXYZ *abcdefghijklmnopqrstuvwxyz 1234567890* **abcdefghijklmnopqrstuvwxyz 123·**
abcdefghijklmnopqrstuvwxyz 1234567890 []%†§‡¶*()$,.-;‘:’!?&⅛¼⅜½⅝¾⅞ []%†§‡¶*()$,.-;‘:’!?&⅛¼⅜½⅝
[]%†§‡¶*()$,.-;‘:’!?&⅛¼⅜½⅝¾⅞

ABCDEFGHIJKLMNOPQRSTUVWXYZ   1234657890
ABCDEFGHIJKLMNOPQRSTUVWXYZ   *1234657890*

ABCDEFGHIJKLMNOPQRSTUVWXYZ &ÆŒ

abcdefghijklmnopqrstuvwxyz   fi fl ff ffi ffl,.-;‘:’!?()$&|*
abcdefghijklmnopqrstuvwxyz   fi fl ff ffi ffl,.-;‘:’!?()$&|

ÆŒæœ[]†‖‡§¶%@tb--—£¢/⅛¼⅜½⅝¾⅞⅓⅔
ÆŒæœ[]†‖‡§¶%@tb--—£¢/⅛¼⅜½⅝¾⅞⅓⅔

ABCDEFGHIJKLMNOPQRSTUVWXYZ   1234567890
ABCDEFGHIJKLMNOPQRSTUVWXYZ   1234567890

abcdefghijklmnopqrstuvwxyz   fi fl ff ffi ffl,.-;‘:’!?()$&|*
abcdefghijklmnopqrstuvwxyz   fi fl ff ffi ffl,.-;‘:’!?()$&|*

ÆŒæœ[]†‖‡§¶%@tb--—£¢/⅛¼⅜½⅝¾⅞⅓⅔
ÆŒæœ[]†‖‡§¶%@tb--—£¢/⅛¼⅜½⅝¾⅞⅓⅔

182

HUNNEWELL was produced by Hansen Type Foundry in 1907 or earlier. It is very similar to *Cushing No. 2* (q.v.), but the roman lowercase is a little narrower.

Hunnewell, Hansen (6-48pt)
Hunnewell Italic, Hansen (6-18pt)

HUNT ROMAN was designed in 1961 by Hermann Zapf, cut and cast privately by Stempel for the Hunt Institute Botanical Library at Carnegie Institute of Technology (later Hunt Institute for Botanical Documentation, Carnegie-Mellon University), Pittsburgh, Pennsylvania, which also features fine books and bindings. It was determined that this new type should accompany the library's use of *Spectrum,* an English Monotype face, to make its publications more elegant and graceful. It is intended for display use, but on occasion has been used for limited settings of text, and is a crisp blend of transitional and contemporary letter forms. Later Zapf designs for digital typesetting are rather similar.

Hunt Roman, Stempel, private (14-24pt)

HUXLEY VERTICAL is a font of delicate capitals designed by Walter Huxley in 1935 for ATF, expressing the smart modernism of the day. Strokes are uniformly light throughout, center strokes are low and extended to the left, and there are alternate round versions of several letters. Compare *Agency Gothic, Vernen.*

Huxley Vertical, ATF 596 (18-120pt)

IDEAL (originally called *Ideal News*) was designed by Herman R. Freund for Intertype in 1926, for the New York *Times.* It has much the appearance of *Century Schoolbook,* but with shorter ascenders and squattier capitals. The italic is a little closer to *Century Expanded Italic,* providing more contrast with the roman. Sturdy serifs, substantial hairlines, and open loops make it a practical face for the demanding production requirements of high-speed newspaper use. *Ideal Bold* is heavier than the Century bold faces.

Ideal [News] and Italic and Bold, Inter (5½-14pt)

IHLENBURG—see *Bradley.*

IMPERIAL was designed by Edwin W. Shaar in 1954 as a newspaper text face. Like most other news faces it has a large x-height with short descenders, but unlike most news faces of the time, it blends certain oldstyle and contemporary characteristics, and is a little narrower and more closely fitted. This gives a feeling of friendliness and warmth, but retains a high degree of legibility.

Imperial and Italic and Bold, Inter (5½-14pt)

IMPERIAL (other)—see *Emperor;* also *Wide Latin* under Imports in the Appendix.
INCLINED GOTHIC—see *Gothic Inclined.*
INCLINED GOTHIC BOLD—see *Modern Gothic Italic.*
INFORMATION—see Imports in Appendix.
INLAND—see *Bizarre Bold.*

INLAND COPPERPLATE, 24-pt.

𝕬𝕭𝕮𝕯𝕰𝕱𝕲𝕳𝕴𝕵𝕶𝕷𝕸𝕹𝕺𝕻𝕼𝕽𝕾𝕿𝖀𝖁𝖂𝖃𝖄𝖅&
abcdefghijklmnopqrstuvwxyz $1234567890 .,-:;'!?

INVITATION SCRIPT, Inland 24-pt. (Dave Greer)

ABCDEFGHIJKLMNOPQRSTUVWXYZ&

abcdefghijklmnopqrstuvwxyz $1234567890 .,-:;'!!..oćś,-

INVITATION, ATF 24-pt. (Lauren Geringer, Rick von Holdt)

ABCDEFGHIJKLMNOPQRSTUVWXYZ.,;:-'!?&
abcdefghijklmnopqrstuvwxyzfffiflffiffl$1234567890

INVITATION SHADED, ATF 24-pt.

ABCDEFGHIJKLMNOPQRSTUVWXYZ& .,-:;'!?
abcdefghijklmnopqrstuvwxyz $1234567890

INVITATION TEXT, BB&S 24-pt. (part reduced)

American Secretary Report Marital Rite Now Legally Performed

IONIC NO. 5 & ITALIC, Lino 12-pt.

ABCDEFGHIJKLMNOPQRSTUVWXYZ&ÆŒ ABCDEFGHIJKLMNOPQRSTUVWXYZ&ÆŒ
ABCDEFGHIJKLMNOPQRSTUVWXYZ&ÆŒ
abcdefghijklmnopqrstuvwxyzæœfiflffffiffl 1234567890 $£,.:;-"?! ()@℔*†‡¶§[]% ⅛¼⅜½⅝¾⅞
abcdefghijklmnopqrstuvwxyzæœfiflffffiffl 1234567890 $£,.:;-"?! ()@℔ †‡¶§[]% ⅛¼⅜½⅝¾⅞

IONIC CONDENSED, Lino 18-pt.

ABCDEFGHIJKLMNOPQRSTUVWXYZ& abcdefghijklmnopqrstuvwxyz fiflffffiffl 1234567890 ($,.:;-'?!) ⅛¼⅜½⅝

IRVIN, Mono private 24-pt.

ABCDEFGHIJKLMNOPQRSTUVWXYZ&
~$1234567890?!()[]¢.,"

Name in parentheses after some specimens
indicates person who has set that specimen,
in whole or in part, to our format.

184

INLAND COPPERPLATE is a shaded Old English typeface, first shown by Inland Type Foundry in November 1901. It is similar to *Typo Text* (q.v.), although the specimen here, reproduced from an over-inked showing, doesn't reveal the shading.

Inland Copperplate, Inland-ATF 202 (8-36pt)

INLAND FRENCH SCRIPT, etc.—see *French Script,* etc.
INLAND GOTHIC, INLAND CONDENSED GOTHIC—see *Gothic No. 6, Gothic Condensed.*
INSERAT—see *Aurora* under Imports in Appendix.
INTERSCRIPT—see *Typo Upright.*

INVITATION SCRIPT was cut by Inland in 1896. It is a connected style similar to *Typo Script Extended.*

Invitation Script, Inland (12-48pt)

INVITATION SHADED is a unique shaded roman letter with unusual triangular serifs on some of the letters, designed in 1916 by Morris F. Benton for ATF. *Invitation,* a solid version, was made by the same designer in 1917. The shaded version was one of a long series of shaded faces produced by ATF from 1913 on; these faces, as the name implies, were intended for use in fine invitations and announcements, following the style of engraved work.

Invitation, ATF 457 (6-24pt)
Invitation Shaded, ATF 217 (8-24pt)

INVITATION TEXT was designed by Robert Wiebking for BB&S in 1914. It is a comparatively light Old English style, similar to *Wedding Text* (q.v.). Also see *Typo Text.*

Invitation Text, BB&S-ATF 1693 (6-48pt)

IONIC is a general name for a style of typeface which is closely related to the Clarendons (q.v.). Plain, sturdy designs with strong serifs and little contrast, the Ionics were popular in the latter part of the nineteenth century. Although many founders offered them, they were generally gone by early in this century. A few received a new lease on life when they were copied by Monotype, Linotype, or Intertype.

Two new Ionics appeared in this century. *Ionic No. 5* was designed by C. H. Griffith in 1926 for Linotype, as a newspaper text face. It features a large lowercase with short ascenders and descenders, with no fine lines or serifs to break down in stereotyping, and no small openings to fill up with ink. This is one of a few faces made in many closely graded sizes: 5-, 5½-, 6-, 6½-, 6¾-, 7-, 7½-, 8-, 9-, 10-, and 12-point. Intertype's *Windsor,* developed in 1959, is comparable. *Ionic Condensed* was designed by Griffith in 1927, also for Linotype. It is a refinement of traditional designs, intended for newspaper headings, and has most of the general characteristics of the text face. *Ionic Extra Condensed* is essentially the same, a little narrower and without lowercase, also for newspaper headlines.

Ionic No. 522, ATF 272 (5-18pt); Ionic, BB&S (6-24pt); Keystone (12-36pt); Mono 62 (18-36pt); Clarendon Medium or Caledonian No. 5, BB&S-ATF 1581 (5-48pt)
Ionic, Mono 56J (5-8pt)
Ionic No. 5 and Italic, Lino (5-12pt); Windsor and Italic and Bold, Inter (8½,9pt)
Ionic Condensed, Lino (18-36pt)
Ionic Extra Condensed, Lino (42pt)
Round Ionic, Mono 156J (5,6pt)
Wide Ionic, Mono 256J (6pt)
Ionic (Consort) is known as Egiziano in Italy.

IONIC SHADED—see Antiques in Appendix.

IRVIN is a very unusual typeface, used for many years for the distinctive heads in the *New Yorker* magazine. It was designed in 1925 by Rea Irvin, first art director of the magazine, and mats were made by Monotype for private use by the magazine's printers. The design features irregular letter shapes, proportions, and spacing, as though hastily lettered.

Irvin, Mono (8-30pt), private

ITALIA CONDENSED, Keystone (30-pt. at 80%) (Alan Waring)

ABCDEFGHIJKLMNOPQRSTUVWXYZ&ÆŒ$£1234567890

abcdefghijklmnopqrstuvwxyzfffifflflffffi.,-:;'!?

ITALIAN OLDSTYLE, Mono 24-pt.

ABCDEFGHIJKLMNOPQRSTUVWXYZ&

abcdefghijklmnopqrstuvwxyz $1234567890 .,-:;'!?

fifffl ffiffl st ct ℂ $1234567890

ITALIAN OLDSTYLE ITALIC, Mono 24-pt.

ABCDEFGHIJKLMNOPQRSTUVWXYZ& C E L Q TU

abcdefghijklmnopqrstuvwxyz $1234567890 .,-:;'!? fiflffffiffl &s

ITALIAN OLDSTYLE WIDE, Mono 18-pt. (Guy Botterill)

ABCDEFGHIJKLMNOPQRSTUVWXYZ

abcdefghijklmnopqrstuvwxyzfffififlffiffl &1234567890$.,-:;!?'ℂ)

IVANHOE, Keystone 18-pt.

ABCDEFGHIJKLMNOPQRSTUVWXYZ

abcdefghijklmnopqrstuvwxyz 1234567890

JANSON, Mono 24-pt.

ABCDEFGHIJKLMNOPQRSTUVWXYZ $1234567890

abcdefghijklmnopqrstuvwxyz fifflflffiffl .,-:;"!?&$1234567890

JANSON ITALIC, Mono 24-pt.

ABCDEFGHIJKLMNOPQRSTVUWXYZ A B D P R Y

abcdefghijklmnopqrstuvwxyz fi fl ff ffi ffl gy .,-:;"!?&$1234567890

JAPANET, BB&S 24-pt. (Stephen H. Derring)

ABCDEFGHIJKLMNOPQRSTUVWXYZ

abcdefghijklmnopqrstuvwxyz1234567890 &$.,-:;!?

JEFFERSON GOTHIC, Mono 24-pt.

ABCDEFGHIJKLMNOPQRSTUVWXYZ& $1234567890 .,-:;'!?

186

ITALIA CONDENSED is a very narrow thick-and-thin face advertised by Keystone in 1900, although it is probably of earlier origin. A number of the caps and a few lowercase letters have flourishes. Compare *Onyx, Compact.*

Italia Condensed, Keystone (12-48pt)

ITALIAN CONDENSED—see *P. T. Barnum.*

ITALIAN OLD STYLE was designed by Frederic W. Goudy for Lanston Monotype in 1924. It is based on early Venetian types of the latter part of the fifteenth century. Bruce Rogers, in a handsome booklet introducing the face, says it "reminds me most strongly and admirably of Ratdolt's fine Roman." However, Goudy says this was not the source. Goudy also says he persuaded Monotype to cut this original rendition rather than copy ATF's *Cloister Oldstyle,* which was quite popular then, and which was based on similar sources. This face is a little more delicate and individual than *Cloister,* and is larger in relation to the body size, but makes a very distinctive and impressive page. Compare *Centaur.*

Italian Old Style, Mono 243 (8-36pt)
Italian Old Style Italic, Mono 2431 (8-36pt)
Italian Old Style Wide, Mono 443 (14-36pt)

Italian Old Style Wide was drawn by Sol Hess, also in 1924. It is slightly heavier and substantially wider than Goudy's design.

ITALIAN ORNATE—see *Latin Ornate* under Antiques in Appendix.

IVANHOE was introduced by Keystone Type Foundry about 1915, a copy of the face designed by Edward Shanks for the P. M. Shanks Foundry in England in 1912. It is a rather neat but undistinguished face, similar to classic fifteenth-century Italian designs.

Ivanhoe, Keystone (6-48pt)

JANSON is adapted from types often attributed to Anton Janson, seventeenth-century Dutch letter founder, although researchers have shown that the originals were cut by Nicolas Kis, a Hungarian punchcutter and printer. The Linotype version was done in 1932 under the direction of C. H. Griffith, based on the 14-point size of about 1660. The Monotype version was adapted by Sol Hess in 1936, in collaboration with Bruce Rogers. Both versions are sharp and clear cut, and rather compact. They bear some resemblance to the types of William Caslon, which were based on later, similar Dutch types.

Janson and Italic, Lino (8-14pt); Mono 401-4011 (8-36pt)

JAPANET was originally *Wedge Gothic,* cut by BB&S in 1893 for the Chicago *Herald.* It was renamed for the 1925 specimen book of the founder. It was recast by ATF in 1954.

Japanet, BB&S-ATF 1694 (8-48pt); LATF (18pt)

JEFFERSON GOTHIC was originally Monotype's copy of *News Gothic Extra Condensed,* using the same foundry name. In 1916 Sol Hess designed several alternate round capitals; matrix fonts include both styles of these letters, but no lowercase. Baltimore Type called it *Tourist Extra Condensed.* Compare *Phenix.*

Jefferson Gothic, Mono 227 (14-72pt)

ABCDEFGHIJKLMNOPQRSTUVWXYZ&
abcdefghijklmnopqrstuvwxyz$;:,?-1234567890.'!

ABCDEFGHIJKLMNOPQRSTUVWXYZ1234567890.,;:'!?$
abcdefghijklmnopqrstuvwxyz

ABCDEFGHIJKLMNOPQRSTUVWXYZ
abcdefghijklmnopqrstuvwxyz

REWARD FOR BEST LINE CUSTOMERS
Appreciate Progressive Printers in 53 Modern Letters

ABCDEFGHIJKLMNOPQRSTUVWXYZ abcdefghijklmnopqrstuvwxyz &!?$ 1234567890 .,-:;'

ABCDEFGHIJKLMNOPQRSTUVWXYZ&
$1234567890 .,-:;'!?

LIGHT HOUSE MARKET
Mariners Storm Bound Cars Pass Street

ABCDEFGHIJKLMNOPQRRSTUVWXYZ&.,-;'!?
abcdefghijklmnopqrstuvwxyz $1234567890

ABCDEFGHIJKLMNOPQRSTUVWXYZ& abcdefghijklmnopqrstuvwxyz $1234567890

BRIGHT STARS
Aid the wandering pedestrians. $67890

JENSON OLDSTYLE, though a comparatively crude face in itself, did much to start the late nineteenth-century move toward better types and typography. Designed by J. W. Phinney of the Dickinson Type Foundry (ATF) and cut by John F. Cumming in 1893, it was based on the *Golden Type* of William Morris for the Kelmscott Press in 1890; that in turn was based on the 1470-76 types of Nicolas Jenson. Morris had established standards for fine printing, in spite of the fact that he did not design really fine types. Serifs in particular are clumsy, but the Jenson types quickly became popular. BB&S introduced *Mazarin* in 1895-96, as "a revival of the Golden type, redesigned by our artist." But it was a poor copy, and was replaced by *Morris Jensonian.* Inland's *Kelmscott,* shown in 1897, was acquired by BB&S and renamed *Morris Jensonian* in 1912; Keystone had *Ancient Roman* (q.v.); Crescent Type Foundry had *Morris Old Style;* Hansen had *Hansen Old Style* (q.v.); and other founders had several other faces, all nearly like *Jenson.*

It is hard to realize that *Jenson* was inspired by the same historic type as the later and more refined *Centaur, Cloister,* and *Eusebius.*

ATF spelled the name "Jensen" in some early specimens, and added "No. 2" to the series, the latter presumably when it was adapted to standard alignment or when minor changes were made in the design. *Jenson Italic* was introduced at the same time as the roman. ATF advertised Phinney's *Jenson Heavyface* in 1899 as "new and novel—should have been here long ago." *Jenson Condensed* and *Bold Condensed* were introduced in 1901.

Jenson Oldstyle [No. 2], ATF 276 (6-72pt); Mono 58 (6-36pt); Jenson, Lino (6-14pt); Morris Jensonian, BB&S-ATF 1790 (6-48pt); Mazarin [No. 5], BB&S-ATF 1771 (6-60pt); Hansen Old Style No. 40, Hansen (6-36pt)
Jenson Italic [No. 2], ATF 275 (6-72pt); Lino (8pt); Mazarin Italic, BB&S
Jenson Condensed, ATF 219 (6-144pt); Mono 258 (10-36pt); Lino (18pt)
Jenson Heavyface, ATF (12-120pt); Jenson Bold, Lino (18-30pt)
Jenson Bold Condensed, ATF 218 (6-144pt); Jenson Condensed, Lino (24pt)

JIM CROW is ATF's 1933 and 1949 recasting of *Gothic Shade,* originally by Dickinson Type Foundry, a predecessor, about 1850. It has also been called *Tombstone.* Additional sizes were cut by Los Angeles Type Foundry.

Jim Crow, ATF (24pt); TF-P (24pt); LATF (18-30pt)

JOHN ALDEN is a novelty face with a supposed Colonial flavor, introduced by Keystone in 1901. It has some of the quaint details, but not the irregular edges, featured by a number of faces of the period. The matching italic is named *Priscilla* (q.v.). They are apparently the first faces to introduce reverse apostrophes (") as modern quotation marks.

John Alden, Keystone (6-60pt)

JOHN HANCOCK series was originated by Keystone Type Foundry and introduced in 1903; however, it was patented in 1907, with the patent assigned to Charles William Smith, probably the designer. It was named for the president of the Continental Congress and first signer of the Declaration of Independence. It is a plain, no-frills, hard-working typeface, modern in character but without the hairlines of Bodoni. Serifs are short and square, but those on the lighter strokes have diagonal brackets. The lowercase is large, with short ascenders and descenders. Letters are normal roman shapes, except for the open-tailed *g,* and the *e* with its slanted crossbar. There are two cap *R*'s in the regular width, and two *m*'s in regular and *Extended*—the round-top version is unusual.

The Monotype copies of 1912 follow the general character of the faces, but *e* has a horizontal crossbar, alternate characters are omitted, and proportions are changed somewhat; *Condensed* has slightly rounded fillets on some serifs. The *Outline* goes unusually small, but in small sizes the thin strokes are not opened. Compare *Bold Antique; Contact Bold Condensed; Hampton; Lowell.*

John Hancock, Keystone-ATF 861 (6-72pt); Mono 142 (5½-12pt); Bold Face No. 6, Lino (10-14pt)
John Hancock Condensed, Keystone-ATF 862 (6-120pt); Mono 245 (14-36pt)
John Hancock Extended, Keystone-ATF 863 (6-60pt)
John Hancock Outline, Keystone-ATF 864 (6-72pt)

JOHN HANCOCK EXTENDED, ATF 18-pt. (Dave Norton)

ABCDEFGHIJKLMNOPQRSTUVWXY
abcdefghijklmnopqrstuvwxyz m   Z&
.,-:;'!?""''$1234567890

JOURNAL HEADLETTER, private (Rick von Holdt)

New Heading Letter Traveling With the Baby
Table of Contents We Test Our Readers' Recipes

JULIANA OLDSTYLE, Rimmer 18-pt. (Jim Rimmer)

ABCDEFGHIJKLMNOPQRSTUVWXYZ&

abcdefghijklmnopqrstuvwxyzff fi fl ffi ffl ct st.,'; :!?1234567890$

JUMBO TYPEWRITER, ATF 24-pt.

ABCDEFGHIJKLMNOPQRSTUVWXYZ&
$1234567890.,-'":;!?(

KAATSKILL, Goudy, private 18-pt.

ABCDEFGHIJKLMNOPQRSTUVWXYZ&1234567890

ABCDEFGHIJKLMNOPQRSTUVWXYZ&

abcdefghijklmnopqrstuvwxyz ct fi ff ffi fl ffl .,';:!?-

Commas, / Quotes," and "Uniquotes"

Fonts of metal foundry type traditionally had no opening quotation marks. There was no need for them, as hand compositors could easily invert commas for that purpose (A).

"A" "B" "C" 66 "" "

Keyboard operators could not do that, of course, so typesetting machines such as Linotype and Monotype included opening quotes. These were single marks, with double quotes being formed by two single opening quote marks or two apostrophes.

On older typewriters, which produced a comparatively crude substitute for typesetting, the uniform width for all characters made two single quotes too far apart, so for the sake of simplicity, typewriters always had "uniquotes," to coin a word—the same character for both opening and closing use—with one single character and one double

character. (Actually, these are more properly known as single and double prime marks.)

Meanwhile, because inverted commas in long descender typefaces (B) were too low for good appearance, "modern" quotes (C) were developed, with the apostrophe design reversed. (See *John Alden*.) These were subsequently made by the founders for many faces, including some short descender designs, and often in both single and double characters. They are shown in this book as far as possible.

Commas of shadow designs (D) can't be inverted without displacing the shadow. For such faces (E), opening quotation marks are a necessity.

As typewriters were improved, they retained their uniquotes. Modern word processor keyboards do likewise, but true quotation marks can usually be obtained—commonly with an extra operation which "desktop publishers" often do not use. Most professional typographers, though, routinely use the true forms.

JOURNAL HEADLETTER was designed and privately cast in 1929 for use as heads by the *Ladies' Home Journal.* There are several sizes, with several logotypes and a number of alternate characters.

JULIANA OLDSTYLE was designed and cut by Jim Rimmer in Vancouver in 1984, as a private type. He says, "It represents my first attempt at cutting a metal type. I drew my letters completely freehand, hoping to capture a punch-cut look. My artwork was then reduced and made into a dry transfer sheet, which I rubbed onto type-high typemetal blanks. I then cut the letters and electroformed copper matrices."

Juliana Oldstyle, Rimmer (18pt) private

JUMBO TYPEWRITER is included here because it is one of the very few typewriter faces made in display sizes. It is an ATF face, issued about 1934, following the typewriter characteristic of a single width for all letters, and is made only in the size shown. The specimen here shows the complete font. Compare *Bulletin Typewriter*.

Jumbo Typewriter, ATF 590 (24pt)

KAATSKILL is a private typeface designed and cut by Frederic W. Goudy for use in an edition of *Rip Van Winkle* which he made for The Limited Editions Club, in 1929. Goudy says that what he had in mind was merely to design a type "as simple, legible, vigorous, clear, and effective in detail as I could, and which would at the same time show no note of strangeness in the mass. . . . I feel that *Kaatskill* owes nothing in its design to any existing face, and the type therefore is as truly an American type as anything so hidebound by tradition as type can be." It is named for the Catskill mountains, which were the locale of Goudy's home and workshop as well as of the story. See *Trajan Title*.

Kaatskill, Goudy, private (12-18pt)

KABEL—see *Sans Serif;* also *Tempo, Vogue.*

ABCDEFGHIJKLMNOPQRSTUVWXYZ$1234567890
abcdefghijklmnopqrstuvwxyz'.,-:;''!?[]()&%+
ÆŒMNW

ABCDEFGHIJKLMNOPQRSTUVWXYZ&
abcdefghijklmnopqrstuvwxyz 1234567890
⅔ ½ ¼ ⅓ ¾ %

ABCDEFGHIJKLMNOPQRSTUVWXYZ&.,-:;''!?()[]
abcdefghijklmnopqrstuvwxyz 1234567890+—
% ¼ ⅓ ½ ⅔ ¾

ABCDEFGHIJKLMNOPQRSTUVWXYZ
abcdefghijklmnopqrstuvwxyz.,-:;''!?[]()&+
$1234567890 ÆŒMNW

ABCDEFGHIJKLMNOPQRSTUVWXYZ&
abcdefghijklmnopqrstuvwxyz 1234567890

ABCDEFGHIJKLMNOPQRSTUVWXYZ& abcdefghijklmnopqrstuvwxyz 1234567890 ÆŒMNW
¾⅔ ½¼⅓⅔%

ABCDEFGHIJKLMNOPQRSTUVWXYZ
abcdefghijklmnopqrstuvwxyz +[](),.-':';!?—&
$1234567890 %¼⅓½¾⅔

KARNAK is a family of square-serif types designed by Robert H. Middleton for Ludlow, beginning in 1931, when the light and medium weights were introduced, with other weights and widths announced as late as 1942. Like *Stymie*, the other extensive American square-serif series, it is derived from *Memphis*, and all three series are very similar. Most members of the Karnak family are most easily distinguished by the cap *G*; Karnak italics are also distinguished by a greater slant to fit Ludlow's 17-degree matrices, except 14-point and smaller in *Karnak Intermediate Italic* and *Medium Italic*, which are made on straight matrices and slant about 10 degrees. Light and medium weights have several alternate round capitals as shown; the very narrow *Karnak Obelisk* also has comparable alternate round *AEMNW*. Compare *Cairo, Memphis, Stymie*. One magazine article speaks of *Karnak Open*, but this has not been found in any Ludlow literature.

Karnak Light, Ludlow 30-L (6-72pt)
Karnak Intermediate, Ludlow 30-LM (6-72pt)
Karnak Intermediate Italic, Ludlow 30-LMI (8-48pt)
Karnak Medium, Ludlow 30-M (6-72pt)
Karnak Medium Italic, Ludlow 30-MI (8-48pt)
Karnak Obelisk, Ludlow 30-MEC (14-72pt)
Karnak Black, Ludlow 30-H (10-72pt)
Karnak Black Italic, Ludlow 30-HI (14-72pt)
Karnak Black Condensed, Ludlow 30-HC (14-144pt)
Karnak Black Condensed Italic, Ludlow 30-HCI (14-72pt)

KAUFMANN SCRIPT and *Kaufmann Bold* are a pair of monotone connecting scripts designed by Max R. Kaufmann for ATF in 1936. The joints are well managed to provide the appearance of smooth, flowing handlettering, while presenting a contemporary look and a high degree of legibility. *Swing Bold* on Monotype appears to be an exact copy of *Kaufmann Bold*, and its availability on that system has increased its popularity and usefulness. Compare *Gillies Gothic; Brush*. Also see *Balloon*.

Kaufmann Script, ATF 652 (10-96pt); (Univ 12-24pt)
Kaufmann Bold, ATF 657 (10-96pt); Swing Bold, Mono 217 (14-72pt)

KARNAK BLACK ITALIC, Ludlow 24-pt.

ABCDEFGHIJKLMNOPQRSTUVWXYZ
abcdefghijklmnopqrstuvwxyz.,-:;"!?()[]
$1234567890—+½¼¾⅓⅔%

KARNAK BLACK CONDENSED, Ludlow 24-pt.

ABCDEFGHIJKLMNOPQRSTUVWXYZ $1234567890
abcdefghijklmnopqrstuvwxyz +[](),.-':;!?—& %¼⅓½¾⅔

KARNAK BLACK CONDENSED ITALIC, Ludlow 24-pt.

ABCDEFGHIJKLMNOPQRSTUVWXYZ& ⅓ ½ ¼ ¾ ⅔ %
abcdefghijklmnopqrstuvwxyz 1234567890 .,-:;'!?()[]—

KAUFMANN SCRIPT, ATF 24-pt.

ABCDEFGHIJKLMNOPQRSTUVWXYZ
abcdefghijklmnopqrstuvwxyz's 1234567890&$.,-'""';!?¢

KAUFMANN BOLD, ATF 24-pt.

ABCDEFGHIJKLMNOPQRSTUVWXYZ
abcdefghijklmnopqrstuvwxyz's 1234567890&$.,-'""';!?¢

KENILWORTH, Inland 18-pt.

ABCDEFGHIJKLMNOPQRSTUVWXYZ& 1234567890
abcdefghijklmnopqrstuvwxyz

KENILWORTH ITALIC, Inland 18-pt.

THE MECHANICAL PERFECTION 23 AMONG SLANTS
And Artistic Zenith of Modern Typefounding Are Found in the Inland Productions

KENNERLEY OLDSTYLE, Mono 24-pt. (William Danner)

ABCDEFGHIJKLMNOPQRSTUVWXYZ& $1234567890
abcdefghijklmnopqrstuvwxyz .,-:;'!? ff fiflffiffl ctst ℂ] ❀ 12345

KENNERLEY ITALIC, Mono 24-pt.

ABCDEFGHIJKLMNOPQRSTUVWXYZ& 1234567890$
abcdefghijklmnopqrstuvwxyz .,-:;'!? ABCDEMPRCUNQTYZ

Intertype

KENNERLEY BOLD, Mono 24-pt. (Fred Sholty, Rich Hopkins)

ABCDEFGHIJKLMNOPQRSTUVWXYZ&
abcdefgghijjklmnoppqqrstuvwxyz fiffflffiffl ctst .,-;:'!?
$12345678901234567890

KENNERLEY BOLD ITALIC, Mono 24-pt. (Fred Sholty)

ABCCDEEFGGHIJKLMNOPQRSTCUUVWXYZ
abcdefghijkl mnopqrstuvwxyz ctstffifflfffl fi ?!.,-;:'
&1234567890$1234567890

KENNERLEY OPEN CAPS, Mono (36H4 at 67%) (Rick von Holdt)

ABCDEFGHIJKLMNOP
QRSTUVWXYZ& .,$1234567890

KEYNOTE, ATF 24-pt.

ABCDEFGHIJKLMNOPQRSTUVWXYZ&Th
abcdefghijklmnopqrstuvwxyziseresorosthtt ,;:.-'!!' $1234567890£

194

KELMSCOTT—see *Jenson Oldstyle.*

KENILWORTH was introduced by Inland Type Foundry in 1904. It is similar to *Cheltenham Oldstyle.* Mats for the italic, at least, were later acquired by BB&S but apparently not used there; only the italic mats ended up in the vaults of ATF. Compare *Lowell.*

Kenilworth, Inland (6-84pt)
Kenilworth Italic, Inland-BB&S-ATF 1695 (6-48pt)

KENNERLEY OLD STYLE. Like many types designed by Frederic W. Goudy, *Kennerley* was executed in response to a particular need. In 1911, Mitchell Kennerley, a New York publisher, asked Goudy to design a book, *The Door in the Wall,* by H. G. Wells. Goudy had some trial pages set in *Caslon Oldstyle*—Goudy refers to it as *Caslon Old Face,* but a reproduced example is the looser *Caslon Oldstyle.* If Goudy or Kennerley had used the tighter English version of Caslon, perhaps this face would not have been designed. But as the effect did not satisfy Goudy, he obtained the publisher's permission to design and cut a new typeface which he would later cast and attempt to sell to "discriminating printers" to recoup at least part of the expense of producing it.

Kennerley, named for the publisher, has much less contrast and angularity than Caslon, and sets very compactly, giving a solid appearance to a page. It far exceeded Goudy's expectations for popularity, and he gradually added other sizes for his own sales. In 1920 he sold reproduction rights in this country to Lanston Monotype. Meanwhile, in 1915 Goudy had drawn a companion italic (it was shown in that year, although Goudy later gave the date as 1918). In the specimen here, the *NQTYZ* shown separately are offered as alternates by Intertype only. Sol Hess provided *Kennerley Open Capitals* for Lanston in 1925 by opening each letter with a white line.

In 1924 Goudy designed bold and bold italic for *Kennerley,* at the request of Monotype. Goudy was never enthusiastic about bold typefaces, but says, "I think I kept the Kennerley character in my bold rendition as well as could have been done." The lowercase of this face was later used with *Hadriano* capitals.

Intertype adapted *Kennerley* to its machine in 1923, first announcing it under the same name. A little later this name was changed to *Kenntonian.*

Kennerley Old Style, Goudy; Mono 268 (6-72pt); Kenntonian, Inter (6-36pt)
Kennerley Italic, Goudy; Mono 2681 (6-72pt); Kenntonian Italic, Inter (6-24pt)
Kennerley Bold, Mono 269 (6-72pt)
Kennerley Bold Italic, Mono 2691 (6-72pt)
Kennerley Open Capitals or Kennerley Open Shaded, Mono 368 (36H4pt)

KEYNOTE is an informal brush script, designed by Willard T. Sniffin for ATF in 1933. Its name was suggested by the political campaigns of the previous year. There is variation in weight of strokes, and letters are unconnected, but there are a number of logotypes of connecting pairs of letters. Inclination is slight, permitting it to be cast on straight bodies with little overhang. Compare *Raleigh Cursive* by the same designer.

Keynote, ATF 579 (24-96pt); (Univ 24-72pt)

KEYSTONE EXPANDED—see *Latin Expanded.*
KEYSTONE OLD STYLE—see *Ronaldson.*
KEYSTONE VICTORIA—see *Victoria Italic.*

"A WARNING SIGNAL must not only waves on the drum of the ear, but it mind behind the ear and cause volitional signal should carry its alarm notice over the least one block, to even a deaf or slow-moving

KORINNA & BOLD, Inter 14-pt.

ABCDEFGHIJKLMNOPQRSTUVWXYZ % [ ] * † | ‡ || § ¶ – — ⅛ ¼ ⅜ ½ ⅝ ¾ ⅞

ABCDEFGHIJKLMNOPQRSTUVWXYZ % [ ] * † | ‡ || § ¶ – — ⅛ ¼ ⅜ ½ ⅝ ¾ ⅞

abcdefghijklmnopqrstuvwxyz fiflffffiffl,.-;':'!?() @tb $1234567890 æœÆŒ&£

abcdefghijklmnopqrstuvwxyz fiflffffiffl,.-;':'!?() @tb $1234567890 æœÆŒ&£

LAFAYETTE EXTRA CONDENSED, Ludlow 24-pt.

ABCDEFGHIJKLMNOPQRSTUVWXYZ& abcdefghijklmnopqrstuvwxyz $1234567890 . : , ; - — ' ' ! ? ( )

LAFAYETTE TEXT, Hansen 24-pt.

Annual Graduating Exercises of Harvard College 123467890

LANSTON 125 & ITALIC & BOLD, Mono 11-pt.

abcdefghijklmnopqrstuvwxyz 1234567890$
ABCDEFGHIJKLMNOPQRSTUVWXYZ&

abcdefghijklmnopqrstuvwxyz 1234567890$
ABCDEFGHIJKLMNOPQRSTUVWXYZ&

abcdefghijklmnopqrstuvwxyz 1234567890$
ABCDEFGHIJKLMNOPQRSTUVWXYZ&

LARIAT, Phoenix 24-pt.

ABCDEFGHIJKLMNOPQRSTUVWXYZ $1234567890

abcdefghijklmnopqrstuvwxyz.,!?';:-

196

KLAXON was designed by Frederic W. Goudy in 1914 as a private type for the manufacturers of the Klaxon Auto Warning Signal, an accessory auto horn in the days when this item was not standard equipment. The type is suggestive of *Kennerley,* but slightly heavier, with some little quirks of design that make it more successful for its intended use as a publicity type rather than for book work. Matrices, which were cut by Robert Wiebking, were lost in Goudy's fire of 1939.

Klaxon, Goudy, private

KLONDIKE—see *Gold Rush.*

KORINNA and *Korinna Bold* were cut by Intertype in 1934 from a German foundry face. They remained in a novelty class and saw comparatively little use in metal, but have become much more popular in electronic typesetting.

Korinna, Inter (6-18pt)
Korinna Bold, Inter (6-14pt)

LACLEDE OLDSTYLE—see *Munder Venezian.*

LAFAYETTE EXTRA CONDENSED is a Ludlow face designed by Robert H. Middleton in 1932. It is almost monotone in weight, but has very small serifs and is more roman than gothic in appearance. It was intended for newspaper heads, but was not shown after the 1940s. Compare *Compact.*

Lafayette Extra Condensed, Ludlow 35-EC (18-48pt)

LAFAYETTE TEXT was shown by Hansen in 1908. It is very similar to *Engravers Old English,* differing most noticeably in the fine vertical line that drops below the base line in some of the capitals.

Lafayette Text, Hansen (8-36pt)

LANSTON 125 and *Lanston Bold* are Monotype copies of *Melior,* the popular German foundry face designed by Hermann Zapf, although modified somewhat. The specimens shown here are slurred and heavied.

Lanston and Italic, Mono 125 (6-11pt)
Lanston Bold, Mono 180 (7-11pt)

LARGO—see Imports in Appendix.

LARIAT was designed by Helmith Thoms in 1963 for Typefounders of Phoenix, but released in 1965. It is an upright, connected script with a rope-like face.

Lariat, TFP, LATF (24-48pt)

LATIN ANTIQUE, BB&S 24-pt. (Dave Greer)

ABCDEFGHIJKLMNOPQRSTUVWXYZ&
abcdefghijklmnopqrstuvwxyz .,-:;'!?
£$1234567890 ÆæŒœ

LATIN BOLD CONDENSED, 24-pt.

ABCDEFGHIJKLMNOPQRSTUVWXYZ $1234567890
abcdefghijklmnopqrstuvwxyz   [] (),.-;:'!?&   ff fi ffi fl ffl

ELONGATED LATIN or CONDENSED LATIN, 24-pt. (Guy Botterill)

ABCDEFGHIJKLMNOPQRSTUVWXYZ& abcdefghijklmnopqrstuvwxyz.,-:;!?'$1234567890

LATIN EXPANDED (GUARD, BB&S, 36-pt. at 67%) (Stan Kroeger)

ABCDEFGHIJKLMNOPQRSTUVWX
abcdefghijklmnopqrstuvwxyzZ &$,.-:;'!'
1234567890

LATIN LIGHTFACE, BB&S 24-pt.

HOME SECURED Imported Material

LATIN OLDSTYLE BOLD (MODERN TITLE), BB&S 18-pt.

ABCDEFGHIJKLMNOPQRSTUVWXYZ&ÆŒ.,-:;'!?
abcdefghijklmnopqrstuvwxyzfiflæœ$1234567890

LAUREATE, Keystone 24-pt. (Dave Norton)

ABCDEFGHIJKLMNOPQRSTUVWXYZ&
abcdefghijklmnopqrstuvwxyz $1234567890£
.,=:;'!? " ", Æ æ Œ œ QU Qu Co Th ❧ ✿

LAW ITALIC NO. 520, ATF 14-pt.

ABCDEFGHIJKLMNOPQRSTUVWXYZ& .,-:;?!'
abcdefghijklmnopqrstuvwxyz fffiflfffiffl 1234567890$

LAW ITALIC NO. 23K, Mono 12-pt.

ABCDEFGHIJKLMNOPQRSTUVWXYZ&
abcdefghijklmnopqrstuvwxyz fffiffifffiflffl $1234567890 .,-:;'!?

198

LATIN is a general name for a number of typefaces which originated in the 1880s or earlier. Most of them were made by various foundries, sometimes under other names. Some had little or no apparent design relationship to each other.

ATF's *Latin Antique No. 520* was Marder, Luse's *Latin Antique No. 120;* other founders had it simply as *Latin Antique,* though BB&S originally called it *Latin No. 5.* It is a wide, medium-weight face with very small, rounded serifs, and lacks the curlicues of *Latin Modern* or *Modern Antique.*

Latin Bold Condensed is now the most common name of the most prominent survivor of this group, but most recent fonts were imported from England, although ATF had at least two sets of matrices in its vaults for many years. ATF formerly made the face as *Modern Antique No. 2,* originating at Cincinnati Type Foundry. BB&S in its later years called the same face *Latin Modern,* but earlier had also called it *Latin Antique.* Inland simply called it *Latin* series. From whatever source, it is a bold, compact display face, characterized by heavy, triangular serifs. The strokes of several lowercase letters terminate in pointed curlicues. In the 1950s or 1960s, fonts imported from Stephenson Blake achieved some popularity; this is the source of the specimen shown here.

Latin Condensed, Extra Condensed, Elongated, and *Compressed* are much narrower versions of this design, though a little lighter and with fewer curlicues. The New York *Times* has used a version of *Latin Condensed* for news heads for many years. In its 1898 book, ATF applied the name "Baskerville" to Latin Condensed!

Light Modern has curlicues and long triangular serifs but is much lighter, while *Latin Expanded* (formerly called *Guard*) is the same but wider. ATF called the latter design *Lightface Celtic No. 40,* shown in 1886 by Marder, Luse, while Keystone had a similar *Keystone Expanded,* and Linotype had *Celtic No. 1.*

The BB&S *Latin Lightface* is a much lighter version of *Latin Antique;* it was formerly called *Light Latin. Latin Oldstyle Bold* has the least relationship to other Latin faces. It was formerly known as *Modern Title,* and before that *Monarch,* shown in 1893 or earlier; ATF called the same face *Eastman Oldstyle.*

Also see *Emperor.*

Latin Antique No. 520, ATF 278 (5-30pt); Latin Antique, BB&S-ATF 1697 (6-48pt); Mono 63 (6-36pt); Lino (8-12pt); Keystone (5-48pt); Inland (6-48pt); Latin Antique No. 3, Hansen (6-48pt)
(Latin Bold Condensed); Latin Modern, BB&S-ATF 1701 (6-72pt); Modern Antique No. 2, ATF (6-72pt); Latin, Inland (6-36pt); Modern Antique No. 3, Hansen (6-72pt)
Latin Condensed No. 550, ATF 279 (10-72pt); Latin Condensed, BB&S-ATF 1698 (10-72pt); Mono 94 (18-36pt); Mono 247 (30pt); Lino = Inter (18-36pt); Keystone (10-72pt)
Latin Extra Condensed, Lino = Inter (30pt); Latin Condensed No. 3, Hansen (10-48pt)
Latin Compressed, Lino (30pt)
Light Modern, BB&S-ATF 1745 (24-48pt)
Latin Expanded, BB&S-ATF 1699 (6-48pt); Celtic No. 1, Lino (8pt); Lightface Celtic, Marder Luse (6-48pt)
Latin Lightface, BB&S-ATF 1700 (6-48pt)
Latin Oldstyle Bold, BB&S-ATF 1703 (6-72pt); Eastman Oldstyle, ATF (6-72pt)
Also see Wide Latin under Imports in Appendix.

LATIN ORNATE—see Antiques in Appendix.

LAUREATE is a novel roman design issued by Keystone Type Foundry in 1901, and latter issued by Ludlow. It is a medium weight roman, with bracketed serifs tapering to sharp points; except for the shape of the serifs it is much like *Venezia* (q.v.), produced by Keystone a year earlier. Also compare *Grasset.*

Laureate, Keystone (6-72pt); Ludlow 7 (18-36pt); Title No. 5, Lino (12pt)

LAURENTIAN—see *Humanistic.*

LAW ITALIC is said to have originated as an imitation of formal styles of penmanship used for legal documents. The most common of several substantially different varieties is ATF's *Law Italic No. 520,* which originated with Marder, Luse about 1870. Several of the capitals are swash-like, while lowercase *f* and *g* have distinctive shapes. It has long thin serifs and sharp contrast between thick and thin strokes. Inland called the same design *Caledonian Italic;* Hansen had *Barrister Italic.*

Monotype's *Law Italic No. 23* is a sloped roman, somewhat similar to *Ronaldson.* Other *Law Italics* are obsolete.

Law Italic No. 520, ATF 280 (8-14pt); Law Italic No. 5, BB&S (8-14pt); Law Italic, Mono 115C (8-12pt); Lino (10,12pt); Keystone (8-14pt); Barrister Italic, Hansen (6-12pt)
Law Italic, Mono 23K (6-12pt)

ABCDEFGHIJKLMNOPQ ABCDEFGHIJKLMNO ABCDEFGHIJKLMN
abcdefghijklmnopq abcdefghijklmno abcdefghijklm

ABCDEFGHIJKLMNOPQR ABCDEFGHIJKLMNO
abcdefghijklmnopq abcdefghijklmno

LEXINGTON, ATF 24-pt.

ABCDEFGHIJKLMNOPQRSTUVW
XYZ.,-:;"'!?& $1234567890

LIBERTY, ATF 24-pt. (Herb Harnish)

ABCDEFGHIJKLMNOPQRSTUVWXYZ&
abcdefghijklmnopqrstuvwxyz $1234567890 .,-:;'!?
C

LIGHT OLDSTYLE, ATF 24-pt. (Mark Ardagna)

ABCDEFGHIJKLMNOPQRSTUVWXYZ&
abcdefghijklmnopqrstuvwxyz.,-:;'!?$1234567890

LIGHTLINE GOTHIC, ATF 24-pt.

ABCDEFGHIJKLMNOPQRSTUVWXYZ
abcdefghijklmnopqrstuvwxyz$1234567890&.:;-,'?!

Legibility Group

In the 1920s advances in the mechanical production of newspapers required more suitable typefaces than the weak modern romans then in common use. Mergenthaler Linotype designers experimented with other letter forms, and produced *Ionic No. 5,* based on the Clarendon style of mid-nineteenth century. It featured larger x-height, well-bracketed serifs, and a nearly uniform weight. It was first used by the Newark *Evening News,* where it was very successful, and within a year had been adopted by three thousand newspapers around the world.

Mergenthaler sponsored research in legibility, under the direction of C. H. Griffith, and introduced the Legibility Group of typefaces. *Excelsior* featured more open counters; *Opticon* was thickened for use on less absorbent papers; *Paragon* was produced for specialized tabloid conditions. *Corona* was introduced in 1941 to avoid distortions of mat shrinkage, and soon became most widely used; fully half of American newspapers were said to be using it by the 1970s.

Intertype *Ideal* is similar to *Ionic. Regal,* produced about 1935 for the Chicago *Tribune,* is similar to *Excelsior.* In 1939 *Rex* was produced for the Milwaukee *Journal;* it is similar to *Regal* but narrower. In 1957 Edwin Shaar, director of typography for Intertype, produced *Imperial,* another close-fitting legibility letter which became very successful, and was adopted by many newspapers including the New York *Times.* Intertype copied *Corona* in 1960 as *Royal.* See these various faces as listed alphabetically.

LAYOUT GOTHIC was an attempt to do in metal some of the things that advertising artists were demanding of photolettering with its new-found "freedom" of tight spacing. Roy Rothstein, a Cleveland typographer, redesigned several characters for the *Alternate Gothics;* these were specially cast by ATF about 1959, and other characters were trimmed for very close fitting. Similar heavier gothics had been made about 1951: *Roys Gothic No. 2* by Rothstein in collaboration with Jack Forman, *Roys Gothic No. 3* by Rothstein, and *Roys Gothic No. 4,* an adaptation of *Helvetica Extra Bold Condensed,* imported from Germany. All this was done in the 60-point size; other sizes were furnished photographically.

Layout Gothic No. 1, 2, and 3; Roys Gothic No. 2, 3, and 4, ATF private (60pt)

LE MERCURE—see *Nicolas Cochin;* also Imports in Appendix.
LEGEND—see Imports in Appendix.

LEXINGTON is a font of shaded and decorated letters and figures, drawn for ATF by Wadsworth A. Parker in 1926, from a design by Clarence P. Hornung. It is an ornamental form of roman letter, with curly serifs, and tendrils at the ends of light strokes. It was recast in 1954, and copied in one size by Los Angeles Type.

Lexington, ATF 571 (24-72pt); LATF (24pt)

LIBERTY was designed for ATF by Willard T. Sniffin in 1927, presumably to counter the importation of *Bernhard Cursive,* which it greatly resembles. It differs in the crossbars of *A* and *H,* which have loops in them, the hooked ascenders of *bdhl,* and some lesser details, but it is a delicately handsome, unconnected script, with very small lowercase and very tall ascenders. On Intertype it is known as *Lotus.* Also compare *Pompeian Cursive.*

Liberty, ATF 511 (12-72pt); (Univ 12-48pt); Lotus, Inter (10-18pt)

LIBRA—see Imports in Appendix.
LIGHTFACE—see *Modern Roman Lightface.*
LIGHT MODERN—see *Latin.*

LIGHT OLDSTYLE is a very light roman with mixed oldstyle and modern characteristics. It has very thin hairlines and very small bracketed serifs. ATF says it originated with Inland Type Foundry, but Steve Watts says it was designed by Morris Benton for ATF in 1916, four years after Inland merged with ATF. It seems to be displayed only in the 1923 ATF specimen book.

Light Oldstyle, ATF 225 (6-48pt)

LIGHTLINE GOTHIC (originally called simply *Lightline*) was designed by Morris F. Benton in 1908 for ATF. It is essentially a lighter version of *News Gothic,* as there are no important differences in shape except *M* with a shorter vertex and *Q* with a different tail. It represents a modernization of light nineteenth-century gothics, with much greater refinement of draftsmanship and precision of cutting and casting.

Lightline Gothic, ATF 222 (6s-36pt); Mono 452 (6s-12pt); also Lightline Title Gothic, ATF 480 (6s-12L); Mono 352 (6s-6L)

From the beginning, *Lightline* was made in four sizes on 6-point body, with only the two larger sizes having lowercase. In 1921 Benton devised *Lightline Title Gothic,* taking the four 6-point sizes, without lowercase, and casting the 8-, 10-, 12-, and 14-point sizes, also without lowercase, to title alignment on 12-point body, in the manner of *Copperplate Gothics.*

Compare *Trade Gothic Light;* also *News Gothic, Blair Condensed, Record Gothic Thinline Condensed.* Also see *Boxhead Gothics, Typotabular Gothics.*

COMPRISING MODERN SPECIMEN
Design Charms Containing Characteristic

ABCDEFGHIJKLMNOPQRSTUVWXYZ&
abcdefghijklmnopqrstuvwxyz.,-:;'!?$1234567890

ABCDEFGHIJKLMNOPQRSTUVWXYZ&
abcdefghijklmnopqrstuvwxyz
$1234567890 .,-:;'!?

ABCDEFGHIJKLMNOPQRSTUVWXYZ&
abcdefghijklmnopqrstuvwxyz $1234567890 .,-:;'!?

ABCDEFGHIJKLMNOPQRSTUVWXYZ&
abcdefghijklmnopqrstuvwxyz $1234567890 .,-:;'!?

ABCDEFGHIJKLMNOPQRSTUVWXYZ&
abcdefghijklmnopqrstuvwxyz
$1234567890 .,-:;'!?

ABCDEFGHIJKLMNOPQRSTUV
abcdefghijklmnopqrstuvwxyz
$1234567890 .,-:;'!?   WXYZ&

ABCDEFGHIJKLMNOPQRSTUVWXYZ
$1234567890 .,"'!?-:;&

LILITH—see Imports in Appendix.

LINING CAIRO, LINING GOTHIC, LINING MEMPHIS, etc.—see under Cairo, Gothic, Memphis, etc.

LINO SCRIPT—see *Typo Upright.*

LINO TEXT—see *Wedding Text.*

LITHO ANTIQUE—see *Rockwell.*

LITHO GOTHIC and *Light Litho Gothic* were issued by Inland Type Foundry in 1911 and 1910 respectively. *Litho Gothic* is light, but *Light Litho Gothic* has an extremely thin line, possibly the lightest typeface made. Both are very plain, wide, and loosely set. *Blair* is the same as *Litho Gothic,* but cast as a title face without lowercase. There is also an *Offset Light Litho Gothic,* the same design but cut in reverse of normal, used for transferring small type to lithographic stones before photolithography was developed.

Litho Gothic, Inland-ATF 313 (5-36pt);
  Blair (title), Inland-ATF 19 (6s-24L)
Light Litho Gothic, Inland-ATF 224 (6s-24pt); Offset Light Litho Gothic, Inland-ATF 342 (5-12pt); Light Litho Gothic Title, ATF 394 (6s-6L); also Offset Title Light Litho Gothic, Inland-ATF 595 (6s-6L)

LITHO ROMAN was designed by Inland Type Foundry in 1907, and a number of variations followed during the next four years. When Inland merged with ATF in 1912, all these faces went along and were shown in the ATF book of that year. They are intended to imitate a style of lettering popular with lithographers in the days when lettering and designs were carefully drawn on lithographic stones. This process was especially in demand for high-quality stationery and announcements. The original *Litho Roman* is rather heavy, with fine hairlines. Serifs on heavy strokes are slightly filleted, while those on hairlines are heavy triangles. The ear of the *g* starts straight up from within the bowl, and in some series the tail of the cap *R* is not quite connected to the bowl.

Title Shaded Litho, introduced by Inland in 1911, features horizontal shading, rather than the diagonal shading of almost all other such faces.

Several versions have a title series, lacking lowercase and otherwise larger on the body, except in 6-point where caps are identical in the larger sizes but with additional smaller sizes. In 1917 two of these title series were modified by Morris F. Benton and reissued as *Card Litho* and *Card Light Litho.* The latter became the last survivor of the family, being shown by ATF as late as 1979 specimens. However, the Monotype copy of *Light Litho* may still be available elsewhere.

Litho Light and *Litho Bold* were issued by Ludlow in 1941; they are essentially the same as *Title Light Litho* and *Title Litho Roman* (no lowercase), but the tail of the *R* connects and the lower end of the *C* does not turn inward, although an alternate *C* matches the foundry letter.

Rimmed Litho is basically the same design, including lowercase, but with a fine line surrounding each character.

Compare *Engravers Roman* series; *Masterman.*

Litho Roman, Inland-ATF 314 (6-72pt);
  Title Litho Roman, Inland-ATF 395 (6s-60pt); Card Litho (title), ATF 44 (6s-6L); Litho Bold (title), Ludlow 45-B (6s-18L)
Condensed Litho, Inland-ATF 118 (6-72pt);
  Condensed Title Litho, Inland-ATF 124 (6-72pt)
Compressed Litho, Inland-ATF (5-60pt)
Light Litho, Inland-ATF 223 (5-48pt);
  Light Litho Roman, Mono 162 (5-36pt); Title Light Litho, Inland-ATF 393 (6s-24pt); Card Light Litho, ATF 45 (6s-12L); Litho Light (title), Ludlow 45-L (6s-18L)
Bold Litho, Inland-ATF 31 (6-48pt)
Title Shaded Litho, Inland-ATF 396 (6s-24L); Title Litho Shaded, Mono 246 (12s-18pt)
Rimmed Litho, Inland-ATF 369 (8-48pt)

RIMMED LITHO, 24-pt. (Elizabeth Nevin)

ABCDEFGHIJKLMNOPQRSTUVWXYZ
abcdefghijklmnopqrstuvwxyz
1234567890!?',.;:-$&

LITHOGRAPH SHADED, ATF 18L

ABCDEFGHIJKLMNOPQRSTUVW
$1234567890 .,-:;'!? XYZ&

LOMBARDIC CAPITALS, Mono 24-pt.

ABCDEFGHIJKLMNOPQRSTUVWXYZ ✛

LONDON GOTHIC, Keystone 24-pt.

NEW CONTINENTAL LINE TOURS
Nothing is more beneficial to New York. $567

LORIMER & ITALIC, Inter 12-pt.

ABCDEFGHIJKLMNOPQRSTUVWXYZ $1234567890 ABCDEFGHIJKLMNOPQRSTUVWXYZ
ABCDEFGHIJKLMNOPQRSTUVWXYZ $1234567890

abcdefghijklmnopqrstuvwxyz fifl ff ffi ffl ,.-;':'!?( ) @ lb &£ æœÆŒ Æ Œ & [ ] * † | ‡ ‖ § ¶ ⅛ ¼ ⅜ ½ ⅝ ¾ ⅞
abcdefghijklmnopqrstuvwxyz fiflff ffi ffl ,.-;':'!?( ) @ lb &£ æœÆŒ

LOUVAINE LIGHT, ATF (36-pt. at 67%) (Herb Harnish)

ABCDEFGHIJKLMNOPQRSTUVWXYZ&$
abcdefghijklmnopqrstuvwxyz.,-:;'!? 1234567890

LOUVAINE LIGHT ITALIC, ATF 24-pt. (Walter Brovald)

ABCDEFGHIJKLMNOPQRSTUVWXYZ&
abcdefghijklmnopqrstuvwxyzffffiflffiffl ,-:;'!?$1234567890

LOUVAINE MEDIUM, ATF 24-pt.

ABCDEFGHIJKLMNOPQRSTUVWXYZ& ,:;.-'!?""''
abcdefghijklmnopqrstuvwxyzfifffflffiffl $1234567890

LOUVAINE MEDIUM ITALIC, ATF 24-pt.

ABCDEFGHIJKLMNOPQRSTUVWXYZ& ,:;.-'!?
abcdefghijklmnopqrstuvwxyzfifffflffiffl $1234567890

LOUVAINE BOLD, ATF 24-pt.

ABCDEFGHIJKLMNOPQRSTUVWXYZ& ,:;.-'!?
abcdefghijklmnopqrstuvwxyzfifffflffiffl $1234567890

LITHOGRAPH SHADED was designed by Morris F. Benton and W. F. Capitain in 1914. It is the same design as *Engravers Shaded* (q.v.), except for the unusual shading which is heavier at the top. As Capitain was primarily a punch-cutter, this was probably an experiment on his part, using the shading machine invented by Linn Boyd Benton a few years earlier. This feature has not been found on any other face, nor has any showing of this face after 1923.

Lithograph Shaded, ATF 315 (6s-18L)

LOG CABIN—see *Rustic* under Antiques in Appendix.

LOMBARDIC CAPITALS were cut by Frederic W. Goudy in 1929, based on drawings he had made eight years earlier. They were derived from early Italian decorative letter forms, and designed to serve especially as alternate capitals with the lowercase of *Goudy Text*. For this purpose, or as initials at the beginning of text, they provide a touch of elegance, more so than when used by themselves to form words.

Lombardic Capitals, Goudy; Mono 310 (18-72pt)

LONDON GOTHIC was issued by Keystone Type Foundry in 1910 or earlier, but is virtually a duplicate of *Royal Gothic,* shown by Marder, Luse & Co. in 1887. It is similar to the same founder's *Charter Oak* series, but upright. Although the italic face survived Keystone's acquisition by ATF in 1919, *London Gothic* does not appear to have done so. See *Charter Oak.*

London Gothic, Keystone (8-72pt)

LORIMER was adapted by Intertype from *Romaansch,* as cast by a German typefoundry, and is similar to *Elzevir* or *French Oldstyle.* Keystone's *Paul Revere* is practically the same face. Intertype's *Remson Bold* comes from *Romaansch Bold.* Compare *Dickens;* also see *Berlin Antique.*

Lorimer and Italic, Inter (6-12pt); Paul Revere and Italic, Keystone (6-72pt)

LORRAINE—see *Venus* under Imports in Appendix.
LOTUS—see *Liberty.*

LOUVAINE series was designed by Morris F. Benton for ATF in 1928. It is an adaptation of *Bodoni* (the working title was *Modern Bodoni*), and many of the characters are identical. Only *g* and *y* are basically different; otherwise the distinction is in the more abrupt transition from thick to thin strokes in this series. In this respect, *Ultra Bodoni* has more affinity to *Louvaine* than to the other *Bodoni* weights. The three weights of *Louvaine* correspond to *Bodoni Book,* regular, and *Bold.* This series did not last long enough to appear in the 1934 ATF specimen book, the next complete one after its introduction. Compare *Tippecanoe.*

Louvaine Light, ATF 519 (6-48pt)
Louvaine Light Italic, ATF 520 (6-36pt)
Louvaine Medium, ATF 521 (6-72pt)
Louvaine Medium Italic, ATF 522 (6-72pt)
Louvaine Bold, ATF 523 (6-72pt)
Louvaine Bold Italic, ATF 524 (6-72pt)

LOUVAINE BOLD ITALIC, ATF 24-pt.

ABCDEFGHIJKLMNOPQRSTUVWXYZ& ,;:.-'!?'
abcdefghijklmnopqrstuvwxyz $1234567890

LOWELL (48pt. at 50%) (Dave Norton)

ABCDEFGHIJKLMNOPQRSTUVWXYZ$1234567890.,-:;'!?

abcdefghijklmnopqrstuvwxyz

LUDLOW BLACK, Ludlow 24-pt.

ABCDEFGHIJKLMNOPQRSTUVWXYZ.,";?!

abcdefghijklmnopqrstuvwxyz 1234567

LUDLOW BLACK ITALIC, Ludlow 24-pt.

ABCDEFGHIJKLMNOPQRSTUVWXYZ

abcdefghijklmnopqrstuvwxyz 12345

LYDIAN, ATF 24-pt.

AABCDEFGHIJKLMNOPQRSTUVWXYZ&

abcdefghijklmnopqrstuvwxyz 1234567890$.,-:;'!?'

LYDIAN ITALIC, ATF 24-pt.

ABCDEFGHIJKLMNOPQRSTUVWXYZ&

abcdefghijklmnopqrstuvwxyz $1234567890 .,-:;'!?'

LYDIAN BOLD, ATF 24-pt.

AABCDEFGHIJKLMNOPQRSTUVWXYZ

abcdefghijklmnopqrstuvwxyz$1234567890¢&.,-:;"!?

LYDIAN BOLD ITALIC, ATF 24-pt.

ABCDEFGHIJKLMNOPQRSTUVWXYZ

abcdefghijklmnopqrstuvwxyz$1234567890¢&.,-:;"!?

LYDIAN BOLD CONDENSED, ATF 24-pt.

ABCDEFGHIJKLMNOPQRSTUVWXYZ&

abcdefghijklmnopqrstuvwxyz $1234567890 .,-:;'!?' ¢

LYDIAN BOLD CONDENSED ITALIC, ATF 24-pt.

ABCDEFGHIJKLMNOPQRSTUVWXYZ

abcdefghijklmnopqrstuvwxyz 1234567890 .,-:;"!?&¢

LOWELL was introduced by Keystone Type Foundry in 1905. The patent was issued to Charles W. Smith, probably the designer. It is somewhat similar to *Cheltenham Oldstyle,* but much more mechanical, with small square serifs which are unbracketed except on the arms of *EFLTZ.* It has many of the characteristics of the same founder's much heavier *John Hancock.* Compare *Kenilworth.*

Lowell, Keystone (6-84pt)

LUCIAN—see Imports in Appendix.

LUDLOW BLACK was designed by Robert H. Middleton for Ludlow in 1924. It is very similar to *Cooper Black,* the most apparent differences being the concave serifs and the greater slant of the italic. Also compare *Pabst Extra Bold.*

Ludlow Black, Ludlow 15 (8-48pt)
Ludlow Black Italic, Ludlow 15-I (12-48pt)

LYDIAN series is a brilliant and popular calligraphic style designed by Warren Chappell for ATF. The lighter weight and italic were designed in 1938; bold and italic in 1939. They have the appearance of being lettered with a broad pen held at a 45-degree angle, but the ends of vertical strokes are square, improving legibility and stability. This is probably the most popular thick-and-thin serifless letter of American origin, though the concept is more popular in Europe. Oldstyle figures were made for these four Lydians, but were fonted separately and very rarely used. These four faces were copied by Intertype in an unusually large range of sizes for a slug machine, and from these matrices some suppliers cast fonts of type for handsetting. Lydian is named for the designer's wife, Lydia. Compare *Czarin, Stellar, Radiant, Optima, Samson, Valiant.*

Lydian Cursive was drawn by the same designer in 1940. Although it gives the appearance of having been drawn with the same sort of pen as the regular series, it is much freer and more calligraphic, with a style unmatched by any other American script or cursive face.

Lydian Bold Condensed was designed in 1946, also by Chappell, but not marketed until 1949. It has the general character of the earlier faces, but with much more emphasis on the vertical strokes. This gives the lowercase a suggestion of the effect of a simplified German blackletter.

Lydian, ATF 666 (10-96pt); Inter (8-36pt)
Lydian Italic, ATF 667 (10-96pt); Inter (8-36pt)
Lydian Bold, ATF 673 (10-96pt); Inter (8-36pt)
Lydian Bold Italic, ATF 674 (10-96pt); Inter (8-36pt)
Lydian Bold Condensed, ATF 692 (10-72pt)
Lydian Bold Condensed Italic, ATF 693 (10-72pt)
Lydian Cursive, ATF 682 (18-72pt)

LYRIC—see *Greeting Card.*

LYDIAN CURSIVE, ATF 24-pt.

ABCDEFGHIJKLMNOPQRSTUVWXYZ$1234567890
abcdefghijklmnopqrstuvwxyz.,-:;'""!?¢£&

MacFARLAND, Inland 24-pt. (Steve Boerner)

ABCDEFGHIJKLMNOPQRSTUVWXYZ
abcdefghijklmnopqrstuvwxyz&1234567890$.,-:;'!?

MacFARLAND ITALIC, 24-pt.

ABCDEFGHIJKLMNOPQRSTUVWXYZ .,'-;:!?
abcdefghijklmnopqrstuvwxyz 1234567890&$

CONDENSED MacFARLAND, ATF 24-pt. (Mac Gardner)

ABCDEFGHIJKLMNOPQRSTUVWXYZ$!?-.
abcdefghijklmnopqrstuvwxyz1234567890:;;

MADEMOISELLE, Balto 24-pt.

ABCDEFGHIJKLMNOPQRSTUVWXYZ 1234790
abcdefghijklmnopqrstuvwxyz .,:'-&()!? $1234567890

MAJESTIC & BOLD, Lino 9-pt. & ITALIC, 8-pt.

ABCDEFGHIJKLMNOPQRSTUVWXYZ& abcdefghijklmnopqrstuvwxyz fiflffffiffl 1234567890 [($£,.:;'-'?!*†‡§¶)]
ABCDEFGHIJKLMNOPQRSTUVWXYZ& abcdefghijklmnopqrstuvwxyz fiflffffiffl 1234567890 [($£,.:;'-'?!*†‡§¶)]
ABCDEFGHIJKLMNOPQRSTUVWXYZ& abcdefghijklmnopqrstuvwxyz 1234567890 [($£,.:;'-'?!†‡§¶)]*

MANDATE, Ludlow 24-pt.

ABCDEFGHIJKLMNOPQRSTUVWXYZ
abcdefghijklmnopqrstuvwxyz.,-:;"!?&()[]on or of t's'
$1234567890 % CEFIQT

MANHATTAN, 24-pt. (Dave Greer)

ABCDEFGHIJKLMNOPQRSTUVWXYZ&
abcdefghijklmnopqrstuvwxyzœœ .,-:;'!? £$1234567890

MANILA, Inland 24-pt. (part reduced) (Stanley Kroeger)

QUICK LINING RECOMMEND
Banished Results 38 Exact Cutting 45

MacFARLAND was cut in 1899 by Inland Type Foundry, adapted from *Römische Antiqua* of Genzsch & Heyse in Germany. It is named in honor of Mr. J. Horace MacFarland, prominent printer of Harrisburg, Pennsylvania. At about the same time, the foundry of A. D. Farmer & Son cut essentially the same face from the same source, naming it *Bradford* after the first noted printer of New York; and Hansen issued *Crawford,* another look-alike. The Inland faces, along with *Condensed MacFarland* designed and cut in 1903, went to ATF when that foundry acquired Inland in 1912. The faces have some relationship to *Elzevir* or *French Old Style,* but are heavier, though not as heavy as the related DeVinne series. Lacking the eccentricities of some characters of *DeVinne,* these faces became popular for book titles and other work for which *DeVinne* was considered unsuitable. Keystone's *Dickens* is very similar but a little lighter; it is known as *Classic* on Linotype, but 18-point *Classic Italic* is the equivalent of *MacFarland Italic.* Compare *Lorimer.*

MacFarland, Inland-ATF 316 (5-84pt); Mono 68 (6-36pt); Crawford, Hansen (6-48pt); also Dickens, Keystone (6-12pt); Classic, Lino (6-14pt)

MacFarland Italic, Inland-ATF 317 (6-48pt); Mono 681 (6-36pt); Crawford Italic, Hansen (6-48pt); also Dickens Italic, Keystone (6-12pt); Classic Italic, Lino (6-18pt)

Condensed MacFarland, Inland-ATF 119 (6-84pt)

MADEMOISELLE was designed by Tommy Thompson in 1953 as a display face for *Mademoiselle* magazine. It was cut by Herman Schnoor at Baltimore Type, which also offered fonts for general sale. It is a delicate, narrow modern roman, with long ascenders and short descenders, rather loosely fitted, and works well for display with transitional text faces such as *Bulmer* and *Scotch Roman.* Both lining and oldstyle figures are provided, along with several pointing hands as shown.

Mademoiselle, Balto 221 (24-48pt)

MAJESTIC is a newspaper face produced by Linotype staff designers in 1955. It is similar to *Corona,* but was made in very few sizes.

Majestic and Italic, Lino (8pt)
Majestic and Bold, Lino (8,9pt)

MANDARIN—see Antiques in Appendix.

MANDATE is a connecting script designed by Robert H. Middleton for Ludlow in 1934. It has a rough-and-ready sort of handwritten appearance, more informal and unstudied than the somewhat similar *Kaufmann Bold* and *Brush* (q.v.). Some of the capitals have extra height, extending below the base line. In the specimen shown here, a number of capitals, as well as *z* and the logotypes, have been lengthened with the additional terminal stroke.

Mandate, Ludlow 36-BIC (14-72pt)

MANHATTAN was introduced by ATF in 1904 or earlier. An ad at that time said it was "for any form of display requiring strength, legibility, and beauty." It was shown in the 1906 specimen book but was gone by 1912. It is a heavy, vertical, semi-calligraphic face, with horizontal ends on the majority of the main stems but not all.

Manhattan, ATF (10-72pt)

MANILA is an adaptation of nineteenth-century antiques known generally as *Clarendon, Doric,* or *Ionic.* Inland Type Foundry introduced a series under this name in 1899, and Monotype in 1909 produced a *Manila,* probably adapted from another foundry source, but differing somewhat from the Inland face. Both have the same general character, but the Monotype face is a little narrower. The Inland face apparently was not continued after ATF took over the foundry in 1912, perhaps because of its similarity to ATF's *Doric No. 520.* A completely different face with the same name was brought out by A. D. Farmer & Son, also in 1899; both series were named for the victory of Admiral Dewey over the Spanish at Manila in the Philippine Islands the previous year.

Manila, Inland (6-48pt); Manila, Mono 92 (5½-12pt)

MARBLE HEART, ATF (42-pt. at 57%)

ABCDEFGHIJKLMNOPQRSTUVWXYZ.,;:-'!? 1234567890$

MARLBOROUGH, Goudy 16-pt.

A B C D E F G H I J K L M N O P Q R S T U V W X Y Z &.,';:!?-
a b c d e f g h i j k l m n o p q r s t u v w x y z æ œ fi ff ffi fl ffl & $ 1 2 3 4 5 6 7 8 9 0

MASTERMAN, Mono 24-pt.

ABCDEFGHIJKLMNOPQRSTUVWXYZ&
abcdefghijklmnopqrstuvwxyz fi fl ff ffi ffl æ œ
$1234567890.,-:;'!?

MASTODON, Hansen 24-pt.

HISTORY OF THE MERCHANT MARINE 12345
Foreign products obtained at great risk 67890

MATTHEWS, ATF 24-pt. (Bob Orbach)

ABCDEFGHIJKLMNOPQRSTUVWXYZ&$.,:;!?
abcdefghijklmnopqrstuvwxyz1234567890

CONDENSED MATTHEWS, ATF 24-pt.

REFINING CHARACTER Bought Exquisite Types

MAYFAIR CURSIVE, Ludlow 24-pt. (part reduced) (Phil Ambrosi)

AABCDEFGHIJKLMNOPQRSTUVWXYZ
abcdefghijklmnopqrstuvwxyz   1234567890$ &$—.,;:-''?! FQJT %

MARBLE HEART is an ATF reissue, in 1933 and several later times, of *Gothic Double Shade,* an 1870s face of Boston Type Foundry, one of ATF's predecessors. The ATF casting was later plated and issued by John Carroll and others, and cut in smaller sizes by Los Angeles Type Foundry.

Marble Heart, ATF (42pt); Carroll-TFP-Triangle (42); LATF (18-42)

MARKET GOTHIC—see *Bell Gothic.*

MARLBOROUGH was designed in 1925 by Frederic W. Goudy for a printer who lost interest before it was completed. As matrices for the 16-point size had been cut by Robert Wiebking, Goudy cast a few fonts, but was not pleased with the results. Revisions were drawn, but were not completed before his workshop was destroyed by fire in 1939. In 1942 the design was sold to Monotype, but there is no evidence that they did anything with it. The name is from the town in New York where Goudy lived and worked.

Marlborough, Goudy (16pt)

MARTIN and *Italic* are listed as a Monotype production of 1945, adapted by Sol Hess from old sources, but no specimen or further information has been found.

MASTERMAN was put on Monotype in 1909, but it originated with Hansen some time before that. It is a modification of earlier faces known generally as *Title* before type names as we know them became common, and is similar to some of the faces in the Engravers and Litho families (q.v.). The characters have high contrast, and lowercase has fairly long ascenders. The basic character is a plain, severe roman shape. It was popular as an early advertising display face.

Masterman, Hansen (6-48pt); Mono 158 (5-36pt)

MASTODON is a heavy roman issued by Hansen early in the century. The founder called it "a strong, distinctive face that compels attention."

Mastodon, Hansen (8-72pt)

MATSON—see *Modern Roman Extra Condensed.*

MATTHEWS is a very heavy, thick-and-thin, serifless type introduced by Inland Type Foundry in 1901. It is somewhat similar to the later *Globe Gothic Bold*—in fact it is more carefully designed and seems to agree better with the lighter Globe Gothics than the latter face does. ATF cast both faces for a while after acquiring Inland in 1912, as well as *Condensed Matthews,* which Inland had introduced in 1903 as "a new gothic letter." The specimen of *Matthews* shown here is from a font showing considerable wear, with rounded corners. Compare *Radiant Heavy.*

Matthews, Inland-ATF 319 (6-72pt)
Condensed Matthews, Inland-ATF 120 (6-72pt)

MATURA, MAXIME—see Imports in Appendix.

MAYFAIR CURSIVE is a precise script designed by R. Hunter Middleton for Ludlow in 1932. Letters are not connected, although some of them have starting or finishing strokes that almost meet. It is more severe than *Coronet,* designed a few years later by the same artist, and never achieved the widespread popularity of the latter face. Also compare *Liberty, Bernhard Tango.*

Mayfair Cursive, Ludlow 31-MIC (14-72pt)

ATTRACTIVE BEDSTEADS
Steel Springs and 28 Chilled Iron Shafts

ABCDEFGHIJKLMNOPQRSTUVWXYZ;&-!'?£$
abcdefghijklmnopqrsf tuvwxyz 1234567890

SPRING OPENING Prominent Contrast
EUROPEAN MEMBERS Returning Home Shortly

ABCDEFGHIJKLMNOPQRSTUVWXYZ .,-
1234567890.,-;;'!?

ABCDEFGHIJKLMNOPQRSTUVWXYZ&
abcdefghijklmnopqrstuvwxyz?!-;:.,'$1234567890

ABCDEFGHIJKLMNOPQRSTUVWXYZ&EFGHIS
abcdefghijklmnopqrstuvwxyzff fiflffifflﬔﬕ$1234567890.,-:;'!?

American Type Founders Company
Made in 24-Point, for your approval A.D. 1909

ABCDEFGHIJKLMNOPQRSTUVWXYZ $1234567890   ABCDEFGHIJKLMNOPQRSTUVWXYZ
ABCDEFGHIJKLMNOPQRSTUVWXYZ $1234567890   æœÆŒ æœÆŒ
abcdefghijklmnopqrstuvwxyz fiflff ffiffl ,.-;':'!? ( ) @ ℔&£ * † | ‡ || § ¶ -- ⅛ ¼ ⅜ ½
abcdefghijklmnopqrstuvwxyz fiflff ffiffl ,.-;':'!? ( ) @℔&£

ABCDEFGHIJKLMNOPQRSTUVWXYZ
abcdefghijklmnopqrstuvwxyz $1234567890

212

MAZARIN was introduced by BB&S in 1895, redesigned from the *Golden Type* of William Morris. *Mazarin Italic* was introduced a year later, but neither face lasted long. See *Jenson Oldstyle*.

Mazarin No. 5, BB&S (6-60pt)
Mazarin Italic, BB&S (6-48pt)

McCLURE was introduced by Inland Type Foundry in 1902 as "a sturdy, unique, and characterful design . . . named for S. S. McClure, publisher of *McClure's* magazine." It is a medium-weight roman with the triangular serifs of some of the faces in the Latin family; contrast between thicks and thins is only moderate. It was cast for a time by ATF after that foundry absorbed Inland.

McClure, Inland-ATF 325 (6-72pt)

McFARLAND—see *MacFarland*.

McMURTRIE TITLE was designed in 1922 by Douglas C. McMurtrie. It is a font of highlighted roman capitals, based on a face created by the eighteenth-century Dutch founder, J. F. Rosart. The source of the first line of the specimen, a major typographer, shows no characters except the alphabet and three points. But the cases of a prominent printer include the points and figures shown on the second line. Although the letters seem to be identical, each size is on the next larger body compared to the first showing (thus the second specimen line is on 30-point body). The second line seems to be a little less compatible with the capitals, and perhaps was substituted from another source. Compare *Caslon Shaded, Cameo*.

McMurtrie Title, Continental Typefounders (18-30pt)

McNALLY is an Inland face that was first shown in 1905. It is very similar to *DeVinne,* but with heavier hairlines. It does not appear in ATF specimen books after that foundry acquired Inland in 1912.

McNally, Inland (5-84pt)

MEDIAEVAL is an unusual typeface designed by Frederic W. Goudy in 1930. He says that it is based on a twelfth-century South German manuscript hand, with the lowercase borrowing the freedom of the scribe's pen of the Renaissance, but with capitals being more or less composites of monastic manuscript and Lombardic painted forms. The result is a unique but very readable version of the traditional "Old English" letter, somewhat romanized.

Mediaeval: Goudy (14-48pt)

MEDIAL SCRIPT is a simple, connecting design issued by ATF in 1909, and shown only in one size. It may be a revival of an earlier face.

Medial Script, ATF (24pt)

MEDIEVAL was introduced by Intertype in 1929 as a copy of "Holland's most popular type," designed by S. H. DeRoos. It is based on the same Venetian type of 1470 as *Centaur, Cloister,* and others, but with several distinctive characters including cap *A* with a prominent single serif at the apex, *M* with double serifs at the apex, *P* and *R* with large bowls, cap *U* with lowercase form, single-bowl *g* with open tail, and in the italic an unusual lowercase *f*. There is also *Medieval Bold* and *Italic,* and a wide version in 6-point only. Notice the difference in spelling between this face and Goudy's entirely different *Mediaeval*. Compare *Benedictine*.

Medieval and Italic, Inter (6-24, 6-14pt)
Medieval Bold and Italic, Inter (6-24, 6-14pt)
Medieval Expanded, Inter (6pt)

MEDIUM CONDENSED GOTHIC—see *Gothic, Medium Condensed*.
MEDIUM GOTHIC NO. 7—see *Boston Gothic, Mid-Gothic*.
MELIOR—see *Lanston;* also see Imports in Appendix.

MEMPHIS LIGHT & ITALIC, Lino 14-pt.

ABCDEFGHIJKLMNOPQRSTUVWXYZ ff fi ffi fl ffl ABCDEFGHIJKLMNOPQRSTUVWXYZ . A a f
abcdefghijklmnopqrstuvwxyz −% *(),.-;':'!?—&& $1234567890 ⅛ ¼ ⅜ ½ ⅝ ¾ ⅞
ABCDEFGHIJKLMNOPQRSTUVWXYZ ff fi ffi fl ffl
*abcdefghijklmnopqrstuvwxyz −% *(),.-;':'!?—& $1234567890* Є К m n U
Є К m n U

MEMPHIS MEDIUM & ITALIC, Lino 14-pt.

AABCDEFGHIJKLMNOPQRSTUVWXYZ& ABCDEFGHIJKLMNOPQRSTUVWXYZ&
aabcdeffghijklmnopqrstuvwxyz 1234567890 ($£,.:;-'?!«»'*†)
AABCDEFGHIJKLMNOPQRSTUVWXYZ& ABCDEFGHIJKLMNOPQRSTUVWXYZ&
aabcdeffghijklmnopqrstuvwxyz 1234567890 ($£,.:;-'?!«»†)*

MEMPHIS BOLD & ITALIC, Lino 14-pt.

AABCDEFGHIJKLMNOPQRSTUVWXYZ& $£..:;-'?!«»—|—ÆŒæœ Є К m n W
AABCDEFGHIJKLMNOPQRSTUVWXYZ& $£..:;-'?!«»—— ÆŒæœ Є К m n W
aabcdeffghijklmnopqrstuvwxyz 1234567890 ()*†‡§¶[]@℔% ⅛¼⅜½⅝¾⅞
aabcdeffghijklmnopqrstuvwxyz 1234567890 ()*†‡§¶[]@℔% ⅛¼⅜½⅝¾⅞

LINING MEMPHIS LIGHT & BOLD, Lino 12L

ABCDEFGHIJKLMNOPQRSTUVWXYZÆŒ 1234
ABCDEFGHIJKLMNOPQRSTUVWXYZÆŒ 1234

MEMPHIS EXTRA BOLD & ITALIC, Lino 14-pt.

AABCDEFGHIJKLMNOPQRSTUVWXYZ&
AABCDEFGHIJKLMNOPQRSTUVWXYZ&
aabcdeffghijklmnopqrstuvwxyz 1234567 ($£,.:;-'?!«»*†)
aabcdeffghijklmnopqrstuvwxyz 1234567 ($£,.:;-'?!«»*†)

MEMPHIS MEDIUM CONDENSED, BOLD CONDENSED & EXTRA BOLD CONDENSED, Lino 14-pt.

ABCDEFGHIJKLMNOPQRSTUVWXYZ&   ABCDEFGHIJKLMNOPQRSTUVWXYZ&
ABCDEFGHIJKLMNOPQRSTUVWXYZ&   **ABCDEFGHIJKLMNOPQRSTUVWXYZ&**
abcdefghijklmnopqrstuvwxyz   abcdefghijklmnopqrstuvwxyz
abcdefghijklmnopqrstuvwxyz   **abcdefghijklmnopqrstuvwxyz**
12345 ($£,.:;'-'?!*†‡§¶fiflfffffiffl) 67890   12345 ($£,.:;'-'?!*†‡§¶fiflfffffiffl) 67890
12345 ($£,.:;'-'?!*†‡§¶fiflfffffiffl) 67890   **12345 ($£,.:;'-'?!*†‡§¶fiflfffffiffl) 67890**

MENU ROMAN, BB&S 24-pt.

PRINTER and Client Pleased

MENU SHADED, BB&S 18-pt. (Roger Frith)

ABCDEFGHIJKLMNOPQRSTUVWXYZ& .,=;:!?'
abcdefghijklmnopqrstuvwxyz $1234567890

214

MEMPHIS is the Linotype copy of the popular German square-serif face known as *Memphis* or *Girder,* designed by Rudolf Weiss about 1929, which did much to revive interest in this old style. *Memphis Light* and *Bold* were introduced by Linotype in 1933, Italics and Unique Caps in 1934, *Medium* in 1935, and other variations up to 1938. The *Extra Bold* versions were designed by C. H. Griffith. Alternate characters are available in some versions to more nearly approximate the appearance of *Stymie* or *Beton* (q.v.). The *Lining* versions are comparable to small caps in the regular versions, being proportionately wider and heavier than caps, and have no lowercase; there are several sizes each in 6- and 12-point, permitting various cap-and-small-cap combinations, in the manner of *Copperplate Gothic.* Also see *Ward;* compare *Cairo, Karnak.*

Memphis Light, Lino (6-36pt); APL (6-144pt)
Memphis Light Italic, Lino (6-14pt)
Memphis Medium, Lino (6-36pt); APL (18-72pt)
Memphis Medium Italic, Lino (6-30pt); APL (24-48pt)
Memphis Bold, Lino (6-36pt); APL (6-144pt)
Memphis Bold Italic, Lino (6-30pt)
Lining Memphis Light and Bold, Lino (6s-12L)
Memphis Extra Bold, Lino (8-30pt); APL (18-144pt)
Memphis Extra Bold Italic, Lino (8-18pt)
Memphis Medium Condensed, Lino (8-36pt); APL (96-144pt)
Memphis Bold Condensed, Lino (10-36pt)
Memphis Extra Bold Condensed, Lino (8-36pt); APL (96-144pt)

MENU ROMAN is the BB&S rename, for the 1925 specimen book, of *Skinner,* which was shown by Inland Type Foundry about 1885, and ascribed to John K. Rogers as well as to Nicholas J. Werner. *Menu Title,* formerly *Lining Menu,* was Inland's *Bruce Title,* by Werner. *Menu Shaded* was *Acme,* designed in 1886 or earlier. The latter has only a very general relationship to the other faces which are nearly monotone, with long serifs tapering to sharp points. Compare *Paragon.*

Menu Roman, BB&S-ATF 1773 (6-30pt); also Menu Title, BB&S-ATF 1775 (6-24pt)
Menu Shaded, BB&S (6-30pt)

MERIONTYPE was designed by William Martin Johnson about 1905 or earlier and cast by ATF for use in *Ladies' Home Journal.* ATF says, "The requirements called for a composite modernization of popular oldstyle faces, retaining all of their desirable features, while eliminating those proven undesirable. It was further stipulated that the *Meriontype* letters must be interusable with the letters of *Bulfinch,* or sister series." Some letters appear to be identical in the two series, others are similar, although the serifs of *Meriontype* are generally a little larger and more angular. The lowercase *g* of the latter face has the appearance of being reversed.

Meriontype, ATF (6-72pt)

MERRYMOUNT was designed by Bertram G. Goodhue for Daniel B. Updike's Merrymount Press in Boston, and was cut only in 18-point. This was used in an impressive Altar Book, which established the reputation of Updike and his Press. Steve Watts says the face was cut by Mr. [August] Woerner of A. D. Farmer & Son Type Foundry in New York. The original punches and matrices are preserved by the Providence (Rhode Island) Public Library as part of its extensive Updike Collection, where a note with the mats says, "Cut by A. Woener (sic), June 21st, 1895."

Merrymount, private (18pt)

MERIONTYPE, ATF 12-pt. (Ralph Babcock)

ABCDEFGHIJKLMNOPQRSTUVWXYZ&
abcdefghijklmnopqrstuvwxyz $1234567890 .,-';:!?

MERRYMOUNT, 18-pt. (Providence Public Library)

ABCDEFGHIJKLMNOPRQSTUVWXYZ 1234567890 ([-$£.',.:;?!·&ct—
abcdefghijklmnopqrstuvwxyz ŒÆæœffffiflffiffl JESUS LORD ℞ ℣ ¶

METROTHIN NO. 2, Lino 14-pt.

ABCDEFGHIJKLMNOPQRSTUVWXYZ& ABCDEFGHIJKLMNOPQRSTUVWXYZ&
abcdefghijklmnopqrstuvwxyz 1234567890($£,.:;'-'?!*†) 1234567890 A E F G K M N S W Y

Gothic 42

METROTHIN NO. 2 ITALIC, Lino (24-pt. at 57%)

ABCDEFGHIJKLMNOPQRSTUVWXYZ&ÆŒ abcdefghijklmnopqrstuvwxyzæœ 1234567890$/,.:;-"?!–()%

METROLITE NO. 2 & ITALIC, Lino 14-pt.

ABCDEFGHIJKLMNOPQRSTUVWXYZ& AGJMNVWagvw,;''
ABCDEFGHIJKLMNOPQRSTUVWXYZ&
abcdefghijklmnopqrstuvwxyz 1234567890 ($£,.:;'-'?!*†)
abcdefghijklmnopqrstuvwxyz 1234567890 ($£,.:;'-'?!†)*

Original

METROMEDIUM NO. 2 & ITALIC, Lino 14-pt.

ABCDEFGHIJKLMNOPQRSTUVWXYZ& ABCDEFGHIJKLMNOPQRSTUVWXYZ& Q aefjt&$
ABCDEFGHIJKLMNOPQRSTUVWXYZ&
abcdefghijklmnopqrstuvwxyz 1234567890 ($£,.:;'-'?!*†) 1234567890 A E F G K M N S W Y
abcdefghijklmnopqrstuvwxyz 1234567890 ($£,.:;'-'?!†)*

Gothic 44

METROBLACK NO. 2 & ITALIC, Lino 14-pt.

ABCDEFGHIJKLMNOPQRSTUVWXYZ& **AGJMNVWagvw,;''**
ABCDEFGHIJKLMNOPQRSTUVWXYZ& ***AGNVagvw,;'***
abcdefghijklmnopqrstuvwxyz 1234567890 ($£,.:;'-'?!*†)
abcdefghijklmnopqrstuvwxyz 1234567890 ($£,.:;'-'?!*†)

Original

LINING METROMEDIUM & METROTHIN, Lino 12L

ABCDEFGHIJKLMNOPQRSTUVWXYZ&ÆŒ 1234567890
ABCDEFGHIJKLMNOPQRSTUVWXYZ&ÆŒ 1234567890

MID-GOTHIC NO. 52, Mono 176 24-pt.

ABCDEFGHIJKLMNOPQRSTUVWXYZ&
abcdefghijklmnopqrstuvwxyz $1234567890 .,-:;'!?

MID-GOTHIC NO. 52, Mono 276 24-pt.

ABCDEFGHIJKLMNOPQRSTUVWXYZ&
abcdefghijklmnopqrstuvwxyz $1234567890 .,-:;'!?

MIEHLE EXTRA CONDENSED, ATF (48-pt. at 50%) (Rick von Holdt)

ABCDEFGHIJKLMNOPQRSTUVWXYZ&.,-:;'!? abcdefghijklmnopqrstuvwxyzfffififfffiffl$1234567890

MISSAL INITIALS, ATF 18-pt. (Cliff Helbert)

ABCDEFGHIJKLMNOPQRSTUVWXYZ

METROLITE and *Metroblack* were designed by William A. Dwiggins and introduced by Linotype in January 1930, as the first American faces to join the trend to sans serif started by Futura and Kabel. These faces are less mechanical than the European imports, and were promoted as being less monotonous and illegible. The first two weights were soon followed by *Metrothin* and *Metromedium*. In 1932 several characters were redesigned; thereafter the series was promoted as *Metrothin No. 2, Metrolite No. 2, Metromedium No. 2,* and *Metroblack No. 2,* including the redesigned characters, but the original characters were available as extras—these are shown at the right of the *Metrolite* and *Metroblack* specimens, and partially for *Metroblack Italic*. APL matrices were made only for the No. 2 version.

    Metrolite No. 2 Italic was shown in 1935, along with *Lining Metrothin* and *Lining Metromedium,* which are like the small caps of the regular faces. Italics for *Metromedium No. 2* and *Metroblack No. 2* were shown in 1937. *Metrolite No. 4 Italic* and *Metrothin No. 4 Italic* are essentially the same design but narrower, for mechanical purposes. Unique Capitals are made for some sizes of *Metrothin* and *Metromedium.*

    Alternative figures are made as follows:
Gothic No. 39, for *Metrothin No. 2,* similar to *Spartan Light.*
Gothic No. 40, for *Metrolite No. 2,* similar to *Spartan Medium.*
Gothic No. 41, for *Metroblack No. 2,* similar to *Spartan Black.*
Gothic No. 42, for *Metrothin No. 2,* similar to *Kabel Light.*
Gothic No. 43, for *Metrolite No. 2,* similar to *Kabel Medium.*
Gothic No. 44, for *Metromedium No. 2,* similar to *Kabel Bold.*
Gothic No. 45, for *Metroblack No. 2,* similar to *Sans Serif Extra Bold.*

METROPOLIS, MICHELANGELO—see Imports in Appendix.
MICROGRAMMA—see *Eurostile* under Imports in Appendix.

MID-GOTHIC was designed by Nicholas J. Werner for Central Type Foundry, probably just before that St. Louis foundry joined the merger that formed American Type Founders in 1892. It is an undistinguished gothic of nineteenth-century style, but is an interesting example of the way many of the earlier types were modified for Monotype. The original copy of this face for machine typesetting (6- to 12-point) was necessarily reproportioned to meet mechanical requirements; the same patterns were then used for display sizes and the result is series 176. Later the foundry design was copied much more exactly, with little or no modification, as series 276. Both versions have been shown in Monotype literature as *Lining Gothic, Mid-Gothic,* or *Mid-Gothic No. 2* at various times. The No. 2 designation was applied to many foundry faces around the turn of the century when they were adapted to standard alignment or when other slight changes were made. Hansen copied this face as *Medium Gothic No. 7,* and made an inline version as *Boston Gothic* (q.v.).

MIEHLE EXTRA CONDENSED was designed by Morris F. Benton for ATF in 1906. It is a very narrow face with large x-height, and has very short, blunt serifs and little contrast between thick and thin strokes. It was intended for use in newspapers for headlines. Normal and Condensed widths were drawn but apparently not completed. Compare *Compact,* a more thick-and-thin face of similar proportions.

MINUET—see *Piranesi Italic.*

MISSAL INITIALS were issued by ATF in 1904; their design has been ascribed to Will Bradley. Derived from fifteenth-century sources, each letter is designed to fill a square area. Compare *Caxton Initials, Lombardic Initials.*

Metrothin [No. 2], Lino (6-36pt); APL (6-144pt)
Metrothin No. 2 Italic, Lino (24,30pt)
Metrothin No. 4 Italic, Lino (24,30pt)
Metrolite [No. 2], Lino (6-36pt); APL (6-144pt)
Metrolite No. 2 Italic, Lino (6-30pt)
Metrolite No. 4 Italic, Lino (24,30pt)
Metromedium [No. 2], Lino (6-36pt); APL (6-144pt)
Metromedium No. 2 Italic, Lino (6-36pt)
Metroblack [No. 2], Lino (6-42pt); APL (6-144pt)
Metroblack No. 2 Italic, Lino (6-24pt)
Lining Metrothin and Metromedium, Lino (6s-12L)

Mid-Gothic [No. 2], Central-ATF 285 (6-72pt); same or Lining Gothic, Mono 176 (6-36pt); Mono 276 (14-36pt); Medium Gothic No. 7, Hansen (6-72pt)

Miehle Extra Condensed, ATF 326 (6-120pt); also Miehle Extra Condensed Title, ATF 327 (6-96pt)

Missal Initials, ATF (10-60pt)
Missal Text, BB&S (8-36pt)

MISSION, 18-pt. (Duane Scott)

ABCDEFGHIJKLMNOPQRSTUVWXYZ&$.,:'-?!
abcdefghijklmnopqrstuvwxyz1234567890ffifl

MITCHELL, Inland 24s (Dan X. Solo)

ABCDEFGHIJKLMNOPQRSTU
VWXYZ 1234567890 $&!?

MODERN ANTIQUE (NO. 2), Mono 12-pt.

ABCDEFGHIJKLMNOPQRSTUVWXYZ&$1234567890.,-:;''?!
abcdefghijklmnopqrstuvwxyz flfffiflffi

MODERN ANTIQUE CONDENSED, Mono 12-pt.

ABCDEFGHIJKLMNOPQRSTUVWXYZ&ÆŒ
abcdefghijklmnopqrstuvwxyzæœfifffiflffi 1234567890 $.,-'':;!?

MODERN GOTHIC, BB&S 24-pt.

ABCDEFGHIJKLMNOPQRSTUVWXYZ&
Elocutionist Generously $1234567890 .,-:;'!?

MODERN GOTHIC ITALIC, BB&S 24-pt. (part reduced) (Sheldon Wesson)

ABCDEFGHIJKLMNOPQRSTUVWXYZ
abcdefghijklmnopqrstuvwxyz .,-:;'!?
1234567890$& ÆŒ œæ fffififlffiffi

MODERN GOTHIC CONDENSED, Mono 24-pt.

ABCDEFGHIJKLMNOPQRSTUVWXYZ&
abcdefghijklmnopqrstuvwxyz   .,:;-!?   1234567890$

MISSAL TEXT—see *Faust Text.*

MISSION was designed for BB&S by Sidney Gaunt in 1905, but patented by George Oswald Ottley. It is a rather novel face, with long ascenders and short descenders. Serifs are triangular, like some members of the Latin series. Most noticeable is the way some strokes in the capital letters are joined with fillet curves, especially in the *B*. Compare *Viking.*

Mission, BB&S-ATF 1778 (6-48pt)

MISTRAL—see Imports in Appendix.

MITCHELL is a plain, wide gothic, introduced by Inland Type Foundry in 1906. It is very similar to *Blair* (q.v.), but heavier.

Mitchell, Inland-ATF 328 (6s-36pt)

MODERN ANTIQUE and *Modern Antique Condensed* were adapted to Monotype in 1909 from traditional faces dating from about 1820, commonly known simply as Antiques or Egyptians. They were forerunners of the square serifs, but closer to romans in general appearance, and were usually used for boldface emphasis with roman types, particularly modern romans. In most sizes these two Monotype faces are the same set width as each other, and have the same figures and points. Otherwise they differ only in the proportions of the C2 and C1 arrangements, being good examples of adaptations to the basic Monotype unit system. (See "Practical Design Limitations" in Introduction.) Also see *Bold Antique;* and *Latin Modern* under *Latin Bold Condensed.*

Modern Antique, Mono 26 (5-12pt); Antique No. 4, Lino (8pt) (see Ionic No. 4)
Modern Antique Condensed, Mono 76 (5-12pt); Antique No. 3, Lino = Inter

MODERN BODONI—see *Louvaine.*
MODERN CASLON—see *Caslon Medium.*

MODERN GOTHIC originated with BB&S about 1897. It appears to be a modernization of older nineteenth-century gothics, although it has considerable resemblance to the much later European design, *Helvetica Bold.* It has the horizontal endings to curved strokes which typify *Helvetica,* but the more typically American double-bowl *g*. However, it is much more loosely fitted and not as refined as either *Helvetica* or the American *Franklin Gothic,* which originated in 1902. The entire series is called *Gothic Modern* in some specimens.

Modern Condensed Gothic is probably the best member of this family. It was copied by Monotype at an early date, with 6- to 12-point sizes substantially modified to fit the unit system; however, unlike many early Monotype copies, display sizes are virtually exact copies of the foundry original. In 1928 Sol Hess drew a set of alternate capitals for this face, and the name was changed to *Tourist Gothic* (q.v.) in display sizes, 14-point and larger. This face is often called *Franklin Gothic Condensed,* but this is not correct as there is only a general resemblance. *Medium Condensed Gothic Outline,* cut by Triangle Type Foundry in Chicago, is an open version, without lowercase, of this face; some other sources inaccurately call it *Franklin Gothic Condensed Outline* (q.v.).

The larger sizes of *Gothic No. 13* (q.v.) on Linotype and Intertype are very similar. Monotype also has *Tourist Gothic Italic,* and an adaptation of *Modern Gothic Italic* under the name of *Bold Inclined Gothic.*

Modern Gothic [or Gothic Modern], BB&S-ATF 1662 (5-96pt); also Modern Gothic Title, BB&S-ATF 1666 (6-84pt)
Modern Gothic Italic, BB&S-ATF 1665 (5-72pt); Bold Inclined Gothic, Mono 132K (6-12pt)
Modern Condensed Gothic, BB&S-ATF 1663 (6-72pt); Mono 140 (6-72H4); also Modern Condensed Gothic Title, BB&S-ATF 1664 (6-120pt)
Outline Gothic Medium Condensed, Triangle (18-48pt); Franklin Gothic Condensed Outline, Baltimore etc. (24-60pt)

MODERN NO. 20—see Imports in Appendix.

MODERN NO. 8 & ITALIC, Mono 12-pt.

ABCDEFGHIJKLMNOPQRSTUVWXYZ&ÆŒ   ABCDEFGHIJKLMNOPQRSTUVWXYZ&ÆŒ
ABCDEFGHIJKLMNOPQRSTUVWXYZ&ÆŒ

abcdefghijklmnopqrstuvwxyzæœfifflflffiffl 1234567890 $.,-'':;!?
abcdefghijklmnopqrstuvwxyzæœfifflflffiffl 1234567890 $:;!?

MODERN CONDENSED & ITALIC, Mono 1ABC 10-pt.

ABCDEFGHIJKLMNOPQRSTUVWXYZ&ÆŒ ABCDEFGHIJKLMNOPQRSTUVWXYZ&ÆŒ
abcdefghijklmnopqrstuvwxyzæœ fiflffffiffl   *abcdefghijklmnopqrstuvwxyzæœ fiflffffiffl*
$1234567890 .,-'':;!?   *$1234567890 :;!?*
ABCDEFGHIJKLMNOPQRSTUVWXYZ&ÆŒ

MODERN & ITALIC, Mono 34ABC, 8-pt.

ABCDEFGHIJKLMNOPQRSTUVWXYZ&ÆŒ ABCDEFGHIJKLMNOPQRSTUVWXYZ&ÆŒ
abcdefghijklmnopqrstuvwxyzæœ fiflffffiffl   *abcdefghijklmnopqrstuvwxyzæœ fiflffffiffl*
$1234567890 .,-'':;!?   *$1234567890 :;!?*
ABCDEFGHIJKLMNOPQRSTUVWXYZ&ÆŒ

MODERN EXTENDED & ITALIC, Mono 5AC 9-pt.

abcdefghijklmnopqrstuvwxyz 1234567890$ *abcdefghijklmnopqrstuvwxyz 1234567890$*
ABCDEFGHIJKLMNOPQRSTUVWXYZ&   *ABCDEFGHIJKLMNOPQRSTUVWXYZ&*

MODERN ROMAN EXTRA CONDENSED (MATSON, Lino) (30-pt. at 80%)

ABCDEFGHIJKLMNOPQRSTUVWXYZ& ,.:;?!()"--ÆŒ$1234567890

MODERN ROMAN BOLD CONDENSED (TITLE CONDENSED NO. 75, Hansen) 24-pt. (Herb Harnish)

ABCDEFGHIJKLMNOPQRSTUVWXYZ&
abcdefghijklmnopqrstuvwxyz 1234567890

MODERN ROMAN BOLD EXTRA CONDENSED, BB&S 24-pt.

COMPOSITION Proved Exceptional

MODERN ROMAN CONDENSED, Mono 146 18-pt.

ABCDEFGHIJKLMNOPQRSTUVWXYZ
abcdefghijklmnopqrstuvwxyzfifflflffiffl1234567890&$.,-':;!?

MODERN NO. 3 EXTRA CONDENSED, Mono 216A 8-pt.

ABCDEFGHIJKLMNOPQRSTUVWXYZ& abcdefghijklmnopqrstuvwxyz fififlffiffl $1234567890 .,-:;'!?

MODERN ROMAN ITALIC, BB&S 12-pt.

MODERN ROMAN ITALIC Marked Character CREATES

MODERN ROMAN LIGHTFACE, BB&S 24-pt.

DRUG Employed ENTHUSIASM
Stirring Addresses to great throngs of men

220

MODERN ROMAN or *Modern* is a general term for faces drawn with greater precision and greater contrast between thick and thin strokes than the earlier Old Style faces. The trend began with the work of Bodoni and Didot in the latter part of the eighteenth century; modern faces derived from Bodoni's designs in particular now typify the modern romans. The first extra condensed face of the sort with lowercase appears to be Figgins' *Narrow Gauge* of about 1850; it was duplicated by ATF's *Extra Condensed No. 40*, which didn't last into the twentieth century, but which was nearly duplicated by the *Modern Roman Extra Condensed* of others.

In the nineteenth century the name *Aldine* was applied to some bold condensed versions of modern roman; *Aldine Condensed* was produced by Heinrich Flinsch in 1871. In this century modern roman faces as well as virtually all other faces have distinctive family names; earlier types to a great extent had only generic names and identifying numbers.

In the early 1900s Monotype adapted a number of modern roman text faces to its system, mostly in a few small sizes only; some of them differ from each other only in slight changes of proportions. BB&S still showed a number of Modern Romans as late as their last specimen book in 1925; by that time ATF had replaced most of its corresponding faces with more contemporary designs.

Modern Roman Bold Extra Condensed is obviously the forerunner of *Onyx*, differing mainly in the circular shapes.

The faces listed here are representative of some of those offered, including some that have been identified as being essentially the same from two or more sources. Former names are in parentheses. Compare *Bodoni, Century Expanded, Scotch Roman, Mademoiselle, Onyx*, etc. Also see *Atlantic, Bold Face, Compressed No. 30, Latin Old Style Bold, Numbered Faces*.

Modern and Italic, Mono 8ABC (4-18pt)

Modern Condensed and Italic, Mono 1ABC (6-10pt)

Modern No. 4 and Italic, BB&S; Mono 34ABC (6-12pt)

Modern Roman Bold Condensed (Lining Aldine), BB&S-ATF 1780 (5-48pt); Lining Condensed Title No. 523, ATF 239 (5-54pt); Aldine, Mono 33 (6,8pt); Aldine No. 1 (6-10pt); Title Condensed No. 75, Hansen (24pt)

Modern Roman Bold Extra Condensed (Lining Aldine Condensed), BB&S-ATF 1781 (6-48pt)

Modern Roman Condensed (Condensed No. 54), BB&S-ATF 1782 (6-48pt); Mono 146 (8-36pt); also Condensed Title No. 1, Lino

Modern Roman Extra Condensed (Extra Condensed No. 56), BB&S-ATF 1783 (6-54pt); Extra Condensed, Keystone (12-42pt); Matson, Lino (30,36pt); Modern No. 3 Extra Condensed, Mono 216A (8pt)

Modern Roman Italic (Title Italic No. 10), BB&S-ATF 1784 (6-12pt); Boldface Italic No. 520, ATF (6-12pt)

Modern Roman Lightface (Lightface No. 7), BB&S-ATF 1785; [Lining] Lightface No. 558, ATF (6-30pt); Lightface No. 5, Keystone (6-30pt); also Title No. 551, ATF (10-24pt)

Modern Roman Medium (Title No. 5), BB&S-ATF 1786 (5-48pt); Boldface No. 520, ATF 230 (5-12pt)

Modern Roman Wide (Expanded No. 5 or Title Expanded), BB&S-ATF 1787 (6-16pt)

Modern Roman No. 64 and Italic, BB&S-ATF [Nos.] 1916, 1914 (5-18pt)

Modern Roman No. 80 and Italic, BB&S-ATF [Nos.] 1918, 1915 (6-12pt)

MODERN ROMAN MEDIUM, BB&S 24-pt.

BINDER Has Strength

MODERN ROMAN WIDE, BB&S 16-pt.

Stop Normandy CHIMES RINGS

MODERN ROMAN NO. 64 & ITALIC, BB&S 10-pt.

ABCDEFGHIJKLMNOPQRSTUVWXYZ&ÆŒ .,'-:;!?()[]— $1234567890£

ABCDEFGHIJKLMNOPQRSTUVWXYZ&ÆŒ abcdefghijklmnopqrstuvwxyzæœ ff fi ffi fl ffl

ABCDEFGHIJKLMNOPQRSTUVWXYZ&ÆŒ .,'-:;!? $1234567890£

abcdefghijklmnopqrstuvwxyzœœ ff fi ffi fl ffl

MODERN ROMAN NO. 80 & ITALIC, BB&S 10-pt.

ABCDEFGHIJKLMNOPQRSTUVWXYZ&ÆŒ .,'-:;!?()[]— $1234567890£

ABCDEFGHIJKLMNOPQRSTUVWXYZ& abcdefghijklmnopqrstuvwxyzæœ fffiffiflffl

ABCDEFGHIJKLMNOPQRSTUVWXYZ&ÆŒ .,'-:;!? fffiffiflffl $1234567890£

abcdefghijklmnopqrstuvwxyzœœ

MODERN TEXT, BB&S 24-pt. (part reduced)

Eighth National Bank Wind Blows Fresh
Regards Designing Practical

MODERNIQUE, ATF 24-pt. (part spaced)

ABCDEFGHIJKLMNOPQRSTUVWXYZ
abcdefghijklmnopqrstuvwxyz
$1234567890 &.,-:;ᵉ'!?

MODERNISTIC, Mono 18-pt.

ABCDEFGHIJKLMNOPQRSTUVWXYZ&
$1234567890 .,-:;"!?∾ ʰ ʼ

MONOTONE GOTHIC, ATF 24-pt.

ABCDEFGHIJKLMNOPQRSTUVWXYZ&
abcdefghijklmnopqrstuvwxyz $1234567890 .,-:;'!?

MONTALLEGRO, 14-pt. (Providence Public Library)

ABCDEFGHIJKLMNOPQRSTUVWXYZ &?£',.:![($-- 1234567890
adcbefghijklmnopqrstuvwxyz ÆŒæœgaravawayafiffflffiffl

Light Type

At a quarter pound per square inch of printed surface, type is heavy. One approach to lightening it was the use of APL, the All Purpose Linotype, to cast large sizes. In the 1930s, one supplier offered fonts of separate letters of selected faces in the Bodoni, Garamond, Gothic, and Memphis families, as "O.K. Light Type," with sizes ranging from 42- to 144-point. The smaller sizes were cast on 12-point slugs, larger ones on 30-point, with individual letters being sawed out of the slugs and sold in fonts. This drastically reduced the weight of the fonts themselves, but required underpinning. Here the use of hollow metal furniture or slugs still retained worthwhile savings of weight, but the idea doesn't appear to have been widely used.

MODERN TEXT is a conventional Old English design, somewhat more ornate than *Engravers Old English* which is about the same weight, more like a heavier weight of *Wedding Text*. It was first shown by Robert Wiebking's Advance Type Foundry in Chicago, in 1913, so was probably designed by Wiebking. Advance was soon absorbed by Western and later by BB&S, and this face and others were continued by that foundry; matrices eventually went to ATF but there is no record of this face having been cast by that foundry.

Modern Text, BB&S-ATF 1788 (6-36pt)

MODERNIQUE is a novelty face designed by Morris F. Benton for ATF in 1928. It features extreme contrast of very heavy main strokes and thin hairlines, with strong vertical emphasis. Ascenders and descenders are short, and it is very close fitting. Dots on the *i* and *j* are semi-circles. It was gone before ATF issued its next complete specimen book in 1934. The specimen shows the complete font. Compare *Stygian Black, Matthews, Radiant Heavy*.

Modernique, ATF 517 (6-72pt)

MODERNISTIC was designed by Wadsworth A. Parker for ATF in 1928, and copied by Monotype the same year. It is a novelty face of high contrast, with delicate hairlines and decorated heavy strokes. It has small conventional horizontal serifs, but no vertical serifs.

Modernistic, ATF 507 (18-72pt); Mono 297 (18-36pt); (Univ 18-72pt)

MODERNIZED GOTHIC—see *Alternate Gothic No. 1.*
MOLÉ FOLIATE—see Imports in Appendix.
MONARCH—see *Latin Oldstyle Bold.*
MONITOR—see *Bookman.*
MONOLINE SCRIPT—see Imports in Appendix.

MONOTONE GOTHIC was designed by Morris F. Benton for ATF in 1907. It is virtually the same as *News Gothic,* but wider and a little lighter; only the *M* and *Q* are noticeably different otherwise. Compare *News Gothic Extended, Trade Gothic Extended;* also *Lightline Gothic, Franklin Gothic, Record Gothic Extended.*

Monotone Gothic, ATF 329 (6s-48pt); also Monotone Title, ATF 330 (6s-36pt)

MONOTYPE 38E—see *Goudy Light Old Style.*

MONTAIGNE was designed by Bruce Rogers in 1901, and privately cast for the Riverside Press in Cambridge, Massachusetts. It was derived from one page printed in the noted type of Nicolas Jenson, and made in one size only, approximately 16-point, with punches cut by John Cumming of Worcester, Massachusetts. Compare *Jenson, Cloister, Centaur, Eusebius.*

Montaigne, private (16pt)

MONTALLEGRO was designed by Herbert Horne and privately cast for the Merrymount Press, Boston, in 1904. D. B. Updike in his *Printing Types* says, "Herbert P. Horne designed three types of importance . . . *Montallegro* came first. This type was modelled on an early Florentine font, and was intended to be a good 'reading type,' which should have rather more flexibility and grace than the fonts based on older Italian forms. It was first used in Condivi's *Life of Michelagnolo Buonarroti* by the Merrymount Press. This type was cut under Mr. Horne's direction by E. P. Prince of London, an English craftsman of great ability. . . ." Punches and matrices are preserved in the Updike Room of the Providence Public Library.

Montallegro, private (14pt)

MONTICELLO & ITALIC, Lino 14-pt.

ABCDEFGHIJKLMNOPQRSTUVWXYZ&ÆŒ ABCDEFGHIJKLMNOPQRSTUVWXYZ&ÆŒ
ABCDEFGHIJKLMNOPQRSTUVWXYZ&ÆŒ
abcdefghijklmnopqrstuvwxyzæœfiflffffiffl 1234567890$£,.:;'-'?!()*†‡¶§[]%
abcdefghijklmnopqrstuvwxyzæœfiflffffiffl 1234567890$£,.:;'-'?!()†‡¶§[]%*

MORRIS JENSONIAN, BB&S 18-pt. (Darrell Hyder)

ABCDEFGHIJKLMNOPQRSTUVWXYZ&
abcdefghijklmnopqrstuvwxyz $1234567890.-,':;?!

MORRIS ROMANIZED BLACK (TELL TEXT), BB&S 18-pt. (Dave Norton)

ABCDEFGHIJKLMNOPQRSTUVWXYZ&.,-:;'!?
abcdefghijklmnopqrstuvwxyzfffiflffiffl æœ$1234567890£

MOTTO, ATF 24-pt.

ABCDEFGHIJKLMNOPQRSTUVWXYZ&
abcdefghijklmnopqrstuvwxyz $1234567890 .,-:;'!?

MOUNTAIN HOUSE PRESS TYPE, Hunter 18-pt. private

LALANDE, JOSEPH JÉRÔME LE FRANÇAIS DE, 1732-1807.
Art de faire le papier. In: Description des arts et métiers, published by
the Académie des sciences. Volume 4. Paris, 1761. 29 x 45 cm.

MOUNTAIN HOUSE PRESS TYPE II, Hunter 18-pt. private

DARD HUNTER, II ⚘ Post Office Box 771
Chillicothe, Ohio 45601 ⚘ United States of America

MONTGOMERY WARD—see *Ward.*

MONTICELLO is a Linotype recreation of America's first great typeface, Binny & Ronaldson's *Roman No. 1,* cut about 1796 by Archibald Binny in Philadelphia. His was the first permanent American type foundry. After about 30 years, the Binny face fell into disuse. The matrices survived, though, and a few fonts were cast about 1892 and the face was renamed *Oxford* (q.v.).

In 1943 Princeton University Press announced plans for publishing a 52-volume edition of *The Papers of Thomas Jefferson.* As President, Jefferson had personally written to friends in France, introducing a Binny & Ronaldson representative who was seeking a source of antimony to replenish the shortage which threatened the young typefounding industry in this country. Jefferson also referred in this letter to the importance of type to civilization and freedom. In addition, the popularity of this typeface coincided with the most prominent years of Jefferson's life. Therefore Linotype suggested that a recutting of the face would be most appropriate for the Jefferson books, and the publisher heartily agreed. C. H. Griffith, Linotype typographic consultant, made a detailed study of Binny's type and redrew it in 1946 for the requirements of Linotype composition and modern printing conditions. It is a vigorous transitional face, somewhat similar to Baskerville but slightly heavier and a little crisper.

Monticello and Italic, Lino (7-14pt)

MORRIS JENSONIAN, MORRIS OLD STYLE—see *Jenson Oldstyle.*

MORRIS ROMANIZED BLACK is an adaptation of the *Troy* and *Chaucer* types designed by William Morris for his Kelmscott Press. This adaptation first appeared under the name *Tell Text* about 1895, and was renamed in 1925. *Troy* and *Chaucer* were two sizes of one style, approximately 18- and 12-point respectively. William Morris had previously designed a roman type which became popular commercially as *Jenson Oldstyle* (q.v.); of this design he says, "After a while I felt that I must have a Gothic [in the sense of Black-letter or Old English] as well as a Roman, and herein the task I set myself was to redeem the Gothic character from the charge of unreadableness. . . . Keeping my end steadily in view, I designed a blackletter type which I think I may claim to be as readable as a Roman one, and to say the truth, I prefer it to the Roman." Compare *Satanick.*

Morris Romanized Black, BB&S-ATF 1791 (6-60pt)

MOTTO is a calligraphic typeface designed by Morris F. Benton for ATF in 1915. It is similar to the same designer's *Freehand,* drawn a couple of years later, but has plainer capitals, heavier thin strokes, and shorter descenders. But letters combine into legible words with a pleasant, hand-lettered appearance. Also compare *Humanistic, Verona.*

Motto, ATF 447 (6-48pt)

MOTTO (other)—see Antiques in Appendix.

MOUNTAIN HOUSE PRESS TYPES were designed and cut by Dard Hunter between 1912 and 1915, and by Dard Hunter Jr. in 1937-39, for the private use of their Mountain House Press.

Mountain House Press Type, Hunter (18pt)
Mountain House Press Type II, Hunter (18pt)

MOUNTJOYE—see *Bell.*

MUNDER VENEZIAN, BB&S 24-pt. & 18-pt. Special Characters (Rick von Holdt)

ABCDEFGHIJKLMNOPQRSTUVWXYZ
abcdefghijklmnopqrstuvwxyz 1234567890$& C R U ct st

MUNDER ITALIC, BB&S 24-pt.

ABCDEFGHIJKLMNOPQRSTUVWXYZ&
abcdefghijklmnopqrstuvwxyz $1234567890 .,-:;'!? " "

MUNDER BOLD, BB&S (42-pt. at 57%) & 18-pt. Special Characters (Rick von Holdt)

ABCDEFGHIJKLMNOPQRSTUVWXYZ CRU
abcdefghijklmnopqrstuvwxyz1234567890$&

MUNDER BOLD ITALIC, BB&S (30-pt. at 80%) (Rick von Holdt)

ABCDEFGHIJKLMNOPQRSTUV
abcdefghijklmnopqrstuvwxyz 12345678

MURRAY HILL, ATF 24-pt.

ABCDEFGHIJKLMNOPQRSTUVWXYZ
abcdefghijklmnopqrstuvwxyz..:;--""'!?&()%$1234567890¢*

MURRAY HILL BOLD, ATF 24-pt.

ABCDEFGHIJKLMNOPQRSTUVWXYZ
abcdefghijklmnopqrstuvwxyz.,.:;--'""'!?&()%$1234567890¢*

NABISCO, Goudy 18-pt.

ABCDEFGHIJKLMNOPQRSTUVWXYZ
abcdefghijklmnopqrstuvwxyz $&?!'-.:;,, 1 2 3 4 5 6 7 8 9 0

NARCISS, Lino 18-pt.

ABCDEFGHIJKLMNOPQRSTUVWXYZ&
abcdefghijklmnopqrstuvwxyz1234567890 ($,.:;'-'?!)

NATIONAL OLDSTYLE, ATF 18-pt.

ABCDEFGHIJKLMNOPQRSTUVWXYZ&.,;':!?-$
abcdefghijklmnopqrstuvwxyzfiffflffiffl1234567890

MUNDER VENEZIAN was designed by Robert Wiebking and first shown as *Laclede Oldstyle* by the Laclede Type Foundry in St. Louis, in 1922. That foundry was acquired by BB&S shortly thereafter, and this face was recut under the Munder name, in honor of Norman T. A. Munder, Baltimore "dean of printers." It is a classic roman face, similar in some ways to *Forum, Goudy Oldstyle, Kennerley,* and other faces by Goudy. Wiebking had been the engraver of Goudy's designs since 1911 and of Bruce Rogers' *Centaur* in 1914. *Laclede* or *Munder* was probably the most elegant face of his own design.

In 1925-27 Wiebking added *Munder Italic, Munder Bold,* and *Munder Bold Italic,* all for BB&S. Together they form a handsome family, not copied by any other American manufacturer. However, Stephenson Blake in England copied *Munder Venezian* under the name *Verona,* but drew different italic and bold versions (see Imports in Appendix).

Munder Venezian, BB&S-ATF 1795 (6-72pt)
Munder Italic, BB&S-ATF 1794 (6-72pt)
Munder Bold, BB&S-ATF 1792 (6-72pt)
Munder Bold Italic, BB&S-ATF 1793 (6-72pt)

MURRAY HILL and *Murray Hill Bold* were designed by Emil Klumpp for ATF about 1956. They are smart, free flowing, modern scripts, nearly vertical, and letters are not connected. Their refreshing informality has made them popular for advertising as well as for stationery and announcements, while their nearly complete lack of kerns has made them durable, practical, and easy to set. The name, incidentally, is said to have come from a New York telephone exchange, before the days of all-numeric dialing, serving an area of the same name in which many large advertising agencies were located.

Murray Hill, ATF 711 (14-72pt)
Murray Hill Bold, ATF 713 (14-72pt)

NABISCO was designed by Frederic W. Goudy in 1921 as a private type for National Biscuit Company, based on hand-lettering of the company name he had done about twenty years earlier. As he had in the meantime drawn *National Oldstyle* (q.v.) for ATF, based on the same lettering, this face is consciously different although retaining the same general characteristics. Several sizes were cut by Robert Wiebking. The baking company was pleased, and used it frequently for several years.

Nabisco, Goudy, private

NARCISS is an adaptation by Linotype in 1925 of *Narcissus,* designed by Walter Tiemann in 1921 for the Klingspor foundry in Germany, based on a face which Fournier had cut about 1745. It is a fairly heavy shaded roman, very similar to *Cameo* and *Gravure,* and somewhat similar to *Caslon Shaded, Caslon Openface, Goudy Open,* etc. (q.v.). This face is rather wide, and the white line that gives the shaded effect is narrow. Each size is undersize, about as big as the next smaller size should be.

Narciss, Lino (10-36pt); APL (18-36pt)

NARROW SANS ITALIC—see Imports in Appendix.

NATIONAL OLDSTYLE was designed by Frederic W. Goudy for ATF in 1916. It is based on lettering he had done about fifteen years earlier for National Biscuit Company, hence the name. It was moderately popular for a while for publication and advertising display work, and for titles for silent motion pictures. Compare *Nabisco.*

National Oldstyle, ATF 472 (6-48pt)

NATIONAL ROMAN—see *Scotch Roman.*

NEON, Neon 24-pt.

ABCDEFGHIJKLMNOPQRSTUVWXYZ .„!?&
❖ () $1234567890

NEPHI MEDIAEVAL, Rimmer 18-pt. (Jim Rimmer)

ABCDEFGHIJKLMNOPQuRSTUVWXYZ&
abcdefghijklmnopqrstuvwxyzffffifflffiflfflcttatitutt.,-:;:!?1234567890$&

NEULAND INLINE, Balto 24-pt.

ABCDEFGHIJKLMNOPQRSTUVWXYZ
&1234567890$.,-:;!?`'S/)+★

NEWPORT, ATF 18-pt. (Dave Churchman)

ABCDEFGHIJKLMNOPQRSTUVWXYZ MW&abcdefghijklmnopqrstuvwxyz$1234567890.,-:;"!?

NEWS WITH CLARENDON, Lino 9-pt.

ABCDEFGHIJKLMNOPQRSTUVWXYZ&	abcdefghijklmnopqrstuvwxyz	1234567890	($£,.:;'-'?!*)	⅛ ¼ ⅜ ½ ⅝ ¾ ⅞ ⅓ ⅔
ABCDEFGHIJKLMNOPQRSTUVWXYZ&	**abcdefghijklmnopqrstuvwxyz**	**1234567890**	**($£,.:;'-'?!*)**	**⅛ ¼ ⅜ ½ ⅝ ¾ ⅞ ⅓ ⅔**

Comparison of Some Serif Styles

Hh Hh Hh Hh Hh Hh **Hh** Hh
1   2   3   4   5   6   7   8

Serifs are one of the most important factors in creating the character of a typeface and in recognizing the design. Some typical serif styles are shown here, but many others could be identified.

Venetian old style serifs, typified by Garamond (1), are bracketed, that is, joined to the stem with curves or fillets; top serifs on lowercase letters are inclined. Dutch-English old style serifs, represented by Caslon (2), are thinner and more pointed.

Transitional serifs, shown by Baskerville (3), are between old style and modern characteristics.

Modern serifs, characterized by Bodoni (4), are either unbracketed or slightly bracketed on the hairlines, with top brackets on lowercase letters flat or nearly so.

Egyptian serifs, shown by Craw Clarendon Book (5), are bracketed, but are much heavier than old style serifs.

Square or slab serifs, as in Stymie Medium (6), are unbracketed but heavier than modern.

The Latin serifs of Latin Bold Condensed (7), are wedge-shaped.

News Gothic (8) and other serifless types have no serifs, of course. See Gothic and Sans Serif in the main text.

Other serifs are combinations or modifffications of these forms, or vary otherwise.

228

NEON is a three-dimensional sans-serif alphabet of inline capitals with a deep shadow, designed in 1936 by Willy Schaefer for the C. E. Weber foundry in Germany and copied in this country by Pittsburgh's National Type Foundry, which later became Neon Type Foundry. Compare *Umbra*. The left-hand shadow is unusual.

Neon, Neon Type Foundry (18-54pt)

NEPHI MEDIAEVAL was designed and cut by Jim Rimmer in Vancouver in 1986, for private use. He says it "was inspired by the Subiaco type of the Ashendene Press and by its inspiration, the type of Sweynheym and Pannartz. My design breaks away from those types slightly in form and is softer in general feeling. In time I will cut other sizes."

Nephi Mediaeval, Rimmer (18pt) private

NEULAND and *Neuland Inline* were originally handcut by Rudolf Koch for Klingspor foundry in Germany, about 1923. Being handcut, each size differed somewhat from others, and the *Inline* differed from the regular. The copies cast by Baltimore Type were recut by pantagraph from one size of the regular, and thus are uniform from one size to another. The white inline was added to this same recutting, and is slightly wider than in the German version.

Neuland, Balto 703 (14-36pt)
Neuland Inline, Balto 704 (14-36pt)

NEW BOOKMAN, NEW CASLON, etc.—see *Bookman, Caslon,* etc.
NEW CAMBRIDGE—see *Cambridge.*
NEW GOTHIC CONDENSED—see under *Gothics, Condensed.*
NEW VILLAGE TEXT—see *Village Text.*
NEW YORK GOTHIC—see *Gothic No. 545.*

NEWPORT is an extra condensed novelty gothic, designed by Willard T. Sniffin for ATF in 1932. Caps occupy almost the entire body, and lowercase letters are tall, with short ascenders and very short descenders. In 48-, 60-, and 72-point sizes, descenders are cast on bodies 6 points larger. The round capitals *CDGPR* include arcs that are less than half a circle, joining stems at an acute angle. *AEFH* feature very low crossbars. The normal *M* is splayed, with the vertex ending short of the baseline, and is the *W* inverted. There are also an alternate *M* and *W*, consisting of three parallel lines with rounded top or bottom. In addition to characters shown in the specimen here, there are a cent mark and a small superior dollar mark, made only in 24-point and larger. Compare *Jefferson Gothic, Phenix.*

Newport, ATF 560 (6-72pt)

NEWS WITH CLARENDON is a typical newspaper text, but duplexed with an attractive version of *Clarendon* instead of the usual bold face. It was cut by Linotype, apparently only in 9-point, and was nicknamed *Cascade.*

News with Clarendon, Lino (9pt)

NEWS GOTHIC, ATF 24-pt.

ABCDEFGHIJKLMNOPQRSTUVWXYZ&
abcdefghijklmnopqrstuvwxyz.,:;-!?1234567890$ fi fl ff

Mono

NEWS GOTHIC ITALIC, Mono 12-pt.

ABCDEFGHIJKLMNOPQRSTUVWXYZ&
abcdefghijklmnopqrstuvwxyz.,-:;"!?— $1234567890

NEWS GOTHIC CONDENSED, Mono 24-pt.

ABCDEFGHIJKLMNOPQRSTUVWXYZ&
abcdefghijklmnopqrstuvwxyz.,:;-!? 1234567890$ fi fl ff ffi ffl Æ Œ æ œ

NEWS GOTHIC EXTRA CONDENSED, ATF 24-pt.

ABCDEFGHIJKLMNOPQRSTUVWXYZ& abcdefghijklmnopqrstuvwxyz .,:;-!? 1234567890$

NEWS GOTHIC EXTENDED, Inter 14-pt.

ABCDEFGHIJKLMNOPQRSTUVWXYZ ?&†‡§[]%–*¶‖
abcdefghijklmnopqrstuvwxyz$1234567890 ℔@⅛⅜⅝⅞¼¾½⅓⅔

NEWS GOTHIC BOLD, ATF 24-pt. (third line Mono)

ABCDEFGHIJKLMNOPQRSTUVWXYZ $1234567890
abcdefghijklmnopqrstuvwxyzg .,:;-"–!?&¢
ABCDEFGHIJKLMNOPQRSTUVWXYZ rstuvwxy

NEWS GOTHIC BOLD ITALIC, Inter 14-pt.

ABCDEFGHIJKLMNOPQRSTUVWXYZ
abcdefghijklmnopqrstuvwxyz $1234567890

NEWS GOTHIC BOLD EXTENDED, Inter 14-pt.

ABCDEFGHIJKLMNOPQRSTUVWXYZ ?&†‡§[]%–*¶
abcdefghijklmnopqrstuvwxyz$1234567890 ℔@⅛⅜⅝⅞¼¾½⅓⅔

NEWS GOTHIC CONDENSED BOLD, ATF 24-pt.

ABCDEFGHIJKLMNOPQRSTUVWXYZ& $1234567890
abcdefghijklmnopqrstuvwxyz .,-::;'!?()[] – – * % " " " " ¢ $ £ · · ' " g

230

NEWS GOTHIC was designed by Morris F. Benton for ATF in 1908, in regular, condensed, and extra condensed widths, as part of his assignment to modernize the nineteenth-century gothics inherited from the foundry's predecessors. *News Gothic,* with its much finer rendering, is part of what might be called a family of basic American gothics, for it is essentially a light version of *Franklin Gothic. Lightline Gothic* is still lighter and *Monotone Gothic* is wider, but all of them, with the variations of News and Franklin Gothics, are as closely related as are members of most other type families. However, the flat-sided extra condensed is more similar to the style of the Alternate Gothics.

These American gothics were pushed into obsolescence by the popularity of the German sans serifs, such as *Futura* and *Kabel,* in the 1930s. But they were rediscovered in the late 1940s, and made a strong come-back. Linotype introduced its comparable *Trade Gothic* family (q.v.) early in the 1950s; Intertype cut *News Gothic* and *News Gothic Bold* in 1955; Ludlow began to expand its *Record Gothic* family (q.v.); and ATF and Monotype added to their families of *News Gothic.* Bud Renshaw drew ATF's version of *News Gothic Bold* in 1958, while a third version of the same face was offered by Monotype. Intertype offered *News Gothic Extended* with bold extended in 1961. ATF had drawings for *News Gothic Italic* as early as 1912, and reconsidered the face in 1965, but we have no record of its production; Monotype and Intertype brought out their own versions of italic, similar to each other except that the former has slightly greater slant. ATF introduced *News Gothic Condensed Bold,* by Frank Bartuska, in 1965, while Monotype and Intertype used the name *News Gothic Bold Condensed* for their earlier versions.

Baltimore Type's "News Gothic" is actually *Inland Gothic No. 6,* Mono 149, while "Balto Gothic," with Italic and Bold, is *News Gothic.*

Compare *Franklin Gothic, Lightline Gothic, Monotone Gothic;* also *Trade Gothic, Record Gothic.* Also see *Phenix, Jefferson Gothic.*

News Gothic, ATF 338 (5-72pt); Mono 206 (5-36pt); Inter (6-24pt)

News Gothic Italic, Mono 206K (6-12pt); Inter (6-14pt)

News Gothic Condensed, ATF 339 (6-72pt); Mono 204 (5-24pt); Inter (6-24pt); Gothic No. 18, Lino (18,24pt)

News Gothic Extra Condensed, ATF 340 (6-72pt); same or Jefferson Gothic, Mono 227 (14-72pt); also News Gothic Extra Condensed Title, ATF 341 (6-72pt)

News Gothic Extended and Bold Extended, Inter (6-24pt)

News Gothic Bold, ATF 715 (6-72pt); Mono 93 (5-36pt); Inter (6-24pt)

News Gothic Bold Italic, Inter (6-14pt)

News Gothic Condensed Bold, ATF 724 (8-72pt); News Gothic Bold Condensed, Mono 205 (6-36pt); Inter (6-24pt)

NEWSFACE—see *Hingham.*
NEWTON SCRIPT—see *Royal Script.*

NICOLAS COCHIN, ATF 24-pt.

ABCDEFGHIJKLMNOPQRSTUVWXYZ—&
abcdefghijklmnopqrstuvwxyzffffifffflffl « » ""(),.~;:'!?$1234567890
1 2 3 4 5 6 7 8 9 0

NICOLAS COCHIN ITALIC, ATF 24-pt.

ABCDEFGHIJKLMNOPQRSTUVWXYZ,.~;:'!?&
abcdefghijklmnopqrstuvwxyzff fiffiflffl&enrt$1234567890 « »()
1 2 3 4 5 6 7 8 9 0

NICHOLAS COCHIN BOLD, 24-pt.

ABCDEFGHIJKLMNOPQRSTUVWXYZ&
abcdefghijklmnopqrstuvwxyz "".' ;:?!-) $1234567890

NORMAN CAPITALS. ATF private

ABCDEFGHIJKLMNOPQRSTUVWXYZ

NORWOOD ROMAN, ATF 12-pt.

ABCDEFGHIJKLMNOPQRSTUVWXYZ   1234567890
abcdefghijklmnopqrstuvwxyz
ABCDEFGHIJKLMNOPQRSTUVWXYZ

NOVA SCRIPT, Inter 18-pt.

ABCDEFGHIJKLMNOPQRSTUVWXYZ abcdefghijklmnopqrstuvwxya 1234567890$
()$,.-;:'!?& z fiflffffifffl

NOVEL GOTHIC, ATF 18-pt.

ABCDEFGHIJKLMNOPQRSTUVWXYZ& : ; ! ? " " ˅ ⟶ ✦
abcdefghijklmnopqrstuvwxyz $1234567890 . , - ' '

NICOLAS COCHIN was cut by ATF about 1926, and by Monotype in 1929, from the face originated about 1912 by the Peignot foundry in France, designed by Georges Peignot. It is based on the distinctive lettering employed by a group of French copperplate engravers of the seventeenth and eighteenth centuries. It is named for Charles Nicolas Cochin, one of the more eminent artists and engravers of the period, although it is not a copy of his specific work, but rather an interpretation of the best work of the time. This typeface features a very small x-height, with long ascenders and short descenders, and long, sharply defined serifs. Lining figures were added to meet the requirements of the American printer, but ATF also duplicated the original French figures. Fonts also contained French quotation marks in both roman and italic, and several lowercase swash terminal characters in italic. Also see *Cochin*.

Nicolas Cochin, ATF 483 (6-72pt); Mono 461 (14-36pt)
Nicolas Cochin Italic, ATF 487 (6-48pt); Mono 4611 (14-36pt)
Nicholas Cochin Bold, Balto 105 (12-48pt)

Because of the difference in the European and American point systems, European faces are slightly larger for the same nominal size. When they are copied by American founders they are usually cast on larger, oversize bodies; sometimes descenders are shortened to fit. Nicolas Cochin is an exception; it is made to the full European size, with descenders overhanging the body slightly in some of the larger sizes.

Nicholas Cochin Bold (with the surplus *h*) was made by Baltimore Type, presumably copied from the same French source. *Le Mercure,* an open version, is shown under Imports in the Appendix.

NICOLAS JENSON—see *Eusebius*.
NITETIME, NOONTIME—see *Venus* under Imports in Appendix.

NORMAN CAPITALS were designed by Frederic W. Goudy in 1910 and named for Norman T. A. Munder, prominent Baltimore printer. Goudy had designed a printing-ink catalog for Munder, for the George H. Morrill Company of Boston, with lettered headings. As the company name recurred frequently, Goudy designed and cast the letters necessary for that name, later adding the remainder of the alphabet. Mats were engraved by Robert Wiebking, but fonts were privately cast by ATF. The face has no relation to various nineteenth-century Norman types.

Norman Capitals, ATF, private (24pt)

NORMANDE, NORMANDIA OUTLINE—see Imports in Appendix.

NORWOOD ROMAN was designed for ATF in 1906 by Morris F. Benton, at the suggestion of J. S. Cushing. It was originally called *Cushing Roman,* but was renamed for Cushing's Norwood Press Co. in Norwood, Massachusetts. It is a rather narrow, moderately heavy modern roman, with the modern characteristics softened a bit toward the oldstyle. It was made only in text sizes, and there was no italic. Compare *Century Oldstyle*.

Norwood Roman, ATF 431 (6-12pt)

NOVA SCRIPT was designed by George F. Trenholm in 1937 for Intertype. It is a monotone cursive design, with narrow lowercase and unusual capitals, and has small serifs on some of the letters. The inclination is slight, to keep it within the limitations of straight matrices, and it was made only in one size. Compare *Camera, Card Italic*.

Nova Script, Inter (18pt)

NOVEL GOTHIC was an attempt at modernism, originated by Charles H. Becker, a hand engraver in the matrix cutting department of ATF, whose regular job was putting the finishing refinements on matrix patterns. It was completed by Morris F. Benton and introduced in 1928. Compare *Eagle Bold*.

Novel Gothic, ATF 512 (6-72pt)

233

NUBIAN, ATF 18-pt.

ABCDEFGHIJKLMNOPQRSTUVWX
abcdefghijklmnopqrstuvwxyz ſ YZ
1234567890.,-ʻʼ!?$&

NO. 1 & ITALIC, Lino 12-pt.

ABCDEFGHIJKLMNOPQRSTUVWXYZ&   ABCDEFGHIJKLMNOPQRSTUVWXYZ&
ABCDEFGHIJKLMNOPQRSTUVWXYZ&
abcdefghijklmnopqrstuvwxyzfiflffffiffl 1234567890($£,.:;ʻʼ?!*†)
abcdefghijklmnopqrstuvwxyzfiflffffiffl 1234567890($£,.:;ʻʼ?! †)

NO. 2 & GOTHIC NO. 3, Lino 10-pt.

ABCDEFGHIJKLMNOPQRSTUVWXYZ&
ABCDEFGHIJKLMNOPQRSTUVWXYZ&

abcdefghijklmnopqrstuvwxyz fiflffffiffl   1234567890 [($£ £,.:;ʻ-ʼ?!*†‡§¶)]
abcdefghijklmnopqrstuvwxyz fiflffffiffl   1234567890 [($£ £,.:;ʻ-ʼ?!*†‡§¶)]

NO. 11 & GOTHIC CONDENSED NO. 4, Lino 6-pt.

ABCDEFGHIJKLMNOPQRSTUVWXYZ&   abcdefghijklmnopqrstuvwxyzfiflffffiffl 1234567890($£,.:;ʻ-ʼ?!*†)
ABCDEFGHIJKLMNOPQRSTUVWXYZ&   abcdefghijklmnopqrstuvwxyzfiflffffiffl 1234567890($£,.:;ʻ-ʼ?!*†)

NO. 12 & GOTHIC CONDENSED NO. 11, Lino 8-pt.

ABCDEFGHIJKLMNOPQRSTUVWXYZ&   abcdefghijklmnopqrstuvwxyzfiflffffiffl 1234567890($£,.:;ʻ-ʼ?!*†)
ABCDEFGHIJKLMNOPQRSTUVWXYZ&   abcdefghijklmnopqrstuvwxyzfiflffffiffl 1234567890($£,.:;ʻ-ʼ?!*†)

NO. 16 & ITALIC, Lino 14-pt.

ABCDEFGHIJKLMNOPQRSTUVWXYZ&   ABCDEFGHIJKLMNOPQRSTUVWXYZ&
ABCDEFGHIJKLMNOPQRSTUVWXYZ&
abcdefghijklmnopqrstuvwxyzfiflffffiffl ($£:;ʻ-ʼ?*†) 123
abcdefghijklmnopqrstuvwxyzfiflffffiffl ($£:;ʻ-ʼ? †) 123

NO. 21 & ITALIC, Lino 12-pt.

ABCDEFGHIJKLMNOPQRSTUVWXYZ&ÆŒ   ABCDEFGHIJKLMNOPQRSTUVWXYZÆŒ
ABCDEFGHIJKLMNOPQRSTUVWXYZ&ÆŒ
abcdefghijklmnopqrstuvwxyzæœfiffflffiffl   [($.,-ʻʼ:;!?-—)] 1234567890
abcdefghijklmnopqrstuvwxyzæœfiffflffiffl   [($.,-ʻʼ:;!?-—)] 1234567890

OCTIC GOTHIC, Mono 366 18-pt. (Henry Weiland)

ABCDEFGHIJKLMNOPQRSTUVW
YXZ $1234567890 .,-:;'?!

OFFSET GOTHIC CLEARCUT TITLE, ATF 12-pt.

PACK MY BOX WITH FIVE DOLLS

OFFSET PASTEL CONDENSED, ATF 24-pt.

PACK MY BOX WITH FIVE D pack my box with five dozel|12

234

NOVELTY GOTHIC—see *Gothics, Miscellaneous;* also *Bernhard Gothic.*

NUBIAN was designed for ATF in 1928 by Willard T. Sniffin. It is a wide, very heavy design with extreme contrast of thick and thin strokes, and has very short serifs. The lowercase *g* has an uncompleted tail, and the *i* and *j* have semicircular dots. Compare *Ultra Bodoni, Cooper Modern.*

Nubian, ATF 510 (6-72pt); (Univ 6-24pt)

NUMBERED FACES generally are holdovers from the nineteenth century, before distinctive names became common. A number of Linotype and Intertype faces never had names, though, and were always designated simply by number; they are probably adapted from older foundry faces. There is little difference between them, except for weight and width; some are made only in one or two small sizes, only *No. 16* and *No. 36* are made as large as 14-point. Only a few of the more commonly used faces of this sort are shown here. Comparable faces on Monotype are generally called "Modern Roman" (q.v.), with distinguishing numbers.

No. 1 and Italic, Lino = Inter (5½-12pt)
No. 11, Lino = Inter (5½-6pt)
No. 12 and Italic, Lino = Inter (6-8pt)
No. 16 and Italic, Lino = Inter (6-14pt)
No. 21 and Italic, Lino = Inter (6-12pt)
No. 36 and Italic, Lino (12,14pt)

   No. 1 was introduced by Linotype in 1903 as their latest face. *No. 11* and *No. 12* were used extensively for telephone directories before the inception of *Bell Gothic; No. 11* is very compact while *No. 12* is nearer to normal width. *No. 16* is a copy of "Serie 16," a popular French face early in the century, and introduced by Linotype in 1910; it is similar to *French Round Face* but heavier. *No. 36* was also made as *Congressional* (q.v.).

   As an exception, *Number 11* series is the Ludlow copy of the *Goudy Oldstyle* family (q.v.).

OCTIC GOTHIC was a nineteenth-century style. In the Monotype copy, many characters were identical to *Gothic No. 545* (Mono 66); in others curves were replaced by diagonal lines. The name probably comes from the octagon shape. Compare *Chamfer Gothic.*

Octic Gothic, Mono 366 (10-30pt)
Octic Gothic No. 2, Mono 566 (12-36pt)

OFFSET FACES. Around the turn of the century, a number of faces were cut in reverse—that is, reading from right to left—for a process of transferring small types to lithographic stones before the development of photolithography and rotary offset printing. *Engravers Roman* and various gothics were among those cut this way in addition to their normal forms. Some were available until 1950. The only such face in more recent times—for marking negatives and other uses—was *Record Gothic Offset* (q.v.).

Offset Engravers Roman, ATF 1798 (6s-18pt)
Offset Engravers Title, ATF 1799 (6s-18pt)
Offset Gothic Clearcut Title, ATF 1797 (6,12pt)
Offset Gothic Title No. 60, ATF 1800 (6-10pt)
Offset Lining Gothic No. 47, ATF 1802 (6-12pt)
Offset Pastel Condensed, ATF 1801 (24pt)

OLD BAILEY—see *Ionic Shaded* under Antiques in Appendix.

OLD BOWERY is an ATF revival, in 1933 and again in 1949, of *Round Shade No. 2,* originated by Bruce, one of its predecessor companies, about 1854, as *Ornamented No. 1007.*

Old Bowery, ATF 943 (30pt); Carroll, TFP, LATF, Triangle (30pt)

OLD BOWERY, ATF 30-pt.

ABCDEFGHIJKMNOPQRSTUVWXYZ&

OLD DUTCH, BB&S 14-pt. (Ralph Babcock, Rick von Holdt)

ABCDEFGHIJKLMNOPQRSTUVWXYZ¢&$1234567890.,-:;'!?

[CASLON] OLD ROMAN, BB&S 18-pt. (Dave Greer)

ABCDEFGHIJKLMNOPQRSTUVWXYZ&
abcdefghijklmnopqrstuvwxyz $1234567890 .,-:;'!?
ABCDEFGHIJKLMNOPQRSTUV

[CASLON] OLD ROMAN ITALIC, BB&S 24-pt. (Stan Kroeger)

ABCDEFGHIJKLMNOPQRSTUVWXYZ&
abcdefghijklmnopqrstuvwxyz$.,-:;!?1234567890

OLD ROMAN CONDENSED, BB&S 24-pt.

HONORED EDITION Select Studies Needful

OLD ROMAN BOLD, BB&S 24-pt.

EXQUISITE BEADS National Department

OLD ROMAN BOLD CONDENSED, BB&S 18-pt. (Herb Harnish)

ABCDEFGHIJKLMNOPQRSTUVWXYZ&$1234567890
abcdefghijklmnopqrstuvwxyz.,-'!?

OLD ROMAN BLACK, BB&S 24-pt. (Herb Harnish)

ABCDEFGHIJKLMNOPQRSTUVWXYZ&$
abcdefghijklmnopqrstuvwxyz.,-:;!?1234567890

OLD ROMAN BLACK ITALIC, BB&S 24-pt. (part reduced)

DESIRE RECORD ENTERPRISE
New Business Standards Considered The

OLD ROMAN SEMITONE, BB&S 24-pt.

CLOSING SALE Quality Displays

OLD STYLE ANTIQUE, Keystone 24-pt.

DECORATION Fashionables Amazed

OLD DUTCH was designed in 1925 for BB&S by Richard N. McArthur, who was then advertising manager of the foundry. It is a font of shaded capitals, decorated with a circle set into each main stroke, and is probably derived from eighteenth-century sources. It was recast by ATF in 1954. *Colonial* is similar, but with conventional serifs. Also compare *Dresden*.

Old Dutch, BB&S-ATF 1803 (8-48pt)

OLD ENGLISH—see *Engravers Old English;* also *Cloister Black, Goudy Text, Wedding Text,* etc.

OLD GOTHIC BOLD ITALIC—see *Doric Italic.*

OLD ROMAN was designed about 1895 by T. W. Smith, manager of the foundry of H. W. Caslon & Company in England, where it was cast in small sizes, and copied by BB&S about 1903 with Caslon's permission. Sizes above 16-point were originated by BB&S. It is a modernized antique letter, with a little more weight than many romans, and became popular for advertising, especially for work that was to be reduced or reproduced photographically, before photolithography or etched letterpress plates had been developed to the point of sharp, accurate reproduction of typefaces. It has somewhat the feeling of *Bookman,* but serifs are unbracketed and longer with rounded ends, and some characters are less formal. This face was called *Caslon Old Roman* in some BB&S specimens, and copied by Monotype only under that name. Some versions were put on Linotype in 1913.

Old Roman or Caslon Old Roman, BB&S-ATF 1804 (6-72pt); Old Roman, Lino (8-14pt); Caslon Old Roman, Mono 78 (6-36pt)

Old Roman Italic or Caslon Old Roman Italic, BB&S-ATF 1810 (6-48pt); Old Roman Italic, Lino (8-14pt); Caslon Old Roman Italic, Mono 781 (6-36pt)

Old Roman Condensed, BB&S-ATF 1809 (6-72pt)

Old Roman Bold, BB&S-ATF 1807 (6-72pt)

Old Roman Bold Condensed, BB&S-ATF 1808 (6-120pt); Roman Bold Condensed, Lino (12-24pt)

Old Roman Black, BB&S-ATF 1805 (6-72pt)

Old Roman Black Italic, BB&S-ATF 1806 (6-48pt)

Old Roman Semitone, BB&S-ATF 1811 (18-60pt)

A number of variations of this face were drawn by Sidney Gaunt for BB&S in 1907 to 1909, making a substantial and popular family, especially for display advertising. These variations include *Old Roman Condensed; Bold,* which is about the proportion of Condensed; *Bold Condensed,* which is much narrower and heavier; *Black* and *Black Italic,* which are about the proportion of the original faces; and a unique *Semitone,* which is the *Bold* with a series of diagonal white lines cut through all strokes without an outline, making a shaded effect. This *Semitone* is also unusual among shaded faces in that the number of white lines is the same for any given letter, regardless of size; thus the shading is coarse in large sizes and fine in small sizes.

OLD STYLE ANTIQUE [NO. 560] was the face on which *Bookman* (q.v.) was based. It was cast by a number of founders, of which Keystone continued to cast it into this century. Also see *Stratford.*

Old Style Antique, Keystone (6-48pt)

OLDSTYLE NO. 1 & ITALIC, Lino 14-pt. (Ronaldson Alternates No. 1, 12-pt.)

ABCDEFGHIJKLMNOPQRSTUVWXYZ& ABCDEFGHIJKLMNOPQRSTUVWXYZ&
ABCDEFGHIJKLMNOPQRSTUVWXYZ&

abcdefghijklmnopqrstuvwxyz1234567($£,.:;'-'?!*†)1234567 C E F G L S T Æ Œ 3 5 6 7 . : 9 æ œ ct
abcdefghijklmnopqrstuvwxyz1234567($£,.:;'-'?! †)1234567 C E F G L S T Æ Œ C E F G L S T Æ Œ ct

OLDSTYLE NO. 3 & ITALIC, Lino 12-pt.

ABCDEFGHIJKLMNOPQRSTUVWXYZ& ABCDEFGHIJKLMNOPQRSTUVWXYZ&
ABCDEFGHIJKLMNOPQRSTUVWXYZ&

abcdefghijklmnopqrstuvwxyzfiflffffiffl12345678($£,.:;'-'?!*†)12345678
abcdefghijklmnopqrstuvwxyzfiflffffiffl12345678($£,.:;'-'?! †)12345678

OLDSTYLE NO. 7 & ITALIC, Lino 14-pt.

ABCDEFGHIJKLMNOPQRSTUVWXYZ&ÆŒ ABCDEFGHIJKLMNOPQRSTUVWXYZ&ÆŒ
ABCDEFGHIJKLMNOPQRSTUVWXYZ&ÆŒ

abcdefghijklmnopqrstuvwxyzæœfifffflffiffl 1234567890 [($.,-'':;!?-—)] 1234567890
abcdefghijklmnopqrstuvwxyzæœfifffflffiffl 1234567890 [($.,-'':;!?-—)] 1234567890

OLDTYME OUTLINE, Triangle (72-pt. at 50%); OUTLINE, Triangle 24-pt. #1

OLYMPIAN & ITALIC & BOLD, Lino 10-pt.

ABCDEFGHIJKLMNOPQRSTUVWXYZ&   ABCDEFGHIJKLMNOPQRSTUVWXYZ&
ABCDEFGHIJKLMNOPQRSTUVWXYZ&   **ABCDEFGHIJKLMNOPQRSTUVWXYZ&**
abcdefghijklmnopqrstuvwxyz   abcdefghijklmnopqrstuvwxyz
abcdefghijklmnopqrstuvwxyz   **abcdefghijklmnopqrstuvwxyz**
1234567890$,.:;'-'?!—()   1234567890$,.:;'-'?!—()
1234567890$,.:;'-'?!—()   **1234567890$,.:;'-'?!—()**
⅛ ¼ ⅜ ½ ⅝ ¾ ⅞   2⅛ 3¼   ⅛ ¼ ⅜ ½ ⅝ ¾ ⅞   2⅛ 3¼
⅛ ¼ ⅜ ½ ⅝ ¾ ⅞   2⅛ 3¼   **⅛ ¼ ⅜ ½ ⅝ ¾ ⅞   2⅛ 3¼**

ONYX, Mono 24-pt.

ABCDEFGHIJKLMNOPQRSTUVWXYZ.,-:;"0!?&%$$1234567890
abcdefghijklmnopqrstuvwxyz

ONYX ITALIC, Mono 24-pt.

ABCDEFGHIJKLMNOPQRSTUVWXYZ$1234567890
abcdefghijklmnopqrstuvwxyz.,-:;"!?&

238

OLD STYLE numbered faces are mostly of nineteenth-century origin, when most typefaces had generic names of this sort rather than more individual names. A few such foundry faces survived into the twentieth century, but most endured as copies or adaptations by the composing machine companies. Incidentally, ATF commonly uses *Oldstyle* as one word; others generally prefer two words. This book tries to follow the style of the principal source of each face. There were many such faces, including condensed and title versions, but only a few of the most notable and lasting have survived to be listed here.

Linotype's *Old Style No. 1* is of English origin, and has long been popular for periodical and book work. Although it was adapted from a face offered by the MS&J foundry, predecessors of ATF, it was duplicated by ATF as *Oldstyle No. 583,* using strikes furnished by the Mergenthaler company, so printers could handset corrections to material set on the slug machines. This face is similar to *Binny;* with the substitution of a number of conversion characters it is known on Linotype as *Ronaldson* (q.v.).

Old Style No. 3, Linotype, is copied from *Old Style No. 20* of the Bruce Typefoundry, and is also cut by Monotype as *Bruce Old Style No. 20* (q.v.). *Old Style No. 7,* Linotype, is also based on a Bruce face—one from the early 1870s that in turn was derived from a face designed and cut some years earlier by Miller and Richard, the noted Edinburgh typefounders. It also has a set of *Ronaldson* conversion characters, although it differs somewhat from the face mentioned above. In 24-point only, Linotype's *Old Style No. 7* is a faithful copy of ATF's *Century Oldstyle,* and was originally offered under that name. Intertype, meanwhile, copied Monotype's version of *Century Old Style* as *Old Style No. 9.* Also see *Clearcut Oldstyle.* Compare *Binny, Franklin Old Style.*

Old Style No. 1 and Italic, Lino = Inter (5-18pt); Oldstyle No. 583, ATF 345 (6-11pt)
Old Style No. 3 and Italic, Lino (6-12pt); Bruce Old Style No. 20, Mono 31EFG (6-12pt)
Old Style No. 7 and Italic, Lino = Inter (6-18, see text)
Old Style No. 9 and Italic, Inter (8-10, see text)

OLD TOWN—see *Figaro* under Imports in Appendix.

OLDTYME OUTLINE was cut by Triangle Type Foundry in Chicago for makers of rubber stamps. There were variations, *No. 2* being slightly narrower; the specimens shown here are typical. In small sizes, the comparable face is known simply as *Outline.* Triangle also had *Slim Outline,* in the general style of *Chamfer Gothic.* All these faces were rather crudely drawn.

Oldtyme Outline No. 1, Triangle (60,72pt); Oldtyme Outline No. 2, Triangle (60pt)
Outline No. 1, Triangle (24pt); Outline No. 2, Triangle (24pt)
Slim Outline, Triangle (60,72pt)

OLIPHANT—see *Advertisers Upright Script.*
OLYMPIA—see *Typo Gothic.*

OLYMPIAN is a newspaper text face, designed by Matthew Carter for Linotype in 1970, and is one of the last faces cut for metal typecasting on that machine. In fact it was also made for phototypesetting at the same time. It differs from the usual newspaper faces, having a little more hint of oldstyle characteristics.

Olympian and Italic and Bold, Lino (8-10pt)

ONDINE—see Imports in Appendix.

ONYX was designed by Gerry Powell for ATF in 1937. It is essentially a modernization of *Modern Roman Bold Extra Condensed,* and could well be called an extra condensed version of *Ultra Bodoni.* Linotype classifies the face with *Poster Bodoni,* their equivalent to *Ultra Bodoni. Onyx Italic* was designed by Sol Hess for Monotype in 1939, and is made as mats only by that company. *Onyx* is also cast by the Amsterdam foundry as *Arsis.*

Onyx, ATF 661 (18-120pt); Mono 404 (18-72H4); Poster Bodoni Compressed, Lino (18-36pt)
Onyx Italic, Mono 4041 (24-72pt)

OPTICON & ITALIC, Lino 11-pt.

ABCDEFGHIJKLMNOPQRSTUVWXYZ& ABCDEFGHIJKLMNOPQRSTUVWXYZ&
ABCDEFGHIJKLMNOPQRSTUVWXYZ&
abcdefghijklmnopqrstuvwxyz 12345 ($£,.:;'-'?!*†‡§¶fiflffffifffffiffl) 67890
abcdefghijklmnopqrstuvwxyz 12345 ($£,.:;'-'?! †‡§¶fiflffffifffffiffl) 67890

OPTIMA MEDIUM & ITALIC, Lino 12-pt.

ABCDEFGHIJKLMNOPQRSTUVWXYZ&ÆŒ 1234567890$£,.:;'-'?!-|— ...()@℔¢*†‡¶§[]%/
ABCDEFGHIJKLMNOPQRSTUVWXYZ&ÆŒ 1234567890$£,.:;'-'?!-|—... ()@℔¢*†‡¢§[]%/
abcdefghijklmnopqrstuvwxyzæœfiflffffffiffl gjpqy ⅛¼⅜½⅝¾⅞⅓⅔⅕⅖⅗⅘⅙⅚ 2⅛3¼
abcdefghijklmnopqrstuvwxyzæœfiflffffffiffl gjpqy ⅛¼⅜½⅝¾⅞⅓⅔⅕⅖⅗⅘⅙⅚ 2⅛3¼

OPTIMA MEDIUM & BLACK, Lino 12-pt.

ABCDEFGHIJKLMNOPQRSTUVWXYZ&ÆŒ 1234567890$£,.:;'-'?!-|— ...()@℔¢*†‡¶§[]%/
ABCDEFGHIJKLMNOPQRSTUVWXYZ&ÆŒ 1234567890$£,.:;'-'?!-|—... ()@℔¢*†‡¶§[]%/
abcdefghijklmnopqrstuvwxyzæœfiflffffffiffl gjpqy ⅛¼⅜½⅝¾⅞⅓⅔⅕⅖⅗⅘⅙⅚ 2⅛3¼
abcdefghijklmnopqrstuvwxyzæœfiflffffffiffl gjpqy ⅛¼⅜½⅝¾⅞⅓⅔⅕⅖⅗⅘⅙⅚ 2⅛3¼

ORIGINAL OLD STYLE ITALIC, ATF 18-pt.

ABCDEFGHIJKLMNOPQRSTUVWXYZ& HNQ $1234567890
abcdefghijklmnopqrstuvwxyz fffiflffiffffla .,-:;'?! aeo æœ ſſſiſ

ORIGINAL OLD STYLE & ITALIC, Lino 14-pt.

ABCDEFGHIJKLMNOPQRSTUVWXYZ& ABCDEFGHIJKLMNOPQRSTUVWXYZ&
ABCDEFGHIJKLMNOPQRSTUVWXYZ&
abcdefghijklmnopqrstuvwxyzfiflffffffiffl 123 ($£:;'-'?!*†‡§¶) 123
abcdefghijklmnopqrstuvwxyzfiflffffffiffl 123 ($£:;'-'?!) 123

OTHELLO, ATF 24-pt.

ABCDEFGHIJKLMNOPQRSTUVWXYZ& N
abcdefghijklmnopqrstuvwxyz $1234567890 '.,-:;'!?

240

OPTICON was designed in 1935 by C. H. Griffith for Linotype. It is a member of what that supplier calls its Legibility Group of faces designed primarily for newspaper use. It is essentially the same as *Excelsior,* but with stems and thick lines weighted slightly, for printing on hard-surfaced paper.

Opticon and Italic, Lino (5½-12pt)

OPTIMA is one of the most popular creations of the noted German type designer, Hermann Zapf. This face is most often represented in this country by imported foundry type or imported Linotype matrices, made to European alignment standards. But Mergenthaler Linotype cut two weights—not those most often used—on American alignment, in 1968. It is a thick-and-thin serifless face, combining the best of roman and gothic forms, representing contemporary style without the severity of gothic. Compare *Stellar, Lydian, Radiant,* etc.

Optima Medium and Italic, Lino (6-12pt)
Optima Black, Lino (6-12pt)

ORIGINAL OLD STYLE ITALIC was cut in 1858 in four sizes by Elihu White's Type Foundry in New York, which became Farmer, Little & Company and later A. D. Farmer & Son Type Foundry, which in turn was sold to ATF in 1909. In 1911 ATF resurrected the 18-point size of this face, the only size that had sold well, and recut the letters *a, e,* and *o,* which were oversize in the original cutting. At other times it was again made available, but only in weight fonts and on special order. The three swash caps, the oversize vowels, and the long *s* and its ligatures were sold separately.

Original Old Style Italic, ATF (18pt)
Original Old Style and Italic, Lino (6-14pt)

Original Old Style and *Italic* were cut by Linotype about 1920, based on the Farmer face, which was derived from a late eighteenth-century English modernization of Caslon. It has much of the character of Caslon, but the roman capitals are a little heavier. Serifs are generally less bracketed, especially at the foot of lowercase letters, and contrast between thick and thin lines is increased a bit. The italic is lighter than the roman. For those who dislike the spottiness resulting from the heavier capitals, Linotype suggested the substitution of *Caslon Old Face* capitals. Compare *Scotch Roman, Oxford;* also see *Caslon.*

ORNAMENTED—see various faces under Antiques in Appendix.
ORNATA—see Imports in Appendix.
ORNATE—see *Romantiques* and *Tuscans* under Antiques in Appendix.
ORNATE TITLE—see *Goudy Ornate.*
ORPLID—see Imports in Appendix.

OTHELLO is a very heavy, squarish, narrow gothic letter, designed in 1934 by Morris F. Benton for ATF, as a revision of an 1884 face of the same name issued by Central Type Foundry in St. Louis, and inherited by ATF in 1892. It is distinguished by the diagonal ends on a number of strokes, the lowercase forms of the capitals *M, N,* and *Y,* and several other unusual characters. An alternate *N* appeared only in early showings. Compare *Heading.* A different *Othello* is shown under Imports in Appendix.

Othello, ATF 594 (18-72pt)

OUTLINE—see *Oldtyme Outline; Contour;* other faces under family names.
OUTLINE GOTHIC MEDIUM CONDENSED—see *Tourist Gothic.*
OVERGROWN—see *Binny.*

OXFORD & ITALIC, ATF 12-pt. (Ralph Babcock)

ABCDEFGHIJKLMNOPQRSTUVWXYZ&
abcdefghijklmnopqrstuvwxyz $1234567890 .,-:;'!?(] fifflffiffl

ABCDEFGHIJKLMNOPQRSTUVWXYZ&
abcdefghijklmnopqrstuvwxyz .,-:;'!? fi ff fl ffi ffl

PABST OLDSTYLE, ATF (30-pt. at 80%) (Edward M. Lewis)

ABCDEFGHIJKLMNOPQRSTUVWXYZ&$
abcdefghijklmnopqrstuvwxyz.,-:;'!?1234567890 ft *The and of*

PABST OLDSTYLE, Mono 24-pt. (Rick von Holdt)

ABCDEFGHIJKLMNOPQRSTUVWXYZ
abcdefghijklmnopqrstuvwxyz.,-:;'!?1234567890&$

PABST OLDSTYLE ITALIC, ATF 18-pt. (part reduced) (Dave Greer)

ABBCDDEFGGHIJKLMMNNOPPQQu RRSTTUVWX
abcdefghijklmnopqrstuvwxyz$£ff1234567890 .,-:;'!? fffhflffhffl   *YZ&*

PABST EXTRA BOLD & ITALIC, Lino 14-pt.

ABCDEFGHIJKLMNOPQRSTUVWXYZ& 1234567890
ABCDEFGHIJKLMNOPQRSTUVWXYZ& 1234567890
abcdefghijklmnopqrstuvwxyz ($£,.:;'-'?!*)
abcdefghijklmnopqrstuvwxyz ($£,.:;'-'?!*)

PABST EXTRA BOLD CONDENSED & ITALIC, Lino 14-pt.

ABCDEFGHIJKLMNOPQRSTUVWXYZ&
ABCDEFGHIJKLMNOPQRSTUVWXYZ&
abcdefghijklmnopqrstuvwxyz 1234567890($£,.:;'-'?!*)
abcdefghijklmnopqrstuvwxyz 1234567890($£,.:;'-'?!*)

Name in parentheses after some specimens
indicates person who has set that specimen,
in whole or in part, to our format.

OXFORD and *Italic* were designed and cut by Archibald Binny of the firm of Binny & Ronaldson, Philadelphia, the first lasting American type foundry. These were the first body types made by this firm when it began to cast types in 1796, and were called simply *Roman No. 1* and *Italic*. The matrices were preserved through a succession of founders, leading to the formation of American Type Founders in 1892. Joseph W. Phinney, vice president of the company, had trial fonts cast from these matrices and prepared a specimen sheet, giving the types the name of *Oxford*. The type has seen limited use by several printers specializing in fine printing, notably by D. B. Updike of The Merrymount Press in Boston, who selected it for his monumental 2-volume work, *Printing Types: Their History, Forms, and Use,* volumes which were completely handset in this face. There are no italic figures for this face.

Oxford was never included in ATF's general specimen books, but was available on special order. The 9- to 12-point sizes were available in full; in 8-point only the roman lowercase and figures survived; *Baskerville* caps and complete italic were substituted. In the 1950s Steve Watts, retired sales promotion manager of the foundry, sponsored a group-order program which made the type available at less than usual special-order prices; a number of hobbyists and private press proprietors took advantage of this—in fact one of them supplied the specimen herewith.

Meanwhile, Linotype adapted and reissued the face under the name *Monticello* (q.v.) in 1943. Also compare *Baskerville, Original Old Style.*

Oxford, ATF 708 (8-12, see text)
Oxford Italic, ATF 709 (9-12pt)

PABST OLDSTYLE or *Pabst Roman* is an early design by Frederic W. Goudy. Lettering he had done for advertisements of Pabst Brewing Company attracted the attention of the advertising manager of a Chicago department store, who asked Goudy to design a typeface based on that lettering. Drawings were delivered and paid for, but owing to the cost of engraving matrices and producing type, the project was abandoned at that point. Later an arrangement was made with ATF, whereby several sizes were cut, with the department store having exclusive use of it for a limited time, after which it became the property of the foundry and was offered for general sale. It was named, however, for Col. Fred Pabst of the brewing company.

In a popular style of the day, *Pabst* retains a hand-lettered feeling through slight irregularities in the edges of lines, carefully preserved in the metal. It also features italic logotypes *The, and,* and *of* in the roman font. *Pabst* was designed in 1902, and the following year ATF commissioned Goudy to draw an italic to accompany it. Matrices for both designs were cut by Robert Wiebking for the foundry, Goudy's first business contact with the man who was to cut many of his types over the next two decades.

Caps of the Monotype copy of *Pabst Oldstyle,* released in 1912, are a little narrower than the foundry original. *Pabst Old Style Condensed* is a modification by Linotype; it is very similar to the proportions of the Monotype copy of the regular face. Compare *Avil, Powell.*

Pabst Oldstyle, ATF 347 (6-72pt); Mono 45 (6-36pt); Lino (10-14pt)
Pabst Italic, ATF 346 (6-72pt); Lino (10-14pt)
Pabst Old Style Condensed, Lino (18pt)

PABST EXTRA BOLD is not related to *Pabst Oldstyle.* This family was designed for Linotype in 1928, and the condensed version in 1931, by C. H. Griffith, as an interpretation of the extra bold letter typified by *Cooper Black.* There is considerable resemblance, but in this face the tops and bottoms of serifs are flat instead of rounded. Also compare *Ludlow Black.*

Pabst Extra Bold and Italic, Lino (8-24, 8-18pt); APL (18-120, 18-48pt)
Pabst Extra Bold Condensed and Italic, Lino (10-48, 10-24pt); APL (18-72pt roman)

PACIFIC—see Antiques in Appendix.

PACKARD, ATF 24-pt. (Dave Greer)

ABCDEFGHIJKLMNOPQRSSTUVWXYZ&ThฟินtY

abcdefghijklmnopqrstuvᴠwwxyyz .,-:;'!? $1234567890 ffฟิฟีffifffifft

PACKARD BOLD, ATF (30-pt. at 80%)

ABCDEFGHIJKLMNOPQRSTUVWXYZ&1234567890

abcdefghijklmnopqrstuvwxyz ff fi fl ffi ffl th ty Th.,-':;!?

PANTAGRAPH SCRIPT, BB&S 24-pt. (Herb Harnish)

ABCDEFGHIJKLMNOPQRSTUVWXYZ

abcdefghijklmnopqrstuvwxyz .,-':;!?℀ ℔ $1234567890

PARAGON & ITALIC, Lino 10-pt.

ABCDEFGHIJKLMNOPQRSTUVWXYZ&   ABCDEFGHIJKLMNOPQRSTUVWXYZ&
ABCDEFGHIJKLMNOPQRSTUVWXYZ&
abcdefghijklmnopqrstuvwxyz fiflffffiffl   1234567890 [($£,.:;'-'?!*†‡§¶)]   ⅛ ¼ ⅜ ½ ⅝ ¾ ⅞
abcdefghijklmnopqrstuvwxyz fiflffffiffl   1234567890 [($£,.:;'-'?!†‡§¶)]   ⅛ ¼ ⅜ ½ ⅝ ¾ ⅞*

PARAGON PLATE, BB&S 24-pt.

ABCDEFGHIJKLMNOPQRSTUVWXYZ&

abcdefghijklmnopqrstuvwxyz.,-:;'!?$1234567890

PARAGON PLATE ITALIC, BB&S 24-pt.

Skillful Talent Demand ELEGIBLE

PARAMOUNT, ATF 24-pt.

ABCDEFGHIJKLMNOPQRSTUVWXYZ

a b c d e f g h i j k l m n o p q r s t u v w x y z

$ 1 2 3 4 5 6 7 8 9 0 & . , : ; - ' ' ! ? ( )

PARISIAN, ATF (30-pt. at 80%)

ABCDEFGHIJKLMNOPQRSTUVWXYZ& EMS

abcdefghijklmnopqrstuvwxyz $1234567890 .,-:;'!? '

244

PACKARD is ATF's adaptation of a distinctive style of lettering done by Oswald Cooper in advertisements for the Packard Motor Car Company, in 1913. *Packard Bold* followed in 1916. The latter is credited to Morris Benton, again closely following Cooper's original lettering, and it is quite likely that Benton did the actual adaptation of the first face also. These faces retain a handlettered appearance partly by the slightly irregular edges of strokes, partly by a number of alternate characters. Both were quite popular for several years.

Packard, ATF 348 (6-48pt)
Packard Bold, ATF 453 (6-48pt)

PAGODA—see *Matura* under Imports in Appendix.
PALATINO, PALETTE—see Imports in Appendix.
PALISADE—see *Bodoni Campanile.*
PALMER—see *Stationers Semiscript.*

PANTAGRAPH SCRIPT is an upright connecting script introduced by BB&S in 1893 but shown as late as 1925. It is distinguished by very long starting strokes on the capitals.

Pantagraph Script, BB&S-ATF 1816 (12-60pt)

PARAGON was designed by C. H. Griffith for Linotype in 1935. It is a member of that company's Legibility Group of typefaces, planned primarily for sharp and clean printing under the difficult inking and printing conditions of newspaper production, but also useful and popular for other periodical work. This face is lighter and airier than most such faces; otherwise it is much the same style. Compare *Excelsior, Ionic, Opticon, Textype;* also see *Classified.*

Paragon and Italic, Lino (6-10pt)
Paragon and Paragon Bold, Lino (5½-10pt)

PARAGON or *Paragon Plate* is a light, monotone face with long, pointed serifs, introduced by BB&S in 1901, and is completely unrelated to the face above. Originally it had the single name, the other being added later. It was useful primarily for stationery and announcements. *Paragon [Plate] Italic,* introduced in 1902, is essentially a sloped version of the roman, and was also offered in a title version as *Program Italic.* Compare *Victoria Italic, Menu.*

Paragon [Plate], BB&S-ATF 1817 (6-24pt)
Paragon [Plate] Italic, BB&S-ATF 1818 (6-24pt); also Program Italic (title), BB&S-ATF 1848 (6s-24L)

PARAGON GOTHIC—see *Gothic No. 578.*

PARAMOUNT was designed by Morris Benton in 1930 for ATF. It is basically a heavier companion to *Rivoli* (q.v.), which in turn is based on *Eve,* an importation from Germany, but is heavier than *Eve Bold.* It is an informal face with a crisp, pen-drawn appearance. Lowercase is small, with long ascenders and short descenders. Vertical strokes taper, being wider at the top. It was popular for a time as an advertising and announcement type.

Paramount, ATF 536 (6-72pt)

PARISIAN was designed for ATF in 1928 by Morris F. Benton. It is a frivolous thick-and-thin seriless design, with small lowercase and long ascenders. It has some general resemblance to *Broadway,* in the severe contrast of its thick and thin lines, but is much lighter and more informal. It is obviously a face for limited use, but has been popular for stationery and announcements. It was copied quite exactly by Intertype, which is surprising because on that machine it was duplexed with *Rivoli,* which means that the brass or body width of each corresponding character for each face is identical. The Intertype face was popular with companies specializing in mass production of personal stationery. Lowercase was not made for the 6- and 8-point sizes of foundry type.

Parisian, ATF 513 (6-72pt); Inter (10-18pt); (Univ 10-24pt)

PARK AVENUE, ATF 24-pt., Inter 14-pt.

ABCDEFGHIJKLMNOPQRSTUVWXYZ

abcdefghijklmnopqrstuvwxyz.,-:; "!?&£eres $1234567890

ABCDEFGHIJKLMN OP QRSTUVWXYZ$1234567890 abcdefghijklmnopqrstuvwxyz.,-:;'""!?

PARKWAY SCRIPT, Ludlow 24-pt. (part reduced) (Phil Ambrosi)

ABCDEFGHIJKLMNOPQRSTUVWXYZ&

abcdefghijklmnopqrstuvwxyz 1234567890$&?!.,-"::()[]— FTÆŒæœ£'ijß%

PARMA & ITALIC, Lino 12-pt.

ABCDEFGHIJKLMNOPQRSTUVWXYZ&ÆŒ 1234567890$£,.:;-"?!
ABCDEFGHIJKLMNOPQRSTUVWXYZ&ÆŒ 1234567890$£,.:;-"?!
ABCDEFGHIJKLMNOPQRSTUVWXYZ&ÆŒ
abcdefghijklmnopqrstuvwxyzæœfiflffffiffl ()@lb*†‡¶§||%⅛¼⅜½⅝¾⅞
abcdefghijklmnopqrstuvwxyzæœfiflffffiffl ()@lb†‡¶§||%⅛¼⅜½⅝¾⅞*

PARSONS, 24-pt. (Rich Hopkins)

ABCDEFGHIJKLMNOPQRSTUVWXYZ
abcdefghijklmnopqrstuvwxyz AMNT GJbdghklpy
1234567890$& .,-:;'!?—[]

PARSONS ITALIC, 24-pt. (part reduced)

ABCDEFGHIJKLMNOPQRSTUVWXYZ&
abcdefghijklmnopqrstuvwxyz fffifffiflffl .,-:;'!?bghky[]—
$1234567890 AMNT ThTo

PARSONS BOLD, 24-pt. (Herb Harnish)

ABCDEFGHIJKLMNOPQRSTUVWXYZ
abcdefghijklmnopqrstuvwxyz AMNT bdghklpy
$1234567890&.,-:;'!?[]GJ—

PARSONS SWASH INITIALS, BB&S 24-pt. (Rich Hopkins)

ABCDEFGHIJKLMNOPQRSTUVWY

PARK AVENUE is a distinctive script design by Robert E. Smith, cut by ATF about 1933. It is not quite a joining script, although some letter combinations seem to do so. Lowercase is rather small, with long ascenders, some of which have an open loop. This is probably one of the most successful designs in the founder's project of replacing the delicate traditional scripts with more contemporary interpretations. It was adapted to Intertype in 1939, in a version that departs remarkably little from the original, considering that it is duplexed with the totally dissimilar *Bernhard Fashion,* the only obvious differences being the lining figures, the narrowing of a few capitals, and straightening of the lowercase *f* and *l* to fit the straight, non-kerning matrices. However, some capitals have excess blank space on the left side. It is popular for stationery and announcements. Baltimore copied the foundry version as *Belair,* while several other suppliers cast fonts from Intertype matrices. Compare *Parkway Script, Piranesi Italic, Raleigh Cursive.*

Park Avenue, ATF 577 (12-72pt); Inter (12-18pt); (Univ 14-24pt); Belair, Balto 417 (12-24pt)

PARKWAY SCRIPT was designed by Emil Hirt for Ludlow in 1964. It has much the same character as *Park Avenue,* but is a little softer and more reserved, with a little less appearance of joining. It has virtually the same uses.

Parkway Script, Ludlow 57-MIC (12-36pt)

PARMA, with *Italic* and *Bold,* was cut by Linotype in 1930, as an adaptation of *Ratio-Latein,* designed in Germany by Friedrich Wilhelm Kleukens for the Stempel typefoundry. It is cut to German standards of alignment, raising doubt as to whether it was also actually cut in America, but it was shown on a standard American advance proof sheet.

Parma and Italic and Bold, Lino (8-12pt)

PARSONS was designed for BB&S in 1917 by Will Ransom, Chicago artist, based on the distinctive style of lettering he had been doing for advertisers in that city, and was named for I. R. Parsons, advertising manager of a Chicago department store. It is nearly monotone, but with a hand-lettered quality. It has unusual half-serifs and unique forms to a number of letters. The caps *MNUY* have a lowercase design, but at the insistence of users a more conventional form of *M* and *N* was added by the foundry, to the distress of the designer. *Parsons Italic* and *Parsons Bold* were added in 1918 by the same artist.

Parsons, BB&S-ATF 1819 (6-72pt); (Univ 6-48pt)
Parsons Italic, BB&S-ATF 1821 (6-48pt); (Univ 6-48pt)
Parsons Bold, BB&S-ATF 1820 (6-72pt); Mono 431 (see text)
Parsons Swash Initials, BB&S (18-48pt)

Oversize ascenders and descenders are one of the most notable features of this type, but Ransom was reluctant to let the foundry cut them. At his insistence the foundry included with specimens a warning that generally only one such letter should be used in a line, and suggesting other restrictions. The type was a great success but the suggestions were commonly ignored, and advertising bristled with groves of tall letters. It is said that this display of bad taste in the use of his design dismayed Ransom so much that he abandoned the idea of designing other typefaces. Only *Clearcut Shaded Capitals,* in 1924, are later credited to him, aside from decorative material. *Parsons* is believed to be the first face to feature long characters of this sort, although several artists had used them in distinctive hand-lettering. At least one typeface—*Pencraft* (q.v.)—had earlier supplied flourishes which could be added to special ascenders and descenders. *Stymie Bold* (q.v.) resurrected the idea later but less successfully. The *Parsons* long characters were included in all fonts; f-ligatures were made for all sizes of italic, but only up to 18-point in the roman and not at all for the bold.

Monotype lists "Parson's Bold" in some of its literature; this is presumed to be the same face but no confirmation or specimen has been found.

Parsons Swash Initials were designed by Sidney Gaunt; some of them were not approved by Ransom but were cast anyway.

PASTEL, BB&S (36-pt. at 67%) (Schuyler Shipley)

ABCDEFGHIJKLMNOPQRSTUVWXYZ&
abcdefghijklmnopqrstuvwxyz.,-:;'!?
$1234567890 AFHKRfhkmn

PASTEL BOLD, BB&S (60-pt. at 40%) (Gary Hantke)

ABCDEFGHIJKLMNOPQRSTUVWXYZ&.,-:;'?
abcdefghijklmnopqrstuvwxyz$1234567890

PASTEL CONDENSED, BB&S 24- & 18-pt. (part reduced)

Regimental HONORS BUILDING Styles Greatest A F H K R h k m n
ABCDEFGHIJKLMNOPQRSTUVWXYZ&.,:;-'!? $1234567890

PASTEL [ERA] OPEN, BB&S 24- & 18-pt. (Dave Norton)

ABCDEFGHIJKLMNOPQRSTUVWXYZ&
abcdefghijklmnopqrstuvwxyz.,-:;'!?$1234567890
AFHKRfhkmn

PASTEL, Inter (30-pt. at 80%); PASTEL LIGHTFACE Auxiliaries, BB&S 18-pt.

ABCDEFGHIJKLMNOPQRSTUVWXYZ A F H K R
abcdefghijklmnopqrstuv $1234567890 f h k m n

PASTEL ITALIC, Inter (30-pt. at 50%)

ABCDEFGHIJKLMNOPQRSTUVWXYZabcdefghijklmnopqrstuv$1234567890

PAUL REVERE, Keystone 18-pt. (John Horn)

ABCDEFGHIJKLMNOPQRSTUVWXYZ&ÆŒ-,.;':?!
abcdefghijklmnopqrstuvwxyzæœ$1234567890

PEIGNOT, ATF 24-pt.

ANOTHER METHOD Approvement considered

PEKIN, 30-pt. with 18-pt. Alternates

ABCDEFGHIJKLMNOPQRSTUVWXYZ& E H M h m n r t
abcdefghijklmnopqrstuvwxyz $1234567890 .,-:;'!?

248

PASTEL began as *Era,* designed for BB&S about 1892 by Nicholas J. Werner and Gustav Schroeder. *Lightface Era* and *Era Open* were added about 1895, and *Era Condensed* about 1898. Around the turn of the century the name was changed to *Pastel,* perhaps when *Pastel Bold* was added in 1903. *Era* and *Pastel* are identical, except that *Era* had only the characters with extended strokes, shown as Auxiliaries with *Pastel,* where they were replaced with more conventional characters in regular fonts. *Pastel* is virtually a monotone design, with tiny, pointed serifs. There are several unusual characters, including the splayed *M* and the *N* with the curved diagonal. *Pastel* was quite popular for subtitles in motion pictures, before the advent of sound. It was recast by ATF in 1954.

Intertype's cutting of *Pastel* is essentially the same as the foundry's *Pastel Lightface;* Intertype also cut a sloped version as *Pastel Italic.*

PAUL REVERE—see *Lorimer.*

PEIGNOT. ATF advertised this face in 1913. It was similar to *Auriol* (q.v.), but no complete specimen of it has been found. Undoubtedly it was obtained from the Peignot foundry in France, but has no similarity to the later face of the same name, which is shown under Imports in Appendix.

PEKIN is one of many faces renamed by BB&S for their 1925 specimen book. Its original name was *Dormer,* patented by the Great Western foundry in 1888 and credited to Ernst Lauschke. It is a very novel face, basically a fine-line letter with most characters having a heavier accented portion in an unconventional place. Vertical strokes on some of the capitals extend downward like descenders. It was made only in two sizes, one of which was later plated by Type Founders of Phoenix, after ATF had recast it in 1954.

PEN PRINT and *Pen Print Bold* were introduced by Inland Type Foundry in 1911, with the latter thought to have been the last face cut by that foundry before its sale to ATF. *Pen Print Open* was designed for ATF in 1921 by Morris Benton, and includes open versions of all the characters shown for the bold. The series has more the appearance of rather crude brush lettering than pen "printing," but the inclusion of an open version is contrary to the conception; perhaps it was intended for two-color printing. The letters have a slight backslant. The bold was also cut by Intertype, in 1927. Compare *Dom Casual.*

Pastel, BB&S-ATF 1822 (6-72pt)
Pastel Condensed, BB&S-ATF 1824 (8-72pt); also Offset Pastel Condensed, BB&S-ATF 1801 (24-72pt)
Pastel Lightface, BB&S-ATF 1825 (6-72pt); Pastel and Italic, Inter (30pt)
Pastel Bold, BB&S-ATF 1823 (5-72pt)
Pastel Open, BB&S-ATF 1826 (12-60pt)

Peignot, ATF 349 (12-60pt)

Pekin, BB&S-ATF 1827 (18,30pt); TFP-LATF (18pt)

Pen Print, Inland-ATF 350 (6-60pt)
Pen Print Bold, Inland-ATF 351 (6-60pt); Pen Bold, Inter (10-36pt)
Pen Print Open, ATF 466 (18-48pt)

PEN PRINT, ATF 18-pt.

ABCDEFGHIJKLMNOPQRSTUVWXYZ?
abcdefghijklmnopqrstuvwxyz&1234567890$.,:;-'!

PEN PRINT BOLD, ATF 24-pt.

ABCDEFGHIJKLMNOPQRSTUVWXYZ&
abcdefghijklmnopqrstuvwxyz $1234567890 .,-:;'!?

PEN PRINT OPEN, ATF (48-pt. at 50%) (Alfred Babcock, Dave Churchman)

ABCDEFGHIJKLMNOPQRSTUVWXYZ
abcdefghijklmnopqrstuvwxyz 1234567890$&

PENCRAFT OLD STYLE, BB&S (30-pt. at 80%), 18-pt. Ligatures, Auxiliaries, Specials (Rick von Holdt, Ward Schori)

ABCDEFGHIJKLMNNOPQRSTUVWXYZ&

abcdefghijklmnopqrstuvwxyz.,:;'?!-~$1234567890

fffiflffiffl The bdfhklpqγ~

of ∴ · ⁼ ⁓ by and

Specials

Examples of use

PENCRAFT ITALIC, BB&S 24-pt., 18-pt. Auxiliaries (Rick von Holdt)

ABCDEFGHIJKLMNOPQRSTUVWXYZ&

abcdefghijklmnopqrstuvwxyzfffifflffiffl.,:;'-?!

$1234567890 a e n s c w ch qu h ly ng s ſt th

PENCRAFT OLD STYLE BOLD, BB&S 18-pt. (Lucy S. Douglas)

ABCDEFGHIJKLMNOPQRSTUVWXYZ

abcdefghijklmnopqrstuvwxyz 1234567890 -;:,'!?&$

The and · ⁼ ÷ of by

PENCRAFT SHADED, BB&S 24-pt.

STRIKING EFFECTS ARE GOOD
Displaying Characters $1234567890

PENCRAFT TEXT, BB&S 18-pt. (Rick von Holdt)

ABCDEFGHIJKLMNOPQRSTUVWXYZ abcdefghijklmnopqrstuvwxyz 1234567890

PENDRAWN, Mono (36-pt. at 67%)

A A B C D E F G H I J K L M N O P Q R S T U V W X
Y Z & $ 1 2 3 4 5 6 7 8 9 0 . , - ' : ; ! ?
a b c d e e f g h i j k l m n o p q r s t u v w x y z fi fl ff ffi ffl

PENN GOTHIC, Keystone 12-pt.

MENU USEFUL FOR BEST KIND OF PRINT. $12

PERICLES, ATF 18-pt.

ABCDEFGHIJKLMNOPQRSTUV& $123456
ℇ R W X Y Z 7 8 9 0 . , ⁼ ' „ " : ; ! ? · ç ★

PEN TEXT—see *Engravers Upright Script.*

PENCRAFT OLDSTYLE and *Pencraft Italic* were designed by Sidney Gaunt for BB&S in 1914, with the bold and shaded versions following over the next two years. The *Oldstyle* is a rather charming interpretation of lettering styles popular at that time, but the other versions are not as impressive. *Pencraft Oldstyle* is notable for the large number of Auxiliary characters, some of which were commonly included with other similar faces, and the unique *Pencraft Specials,* which consisted of a variety of swash strokes to be used to extend the special ascending and descending letters. *Pencraft Italic* included several swash caps among its Auxiliaries, and *Pencraft Bold* had Auxiliaries comparable to the roman, but without the flourishes or Specials. Compare the long ascenders and descenders of *Parsons* and *Stymie.*

Pencraft Oldstyle, BB&S-ATF 1829 (6-72pt); also Pencraft Title, BB&S-ATF 1834 (6s-42pt)
Pencraft Italic, BB&S-ATF 1828 (6-48pt)
Pencraft Oldstyle Bold, BB&S-ATF 1830 (6-72pt)
Pencraft Oldstyle Bold Condensed, BB&S-ATF 1831 (6-72pt)
Pencraft Shaded, BB&S-ATF 1832 (24-48pt)

PENCRAFT TEXT was designed by Sidney Gaunt for BB&S in 1916. It has somewhat the character of *Pencraft Oldstyle,* by the same artist at about the same time, but it can hardly be considered a part of that family. It has just a suggestion of the angularity of Text or Old English faces, but retains more of the character of simple hand-lettering.

Pencraft Text, BB&S-ATF 1833 (12-48pt)

PENDRAWN was designed for Monotype about 1933 by Sol Hess. It retains much of the quality of sixteenth-century hand-lettering, and is generally modern in character without the severity typical of most modern types. Serifs are long and thin, slightly concave, but those at the top of lowercase stems are slanted as in oldstyle types. Stems taper slightly toward the ends, and figures are hanging. Round letters tend toward an egg shape, with the small end down. It has been made only in two sizes: regular 36-point as a complete font, and 36H4 as oversize capitals only.

Pendrawn, Mono 358 (36,36H4)

PENN GOTHIC is a wide, serifless capital font with thick-and-thin contrast, shown by Keystone Type Foundry in 1905.

Penn Gothic, Keystone (6s-24pt)

PERICLES is a distinctive font of sans-serif capitals designed in 1934 for ATF by Robert Foster, based on hand-lettering he had been doing for several years for magazine and advertising headlines. It is much more informal than other sans serifs of the time, such as *Futura* or *Bernhard Gothic,* with more of an inscriptional feeling. Some characters are derived from classical Greek forms. A 72-point size is said to have been cut but never issued.

Pericles, ATF 583 (18-60pt)

PERPETUA—see Imports in Appendix.
PERRY—see *Steelplate Gothic.*

PHENIX (ATF's spelling) was designed by Morris F. Benton for ATF in 1935. It is the same founder's and designer's *News Gothic Extra Condensed,* with several characters redesigned in the "round" fashion of the time. It is similar to *Jefferson Gothic,* derived earlier from the same source by Monotype. Baltimore Type called it *Tourist Extra Condensed.*

Phenix, ATF 651 (24-72pt)

PHIDIAN—see Antiques in Appendix.

PHENIX, ATF 24-pt.

ABCDEFGHIJKLMNOPQRSTUVWXYZ& abcdefghijklmnopqrstuvwxyz $1234567890 .,-:;'!?

ABCDEFGHIJKLMNOPQRSTUVWXYZ&
abcdefghijklmnopqrstuvwxyz $1234567890 .,-:;'!?

ABCDEFGHIJKLMNOPQRSTUVWXYZ&
abcdefghijklmnopqrstuvwxyz $1234567890 .,-:;'!?`

ABCDEFGHIJKLMNOPQRSTUVWXYZ&
abcdefghijklmnopqrstt_uvwxyzctst $1234567890 .,=:;"!?
ABCDEFGHIJKLMNOPQRSTUVWXYZ&

ABCDEFGHIJKLMNOPQRSTUVWXYZ
abcdefghijklmnopqrstuvwxyz$1234567890.,-:;"!?&

ABCDEFGHIJKLMNOPQRSTUVWXYZ
abcdefghijklmnopqrstuvwxyz &.,;:-!?" $£stct 1234567890
A B C D E F G H I J K L M N O P Q R
S T U V W X Y Z &

ABCDEFGHIJKLMNOPQRSTUVWXYZ&
abcdefghijklmnopqrstuvwxyz 1234567890

ABCDEFGHIJKLMNOPQRSTUVWXYZ&   *abcdefghijklmnopqrstuvwxyz*   *1234567890*

ABCDEFGHIJKLMNOPQRSTUVWXYZ&
abcdefghijklmnopqrstuvwxyz 1234567890

ABCDEFGHIJKLMNOPQRSTUVWXYZ
&$1234567890.,-:;"!?°ATAYLTLY

PHILADELPHIA LINING GOTHIC is a late-nineteenth-century face originating with MS&J, which cut it in several widths and weights. In 1912 Monotype copied one of these, which would have been known as *Bold Condensed* except that the foundry designated variations only by numbers; this was No. 8. As a foundry type it was notable for the number of versions available; as a single Monotype face it is undistinguished. ATF continued to cast the family for a decade or so after the merger in 1892, then replaced these faces with the *News, Alternate,* and *Franklin Gothic* families. The Monotype copy lasted much longer. Hansen's *Extended Lining Gothic* was a copy of *Philadelphia Lining Gothic No. 14.* Compare *Mid-Gothic, Wide Line Gothic.*

Philadelphia Lining Gothic, MS&J-ATF (6-48pt); Mono 52 (6-36pt)
Extended Lining Gothic, Hansen (6-30pt)

PIRANESI was designed by Willard T. Sniffin for ATF in 1930. It is a very delicate roman, with long ascenders and rather short descenders, and is named for an eighteenth-century Italian engraver. Other versions were added by Morris Benton: *Piranesi Italic,* also in 1930; *Piranesi Bold Italic* in 1931; and *Piranesi Bold* roman in 1933. The italics are more characterful and have more of a calligraphic feeling, especially in the cursive capitals, but a separate set of Plain Capitals—essentially a slanted version of the roman—was produced for each of the italics. Oldstyle figures were made for all versions, and lining figures were also available for the bold roman. Both romans and both sets of italic plain capitals were still shown by ATF in recent specimens. There seems to be no explanation for the high series number of *Piranesi Italic Plain Caps,* but that is how it appears in ATF literature. *Piranesi Italic,* with regular cursive capitals, was also made by Intertype under the name *Minuet.*

Piranesi, ATF 538 (8-72pt)
Piranesi Italic, ATF 547 (8-48pt); Minuet, Inter (10-18pt); Piranesi Italic Plain Caps, ATF 1974 (8-48pt)
Piranesi Bold, ATF 569 (6-72pt)
Piranesi Bold Italic, ATF 570 (8-72pt); Piranesi Bold Italic Plain Caps, ATF 572 (8-72pt)

PLANTIN is a popular roman face cut by the English Monotype company in 1913, derived from prints of an old-face design cut during the sixteenth century by Robert Granjon for the famous Dutch printer, Christophe Plantin. It was copied in 1937 by Ludlow in three versions, and also by Intertype in roman and italic. It has somewhat the letter forms of the French oldstyle faces that inspired *Times Roman,* but wider and with sturdier hairlines.

Plantin, Ludlow 39-L (6-24pt); Inter (11,18pt)
Plantin Italic, Ludlow 39-LI (6-12pt); Inter (11,18pt)
Plantin Bold, Ludlow 39-B (6-24pt)
English Monotype also has Plantin Light & Italic, Bold Italic, Bold Condensed.

PLATE GOTHIC was advertised by BB&S as "new" in 1900, and other versions were added within several years. It is somewhat similar to *Copperplate Gothic,* but not as well proportioned, and has even tinier serifs. Some members of the *Steelplate Gothic* family (q.v.) of the same foundry have the same characteristics, and appear to be a rename or at least a replacement for members of this family. Note that the colon and semicolon are full cap height, which is very unusual. *Plate Gothic* is also Ludlow's name for *Copperplate Gothic* (q.v.).

Plate Gothic, BB&S-ATF 1836 (6s-36pt); Card Gothic No. 3, Hansen (6s-24pt)
Plate Gothic Condensed, BB&S-ATF 1838 (6s-36pt)
Plate Gothic Light, BB&S-ATF 1839 (6s-36pt)
Plate Gothic Light Condensed, BB&S-ATF 1840 (6s-36pt)
Plate Gothic Bold, BB&S-ATF 1837 (6s-12pt)

PLATE ROMAN—see *Brandon.*

PLATE SCRIPT was a BB&S series from 1897, very similar to *Typo Script.* There were three sets of lowercase, *No. 2* and *No. 3* being very slightly heavier than the regular; all were identical otherwise.

Plate Script, BB&S-ATF 1841 (14-48pt)
Plate Script No. 2, BB&S-ATF 1752 (14-48pt)
Plate Script No. 3, BB&S-ATF 1753 (14-48pt)

PLATE GOTHIC BOLD, BB&S 12L (Rick von Holdt)

ABCDEFGHIJKLMNOPQRSTUVWXYZ & $1234567890 .,-'":;!? AT AY LT LY ©

PLATE SCRIPT, BB&S 24-pt.

Eight Models with the Requested Desired Effect Properly Shipped

PLATE TEXT, BB&S 18-pt. (Leonard Bahr)

ABCDEFGHIJKLMNOPQRSTUVWXYZ&
abcdefghijklmnopqrstuvwxyz .,:;-'!?$ 1234567890

PLATE TEXT NO. 4, BB&S 24-pt.

ABCDEFGHIJKLMNOPQRSTUVWXYZ .,~:;'!?
abcdefghijklmnopqrstuvwxyz h $1234567890

PLYMOUTH, 24-pt. (William M. Danner)

ABCDEFGHIJKLMNOPQRSTUVWXYZ
abcdefghijklmnopqrstuvwxyzRahmnu
&of&1234567890$.,-:;!?'

PLYMOUTH ITALIC, BB&S 24-pt. (part reduced)

ABCDEFGHIJKLMYZ@ ORANGE
Civilization's history of 1234567890
A S R T W & A Y

PLYMOUTH CONDENSED, BB&S 24-pt.

ABCDEFGHIJKLMNOPQRSTUVWXYZ@$1234567890
abcdefghijklmnopqrstuvwxyz .,-:;'!? a g h m n u R U of The

PLYMOUTH BOLD, BB&S 24-pt. (Dave Greer)

ABCDEFGHIJKLMNOPQRSTUV
abcdefghijklmnopqrstuvwxyz
$1234567890.,:;'!?- WXYZ@

POMPEIAN CURSIVE, BB&S (54-pt. at 50%)

ABCDEFGHIJKLMNOPQRST
UVWXYZ& Sh Sk St ff fl ffi $1234567890
abcdefghijklmnopqrrstt uvwxyz .,-;:'!?fi

PONTIAC, ATF 24-pt. (John Horn, Dave Greer)

ABCDEFGHIJKLMNOPQRSTUVWXYZ&.,-:;'!?
abcdefghijklmnopqrstuvwxyz£$1234567890

254

PLATE TEXT is an Old English design made in several varieties by BB&S about 1902. *Plate Text* itself is a shaded face, similar to *Typo Text* (q.v.); *Plate Text No. 4* is a fairly light design, just a little heavier than *Wedding Text* (q.v.), but not as well drawn. Compare *Shaw Text.*

Plate Text, BB&S (8-18pt)
Plate Text No. 2, BB&S
Plate Text No. 3, BB&S
Plate Text No. 4, BB&S (8-36pt)

PLAYBILL—see Imports in Appendix.

PLYMOUTH and *Plymouth Italic* were cut by BB&S in 1900 with *Plymouth Condensed* and *Plymouth Bold* following in 1901. They are prime examples of the "rugged" style popular at that time, and are said to have been based on lettering being used for headings by the Curtis Publishing Company (see *Post*). The italic is freely drawn, with a number of swash-like characters, and is even more rugged than the roman. The condensed is simply a narrow version of *Plymouth,* but the bold is also more rugged or irregular.

Plymouth was later known as *Rugged Black,* while *Plymouth Bold* became *Rugged Extra Black* and later *Adcraft Black* (q.v.). *Plymouth* and *Plymouth Italic* were adapted by Monotype in 1913, with the keyboard sizes (6- to 12-point) being modified as usual to fit mechanical requirements. Monotype display sizes of *Plymouth* appear to match the foundry original, but the so-called *Plymouth Italic* on Monotype (14- to 36-point) is a copy of ATF's *Post Oldstyle Italic,* probably due to a misidentification when punches were prepared.

Plymouth or Rugged Black or Adcraft Bold, BB&S (6-120pt); Plymouth, Mono 60 (6-36pt)
Plymouth Italic, BB&S (6-72pt); Mono 601 (see text)
Plymouth Condensed, BB&S (6-72pt)
Plymouth Bold or Adcraft Black, BB&S-ATF 1500 (6-72pt)

POMPEIAN CURSIVE was drawn for BB&S in 1927 by Oswald Cooper, to provide an American alternative to *Bernhard Cursive,* the popular German face which had been most instrumental in opening the doors to the importation of foreign typefaces. Cooper at first had drawn a substantially different cursive, but reluctantly and at the insistence of the foundry redrew it more like the German face but with just enough differences to make it distinctive. But Cooper insisted on avoiding the obvious name "Barnhart Cursive." The name with an Italian connotation was chosen because the style was said to have been based on eighteenth-century Italian copperplate lettering. Soon thereafter BB&S merged into ATF, and this face was not shown in subsequent ATF specimen books. Compare *Liberty.*

Pompeian Cursive, BB&S (12-54pt)

PONTIAC is a thick-and-thin, serifless face, almost a condensed version of *Quentell,* and was advertised by ATF in 1902. It must be older, though, because it is similar but inferior to *Globe Gothic Condensed,* designed for the same foundry in 1900.

Pontiac, ATF 352 (6-72pt)

POOR RICHARD is a rather novel roman, issued by Keystone Type Foundry in 1919. It has slight contrast and long ascenders, with unusual forms to several characters. It does not seem to have survived when Keystone merged with ATF that year.

Poor Richard, Keystone (6-72pt)

POOR RICHARD, Keystone 24-pt. (Duane Scott)

ABCDEFGHIJKLMNOPQRSTUVWXYZ&
abcdefghijklmnopqrstuvwxyz 1234567890.,;:""""?!$-

POST CONDENSED, 24-pt. (Jane Roberts)

ABCDEFGHIJKLMNOPQRSTUVWXYZ
abcdefghijklmnopqrstuvwxyz&1234567890$.,;:-'!?

POST MONOTONE, 24-pt. (Herb Harnish)

ABCDEFGHIJKLMNOPQRSTUVWXYZ&$
abcdefghijklmnopqrstuvwxyzfffiflffiffl.,-:;'!?
1234567890 The of ahmnouE

POST MONOTONE NO. 2, 24-pt. (Herb Harnish)

ABCDEFGHIJKLMNOPQRSTUVWXYZ&$12345
abcdefghijklmnopqrstuvwxyzfffiflffiffl.,-:;'!? 67890

POST OLDSTYLE ROMAN NO. 1, ATF 24-pt. (Elizabeth Nevin)

ABCDEFGHIJKLMNOPQRSTUVWXYZ
abcdefghijklmnopqrstuvwxyzfffiflffiffl
&1234567890$.,-:;!?' ✿ ✐ The of

POST OLDSTYLE ROMAN NO. 2, ATF 14-pt. (Herb Harnish)

ABCDEFGHIJKLMNOPQRSTUVWXYZ&$1234567890 ✐✿☙
abcdefghijklmnopqrstuvwxyzfffiflffiffl.,-:;'!?Thect ofofffiflEORS

POST OLDSTYLE ITALIC, Mono 18-pt. (see text)

ABCDEFGHIJKLMNOPQRSTUVWXYZ
abcdefghijklmnopqrstuvwxyz £$&1234567890 ;:.,'=!?

POST TEXT & ITALIC, Mono 11-pt.

ABCDEFGHIJKLMNOPQRSTUVWXYZ&ÆŒ   *ABCDEFGHIJKLMNOPQRSTUVWXYZ&ÆŒ*
abcdefghijklmnopqrstuvwxyzæœ   fiflffffiffl   *abcdefghijklmnopqrstuvwxyzæœ   fiflffffiffl*
$1234567890   .,-'':;!?   *$1234567890   :;!?*
ABCDEFGHIJKLMNOPQRSTUVWXYZ&ÆŒ

POST SHADED ITALIC, ATF private 30-pt.

ABCDEFGHIJKLMN
OPQRSTUVWXYZ

256

POST. The various faces bearing this name are all believed to have been designed for or inspired by the Curtis Publishing Company and its *Saturday Evening Post* magazine. *Post Oldstyle Roman No. 1* and *No. 2* were designed in 1900 by E. J. Kitson, *Saturday Evening Post* artist, who had previously drawn each heading separately, and cast by ATF, while *Post Oldstyle Italic* was patented by Herman Ihlenburg in 1903. They are based on the lettering of Guernsey Moore, No. 2 being a heavier version of No. 1, with the italic being about the weight of No. 1. They are rugged or irregular faces, in the popular style of the day, and are similar to such faces as *Blanchard, Buffalo,* and *Plymouth,* produced by other foundries about the same time. *Post Condensed* is the weight of No. 2, and is comparable in design but lacks the irregular edges. This condensed face was copied by Monotype and Linotype, the latter giving it the name "Baskerville Condensed"! Display sizes of *Post Italic* were made by Monotype under the name of *Plymouth Italic* (q.v.).

Post Monotone was issued by ATF in 1903. It is a wide face, following the general design characteristics of *Post Oldstyle,* but the strokes are monotone rather than thick-and-thin, and do not have the irregularities of its older counterpart. The greater width is due in part to a greater x-height, with short ascenders as well as descenders. *Post Monotone No. 2,* a narrower version of the same design, appeared later.

Post Text was cut for Monotype in 1902, and at times has also been known as *Easyread* or *Extended Modern.* It was used as a text face by the *Saturday Evening Post* for a number of years beginning in 1930. It is essentially the same as the faces known generally as *Modern,* but is wider than most of them. Also see *Curtis Post, Curtis Shaded Italic.*

* * *

Other Post Faces were produced privately for the exclusive use of the magazine. *Post Shaded Italic* was cut by ATF in 1910, and used for headings for many years from that time. In 1939 a new typographic styling of the magazine was undertaken, under the direction of Sol Hess, Monotype art director, and two new faces were produced. *Post-Stout Italic* was a filled-in version of the earlier face, with some characters redesigned. A greater modification, *Postblack,* was tried in both roman and italic, but the roman was abandoned after trials, and only the *Postblack Italic* was produced. It and *Post-Stout Italic* were adopted by the magazine in 1939 and used extensively.

One authority lists *Post Roman Heading Letter* or *Post Headletter* as having been designed by Tommy Thompson in 1943 for the *Saturday Evening Post,* and privately cut by Monotype for the publication. Whether this is a reference to the face shown in the specimen here, or to *Postblack* and *Italic,* in spite of the conflict of dates, is uncertain. Also see *Curtis Post.*

Post Oldstyle Roman No. 1, ATF 358 (6-72pt)
Post Oldstyle Roman No. 2, ATF 359 (6-72pt)
Post Oldstyle Italic, ATF 357 (6-60pt); Plymouth Italic (q.v.), Mono 601
Post Condensed, ATF 354 (6-72pt); Mono 360 (6-36pt); Baskerville Condensed, Lino (12,14pt)
Post Monotone, ATF 355 (5-36pt)
Post Monotone No. 2, ATF 356 (6-36pt)
Post Text and Italic, Mono 5ABC (5½-12pt)

Post Shaded Italic, ATF (private)
Post-Stout Italic, Mono (17-33pt, private)
Postblack Italic, Mono (7-30pt, private)
Post Roman Heading Letter or Post Headletter, Mono 458 (private)

POST ROMAN (other)—see Imports in Appendix.

POST STOUT ITALIC, private 28-pt.

ABCDEFGHIJKLMNOPQRSTUVWXYZ

POSTBLACK ITALIC, private 30-pt.

ABCDEFGHIJKLMNOPQRSTUVW
abcdefghijklmnopqrstuvwxyz XYZ

POSTER, Mono 24-pt.

ABCDEFGHIJKLMNOPQRSTUVWXYZ&
abcdefghijklmnopqrstuvwxyz 1234567890$.,-:;'!?()

POSTER GOTHIC, ATF 24-pt.

ABCDEFGHIJKLMNOPQRSTUVWXYZ&
1234567890 $?!.,::;'-

POWELL, Mono 24-pt.

ABCDEFGHIJKLMNOPQRSTUVWXYZ&-:;'!?
abcdefghijklmnopqrstuvwxyz fffifl $1234567890 .,
The and & ft é ¢ of

POWELL ITALIC, Mono 24-pt.

ABCDEFGHIJKLMNOPQRSTUVWXYZ&
abcdefghijklmnopqrstuvwxyz .,-:;'!? fifffflffifffl
$1234567890

PRIMER & ITALIC, Lino 14-pt.

ABCDEFGHIJKLMNOPQRSTUVWXYZ& (234567 |0 .ffl&*$)8:9Z1ffi fl 1234567890
ABCDEFGHIJKLMNOPQRSTUVWXYZ& ABCDEFGHIJKLMNOPQRSTUVWXYZ& *1234567890*

abcdefghijklmnopqrstuvwxyzfffififlfffiffl .,-:;"!?*†‡§◖/@()[] $1234567890£⅛¼⅜½⅝¾⅞%
abcdefghijklmnopqrstuvwxyzfffififlfffiffl .,-:;"!?o†‡§◖/@()[] $1234567890£⅛¼⅜½⅝¾⅞%

PRIORY BLACK TEXT, BB&S 24-pt. (part reduced) (Ivan Snyder)

𝔄𝔅ℭ𝔇𝔈𝔉𝔊𝔥𝔍𝔍𝔎𝔏𝔐𝔑𝔒𝔓𝔔ℜ𝔖𝔗𝔘𝔙𝔚𝔛𝔜ℨ&$
abcdefghijklmnopqrstuvwxyz &$l.,:;'!?

Name in parentheses after some specimens
indicates person who has set that specimen,
in whole or in part, to our format.

POSTER is a heavy, narrow, very compact gothic designed by Sol Hess for Monotype. Its general appearance suggests a contemporary serifless design, but in fact there is a slight hint of serifs. The slightly splayed *M* and the single-bowl *g* are suggestive of British grotesques. Ascenders and descenders are short, giving a large x-height, and the face is closely fitted. Some literature calls it *Hess Poster.*

Poster, Mono 700 (14-36pt)

POSTER BODONI—see *Ultra Bodoni* under Bodoni.
POSTER BODONI COMPRESSED—see *Onyx.*

POSTER GOTHIC was designed by Morris Benton for ATF in 1934. It is essentially a continuation into larger sizes of *Bank Gothic Condensed Medium* (q.v.), but is more closely fitted, as a large face should be.

Poster Gothic, ATF 592 (24-96pt)

POWELL. Shortly after the successful introduction of *Pabst Oldstyle,* the department store advertising manager who had commissioned that type—a Mr. Powell—left that store and became ad manager of another large store. Again he approached Frederic W. Goudy to design a type for him, similar to *Pabst* but necessarily somewhat different. The result this time was named *Powell.* Caps are much like those of *Pabst,* but the lowercase, instead of being very small with long ascenders as in that face, is larger with more normal ascenders. *Powell* was cut by Keystone Type Foundry and released in 1903. Compare *Pabst, Hearst.*

The foundry later designed a companion italic, ignoring Goudy's suggestion that he do so. *Powell Italic* was advertised in June 1908 as the first "non-kerning" italic, in which no characters overhang the rectangular type body. Favorable reception to this idea encouraged the foundry to cut several other non-kerning series.

Powell, Keystone (6-72pt); Mono 97 (6-36pt); Ludlow 9 (14-48pt)
Powell Italic, Keystone (6-72pt); Mono 971 (6-36pt)

PRIMER was designed by Rudolph Ruzicka for Linotype and introduced in 1953. A half-dozen years earlier Linotype had commissioned this noted artist and engraver to design a face to replace *Century Schoolbook.* Legibility was the primary consideration, along with more contemporary styling. It is designed for a crisper feeling, and offers a choice of either long or short descenders, as well as lining or oldstyle figures. The italic is specifically drawn within the mechanical restrictions of slug-machine matrices. Although a great many typefaces increase their proportionate width in small sizes, *Primer* carries this reproportioning a little further than most, resulting in an unusually legible and stylish face, even in 6-point. It is popular for advertising and general book work as well as for educational materials.

In the specimen shown here, the characters shown immediately above the small caps are those normally combined with these letters. These figures and other characters are also made in combination with their italic counterparts for insertion of matrices by hand, or can be cut to replace small caps on the keyboard.

Primer and Italic, Lino (6-14pt)

PRIORY TEXT was the blackletter of the Fry Foundry in England, with some sizes dating back to about 1600, and most sizes shown in 1785. It was revived by Talbot Baines Reed for his *History of the Old English Letterfoundries* in 1887, and DeVinne used it for his edition of *Philobiblon* in 1889. The Dickinson foundry, a forerunner of ATF, issued it as *Priory Text* about that time. It is very similar to *Caslon Text* (q.v.). BB&S made a near-duplicate type, originally called *Reed Text,* but later shown as *Priory Black Text.* Although the latter was shown as late as 1925, these faces had generally been replaced earlier by *Cloister Black* (q.v.) and other Old English faces with more refined draftsmanship.

Priory Text, ATF (8-36pt); Priory Black Text, BB&S-ATF 1847 (8-48pt)

ORNAMENTS RECEDING HUNGER Killed
For Arts and all Kinds Sails of The Vessel the Bear

PROCESS & ITALIC, Mono 9-pt.

ABCDEFGHIJKLMNOPQRSTUVWXYZ& abcdefghijklmnopqrstuvwxyz fffiffiflffl $1234567890 .,-:;'!?( )   ABCDEFGHIJKLMNOPQRSTUVWXYZ&

ABCDEFGHIJKLMNOPQRSTUVWXYZ& abcdefghijklmnopqrstuvwxyz fffiffiflffl .,-:;'!?( )

PUBLICITY GOTHIC, 24-pt. (Dave Greer)

ABCDEFGHIJKLMNOPQRSTUVWXY
abcdefghijklmnopqrstuvwxyz &Z
.,-:;!? $1234567890LY ST CºR.ſ▪ᵥ◾◢

QUADRATA II, Duensing 12/14-pt.

ABCC DEFGHIJK L M NOP QU R RST T uvW XYZ

+ ⊕ ÆŒ 1234567890 [.,:;'-/!?*]

QUENTELL, ATF 24-pt. #2

ABCDEFGHIJKLMNOPQRSTUVWXYZ& $1234567890
abcdefghijklmnopqrstuvwxyz fffiffiflffl .,-:;'!?

260

PRISCILLA was introduced by Keystone Type Foundry in 1901, and first shown with *Ben Franklin*. Later the same year, though, it was advertised with *John Alden,* which it more nearly resembles. Both are quaint designs, supposedly typical of Colonial types; both have swash-like serifs on some of the caps, equal weighting on both sides of the cap *U,* and weighting on the wrong side of the cap *Y.* Both faces were shown by Keystone as late as 1919, just before its merger with ATF.

Priscilla, Keystone (6-60pt)

PRISMA—see Imports in Appendix.

PROCESS was designed by Monotype for the Crowell Publishing Company, and produced about 1939. It was intended for clarity in reproduction by gravure, and was based on *Goudy Light.* Thin lines and serifs were thickened, and a monotone weight was preserved throughout. The pointed parts of letters were rounded, the counters of certain characters were opened up, and the general fitting was increased. Only one size was cut.

Process and Italic, Mono 138EFG (9pt)

PROFIL—see Imports in Appendix.
PROGRAM ITALIC—see *Paragon Plate Italic.*

PUBLICITY GOTHIC was designed by Sidney Gaunt in 1916 for BB&S. It is basically a bold gothic, but with many deep irregularities designed into the edges of strokes, which are the same in all sizes. There are no descenders, characters which normally have descenders being designed within the x-height. Caps and ascenders are nearly the full body size, making the face considerably oversize by usual standards. Lowercase *q* has a capital form and is made only in combination with *u.* The colon and semicolon are full cap height, and there are a number of special characters as shown. ATF revived it for a short time about 1933. Compare *Advertisers Gothic.*

Publicity Gothic, BB&S-ATF 1849 (6-120pt)

PUNCH—see *Signal Black* under Imports in Appendix.
PURITAN—see *Adcraft.*

QUADRATA is a recreation of an uncial form, designed in 1970 by Paul Duensing. The first experimental version was smoothly modeled; later it was modified, especially with the irregular edges, and completed as *Quadrata II* and cast by the designer at his Private Press and Typefoundry.

Quadrata II, Duensing (12-24pt)

QUENTELL was drawn for ATF's Central Type Foundry branch in St. Louis; it has been ascribed to N. J. Werner, but a design patent was issued in 1895 to William S. Quentell, advertising manager of Armour & Company of Chicago, for whom the face was made. Two years later it was redrawn as *Taylor Gothic* by Joseph W. Phinney for ATF, and later redesigned as *Globe Gothic* (q.v.). Meanwhile, the original *Quentell* was slightly modified as *Quentell No. 2,* and in that form continued to be shown in specimens along with its altered forms. See *Pontiac.*

Quentell No. 2, ATF 295 (6-72pt)

IDEAL SAMPLES *EXPERT IN TRADE* **BALANCE SHEETS**
The men who want *Interesting lecture on* **Saving a few minutes**
to achieve success *better printing by the* **every hour is effected**

QUILL, Keystone 24-pt. (William Wokoun)

AABCDEFGHIJKLMNOPQRSSTUVWXYZ
abcdefghijklmnopqrstuvwxyz &I2345678890$.,-:;!?'

QUILL OUTLINE, Keystone 24-pt. (Dave Greer)

AABCDEFGHIJKLMNOPQRSSTUVWXYZ&
abcdefghijklmnopqrstuvwxyz .,-:;'!? $I234567890

RADIANT MEDIUM, Ludlow 24-pt.

ABCDEFGHIJKLMNOPQRSTUVWXYZ& .,-:;'!?()[]—""
abcdefghijklmnopqrstuvwxyz 1234567890 A K M N R W

RADIANT MEDIUM ITALIC, Ludlow 24- & 18-pt.

ABCDEFGHIJKLMNOPQRSTUVWXYZ& $.,-:;"!?
abcdefghijklmnopqrstuvwxyz 1234567890

RADIANT BOLD, Ludlow 24-pt.

ABCDEFGHIJKLMNOPQRSTUVWXYZ& .,-:;'!?()[]—'%
abcdefghijklmnopqrstuvwxyz 1234567890¼⅔⅓½¾
A K M N R W

RADIANT BOLD CONDENSED, Ludlow 24-pt.

ABCDEFGHIJKLMNOPQRSTUVWXYZ AKMNRW
abcdefghijklmnopqrstuvwxyz.,-:;"!?()[]&. $$1234567890ᶜ

RADIANT BOLD CONDENSED ITALIC, Ludlow 24-pt.

ABCDEFGHIJKLMNOPQRSTUVWXYZ&
abcdefghiklmnopqrstuvwxyz 1234567890

QUICK-SET ROMAN was designed in 1918 for ATF, and ascribed to Capitan and Becker. ATF does not identify these persons further, but they may have been W. F. Capitaine, who had designed a few nineteenth-century faces for predecessors of ATF, and Charles W. Becker, a hand engraver in the matrix cutting department who had also participated in the design of some other faces. These types were designed so that there are only four different widths of characters in each size, and all widths are multiples of points or half points. All three series are the same width, size for size. This makes justification faster and easier, and is especially useful for timetables and other work requiring justification in narrow columns. This is the principle of a series of Self-Spacing faces designed by Linn Boyd Benton in 1883, also of most proportionally-spacing typewriters. Linotype has several faces, known collectively as *Self Spacing Faces,* adapted to the same principle. Also see *Typotabular Gothic.*

Quick-Set Roman, ATF 361 (6-18pt)
Quick-Set Italic, ATF 362 (6-18pt)
Quick-Set Bold, ATF 363 (6-18pt)

QUILL was issued by Keystone Type Foundry in 1899 or earlier. It is a heavy, cursive display font. Many strokes, especially in the lowercase, end in blobs that would suggest brush work, but elsewhere strokes are squared off too much for that. The lowercase is generally regular, but many capitals have heavier portions that tend to make a spotty appearance. There was also *Quill Outline,* about 1900.

Quill, Keystone (12-72pt)
Quill Outline, Keystone (12-48pt)

QUILLSCRIPT—see *Thompson Quillscript.*
RACINE—see *Sketch Title.*

RADIANT was designed by Robert H. Middleton for Ludlow, and introduced in 1938, with additional members of the family being added over the following two or three years. It is a precise, thick-and-thin, serifless style, expressing the modern spirit of the forties while breaking away from the ubiquitous monotone sans-serifs. *Radiant Medium* is actually about as light as possible to maintain thick-and-thin contrast, but bold and heavy weights offer substantial contrast. All upright versions have as alternates the round forms of *AKMNRW,* as shown with some of the specimens. Italics have the standard 17-degree slant of Ludlow italic mats, which is rather extreme for serifless faces, except for small sizes of *Medium Italic,* which are made on straight mats and are redesigned with about 10-degree slope. Like most Ludlow faces, all versions of this face have fractions and percent marks available as extras.

Thick-and-thin serifless faces are rare in this country. Compare the older *Globe Gothic;* also *Empire, Stellar, Lydian, Optima,* and *Czarin,* which aren't really in the same category.

Radiant Medium, Ludlow 43-M (6-72pt)
Radiant Medium Italic, Ludlow 43-MI (8-48pt)
Radiant Bold, Ludlow 43-B (6-72pt)
Radiant Bold Condensed, Ludlow 43-BC (12-72pt)
Radiant Bold Condensed Italic, Ludlow 43-BCI (18-72pt)
Radiant Bold Extra Condensed, Ludlow 43-BEC (14-96pt)
Radiant Heavy, Ludlow 43-H (10-72pt)

RADIANT BOLD EXTRA CONDENSED, Ludlow 24-pt.

ABCDEFGHIJKLMNOPQRSTUVWXYZ& abcdefghijklmnopqrstuvwxyz $1234567890 .,-:;'!?()[]—'
¼½¾⅓⅔% AKMNW

RADIANT HEAVY, Ludlow 24-pt.

ABCDEFGHIJKLMNOPQRSTUVWXYZ&$.,-:;"'!?()[]·
abcdefghijklmnopqrstuvwxyz 1234567890
AKMNRW ¼ ½ ¾ ⅓ ⅔ %

RAILROAD GOTHIC, ATF 24-pt. (part reduced)

ABCDEFGHIJKLMNOPQRSTUVWXYZ1234567890$&?!.,:

RALEIGH CURSIVE, ATF 24-pt.

ABCDEFGHIJKLMNOPQRRSTUVWXYZ

abcdefghijklmnopqrstuvwxyz 1234567890$.,-:;"!? arerirasesisus&

RALEIGH INITIALS, ATF (36-pt. at 67%)

A B C D E F G H I J K L M N O

P Q R S T U V W X Y Z

RALEIGH GOTHIC CONDENSED, ATF (72-pt. at 50%)

ABCDEFGHIJKLMNOPQRSTUVWXYZ$1234567890&..:;-'?!AKMNS

RECORD GOTHIC, Ludlow 24-pt.

ABCDEFGHIJKLMNOPQRSTUVWXYZ 1 $1234567890

abcdefghijklmnopqrstuvwxyz g%·[](),.-;':'!?—&¼⅓½⅔

RECORD GOTHIC CONDENSED, Ludlow 24-pt.

ABCDEFGHIJKLMNOPQRSTUVWXYZ 1 $1234567890

abcdefghijklmnopqrstuvwxyz g %·[](),.-;':'!?—&¼⅓½⅔¾

RECORD GOTHIC CONDENSED ITALIC, Ludlow 24-pt.

ABCDEFGHIJKLMNOPQRSTUVWXYZ&

abcdefghijklmnopqrstuvwxyz 1234567890 % ¼ ⅓ ½ ⅔ ¾

RECORD GOTHIC EXTRA CONDENSED, Ludlow 24-pt.

ABCDEFGHIJKLMNOPQRSTUVWXYZ& abcdefghijklmnopqrstuvwxyz 1234567890 . : , ; - ' ' ! ? ( ) [ ] — ·

% ¼ ⅓ ½ ⅔ ¾

RECORD GOTHIC OFFSET, Ludlow 8-pt.

ABCDEFGHIJKLMNOPQRSTUVWXYZ& abcdefghijklmnopqrstuvwxyz 1234567890

RAILROAD GOTHIC is a plain, traditional form of heavy, condensed gothic, first shown by ATF early in the century, although it has the appearance of a nineteenth-century face, as some characters seem disproportionate to the others. There is no lowercase. It has long been popular for newspaper headlines, especially in the very large sizes, some of which continue to be shown in recent ATF lists. Ludlow makes the same design in some large sizes as *Gothic Bold Condensed Title*. Compare *Headline Gothic* (ATF).

Railroad Gothic, ATF 364 (6s-120pt); Gothic Bold Condensed Title, Ludlow 6-BCT (60-96pt)

RALEIGH CURSIVE is a spirited design by Willard T. Sniffin, drawn in 1929 for ATF but introduced in 1930. It has a pen-drawn quality, with precise lowercase letters which don't quite connect, and flourished capitals. There are two versions of cap *R* and *T,* and several lowercase ligatures, as shown. Sizes over 36-point were discontinued in the late 1940s.

Raleigh Initials were designed by the same artist at about the same time. They closely follow the style of *Raleigh Cursive*, but are more freely drawn. For each size, *J* and *Q* are cast on the next larger body size. Compare *Park Avenue, Piranesi Bold Italic.*

Raleigh Cursive, ATF 531 (10-72pt)
Raleigh Initials, ATF (36-96pt)

RALEIGH GOTHIC [CONDENSED] was designed by Morris F. Benton for ATF in 1932. It is a prim, narrow, medium weight gothic face, with normally round characters being squared except for short arcs on the outside of corners. The alternate characters *AKMNS* give an even greater vertical appearance than usual. At first, this face was promoted with *Raleigh Cursive* as a stylish companion face, although there is no apparent relationship other than the name. Compare *Phenix, Alternate Gothic, Agency Gothic.*

Raleigh Gothic Condensed, ATF 564 (72-144pt)

RANSOM SHADED INITIALS—see *Clearcut Shaded Caps.*
RATDOLT—see *Goudy Lanston.*
RATIO-LATEIN—see *Parma.*

Record Gothic, Ludlow 6-R (6-48pt); News Gothic (q.v.)
Record Gothic Condensed, Ludlow 6-RC (6-72pt); News Gothic Condensed (q.v.)
Record Gothic Extra Condensed, Ludlow 6-REC (10-48pt); News Gothic Extra Condensed (q.v.)
Record Gothic Offset, Ludlow 6-ROF (8pt)
Record Gothic Condensed Italic, Ludlow 6-RCI (8-48pt)
Record Gothic Extended, Ludlow 6-RE (6-48pt)
Record Gothic Extended Italic, Ludlow 6-REI (12-48pt)
Record Gothic Bold, Ludlow 6-RB (6-72pt)

RECORD GOTHIC was made on Ludlow before 1930, but originally only in small sizes and in regular weight and width. As such it was a copy of *News Gothic,* useful for small headings on ruled record sheets, hence probably the name. But faces such as *News Gothic* were by then being pushed aside by the new wave of sans serifs, inspired by *Futura,* and nothing was added to this

(Record Gothic continues)

RECORD GOTHIC EXTENDED, Ludlow 24-pt.

ABCDEFGHIJKLMNOPQRSTUVWXYZ&
abcdefghijklmnopqrstuvwxyz 12345678

RECORD GOTHIC EXTENDED ITALIC, Ludlow 24-pt.

ABCDEFGHIJKLMNOPQRSTUVWXYZ&
abcdefghijklmnopqrstuvwxyz 1234567

RECORD GOTHIC BOLD, Ludlow 24-pt.

ABCDEFGHIJKLMNOPQRSTUVWXYZ$1234567890
abcdefghijklmnopqrstuvwxyz (.,-)"&"[:;!?]¼½⅓⅔¾%·1g

RECORD GOTHIC BOLD ITALIC, Ludlow 24-pt.

ABCDEFGHIJKLMNOPQRSTUVWXYZ$1234567890
abcdefghijklmnopqrstuvwxyz(.,-)'&'[:;!?]¼½⅓⅔¾%·1g

RECORD GOTHIC BOLD CONDENSED, Ludlow 24-pt.

ABCDEFGHIJKLMNOPQRSTUVWXYZ&
abcdefghijklmnopqrstuvwyxz .:.,;-"()[]!?—· $1234567890

RECORD GOTHIC BOLD EXTENDED, Ludlow 24-pt. (Herb Harnish)

ABCDEFGHIJKLMNOPQRSTUVWXYZ&
abcdefghijklmnopqrstuvwxyz .,-:;"!?()[]·—
$1234567890 ¼½¾⅓⅔ QRg17

RECORD GOTHIC BOLD EXTENDED REVERSE, Ludlow 18-pt.

ABCDEFGHIJKLMNOPQRSTUVWXYZ& **1234567890**

RECORD GOTHIC BOLD EXTENDED ITALIC, Ludlow 24-pt.

ABCDEFGHIJKLMNOPQRSTUVWXYZ&
abcdefghijklmnopqrstuvwxyz 12345

RECORD GOTHIC THINLINE CONDENSED, Ludlow 24-pt.

ABCDEFGHIJKLMNOPQRSTUVWXYZ&
abcdefghijklmnopqrstuvwxyz 1234567890

RECORD GOTHIC HEAVY CONDENSED, Ludlow 24-pt.

ABCDEFGHIJKLMNOPQRSTUVWXYZ& Rg17
abcdefghijklmnopqrstuvwxyz $1234567890 .:.,;-"()[]!?—·

RECORD GOTHIC LIGHT MEDIUM-EXTENDED, Ludlow 24- & 18-pt.

ABCDEFGHIJKLMNOPQRSTUVWXYZ& .:.,;-"!?()[]—·
abcdefghijklmnopqrstuvwxyz 1234567890$ RQ17g

series until the early 1950s, when typographers rediscovered the traditional American gothics. Then Ludlow added larger sizes of *Record Gothic*, and cut *Record Gothic Condensed,* followed by *Record Gothic Extra Condensed;* these were likewise copied from their News Gothic prototypes.

In 1956, Robert H. Middleton, director of Ludlow's department of typeface design, began a series of original additions to this family, which eventually included twenty members. First came *Record Gothic Condensed Italic* and *Record Gothic Bold;* then *Bold Extended* and other variations as shown. *Record Gothic Medium-Extended* was an innovation; the name indicates semi-wide. It was that, and it retained general family characteristics, but it also had much of the appearance of the new grotesques such as *Helvetica* which were beginning to come over from Europe. Eventually there were four weights of *Medium-Extended* plus an italic, forming a family within a family, and making *Record Gothic* probably the only family available in five widths.

Record Gothic Thinline Condensed was another innovation, on the order of a condensed version of *Lightline Gothic. Record Gothic Bold Condensed* and *Heavy Condensed,* done in 1969, show the influence of European grotesques. Most unusual is *Record Gothic Bold Extended Reverse,* which features white letters on a black band, complete with several optional endings for the band. And *Record Gothic Offset,* a reverse-reading face for titling photographs and marking electronic parts. (See Offset Faces.)

All Record Gothic italics are cut for Ludlow's 17-degree italic matrices; most serifless italics slope about 8 to 12 degrees. While not the greatest angle, 17 degrees is rather extreme, and results in some awkward character shapes.

Nearly all versions of *Record Gothic* have as alternate characters a single-bowl lowercase *g* and a figure *1* without bottom serifs. Most also have fractions and percent mark available; a few have other alternate characters. Compare *News Gothic* and *Trade Gothic* families, *Alternate Gothic, Helvetica.*

Record Gothic Bold Italic, Ludlow 6-RBI (8-72pt)
Record Gothic Bold Condensed, Ludlow 6-RBC (12-72pt)
Record Gothic Bold Extended, Ludlow 6-RBE (6-72pt)
Record Gothic Bold Extended Reverse, Ludlow 6-RBEV (18pt)
Record Gothic Bold Extended Italic, Ludlow 6-RBEI (8-72pt)
Record Gothic Thinline Condensed, Ludlow 6-RTC (14-72pt)
Record Gothic Heavy Condensed, Ludlow 6-RHC (14-48pt)
Record Gothic Light Medium-Extended, Ludlow 6-RLME (6-36pt)
Record Gothic Medium-Extended, Ludlow 6-RME (6-72pt)
Record Gothic Medium-Extended Italic, Ludlow 6-RMEI (6-36pt)
Record Gothic Bold Medium-Extended, Ludlow 6-RBME (6-72pt)
Record Gothic Heavy Medium-Extended, Ludlow 6-RHME (6-72pt)

RECORD GOTHIC MEDIUM-EXTENDED, Ludlow 24-pt.

ABCDEFGHIJKLMNOPQRSTUVWXYZ&
abcdefghijklmnopqrstuvwxyz .:,;-''!?()[] — ·
$1234567890 % ¼ ⅓ ½ ⅔ ¾

RECORD GOTHIC MEDIUM-EXTENDED ITALIC, Ludlow 24-pt.

ABCDEFGHIJKLMNOPQRSTUVWXYZ&
abcdefghijklmnopqrstuvwxyz 1234567890

RECORD GOTHIC BOLD MEDIUM-EXTENDED, Ludlow 24-pt.

ABCDEFGHIJKLMNOPQRSTUVWXYZ&
abcdefghijklmnopqrstuvwxyz 1234567890

RECORD GOTHIC HEAVY MEDIUM-EXTENDED, Ludlow 24-pt. (Herb Harnish)

ABCDEFGHIJKLMNOPQRSTUVWXYZ&
abcdefghijklmnopqrstuvwxyz .,-:;"!?()[]·—
$1234567890 QRg1

ABCDEFGHIJKLMNOPQRRSTUVW XYZ&:1234567890;··

ABCDEFGHIJKLMNOPQRSTUVWXYZ *ABCDEFGHIJKLMNOPQRSTUVWXYZ* **ABCDEFGHIJKLMNOPQRSTUVW**

ABCDEFGHIJKLMNOPQRSTUVWXYZ *abcdefghijklmnopqrstuvwxyz* *123456789* **abcdefghijklmnopqrstuvwxyz** **1234**

abcdefghijklmnopqrstuvwxyz 123456789 [ ]%†§‡¶*()$,.-;‘:’!?&⅛¼⅜½⅝¾⅞ [ ]%†§‡¶*()$,.-;‘:’!?&⅛¼⅜½⅝

[ ]%†§‡¶*()$,.-;‘:’!?&⅛¼⅜½⅝¾⅞

THE TYPECASTING PROPOSITION Is an Important Development of the Monotype, and is but One of its Many Strong and Desirable Features $1234567890

ABCDEFGHIJKLMNOPQRSTUVWXYZ

abcdefghijklmnopqrstuvwxyz,.:;-""'!?&()%$1234567890¢,—

ABCDEFGHIJ-1234567   ABCDEFGHIJKLMNOPQR.-1234567890

The California Type Case

Often called the *California Job Case,* this is one of many type case arrangements, but probably the one most commonly used.

Authorities differ as to the origin of the name. Some say the design was developed *in* California, others say it was created to simplify the equipment of the printer traveling overland *to* California during the mid-nineteenth century Gold Rush.

The left two-thirds of the California case is the same layout as the lower case of an earlier era, when type for setting extensive text matter was kept in pairs of cases. The right third of the California case is equivalent to half of the old upper case, which also housed small caps and additional miscellaneous characters.

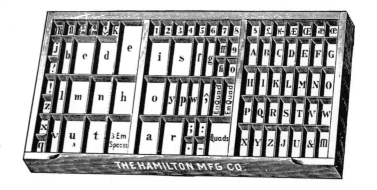

RECORD TITLE was designed in 1927 by Frederic W. Goudy as a private type for *The Architectural Record* magazine, commissioned by Charles De-Vinne, art director of the magazine and grandson of Theodore L. DeVinne. Goudy based his work on a treatise on classic letter design printed at Parma by Damianus Moyllus in 1480, but soon found that the geometrical proportions advocated by that work had to be modified considerably for good appearance as type. But Goudy considered this one of the most satisfactory commissions of his career. The magazine used the type for several years, until the popularity of sans serifs displaced such classic roman letters.

Record Title, Goudy (12-24pt) private

RECUT CASLON, RECUT DeVINNE, etc.—see under *Caslon, DeVinne,* etc.

REED TEXT—see *Priory Text.*

REGAL was created for the Chicago *Tribune,* designed by Herman R. Freund and introduced by Intertype in 1935, with *Regal Bold* following in 1937. This is primarily a newspaper face, rather wide, with large x-height and short ascenders and descenders, similar to *Ideal* but a little lighter. Also compare *Paragon.*

Regal and Italic and Bold, Inter (5-14pt)

REGAL ITALIC (other)—see *Victoria Italic.*

REGINA, REINER SCRIPT—see Imports in Appendix.

RELIEVO—see Antiques in Appendix.

REMSON BOLD—see *Lorimer, Berlin Antique.*

RENNER. Theodore L. DeVinne says of this face: "Renner is a fair copy, but not a servile imitation, of the style of type devised by Franz Renner of Venice, and first used by him in his edition of the 'Quadragesimale' of 1472. It was made in 1899 (by the Bruce Typefoundry division of ATF) for the service of the DeVinne Press, to exemplify the belief of the writer that the legibility of print does not depend so much upon an increase of blackness or thickness of its stems as on the entire and instant visibility of every line in every character." In spite of DeVinne's enthusiasm for it, *Renner* is a quaint, now dated face. But it is notable for having an *Underscore* version for emphasis, although an italic was made by Bruce. The underscore consists of a series of short strokes, one to four under each character, cutting through descenders. Because of the varying width of characters, strokes vary somewhat in length. It was copied by Monotype, which extended its life, but has long been obsolete now.

Renner, ATF; Mono 173 (6-12pt)
Renner Underscore, ATF; Mono 174 (10,14pt)

REPRO SCRIPT was designed for ATF in 1953 by Jerry Mullen. It is a continuous script except for a few letter combinations, nearly monotone in weight, and narrow. It is informal, but not as much so as *Brody,* which is another of the foundry's attempts to replace its delicate old traditional scripts with contemporary faces. Steve Watts says it was designed to work with *News Gothic Condensed* and other plain sans serifs, but the connection is not apparent. Compare *Brody, Brush, Kaufmann Script.*

Repro Script, ATF 705 (18-60pt)

REVERSE FACES. Service Engravers in New York City made matrices for several faces for casting on the Ludlow machine, with the unusual feature of white letters on a solid background. These include *Reverse Extended,* which was similar to *Gothic No. 545,* and *Reverse Condensed,* which differed in various sizes but was similar to nineteenth-century gothics. The 36- and 48-point sizes were considerably heavier than smaller sizes. Fonts include the usual capitals, figures and punctuation marks; a number of decorative end pieces were available separately. Also see *Record Gothic Bold Extended Reverse; Adstyle Borders.*

Reverse Extended, Service (12-24pt)
Reverse Condensed, Service (12-48pt)

ABCDEFGHIJKLMNOPQRSTUVWXYZ *ABCDEFGHIJKLMNOPQRSTUVWXYZ* **ABCDEFGHIJKLMNOPQRSTUVW**

ABCDEFGHIJKLMNOPQRSTUVWXYZ *abcdefghijklmnopqrstuvwxyz* *123456789* **abcdefghijklmnopqrstuvwxyz** **1234**

abcdefghijklmnopqrstuvwxyz 123456789 *[ ]%†§‡¶*( )$,.-;':'!?&⅛¼⅜½⅝¾⅞* **[ ]%†§‡¶*( )$,.-;':'!?&⅛¼⅜½⅝**

[ ]%†§‡¶*( )$,.-;':'!?&⅛¼⅜½⅝¾⅞

RIVOLI, ATF 24-pt.

ABCDEFGHIJKLMNOPQRSTUVWXYZ

abcdefghijklmnopqrstuvwxyz $1234567890 & .,:;="!?

RIVOLI ITALIC, ATF (30-pt. at 80%)

ABCDEFGHIJKLMNOPQRSTUVWXYZ&ABEGH

abcdefghijklmnopqrstuvwxyzct(.,=:;"!?)$£1234567890 JKLMR

ROBIN, Nelson private (Stan Nelson)

ABCDEFGHIJKLMNOPQRSTTVW YZ

abcdefgghijklmnnopqrstuvwxyz& .,';?-~ s-éeflf✝℀

ROCKWELL ANTIQUE, Mono 24-pt.

ABCDEFGHIJKLMNOPQRSTUVWXYZ& !?

abcdefghijklmnopqrstuvwxyz$1234567890.,-:;'

AAJKafkrty

ROGERS, Inland 24-pt. (Dan X. Solo)

ABBCDDEFGHIJKLMNOPPQRRSS

TUVWXYZ 1234567890

aabcdefghijklmmnnopqrstuuvwxyz

REX is a newspaper face, cut by Intertype about 1938. It has smaller x-height and longer ascenders than most such faces, but otherwise is typical. Compare *Textype.*

Rex and Italic and Bold, Inter (4-14, 6-10, 5-14pt)

RHAPSODIE—see Imports in Appendix.
RHUMBA—see *Gill Sans Shadow* under Imports in Appendix.
RICCARDO—see Imports in Appendix.
RICHELIEU—see *Cushing Oldstyle.*
RIMMED LITHO—see *Litho Roman* series.

RIVOLI and *Rivoli Italic* were designed for ATF by Willard T. Sniffin about 1928. They are delicate faces with a nervous, pen-drawn quality, and are very similar to *Eve* and *Eve Italic,* designed by Rudolf Koch in Germany a few years earlier. However, *Rivoli* has the extra hairline on all sizes of caps in both roman and italic, whereas *Eve* has this line only on italic caps in sizes from 14-point up. Compare *Paramount,* which is essentially a bold version of *Rivoli.*

Rivoli, ATF 515 (10-48pt); Inter (10-18pt); (Univ 10-48pt)
Rivoli Italic, ATF 526 (10-48pt); (Univ 10-48pt)

ROBIN was designed and privately cast by R. Stanley Nelson, private press operator in Maryland. The designer says, "Like blackletter fonts this is really a minuscule with a set of uppercase forms attached. I plan to cut lombardic caps as well, and other lowercase letters in the future. . . . The rustic caps are not complete but there are a lot of problems with them. . . . The face is experimental and not in its final form."

Robin, Nelson, Private (24pt)

ROCKWELL ANTIQUE was a reissue of *Litho Antique,* cut by William Schraubstädter for Inland Type Foundry and introduced in January 1910, when it was advertised as the "newest typeface; one of our best; closely imitating steelplate and lithography." In the late 1920s similar faces became popular in Europe, and some were imported into the United States. Morris Benton of ATF added several characters to the old Inland face, matrices of which were then in ATF's vaults, and it was reissued in 1931 as *Rockwell Antique.* But Benton saw that something more was needed, and redrew it as *Stymie Bold* (q.v.) in the same year. The alternate characters which were added to *Rockwell* are the same ones now shown with *Stymie Bold.*

Rockwell Antique or Litho Antique, ATF 312 (6-60pt); Rockwell Antique or Rockwell, Mono 189 (6-72H4)

Monotype copied *Rockwell* but erroneously called it *Stymie Bold* in some literature, and there has been confusion between the two faces ever since; the latter name is often applied to fonts of *Rockwell* cast on Monotype machines by secondary suppliers. Indicative of this confusion, *Stymie Bold Italic* on Mono is series 1891, corresponding to *Rockwell* series 189, while *Stymie Bold* is 790.

English Monotype has several weights of *Rockwell,* a square serif family which differs from this face and should not be confused with it; see Imports in Appendix.

Antique Shaded (q.v.) is sometimes called *Rockwell Antique Shaded.*

ROGERS was advertised by Inland Typefoundry in 1902 as "one of our most recent novelties." It was designed by A. V. Haight. Compare *Bewick, Vanden Houten.*

Rogers, Inland (6-72pt)

ROGERS ROMAN—see *Engravers Litho Bold.*
ROMAN COMPRESSED—see Imports in Appendix.
ROMANA—see *Berlin Antique.*
ROMANTIC—see *Tokio.*
ROMANTIQUES—see Antiques in Appendix; also *Tuscans* in the same section.

ROMANY, ATF 24-pt.

ABCDEFGHIJKLMNOPQRSTUVWXYZ& Q

abcdeofghijklmnopqrstuvwxyz 1234567890 $?!.,:;'-`

RONALDSON & ITALIC, Mono 12-pt.

ABCDEFGHIJKLMNOPQRSTUVWXYZ&ÆŒ *ABCDEFGHIJKLMNOPQRSTUVWXYZ&ÆŒ*

abcdefghijklmnopqrstuvwxyzæœ fiflffffiffl *abcdefghijklmnopqrstuvwxyzæœ fiflffffiffl*

$1234567890£ .,-":;!? $1234567890 *$1234567890 :;!? $1234567890*

ABCDEFGHIJKLMNOPQRSTUVWXYZ&ÆŒ

ROSETTI, ATF (30-pt. at 80%) (Duane Scott)

AABBCDDECEFFGHIJKLMCMNCNOPPQRRRSTTUVWCV

aabcdefghijklmnopqrstuvwxyz&ctst.,:;'-?1234567890 XYYZ$

ROUNDHAND, 24-pt.

ABCDEFGHIJKLMNOPQRSTUVWXYZ&

abcdefghijklmnopqrstuvwxyz!? $1234567890

ROYAL SCRIPT, 24-pt. #1 & #2

ABCDEFGHIJKLMNOPQRSTUVWXYZ&

abcdefghijklmnopqrstuvwxyz $1234567890 .,=:;'!? abcdefghijklmnopqrstuvwxyz

---

Majuscules and Minuscules

Majuscules are called *caps* or *capitals,* or sometimes *upper case.* Minuscules are called *lower case,* or sometimes *small letters,* although that latter term is vague.

The *upper-* and *lower-case* names come from the pairs of type cases used in the days when all type was set by hand. Literally the lower case, nearer the compositor, held the minuscules, figures, and punctuation marks, while the upper case had capitals, along with small capitals and miscellany.

As machine typesetting replaced hand composition, these pairs of cases were generally replaced with single cases of various designs, mostly the California case, which accommodated majuscules and minuscules in one layout.

* * *

The "Colonial printer" here is representative of hundreds of "stock cuts" once available from typefounders. Most were cast in type molds, the same as regular type, although large sizes were electrotyped.

ROMANY is a simple monotone script, designed by Alfred R. Bosco for ATF about 1934. It is vertical, rather wide, and characters don't quite connect. There is an alternate *e* as shown, also an alternate *A* which is similar to the lowercase form. The *F* has no crossbar and could be taken for a *T* except by context. Compare *Keynote, Brody, Repro Script.*

Romany, ATF 585 (12-72pt)

RONALDSON OLD STYLE was designed and cut by MS&J in 1884, and subsequently copied by various other foundries. It was notable for the exaggerated serifs on a number of letters, and the name is now associated with these peculiarities, which were also applied to various other faces in the nineteenth century. Monotype cut a reasonably good copy of the foundry face, although modified to fit mechanical requirements, while Linotype cut a set of conversion characters which could be substituted for the regular characters of *Old Style No. 7.* A similar set of conversion characters was cut for Linotype and Intertype *Old Style No. 1* (q.v.), which is a somewhat lighter face. Keystone called its version *Keystone Old Style.* Other versions of Ronaldson did not last long into the twentieth century.

Ronaldson No. 2, ATF (6-42pt); Ronaldson No. 551 and Italic, ATF 298 and 430 (6-12pt); Ronaldson Old Style and Italic, Mono 16EFG (6-12pt); Ronaldson and Italic, Lino = Inter (6-14pt, Old Style No. 1); Ronaldson No. 7 and Italic, Lino (8-11pt, Old Style No. 7); Keystone Old Style, Keystone (6-48pt)

RONDO—see Imports in Appendix.

ROSETTI is a thick-and-thin, serifless face, drawn by Willard T. Sniffin for ATF in 1931. Many of the capitals are informal, and some have an extra swash version. In lowercase letters such as *h* and *m,* the ascending stroke leaves the stem at a low point. Compare *Parisian, Optima, Radiant, Czarin, Lydian.*

Rosetti, ATF 539 (6-72pt)

ROUND SHADE—see *Old Bowery.*

ROUNDHAND was designed for ATF about 1900, and has been ascribed to Herman Ihlenburg. It has the appearance of handwriting with a broad pen, but letters are not quite connected.

Roundhand, ATF 370, (10-60pt)

ROYAL—see *Corona.*
ROYAL GOTHIC—see *London Gothic, Contour No. 1.*

ROYAL SCRIPT originated with the Central Type Foundry branch of ATF in St. Louis in 1893. It is much like the later *Typo Script,* but wider. In spite of that similarity, it appeared in ATF specimen books as late as 1968. In the 24- and 30-point sizes there are normal and small versions of lowercase, caps being the same. Early specimens designated these large and small sizes as No. 1 and No. 2 respectively, later specimens as No. 551 and No. 552. Hansen's *Newton Script* is the same design.

Royal Script, ATF 304 (10-48pt); (Univ 18-24pt); Newton Script, Hansen (12-30pt)

ABCDEFGHIJKLMNOPQRSTUVWXYZ&
abcdefghijklmnopqrstuvwxyz$1234567890£
fifl@ÆŒæœctMRahmntu Thefshfiflst

ABCDEFGHIJKLMNOPQRSTUVWXYZ&$1234567890£@ÆŒ
abcdefghijklmnopqrstuvwxyzfifl.,-:;'!?æœctMRahmntu Thefshfiflst

ABCDEFGHIJKLMNOPQRSTUVWXYZ&.,-:;'!?
abcdefghijklmnopqrstuvwxyzfifl$1234567890

Marks & Herd Honorable Race $51.23
New Design Nome Golf Social Romance

SOUVENIR OF RACES Rockaway 38 Luna
ABCDEFGHIJKLMNOPQRSTUVWXYZ&
aabcdeeffghijklmnopqrsstuvwxyz $1234567890 .,-:;'!?   a e f s t

TALISMAN ITALIC GRAND SCENERY
Series Cannot be 58 Overlooked River Canyon
w y J ω of and the

ROYCROFT was one of the most popular of a number of rugged faces used around the turn of the century, when printing with an antique appearance was in vogue. It was inspired by lettering used by the *Saturday Evening Post,* then a popular weekly magazine, and has been credited to Lewis Buddy, a former *Post* artist and letterer, but ATF says it was designed "partly" by Morris Benton, about 1898. Gerry Powell, director of typographic design for ATF in the 1940s, says, "Roycroft was first known as *Buddy;* changed when it was adopted by Elbert Hubbard for the Roycroft Press." Henry L. Bullen, ATF librarian and historian, says, "The first font of type to be made from matrices directly engraved on the Benton machine was 24-point *Roycroft,* October 4, 1900." While the machine was originally designed in 1884 to cut punches rather than matrices, it is doubtful that no fonts of mats were cut before 1900. *Roycroft* is also said to be the first face for which the large size of 120-point was engraved in type metal, with matrices made by electrotyping.

Many faces of the day had a number of alternate characters. For this face, ATF gave specific instructions for their intended use: "*M* with the short vertex, in words the letters of which are open; *R* with the long tail, as a final letter in all-cap words; the wide *h, m,* and *n,* as a final letter only; *t* with the swash tail, as a final letter but not too frequently; *u* with the descending stroke, in words having no descending letters; *ct* ligature, wherever possible; the long *s* and its combinations, in antique work."

Roycroft Open was cut in 1902, probably from the same patterns as the parent face. *Roycroft Tinted* is a very unusual face, in which the face is engraved with the equivalent of a halftone screen of about 25 percent tone value, with a black shadow on the right side; this face was cut by the Dickinson Type Foundry branch of ATF in Boston, and includes the same special characters as *Roycroft*. Compare *Post Oldstyle*.

Roycroft, ATF 371 (8-120pt)
Roycroft Open, ATF 372 (12-72pt)
Roycroft Tinted, ATF 373 (12-60pt)

ROYS GOTHIC—see *Layout Gothic.*
RUGGED BLACK—see *Cooper Black.*

RUGGED BOLD was issued by ATF in 1902, and later advertised as a "new and strong letter for attractive job work and advertising display." But it is an extreme example of the generally rugged faces which were popular then, having not only irregular edges on the letters, but characters of uneven size and slope, as well as bizarre design. Caps were the usual size for faces on standard alignment, but lowercase *g* had a very short descender and *y* had no descender at all below the base line.

Rugged Bold, ATF 374 (6-72pt)

RUGGED BOLD (not the one mentioned above) was part of a series offered by BB&S about 1911, but the series was actually an assembly of faces originally known by a variety of other names, and some of them were later renamed again. *Rugged Lightface* was originally *Carlton* and later became *Adcraft Lightface* (q.v.). *Rugged Medium* had been *Alfred Medium* and became *Adcraft Medium;* while *Rugged Bold* and *Italic* were formerly *Talisman* and *Italic,* patented by Sidney Gaunt in 1903 and 1904 respectively.

Rugged Black and *Black Condensed* and *Black Italic* were formerly *Plymouth* and *Condensed* and *Italic* and continued to be better known by those names, partly because some were copied by Monotype. *Rugged Extra Black* was formerly *Plymouth Bold* and later became *Adcraft Black.* See *Adcraft, Plymouth.*

Rugged Lightface or Adcraft Lightface, BB&S-ATF 1501 (8-48pt)
Rugged Medium or Adcraft Medium, BB&S-ATF 1502 (6-72pt)
Rugged Bold or Talisman, BB&S (6-72pt)
Rugged Bold Italic or Talisman Italic, BB&S (6-72pt)
Rugged Black or Plymouth, BB&S (6-120pt)
Rugged Black Italic or Plymouth Italic, BB&S (6-72pt)
Rugged Black Condensed or Plymouth Condensed, BB&S (6-72pt)
Rugged Extra Black or Plymouth Bold or Adcraft Black, BB&S-ATF 1500 (6-72pt)

DISCOURAGE· THOREY MOTOR COMPANY PROPOSE
Unique Actions Great Selling Force–Printing ThirstyChild

ΛBCDEFGHIJKLMNOPQRSTUVWXYZ,.-''

ABCDEFGHIJKLMNOPQRSTUVWXYZ& 1234567890
abcdefghijklmnopqrstuvwxyz $\frac{1}{8}\frac{1}{4}\frac{3}{8}\frac{1}{2}\frac{5}{8}\frac{3}{4}\frac{7}{8}$ **($,.:;'-'?!-.)**

ABCDEFGHIJKLMNOPQRSTUVWXYZ&.,';:!?·1234567890
abcdefghijklmnopqrstuvwxyz fi ff ffi fl ffl & ABCDEFGHIJKLMNOPQRSTUVWXYZ&

ABCDEFGHIJKLMNOPQRSTUVWXYZ&.,';:!?·
abcdefghijklmnopqrstuvwxyz ABCDEGPRT fiffffiflffl ft &

ABCDEFGHIJKLMNOPQRSTUVWXYZ&.,'·

ABCDEFGHIJKLMNOPQRSTUVWXYZ&
abcdefghijklmnopqrstuvwxyz$1234567890.,-:;'!?

ABCDEFGHIJKLMNOPQRSTUVWXYZ& R
abcdefghijklmnopqrstuvwxyz $1234567890
.:,;-''!?()[]—· ½ ⅓ ⅔ ¼ ¾ %

RUGGED ROMAN was designed for ATF by Morris F. Benton in 1909-11. It was patented in 1915, but the earliest showing seems to have appeared in 1917. It is a rugged face, as the name says, of the sort that was popular early in the century, but appears to have no relation to other faces having the name "Rugged." It somewhat resembles *Roycroft,* but is lighter. But to add to the uncertainty, fonts contained a number of ligatures of the kind which were more common in the early 1900s, in addition to the usual f-ligatures.

Rugged Roman, ATF 375 (6-72pt)

RUSTIC—see Antiques in Appendix.
RUSTIC ORNAMENTED SHADED—see *Bruce Mikita* under Antiques in Appendix.

RUSTICA was designed, cut in 1965, and privately cast by Paul Hayden Duensing, operator of his own private press and typefoundry. It is patterned on the work of scribes of the third and fourth centuries. The crossbar of the cap *A* is intentionally omitted for authenticity.

Rustica, Duensing (12-24pt)

RYERSON CONDENSED was designed by C. H. Griffith in 1940 for Linotype, as a modernization of *Globe Gothic Condensed* (q.v.).

Ryerson Condensed, Lino (18-36pt)

SAINT JOHN—see *Bradley.*

SAKS GOUDY and *Italic* were designed and cut by Frederic W. Goudy in 1934 as private types for the Saks Fifth Avenue department store in New York. Although having the classic proportions of most of this designer's romans and italics, these faces achieve distinction through many small details, such as the tapered strokes of *K, R, V, W,* etc. As the small caps were quite small in relation to the regular caps, Goudy used their patterns to cut caps of full height, thus producing a bold face. No record has been found of the sizes produced.

Saks Goudy, Goudy, private
Saks Goudy Italic, Goudy, private
Saks Goudy Bold, Goudy, private

SALEM was introduced by Keystone Type Foundry in 1901, the initial ad calling it "a witchey typeface." Later specimens called it "one of our most useful and prominent typefaces . . . may be used to great advantage in any and all the finest productions of art display work." To later tastes it is quaint and bizarre. The Monotype copy shown in the specimen here appears to be quite faithful to the original, more so than many early copies of foundry faces.

Salem, Keystone (6-72pt); Mono 220 (10-36pt)

SALTO, SALTINO—see Imports in Appendix.

SAMSON is a very bold, sturdy face designed by R. Hunter Middleton in 1940 for Ludlow. It is derived from lettering done with a broad pen, and retains much of that feeling. The name was chosen to denote power and strength. It has been popular for newspaper advertising in particular. Compare *Lydian, Valiant.*

Samson, Ludlow 47-H (24-72pt)

SAMSON UNCIAL—see *Hammer Samson Uncial.*

SANS SERIF LIGHT, Mono 24-pt., with 18-H91, 18-H92, 24-H93 Alternates

ABCDEFGHIJKLMNOPQRSTUVWXYZ

abcdefghijklmnopqrstuvwxyzfffifl $1234567890&«».,-:;'!?()

AJWYaegitu   AEFKMNRSWeks   ABCDEFGHIJKLMNOPQRSTU

SANS SERIF LIGHT ITALIC, Mono 24-pt., with 18-H91 Alternates

ABCDEFGHIJKLMNOPQRSTUVWXYZ&

abcdefghijklmnopqrstuvwxyz $1234567890 .,-:;'!?()

ACGWabegjtu

SANS SERIF LIGHT CONDENSED, Mono (30-pt. at 80%)

ABCDEFGHIJKLMNOPQRSTUVWXYZ&

abcdefghijklmnopqrstuvwxyz $1234567890

SANS SERIF MEDIUM, Mono 24-pt., with 18-H91, 24-H92 Alternates

ABCDEFGHIJKLMNOPQRSTUVWXYZ&

abcdefghijklmnopqrstuvwxyz fffifl $1234567890 .,-:;'!?() «»

AJWYaegitu   AEFKMNRSW eks

SANS SERIF MEDIUM CONDENSED, Mono 24-pt.

ABCDEFGHIJKLMNOPQRSTUVWXYZ&

abcdefghijklmnopqrstuvwxyz $1234567890 .,-:;'!?() '

SANS SERIF BOLD, Mono 24-pt., with 24-H91, 18-H92, 18-H9 Alternates

ABCDEFGHIJKLMNOPQRSTUVWXYZ

abcdefghijklmnopqrstuvwxyz fffi 1234567890(&$.-':;!?)«»◆¢¶|¢

AJWY'aegtu   AEFKMNRSWeks   ACEFGHYaefgijrstu

SANS SERIF BOLD ITALIC, Mono 24-pt., with 18-H91 Alternates

ABCDEFGHIJKLMNOPQRSTUVWXYZ

abcdefghijklmnopqrstuvwxyz 1234567890(&$.,-':;!?)«»

ACGWabegjtu

SANS SERIF is a general term for serifless types, particularly the newly proportioned faces of that sort which originated in Germany in the 1920s, as opposed to the older, traditional gothics. It is also the unimaginative name for Monotype's extensive series which began as a copy of one of the most popular of the German faces, Rudolf Koch's *Kabel,* sometimes called *Cable,* named in celebration of the opening of the trans-Atlantic telephone cable connecting America and Europe. Koch's face appeared about 1927, with Monotype copying the *Light* and *Bold* in 1930. These two weights and their italics are virtually exact copies of the originals. Over the next three years Sol Hess designed a number of variations for Monotype, which differ more or less from their German counterparts, especially in the heavy weights. *Light Condensed, Medium, Medium Condensed, Extrabold* and *Italic* and *Condensed,* and *Lined* filled out the family.

From this point Monotype went on to explore a new dimension in type design with the introduction of a novel idea in alternate characters. By the substitution of a dozen characters, more or less, for those in the standard font, the Monotype user could have "three type faces from one," as the advertising said. With one set of alternates, available for most members of the family and designated H91 (suffixed to the series number), *Sans Serif* could be transformed into an approximation of *Futura;* another set (H92) contained the round capitals then popular. A set for *Sans Serif Bold* suggested *Bernhard Gothic Medium* (H9), while a somewhat similar but maverick set was made for *Light* (H93). The various condensed faces include *aegjtu* alternates, comparable to H91, in the regular matrix fonts, but they are missing from the specimens here. It was an unusual and useful idea, but some users of Monotype matrices have been careless about mixing parts of sets with regular characters, or of inconsistent use of alternates in various sizes of a series.

In general, the basic *Kabel* is less mechanical than *Futura,* and has longer ascenders with smaller x-height. Introduced into the United States at about the same time as *Futura, Kabel* probably had greater initial impact, but in the long run *Futura* (q.v.) and its counterparts became more popular and lasting. Also see *Bernhard Gothic, Goudy Sans Serif, Metro, Tempo, Vogue;* also *Prisma* under Imports in Appendix.

Sans Serif Light, Mono 329 (6-72H4)
Sans Serif Light Italic, Mono 3291 (6-72pt)
Sans Serif Light Condensed, Mono 357 (14-72pt)
Sans Serif Medium, Mono 331 (6-72pt)
Sans Serif Medium Condensed, Mono 354 (14-72pt)
Sans Serif Bold, Mono 330 (6-72H4)
Sans Serif Bold Italic, Mono 3301 (6-72pt)
Sans Serif Extrabold, Mono 332 (6-72H4)
Sans Serif Extrabold Italic, Mono 3321 (8-72pt)
Sans Serif Extrabold Condensed, Mono 333 (14-72H4)
Sans Serif Lined, Mono 430 (24-36pt)

SANS SERIF EXTRABOLD, Mono 24-pt., with 18-H91 Alternates

ABCDEFGHIJKLMNOPQRSTUVWXYZ !?
abcdefghijklmnopqrstuvwxyzfifffl1234567890(&$.,-':;)«»
AJYaegjtu

SANS SERIF EXTRABOLD ITALIC, Mono 24-pt.

ABCDEFGHIJKLMNOPQRSTUVWXYZ& $1234567890
abcdefghijklmnopqrstuvwxyz fffifl .,-:;'!?() " " « »

SANS SERIF EXTRABOLD CONDENSED, Mono 14-pt.

ABCDEFGHIJKLMNOPQRSTUVWXYZ& abcdeefghijklmnopqrstuvwxyz $1234567890.,:;-"'!?

SANS SERIF LINED, Mono 24-pt.

ABCDEFGHIJKLMNOPQRSTUVWXYZ& $1234567890 .,-':;!?

279

SATANICK (30-pt. at 80%) (Guy Botterill, Charles Bush)

ABCDEFGHIJKLMNOPQRSTUVWXYZ
abcdefghijklmnopqrstuvwxyz & 1234567890$.,-:;!?')£✿

SATANICK OUTLINE, (36-pt. at 67%) (Dave Greer)

ABCDEFGHIJKLMNOPQRSTUVWXYZ&
abcdefghijklmnopqrstuvwxyz&.,-:;!?|£$1234567890

SATELLITE & ITALIC & BOLD, Inter 8½-pt.

ABCDEFGHIJKLMNOPQRSTUVWXYZ abcdefghijklmnopqrstuvwxyz fi fl ff ffiffl ,.-;':'!?|() @ ℔ & — $1234567890
ABCDEFGHIJKLMNOPQRSTUVWXYZ abcdefghijklmnopqrstuvwxyz fi fl ff ffiffl ,.-;':'!?|() @ ℔ & — $1234567890
ABCDEFGHIJKLMNOPQRSTUVWXYZ abcdefghijklmnopqrstuvwxyz fi fl ff ffi ffl ,.-;':'!?|() @ ℔ & — $1234567890
ABCDEFGHIJKLMNOPQRSTUVWXYZ abcdefghijklmnopqrstuvwxyz fi fl ff ffi ffl ,.-;':'!?|() @ ℔ & — $1234567890

SCHOEFFER OLDSTYLE, Mono 24-pt. (Henry Weiland)

ABCDEFGHIJKLMNOPQRSTUVWXYZ&$1234567890 47
abcdefghijklmnopqrstuvwxyz .,:;-'!? æœÆŒ GMRS£

SCHOOLBOOK OLDSTYLE, ATF 14-pt.

A B C D E F G H I J K L M N O P Q R S T U V W X Y Z & $
a b c d e f g h i j k l m n o p q r s t u v w x y z ff fi fl ffi ffl
1 2 3 4 5 6 7 8 9 0 . , - ' ' : ; ! ?

SCOTCH ROMAN, Mono 24-pt.

ABCDEFGHIJKLMNOPQRSTUVWXYZÆŒ
abcdefghijklmnopqrstuvwxyzæœfifffflffiffl
1234567890&$.,-':;!?£

SCOTCH ROMAN ITALIC, Mono 24-pt. (Cliff Leonard)

ABCDEFGHIJKLMNOPQRSTUVWXYZ&
abcdefghijklmnopqrstuvwxyz $1234567890 .,-:;'!?
ABCDGKLMNPRTV

SCOTCH NO. 2 & ITALIC, Lino 12-pt.

ABCDEFGHIJKLMNOPQRSTUVWXYZ   ABCDEFGHIJKLMNOPQRSTUVWXYZ
ABCDEFGHIJKLMNOPQRSTUVWXYZ
abcdefghijklmnopqrstuvwxyz $1234567890
abcdefghijklmnopqrstuvwxyz $1234567890

SCOTCH OPEN SHADED ITALIC, Mono (36-pt. at 67%)

ABCDKLMNPRTV

SANS SERIF SHADOW—see *Gill Sans Shadow Titling* under Imports in Appendix.

SANS SERIFS SHADED—see Imports in Appendix.

SANSERIF 52—see *Spartan Black*.

SAPPHIRE—see Imports in Appendix.

SATANICK, issued by ATF in 1896, was called "the invention of John F. Cumming of Worcester, Massachusetts." It has also been credited to Joseph W. Phinney of ATF; probably Cumming cut it from Phinney's drawings. However, it was a close copy, though perhaps a little heavier, of the *Troy* and *Chaucer* types of William Morris. DeVinne called it "a crude amalgamation of Roman with Black-letter, which is said to have been modeled by Morris upon the style made by Mentel of Strasburg in or near the year 1470." See *Morris Romanized Black*.

Satanick, ATF (6-72pt)
Satanick Outline, ATF

SATELLITE is a newspaper face designed by Edwin W. Shaar for Intertype in 1974. With large x-height and sturdy hairlines, especially in the bold version, it is designed for legibility under the rigors of high-speed newspaper production, but without sacrificing a stylish appearance.

Satellite and Italic and Bold, Inter

SAUNDERS—see *DeVinne*.

SCHADOW—see Imports in Appendix.

SCHOEFFER OLDSTYLE [NO. 2] was designed by Herman Ihlenburg for ATF in 1897. It is typical of a number of faces of the day—a plainly lettered roman with small, blunt serifs. Some references list *Schoeffer Condensed*, cut in 1902; this is probably the face shown a little later as *Adver Condensed* (q.v.). On Linotype, *Schoeffer Oldstyle* was called *Elzevir No. 2*.

Schoeffer Oldstyle [No. 2], ATF 305 (8-72pt); Schoeffer, Mono 69 (6-36pt); Elzevir No. 2, Lino (10-36pt)

SCHOOLBOOK OLDSTYLE was designed for ATF about 1924 by Morris F. Benton. It has much of the same character as *Century Catalogue,* but is a little heavier. There is no italic and it has not been made for machine typesetting.

Schoolbook Oldstyle, ATF 484 (6-48pt)

SCOTCH ROMAN is derived from a face cut and cast by the Scotch foundry of Alexander Wilson & Son at Glasgow before 1833, when it was considered a novelty letter. The modern adaptation of the face was first made in 1903 by the foundry of A. D. Farmer & Sons, later part of ATF. It is a modern face, but less mechanical than Bodoni, and has long been popular. Capitals, though, appear heavier than lowercase letters and tend to make a spotty page. Hansen's *National Roman* is virtually the same face, with the added feature of an alternate *r* with raised arm in the manner of *Cheltenham Oldstyle*.

When Monotype copied *Scotch Roman* in 1908, display sizes were cut to match the foundry face, but in keyboard sizes, necessarily modified to fit mechanical requirements, the caps were lightened and the entire face was somewhat regularized. *Scotch Open Shaded Italic,* a partial set of swash initials, was designed by Sol Hess in 1924. Similar swash letters, but not shaded, were also drawn by Hess and made by Monotype for regular *Scotch Roman Italic*.

Linotype had adapted *Scotch Roman* to its system in 1903, retaining the heavier capitals, but in 1931, by special permission of Lanston Monotype, brought out *Scotch No. 2* to match the Monotype version. Compare *Atlantic, Bell, Caledonia, Original Old Style*.

Scotch Roman, ATF 379 (6-72pt); BB&S-ATF 1856 (6-48pt); Mono 36 (6-36pt); Scotch, Lino = Inter (6-30pt); Scotch No. 2, Lino (8-12pt); National Roman, Hansen (6-36pt)
Scotch Roman Italic, ATF 380 (6-48pt); Mono 361 (6-36pt); Scotch Italic, Lino = Inter (6-18pt); Scotch No. 2 Italic, Lino (8-12pt); National Roman Italic, Hansen (6-12pt)
Scotch Open Shaded Italic, Mono 361So (36pt)

SCRIPPS COLLEGE OLD STYLE, Goudy 16-pt.

ABCDEFGHIJKLMNOPQRSTUVWXYZ&.,';:!?-1234567890
abcdefghijklmnopqrstuvwxyzfifffffiflfflctæct ABCDEFGHIJKLMNOPQRSTUVWXYZ&

SCRIPPS COLLEGE ITALIC, Goudy 16-pt.

A B C C E F G H I L N O P Q R S T U
a b c d e f g h i j l m n o p r s t u y ? , ;

SEYMOUR, 16-pt. (Cliff Helbert)

ABCDEFGHIJKLMNOPQRSTUVWXYZ
abcdefghijklmnopqrstuvwxyz&1234567890.,-–:;?`

SHADOW, ATF 24-pt.

ABCDEFGHIJKLMNOPQRSTUVWXYZ& M
$1234567890.,-:;'!?

Intertype

SHAW TEXT, 24-pt.

ABCDEFGHIJKLMNOPQRSTUVWXYZ &
abcdefghijklmnopqrstuvwxyz $1234567890 .,-:;'!?

SHERMAN, ATF 14-pt. private (Dave Norton)

ABCDEFGHIJKLMNOPQRSTUVWXYZ&.,-:;'!?1234567890
abcdefghijklmnopqrstuvwxyzfffiflffiffl

282

SCRIPPS COLLEGE OLD STYLE was designed and cut in 1941 by Frederic W. Goudy, as a private typeface for the school of that name in Claremont, California. Goudy calls it a straightforward, simple design that displays no freakish qualities. It was used by students at the school for experimental design projects which were printed on an old handpress. The italic was cut three years later.

Scripps College Old Style, Goudy (16pt) private
Scripps College Italic, Goudy (16pt) private

SCRIPT, SCRIPT BOLD—see *Broad-Stroke Cursive;* also Imports in Appendix.
SCROLL SHADED—see Antiques in Appendix.
SELF SPACING FACES—see *Quick-Set Roman.*

SEYMOUR is a private press type, designed by Ralph Fletcher Seymour for his Alderbrink Press in Chicago. In a 1945 book, the designer says, "With Goudy's help and Wiebking's matrice cutting and fitting machines I got my first face of type designed, cut, and finally cast . . . and my first book printed from the type." The book he referred to was dated 1902. The type seems never to have been named—it could have been *Seymour* for the designer or *Alderbrink* for the press.

Seymour or Alderbrink, private (10-16pt)

SHADOW was designed in 1934 by Morris F. Benton and released by ATF the following year. It might be called an "invisible" face—the letters are not there, just their shadows. It is typical of the round, condensed gothic style popular at the time, when letters such as *A, M,* and *N* lost their angularity. There is no discernible difference in width or design between look-alikes cap *O* and zero, nor between cap *I* and figure *1*, although a tiny letter cast on the shoulder of these characters indicates what they are. *Shadow* was copied by Intertype in 1936, and some secondary suppliers cast fonts from its matrices. This is distinguished by the lack of the upper upright on *M*, as shown.

Shadow, ATF 589 (24-48pt); Inter (14,36pt)

SHADOW (other)—see *Gill Sans* under Imports in Appendix.

SHAW TEXT was introduced by Inland Type Foundry in 1907 as its "latest novelty," although it is a rather conventional Old English face, a little heavier than *Wedding Text,* and a little lighter and fancier than *Engravers Old English.* After Inland merged with ATF, *Shaw Text* continued to be shown until 1954. Compare *Plate Text.*

Shaw Text, ATF 382 (8-48pt)

SHERMAN was designed in 1912 by Frederic W. Goudy as a private type for Frederick Sherman, a publisher and fine printer. Since Sherman already had an earlier type drawn by Goudy, the designer felt that a new type for him should be decidedly different. While the drawings were pleasing, the type as cut in 14-point was a disappointment to Goudy. Due to his inexperience, he says, he had believed that close fitting was essential to a typeface, and in this design he went to extremes. However, a quantity of the type was cast and shipped to Sherman. This was dumped after Sherman's death. Later a special casting was made by ATF for Syracuse University, where this specimen was obtained.

Sherman, Goudy (14-24pt) private

SHOWBOAT—see *Figaro* under Imports in Appendix.
SIGNAL, SISTINA—see Imports in Appendix.

SIXTEENTH CENTURY ROMAN, Duensing 24-pt.

ABCDEFGHILMNOPQuRSTVVV & 1234567890
abcdefghijlmnopqrstuvvvxz fffiffiﬅ ſ ſʃﬅſiʃsﬃ (.,:°-§)
❡ æctādȩ̄ęïñópq̧q̃ǫ̃íū ✶ JKUXYZ ky $;?!

SKETCH TITLE, BB&S 18-pt.; SKETCH CIRCULAR, 10-pt. (Ed Newman)

ABCDEFGHIJKLMNOPQRSTUVWXYZ1234567890&$
ABCDEFGHIJKLMNOPQRSTUVWXYZ
abcdefghijklmnopqrstuvwxyz1234567890 ♀ ☞&$

SLIMLINE, Mono 24-pt.

AABCDEFGHIJKLMMNOPQRSTUVWXYZ& KY
abcdeefghijklmnopqrstuvwwxyz ak ¢$$1234567890%.,:;-ˇ'!?()

SOUVENIR, ATF 24-pt.

ABCDEFGHIJKLMNOPQRSTUVWXYZ&
abcdefghijklmnopqrstuvwxyz fffiffififlﬄ $1234567890 .,-:;'!?

SOUVENIR & DEMIBOLD, Matro 14-pt. & ITALIC, 12-pt. lc

ABCDEFGHIJKLMNOPQRSTUVWXYZ
abcdefghijklmnopqrstuvwxyz 1234567890
ABCDEFGHIJKLMNOPQRSTUVWXYZ
abcdefghijklmnopqrstuvwxyz 1234567890

ABCDEFGHIJKLMNOPQRSTUVWXYZ
abcdefghijklmnopqrstuvwxyz 1234567890

Name in parentheses after some specimens
indicates person who has set that specimen,
in whole or in part, to our format.

284

SIXTEENTH CENTURY ROMAN is a 1967 recreation by Paul H. Duensing, at his Private Press and Typefoundry, of a face represented by a set of antique punches acquired in Europe. As they were incomplete and unusable as punches, he had to design the missing characters and cut matrices for the entire font, intentionally preserving the ancient appearance. The first half of the last line of the specimen here shows the variety of outmoded characters included in the font; the last half shows the redesigned missing characters, and four characters from *Garamond Bold.*

Sixteenth Century Roman, Duensing (24pt)

SKELETON ANTIQUE—see *Antique Extra Condensed.*

SKETCH CIRCULAR is a novel, outdated style, offered by BB&S for use on announcements and similar work. The companion all-cap face, *Sketch Title,* was formerly known as *Racine,* cut in 1890. Both series lasted into the late 1920s.

Sketch Circular, BB&S-ATF 1859 (8-14pt); also Sketch Title, BB&S-ATF 1860 (6s-30pt)

SKINNER—see *Menu Roman.*
SLIM BODONI—see *Bodoni.*
SLIM OPEN—see *Agency Gothic Open.*
SLIM OUTLINE—see *Oldtyme Outline.*

SLIMLINE was designed by Sol Hess in 1939 for Monotype. It is a lightweight, very narrow, monotone face with tiny serifs and a number of alternate round characters. It has had some use for stationery. Compare *Huxley Vertical.*

Slimline, Mono 241 (24-72pt)

SLOGAN—see Imports in Appendix.
SLOPE GOTHIC—see *Gothic Inclined.*
SOCIETY SCRIPT—see *Typo Upright.*
SOCIETY TEXT—see *Wedding Text.*
SOLEMNIS—see Imports in Appendix.
SOUTHERN CROSS—see Antiques in Appendix.
SOUTHEY—see *Handcraft.*

SOUVENIR was designed by Morris F. Benton in 1914 for ATF. It is an early face to feature rounded serifs and a soft, rubbery look. There is only slight contrast between thick and thin strokes, and the general weight is light. In development the working title was *Round Roman.* Being made in only one weight, with no italic and a limited range of sizes, *Souvenir* achieved little popularity.

Souvenir, ATF 449 (6-36pt)
Souvenir and Italic, Matrotype (8-14pt)
Souvenir Demi Bold and Italic, Matrotype (8-14pt)

With the advent of phototypesetting, two versions of matching heavier weights were made for that medium. One of these, drawn by Ed Benguiat, New York lettering artist, achieved such popularity that it was later cut on matrices for use on Linotype, by Matrotype in England, in regular and demi-bold weights with matching italics. This is one of very few instances of a phototype face being cut in metal. However, the success of the phototype versions prompted ATF to reissue the face for a short time in 1972, and some secondary sources have cast fonts of separate type from the Matrotype matrices.

285

SPARTAN LIGHT, Lino 14-pt.

ABCDEFGHIJKLMNOPQRSTUVWXYZ&
abcdefghijklmnopqrstuvwxyzfiflffffiffl [($£,.:;'-'?!*†‡§¶)] 1234567890

SPARTAN BOOK & ITALIC, Lino 14-pt.

ABCDEFGHIJKLMNOPQRSTUVWXYZ 1234567890 Æ Œ Æ Œ æ œ ABCDEFGHIJKLMNOPQRSTUVWXYZ
ABCDEFGHIJKLMNOPQRSTUVWXYZ 1234567890 Æ Œ æ œ
abcdefghijklmnopqrstuvwxyz fi fl ff ffi ffl £ $ & & ( ) . , : ; ' ' ! ? * - — — [ ] † ‡ § ¶ ⅛ ¼ ⅜ ½ ⅝ ¾ ⅞
abcdefghijklmnopqrstuvwxyz fi fl ff ffi ffl £ $ & ( ) , : ; ' ' ! ? [ ] † ‡ § ¶ ⅛ ¼ ⅜ ½ ⅝ ¾ ⅞

SPARTAN BOOK CONDENSED & HEAVY CONDENSED, Lino 14-pt.

ABCDEFGHIJKLMNOPQRSTUVWXYZ&ÆŒ 1234567890$£,.:;'-'?!–|— . . . ()*†‡¶§[]%
ABCDEFGHIJKLMNOPQRSTUVWXYZ&ÆŒ 1234567890$£,.:;'-'?!–|— . . . ()*†‡¶§[]%
abcdefghijklmnopqrstuvwxyzæœfiflffffiffl ⅛¼⅜½⅝¾⅞⅓⅔⅕⅖⅗⅘⅙⅚ 2⅛3¼
abcdefghijklmnopqrstuvwxyzæœfiflffffiffl ⅛¼⅜½⅝¾⅞⅓⅔⅕⅖⅗⅘⅙⅚ 2⅛3¼

SPARTAN MEDIUM & ITALIC, Lino 14-pt.

ABCDEFGHIJKLMNOPQRSTUVWXYZ&
ABCDEFGHIJKLMNOPQRSTUVWXYZ&
abcdefghijklmnopqrstuvwxyzfiflffffiffl [($£,.:;'-'?!*†‡§¶)] 1234567890
abcdefghijklmnopqrstuvwxyzfiflffffiffl [($£,.:;'-'?!†‡§¶)] 1234567890*

SPARTAN MEDIUM CONDENSED, ATF 24-pt.

ABCDEFGHIJKLMNOPQRSTUVWXYZ
abcdefghijklmnopqrstuvwxyz1234567890(&$.,-'"'":;!?%¢$)

SPARTAN BOLD & ITALIC, Lino 14-pt.

ABCDEFGHIJKLMNOPQRSTUVWXYZ& 1234567890 ⅛ ¼ ⅜ ½ ⅝ ¾ ⅞ ⅓ ⅔ ⅕ ⅖ ⅗ ⅘ ⅙
***ABCDEFGHIJKLMNOPQRSTUVWXYZ& 1234567890* ⅛ ¼ ⅜ ½ ⅝ ¾ ⅞ ⅓ ⅔ ⅕ ⅖ ⅗ ⅘ ⅙**
abcdefghijklmnopqrstuvwxyz fiflffffiffl [($£,.:;'-'?!*†‡§¶)] 1/8 1/4 3/8 1/2 5/8 3/4 7/8 1/3 2/3 1/5 2/5 3/5 4/5 1/6 5/6
abcdefghijklmnopqrstuvwxyz fiflffffiffl [($£,.:;'-'?!*†‡§¶)] a a ' '

SPARTAN BOLD CONDENSED & ITALIC, Lino 14-pt.

ABCDEFGHIJKLMNOPQRSTUVWXYZ& ***ABCDEFGHIJKLMNOPQRSTUVWXYZ&*** **a *a* ' '**
abcdefghijklmnopqrstuvwxyz fiflffffiffl ***abcdefghijklmnopqrstuvwxyz fiflffffiffl***
1234567890 [($£,.:;'-'?!*†‡§¶)] ***1234567890 [($£,.:;'-'?!*†‡§¶)]***
⅛ ¼ ⅜ ½ ⅝ ¾ ⅞ ⅓ ⅔ ***⅛ ¼ ⅜ ½ ⅝ ¾ ⅞ ⅓ ⅔***

SPARTAN HEAVY & ITALIC, Lino 14-pt.

ABCDEFGHIJKLMNOPQRSTUVWXYZ&
ABCDEFGHIJKLMNOPQRSTUVWXYZ&
abcdefghijklmnopqrstuvwxyzfiflffffiffl [($£,.:;'-'?!*†‡§¶)] 1234567890
abcdefghijklmnopqrstuvwxyzfiflffffiffl [($£,.:;'-'?!*†‡§¶)] 1234567890

SPARTAN as produced by Linotype and ATF is equivalent to *Futura* (q.v.). Although it is claimed to have been derived from several similar European faces, the differences between it and *Futura* are so slight that for most practical purposes they are almost interchangeable. Linotype announced *Sanserif 52* and *Italic* early in 1939; later in the same year these faces were offered as *Spartan Black,* along with light, medium, and heavy weights, all with italics. In 1941 ATF cut some of these faces; by arrangement with Mergenthaler the small sizes were cut to match.

Over the following dozen years or more, additional weights and widths were drawn by Bud Renshaw and Gerry Powell for ATF, and by Linotype staff designers. Renshaw's *Spartan Medium Condensed,* drawn in 1953, is wider than the corresponding faces in other families. In 1955 Linotype announced *Spartan Bold,* "the latest member of the Spartan family; slightly larger on the body than *Spartan Heavy* and more compactly fitted." *Spartan Extra Black* is heavier than the comparable faces from other sources. ATF made supplementary Advertising Figures, Decimal Figures, and Fractions for several weights of Spartan.

Spartan Circuit and *Spartan Circuit Heavy* are 1964 adaptations of the design by Linotype for Teletypesetter use, requiring modification of character widths. Compare *Erbar Bold.* Also see *Classified Display, Tempo Alternate, Twentieth Century.*

SPEEDBALL—see *Balloon.*

Spartan Light, Lino (6-24pt)
Spartan Book, ATF 707 (6-36pt), Lino (5½-24pt)
Spartan Book Italic, Lino (6-24pt)
Spartan Book Condensed, Lino (5½-36pt)
Spartan Medium, ATF 680 (6-120pt), Lino (6-36pt)
Spartan Medium Italic, ATF 681 (6-72pt), Lino (6-36pt)
Spartan Medium Condensed, ATF 706 (6-48pt), Lino (5½-24pt)
Spartan Bold, Lino (14-36pt)
Spartan Bold Italic, Lino (14-36pt)
Spartan Bold Condensed, Lino (18-36pt)
Spartan Bold Condensed Italic, Lino (18-24pt)
Spartan Heavy, ATF 685 (6-120pt), Lino (5½-36pt)
Spartan Heavy Italic, ATF 686 (6-72pt), Lino (6-36pt)
Spartan Heavy Condensed, Lino (5½-36pt)
Spartan Black, ATF 683 (6-120pt), Lino (6-36pt)
Spartan Black Italic, ATF 684 (6-72pt), Lino (6-36pt)
Spartan Black Condensed, ATF 687 (10-120pt), Lino (8-36pt)
Spartan Black Condensed Italic, ATF 688 (10-72pt), Lino (8-36pt)
Spartan Extra Black, ATF 694 (10-72pt), Lino (14-24pt)
Spartan Extra Black Italic, Lino (14-24pt)
Spartan Circuit and Heavy, Lino (6pt)
For comparable faces, see list at Futura.

SPARTAN BLACK & ITALIC, Lino 14-pt.

ABCDEFGHIJKLMNOPQRSTUVWXYZ&
ABCDEFGHIJKLMNOPQRSTUVWXYZ&
abcdefghijklmnopqrstuvwxyzfiflffffiffl
abcdefghijklmnopqrstuvwxyzfiflffffiffl
[($£,.:;'-'?!*†‡§¶)] 1234567890
[($£,.:;'-'?!*†‡§¶)] 1234567890

SPARTAN BLACK CONDENSED & ITALIC, Lino 14-pt.

ABCDEFGHIJKLMNOPQRSTUVWXYZ& abcdefghijklmnopqrstuvwxyzfiflffffiffl [($£,.:;'-'?!*†‡§¶)] 1234567890
ABCDEFGHIJKLMNOPQRSTUVWXYZ& abcdefghijklmnopqrstuvwxyzfiflffffiffl [($£,.:;'-'?!†‡§¶)] 1234567890*

SPARTAN EXTRA BLACK, ATF 24-pt.

ABCDEFGHIJKLMNOPQRSTUVWXYZ&.,:;!?()''""-
abcdefghijklmnopqrstuvwxyz 1234567890*¢

SPARTAN EXTRA BLACK ITALIC, Lino (24-pt. at 57%)

ABCDEFGHIJKLMNOPQRSTUVWXYZ& ($,.:;?!'-)
abcdefghijklmnopqrstuvwxyz 1234567890

SPARTAN CIRCUIT & HEAVY, Lino 6-pt.

ABCDEFGHIJKLMNOPQRSTUVWXYZ& abcdefghijklmnopqrstuvwxyz 1234567890$,.:;'-'?!—()*¢§†‡/% ⅛¼⅜½⅝¾⅞⅓⅔⅕⅖⅗⅘⅙⅚ a £
ABCDEFGHIJKLMNOPQRSTUVWXYZ& abcdefghijklmnopqrstuvwxyz 1234567890$,.:;'-'?!—()*¢§†‡/% ⅛¼⅜½⅝¾⅞⅓⅔⅕⅖⅗⅘⅙⅚ a £

SPEIDOTYPE LIGHT & BOLD, Mono 8-pt. (Lewis Mitchell)

ABCDEFGHIJKLMNOPQRSTUVWXYZ& abcdefghijklmnopqrstuvwxyz £$1234567890,. .,-: ; !?'"*()%
ABCDEFGHIJKLMNOPQRSTUVWXYZ& abcdefghijklmnopqrstuvwxyz $1234567890,. .,-: ; ? !'"()%

SPIRE NO. 5, BB&S 24-pt. (part reduced)

SUPERIOR FINISH INSURED Harmonizing Results Praised Noted Generals Invited

SPIRE, Mono 24-pt.

ABCDEFGHIJKLMNOPQRSTUVWXYZ AKMNUW $1234567890ᶜ,-"!?&()[]

SQUARE GOTHIC, Ludlow 24-pt.

ABCDEFGHIJKLMNOPQRSTUVWXYZ& .,:;!?
abcdefghijklmnopqrstuvwxyz 123456789

SQUAREFACE, Mono 14-pt.

A A B C D E F G H I J K L M N O P Q R S T U V W X Y Z &
a a b c d e f g h i j k l m n o p q r s t u v w x y z
.,-`'':;!?[(«» $1234567890

STATIONERS GOTHIC LIGHT, Mono 12L (Rick von Holdt)

ABCDEFGHIJKLMNOPQRSTUVWXYZ 1234567890$.,:;-'''()!?

STATIONERS GOTHIC MEDIUM, Mono 12L

ABCDEFGHIJKLMNOPQRSTUVWXYZ&$1234567890.,:;-'''()!?

STATIONERS GOTHIC BOLD, Mono 18L

ABCDEFGHIJKLMNOPQRSTUVWXYZ
$1234567890&!?.,:-;

288

SPEIDOTYPE is described by Monotype as a set of faces designed for producing railroad tariff and other tabular composition involving the use of characters, spaces, and quads of only four different standard widths. No. 617E has lowercase and punctuation only, made to combine with the caps of No. 417E. The general principle is similar to *Quick-Set Roman* (q.v.), but the only specimen located is like a typewriter face.

Speidotype Light, Mono 417E and 617E (8pt)
Speidotype Bold, Mono 517J (8pt)

SPENCER OLD STYLE. The design of this face by Frederic W. Goudy was begun in 1934 on a commission for a large book-printing plant, which wanted an exclusive type for some of its work. When this deal fell through, after many drawings were completed, Goudy recalled a promise to make a type for Syracuse University, the first educational institution to recognize his work in type design. Some characters were changed, but the project was not completed, according to a spokesman for the school.

SPENSER—see *Handcraft.*
SPIRAL—see *Emerson.*

SPIRE is a modernization of the old modern roman extra-condensed style, drawn by Sol Hess for Monotype in 1937. There is no lowercase, but there are several alternate round characters. Compare *Greenwich, Modern Roman Extra Condensed,* also *Empire, Slimline. Spire* is also the name of a dissimilar BB&S face, cut in 1898 or earlier and shown as late as 1927.

Spire, Mono 377 (24-72pt)
Spire No. 5, BB&S-ATF 1861 (12-72pt)

SQUARE GOTHIC is a medium-weight Ludlow face, similar to *Gothic No. 545* but with a more contemporary feeling and much better draftsmanship. It is also similar to *Gothic No. 3,* advertised by Laclede Type Foundry in St. Louis as original. Since Robert Wiebking worked at times for both Laclede and Ludlow, it is likely that he is the designer of this face, probably around 1920. *Square Gothic Heavy* was the original Ludlow version of *Franklin Gothic* (q.v.).

Square Gothic, Ludlow 6-ZB (4-48pt)

SQUAREFACE was designed by Sol Hess in 1940 as a variation of *Stymie Extrabold.* A number of characters are the same for both faces, but normally round letters have been squared considerably, with only slightly rounded corners. It makes a vigorous display face, and harmonizes well with other square-serif designs.

Squareface, Mono 890 (14-72pt)

STACCATO—see Antiques in Appendix.
STAGG—see *Braggadocio* under Imports in Appendix.
STANDARD—see Imports in Appendix.
STANDARD GOTHIC—see *Gothic No. 578.*
STANDARD LINING ANTIQUE—see *Typo Gothic.*

STATIONERS GOTHIC LIGHT and *Bold* were designed by Sol Hess for Monotype in 1942, and *Medium* in 1944, but wartime and post-war conditions delayed their release until 1948. They are similar to the *Bank Gothics,* following a style of squared letter popular for copperplate engraved stationery and announcements, and in effect constitute a more contemporary form of the style typified by *Copperplate Gothics.* Like the others, there are several sizes on each of several different bodies, making various cap-and-small-cap combinations easily practical.

Stationers Gothic Light, Mono 84 (6s-24pt)
Stationers Gothic Medium, Mono 82 (6s-24pt)
Stationers Gothic Bold, Mono 85 (6s-24pt)

FOREIGN BANKER DOUBLES CHARGE

STATIONERS SEMI-SCRIPT (30-pt. at 80%)

ABCDEFGHIJKLMNOPQRSTUVWXYZ M

abcdefghijklmnopqrstuvwxyz Qu&$ de fllr ſſst ſffſt.,-:; '!?() 1234567890

STEELPLATE GOTHIC FAMILY, BB&S

STEELPLATE GOTHIC HEAVY

STEELPLATE GOTHIC HEAVY EXTENDED

STEELPLATE GOTHIC HEAVY CONDENSED

STEELPLATE GOTHIC LIGHT

STEELPLATE GOTHIC LIGHT EXTENDED

STEELPLATE GOTHIC LIGHT CONDENSED

STEELPLATE GOTHIC ITALIC

STEELPLATE GOTHIC BOLD

STEELPLATE GOTHIC SHADED

STEELPLATE GOTHIC EXTRALIGHT

STEELPLATE GOTHIC BOLD, BB&S (30-pt. at 67%)

ABCDEFGHIJKLMNOPQRSTUVWXYZ&
$1234567890 .,-:;'!?

STEELPLATE GOTHIC SHADED, 18L

ABCDEFGHIJKLMNOPQRSTUVWXYZ&
$1234567890 .,-:;'!?

STEELPLATE SCRIPT, ATF 24L

ABCDEFGHIJKLMNOPQRSTUVWXYZ $1234567890

abcdefghijklmnopqrstuvwxyz. '?!- L

STELLAR, Ludlow 24-pt. (part reduced)

ABCDEFGHIJKLMNOPQRSTUVWXYZ& AE H

abcdefghijklmnopqrstuvwxyz 1234567890-.,:;!"?+)

STELLAR BOLD, Ludlow 24-pt. (part reduced) (Herb Harnish)

ABCDEFGHIJKLMNOPQRSTUVWXYZ&

abcdefghijklmnopqrstuvwxyz 1234567890$.,-:;"!?[]—+

STATIONERS PLATE is a rather wide, light-weight face with long square serifs, cast by BB&S in several sizes of caps on each of three bodies, making various cap-and-small-cap combinations practical in the manner of *Copperplate Gothic*. Though dating from early in the century, it has somewhat the effect of *Stymie*.

Stationers Plate, BB&S-ATF 1862 (6s-18L)

STATIONERS SEMISCRIPT as offered by BB&S was a renaming of *Palmer Series,* introduced by Inland Type Foundry in 1899. It has been ascribed to Sidney Gaunt. It is similar to the BB&S *Wedding Plate Script* in slope, proportions, and general appearance, but characters do not join. There are a number of special characters as shown.

Stationers Semiscript, BB&S-ATF 1863 (12-42pt)

STEELPLATE GOTHIC is the BB&S equivalent of *Copperplate Gothic.* Most of the series came from Western Type Foundry when BB&S acquired that concern in 1918. *Steelplate Gothic Light Extended* was originally Western's *Farley,* advertised in 1907, while *Steelplate Gothic Heavy Extended* was Western's *Perry;* these faces are not quite as wide as the extended *Copperplate Gothics* (q.v.), and differ in minor details. Other light and heavy versions are very nearly duplicates of *Copperplate Gothic.* All were cut by Robert Wiebking. *Steelplate Gothic Shaded* was drawn by Wiebking in 1918; it is uncertain whether he did this for Western just before the takeover, or for BB&S. It has an added fine line to the right and bottom of strokes, and lacks the tiny serifs of the other faces; it was recast by ATF in 1954. *Steelplate Gothic Italic,* which was Western's *Perry Italic,* is nearly like *Copperplate,* but the *G* lacks a crossbar.

Steelplate Gothic Bold comes from the old BB&S *Plate Gothic* series (q.v.), while the extralight version has the same characteristics. All these faces moved on to ATF when BB&S merged with it in 1929. When the *Copperplate Gothics* went through a brief period of revived popularity for advertising use in the 1950s, ATF reinstated the two largest sizes of *Steelplate Gothic Bold,* rather than cutting additional sizes for *Copperplate.*

Steelplate Gothic Extralight, BB&S-ATF 1874 (6s-6L)
Steelplate Gothic Light, BB&S-ATF 1867 (6s-24L)
Steelplate Gothic Light Condensed, BB&S-ATF 1869 (6s-24L)
Steelplate Gothic Light Extended, BB&S-ATF 1865 (6s-24L)
Steelplate Gothic Heavy, BB&S-ATF 1868 (6s-24L)
Steelplate Gothic Heavy Condensed, BB&S-ATF 1870 (6s-24L)
Steelplate Gothic Heavy Extended, BB&S-ATF 1866 (6s-24L)
Steelplate Gothic Bold, BB&S-ATF 1873 (6s-36pt)
Steelplate Gothic Shaded, BB&S-ATF 1872 (6s-24L); (Univ 6s-24L)
Steelplate Gothic Shaded is known as Spartan Outline in England.

STEELPLATE GOTHIC (other)—see *Typo Gothic.*

STEELPLATE SCRIPT was advertised by ATF in 1907 as "equal to copperplate printing." It originated with Central Type Foundry in 1888. It is a very delicate traditional connected script, suggestive of nineteenth-century styles. The lowercase is quite small, but in 24-point there is an alternate lowercase font which is smaller yet.

Steelplate Script, ATF 307 (12-30pt)

STELLAR and *Stellar Bold* were designed by R. Hunter Middleton for Ludlow in 1929 as a less severe alternative to the monotone sans-serifs which were coming into great popularity. There is moderate thick-and-thin contrast, and strokes flare slightly toward the ends, while ascenders and descenders are fairly long; all this gives a feeling of warmth and pleasantness. Cap *M* is widely splayed, and sloping strokes are cut off at an angle. An alternate *A, E,* and *H* in both weights have the crossbar extended beyond the left upright, and there is an alternate *U* without the extended vertical stroke. Compare *Optima, Lydian, Radiant.*

Stellar, Ludlow 27-L (8-72pt)
Stellar Bold, Ludlow 27-B (8-72pt)

STELLAR (other)—see *Tuscan Graille* under Antiques in Appendix.

ABCDEFGHIJKLMNOPQRSTUVWXYZ
$1234567890¢.,-:;"'!?&

ABCDEFGHIJKLMN 1234567890
OPQRSTUVWXYZ&.,-'':;!?—◆$

ABCDEFGHIJKLMNOP THROUGH THE MEDIUM
through the medium of type and 1234567890?!$&

ABCDEFGHIJKLMNOPQRSTUVWXYZQuTh
abcdefghijklmnopqrstuvwxyz.,-:;!?&fiflffffffiffl ∂   1234567890$

ABCDEFGHIJKLMNOPQRSTUVW
$1234567890!?;.:-', ES   XYZ&

STIPPLED GOTHIC HANSEN TYPE FOUNDRY

WHICH, MELLOW'D BY THE STEALING HOURS
happy by his reign. *A M N R & 🌿 r y The and of*

THE ONLY MACHINE Having a Complete and
Varied Assortment of its own Matrices $1234567890

ABCDEFGHIJKLMN
OPQRSTVWXYZ

STENCIL is a heavy roman letter with white breaks in the thinner strokes, as though done with the traditional cut-out stencil. There are two versions of the type, both issued in 1937. The one drawn by R. Hunter Middleton for Ludlow appears to have reached the market first, having been advertised in June of that year. Its basic letter is much like a *Clarendon* (compare *Craw Clarendon*). The ATF version by Gerry Powell was ready the following month; it is narrower but has a bolder effect. Neither font has lowercase, but the ATF face is cut in a range of sizes, while Ludlow offers only one size.

Stencil, Ludlow 41 (36pt)
Stencil, ATF 662 (18-60pt)

STERLING and *Sterling Cursive* were designed by Morris F. Benton for ATF in 1917 and 1919 respectively. They are a delicate and attractive pair of faces, with long descenders, but have a number of unusual little quirks that make them more suited to such printing as announcements and programs than for extended reading. Italic capitals are quite flourished, but there is an additional set of Plain Capitals, fonted separately, which is essentially a slanted version of the roman.

Sterling, ATF 461 (6-48pt)
Sterling Cursive, ATF 473 (6-36pt); (Univ 6-36pt)

STILLSON was introduced by BB&S about 1899, and patented by R. L. Stillson in 1900. It is a set of rather crude caps, thick-and-thin with generally very small serifs. Particularly noticeable are the high crossbars of *E* and *F*, the tall upright stroke on *G*, and the very short vertex on *M*. There are three sizes each of 6- and 12-point.

Stillson, BB&S 1876 (6s-36pt)

STIPPLED GOTHIC was cut by Hansen in 1907 or earlier. It is a heavy, rather clumsy gothic in outline with a stippled field within that line.

Stippled Gothic, Hansen (18-48pt)

STRADIVARIUS—see Imports in Appendix.

STRATFORD OLD STYLE was Hansen's version of the *Old Style Antique* face which was the predecessor of *Bookman,* but has different swash characters from other versions.

Stratford Old Style, Hansen (6-48pt)

STRATHMORE OLDSTYLE was introduced by ATF in 1906, stating: "Strathmore was designed by a well-known Eastern artist who has had much to do with the work on editions de luxe brought out in recent years by some of our greatest publishing houses. He . . . partly adopted a style considerably used by Spanish sculptors and artists hundreds of years ago, then considered paramount in all things pertaining to art." In spite of this build-up, it is a rather clumsy face, with awkwardly short descenders. The Monotype face has modified character proportions.

Strathmore Oldstyle, ATF 386 (6-72pt); Mono 143 (6-36pt)

STREAMLINE BLOCK is *Franklin Gothic* with two groups of fine white lines cut into it. There are no punctuation marks or figures, only the 26 capitals. It is made only in one size.

Streamline Block, Mono 407 (36pt)

STUDIO—see Imports in Appendix.

STUDLEY was introduced by Inland as "original" in 1897, with extended, condensed, and extra condensed versions following within four years. The series is similar to *Globe Gothic,* and was named for a printer in St. Louis.

Studley, Inland-ATF 387 (6-60pt)
Studley Extended, Inland-ATF 152 (6-60pt)
Condensed Studley, Inland-ATF 121 (6-72pt)
Studley Extra Condensed, Inland-ATF 155 (12-72pt)

STUYVESANT & ITALIC, Lino 12-pt.

ABCDEFGHIJKLMNOPQRSTUVWXYZ& abcdefghijklmnopqrstuvwxyz
1234567890 ($,.:'-') ABCDEFGHIJKLMNOPQRSTUVWXYZ
ABCDEFGHIJKLMNOPQRSTUVWXYZ& abcdefghijklmnopqrstuvwxyz

STYGIAN BLACK, Ludlow 24-pt.

ABCDEFGHIJKLMNOPQRSTUVWXYZ–&·])/.,:;'!
abcdefghijklmnopqrstuvwxyz 1234567890

STYGIAN BLACK ITALIC, Ludlow 24-pt.

ABCDEFGHIJKLMNOPQRSTUVWXYZ&
abcdefghijklmnopqrstuvwxyz 1234567890

STYLESCRIPT, Mono 24-pt.

ABCDEFGHIJKLMNOPQRSTUVWXYZ&
abcdefghijklmnopqrstuvwxyz's .,:;-!? 1234567890$

Mechanical Computers

For a century, Linotype and Monotype machines have produced justified lines of type mechanically. The Linotype uses a simple wedge system, while the Monotype uses a mechanical system of computation.

The Monotype system of composition is actually two machines—a keyboard and a caster. The keyboard punches a paper ribbon, which can be used immediately or at any other time or place. The caster, controlled by that ribbon, is a mechanical marvel—for each character it selects the proper matrix out of 225 or more (depending on the model), positions it precisely over the mold and locks it down, adjusts the mold to the proper width, injects molten metal to form the character, cools the cast, trims off the jet, and places the character in sequence in the line. All this in half a second or less. Along with this, word spaces of the proper size are cast in place so that each line comes out even.

This diagram shows the basic matrix-case layout, the "C" arrangement most often used for work combining roman with italics and small caps. Other standard arrangements provide for normal or wide boldfaces and other combinations, with special arrangements for faces not readily adapted to proportions of the standard arrangement.

																Unit value
█	█	l	t	'	'	.	,	█	l	i	]	[	'	|		5
j	f	i	!	:	;	-	j	f	I	/	:	;	█	█		6
c	r	s	e	)	(	'	'	r	s	t	J	v	°	z		7
‡	q	*	b	g	o	?	I	z	c	e	z	s	†	?		8
I	█	9	7	5	3	1	0	.	9	7	5	3	1	0		9
C	█	█	8	6	4	2	$	-	$	8	6	4	2	█		9
x	k	y	d	h	a	x	J	g	o	a	P	F	L	T		9
A	fi	u	n	.	S	v	y	p	u	n	Q	B	O	E		10
D	█	fl	p	fl	fi	q	k	b	h	d	V	Y	G	R		10
H	&	J	S	œ	æ	ff	█	Z	█	ff	x	U	K	N		11
O	L	C	F	w	£	æ	L	P	F	¶	M	Z	Q	G		12
E	&	Q	V	C	B	T	O	E	A	w	P	T	R	B		13
D	A	Y	ffl	ffi	m	œ	Y	U	G	R	Œ	Æ	w	V		14
K	N	H	ffl	ffi	X	D	N	K	H	m	&	℔	X	U		15
Œ	Æ	¾	¼	½	W	M	—	..	M	W	%	Œ	Æ	█		18

STUYVESANT and *Stuyvesant Italic* were designed in 1942-47 by William A. Dwiggins, inspired by a quaint Dutch type cut by J. F. Rosart about 1750, and used in 1949 in *The Shelby Letters, from the California Mines, 1851-1852,* published by Alfred Knopf.

An entirely different *Stuyvesant,* a novelty design, was made by Keystone before 1906, perhaps before 1900.

Stuyvesant and Italic, Lino (12pt) experimental
Stuyvesant, Keystone (6-48pt)

STYGIAN BLACK and *Italic* were introduced by Ludlow in 1929 as "new and dominating." The roman has much the same style as *Modernique,* brought out the previous year, but the lowercase is much smaller, with long ascenders and descenders, and the effect is less rigid. The italic retains the blackness of the roman but is more of a cursive, with flourished caps and small serifs on the lowercase.

Stygian Black, Ludlow 25 (14-48pt)
Stygian Black Italic, Ludlow 25-I (14-48pt)

STYLESCRIPT was designed by Sol Hess for Monotype in 1940. It is a popular bold thick-and-thin cursive style, which has had considerable use in advertising. It is somewhat like the earlier *Coronet Bold* of Ludlow, but heavier and with a greater x-height; some characters seem to make a conscious effort to differ.

Stylescript, Mono 425 (14-72pt)

STYLUS SCRIPT—see *Monoline Script* under Imports in Appendix.

STYMIE LIGHT, ATF 24-pt.

AAABCDEFGHIJKLMNOPQRRSTUVWXYZ&.,-:;'`'!?
aabcdeffghijklmnopqrstuvwxyz 1234567890$$

STYMIE LIGHT ITALIC, ATF 24-pt.

ABCDEFGHIJKLMNOPQRRSTUVWXYZ&»«().,-:;'`'!?
abcdeffghijklmnopqrstuvwxyz 1234567890$$

STYMIE LIGHT CONDENSED, Mono 24-pt.

AABCDEFGHIJKKLMNOPQRRSTUVWXYZ& 1234567890¢
aabcdefghijklmnopqrstuvwxyyz .,-'`:;!?([«»

STYMIE MEDIUM, ATF 24-pt.

AAABCDEFGHIJKLMNOPQRSTUVWXYZ&().,-:;'`'!?
aabcdeffghijklmnopqrrsttuvwxyyz 1234567890

STYMIE MEDIUM ITALIC, ATF 24-pt.

ABCDEFGHIJKLMNOPQRSTUVWXYZ&().,-:;'`'!?
abcdeffghijklmnopqrrstuvwxyz1234567890

STYMIE MEDIUM CONDENSED, Mono 24-pt. (part reduced)

ABCDEFGHIJKLMNOPQRSTUVWXYZ A K R t y
abcdefghijklmnopqrstuvwxyz a $1234567890 $¢«»[]().,-;':'!?&

STYMIE BOLD, ATF 24-pt. (elongated characters reduced)

AAABCDEFGHIJKLMNOPQRRST
aabcdeffghijklmnopqrrsttuvwxyyz
$1234567890 .,-:;'!? ' UVWXYZ&

STYMIE BOLD ITALIC, ATF 24-pt.

ABCDEFGHIJKLMNOPQRSTUVWXYZ.,-:;'`'!?&
abcdeffghijklmnopqrrstuvwxyz1234567890

STYMIE BOLD is a redesign of *Rockwell Antique* (q.v.), which in turn was a reissue of *Litho Antique,* introduced by Inland Type Foundry in 1910. *Rockwell* appeared in 1931, but Morris Benton redesigned it as *Stymie Bold* in the same year, refining some characters and generally tightening the fit. *Stymie Light* and *Medium* and their *Italics* were also drawn by Benton in 1931, and the series quickly became very popular. *Stymie Bold Italic* followed a bit later.

Elongated Ascenders and Descenders for *Stymie Light, Medium,* and *Bold* are a whimsical idea borrowed from the *Parsons* series (q.v.). Eleven characters as shown are offered for each weight from 18-point up, but there are actually only nine different characters, with an extra *b* and *d* in each set to invert for *p* and *q.* The ascenders are cast to proper alignment for reasonably easy use, but the descenders must be carefully justified vertically. They were short-lived.

Monotype exercised its option to copy ATF faces soon after the introduction of these faces—too soon, in fact, because they copied *Rockwell* and in some literature called it *Stymie Bold,* and there has been confusion between the two faces ever since, with some Monotype users applying the latter name to the older face. The actual *Stymie Bold* was duplicated by Monotype about 1936. But Monotype also did its part in expanding the family; Sol Hess designed *Stymie Extrabold* in 1934, a year before Morris Benton drew *Stymie Black.* These heavy versions differ slightly from each other and from the lighter faces; it's a matter of opinion as to which is more compatible with other Stymies.

Sol Hess and Monotype also produced *Stymie Light Condensed, Medium Condensed,* and *Extrabold Condensed,* in 1935 and 1936. Gerry Powell drew the last major member of the family in 1937, with *Stymie Bold Condensed,* which departs a little more than the others from family characteristics. Trials of a medium condensed version at ATF were abandoned in favor of *Tower* (q.v.). Along the way Powell had also engineered the production in 1936 of *Stymie Light Title* and *Stymie Medium Title,* all-cap versions of their respective weights with several sizes cast on 6- and 12-point bodies in the manner of *Copperplate Gothic.*

But there is more to the Stymie story. Shortly after the introduction of the family, perhaps as early as 1932, ATF undertook a program of producing type

(Stymie continues)

Stymie Light, ATF 553 (6-144pt); Mono 190 (6-72pt)
Stymie Light Italic, ATF 554 (6-72pt); Mono 1901 (6-36pt)
Stymie Light Title, ATF 653 (6s-12L)
Stymie Light Condensed, Mono 690 (12-72pt)
Stymie Medium, ATF 552 (6-144pt); Mono 290 (6-72pt)
Stymie Medium Italic, ATF 555 (6-72pt); Mono 2901 (6-36pt)
Stymie Medium Title, ATF 654 (6s-12L)
Stymie Medium Condensed, Mono 590 (14-72pt)
Stymie Bold, ATF 551 (6-144pt); Mono 790 (6-36pt)
Stymie Bold Italic, ATF 561 (6-72pt); Mono 1891 (6-72pt)
Stymie Bold Condensed, ATF 658 (12-72pt)
Stymie Black, ATF 598 (12-72pt)
Stymie Black Italic, ATF 599 (12-72pt)

STYMIE BOLD CONDENSED, ATF 24-pt.

ABCDEFGHIJKLMNOPQRSTUVWXYZ
abcdefghijklmnopqrstuvwxyz 1234567890 .,-:;'"!?&$¢

STYMIE BLACK, ATF 24-pt.

ABCDEFGHIJKLMNOPQRSTUVWXYZ&$?!.,:;'-
abcdefghijklmnopqrstuvwxyz 1234567890

STYMIE BLACK ITALIC, ATF 24-pt.

ABCDEFGHIJKLMNOPQRSTUVWXYZ
abcdefghijklmnopqrstuvwxyz
&$1234567890.,-:;'"!?

STYMIE EXTRABOLD, Mono 24-pt.

ABCDEFGHIJKLMNOPQRSTUVWXYZ
abcdefghijklmnopqrstuvwxyz
$1234567890&.,-:;'"!? $¢Aat

STYMIE EXTRABOLD ITALIC, Mono 24-pt.

ABCDEFGHIJKLMNOPQRSTUVWXYZ
abcdefghijklmnopqrstuvwxyz a
$¢$1234567890 [] (),.-;':'!?&

STYMIE EXTRABOLD CONDENSED, Mono 24-pt.

ABCDEFGHIJKLMNOPQRSTUVWXYZ A
abcdefghijklmnopqrstuvwxyz a 1234567890¢«»[](),.-;':'!?&

STYMIE INLINE TITLE, ATF 24-pt.

ABCDEFGHIJKLM& $$123 4 5 6 7 8
A A N O P Q R R S T U V W X Y Z

STYMIE INTAGLIO FIGURES, ATF 24-pt.

1234567890

STYMIE COMPRESSED, ATF (288-pt. at 11%)

ABCDEFGHIJKLMNOPQRSTUVWXYZ$1234567890&

STYMIE BOLD OPEN CONDENSED, Balto 24s

ABCDEFGHIJKLMNOPQRSTUVWXYZ&
.,-';:?!()¢$1234567890

298

in extra-large sizes. Some of the Stymies were cast up to 144-point, along with a number of other designs, but even that was not enough. *Stymie Compressed* was cast in 288-point from drawings by Wadsworth A. Parker, head of the ATF specimen department. This is believed to be the largest complete font ever cast in regular type molds. However, apparently there never was a 288-point mold. Instead, all characters are designed to cast the long way in smaller molds, from 30-point for the *I* to 144-point for the *W*, each 288 points "wide." Round letters were virtually flush to the edges of the body—4 inches high! Fonts included capitals, figures, and ampersand, with an undersize dollar mark on 120-point body; for punctuation marks the foundry recommended using available sizes of *Stymie Bold* or *Medium*. One type each of all 38 characters weighed about 47 pounds, and sold originally for $28.05. The cap *W* alone weighed about 2 pounds!

Stymie Stylus, the second largest type font, followed. It is an experimental font, with each character including lowercase cast on the minimum body with no unnecessary metal. There are five different body sizes in the one font, ranging from 96-point for lowercase letters without ascenders or descenders to 180-point for caps and 204-point for lowercase *j*. Like the previous face, these characters were cast sideways in smaller molds. Specimens said, "The letters justify quickly with point spacing material." This specimen has type bodies indicated for several letters. *!?)* were the only punctuation marks. And apparently this was the last of the giant faces produced.

Stymie Inline Title was designed by Parker about 1931; it follows the basic *Stymie Bold* pattern but is cast full face, without lowercase. ATF literature lists a *Stymie Open,* but no specimen or other evidence of it has been found. *Stymie Intaglio Figures* are the *Stymie Bold* design reversed on black squares. *Stymie Bold Open* as offered by Baltimore is a copy of *Beton Open* from Germany, while Baltimore's *Stymie Bold Open Condensed* is a modification by pantagraph of the same face, offered in 1948. *Stymie Shaded* or *Rockwell Shaded* as offered by some secondary sources is *Antique Shaded* (q.v.). ATF offered alternate condensed figures for *Stymie Bold,* but these were actually *Foster Condensed* (q.v.), with only a general similarity.

Sixty-point *Litho Antique* as cast by Inland was oversize by about 5 points. This peculiarity is carried over into members of the Stymie family—even on Monotype. But in some versions of ATF Stymie, 60-point after a time was replaced by 66/60-point, wherein descenders are cast on the larger body.

Compare *Beton, Cairo, Karnak, Memphis.*

288-pt STYMIE COMPRESSED (full size)

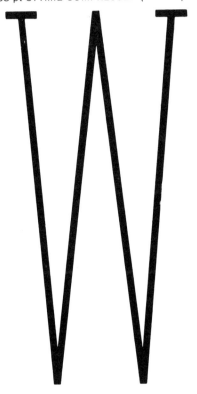

STYMIE STYLUS, ATF (combination sizes—see text—reduced)

299

SUBURBAN FRENCH, Mono 24-pt.

SUBURBAN FRENCH has many characteristics
Is A Book Typeface, But which make it the $67890

SUBURBAN FRENCH ITALIC, Mono 12-pt.

ABCDEFGHIJKLMNOPQRSTUVWXYZ&ÆŒ abcdefghijklmnopqrstuvwxyzæœ fiflffffiffl $1234567890 :;!?

SWAGGER CAPITALS, 36-pt. at 67%

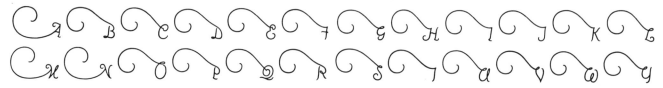

SYLPH INITIALS, Hansen 24-pt. (part reduced)

ABCDEFGHIJKLMNOPQRSTUVWXYZ &
1234567890

TABARD, 24-pt. (Herb Harnish)

ABCDEFGHIJKLMNOPQRSTUVWXYZ& $1234567890
abcdefghijklmnopqrstuvwxyz .,-:;'!? £Thbdefmnoprfy

TALLONE MAX FACTOR, Mono 14-pt. (regular descenders)

ABCDEFGHIJKLMNOPQRSTUVWXYZ&
abcdefghijklmnopqrstuvwxyz fffiffififlffl $1234567890 $1234567890 .,-:;'!?—% "" « »

ABCDEFGHIJKLMNOPQRSTUVWXYZ&
abcdefghijklmnopqrstuvwxyz fffiffififlffl $1234567890 $1234567890 .,-:;'!?« »

Name in parentheses after some specimens
indicates person who has set that specimen,
in whole or in part, to our format.

300

SUBURBAN FRENCH is one of Monotype's first independent recreations of faces from classic sources abroad. It was cut about 1911 at the suggestion of J. Horace MacFarland, prominent Pennsylvania printer, and was adapted to Monotype under the supervision of MacFarland and William Dana Orcutt, a well known typographer and book designer in New England. Its source is said to have been a Didot oldstyle first cut about 1804, but the Monotype face was first introduced under the name of *Bodoni Roman.* The double serifs at the top of lowercase vertical strokes are a distinguishing feature. Compare *French Round Face.*

Suburban French, Mono 172 (6-36pt)
Suburban French Italic, Mono 172G (6-12pt)

SWAGGER CAPITALS or *Swagger Initials* were designed by Carl S. Junge for BB&S in 1925. They are virtually monotone, with an elongated flourish on each of the letters, most of which are cursive in character. There are only twenty-four letters, without *X* or *Z*. The foundry promoted them as being usable as initials with various typefaces.

Swagger Capitals, BB&S (36pt)

SYLPH INITIALS as produced by Hansen include figures and ampersand, but they seem to have little practical use except as initials.

Sylph Initials, Hansen (10-60pt)

SYLVAN—see Imports in Appendix.

TABARD is an irregular face, designed by Lewis Buddy and shown by ATF in 1904 or earlier. It is generally similar to a number of other such faces popular at the time, but narrower, with long ascenders which are less than cap height. There is also less contrast between thick-and-thin strokes than most such faces. Compare *Roycroft, Schoeffer Oldstyle.*

Tabard, ATF (8-72pt)

TALISMAN—see *Rugged Bold.*

TALLONE MAX FACTOR was designed for the cosmetics manufacturer by Alberto Tallone and cut by Monotype in 1956. It is a crisp, contemporary face, with long ascenders and alternate long or short descenders, and both lining and hanging figures.

Tallone Max Factor and Italic, Mono 32-321 (8-14pt)

TANGIER—see Antiques in Appendix.
TANGO—see *Bernhard Tango.*
TASSO—see *Gothic Novelty Title.*
TAYLOR GOTHIC—see *Globe Gothic.*
TEA-CHEST—see Imports in Appendix.
TELL TEXT—see *Morris Romanized Black.*
TEMPLE SCRIPT—see Imports in Appendix.

TEMPO LIGHT, Ludlow 24-pt.

ABCDEFGHIJKLMNOPQRSTUVWXYZ.,-:;"'!?()&—
abcdefghijklmnopqrstuvwxyz $1234567890

TEMPO LIGHT ITALIC, Ludlow 24-pt.

ABCDEFGHIJKLMNOPQRSTUVWXYZ&
abcdefghijklmnopqrstuvwxyz 1234567890 $.,-:;"!?
ABCDEFGHIJKLMNOPQRSTUVWXYZ

TEMPO MEDIUM, Ludlow 24-pt.

ABCDEFGHIJKLMNOPQRSTUVWXYZ.,-:;"'!?&%()[]—+ ½¼⅓¾⅔
abcdefghijklmnopqrstuvwxyz 1234567890c Aa MNVWvw

TEMPO MEDIUM ITALIC, Ludlow 24-pt.

ABCDEFGHIJKLMNOPQRSTUVWXYZ&
abcdefghijklmnopqrstuvwxyz 1234567890 $.,-:;"!?()[]+—
ABCDEFGHIJKLMNOPQRSTUVWYZ
MNUVWadhilmntuvwy j

TEMPO MEDIUM CONDENSED, Ludlow 30-pt.

ABCDEFGHIJKLMNOPQRSTUVWXYZ&.:,;-`´!?()[]—+
abcdefghijklmnopqrstuvwxyz 1234567890 $ %

TEMPO BOLD, Ludlow 24-pt.

ABCDEFGHIJKLMNOPQRSTUVWXYZ.,-'':;!?+ a
abcdefghijklmnopqrstuvwxyz $1234567890%½¼¾

TEMPO BOLD ITALIC, Ludlow 24-pt.

ABCDEFGHIJKLMNOPQRSTUVWXYZ[](),.-;':'!?—&
abcdefghijklmnopqrstuvwxyz $1234567890

TEMPO BOLD CONDENSED, Ludlow 24-pt. (Herb Harnish)

ABCDEFGHIJKLMNOPQRSTUVWXYZ$1234567890&
abcdefghijklmnopqrstuvwxyz.,-:;"'!?%&—½¼¾⅓⅔ a +()[]

TEMPO is Ludlow's answer to the sans serifs which gained popularity in the late 1920s. The entire series was designed by R. Hunter Middleton, director of Ludlow's department of typeface design. The *Light, Medium,* and *Bold* weights were introduced in 1930, *Heavy* and several variations in 1931, and other variations over the next decade or more. They are generally a little different from other sans serifs, and include some innovations not found elsewhere. The most distinctive characteristics are found in the *Light Italic* and *Medium Italic,* which have a somewhat more calligraphic feeling and less stiff formality than other such faces, and which also offer alternate cursive capitals, rare in sans serifs.

But there are more inconsistencies in Tempo than most other families. For instance, the *Light, Medium, Bold,* and *Heavy Italics* are designed with a moderate slope of 10 degrees to fit straight matrices without too much gap between letters; this works well enough in the lighter weights, but produces a loose effect in the more rigid heavier weights. But the two largest sizes of *Tempo Bold Italic* and some of the other italics are designed to fit italic matrices with a slant of 17 degrees, which is rather excessive for sans serifs, especially the condensed versions, although it is handled well. Variant Oblique characters are available for *Medium Italic* which get away from the calligraphic feeling; only these and none of the cursive characters are made in

(Tempo continues)

Tempo Light, Ludlow 28-L (6-72pt)
Tempo Light Italic, Ludlow 28-LI (10-72pt)
Tempo Medium, Ludlow 28-M (6-72pt)
Tempo Medium Italic, Ludlow 28-MI (8-72pt)
Tempo Medium Condensed, Ludlow 28-MC (30-96pt)
Tempo Bold, Ludlow 28-B (6-72pt)
Tempo Bold Italic, Ludlow 28-BI (8-72pt)
Tempo Bold Condensed, Ludlow 28-BC (6-96pt)
Tempo Bold Condensed Italic, Ludlow 28-BCI (8-72pt)
Tempo Bold Extended, Ludlow 28-BE (10-48pt)
Tempo Heavy, Ludlow 28-H (6-96pt)
Tempo Heavy Italic, Ludlow 28-HI (12-72pt)
Tempo Heavy Condensed, Ludlow 28-HC (6-144pt)
Tempo Heavy Condensed Italic, Ludlow 28-HCI (8-72pt)

TEMPO BOLD CONDENSED ITALIC, Ludlow 24-pt.

ABCDEFGHIJKLMNOPQRSTUVWXYZ $1234567890
abcdefghijklmnopqrstuvwxyz.,- ":;!?—&+()[]½ ¼ ¾ ⅓ ⅔

TEMPO BOLD EXTENDED, Ludlow 24-pt. (part reduced)

ABCDEFGHIJKLMNOPQRSTUVWXY
abcdefghijklmnopqrstuvwxyz.,-:;"!?
Z&$1234567890

TEMPO HEAVY, Ludlow 24-pt.

ABCDEFGHIJKLMNOPQRSTUVWXYZ.,-:;"!?()[]%&
abcdefghijklmnopqrstuvwxyz 1234567890ᶜ a
AMNVWvw

TEMPO HEAVY ITALIC, Ludlow 24-pt.

ABCDEFGHIJKLMNOPQRSTUVWXYZ÷[](),.-;':'!?
abcdefghijklmnopqrstuvwxyz& $1234567890
½ ¼ ⅓ ⅔ ¾ %

TEMPO HEAVY CONDENSED, Ludlow 24-pt.

ABCDEFGHIJKLMNOPQRSTUVWXYZ [](),.-;`:'!?—& ¾⅔ ½¼⅓%
abcdefghijklmnopqrstuvwxyz $1234567890 ɑ A M N V W v w

TEMPO HEAVY CONDENSED ITALIC, Ludlow 24-pt.

ABCDEFGHIJKLMNOPQRSTUVWXYZ +[](),.-;':'!?—&
abcdefghijklmnopqrstuvwxyz $1234567890 ⅓¾⅔½¼%

TEMPO BLACK, Ludlow 24-pt.

ABCDEFGHIJKLMNOPQRSTUVWXYZ.,-:;"!?&
abcdefghijklmnopqrstuvwxyz$1234567890

TEMPO BLACK ITALIC, Ludlow 24-pt.

ABCDEFGHIJKLMNOPQRSTUVWXYZ&
abcdefghijklmnopqrstuvwxyz 12345678

TEMPO BLACK CONDENSED, Ludlow 24-pt.

ABCDEFGHIJKLMNOPQRSTUVWXYZ&
abcdefghijklmnopqrstuvwxyz 1234567890

TEMPO BLACK CONDENSED ITALIC, Ludlow 24-pt.

ABCDEFGHIJKLMNOPQRSTUVWXYZ& ½¼⅓¾⅔%
abcdefghijklmnopqrstuvwxyz 1234567890 G t

TEMPO BLACK EXTENDED, Ludlow 24-pt.

ABCDEFGHIJKLMNOPQRSTUVW
abcdefghijklmnopqrstuvwxyz.,-:;
XYZ"!?()[]&—+$1234567890½¼%
CGSacest

Regular characters; alternates in alphabets

TEMPO BLACK EXTENDED ITALIC, Ludlow 24-pt.

ABCDEFGHIJKLMNOPQRSTU
abcdefghijklmnopqrst 12345

304

the largest sizes. *Tempo Bold Extended* and *Black Extended* show the influence of other European grotesques, with much greater x-height and some characters unlike those in the normal and condensed widths.

There are a number of alternate characters for many of the Tempos, especially in the *Medium, Bold,* and *Heavy* weights; their use converts Tempo to an approximation of *Kabel* or other series. But a few alternates are not enough to create the effect of *Futura,* apparently demanded by some users, so *Tempo Alternate* was created in several weights, and introduced about 1960. This is close to *Futura,* except that the italic has Ludlow's 17-degree slant, much greater than *Futura's* usual 8 degrees. This family-within-a-family also has some alternate characters in some weights, to further convert the face into an approximation of other European grotesques. Tempo has been quite popular with newspapers, and to a lesser extent for general commercial printing. Compare *Futura, Sans Serif, Erbar,* etc. Also see *Umbra.*

TEMPO (other)—see *Agency Gothic.*

Tempo Black, Ludlow 28-EH (8-72pt)
Tempo Black Italic, Ludlow 28-EHI (14-72pt)
Tempo Black Condensed, Ludlow 28-EHC (12-96pt)
Tempo Black Condensed Italic, Ludlow 28-EHCI (18-72pt)
Tempo Black Extended, Ludlow 28-EHE (10-72pt)
Tempo Black Extended Italic, Ludlow 28-EHEI (12-48pt)
Tempo Heavy Inline, Ludlow 28-HN (18-48pt)
Tempo Alternate Medium,* Ludlow 28-AM (12-96pt)
Tempo Alternate Bold,* Ludlow 28-AB (6-96pt)
Tempo Alternate Bold Italic,* Ludlow 28-ABI (18-48pt)
Tempo Alternate Heavy,* Ludlow 28-AH (6-72pt)
*For comparable faces, see list at Futura.

TEMPO HEAVY INLINE, Ludlow 24-pt.

ABCDEFGHIJKLMNOPQRSTUVWXYZ&
1234567890$.: , ; - ' ' ! ? — ✚

TEMPO ALTERNATE MEDIUM, Ludlow 24-pt.

ABCDEFGHIJKLMNOPQRSTUVWXYZ&
abcdefghijklmnopqrstuvwxyz 1234567890

TEMPO ALTERNATE BOLD, Ludlow 24-pt.

ABCDEFGHIJKLMNOPQRSTUVWXYZ& $.,-:;"!?()%
abcdefghijklmnopqrstuvwxyz 1234567890

TEMPO ALTERNATE BOLD ITALIC, Ludlow 24-pt.

ABCDEFGHIJKLMNOPQRSTUVWXYZ& $.,-:;"!?()[]
abcdefghijklmnopqrstuvwxyz 1234567890

TEMPO ALTERNATE HEAVY, Ludlow 24-pt.

ABCDEFGHIJKLMNOPQRSTUVWXYZ& .,-:;"!?()[]·
abcdefghijklmnopqrstuvwxyz 1234567890

TEXTYPE & ITALIC, Lino 14-pt.

ABCDEFGHIJKLMNOPQRSTUVWXYZ& abcdefghijklmnopqrstuvwxyz fffiffiflffl
ABCDEFGHIJKLMNOPQRSTUVWXYZ $1234567890 .,-:;'!?()—*% " "
ABCDEFGHIJKLMNOPQRSTUVWXYZ&
abcdefghijklmnopqrstuvwxyz fffiffiflffl $1234567890 .,-:;'!?()

TEXTYPE BOLD & ITALIC, Lino 11-pt.

ABCDEFGHIJKLMNOPQRSTUVWXYZ& abcdefghijklmnopqrstuvwxyzfiflffffifl ($,.:;'-'?!*) 1234567890
ABCDEFGHIJKLMNOPQRSTUVWXYZ& *abcdefghijklmnopqrstuvwxyzfiflffffifl ($,.:;'-'?!*) 1234567890*

THERMOTYPE 100-200-300, ATF 24s; 200, 12-mid

INSTRUCTIONS REMARKING QUALITIES

A B C D E F G H I J K L M N O P Q R S ſ T U V W
X Y Z & $ I 2 3 4 5 6 7 8 9 0 . , - ' ' : ; ! ?

THOMPSON QUILLSCRIPT, ATF 24-pt.

ABCDEFGHIJKLMNOPQRSTUVWXYZ&.,-:;'!?$1234567890
abcdefghijklmnopqrstuvwxyz AAÆFHIJKLMNTVW&fh—""[]()≈/*

TIMES GOTHIC, 48-pt. at 50%

ABCDEF MINER RESIGN
abcd $123 Defective Miter

TIMES GOTHIC ITALIC, 36-pt. at 67%

GOVERNOR RESIGN
Member Questioned

TIMES ROMAN & ITALIC & BOLD, Lino 14-pt.

ABCDEFGHIJKLMNOPQRSTUVWXYZ& abcdefghijklmnopqrstuvwxyz fffiffiflffl
ABCDEFGHIJKLMNOPQRSTUVWXYZ $1234567890 .,-:;'!?()—*% " "
ABCDEFGHIJKLMNOPQRSTUVWXYZ&
abcdefghijklmnopqrstuvwxyz fffiffiflffl $1234567890 .,-:;'!?()
ABCDEFGHIJKLMNOPQRSTUVWXYZ&
abcdefghijklmnopqrstuvwxyz $1234567890 .,-:;'!?()

TIMES NEW ROMAN BOLD ITALIC, Ludlow 24-pt.

ABCDEFGHIJKLMNOPQRSTUVWXYZ&
abcdefghijklmnopqrstuvwxyz 1234567890

TIMES NEW ROMAN HEAVY, Ludlow 24-pt.

ABCDEFGHIJKLMNOPQRSTUVWXY
abcdefghijklmnopqrstuvwxyz 1234

TEXTYPE was designed in 1929 by C. H. Griffith for Linotype. Although intended as a newspaper face, *Textype* with its smaller x-height and longer ascenders than most newspaper faces also became popular for magazines and other publications, as well as for a certain amount of advertising and general printing. There is an 18-point size in roman with italic, also a bold and bold italic. The 18-point size and the bold italic are both rare in newspaper faces. Compare *Excelsior, Ionic, Rex,* etc.

Textype and Italic, Lino (6-18pt)
Textype Bold and Italic, Lino (6-12pt)

THERMO TYPES were designed by Morris F. Benton in 1931 for ATF. They may be said to carry the idea of the Alternate Gothics a step further, with three widths of the same basic design that may be selected to fit the requirements of various layouts. But while the Alternates are intended to be selected only as complete faces, the *Thermo Types* (or *Thermotypes*) are designed so that individual characters can be substituted, without the differences being obvious. The narrow, normal, and wide versions are known as the 100, 200, and 300 series respectively. By 1938 they had been discontinued.

Thermo 100, ATF 548 (6s-24L)
Thermo 200, ATF 549 (6s-24L)
Thermo 300, ATF 550 (6s-24L)

THIRTY-EIGHT-E—see *Goudy Light Old Style.*

THOMPSON QUILLSCRIPT was designed by Tommy Thompson for ATF about 1952. It is an attractive cursive letter with the appearance of lettering with a broad pen. Letters slope moderately and are not joining. The general effect is less formal than most other such faces. Capitals are rather reserved, but a font of alternate characters, mostly more informal capitals, was available separately until 1968. Compare *Heritage, Lydian Cursive, Park Avenue, Raleigh Cursive.*

Thompson Quillscript, ATF 700 (14-48pt)

THORNE SHADED, THOROWGOOD—see Imports in Appendix.
THUNDERBIRD—see Antiques in Appendix.
TIFFANY GOTHIC, TIFFANY SCRIPT, TIFFANY TEXT, etc.—see *Typo Series.*
TIME SCRIPT—see Imports in Appendix.

TIMES GOTHIC and *Italic* were shown by ATF early in the century. They are wide and moderately heavy, with the italic, especially in lowercase, appearing to be not quite as heavy as the upright face. They have some nineteenth-century characteristics, but generally are more carefully cut. On the other hand, curved strokes are cut off horizontally, a characteristic of much more recent faces, and in fact some letters could almost be mistaken for members of the *Helvetica* family. They are likewise almost monotone, but are loosely fitted.

Times Gothic, ATF 389 (6-96pt); Inter (5½pt); (Univ 6-72pt)
Times Gothic Italic, ATF 390 (6-96pt)

TIMES ROMAN or *Times New Roman* was designed under the direction of Stanley Morison for the *Times* of London in 1932, breaking away from traditional newspaper types and establishing a new style, derived from French oldstyle faces but with more contrast and a sharper appearance. It is more compact than most previous newspaper faces, with small, pointed serifs, and was developed through much preliminary optical research.

By 1942 it had come to America, where it was adopted as a text face for several magazines, and from there went on to become popular for advertising work, both as a text face and a display face. Within a few years it was cut for all the composing machines, along with bold and italics. Ludlow added *Times New Roman Heavy.* It continues to rank as one of the most popular text faces. On English Monotype, incidentally, it is made from 4¼- to 72-point. Also see *Classified.*

Times New Roman, Mono 362E (6-12pt); Ludlow 54-L (6-72pt); Times Roman, Lino (5½-24pt); Inter (10pt)
Times New Roman Italic, Mono 362G (6-12pt); Ludlow 54-LI (6-72pt); Times Roman Italic, Lino (5½-14pt); Inter (10pt)
Times New Roman Bold, Mono 57J (6-12pt); Ludlow 54-B (6-72pt); Times Bold, Lino (5½-24pt)
Times New Roman Bold Italic, Mono 57K (6-12pt); Ludlow 54-BI (10-72pt)
Times New Roman Heavy, Ludlow 54-H (18-48pt)
English Monotype also has Times New Roman Wide & Italic, Semi-Bold, Titling.

TIPPECANOE & ITALIC, Lino 12-pt.

ABCDEFGHIJKLMNOPQRSTUVWXYZ abcdefghijklmnopqrstuvwxyz (,.:;?"'!
ABCDEFGHIJKLMNOPQRSTUVWXYZ abcdefghijklmnopqrstuvwxyz (,.:;?"'!

TITLE, Mono 28J 10-pt.

ABCDEFGHIJKLMNOPQRSTUVWXYZ&ÆŒ
abcdefghijklmnopqrstuvwxyzæœ fiflffffiffl
$1234567890 .,-'':;!?

TOKIO (ROMANTIC, Universal) 24-pt. (Herb Harnish)

ABCDEFGHIJKLMNOPQRSTUVWXYZ
abcdefghijklmnopqrstuvwxyz.,-:;'!?()£/$&
1234567890

TORY TEXT, Village 24-pt. (Dave Norton)

ABCDEFGHIJKLMNOPQRSTUVWXYZ&
abcdefghijklmnopqrstuvwxyzfffiflffiffllctftTh.,/:;'!?1234567890

TOURIST GOTHIC, Mono 24-pt.

ABCDEFGHIJKLMNOPQRSTUVWXYZ& ACEEFGJKMNRSWXY
abcdefghijklmnopqrstuvwxyz $1234567890 .,-:;'!?

TOURIST GOTHIC ITALIC, Mono 24-pt.

ABCDEFGHIJKLMNOPQRSTUVWXYZ&
abcdefghijklmnopqrstuvwxyz $1234567890 .,-:;'!?

TOWER, ATF 24-pt.

ABCDEFGHIJKLMNOPQRSTUVWXYZ&
abcdefghijklmnopqrstuvwxyz $1234567890 '.,-:;'!?

308

TIPPECANOE was an experimental face designed in 1944-46 by William A. Dwiggins for Mergenthaler, on the Bodoni-Didot theme. It was used in a book by Elizabeth Coatsworth, a friend of Dwiggins, *The Creaking Stair,* published in 1949 by Coward-McCann. Compare *Louvaine Bold.*

Tippecanoe and Italic, Lino (12pt) experimental

"TITLE" has several connotations in the terminology of type. Through the nineteenth century, "Title" was commonly applied to bold heading faces, usually romans, even down to very small sizes for subheads with small text sizes. Hansen's *Title Condensed No. 75* is virtually a duplicate of the BB&S *Modern Roman Bold Condensed* (q.v.). Except for a surviving Monotype face, other such faces are not included here, but some machine-set faces are shown under other names, as follows: *Title No. 1*—see *Cushing Oldstyle. Title No. 2*—see *DeVinne. Title No. 4*—see *DeVinne Recut. Title No. 5*—see *Laureate;* also *Modern Roman Medium. Title Italic*—see *DeVinne Italic. Title Italic No. 10*—see *Modern Roman Italic.* Also see other Modern Romans. *Title Litho Shaded*—see under *Litho Roman.*

Title, Mono 28J (5½-12pt)

More recently the name has been applied to faces without lowercase, having capitals and figures cast nearly full size on the body; these are now almost exclusively gothics, although romans were often cast this way until early in the century. Such faces that have lasted until more recent years are included in this book as secondary to their cap-and-lowercase counterparts, if any, but are cross-referenced if the name is substantially different.

TOKIO was a rather bizarre novelty face issued by Hansen early in the century. It was copied as *Romantic* by the Universal Typefoundry in Hong Kong, the source of the specimen shown here.

Tokio, Hansen (24-48pt); (Romantic, Univ 18-72pt)

TOMBSTONE—see *Jim Crow.*
TOPIC—see *World Gothic;* also Imports in Appendix.
TORCH—see *Flamme* under Imports in Appendix.
TORINO—see Imports in Appendix.

TORY TEXT was a frankly archaic type designed and produced by Frederic W. Goudy in 1935. For a small edition of a twelfth-century story which he intended to print, Goudy chose a sixteenth-century type design to express the qualities he had in mind. This was redrawn in an attempt to make it more legible for modern readers while retaining the ancient spirit. Goudy describes *Tory Text* as one of his favorite types, and says that he enjoyed every minute of its making. See *Village Text.*

Tory Text, Goudy, private (12-24pt)

TOURIST GOTHIC is a Monotype copy of *Modern Condensed Gothic* (q.v.), with a set of several round alternate caps designed by Sol Hess in 1928. (Sizes under 14-point continued under the *Modern Condensed Gothic* name, without the alternates.) In 1938 Hess drew a matching *Tourist Gothic Italic,* which added to the popularity of the face, although it lacks the round characters.

The *Outline Gothic Medium Condensed* (or *Franklin Gothic Condensed Outline*) from some sources is actually an open version of *Tourist Gothic. Tourist Extra Condensed* of Baltimore Type is a copy of *Phenix* (q.v.) in 24- to 48-point sizes, and is *Jefferson Gothic* (q.v.) in larger sizes.

Tourist Gothic, Mono 140 (14-72H4—see text)
Tourist Gothic Italic, Mono 1401 (14-72pt)
Tourist Extra Condensed, Balto 902 (24-72—see text)
Outline Gothic Medium Condensed, Triangle (18-48pt)

TOWER was designed by Morris F. Benton for ATF in 1934. It is similar to *Stymie Medium Condensed* (q.v.), but with straight sides to the round letters, emphasizing the vertical appearance. The name suggests its tallness and slimness, and it is at home with the *Stymie* series. *Tower Bold* was undertaken by the same designer in 1936, but abandoned in favor of *Stymie Bold Condensed. Tower Italic* was designed but not cast.

Tower, ATF 587 (12-72pt)

TRADE GOTHIC & BOLD, Lino 14-pt.

ABCDEFGHIJKLMNOPQRSTUVWXYZ&ÆŒ
ABCDEFGHIJKLMNOPQRSTUVWXYZ&ÆŒ
abcdefghijklmnopqrstuvwxyzæœfifflffiffl [($.,-'':;!?¡¿– —)] 1234567890
abcdefghijklmnopqrstuvwxyzæœfifflffiffl [($.,-'':;!?¡¿– —)] 1234567890

TRADE GOTHIC CONDENSED & BOLD CONDENSED, Lino 14-pt.

ABCDEFGHIJKLMNOPQRSTUVWXYZ 1234567890
ABCDEFGHIJKLMNOPQRSTUVWXYZ& 1234567890
abcdefghijklmnopqrstuvwxyz fiflfffffiffl&$?!%.,:;"-()[]ÆŒæœ/‡†
abcdefghijklmnopqrstuvwxyz fiflfffffiffl$%!?.,:;"-()[]ÆŒæœ‡†

TRADE GOTHIC EXTRA CONDENSED & BOLD EXTRA CONDENSED, Lino 14-pt.

ABCDEFGHIJKLMNOPQRSTUVWXYZ&ÆŒ   1234567890$£,.:;'-'?!-|—   ...0*†‡¶§[]%
ABCDEFGHIJKLMNOPQRSTUVWXYZ&ÆŒ   1234567890$£,.:;'-'?!-|—...   0*†‡¶§[]%
abcdefghijklmnopqrstuvwxyzæœfiflfffffiffl ⅛¼⅜½⅝¾⅞⅓⅔...
abcdefghijklmnopqrstuvwxyzæœfiflfffffiffl ⅛¼⅜½⅝¾⅞⅓⅔...

TRADE GOTHIC EXTENDED & BOLD EXTENDED, Lino 14-pt.

ABCDEFGHIJKLMNOPQRSTUVWXYZ& ()*@℔†‡¶§/[]%
ABCDEFGHIJKLMNOPQRSTUVWXYZ& ()*@℔†‡¶§/[]%
abcdefghijklmnopqrstuvwxyzfiflfffffiffl 1234567890$£,.:;'-'?! —
abcdefghijklmnopqrstuvwxyzfiflfffffiffl 1234567890$£,.:;'-'?! —

TRADE GOTHIC LIGHT & ITALIC, Lino 14-pt.

ABCDEFGHIJKLMNOPQRSTUVWXYZ ·$1234567890
abcdefghijklmnopqrstuvwxyz ff fi ffi fl ffl []%(),.-;':'!?–& ⅛ ¼ ⅜ ½ ⅝ ¾ ⅞ ⅓ ⅔
ABCDEFGHIJKLMNOPQRSTUVWXYZ $1234567890
abcdefghijklmnopqrstuvwxyz ff fi ffi fl ffl []%(),.-;':'!?–& ⅛ ¼ ⅜ ½ ⅝ ¾ ⅞ ⅓ ⅔

TRAFTON SCRIPT, 24-pt.

ABCDEFGHIJKLMNOPQRSTUVWXYZ&
abcdefghijklmnopqrstuvwxyz $1234567890 .,–:;'!?()""

TRAJAN TITLE, Village 24-pt. (Dave Norton)

ABCDEFGHIJKLMNOPQ·RSTUVWXYZ&
1234567890.,-'

TRADE GOTHIC is a Linotype family of gothics designed by Jackson Burke, and is basically very nearly the same as *News Gothic*. An early face on that machine was *Gothic No. 18*, which in small sizes was like a nineteenth-century face, but in large sizes was essentially the same as *News Gothic Condensed*. In 1948, with the return to popularity of American gothics after European sans serifs had replaced them for a while, the small sizes were recut to match the larger ones, and all were paired with *Gothic No. 20*, an adaptation of *Alternate Gothic No. 2*. The following year more condensed versions of both weights were offered as *Gothic No. 17* and *19*. The bolder weight was very similar to *Alternate Gothic No. 1*, but the lighter weight retained its round-sided design, unlike *News Gothic Extra Condensed*.

As the popularity of these faces continued to grow, Linotype changed the name to *Trade Gothic Condensed* and *Extra Condensed*, with their bold faces, and in 1955 added *Trade Gothic* and *Trade Gothic Bold* in normal widths. The light or regular weight is virtually the same as *News Gothic*, but the bold weight has flat sides on its round letters, making it a wider version of *Alternate Gothic*, unlike the *News Gothic Bold* developed about the same time by Intertype and a little later by other sources. (In a 1977 Linotype specimen book, the names reverted to *Gothic Nos. 17 to 20*.)

Trade Gothic Extended and *Bold Extended* were announced early in 1959; for this bold weight the flat sides finally gave way to round sides, more like the *News Gothics* from other sources. Compare *Monotone Gothic*, which is essentially a wide version of *News Gothic*. In 1962 the last of this family appeared as *Trade Gothic Light* and *Italic*, the upright face being similar to *Lightline Gothic*. Unfortunately, *Trade Gothic* regular had been called *Light* (in distinction from its bold mate) in some Linotype literature, leading to some confusion when the actually lighter version appeared later.

Altogether it has been a very popular and widely used series. Compare *News Gothic, Alternate Gothic, Monotone Gothic, Lightline Gothic;* also *Record Gothic.*

Trade Gothic and Bold, Lino (4½-18pt)
Trade Gothic Condensed and Bold Condensed, or Gothic 18 and 20, Lino (6-24pt)
Trade Gothic Extra Condensed and Bold Extra Condensed, or Gothic 17 and 19, Lino (6-36, 6-24pt)
Trade Gothic Extended and Bold Extended, Lino (6-14pt)
Trade Gothic Light and Italic, Lino (6-14pt)

TRAFTON SCRIPT was designed by Howard Allen Trafton, New York artist and designer, in 1933, and cut by Bauer Type Foundry in Germany. It is a delicate script with letters not quite connected, having large, flourished capitals and small lowercase with long ascenders and descenders. It has a crisp, precise appearance, but is not rigidly formal. Early advertising paired it with light monotone romans, but it is more at home with modern or transitional faces, and is one of the more popular contemporary scripts. Compare *Coronet.*

Trafton Script, Bauer (14-84pt)

TRAJAN TITLE was designed by Frederic W. Goudy in 1930 to fulfill a commission to print a list of subscribers to the building of the community house in his old home town of Forest Hills Gardens, Long Island. The previous year, Goudy had lettered the principal line on the title page of a limited edition of *Rip Van Winkle,* for which he had designed the typeface *Kaatskill* (q.v.). Now he completed that alphabet, feeling that it would be ideal for this purpose.

Goudy calls this one of his favorite designs, and it is indeed an impressive inscriptional style of letter. It is based on letters inscribed at the base of the Trajan Column at Rome, erected about 114 A.D., but not copied slavishly. He cut several sizes, and states that it has been widely used. English and Continental rights were sold to the English Monotype Company.

Trajan Title, Goudy (12-48pt)

TRAJANUS, (30-pt. at 80%) (Guy Botterill)

ABCDEFGHIJKLMNOPQRSTUVWXYZ
abcdefghijklmnopqrstuvwxyz&⟨$1234567890fffifl.,-:;!?'""

TRAJANUS ITALIC, (30-pt. at 80%)

ABCDEFGHIJKLMNOPQRSTUVWXYZ
abcdefghijklmnopqrstuvwxyz e&&⚡$1234567890

TRAJANUS BOLD, (30-pt. at 80%)

ABCDEFGHIJKLMNOPQRSTUVWXYZ
abcdefghijklmnopqrstuvwxyz&⚡$1234567890

TREND, Balto 24-pt.

ABCDEFGHIJKLMNOPQRSTUVWXYZ& $1234567890
abcdefghijklmnopqrstuvwxyz.,-;:''!?$%Th

TRENHOLM OLDSTYLE, BB&S, 18-pt.

A B C D E F G H I J K L M N O P Q R S T U V W X Y Z &
a b c d e f g h i j k l m n o p q r s t u v w x y z . , : ; - ' – ! ?
$ 1 2 3 4 5 6 7 8 9 0 ⁊ ¶ { }

TRENHOLM CURSIVE, BB&S 18-pt.

A B C D E F G H I J K L M N O P Q R S T U V W X Y Z
a b c d e f g h i j k l m n o p q r s t u v w x y z fi fl ff ffi ffl
& $ 1 2 3 4 5 6 7 8 9 0 — . , ; : - ' ! ? ⟨⟨

TRENHOLM SHADED CAPS & TRENHOLM BOLD, BB&S 24-pt.

Trenholm Shaded Capitals **Trenholm Bold**

TRUESDELL, Village 16-pt. (Dave Norton)

ABCDEHIJMORSTUabcdefghijklmnopqrstuvwxyzfiflffi1234590.,-:;'?

TRUESDELL ITALIC, Village 16-pt.

A B C D E F G H I J K L M N O P Q R S T U V W X Y Z & A B C D E G K L P R
a b c d e f g h i j k l m n o p q r s t u v w x y z v y fi ff fl ffl ct st . , ' ; : ! ? - T U W Y Th ⚡

TRYLON SHADED, Balto 24-pt.

ABCDEFGHIJKLMNOPQRSTUVWXYZ $1234567890°.,-:;""!?&

TRAJANUS was designed by Warren Chappell, New York illustrator and letterer, in 1939, and cast by Stempel in Germany. It has the basic form of classic Venetian letters, but with a nervous, pen-drawn, contemporary quality. Ascenders are fairly long but descenders are short. The narrow italic lowercase shows a calligraphic quality in particular. There is an extra little flick of the pen at the end of crossbars of *f* and *t;* caps *M* and *N* have no serifs on their apexes; and cap *U* is lowercase in form. *Trajanus* is named for the Roman emperor whose accomplishments are immortalized in classic letters on the Trajan column. The three versions are also made by German Linotype, but have not received much attention in America.

Trajanus, Stempel (6-48pt)
Trajanus Kursiv or Italic, Stempel (6-48pt)
Trajanus Halbfett or Bold, Stempel (6-48pt)

TREND is a brush-lettered face cut by Baltimore in 1953. It is very similar to *Dom Casual* (q.v.), but has a slight back slant.

Trend, Baltimore 573 (24-72pt)

TRENHOLM is an oldstyle type family designed by George F. Trenholm, Boston artist and designer, for BB&S. That company's specimen book of 1925 shows the series as being in preparation, but it was 1927 before the roman and bold were advertised as being completed, and at that time the *Cursive* was still being cut. In 1928 the *Shaded Capitals* were still listed as being cut. In 1929 BB&S was merged with ATF, and no evidence that this series was cast by ATF after that time has been found, although matrices were later listed in ATF's vaults.

The roman and bold were rather conventional oldstyle designs, with sharply inclined serifs on the top of lowercase strokes, but no great distinction. The cursive was a mixture of that and italic, with no serifs at the top of ascenders. Cursive caps were distinctly that, and the shaded capitals even more so. Perhaps the series would have been successful if it had been available for a longer time, but it quickly became a rarity.

Trenholm Oldstyle, BB&S-ATF 1886 (6-72pt)
Trenholm Cursive, BB&S-ATF 1885 (6-48pt)
Trenholm Bold, BB&S-ATF 1884 (6-96pt)
Trenholm Shaded Capitals, BB&S-ATF 1887 (12-48pt)

TROCADERO—see Antiques in Appendix.
TROY—see *Morris Romanized Black*.
TRUE-CUT BODONI, CASLON, etc.—see under *Bodoni, Caslon,* etc.

TRUESDELL and *Italic* were designed and cut by Frederic W. Goudy in 1930-31, for setting a prefatory note he had written to an article to appear in "The Colophon." The article itself was set in Goudy's *Mediaeval.* Truesdell was his mother's maiden name.

Truesdell, Goudy (16pt)
Truesdell Italic, Goudy (16pt)

TRUMP—see Imports in Appendix.

TRYLON as made by Baltimore Type was a 1949 copy of Stephenson Blake's *Playbill* (see Imports in Appendix), but *Trylon Shaded* and *Trylon Shaded Oblique* were designed and cut by George Battee of the Baltimore foundry. The solid version has lowercase in some sizes; it is somewhat similar to *P. T. Barnum,* with greatly exaggerated horizontal strokes and serifs at top and bottom, but is heavier and narrower. The *Shaded* versions are more properly outlines of the same design, with a small shadow effect at the top (which is unusual) and right of each letter, but without lowercase.

Trylon, Baltimore 801 (24-84/72pt)
Trylon Shaded, Baltimore 821 (24-72pt)
Trylon Shaded Oblique, Baltimore 8211 (24-72pt)

TRYLON SHADED OBLIQUE, Balto 24-pt.

ABCDEFGHIJKLMNOPQRSTUVW& $1234567890.,-''"",;:!?''§""

TUDOR BLACK, BB&S 20L/24-pt.

ABCDEFGHIJKLMNOPQRSTUVWXYZ& Th I M

abcdefghijklmnopqrstuvwxyz $1234567890 .,=:;'!? N

TUDOR MEDIUM & ITALIC, 24-pt.

This is the FO *Also in the IT*

TWENTIETH CENTURY LIGHT, Mono 24-pt.

ABCDEFGHIJKLMNOPQRSTUVWXYZ

abcdefghijklmnopqrstuvwxyzfifffl 1234567890(&$.,-'':;!?)

TWENTIETH CENTURY LIGHT ITALIC, Mono 24-pt.

ABCDEFGHIJKLMNOPQRSTUVWXYZ&

abcdefghijklmnopqrstuvwxyz $1234567890 .,-:;'!? ()

TWENTIETH CENTURY SEMI-MEDIUM & ITALIC, Mono 12-pt.

ABCDEFGHIJKLMNOPQRSTUVWXYZ&   *ABCDEFGHIJKLMNOPQRSTUVWXYZ&*

abcdefghijklmnopqrstuvwxyz   fiflff   *abcdefghijklmnopqrstuvwxyz   fiflff*

$1234567890   .,-'':;!?()   *$1234567890   .,-'':;!?()*

TWENTIETH CENTURY MEDIUM, Mono 24-pt.

ABCDEFGHIJKLMNOPQRSTUVWXYZ ⅛⅙¼⅓⅜½⅝⅔¾⅞

abcdefghijklmnopqrstuvwxyzfifffl 1234567890(&$.,-''':;!?)

TWENTIETH CENTURY MEDIUM ITALIC, Mono 24-pt.

ABCDEFGHIJKLMNOPQRSTUVWXYZ

abcdefghijklmnopqrstuvwxyzfifffl 1234567890(&$.,-':;!?)

TWENTIETH CENTURY MEDIUM CONDENSED, Mono 24-pt.

ABCDEFGHIJKLMNOPQRSTUVWXYZabcdefghijklmnopqrstuvwxyzfifffl1234567890&$.,-:;'!?

TWENTIETH CENTURY MEDIUM CONDENSED ITALIC, Mono 24-pt.

ABCDEFGHIJKLMNOPQRSTUVWXYZ&

abcdefghijklmnopqrstuvwxyz $1234567890'".,-:;'!?()

TUDOR BLACK is a nineteenth-century face that was cut by many founders. D. B. Updike, in his monumental *Printing Types,* says it was cut for Miller & Richard, the former Scottish foundry, recalling round italic gothic types. It appeared in this country in 1889 or earlier, with no distinction between the caps *I* and *J* until about 1900. The modernized capitals *HIMN* were first shown in 1906.

Tudor Black [No. 2], ATF 310 (6-72pt); Tudor Black No. 3, Hansen (6-48pt); Tudor Black, Keystone (6-72pt); (Univ 6-48pt)
Tudor Black Outline, Keystone (12-72pt)
Tudor Black Condensed, Keystone (12-48pt)
Tudor Black is known as Gotico Neretta in Italy.

TUDOR MEDIUM was designed by Charles Tudor for *Life* magazine, and privately cut by Monotype, in the mid-1950s. It is derived from *News Gothic,* but slightly heavier and showing some influence of German grotesques. The upright was cut in a wide range of sizes, but the italic was made only in a few display sizes.

Tudor Medium, Mono (5-60pt) private
Tudor Medium Italic, Mono (16-30pt) private

TUDORESQUE—see *Ecclesiastic* under Antiques in Appendix.
TUSCAN—see Antiques in Appendix.

TWENTIETH CENTURY is Monotype's copy of *Futura* (q.v.), and in display sizes is essentially an exact copy, while composition sizes are only slightly modified. Several additional versions were drawn for Monotype by Sol Hess, including *Twentieth Century Bold Italic* and *Extrabold Italic* in 1937, *Extrabold Condensed Italic* in 1938, *Ultrabold* in 1941, *Ultrabold Condensed* in 1944, and *Medium Condensed Italic* and *Ultrabold Italic* in 1947. Some of these weights have different names than their counterparts in the original *Futura* series or other copies; see the list under *Futura* for comparison of these names as well as technical data.

Twentieth Century Light, Mono 606 (6-72pt)
Twentieth Century Light Italic, Mono 6061 (6-72pt)
Twentieth Century Semi-Medium, Mono 613 (6-12pt)
Twentieth Century Semi-Medium Italic 613K (6-12pt)
Twentieth Century Medium, Mono 605 (6-72pt)

(Twentieth Century continues)

TWENTIETH CENTURY BOLD, Mono 24-pt.

ABCDEFGHIJKLMNOPQRSTUVWXYZ ⅛⅙¼⅓⅜½⅝⅔¾
abcdefghijklmnopqrstuvwxyzfifffl 1234567890(&$.,-":;!?'"/$)

TWENTIETH CENTURY BOLD ITALIC, Mono 24-pt.

ABCDEFGHIJKLMNOPQRSTUVWXYZ&
abcdefghijklmnopqrstuvwxyz $1234567890 .,-:;'!?()''

TWENTIETH CENTURY BOLD CONDENSED, Mono 24-pt.

ABCDEFGHIJKLMNOPQRSTUVWXYZ&
abcdefghijklmnopqrstuvwxyz $1234567890 .,-:;"!?( )—%

TWENTIETH CENTURY EXTRABOLD, Mono 24-pt.

ABCDEFGHIJKLMNOPQRSTUVWXYZ
abcdefghijklmnopqrstuvwxyz1234567890&$.,-':;!?

TWENTIETH CENTURY EXTRABOLD ITALIC, Mono 24-pt.

ABCDEFGHIJKLMNOPQRSTUVWXYZ&
abcdefghijklmnopqrstuvwxyz $1234567890 '.,-:;'!?()

TWENTIETH CENTURY EXTRABOLD CONDENSED, Mono 24-pt.

ABCDEFGHIJKLMNOPQRSTUVWXYZ&
abcdefghijklmnopqrstuvwxyz $1234567890 '.,-:;'!?()—%

TWENTIETH CENTURY EXTRABOLD CONDENSED ITALIC, Mono 24-pt.

ABCDEFGHIJKLMNOPQRSTUVWXYZ&
abcdefghijklmnopqrstuvwxyz $1234567890 '.,-:;'!?()

TWENTIETH CENTURY ULTRABOLD, Mono 24-pt.

ABCDEFGHIJKLMNOPQRSTUVWXYZ&.,-:;''!?()
abcdefghijklmnopqrstuvwxyz $1234567890

TWENTIETH CENTURY ULTRABOLD ITALIC, Mono 24-pt.

ABCDEFGHIJKLMNOPQRSTUVWXYZ&.,-:;''!?()
abcdefghijklmnopqrstuvwxyz $1234567890

TWENTIETH CENTURY ULTRABOLD CONDENSED, Mono 24-pt.

ABCDEFGHIJKLMNOPQRSTUVWXYZ&
abcdefghijklmnopqrstuvwxyz $1234567890 '.,-:;'!?()—%

TWENTIETH CENTURY ULTRABOLD CONDENSED ITALIC, Mono 24-pt.

ABCDEFGHIJKLMNOPQRSTUVWXYZ&
abcdefghijklmnopqrstuvwxyz $1234567890 '.,-:;'!?()

Twentieth Century Medium Italic, Mono 6051 (6-72pt)

Twentieth Century Medium Condensed, Mono 608 (10-72pt)

Twentieth Century Medium Condensed Italic, Mono 6081 (10-36pt)

Twentieth Century Bold, Mono 604 (6-72pt)

Twentieth Century Bold Italic, Mono 6041 (6-72pt)

Twentieth Century Bold Condensed, Mono 612 (14-36pt)

Twentieth Century Extrabold, Mono 603 (6-72pt)

Twentieth Century Extrabold Italic, Mono 6031 (6-72pt)

Twentieth Century Extrabold Condensed, Mono 607 (8-72H4)

Twentieth Century Extrabold Condensed Italic, Mono 6071 (8-72H4)

Twentieth Century Ultrabold, Mono 609 (8-72pt)

Twentieth Century Ultrabold Italic, Mono 6091 (8-72pt)

Twentieth Century Ultrabold Condensed, Mono 610 (8-72pt)

Twentieth Century Ultrabold Condensed Italic, Mono 6101 (14-72pt)

Twentieth Century Ultrabold Extended, Mono 614 (14-48pt)

For comparable faces, see list at Futura.

TYPEWRITER FACES. The faces of many typewriter manufacturers were cut in type by most founders and composing-machine companies, to enable the printer to produce form letters which simulated typewriting before the days of photo-offset printing and photocopying machines—in fact before typewriters and ribbons yielded results that would reproduce well even under present conditions. Typical fonts are shown here, but it is not practical to show all the reproductions. The list below includes typical faces from major sources, but does not attempt to be comprehensive. Also see *Bulletin Typewriter, Giant Typewriter, Goudy Remington Typewriter, Jumbo Typewriter.*

American Typewriter, ATF 11 (6,10pt)

Barnhart Utility Typewriter, BB&S-ATF 1894

Burroughs O2 Elite Typewriter, Mono 271L (10pt)

Improved Typewriter, BB&S-ATF 1895

Mailing List Typewriter, Mono 74L (8,10pt)

Oliver Typewriter, ATF 146, 344 (10pt)

Oliver Printype Typewriter, ATF 343, BB&S-ATF 1897; Mono 259L (12pt)

Oliver Standard Silk Typewriter, BB&S-ATF 1898

Remington Typewriter, ATF 297, 929 (12pt); BB&S-ATF 1899, 1901; Mono 70L (10,12,24pt)

Remington Underscored, Mono 370L (10,12pt)

Remington Typewriter with Underscore, Lino=Inter (8-12pt)

Remington Noiseless Elite Typewriter, Mono 471L (10pt)

Remington Noiseless Elite Underscored, Mono 571L (10pt)

Remington Ribbon Typewriter, Mono 17L (11pt)

New Model Remington Typewriter, ATF 333, 334, 925 (10,12pt)

Silk Remington Typewriter, ATF 383 (12pt); BB&S-ATF 1900

Silk Remington Underscored Typewriter, ATF 455

Remington Standard Typewriter, ATF 615

Reproducing Typewriter, ATF 367 (6-10pt); Mono 72L (6-12pt)

Reproducing Underscored, Mono 372L (6-12pt)

Reproducing Bold Typewriter (Broadface), Mono 572L (8pt)

Reproduction Typewriter, BB&S-ATF 1902 (8pt)

Ribbon-Face Typewriter, ATF 368 (12pt)

Royal Typewriter, Mono 272L (10,12pt)

Royal Underscored, Mono 472L (10,12pt)

New Royal Typewriter, Mono 171L (10pt)

New Royal Typewriter Underscored, Mono 671L (10pt)

Smith Premier Typewriter, ATF 306, 622, 928; Mono 170L (12pt)

New Model Smith Premier Typewriter, ATF 335, 336

Smith Premier Silk Typewriter, BB&S-ATF 1903 (12pt)

Standard Typewriter, ATF 384 (12pt)

Tariff Typewriter with Bold, Lino (8pt)

Underwood Typewriter, ATF 205, 216 (10,12pt); Mono 270L (10,12pt)

New Model Underwood Typewriter, ATF 337 (12pt)

Underwood New Model Silk Typewriter, BB&S-ATF 1904 (12pt)

Underwood Underscored, Mono 470L (10,12pt)

Underwood Typewriter with Underscore, Lino=Inter (10,12pt)

Underwood Bold Typewriter, Ludlow 23-UB (10pt)

Victoria Underwood Typewriter, ATF 410 (12pt)

Yost Typewriter, BB&S-ATF 1768

TWENTIETH CENTURY ULTRABOLD EXTENDED, Mono 24-pt.

ABCDEFGHIJKLMNOPQRSTUVWX YZ& $1234567890 .,-:;'!?()—% " "
abcdefghijklmnopqrstuvwxyz fi fl ff

UNDERWOOD TYPEWRITER, Mono 270 10-pt.

ABCDEFGHIJKLMNOPQRSTUVWXYZ& abcdefghijklmnopqrstuvwxyz .,-:;!?()'" $1234567890
$\frac{1}{4}\frac{1}{2}\frac{3}{4}$ %%@/¢#+×÷*⁻ —-_   .,-:;'"

REMINGTON TYPEWRITER NO. 4, Lino 12-pt.

ABCDEFGHIJKLMNOPQRSTUVWXYZ& 1234567890$¢/,.:;-'"?!|—()
ABCDEFGHIJKLMNOPQRSTUVWXYZ& 1234567890$¢/,.:;-'"?!|—()

abcdefghijklmnopqrstuvwxyz @*[]#%$\frac{1}{4}\frac{1}{2}\frac{3}{4}$
abcdefghijklmnopqrstuvwxyz @*[]#%$\frac{1}{4}\frac{1}{2}\frac{3}{4}$

TYPO GOTHIC (line 1: FRANKLIN CARD GOTHIC) 24s (Sheldon Wesson, Gary Hantke)

ABCDEFGHIJKLMNOPQRSTUVWXYZ &$1234567890,.-:;'!?

TYPO ROMAN, ATF 24L (second line 24s)

ABCDEFGHIJKLMNOPQRSTUVWXYZ&$1234567890

abcdefghijklmnopqrstnvwxyzﬀﬃﬁﬂﬄﬆ.,-:;'!? go'r.ay ay, ty

TYPO ROMAN LIGHT, Inter 14-pt.

ABCDEFGHIJKLMNOPQRSTUVWXYZ.,-:;'""''!? abcdefghijklmnopqrstuvwxyz$1234567890&

TYPO ROMAN SHADED, ATF 24s

ABCDEFGHIJKLMNOPQRSTUVWXYZ

abcdefghijklmnopqrstuvwxyz ay ay, o'ty r. ﬀﬁﬃﬂﬄ ,.-;':'!?& $1234567890

TYPO SCRIPT, ATF 24-pt. (third line, TYPO SCRIPT EXTENDED)

ABCDEFGHIJKLMNOPQRSTUVWXYZ

abcdefghijklmnopqrstuvwxyz o's '',;;.-;:'!?& *$1234567890*

abcdefghijklmnopqrstuvwxyz

TYPO SHADED, ATF 24L (Dave Greer)

ABCDEFGHIJKLMNOPQRSTUVWXYZ&

abcdefghijklmnopqrstuvwxyz,, : '!?ThTu$1234567890 .,

TYPO SLOPE, ATF 24L

ABCDEFGHIJKLMNOPQRSTUVWXYZ&

abcdefghijklmnopqrstuvwxyz $1234567890 .,-:;'!? ',. *ThTu rs r· r ſ p o's*

TYPO TEXT, ATF 24-pt.

ABCDEFGHIJKLMNOPQRSTUVWXYZ&

abcdefghijklmnopqrstuvwxyz ﬀﬁﬃﬂﬄﬆ $1234567890 .,-:;'!?

TYPO UPRIGHT, ATF 24L

ABCDEFGHIJKLMNOPQRSTUVWXYZ P Th Tu

abcdefghijklmnopqrstuvwxyz dho'rsoſrs .,-;:'!?& *$1234567890*

TYPO is a group of ATF faces, most of which have little or no relation to each other except that all are intended for use on stationery, invitations, and other social printing, and are imitative of the work of copperplate and steelplate engravers. Several members of the group were originally named *Tiffany;* the name apparently was changed late in 1906, although a few faces were still shown with the earlier name as late as 1909.

Typo Gothic is the oldest of the group, and has been made by many founders. It is a plain, square, monotone gothic with very small serifs, cast in several sizes of caps and figures on each of several point sizes. The earliest showing seems to have been offered as *Lining Antique* by Illinois Type Foundry in 1889; Keystone Type Foundry later used the same name. Subsequently it was shown as *Cleveland* by Standard Type Foundry, as *Standard Lining Antique* by Marder, Luse, and as *Olympia* by Inland, all before 1900. ATF showed it as *Tiffany Gothic* from 1901 to 1909 and later as *Typo Gothic*. BB&S took over *Olympia* and renamed it *Engravers Gothic*. Damon & Peets called it *Franklin Card Gothic,* which is the cap alphabet shown in the specimen here. Hansen called it *Steelplate Gothic.* From all sources it is essentially the same design, although there are some slight differences. Some versions have a horizontal crossbar on the *G;* some lack this on certain sizes.

Typo Roman was designed by Morris F. Benton for ATF in 1926; it is a narrow modern roman with small lowercase and very long ascenders. The *M* is splayed with a short vertex. Figures are much the same as *Bodoni. Typo Roman Light* was cut by Intertype in 1939. *Typo Roman Shaded* was the first of this group; it is said to have been designed by Morris F. Benton in 1921, adapted from engravings, but was not released by ATF until 1924.

Typo Script and *Typo Script Extended* were designed by Benton and cut by ATF in 1902, originally as *Tiffany Script* and *Extended,* when they were called "as close a copy as possible to reproduce in type the work of the artist who did much of the copperplate engraving for the Pan-American exposition." But Middleton says *Tiffany Script* was the "first face engraved by Wiebking (and Hardinge) on their engraving machine brought from Germany." They are a refinement of popular nineteenth-century scripts; like some of them, these two faces share the same capitals, figures, and punctuation marks—only the lowercase differs. They are similar to *Bank Script* and *Commercial Script,* but lighter and more delicate. Inland's *Invitation Script* was very similar to *Typo Script Extended.* Also see *American Script, Formal Script, Plate Script.*

Typo Text is a shaded Old English design, first shown by ATF as *Tiffany Text* in 1901, although this may be the same face shown by Bruce Type Foundry as *Invitation Text* a short time earlier, just before that foundry merged with ATF. Hansen copied it as *Card Text.* Also see *Plate Text, Inland Copperplate.*

Typo Upright is Morris Benton's interpretation in 1905 of a popular style of vertical *French Script,* introduced by ATF as *Tiffany Upright.* It is the only such design suitable for adaptation to keyboard slug casting, and is called *Lino Script* and *Interscript* by the two leaders in that field. There is also *Typo Upright Bold* and *Typo Shaded,* both recorded as being designed by Benton in 1906, but only the latter is noted as having the *Tiffany* name originally. These two faces are adaptations of the *Typo Upright* design. Finally there is *Typo Slope,* a sharply inclined version of the same design; it is credited to Benton in 1905, originally as *Tiffany Slope.* The lowercase of this face is more nearly a conventional script, while the caps show the French influence. *Typo Upright* was copied by Western as *Society Script.* Also see *French Plate Script.*

TYPO UPRIGHT BOLD, ATF 24L (part reduced) (David Kent)

ABCDEFGHIJKLMNOPQRSTUVWXYZ Th Tu

abcdefghijklmnopqrstuvwxyz 1234567890$& '5.,-:; '!?

TYPOTABULAR GOTHIC, ATF 6-pt. No. 4 (see text)

A B C D E F G H I J K L M N O P Q R S T U V W X Y Z &
abcdefghijklmnopqrstuvwxyz .,-:;'!? $1234567890

ULTRA-MODERN, Ludlow 24-pt. (Herb Harnish)

ABCDEFGHIJKLMNOPQRSTUVWXYZ!?&%— ſ ſg
abcdefghijklmnopqrstuvwxyz 1234567890 $.,-:;''()[]

ULTRA-MODERN ITALIC, Ludlow 24-pt.

ABCDEFGHIJKLMNOPQRSTUVWXYZ&
abcdefghijklmnopqrstuvwxyz 1234567890

ULTRA-MODERN BOLD, Ludlow 24-pt.

ABCDEFGHIJKLMNOPQRSTUVWXYZ!?&ſ g:;,.—
abcdefghijklmnopqrstuvwxyz 1234567890 $-)['

UMBRA, Ludlow 24-pt.

ABCDEFGHIJKLMNOPQRSTUVWXYZ
$1234567890.,-:;''!?&+

UNCIALA, Duensing 14-pt. (Paul Duensing)

ABCDEFGHIJKLMNOPQRSTUVWXYZ .,:;-'!!$ 1234567890 *&,,"+

UNIVERSITY OLD STYLE, Hansen 24-pt. (part reduced)

SALES INCREASED NEAR HOME NATIONS
Pleasing to Customer Glad Moments Fine Parks

UNIVERSITY OLD STYLE ITALIC, Hansen 12-pt.

LEGIBILITY IS THE KEYNOTE
Of good advertising and printing 25

Name in parentheses after some specimens
indicates person who has set that specimen,
in whole or in part, to our format.

320

TYPOTABULAR GOTHICS are a group of faces on 6-point body specially cast to a minimum number of set widths, from two to four widths per font, introduced by ATF in 1915. Designs include two sizes of *Lightline Gothic* with lowercase for one of them, one size of *Monotone Gothic,* and several other plain gothics, as follows:

Typotabular Gothics, ATF 406 (6pt)

No. 1—6-pt. *Gothic No. 44*
No. 2—6-pt. *Lining Gothic No. 528*
No. 3—unidentified
No. 4—6-4 *Lightline Gothic*
No. 5—6-2 *Lightline Title Gothic*
No. 6—6-4 *Monotone Title Gothic*
No. 7—6-72 *Copperplate Gothic Extended*
No. 8—6-pt. *Alternate Gothic No. 1*

The foundry explains: "These Gothic letters have been selected as representing the faces used on card index and blank form work, and are cast on em body, en body, and ⅔-em body, with a few exceptions. As will be appreciated by every printer, it is not possible to obtain first-class typographical results with letters cast on a uniform set, but the saving in time is so great that in many cases—and especially on low-priced blanks—it is price and not typographical excellence that secures the order." The result in most cases was a spotty appearance, as though the word or line had been irregularly letter-spaced, but it served a purpose. (The specimen is simulated by careful spacing of *Lightline Gothic.*) Compare *Quick-Set Roman.*

ULTRA BODONI—see *Bodoni, Ultra.*

ULTRA-MODERN was designed by Douglas C. McMurtrie in 1928, with the assistance of Aaron Borad and Leslie Sprunger. *Ultra-Modern Bold* was designed by McMurtrie about the same time, and *Ultra-Modern Italic* a year or two later. They are all severe thick-and-thin serifless letters; the *Bold* weight is similar to *Broadway* though not quite as mechanical, but has normal descenders and thus the face is not oversize for the body. Also compare *Modernique, Radiant.*

Ultra-Modern, Ludlow 22-M (12-72pt)
Ultra-Modern [Medium] Italic, Ludlow 22-MI (12-48pt)
Ultra-Modern Bold, Ludlow 22-B (14-72pt)

UMBRA was designed by Robert H. Middleton for Ludlow in 1932. It is essentially a shadow version of *Tempo Light,* in which the basic letter is "invisible" but there is a strong shadow to the lower right of each stroke. Compare *Shadow.*

Umbra, Ludlow 34 (18-72pt)

UNCIALA was cut and cast by Paul H. Duensing, from a Czechoslovakian typeface by Oldrich Menhart.

Unciala, Duensing (10-14pt)

UNCLE SAM—see *Tuscan Outline* under Antiques in Appendix.
UNILINE—see *Cushing Monotone.*
UNION PEARL, UNIVERS—see Imports in Appendix.
UNIVERSAL GOTHIC—see *Gothic Condensed No. 523.*
UNIVERSITY OF CALIFORNIA OLD STYLE—see *Californian.*

UNIVERSITY OLD STYLE was issued by Hansen in the early to mid-1910s. It is very similar to ATF's *Century Oldstyle,* differing most apparently in the serif treatments of *CEFG* and details of *ags* in the roman and *CGg* in the italic.

University Old Style, Hansen (6-48pt)
University Old Style Italic, Hansen (6-12pt)

A A B C D E F G H I J K L M N O P Q R S T U
V W X Y Z Mc Mrs Ft Th Wh Co &Co, & $ 1 2 3 4 5 6 7 8 9 0
a b c d e f g h i j k l m n o p q r s t u v w x y z . , - ' : ; ! ?

VALIANT, Mono 24-pt.

ABCDEFGHIJKLMNOPQRSTUVWXYZ&
aabcdefgghijkklmnopqrstuvwxyz1234567890$?!.,:;'-–$¢%""()

VANDEN HOUTEN, Keystone 24-pt. (Dave Greer)

ABCDEFGHIJKLMNOPQRSTUVWXYZ&.,-:;'!?
abcdefghijklmnopqrstuvwxyz %¢$1234567890

VANITY FAIR, McMurtrie 24-pt.

A B C D E F G H I J K L M N O P Q R S T U
V W X Y Z -- .,

VANITY FAIR CAPITALS, Carroll 24- & 14-pt.

A B C D E F G H I J K L M N O P
Q R S T U V W X Y Z - ., . . . ABCDEFGHIJK

VENETIAN, ATF (36-pt. at 67%) (Cliff Leonard)

ABCDEFGHIJKLMNOPQRSTUVWXYZ&.,-:;'!?
abcdefghijklmnopqrstuvwxyzffffifffiffl$1234567890

VENETIAN ITALIC, ATF 18-pt.

ABCDEFGHIJKLMNOPQRSTUVWXYZ&
abcdefghijklmnopqrstuvwxyz $1234567890

VENETIAN BOLD, ATF 24-pt.

HABERDINE METHODS
Neighborhood Refrigerant Wrought Iron Designs

VENEZIA, Keystone 24-pt. (part reduced)

VENEZIA SERIES QUOTED HELPFUL ℱ 75
The VERY latest Standard Lining Type Features

UNIVERSITY SCRIPT is a Spencerian script design introduced by ATF in 1902. It is similar to *Typo Script Extended* in the lowercase, although not quite as well cut, but the caps have extra flourishes, and there are several logotypes or tied characters.

University Script, ATF 407 (14-30pt)

UTILITY GOTHIC—see *Agency Gothic*.

VALIANT is a vigorous thick-and-thin letter with the appearance of having been lettered quickly but well with a broad pen. It was designed by Edwin W. Shaar for Monotype in 1940, and is similar to *Lydian Bold Condensed,* though a little heavier. It is suggestive of *Samson,* but condensed.

Valiant, Mono 412 (14-72pt)

VANDEN HOUTEN is an unusual display face created by Keystone Type Foundry and patented in 1904 by Gibbs Mason, probably the designer. It is a medium weight roman with bizarre serifs on a number of characters, and other eccentricities. Compare *Rogers, Bewick.*

Vanden Houten, Keystone (8-60pt)

VANITY FAIR CAPITALS were adapted by Douglas C. McMurtrie in 1923, from a type of J. F. Rosart, an eighteenth-century Dutch typefounder, and were privately cast for distribution by Continental Typefounders Association. They are a set of shaded italic capitals, with tendril designs used as serifs and breaking the main stems. John S. Carroll, then operating a private typefoundry in Miami Beach, cut much the same face in 1964-65; the specimens here show both cuttings. Carroll's cutting is closer to the original, and true to the Dutch originals, smaller sizes are simpler, lacking the mid-stem ornamentation.

Vanity Fair Capitals, McMurtrie (24pt);
Vanity Fair, Carroll-LATF (14-24pt)

VAUDEVILLE—see Antiques in Appendix.

VENETIAN and *Italic* were designed by Morris F. Benton for ATF about 1911, with *Venetian Bold* following about two years later. They are rather reserved transitional faces, almost modern, instead of classic designs of Venetian origin as the name implies. The result is closer to Bodoni than to Cloister. The working title was *Cheltenham No. 2,* but the relationship to that family is not apparent. It is carefully and neatly done, but never achieved widespread use. Compare *Benton,* a later face by the same designer, which has similar characteristics but more grace and charm.

Venetian, ATF 408 (6-36pt)
Venetian Italic, ATF 409 (6-36pt)
Venetian Bold, ATF 450 (6-36pt)

VENEZIA was produced by Keystone Type Foundry and first shown in 1899. It appears to have been inspired by the same models as *Jenson Oldstyle,* but features more generously bracketed serifs and a generally more pleasing appearance. Except for the unusual link between the bowls of the *g,* it is very agreeable. For a later modification of this design, see *Laureate.*

Venezia, Keystone (6-72pt)

VENEZIA ITALIC, Eng Lino 18-pt.

ABCDEFGHIJKLMNOPQRSTUVWXYZ *abcdefghijklmnopqrstuvwxyz*

VERNEN, Balto 24-pt.

ABCDEFGHIJKLMNOPQRSTUVWXYZ $1234567890¢

VERONA, ATF 24-pt. (Duane Scott)

ABCDEFGHIJKLMNOPQRSTUVWXYZ
abcdefghijklmnopqrstuvwxyz & ! $? ffffiflffiffl 1234567890.,""":;~

VERTICAL GOTHIC, Lino 12-pt.

ABCDEFGHIJKLMNOPQRSTUVWXYZ

VERTICAL SCRIPT, Hansen 24-pt.

Vertical Spring Sales are Patronized by the multitude
Hansen Unmistakable Bargains on each   1234567890¢

VERTICAL WRITING, Boston 24-pt. (part reduced) (Gary Hantke)

ABCDEFGHIJKLMNOPQRSTUVWXYZ
abcdefghijklmnopqrstuvwxyz,.'-!?&$1234567890-;:

324

VENEZIA ITALIC (quite unlike the preceding face) was designed by Frederic W. Goudy in 1925 to accompany a typeface which George W. Jones, well-known English printer and designer, had drawn for the English Linotype Company. It is somewhat similar to *Cloister,* but with stronger serifs.

Venezia Italic, English Lino

VENEZIAN—see *Munder Venezian.*
VENUS—see Imports in Appendix.

VERNEN is essentially a copy of *Huxley Vertical* (q.v.), but omitting the round characters *AKMNWY* and using the alternate pointed characters instead. In addition, the slight extensions of cross strokes to the left of stems have been omitted, and a few other characters have been redrawn. It was offered by Baltimore in 1953.

Vernen, Balto 114 (14-72pt)

VERONA is ATF's adaptation about 1951 of *Bologna,* which had been cut by Stephenson Blake in England in 1948. It is said to have been cut from Stephenson Blake's drawings, but lining figures were drawn to replace the hanging figures which Stephenson Blake had featured. The name was changed to avoid having disrespectful printers call it "baloney," yet retaining an Italian connotation.

Verona, ATF 695 (8-48pt)

At the time ATF did not realize that Stephenson Blake had in turn adapted the design from an earlier ATF face, *Humanistic* (q.v.), drawn by William Dana Orcutt in 1904. With or without its later modifications, which are minor, this face retains more of the appearance of hand-lettering than almost any other cut in metal, and composes into a beautiful page with properly close spacing. Compare *Freehand, Motto, Heritage, Thompson Quillscript.*

Incidentally, when ATF took *Verona* as a new name for Stephenson Blake's *Bologna,* they also overlooked the fact that Stephenson Blake uses the name *Verona* for their copy of BB&S-ATF's *Munder Venezian*—see Imports in Appendix.

VERTICAL GOTHIC is a special-purpose Linotype face, with characters punched at right-angles to the normal position so they will compose into a vertical line, useful for food-store advertising of the time. It was first shown in 1932. The design is equivalent to ATF's *Gothic Condensed No. 521,* but is made in capitals only. Figures and certain other characters of a few other faces are also made for vertical slug work.

Vertical Gothic, Lino (6-12pt)

VERTICAL SCRIPT is a simple—almost childish—monotone upright script design, produced by Hansen in 1897. Although letters connect, they are widely spaced. The Boston foundry of ATF introduced a similar *Vertical Writing,* shown in 1897 and patented in 1898 by Joseph W. Phinney. Both are oversize for the body, with kerned descenders.

Vertical Script, Hansen (12-36pt)
Vertical Writing, ATF (12-24pt)

VICTORIA—see *Ecclesiastic* under Antiques in Appendix.

VICTORIA ITALIC, 18-pt.

ABCDEFGHIJKLMNOPQRSTUVWXYZ&
$1234597890.,-:;'I?

VIKING, Hansen 18-pt.

ABCDEFGHIJKLMNOPQRSTUVWXYZ&$?!
abcdefghijklmnopqrstuvwxyz-;.',1234567890

VIKING ITALIC, Hansen 24-pt.

THE NEW AND ORIGINAL VIKING ITALIC
Exclusive design by The Hansen Type Foundry

VILLAGE, Goudy 16-pt. (Rick von Holdt)

ABCDEFGHIJKLMNOPQRSTUVWXYZ .,;:='!?&$()—
abcdefghijklmnopqrstuvwxyz fffiflffifflæœctst 1234567890

VILLAGE NO. 2, Goudy 16-pt. (Dave Norton)

ABCDEFGHIJKLMNOPQRSTUVWXYZ&1234567890.,-:;'!?
abcdefghijklmnopqrstuvwxyzfffiflffifflct

VILLAGE ITALIC, Goudy 16-pt. (Dave Norton)

ABCDEFGHIJKLMNOPQRSTUVWXYZ&.,-:;'!?abcdefghijklmnopqrstuvwxyzffflctst

VILLAGE TEXT, Goudy 24-pt.

ABCDEFGHIJKLMNOPQRSTUVWXYZ&1234
Cabcdefghijklmnopqrstuvwxyzflffl «;:'!?.,-» 567890

VISTA, Balto 12-pt.

ABCDEFGHIJKLMNOPQRSTUVWXYZ&$1234567890
abcdefghijklmnopqrstuvwxyz .,-':;!?(a

VICTORIA ITALIC is a nineteenth-century design that retained its popularity for many years, and has been made under several names by a number of sources. ATF's Central Type Foundry branch showed it as early as 1893, in its usual form without lowercase, but with several sizes on each of several bodies in the manner of *Copperplate Gothic*. In 1898 the Pacific States Type Foundry in San Francisco showed the face with lowercase as *Pacific Victoria Italic,* and about the same time ATF showed *Regal Italic* with essentially the same lowercase. *Victoria Italic* without lowercase has also been shown by Keystone and Hansen, as well as Monotype and Ludlow. It is a wide, monotone design with thin, pointed serifs, and was popular for a time for business forms and stationery as well as general printing. Compare *Paragon Plate Italic.* Keystone also had *Keystone Victoria,* a similar upright design, without lowercase.

Victoria Italic, ATF 311 (6s-24L); Hansen (6s-24L); Keystone (6s-24L); Mono 224K (5-10pt); Ludlow 18 (6s-12L)
Keystone Victoria, Keystone (6s-12L)

VIKING was cut by John F. Cumming for Hansen in 1899. It is a medium-weight roman in a popular style of the day, with filleted curves within the letters where strokes meet. Compare *Mission.*

Viking or Viking Old Style No. 3, Hansen (6-48pt)
Viking Italic, Hansen (6-24pt)

VILLAGE was designed by Frederic W. Goudy in 1903 on commission from Kuppenheimer & Company, a clothing store, as a private typeface for their advertising. Drawings were approved and paid for, but no type was produced for this account. Later in that year, Goudy and Will Ransom established a printing business which they called the Village Press. This type design was revised and cast to become the private design of this press, and used as such for several years, while the business was in Park Ridge, Illinois. Though based on the classic Jenson type, this face has a number of novel details. The matrices were later purchased by Frederick Sherman, a publisher and fine printer, who used the face for printing the monumental *Catalog of Dutch Paintings* of the Metropolitan Museum.

Miraculously, the mats survived and were recently used by Theo Rehak of The Dale Guild to cast new fonts, the source of the specimen shown here.

For years Goudy wanted something to replace his Village type—not to duplicate it, but to have something for similar uses. In 1932 he designed and cut another type which he called *Village No. 2,* and a year or two later cut an accompanying italic. These are more mature designs, without the unique details of the original design, and have been used for a number of fine booklets. Monotype obtained reproduction rights to these later faces, and produced them for machine composition in two sizes.

Village, Goudy
Village No. 2, Goudy (12-16pt); Goudy Village, Mono 410 (14,18pt)
Village No. 2 Italic, Goudy (12-16pt); Goudy Village Italic, Mono 410G (14,18pt)

VILLAGE TEXT or *New Village Text.* This typeface by Frederic W. Goudy is really a hybrid, combining the capitals of *Tory Text* with the lowercase of *Deepdene Text.* When the Grabhorn Press in San Francisco ordered a large amount of *Deepdene Text* for a proposed book about Caxton, England's first printer, Goudy was not satisfied that this was the best choice for the subject. After quite a bit of study, he hit upon the idea of substituting the *Tory Text* capitals. Grabhorn approved a proof of this combination.

Earlier, Goudy had applied the name *Village Text* to his redesign and recutting of *Aries,* but Grabhorn renamed it *Franciscan* when they used that face for an award-winning book. This left the name available for the later face.

[New] Village Text, Goudy (24pt) private

VIRTUOSA—see Imports in Appendix.

VISTA is a very wide square-serif face, cut by Baltimore Type in 1956. It is said to be a pantagraphic modification of *Hellenic Wide* from Bauer in Germany (see Imports in Appendix); actually it does not match that face in details, although it has the same general effect.

Vista, Baltimore 690 (10-36pt)

VOGUE & BOLD, Inter 14-pt.

ABCDEFGHIJKLMNOPQRSTUVWXYZ abcdefghijklmnopqrstuvwxyz fiflffffiffl ,.-;':'!?()@tb&£

ABCDEFGHIJKLMNOPQRSTUVWXYZ abcdefghijklmnopqrstuvwxyz fiflffffiffl ,.-;':'!?()@tb&£

$1234567890 æœÆŒ []*†|‡||§¶ --—⅛¼⅜½⅝¾⅞ GJMQ agu CGJMQWY egijrt

$1234567890 æœÆŒ []*†|‡||§¶ --—⅛¼⅜½⅝¾⅞ GJMQ agu CGJMQWY egijrt

k m n r u **k m n r u**

VOGUE OBLIQUE & BOLD OBLIQUE, Inter 14-pt.

ABCDEFGHIJKLMNOPQRSTUVWXYZ abcdefghijklmnopqrstuvwxyz fiflffffiffl ,.-;':'!?( )@tb&£

ABCDEFGHIJKLMNOPQRSTUVWXYZ abcdefghijklmnopqrstuvwxyz fiflffffiffl ,.-;':'!?( )@tb&£

$1234567890 œœÆŒ %[]†|‡||§¶ --— ⅛¼⅜½⅝¾⅞*

$1234567890 œœÆŒ %[]*†‡ §¶ --— ⅛¼⅜½⅝¾⅞

VOGUE EXTRA BOLD & OBLIQUE, Inter 14-pt. (Alternates reduced)

ABCDEFGHIJKLMNOPQRSTUVWXYZ abcdefghijklmnopqrstuvwxyz fiflffffiffl ,.-;':'!?( )

ABCDEFGHIJKLMNOPQRSTUVWXYZ abcdefghijklmnopqrstuvwxyz fiflffffiffl ,.-;':'!?( )

$1234567890 œœÆŒ£ %[]*†|‡||§ ¶ --—⅛¼⅜½⅝¾⅞ @tb&

$1234567890 œœÆŒ£ @tb&

CGJMQWY aegijrt $1234567890 AEJMNVWZ rvwz *CGJMQWY egijrt AEFJMNVWZ rvwz*

VOGUE CONDENSED, Inter 18-pt.

ABCDEFGHIJKLMNOPQRSTUVWXYZ abcdefghijklmnopqrstuvwxyz 1234567890 ( )$,.-;':'!?&

VOGUE MEDIUM CONDENSED, Inter 18-pt.

ABCDEFGHIJKLMNOPQRSTUVWXYZ abcdefghijklmnopqrstuvwxyz 1234567890 ( )$,.-;':'!?&¼½¾

VOGUE BOLD CONDENSED, Inter 14-pt.

ABCDEFGHIJKLMNOPQRSTUVWXYZ&½¼¾⅛⅜⅝⅞% abcdefghijklmnopqrstuvwxyz.,-:;"!?( )—$1234567890

VOGUE BOLD EXTRA CONDENSED, Inter (36-pt. at 67%)

EXACTING AND ZEALOUS RESEARCH HAS BEEN THE K Exacting and zealous research has always been the ke

for improvements in line-composing machine manufacture by Intertype. Progressiveness, bac 1234567890

VOGUE EXTRA BOLD CONDENSED & OBLIQUE, Inter 14-pt. (Alternates reduced)

ABCDEFGHIJKLMNOPQRSTUVWXYZ $1234567890 æœÆŒ CEFGRbcfgijt 1234567890$.:;!?"

ABCDEFGHIJKLMNOPQRSTUVWXYZ $1234567890 œœÆŒ

abcdefghijklmnopqrstuvwxyz fi fl ff ffi ffl ,.-;':'!?( )@tb&£ %[]*†|‡||§¶--—⅛¼⅜½⅝¾⅞

abcdefghijklmnopqrstuvwxyz fi fl ff ffi ffl ,.-;':'!?( )@tb&£ %[]*†|‡||§¶--—⅛¼⅜½⅝¾⅞

LINING VOGUE & BOLD, Inter 12-pt.

ABCDEFGHIJKLMNOPQRSTUVWXYZABCDE **ABCDEFGHIJKLMNOPQRSTUVWXYZABCDE**

1234567890123456789012345 **1234567890123456789012345**

VOGUE is an American sans-serif type, cut by Intertype in light and bold weights early in 1930. It had been created for Condé Nast of *Vogue* magazine, but was released also to the general printing trade. It is generally quite similar to *Futura* (q.v.), but caps are the full height of ascenders, and descenders are a bit longer; most noticeable in the original version are the very long crossbar of *G* and the vertical tail of *Q*. The bold weight is about equivalent to *Futura Medium*. Extra bold, oblique, and condensed versions were added over the next several years, and it became especially popular for newspaper work. *Vogue Extra Condensed* was designed by Edwin Shaar in 1971 for the New York *Times* classified display, and cut in 48-point only.

Several sets of alternate characters in some versions enabled users of this series to simulate the general appearance of *Futura, Kabel,* or *Tempo,* while the light and bold weights also offered unusual squared versions of *kmnru,* derived from early tentative designs for *Futura.* Through an unusual twist of names, *Vogue Medium Condensed* is bolder than *Vogue Bold Condensed.* *Vogue Bold Extra Condensed* (not to be confused with *Vogue Extra Bold Condensed*), is made only in a few large sizes and departs somewhat in design. *Lining Vogue* and *Lining Vogue Bold* are made in several sizes of caps and figures to cast on a 6- or 12-point body in the manner of *Copperplate Gothic;* also one small size of 18-point.

Vogue, Inter (6-60pt)
Vogue Oblique, Inter (6-24pt)
Vogue Condensed, Inter (12-36pt)
Vogue Extra Condensed, Inter (48pt)
Vogue Bold, Inter (6-60pt)
Vogue Bold Oblique, Inter (6-36pt)
Vogue Bold Condensed or Vogue
 Headletter, Inter (8-60pt)
Vogue Medium Condensed, Inter (18-36pt)
Vogue Bold Extra Condensed, Inter (30-
 48pt)
Vogue Extra Bold, Inter (6-60pt)
Vogue Extra Bold Oblique, Inter (6-30pt)
Vogue Extra Bold Condensed, Inter (8-
 60pt)
Vogue Extra Bold Condensed Oblique,
 Inter (10-36pt)
Lining Vogue and Bold, Inter (6s-18pt)

VULCAN BOLD is the Linotype copy in 1929 of a Spanish face more commonly known as *Greco Bold* (q.v.). The roman is virtually the same, but the italic has less slant on Linotype to better fit straight matrices.

Vulcan Bold and Italic, Lino (10-24pt)

WALBAUM—see Imports in Appendix.

WALDORF TEXT is an unusual design produced by BB&S in 1914. It gives the general effect of a shaded Old English face, but is not quite Old English in style. The shading consists of parallel lines in the main strokes, as though it was lettered with a broad pen having a nib divided into several sections. It is derived from a copperplate engraving style. Compare *Dietz Text.*

Waldorf Text, BB&S-ATF 1905 (14-36pt)

VULCAN BOLD & ITALIC, Lino 14-pt.

ABCDEFGHIJKLMNOPQRSTUVWXYZ&
ABCDEFGHIJKLMNOPQRSTUVWXYZ&
abcdefghijklmnopqrstuvwxyz ($£,.:;'-'?!*) 1234567
abcdefghijklmnopqrstuvwxyz ($£,.:;'-'?!) 1234567*

WALDORF TEXT, ATF 24L

ABCDEFGHIJKLMNOPQRSTUVWXYZ&
abcdefghijklmnopqrstuvwxyz $1234567890 .,-:;'!?

ABCDEFGHIJKLMNOPQRSTUVWXYZ&$''()
1234567890abcdefghijklmnopqrstuvwxyz,.-;:'!?
ABCDEFGHIJKLMNOPQRSTUVWXYZ
ABCDEFGHIJKLMNOPQRSTUVWXYZ&
$1234567890abcdefghijklmnopqrstuvwxyz,.-:;!?()

ABCDEFGHIJKLMNOPQRSTUVWXYZ&
abcdefghijklmnopqrstuvwxyz $1234567890.,-:;'!? Æ ffl ſ ſt £
ABCDEFGHIJKLMNOPQRSTUV abcdefghijklmnopqrstuvwxyz $1234567890

ABCDEFGHIJKLMNOPQRSTUVWXYZ&!?
abcdefghijklmnopqrstuvwxyz1234567890.,-;:'$rsro'c

ABCDEFGHIJKLMNOPQRSTUVWXYZ
abcdefghijklmnopqrstuvwxyz 1234567890$&?!.,-":;()[]-'
℃ % ¼ ⅓ ½ ⅔ ¾

ABCDEFGHIJKLMNOPQRSTUVWXYZ 1234567890 ABCDEFGHIJKLMNOPQRSTUVWXYZ
ABCDEFGHIJKLMNOPQRSTUVWXYZ 1234567890
abcdefghijklmnopqrstuvwxyz fi fl ff ffi ffl $ @ ¢ æ œ Æ Œ & & ℔ £ Æ Œ [ ] ( ) ‡ | * ‖ † § ¶ %
abcdefghijklmnopqrstuvwxyz fi fl ff ffi ffl $ @ ¢ æ œ & ℔ £ Æ Œ [ ] ( ) * † ‡ § ¶ %
⅛ ¼ ⅜ ½ ⅝ ,.-;':'!? ¾ ⅞ ⅓ ⅔   Qgjpqy   J K   1234567890
⅛ ¼ ⅜ ½ ⅝ ,.-;':'!? ¾ ⅞ ⅓ ⅔   Qgjpqy   J K   1234567890

ABCDEFGHIJKLMNOPQRSTUVWXYZ&
abcdefghijklmnopqrstuvwxyz .,-:;'!?"" $1234567890
ABCDEFGHIJKLMNOPQRSTUVWXYZ&ÆŒ   fifflffifﬄ

ABCDEFGHIJKLMNOPQRSTUVWXYZ& ŒÆ
abcdefghijklmnopqrstuvwxyz fiflffffiffl !? $1234567890

WARD or *Montgomery Ward* is an adaptation by Sol Hess in 1942 of *Memphis Light,* specially redesigned for use in the large catalogs of that mail-order company. Strokes are lightened a bit, and the x-height is increased slightly. It was cut by Monotype for private use.

One reference says there were light and medium weights; another says there were roman and italic in normal width and also an extended version. The latter account seems more authentic.

Ward and Ward Italic, Mono 505 (5,6pt) private
Ward Extended, Mono 503, private

WASHINGTON TEXT was patented in 1904 by S. M. Weatherly, probably the designer, and introduced by Keystone Type Foundry in 1905. It is distinguished by the long starting strokes on many of the capitals, described by Theodore L. DeVinne as "graceful as an ox of one horn." The Monotype adaptation in keyboard sizes, up to 12-point, shortens the opening strokes considerably to fit predetermined character widths and changes other proportions. The lowercase is a round modification of Old English, and is said to have been influenced by *Bradley* (q.v.). The face is named for George Washington, at a time of heightened interest in historic persons.

In *Washington Text Shaded,* shown about 1908, the lowercase is essentially the same, but some caps are substantially different and none except *A* have the exaggerated opening strokes of the solid version. The California private press operator who furnished this shaded specimen, Gordon L. Sullivan, says that about half the caseful of type has the Keystone foundry pinmark, but the other half has no pinmark; while the two lots have different nicks, although the face appears to be identical. This is not unusual, as Keystone was taken over by ATF in 1919. Some Keystone faces were continued in production, using the same matrices but quite likely with different molds on different casting machines. Gordon also comments that the proof was difficult because the type is used—some very much. This is typical of how specimens of a number of the rarer faces in this book were obtained, and this is a particularly delicate face, so the difficulty is not surprising.

Washington Text, Keystone-ATF 935 (6-96pt); Mono 102 (6-36pt)
Washington Text Shaded, Keystone-ATF 936 (8-48pt)

WAVE was designed for Ludlow in 1962 by Robert H. Middleton. It is a medium-weight script, not quite joining, with a brush-drawn appearance and thick-and-thin contrast. The apparent angle is quite a bit more than the 17-degree slope of Ludlow matrices, but letters fit together compactly without noticeable looseness, and form smoothly flowing words. Compare *Brush, Mandate, Kaufmann Bold.*

Wave, Ludlow 53-BIC (12-72pt)

WAVERLEY was drawn by George Trenholm and introduced by Intertype in 1940 as a modern roman that is less severe than *Bodoni.* It is derived from *Walbaum,* from the Berthold foundry in Germany, but is not a close copy. Alternate characters available include long descenders, oldstyle figures, a slightly descending cap *J,* and a *K* with a curved tail like the *R.* There are also several swash capitals for the italic. Compare *Baskerville, Bell, Bodoni, Caledonia, Clarion, Scotch Roman.*

Waverley and Italic, Inter (6-14pt)

WAYSIDE ROMAN and *Italic* were shown by ATF in 1900, as a handsome interpretation of modern face similar to *Scotch Roman,* but without the heavier capitals of the latter face. Some sources say the designer was Will Bradley, but this is disputed by other authorities, and most likely it is a revival of an older face. It was not in regular production very many years, but special castings have been made at times. Some figures appear to be oversize—*6, 7,* and *9* in the specimen shown here—but this is a characteristic of the font, although not uniform from one size to another.

Also compare *Oxford, Bell.*

Wayside Roman and Italic, ATF 441 (6-12pt)

WEBB, ATF 24-pt.

ABCDEFGHIJKLMNOPQRSTUVWXYZ&
abcdefghijklmnopqrstuvwxyz $1234567890 .,„-:;"!?

WEBB CONDENSED, ATF (30-pt. at 80%) (Yvonne Huntress)

ABCDEFGHIJKLMNOPQRSTUVWXYZ
abcdefghijklmnopqrstuvwxyz &$1234567890 ',„-:;!?

WEDDING GOTHIC, ATF 12-pt. (Stanley Sollid)

ABCDEFGHIJKLMNOPQRSTUVWXYZÆŒ
&!?$1234567890 .,:;'-

WEDDING PLATE SCRIPT, BB&S 24L (Herb Harnish)

ABCDEFGHIJKLMNOPQRSTUVWXYZ&$
abcdefghijklmnopqrstuvwxyz.,-:;'!?1234567890 oc , D — h oc r z ,;

WEDDING TEXT, ATF 24L (Dave Greer)

ABCDEFGHIJKLMNOPQRSTUVWXYZ& H wdrdstth
abcdefghijklmnopqrstuvwxyz $1234567890 .,-:;'!?

WEDDING TEXT SHADED, ATF 18-pt.

ABCDEFGHIJKLMNOPQRSTUVWXYZ
abcdefghijklmnopqrstuvwxyzo'c&$1234567890.,-:;'!?

WEISS & ITALIC, Inter 14-pt.

ABCDEFGHIJKLMNOPQRSTUVWXYZ& abcdefghijklmnopqrstuvwxyz fffiffiflffl $1234567890
ABCDEFGHIJ KLMNOPQRSTUVWXYZ .,-:;'!?()—*% " "
ABCDEFGHIJKLMNOPQRSTUVWXYZ&
abcdefghijklmnopqrstuvwxyz fffiffiflffl $1234567890 .,-:;'!?()—*%

WESTINGHOUSE GOTHIC, Mono 24-pt.

ABCDEFGHIJKLMNOPQRSTUVWXYZ ¢$1234567890
abcdefghijklmnopqrstuvwxyz .,-':;""!?&()st

WESTINGHOUSE GOTHIC LIGHT, Mono 12-pt.

ABCDEFGHIJKLMNOPQRSTUVWXYZ&abcdefghijklmnopqrstuvwxyzst.,-:;'""!?$1234567890¢()

332

WAYZATA—see Antiques in Appendix.

WEBB is an outline version of *Foster* (q.v.). It is cut to register for two-color work; slightly larger so slight misregister will not let the *Foster* show around the edges. It was patented in 1905 by William Schraubstädter, probably the designer, and shown by Inland the same year. *Condensed Webb* was shown shortly after.

Webb, Inland-ATF 412 (12-84pt)
Condensed Webb, Inland-ATF 126 (10-84pt)

WEDDING GOTHIC was shown by ATF in 1901, and called "equal to copperplate printing." It is a wide, very plain gothic without lowercase. Hansen copied it as *Card Gothic*. Compare *Blair*.

Wedding Gothic, ATF 413 (6s-36pt); Card Gothic, Hansen (6s-12pt)

WEDDING PLATE SCRIPT was designed by Sidney Gaunt for BB&S in 1904. It is much like the same founder's *French Plate Script,* but sloped, and similar to *Typo Slope,* produced the following year by ATF.

Wedding Plate Script, BB&S-ATF 1908 (14-36pt)

WEDDING TEXT is a light Old English face, designed by Morris F. Benton and cut by ATF in 1901. It is recorded that the 12-point size was cut in type metal in that year, instead of cutting punches or engraving matrices directly. Electrotype matrices were then made from these cuttings. It is uncertain whether this new method of cutting delicate faces resulted in unusual problems and delays, but the face was hailed as "new" in 1907 and again in 1909. It has been copied by Monotype under the same name, by Linotype as *Lino Text,* and by Hansen and Ludlow as *Society Text,* all virtually the same. *Wedding Text Shaded* was also designed by Benton, and cut by ATF about 1913. Compare *Engravers Old English, Invitation Text, Plate Text.*

Wedding Text, ATF 141 (6-48pt); Mono 388 (8-36pt); Lino Text, Lino (8-36pt); Society Text, Hansen (6-36pt); Ludlow 50 (8-36pt)
Wedding Text Shaded, ATF 415 (8-36pt)

WEDGE GOTHIC—see *Japanet.*

WEISS was cut by Intertype in 1935, as a copy of the same face as designed by E. R. Weiss and cast by the Bauer Type Foundry in Germany. *Weiss* is a contemporary roman with an antique feeling, with fairly long ascenders and short descenders. The *M* is splayed; it and *N* have no serifs at the apex; *U* is lowercase in form. Most of the italic capitals are cursive in style, and italic figures are quite small but ranging. The face is undersize, so that each point size appears to be a size or two smaller. See Imports in Appendix for *Weiss Bold* and *Weiss Extrabold.*

Weiss and Italic, Inter (8-18pt)

WESEL—see *World Gothic.*

WESTERN UNION GOTHIC is listed by Monotype, but no specimen has been found. Presumably it resembles the monowidth style used on telegraphic printers.

Western Union Gothic, Mono 212

WESTINGHOUSE GOTHIC is a contemporary condensed gothic of uniform line weight, developed in 1960 by graphics design consultant Paul Rand for Westinghouse Electric Corporation. It was derived from lettering Rand had done earlier for the company logotype and originally used on signs; that was condensed to save space with the long name. It is distinguished by the unusual *st* ligature, for use in the company name. In 1964 that company had matrices made by Monotype, with exclusive rights to the face for two years. A lighter version was cut a few years later.

Westinghouse Gothic, Mono 479 (12-36pt)
Westinghouse Gothic Light, Mono 489 (6-12pt)

333

WHEDONS GOTHIC OUTLINE, ATF 24-pt.

ABCDEFGHIJKLMNOPQRSTUVWXYZ

abcdefghijklmnopqrstuvwxyz 1234567890 &$¢£%.,-::;"!?.∘-−()*

WHITTIER, Keystone 18L

ABCDEFGHIJKLMNOPQRSTUVWXYZ&
$1234567890 ..-:;'!? " " £

WHITTIER BOLD, Keystone 24s

TYPE FOUNDRY EXCURSION

WIDE LINE GOTHIC, Balto 24-pt.

ABCDEFGHIJKL $ abcdefghijklmn 2

WILSON & ITALIC, Mono 152 10-pt.

12345   abcdefghijklmnopqrstuvwxyz   67890$
ABCDEFGHIJKLMNOPQRSTUVWXYZ
ABCDEFGHIJKLMNOPQRSTUVWXYZ
12345   abcdefghijklmnopqrstuvwxyz   67890$
ABCDEFGHIJKLMNOPQRSTUVWXYZ

WINCHELL, Mono 24-pt.

ABCDEFGHIJKLMNOPQRSTUVWXYZ&.,-:;'!?
abcdefghijklmnopqrstuvwxyz$1234567890

CONDENSED WINCHELL, Mono 24-pt.

ABCDEFGHIJKLMNOPQRSTUVWXYZ&
abcdefghijklmnopqrstuvwxyz $1234567890 .,-:;'!?

WINCHESTER & ITALIC, 12-pt. (Dorothy Abbe)

ABCDEFGHIJKLMNOPQRSTUVWXYZ
abcdefghijklmnopqrstuvwxyz
abcdefghijklmnopqrstuvwxyz
ABCDEFGHIJKLMNOPQRSTUVWXYZ
abcdefghijklmnopqrstuvwxyz

334

WHEDONS GOTHIC OUTLINE was designed by Whedon Davis in 1965 while he was ATF staff designer, as a contemporary interpretation of the gothic letterform. It is a condensed face, with flat-sided round letters which emphasize the vertical appearance, and is nearly the only modern American gothic available in outline form. It also features a number of characters not often included in type fonts, as shown—cent, pound sterling, and percent marks; asterisk and parentheses; and hyphen, short dash and center dot in two sizes to work with either caps or lowercase. A solid version was planned but never completed. Compare *Condensed Gothic Outline* (shown with *Alternate Gothic*), *Outline Gothic Medium Condensed* (shown under *Modern Gothic*).

Whedons Gothic Outline, ATF 722 (18-72pt)

WHITEHALL—see *Benton*.
WHITIN BLACK—see *Bold Antique*.

WHITTIER is a wide, lightface gothic, similar to *Copperplate Gothic Light* but with even tinier serifs. It was introduced by Keystone Type Foundry in 1903. *Whittier Bold* was originated by the same foundry in 1910, and is comparable to *Copperplate Gothic Heavy*. Neither face is as well known as the *Copperplates,* though. Condensed and extrabold versions followed, but were quickly lost in Keystone's merger with ATF. Also compare *Steelplate Gothic*.

Whittier, Keystone (6s-24L)
Whittier Bold, Keystone

WIDE LATIN—see *Emperor*.

WIDE LINE GOTHIC is a creation of Herman Schnoor for Baltimore Type, modified by pantagraph from *Philadelphia Lining Gothic,* increasing the width by about 50 percent. The flat sides of round letters. acceptable in the moderately condensed original, make awkward shapes in this extended version. Compare *Franklin Gothic Wide, Tempo Black Extended*.

Wide Line Gothic, Balto 222 (10-36pt)

WILSON is a conventional modern roman design shown by Monotype only in two sizes.

Wilson and Italic, Mono 152ABC (8,10pt)

WINCHELL was designed by Edward Everett Winchell, art director of the Matthews-Northrup Printing Works in Buffalo, New York, and introduced by Inland Type Foundry in 1903 as "especially adapted for use in fine catalog and booklet printing, as well as for commercial stationery, where something out of the ordinary is demanded." It is a bold, thick-and-thin display face, but more like a nineteenth-century design, with some characters seeming to be poorly proportioned or having awkward shapes. These faults are less noticeable in *Condensed Winchell,* introduced by Inland the following year, but patented by William Schraubstädter in 1905. Neither is a distinguished face by later standards. Compare *John Hancock, Bold Antique*.

Winchell, Inland-ATF 416 (6-72pt); Mono 39 (5-36pt)
Condensed Winchell, Inland-ATF 127 (6-84pt); Winchell Condensed, Mono 119 (6-36pt)

WINCHENDON—see *Clarendon*.

WINCHESTER ROMAN and *Winchester Uncial* with their italics were completed in 1944 by William A. Dwiggins, the *Uncial* being an experiment aimed at making the English language easier to read by eliminating some of the ascenders and descenders typically used in this language. Italic caps and other characters were drawn in 1948 but not cut. Although made on Linotype matrices by Mergenthaler, fonts of hand type were cast and used only by Dwiggins and Dorothy Abbe beginning in 1950 at the Püterschein-Hingham Press, where they were partners until his death in 1956. In the specimen shown here, the uncial *f* appears in both italic alphabets. A regular italic *f* was cut but apparently not cast.

Winchester Roman and Roman Italic, Winchester Uncial and Uncial Italic, Lino (12pt) experimental

WOODWARD CONDENSED, Inland 18-pt. (Dave Greer)

ABCDEFGHIJKLMNOPQRRSTUVWXYZ& abcdefghijklmnopqrstuvwxyz .,-:;'!? $1234567890

WOODWARD EXTRA CONDENSED, Inland (30-pt. at 80%) (Dave Greer)

ABCDEFGHIJKLMNOPQRSTUVWYZ& abcdefghijklmnopqrstuvwxyz $1234567890 .,-:;'!?

WORLD GOTHIC, BB&S 24-pt. (part reduced)

MAKES Quick Result Railroad BRIDGE

WORLD GOTHIC ITALIC, BB&S 24-pt. (part reduced)

Credited SCORE KINDS Restful

WORLD GOTHIC CONDENSED, BB&S 24-pt.

FOR SERVICE, USE WORLD CHECKS MARKING Structural

WORRELL UNCIAL, Lino 12-pt. (Dave Greer)

ABCDEFGHIJKLMNOPQRSTUVWXYZ 1234567890 ($,.:;'-'?!) ᴍ ᴍ ᴀᴛ ᴀʏ ʟʏ

ZAPF CIVILITÉ, Duensing 24D

AABBCDଚDEEFGHAHIJJKRRLLLMNO
PPQRRSSSTUVVWXYZ $ 1234567890 ¢
abbcddefgghijkllmnopqurstuvwxyz
a᷄ᴅée᷄ engn᷄ r᷄ spsttht᷄y᷄ ᵮ («&.,:;'!? &»)

ZEPHYR, Ludlow 24-pt.

ABCDEFGHIJKLMNOPQRSTUVWXYZ&
1234567890 .,:;-""!?-- () []

WINDSOR—see *Ionic No. 5;* also *Cambridge;* also see Imports in Appendix.
WOMAN'S HOME COMPANION FACE—see *Companion.*

WOODWARD was designed for Inland Type Foundry in 1894 by William A. Schraubstädter, and named for a Saint Louis printer. Other versions followed over the next few years. In 1911 Inland was purchased by ATF and its equipment divided between that foundry and BB&S. Some time later BB&S reissued *Woodward* and *Woodward Outline* as *DeVinne Recut* and *DeVinne Recut Outline* (q.v.).

Woodward, Inland (6-60pt); DeVinne Recut, BB&S-ATF 1608 (6-60pt)
Condensed Woodward, Inland (6-72pt)
Extra Condensed Woodward, Inland (12-72pt)
Extended Woodward, Inland (6-60pt)
Woodward Outline, Inland (12-60pt); DeVinne Recut Outline, BB&S-ATF 1609 (12-60pt)

WORLD GOTHIC series is similar to *Globe Gothic,* and is probably so named to compete with the latter face. It has been credited to Robert Wiebking, but as a family it is an assemblage of three faces shown separately in their earlier years. *World Gothic* itself was formerly known as *Wesel,* but its origin has not been found. *World Gothic Italic* was originally *Dewey [No. 5],* named for Admiral George Dewey, popular hero of the Spanish-American War, and introduced by BB&S in 1898. *World Gothic Condensed* was originally *Topic [No. 5],* shown by BB&S in 1897. As a group the three faces have only a general relationship to each other, not the harmony of characteristics found in most type families.

World Gothic, BB&S (6-72pt)
World Gothic Italic, BB&S (6-72pt)
World Gothic Condensed, BB&S (6-96pt)

WORRELL UNCIAL was cut by Linotype from designs originally made by Dr. W. H. Worrell, who had based them on the calligraphy of a fifth-century codex or manuscript book. The font was named in honor of Dr. Worrell and first used for *Coptic Texts in the University of Michigan Collection,* a volume which he edited. There are also Greek and Coptic versions of the face. The alphabet itself is interesting, but the *Caslon No. 3 (New Caslon)* figures and punctuation marks Linotype has included with the font are incongruous.

Worrell Uncial, Lino (9,12pt)

ZAPF CIVILITÉ is perhaps the latest face to be cut as metal type, having been announced in January 1985, although the designer, Hermann Zapf, had made sketches for such a face as early as 1940, with further sketches in 1971. But matrices were not cut until 1983 and 1984. The cutting was done by Paul Hayden Duensing in Kalamazoo, Michigan.

Zapf Civilité, Duensing (24pt)

The first Civilité typeface was cut by Robert Granjon in 1557, based on a popular French handwriting style of the time. Other interpretations have been made from time to time, notably the *Civilité* (q.v.) designed by Morris Benton in 1922 for ATF. The new Zapf design has the same general character, but with a more informal and contemporary feeling. A smooth flow between weights of strokes replaces the stark contrast of thick-and-thin in older interpretations. There are several ligatures, and alternate versions of a number of characters, including several terminals. Only the 24-point Didot size is cut or planned.

ZEPHYR was designed by Michael Harvey in 1964 for Ludlow. It is a freely drawn outline-with-shadow font, slightly inclined, with a serif only at the top left of some strokes. The result is decorative and distinctive, with no other similar American typeface coming to mind.

Zephyr, Ludlow 55-HN (24-48pt)

Appendixes and Indexes

Antique Typefaces

A NUMBER OF TYPEFACES of past centuries have found new popularity and use in this century—Baskerville and Caslon, for instance. Others have been revived for special projects and then forgotten.

Several times during the 1940s and 1950s, American Type Founders recast a number of colorful antique faces for which matrices still remained in its vaults. Several individuals or secondary typefounders were inspired to copy these faces or resurrect other old typefaces. New matrices could be made by electrotyping these revivals, perhaps in some cases other old sets of matrices were found. Usually, though, these resurrections involved redrawing and recutting the characters—more or less accurately—from enlargements of old specimens.

Most of the ATF revivals were done under the direction of Stevens L. Watts. They and some early twentieth century faces, which appear in the main text of this book, include:

P. T. Barnum	Japanet	Old Dutch
Bradley	Jim Crow	Original Old Style Italic
Caslon Antique	Lexington	Pastel
Colonial	Marbleheart	Pekin
Gold Rush	Old Bowery	Steelplate Gothic Shaded

Perhaps the first individual revivalist was *Harry Weidemann* of Nyssa, Oregon, about 1950. About 1955 *John S. Carroll* began operating the *Replica Type Foundry* in New York City and later in Miami Beach. The most prolific was *Charles Broad,* whose operations as *Typefounders of Phoenix (TFP)* in Phoenix, Arizona, earned him the nickname of "Mr. Antique." Others include *Andrew Dunker,* Jackson, Michigan.

Many of the matrices of some of these sources are now at *Los Angeles Type Founders (LATF)*, Whittier, California, where some of the faces are still available.

Pat Taylor, Larchmont, New York, recast several old faces from matrices in the Smithsonian Institution; *Theo Rehak* and the *Dale Guild* in Howell, New Jersey, have recast several obsolete foundry faces; and others have recast from other old sets of matrices.

The following descriptions and specimens include most of the revivals from these sources, but not necessarily all. Some of the notes on origins of the faces are taken from the literature of these sources without further checking.

ANGLO originated with the Great Western Type Foundry, later Barnhart Brothers & Spindler, in Chicago, under the same name, in 1889 or earlier. TFP-LATF (18,24pt).

ABCDEFGHIJKLMNOP
abcdefghijklmnopqrs456

ARBORET, a font of capitals and figures with an elaborate background of leaves, was the MacKellar, Smiths & Jordan foundry's *Arboret No. 2,* designed by Herman Ihlenburg in 1885. TFP-LATF (18,24pt).

ABCDEFGHIJKL

ARGENT, which features a shaded face and a shadow, came from Cleveland Type Foundry in Cleveland, Ohio, about 1885. TFP-LATF (24pt).

ABCDE FG H IJKL M NOPQRSTU
abcdefghijklmnopqrstuvwxyz&1

ARGENTINE was recut by John S. Carroll in 1962. It originated with and was named by Robert Beasley at the Fann Street Foundry in London about 1860, and was also shown by Bruce's New York Type Foundry as *Ornamented No. 1509.* Carroll-LATF (12,18pt).

ABCDEFGHIJKLMNOP

BAILEY SHADED was formerly *Ornamented No. 1513.* It originated about 1854 with the Caslon foundry. LATF (42pt).

ABCDEFGHIJKL

BARNUM HEAVY was Bruce's *Ornamented No. 341,* and is called *Hidalgo* by some other sources. The name obviously comes from *P. T. Barnum,* a similar but lighter face which is shown here in the main text. TFP-LATF (14-36pt).

ABCDEFGHIJKLMNOPQ

BRUCE MIKITA was Bruce's *Ornamented No. 1048,* and has also been known as *Rustic Ornamented Shaded.* It has been credited to Julius Herriet, Sr. in 1867. TFP-LATF (18,24pt).

ABCDEFGHIJKLMNOP

CELTIC ORNATE came from Great Western Type Foundry. TFP-LATF (24pt).

ABCDEFGHIJKLMO

CICERO was Bruce's *Ornamented No. 1032.* It originated with the Besley foundry about 1857. TFP-LATF (18pt).

ABCDEFGHIJKLMNOPI2345

CIRCULAR SCRIPT was produced by MacKellar, Smiths & Jordan, designed by W. W. Jackson in 1883. TFP (14-24pt).

Dear Sir: Having carefully studie

CIRCUS, with a decorated roman upper part of each character and a more fanciful lower part, was Bruce's *Ornamented No. 881,* of about 1865. TFP-LATF (24-48pt).

ABCDEFGHIJKLM

CLAYTONIAN was recut by John S. Carroll in 1964, from an 1881 design of Marder, Luse & Company, Chicago, designed by Carl Moller. Carroll-LATF (12pt).

ABCDEFGHIJKLMNOPQRSTUV123

COLUMBINE was recut by Carroll in 1964 from a 1769 face by J. F. Rosart. Compare *Dresden* in our main text. Carroll-LATF (30pt).

ABCDEFGHIJ

CORDON was recut by Carroll in 1963, based on nine characters in an 1888 specimen from the Conner Type Foundry, New York. The same design had been cut by Bruce as early as 1869, where it was known as *Ornamented No. 18.* The letters in Carroll's version are slightly narrower than in the original, and are copied from *Futura Bold Condensed* or one of its derivatives. Carroll- LATF (24pt).

CORINTHIAN was made by Carroll from *Ornamented No. 44* of the Illinois Type Founding Company, Chicago, originating with the Reed & Fox foundry about 1869. It was also shown by Conner as *Corinthian.* Carroll-TFP-LATF (14pt).

ABCDEFGHIJKLMNOPQRSTU

CRAYONETTE originated with the Keystone Type Foundry in Philadelphia, and has been credited to H. Brehmer in 1890; our specimen is of the original. TFP-LATF (12,18pt).

ABCDEFGHIJKLMNO
abcdefghijklmnopqrstuvwxyz12

DELRAYE was cut by Figgins in 1843 and copied later by foundries in the United States by the then-new process of electrotyping. It had the generic name of *Backslope Ray Shaded* until John S. Carroll recut it in 1965, adding one or two new characters. Carroll-LATF (24pt).

ABCDEFGHIJKLM2

DIAMOND INLAID was Bruce *Ornamented No. 1071,* of about 1872. TFP-LATF (24,36pt).

ABCDEFGHIJKLM

ECCLESIASTIC, also known as *Tudoresque* or *Victoria,* was Bruce's *Ornamented No. 540* of 1876. TFP-LATF (18pt).

ABCDEFGHIJKLMNOPQRSTUV
abcdefghijklmnopqrstuvwxyz $12345

EGYPTIAN SHADED or *Egyptian Shaded Extended* came from Illinois Type Foundry. TFP-LATF (24pt).

ABCDEFGHIJKL
abcdefghijklmnop

FARGO originated with the Dickinson Type Foundry in Boston, about 1850. TFP-LATF (14pt).

ABCDEFGHIJKLMNOPQRSTUVW

FILLIGREE or *Filligree Initials* came from Johnson Type Foundry, and the design was credited to Herman Ihlenburg in 1878. LATF (24pt).

ABCDEFGHIJKLM

FRENCH CLARENDON SHADED was formerly a MacKellar, Smiths & Jordan face, designed by Richard Smith in 1871. TFP-LATF (24pt).

ABCDEFGHIJKLMNOPQRSTUW
abcdefghijklmnopqrstuvwxyz2

GRIMALDI came from Central Type Foundry in St. Louis, originating about 1887. TFP-LATF (24pt).

ABCDEEFGHIJKLLMNOPQRR
abcdefghijklmnopqrstuvwxyth12

HARLEQUIN was recut by John S. Carroll in 1963 from a design by Matthias Rosart in 1768. Carroll says, "We have reproduced it from an excellent specimen. Nonetheless, it is slightly heavier than the original due to the inability of the pantagraph to cut a perfect hairline. On today's smoother, harder papers, the final printed appearance is quite close to what the original looked like, printed by hand on dampened hand-made paper." Carroll-LATF (30pt).

ABCDEFGHIJK

IONIC SHADED or *Old Bailey* was MacKellar, Smiths & Jordan's *Ionic Shaded* of about 1860. TFP-LATF (24pt).

SUMMER Excursions 19

LARIAT was probably the only original production of Charles Broad, and as such is shown in the main text of this book. TFP-LATF (24-48pt).

LATIN ORNATE was originally *Italian Ornate* of James Conner & Son, predecessor of the Conner Type Foundry, about 1875. TFP-LATF (24pt).

MANDARIN was issued in 1883 as *Chinese* by the Cleveland Type Foundry of H. H. Thorpe Mfg. Co. TFP-LATF (10-30pt).

ABCDEFGHIJKLMNOPQRS

MOTTO was cast by Boston Type Foundry and recut by John S. Carroll in 1962. He says it carried patent number 11484, issued November 4, 1879, to John K. Rogers, not necessarily the designer. Carroll-LATF (24pt).

PACIFIC was recut from an American Type Founders face of about 1892. TFP-LATF (18pt).

ABCDEFGHIJKLMNOPQRSTUVWXYZ
abcdefghijklmnopqrstuvw$1234567890

PHIDIAN was recut from a MacKellar face of the same name, and was designed by Herman Ihlenburg in 1870. TFP-LATF (24pt).

ABCDEFGHIJKLMNOPQRSTUVWXYZABCDEFGHIJKLM

abcdefghijklmnopqrstuvwxyz $1234567890

PHIDIAN REVISED was redesigned more recently by Dan X. Solo from *Phidian*. TFP-LATF (36pt).

ABCDEFGHIJKLMNOPQRSTUV

RELIEVO was recut from MacKellar's *Relievo No. 2* of 1878. It was patented by R. Smith and W. W. Jackson, but credited to Herman Ihlenburg. TFP-LATF (18,36pt).

ABCDEFGHIJKLMNOPQRSTU

ROMANTIQUES No. 3 is also known as *Harmony* or *Ornate No. 2*, of about 1850. Wiedemann (24pt).

ROMANTIQUES No. 4 is also known as *Dandy* or *Ornate No. 6*. It originated about 1838 in France. Wiedemann (36pt).

ABCDEFGHIJ

For other Romantiques see Tuscans.

RUSTIC or *Log Cabin* was recut by John S. Carroll in 1962 or earlier from Bruce's *Ornamented No. 864*, but originated with Figgins about 1865. The design differs somewhat in different sizes. Carroll-TFP-LATF (12-36pt).

ABCDEFGHIJKL

SCROLL SHADED was recut by Carroll in 1963 from a face cut in 1841 by Henry Caslon at the Chiswell Street Foundry in London. Intended for book titles and initial letters, Carroll says, it has only the essential punctuation marks; no figures were ever cut. Carroll-LATF (18-30pt).

SOUTHERN CROSS was Bruce's *Ornamented No. 1041*, but originated about 1857 with Miller & Richards. TFP-LATF (12-24pt).

ABCDEFGHIJKLMNOPQR

STACCATO was recut in metal from a face in William H. Page's Wood Type Album. TFP-LATF (24,36pt).

ABCDEFGHI

TANGIER was recut from James Conner & Son's *Ornamented No. 43*, of about 1857. TFP-LATF (36pt).

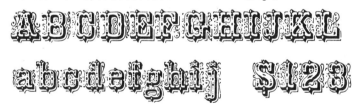

THUNDERBIRD's origin has not been found, but *Thunderbird Extra Condensed* was taken from a face of Charles T. White & Co., New York, in the 1850s or early 1860s. (Thunderbird) TFP-LATF (12-18pt) (Thunderbird Extra Condensed) TFP-LATF (36,48pt).

ABCDEFGHIJK

ABCDEFGHIJKLMNOPQ $12345

TROCADERO is a recutting of *Ornamented No. 25* of Illinois Type Foundry. TFP-LATF (18pt).

ABCDEFGHIJKLM 123

TUSCAN FLORAL was recut by Carroll from a face by Conner. It originated with H. W. Caslon in 1854. The design differs in various sizes. LATF (12-36pt).

ABCDEFGHIJKLM

TUSCAN GRAILLE or *Stellar* was recut by Harry Weidemann (his number 130) from Cincinnati Type Foundry's *Ornamented No. 22J* or Bruce's *Ornamented No. 1046*. It originated about 1860. Weidemann-TFP-LATF (12-30pt).

ABCDEFGHIJKLMNO

TUSCAN OMBREE has several other names: *Romantiques No. 2, Ornate No. 4,* or *Carnival.* It was originally Bruce's *Ornamented No. 847.* It originated about 1849. TFP- LATF (18,24pt).

ABCDEFGHIJ1234

TUSCAN ORNATE was also known as *Romantiques No. 5, Ornate No. 5,* or *Bracelet.* It was originally an English design of about 1850. TFP-LATF (18,24pt).

ABCDEFGHII123

TUSCAN OUTLINE was also known as *Romantiques No. 1, Carnet de Bal, Uncle Sam,* or *Ornate No. 3;* it came from Bruce's *Ornamented No. 851,* and originated about 1830 as the Laurent & Deberny foundry *Ornamented No. 1071.* TFP-LATF (18-30pt).

ABCDEFGHIKLMNOPQRS

VAUDEVILLE's origin has not been found, but it is believed to have been taken from an early photolettering design. TFP-LATF (36pt).

ABCDEFG $12345

WAYZATA was recut from a face by MacKellar. Wayzata is the name of a suburb of Minneapolis, Minn., so perhaps the face originated there. TFP-LATF (30pt).

ABCDEFGHIJKLMN

abcdefghijklmnopqrst

Popular Imports

TYPEFACES HAVE BECOME more international during the twentieth century. The main text of this book, as a general rule, includes faces which were designed in America and/or produced by a *major* American source, with "major" defined for our purposes as one whose productions are mostly original.

But imported types have been sold, copied and used extensively. Even some of the major domestic sources have acted as sales agents for types or matrices from their affiliates or contemporaries abroad. The following list covers many of these, but with no attempt at comprehensiveness.

Many of the following founders or matrix makers are no longer in business, or have been absorbed by others.

Bauer, Frankfurt, Germany.
Berthold, Berlin, Germany.
Deberny & Peignot (D&P), Paris, France.
Richard Gans, Madrid, Spain.
Haas, Basle, Switzerland.
Klingspor, Germany.
Ludwig & Mayer, Frankfurt, Germany.
Nebiolo, Turin, Italy.
Schelter & Giesecke (S&G), Dresden, Germany.
Stephenson Blake Co. (SB), Sheffield, England.
Stempel Typefoundry, Frankfurt, Germany.
Typefoundry Amsterdam (TA), Amsterdam, Netherlands; now has the matrices from a number of other European foundries.
Weber, Stuttgart, Germany.
EMono ("English Monotype") is The Monotype Corporation, Redhill, Surrey, England. A number of secondary American suppliers have English casting machines, or adapters on American machines that permit use of English matrices.
ATF (American Type Founders Co.) was sales agent for types cast to American standards by a number of European founders. Its stock numbers are listed for selected faces.

* * *

Balto (Baltimore Type & Composition Co.); **Castcraft** and **Neon** (divisions of Typefounders of Chicago); and others made electrotype matrices to cast duplicates of faces from other countries, as well as certain domestic faces. Where such faces have been modified or augmented, they are included in the main text of this book. But since it is not always certain whether a supplier is selling copies or imported type, or which supplier has made the copies, we have not generally attempted to state this detail. Furthermore, variations including italics and other weights and widths of some faces shown in our main text have also been imported.

On the following pages, only representative faces are shown for larger families; names of faces shown are in boldface. Where domestic suppliers have applied new names to faces, these names are given in brackets.

ALBERTUS (EMono): **regular** 481, Light 534, Titling 324, **Bold Titling** 538.

ABCDEFGHIJKLMNOPQRSTUVWXYZ&
abcdefghijklmnopqrstuvwxyz

ABCDEFGHIJKLMNOPQRSTUVW

ALLEGRO (TA).

ABCDEFGHIJKLMNOPQRSTUVW.XYZ&
abcdefghijklmnopqrstuvwxyz $12345678

ARISTON (Berthold): Light, **Medium, Bold.**

ABCDEFGHIJKLMNOPQRST
abcdefghijklmnopqrstuvwxyz $123456
ABCDEFGHIJKLMNOP
abcdefghijklmnopqrstuv$12345

AUGUSTEA (Nebiolo): **Neo-Augustea & Augustea Outline.**

ABCDEFGHIJKLMNOPQRSTUVWXY
abcdefghijklmnopqrstuvwxyz 12345678
ABCDEFGHIJKLMNOPQRSTUVWX
YZ& $1234567890

AURORA (Weber): **Condensed** (or Inserat), **Bold Condensed** (or Anzeigen Grotesque), many others.

ABCDEFGHIJKLMNOPQRSTUVWXYZ.,-:;'!?&
abcdefghijklmnopqrstuvwxyz$1234567890

ABCDEFGHIJKLMNOPQRSTUVWXYZ-'!?&
abcdefghijklmnopqrstuvwxyz $123456

BAUER BODONI (Bauer): Roman & Italic, **Bold** & Italic, **Extrabold** & Italic, Title.

ABCDEFGHIJKLMNOPQRSTUVWXY
abcdefghijklmnopqrstuvw$1234567890
ABCDEFGHIJKLMNOPQRSTUVWX
abcdefghijklmnopqrstuvwxyz$123

BAUER CLASSIC (Bauer): **Roman & Italic.**

ABCDEFGHIJKLMNOPQRSTUV
abcdefghijklmnopqrstu $1234567890
ABCDEFGHIJKLMNOPQRSTUV
abcdefghijklmnopqrstuvwxyz $12345

BERNHARD ROMAN & Italic (Bauer), also see Lucian.

ABCDEFGHIJKLMNOPQRSTUVWXY

abcdefghijklmnopqrstuvwxyz $1234567890

ABCDEFGHIJKLMNOPQRSTUVWX

abcdefghijklmnopqrstuvwxyz $1234567890

BERNHARD CURSIVE & Bold (Bauer) [Neon Cursive].

ABCDEFGHIJKLMNOPQRSTU

abcdefghijklmnopqrstuvwxyz   1234567890

ABCDEFGHIJKLMNOPQRSTU

abcdefghijklmnopqrstuvwxyz   fffiflft FlShPhTh .,:;-' " "

BETON (Bauer): **Bold Condensed, Open** [Antique Open, Stymie Open], others (see main text).

ABCDEFGHIJKLMNOPQRS

abcdefghijklmnopqrstuvw

ABCDEFGHIJKLMNOP

BOULEVARD (Berthold).

ABCDEFGHIJKLMN

abcdefghijklmnopqrstuvwxyz

BRAGGADOCIO (EMono): 278 [Stagg].

ABCDEFGHIJKLMNPQRSTUW

abcdefghijklmnopqrstuvwxyz

CAPRICE (Berthold).

ABCDEFGHIJKLM

abcdefghijklmnopqrstuvwxyz $1234567890

CASTELLAR (EMono): 600.

ABCDEFGHIJKL

CHISEL (SB): **regular** and **Wide.** See Latin in main text.

ABCDEFGHIJKLMNOPQRSTUVW
abcdefghijklmnopqrstuvwxyz123
ABCDEFGHIJK
abcdefghijklmno

CITY [CITY COMPACT] (Berthold): Light, **Medium, Bold.**

ABCDEFGHIJKLMNOPQRSTUVWXYZ&
abcdefghijklmnopqrstuvwxyz$1234567

ABCDEFGHIJKLMNOPQRSTUVWXYZ
abcdefghijklmnopqrstuvwxyz$12345

COLUMNA (Bauer).

ABCDEFGHIJKLMNO

CONDENSED SANS SERIFS (SB) **No. 5, Italic,** and others.

ABCDEFGHIJKLMNOPQRSTUVWXYZ
abcdefghijklmnopqrstuvwxyzæœfifffffiffl

ABCDEFGHIJKLMNOPQRSTUVWXYZ
abcdefghijklmnopqrstuvwxyzæœfifffflffiffl

CONSORT (SB): regular, **Italic,** Condensed, Light, Light Condensed, **Bold,** Bold Condensed. See Clarendon in main text.

ABCDEFGHIJKLMNOPQRSTUVWXY
abcdefghijklmnopqrstuvwxyzæœfiffflffiffl

ABCDEFGHIJKLMNOPQRSTUVWXYZ
abcdefghijklmnopqrstuvwxyzæœfiffflffiffl

CORVINUS (Bauer): Light & Italic, Medium & **Italic,** Bold, **Skyline.** See Glamour in main text.

AVWXYZABCDEFGHIJKLMNOPQRST
abcdefghijklmnopqrstuvw $12345678

ABCDEFGHIJKLMNOPQRSTUVWXYZ&$1234567890
abcdefghijklmnopqrstuvwxyz.,:;-'"(fiffl!?

DELPHIN (Weber) **I & II.**

ABCDEFGHIJKLMNOPQRSTUVWXYZ
abcddefgghijklmnopqrstuvwxyz

ABCDEFGHIJKLMNOPQRSTUVWXYZ
abcdefghijklmnopqrstuvwxyz $1234567890 !?&£

DORCHESTER SCRIPT (EMono): 436 or **Grosvenor Script** (EMono—same with very short descenders): 493.

ABCDEFGHIJKLMNOPQRS
TUVWXY abcdefghijklmnopqrstuvwxyz

DYNAMIC (Berthold).

ABCDEFGHIJKLMNOPQRSTUVW
abcdefghijklmnopqrstuvwxyz&†§«»$12345678

EGIZIO (Nebiolo): Medium & **Italic,** Medium Condensed, **Bold & Italic.**

ABCDEFGHIJKLMNOPQRSTUVW&
abcdefghijklmnopqrstuvwxyz $123456

EGYPTIAN BOLD (TA): **Condensed & Extended.**

ABCDEFGHIJKLMNOPQRSTUVWXYZ&
abcdefghijklmnopqrstuvwxyz $123456

ABCDEFGHIJKLMNO
abcdefghijklmnopqrs

EGYPTIAN EXPANDED & Open (SB).

ABCDEFGHIJ XYZ
abcdefghijklmnopq

ELIZABETH ROMAN & Italic (Bauer).

ABCDEFGHIJKLMNOPQRSTUVWXYZ&
abcdefghijklmnopqrstuvwxyz 1234567890$

ABCDEFGHIJKLMNOPQRSTUVWXYZ&&
abcdefghijkklmnopqrstuvwxyzz 1234567890$

ELONGATED ROMAN SHADED (SB).

ABCDEFGHIJKLM $1234

EUROSTILE (Nebiolo) regular, Condensed, **Extended, Bold,** Bold Condensed, Bold Extended, Compact Bold Condensed. Also title version without lowercase: Microgramma light, Extended, Condensed, Bold, Bold Extended.

ABCDEFGHIJKLMNOPQRS
abcdefghijklmnopqrstuvwx

ABCDEFGHIJKLMNOPQRSTUVW
abcdefghijklmnopqrstuvwxyz1234

EVE (Klingspor): **regular** & Italic, Bold & **Italic,** Heavy, Decorative Caps.

ABCDEFGHIJKLMNOPQRSTUVWXYZ
abcdefghijklmnopqrstuvwxyz 1234567890

ABCDEFGHIJKLMNOPQRSTUVWXYZ
abcdefghijklmnopqrstuvwxyz 1234567890

EXCELSIOR (TA): Script, **Semi-Bold.**

ABCDEFGHIJKLMNOP
abcdefghijklmnopqrstuvwxyz $1234567890

FIGARO (EMono): 536 [Old Town or Old Towne, Showboat].

ABCDEFGHIJKLMNOPQRSTUVWXYZ&
abcdefghijklmnopqrstuv4567890.,"-:;!?

FLAMME (S&G) [Bon Aire, Torch].

ABCDEFGHIJKLMNOP
abcdefghijklmnopqrstuvwxyz

FLORIATED CAPITALS (EMono) 431 [Canterbury Capitals, Gill Floriated].

ABCDEFGHIJKLM

FOLIO (Bauer): Light & Italic, Light Condensed, Medium & Italic, Medium Condensed, **Medium Extended** & Italic, Bold, Bold Condensed & Italic, Bold Extra Condensed & Title, Bold Extended, **Extrabold.**

ABCDEFGHIJKLMNOPQRSTUVWXYZR
abcdefghijklmnopqrstuvwxyz4567890

ABCDEFGHIJKLMNOPQRSTUVW
abcdefghijklmnopq$12345678

FORTUNE (Bauer): **Light,** Bold & **Bold Italic,** Extrabold. Later called Fortuna.

ABCDEFGHIJKLMNOPQRSTUVW
abcdefghijklmnopqrstuvwxyz$12345

ABCDEFGHIJKLMNOPQRSTUVW
abcdefghijklmnopqrstuvwxyz123456

FORUM I & II (Weber). See Schadow.

ABCDEFGHIJKLMNOPQR $12345
ABCDEFGHIJKL$1234

FRY'S ORNAMENTED (SB). See *Colonial* in main text.

ABCDEFGHIJK

FUTURA (Bauer) **Black, Display** [Airport Tourist], & **Inline.** See main text.

ABCDEFGHIJKLMNOPQSTUVWXY
abcdefghijklqrstuvwxyz $0126789
ABCDEFGHIJKLMNOPQRSTTUVWXYZ&
abcdefghijklmnopqrstuvwxyz 1234

ABCDEFGHIJKLMNOPQRSTU

GILL SANS (EMono): several weights, widths, italics; and **Cameo** 233, **Cameo Ruled** 299 [Airport Relief, Banner], **Shadow** 406 [Eric Gill Shadow, Rhumba], **Shadow Titling** 304 [Sans Serif Shadow].

ABCDEFGHIJKLMN
ABCDEFGHIJKLMNOP
ABCDEFGHIJKLMN
ABCDEFGHIJKLMN

GLORIA (Gans).

ABCDEFGHIJKLMNOPQRS
abcdefghijklmnopqrstuvwxyz 1234567890

GRAPHIQUE (Haas).

AXYZABCDEFGHIJKLMNO$67890

GRECO ADORNADO (Gans). Also see Greco in main text.

ABCDEFGHIJKLMNOPQRSTU

GROSVENOR SCRIPT—see Dorchester Script.

GROTESQUE (EMono): Light & Italic 126, regular & **Italic** 215, **Bold** 216 (others).

ABCDEFGHIJKLMNOPQRSTUVWXYZ
abcdefghijklmnopqrstuvwxyz 123456
ABCDEFGHIJKLMNOPQRSTUVWXY
abcdefghijklmnopqrstuvwxyz1234567890

GROTESQUE (SB): **No. 8,** No. 9 & **Italic,** and others.

ABCDEFGHIJKLMNOPQRST
abcdefghijklmnopqrstuvwxyz
ABCDEFGHIJKLMNOPQRSTUVWXYZ
abcdefghijklmnopqrstuvwxyz1234567890

HEADLINE & **Headline Open** (TA).

ABCDEFGHIJKLMN**OPQRSTUVWXYZ.,-::'!?**
abcdefghijklmnooppqrstuvwxyyz$1234

HELLENIC WIDE (Bauer).

ABCDEFGHIJKLMNOPQ
abcdefghijklmnopqrstuv

HORIZON (Bauer): Light & Italic, **Medium, Bold,** Bold Condensed.

ABCDEFGHIJKLMNOPQRSTUVWXYZ
abcdefghijklmnopqrstuvwxy $123456789
ABCDEFGHIJKLMNOPQRSTUVWX
abcdefghijklmnopqrstuvwxyz $12345

INFORMATION (Stempel): **Bold Extended** & others.

ABCDEFGHIJKL
abcdefghijklm$

LARGO (TA): **Light, Bold,** Open.

ABCDEFGHIJKLMNOPQRS
ABCDEFGHI $123456789

LATIN WIDE or Wide Latin (SB) [Imperial, Emperor].

ABCDEFGHIJKLM
abcdefghijklmnopqr

LEGEND (Bauer).

ABCDEFGHIJKLMNOPQR
abcdefghijklmnopqrstuvwxyz 1234567890$

LE MERCURE. See Nicolas Cochin in main text.

ABCDEFGHIJKLMN
abcdefghijklmnopqrstuvwxyz

LIBRA (TA): **regular** (ATF imported fonts 5111) & **Light** (ATF 5112).

abcdefghijklmnopqrstuvwxy
abcdefghijklmnopqrstuvwxyzG

LILITH (Bauer).

ABCDEFGHIJKL
abcdefghijklmnop 1234

LUCIAN (Bauer): **regular** (or Bernhard Roman Bold) [Graphic Light], regular Italic, **Bold** [Graphic Bold], Open.

ABCDEFGHIJKLMNOPQRSTUVWXYZ&
abcdefghijklmnopqrstuvwxyz $1234567890.,:;-'""

ABCDEFGHIJKLMNOPQRSTUVWXYZ
abcdefghijklmnopqrstuvwxyz$1234567890.

MATURA (EMono): 496 [Pagoda Bold].

ABCDEFGHIJKLMNOPQ
abcdefghijklmnopqrstuv

MAXIME (Bauer).

ABCDEFGHIJKLMNO
abcdefghijklmnopqrstu$123456

MELIOR (Stempel): **Bold Condensed** & others. See main text.

ABCDEFGHIJKLMNOPQRSTUVWXYZ$1
abcdefghijklmnopqrstuvwxyzfffifl.,-:;

METROPOLIS (Stempel): **Light, Bold,** Shaded. See Homewood in main text.

ABCDEFGHIJKLMNOPQRSTUVWXYZ
abcdefghijklmnopqrstuvwxyz 1234567890

ABCDEFGHIJKLMNOPQRSTU
abcdefghijklmnopqrstuvwxyz

MICHELANGELO (Stempel).

ABCDEFGHIJKLMNOPQRSTUV

MICROGRAMMA—see Eurostile.

MISTRAL (TA).

ABCDEFGHIJKLMNOPQRSTUVW
abcdefghijklmnopqrstuvwxyz.,:;-

MODERN NO. 20 & **Italic** (SB).

ABCDEFGHIJKLMNOPQRSTUVWX
abcdefghijklmnopqrstuvwxyz1234567890
ABCDEFGHIJKLMNOPQRSTUVW
abcdefghijklmnopqrstuvwxyz1234567890

MOLÉ FOLIATE (SB).

ABCDEFGI

MONOLINE SCRIPT (EMono) 351 [Britannic, Stylus Script].

ABCDEFGHIJKLMNOPQRSTUVWXYZ&
abcdefghijklmnopqrstuvwxyz

NARROW SANS ITALIC (SB).

ABCDEFGHIJKLMNOPQRSTUVWXYZÆŒ&,.:;!?'(
abcdefghijklmnopqrstuvwxyzæœ 123456789

NORMANDE (Berthold): **regular** & Italic, **Condensed.**

AXYZABCDEFGHIJKLMN
avwxyzabcdefghijk $1234567
ABCDEFGHIJKLMNabcdefghijklmno $123456

NORMANDIA (Nebiolo): regular & Italic, **Outline,** Extra Condensed.

ABCDEFGHIJKLMNOPQ
abcdefghijklmnopqrstuv

ONDINE (D&P).

ABCDEFGHIJKLMNOPQRSTU
abcdefghijklmnopqrstuvwxyz

ORNATA (Klingspor).

ABCDEFGHIJKLMNO
abcdefghijklmnopqrs

ORPLID (Klingspor).

AABCDEFGHIJKLMMNOPQRST 123456

OTHELLO (EMono) 246. See other in main text; compare Neuland.

ABCDEFGHIJKLMNOPQRSTUVW

PALETTE (Berthold).

ABCDEFGHIJKLMNOPQRS
abcdefghijklmnopqrstuvwxyz

PEIGNOT (D&P): **Light,** Medium, **Bold.**

AEFGHIJKLMNO AOPQRSTUVWXYZ $90123
ALMNOPQRSTUVWXYZABCDE
abcdefghijklmnopqrstuv $12345

PERPETUA (EMono): **regular** & Italic 239, Bold & **Bold Italic** 461, Titling 258, Light Titling 480, Bold Titling 200.

ABCDEFGHIJKLMNOPQRSTUVWXYZ
abcdefghijklmnopqrstuvwxyz $1234567890

ABCDEFGHIJKLMNOPQRSTUVWXYZ&
abcdefghijklmnopqrstuvwxyz

PLAYBILL (SB); see Trylon in main text.

ABCDEFGHIJKLMNOPQRSTUVWXYZÆ
abcdefghijklmnopqrstuvwxyzæœ&1234

POST ROMAN (Berthold): **Light,** Medium, **Bold.**

ABCDEFGHIJKLMNOPQRSTUVWXYZ&
abcdefghijklmnopqrstuvwxyz 1234567890$

ABCDEFGHIJKLMNOPQRSTUVWXY
abcdefghijklmnopqrstuvwxyz 1234567890

PRISMA (Klingspor). See Sans Serif in main text.

ABCDEFGHIJK$1234

PROFIL (Haas).

ABCDEFG

REGINA (Berthold).

ABCDEFGHIJKLMNOPQRST

REINER (TA): **Script** (ATF imported fonts 5165), **Black.**

ABCDEFGHIJKLMNOPQRSTUVW
abcdefghijklmnopqrstuvwxyzfiflff.,-:; " "" !?&st $123
ABCDEFGHIJKLMNOPQRSTUV
abcdefghijklmnopqrstuvwxyz

RHAPSODIE (TA) **Swash** and **regular** caps.

ABCDEFGHIJKL
ABCDEFGHIJKLMNOPQRSTUV
abcdefghijklmnopqrstuvwxyz

RICCARDO (Haas).

ABCDEFGHIJKL $12345

ROCKWELL (EMono): **regular** & Italic 371, **Light** 390, **Bold** & Italic 391, Extra Bold 424, Condensed 414, Bold Condensed 359, Shadow 175.

ABCDEFGHIJKLMNOPQRSTUVWXYZ&
abcdefghijklmnopqrstuvwxyz

ABCDEFGHIJKLMNOPQRSTUVWXY
abcdefghijklmnopqrstuvwxyz

ROMAN COMPRESSED No. 3 (SB).

ABCDEFGHIJKLMNOPQRSTUVWX
abcdefghijklmnopqrstuvwxyz $1234

RONDO (TA): **regular** (ATF imported fonts 5171) & **Bold** (ATF 5172).

ABCDEFGHIJ abcdefghij $12345
ABCDEFGHIJKLMNOP
abcdefghijklmnopqrstuvwxyz$12345678

SALTO & **Saltino** (Klingspor).

ABCDEFGHIJK
ABCDEFGHIJKLMNOPQR
abcdefghijklmnopqrstuvwxyz dj ck ff fi fl ft

SANS SERIFS SHADED (SB).

ABCDEFGHIJKLMNOPQRSTUVWXY
ZÆŒ& 1234567890£$ „.:;-!?'

SAPPHIRE (Stempel).

ABCDEFGHIJKLMNOPQRS
TUVWXYZ $1234567890

SCHADOW (Weber): **regular,** Light & Italic, Semi-Bold, **Bold,** Bold Condensed. See Forum I & II.

ABCDEFGHIJKLMNOPQRSTU
abcdefghijklmnopqrst $12345
ABCDEFGHIJKLMNOPQR
abcdefghijklm$123456789

SCRIPT (EMono): **Light** 475. See Broad-Stroke Cursive in main text.

ABCDEFGHIJKLMNOPQRSTUVWXYZ&
abcdefghijklmnopqrstuvwxyz

SIGNAL (Berthold): **Light,** Medium, **Black** [Punch].

ABCDEFGHIJKLMNOPQRSTUVWXYZ&
abcdefghijklmnopqrstuvwxyz $1234567890
ABCDEFGHIJKLMNOPQRSTUVWXYZ&
abcdefghijklmnopqrstuvwxyz $1234567890

SISTINA (Stempel).

ABCDEFGHIJKLMNOPQRS
TUVWXYZ& $1234567890

SLOGAN (Nebiolo).

ABCDEFGHIJKL
abcdefghijklmnopqrstuvwxyz 1234567

SOLEMNIS (Berthold).

ABCDEFGHIJKLMN$12345

STANDARD (Berthold): many weights & widths including **Extended, Extra Bold Condensed.**

ABCDEFGHIJKLMNOPQRSTUV
abcdefghijklmnopqrstuvwxyz .,:;-
ABCDEFGHIJKLMNOPQRSTUVWXYZ
abcdefghijklmnopqrstuvwxyz123456789

STRADIVARIUS (Bauer).

ABCDEFGHIJKLMNOP
abcdefghijklmnopqrstuvwxyz fifflfft .,:; "-!?& ‹› $12

STUDIO (TA): **regular** (ATF imported fonts 5181) & **Bold.**

ABCDEFGHIJKLMNOPQRSTUVWX
abcdefghijklmnopqrstuvwxyz 123
ABCDEFGHIJKLMNOPQRSTUVW
abcdefghijklmnopqrstuvwxyz 123

SYLVAN or CHAMPLEVÉ (D&P, SB).

ABCDEFGHIJKLM

TEA-CHEST (SB).

ABCDEFGHIJKLM

TEMPLE SCRIPT (EMono): 455.

ABCDEFGHIJKLMNO
abcdefghijklmnopqrstuvw

THORNE SHADED (SB).

ABCDEFGHIJK

THOROWGOOD and Italic (SB).

ABCDEFGHIJKLMN
abcdefghijklm $12345
ABCDEFGHIJKLM
abcdefghijklmnopqrst

TIME SCRIPT (Weber): Light, **Semi-Bold,** Bold.

ABCDEFGHIJKLMNOP
abcdefghijklmnopqr$12345

TOPIC (Bauer): Medium & **Italic, Bold** & Italic.

ABCDEFGHIJKLMNOPQRSTUVWXYZ&
abcdefghijklmnopqrstuvwxyz 1234567890
AABCDEEFGHIJKKLMMNNOPQRSTUV
abcdefghijklmnopqrstuvwxyz 12345

TORINO & **Italic** (Nebiolo).

ABCDEFGHIJKLMNOPQRSTUVWXYZ&.,-
abcdefghijklmnopqrstuvwxyz$1234567890
ABCDEFGHIJKLMNOPQRSTUVWXY
abcdefghijklmnopqrstuvwxyz$123456789

TRUMP (Weber): **Gravure** & **Mediaeval.**

ABCDEFGHIJKLM
ABCDEFGHIJKLMNOPQRSTUVWXY
abcdefghijklmnopqrstuvwxyz 1234567

UNION PEARL (SB).

ABCDEFFGÇHIJKLMNO
PQRSTFUVWXYZQu&,.
abbcddefghhijkllmnopqrsftuvwxyzſhſtj

UNIVERS (D&P—versions identified only by 2-figure number; also cast to American standards for ATF, ATF reference number listed), (EMono—versions named with series numbers): 39 or Extra Light Extra Condensed 684; 45 46 (ATF 1000 1001) or Light & Italic 685; 47 48 (ATF 1002 1003) or Light Condensed & Italic 686; 49 (ATF 1004) or Light Extra Condensed 687; 53 (ATF 1005) or Medium Expanded 688; **55** 56 (ATF 1006 1007) or Medium & Italic 689; 57 58 (ATF 1008 1009) or Medium Condensed & Italic 690; 59 (ATF 1010) or Medium Extra Condensed 691; 63 (1011) or Bold Expanded 692; 65 66 (ATF 1012 1013) or Bold & Italic 693; 67 **68** (1014 1015) or Bold Condensed & Italic 694; 73 (ATF 1016) or Extra Bold Expanded 695; 75 76 (ATF 1017 1018) or Extra Bold & Italic 696; 83 (ATF 1019) or Ultra Bold Expanded 697.

ABCDEFGHIJKLMNOPQRSTUVWXYZ
abcdefghijklmnopqrstuvwxyz$1234567890

ABCDEFGHIJKLMNOPQRSTUVWXYZ.,-:;"!?&()–¢
abcdefghijklmnopqrstuvwxyz$1234567890

VENUS (Bauer): Light, Light Italic, Light Condensed, Light Extended, Medium, Medium Italic, Medium Condensed, **Medium Extended,** Bold, **Bold Italic,** Bold Condensed, Bold Extended [Noontime, Lorraine Medium], Extrabold, Extrabold Condensed, Extrabold Extended [Nitetime, Lorraine Bold].

ABCDEFGHIJKLMNOPQRSTUVW
abcdefghijklmnopqrstuvwxyz .,:;-'!?
ABCDEFGHIJKLMNOPQRSTUVWX
abcdefghijklmnopqrstuvwxyz& $12

VERONA (SB): regular & Italic, Bold & Italic, **Bold Condensed, Extra Bold.** See Munder Venezian in main text.

ABCDEFGHIJKLMNOPQRSTUVWXYZÆ&
abcdefghijklmnopqrstuvwxyzæœ123456789£
ABCDEFGHIJKLMNOPQRSTUW
abcdefghijklmnopqrstuvwxyzæœ123

VIRTUOSA I & II (Stempel), (same lowercase).

ABCDEFGHIJKLM
ABCDEFGHIJKLM
abcdefgghijklmnopqqurstuvwnxyvz æœ ſtfifl

WALBAUM (Berthold & EMono): **regular** & Italic 374, Medium & **Italic** 375.

ABCDEFGHIJKLMNOPQRSTUVWXYZ
abcdefghijklmnopqrstuvwxyz
ABCDEFGHIJKLMNOPQRSTUVW
abcdefghijklmnopqrstuvwxyz

WEISS ROMAN (Bauer): regular & Italic, **Bold, Extrabold.**

ABCDEFGHIJKLMNOPQRSTUVWXY
abcdefghijklmnopqrstuvwxyz$12345678
ABCDEFGHIJKLMNOPQRSTUVWX
abcdefghijklmnopqrstuvwxyz 1234567

WINDSOR (SB): Light, Light Condensed, Medium & Italic, regular, Condensed, **Elongated, Outline.** See Cambridge in main text.

ABCDEFGHIJKLMNOPQRSTUVWXYZÆŒ ,.:;-!
abcdefghijklmnopqrstuvwxyzæœ& 1234567890£
ABCDEFGHIJKLMNOP
abcdefghijklmnopqr$1234

352

Index of Type Designers

AMBERGER, FRITZ L. (c1899-1950)
Artist, printer.
    Bam-Stencil

AURIOL, GEORGES (1863-1938)
[Real name Jean-Georges Huyot]
French lettering artist.
    Auriol

AUSTIN, RICHARD T. (fl. 1788-1830)
19th-century punch-cutter.
    Bell
    Colonial

BARTLETT, EDWARD E. (1863-1942)
Printer; Linotype typographic director.
    Benedictine series
    Elzevir No. 3
    Garamond & Italic
    Garamond Bold & Italic
    Typographic Refinements for many
      faces

BARTUSKA, FRANK (-1975)
Lettering artist.
    Caslon No. 641
    News Gothic Condensed Bold
    Many photolettering faces

BASKERVILLE, JOHN (1706-1775)
English printer & typefounder.
    Baskerville & Italic
    —Bold

BATTEE, GEORGE*
Baltimore Type engraving dept. head.
    Athena
    Trylon Shaded & Oblique

BECKER, CHARLES HERMAN
ATF matrix & pattern maker.
    Cloister Cursive Handtooled
    Goudy Handtooled & Italic
    Novel Gothic
    Quick-Set Roman & Italic
    —Bold

BELL, JOHN (1745-1831)
English printer & typefounder.
    Bell & Italic

BENGUIAT, EDWARD (1914-   )
New York lettering artist.
    Souvenir & Italic
    —Demi Bold & Italic
    Many photolettering faces

BENTON, LINN BOYD (1844-1932)*
Inventor of punch-cutting machine;
ATF director; head, engineering dept.
    Century Roman & Italic
    —Broad-Face & Italic
    —Expanded & Italic
    Self-Spacing Faces

BENTON, MORRIS FULLER
(1872-1948)
Engineer, designer; head, ATF dept. of
typographic design.
    Adscript
    Agency Gothic
    —Open
    Alternate Gothic No. 1
    —No. 2
    —No. 3
    American Backslant
    American Caslon & Italic
    American Text
    Announcement Roman & Italic
    Antique Shaded
    Bank Gothic Light
    —Medium
    —Bold
    —Light Condensed
    —Medium Condensed
    —Bold Condensed
    Baskerville Italic
    Benton (Whitehall) & Italic
    Bodoni & Italic
    —Book & Italic
    —Bold & Italic
    —Bold Shaded
    —Bold Open
    Bold Antique
    —Condensed
    Broadway
    —Condensed
    Bulfinch Oldstyle
    Bulmer & Italic
    Canterbury
    Card Bodoni
    —Bold
    Card Litho
    —Light Litho
    Card Mercantile
    Card Roman
    Century Expanded & Italic
    Century Bold & Italic
    —Bold Condensed
    —Bold Extended
    Century Oldstyle & Italic
    —Bold & Italic
    —Bold Condensed
    Century Catalogue & Italic
    Century Schoolbook & Italic
    —Bold
    Cheltenham Oldstyle & Italic
    —Condensed
    —Wide

    Cheltenham Medium & Italic
    —Medium Condensed
    —Medium Expanded
    —Bold & Italic
    —Bold Condensed & Italic
    —Bold Extra Condensed & Title
    —Bold Extended
    —Extrabold
    —Bold Outline
    —Bold Shaded & Italic
    —Extrabold Shaded
    —Inline
    —Inline Extra Condensed
    —Inline Extended
    Chic
    Civilité
    Clearface & Italic
    —Bold & Italic
    —Heavy & Italic
    Clearface Gothic
    Cloister Black
    Cloister Oldstyle & Italic
    —Lightface & Italic
    —Bold & Italic
    —Bold Condensed
    —Cursive
    —Cursive Handtooled
    —Title & Bold Title
    Commercial Script
    Copperplate Gothic Shaded
    Cromwell
    Cushing Antique
    Della Robbia Light
    Dynamic Medium
    Eagle Bold
    Empire
    Engravers Bodoni
    Engravers Old English
    —Bold
    Engravers Bold
    Engravers Shaded
    Engravers Text
    Franklin Gothic & Italic
    —Condensed
    —Extra Condensed
    —Condensed Shaded
    Freehand
    Garamond & Italic
    —Bold & Italic
    —Open
    Globe Gothic
    —Condensed
    —Extra Condensed
    —Extended
    —Bold & Italic
    Goudy Bold & Italic
    —Catalogue & Italic
    —Extrabold & Italic
    —Handtooled & Italic
    —Title
    Gravure
    Greeting Monotone

BENTON, MORRIS F. *(continued)*
Headline Gothic
Hobo & Light Hobo
Invitation
—Shaded
Light Oldstyle
Lightline Gothic & Title
Lithograph Shaded
Louvaine Light & Italic
—Medium & Italic
—Bold & Italic
Miehle Extra Condensed & Title
Modernique
Monotone Gothic & Title
Motto
News Gothic
—Condensed
—Extra Condensed & Title
Norwood Roman
Novel Gothic
Othello
Packard
—Bold
Paramount
Parisian
Pen Print Open
Phenix
Piranesi Italic
—Italic Plain Caps
—Bold & Italic
—Bold Italic Plain Caps
Poster Gothic
Raleigh Gothic Condensed
Rockwell Antique
Roycroft
Rugged Roman
Schoolbook Oldstyle
Shadow
Souvenir
Sterling & Cursive
Stymie Light & Italic
—Medium & Italic
—Bold & Italic
—Black & Italic
Thermotypes
Tower
Typo Roman & Shaded
Typo Script & Extended
Typo Shaded
Typo Slope
Typo Upright & Bold
Ultra Bodoni & Italic
—Condensed
—Extra Condensed
Venetian & Italic
—Bold
Wedding Text & Shaded

BERNHARD, LUCIAN (1885-1972)
New York designer, lettering artist.
Bernhard Booklet & Italic
Bernhard Fashion
Bernhard Gothic Light & Italic
—Medium & Italic
—Medium Condensed
—Heavy
—Extra Heavy
Bernhard Modern Roman & Italic
—Bold & Italic
Bernhard Tango
—Swash
Many faces in Germany

BINNY, ARCHIBALD (1762-1838)
Early American typefounder.
Binny
Monticello & Italic
Oxford & Italic

BIXLER, MIKE
Private printer.
Bixler Roman

BLAKEFIELD, WILLIAM
Airport Black

BLUMENTHAL, JOSEPH
(1897-1990)
New York printer, teacher, designer.
Emerson & Italic
Spiral

BODONI, GIAMBATTISTA
(1740-1813)
Italian master printer & typefounder.
Bodoni

BORAD, AARON
Ultra-Modern

BOSCO, ALFRED R. (1901-   )
Artist, typographer.
Romany

BRADLEY, WILLIAM H. (1868-1962)
Printer, publisher, artist, typographer.
Bewick Roman
Bradley
Missal Initials
Wayside Roman & Italic

BRODERSEN, HAROLD (1913-   )
Brody

BUDDY, LEWIS III (c1872-1941)
Magazine artist & letterer.
Roycroft
Tabard

BULMER, WILLIAM (1757-1830)
Printer, designer.
Bulmer & Italic

BURFEIND, R. F.
Caslon Adbold series

BURKE, JACKSON (1908-1975)
Director of typographic development,
Linotype.
Aurora & Italic
Trade Gothic & Bold
—Condensed & Bold
—Extra Condensed & Bold
—Extended & Bold
—Light & Italic

CAPITAINE, W. F. (1851-   )
Punch-cutter.
Several 19th-century faces
Adtype & Italic
Caslon Shaded
Lithograph Shaded
Quick-Set Roman & Italic
—Bold

CARROLL, JOHN S. (-1982)*
Typefounder.
Vanity Fair
Early faces recreated

CARTER, MATTHEW (1937-   )
Linotype type designer.
Olympian & Italic
Various phototype faces

CARTER, WILLIAM
English designer.
Dartmouth

CASLON, WILLIAM (1692-1766)
English typefounder.
Caslon & Italic
Caslon Text

CHAPPELL, WARREN (1904-1991)
Typographer, illustrator, letterer.
Lydian & Italic
—Bold & Italic
—Cursive
—Bold Condensed & Italic
Trajanus & Italic
—Bold

CLELAND, THOMAS MAITLAND
(1880-1964)
Painter, designer, illustrator,
typographer.
Caslon Swash
Della Robbia
Garamond & Italic

COLWELL, M. ELIZABETH
Chicago lettering artist.
Colwell Handletter & Italic

COOPER, OSWALD BRUCE
(1879-1940)*
Chicago lettering artist, designer.
Boul Mich
Cooper & Italic
—Black & Italic
—Black Condensed
—Fullface or Modern
—Hilite
Dietz Text
Packard
Pompeian Cursive

COWAN, —
Engravers Old English

CRAW, FREEMAN GODFREY
(JERRY) (1917-   )
Typographer, letterer, art director.
Ad Lib
Craw Clarendon
—Book
—Condensed
Craw Modern & Italic
—Bold
Several photolettering faces

CUMMING, JOHN F. (1852-   )*
Massachusetts punch-cutter.
Jenson Old Style
Satanick
Viking

DAVIS, WHEDON (1933-   )*
ATF sales manager & director of
    typeface design.
    Franklin Gothic Condensed Italic
    Whedons Gothic Outline

DeBENEDICTIS, PLATO
15th-century Italian printer &
typefounder.
    Benedictine series

DEMETER, PETER A. (1875-1939)
German designer.
    Demeter
    Dresden

DeROOS, SJOERD HENDRIK
(1877-1962)
    Card Italic
    DeRoos & Italic
    Egmont & Italic
    —Medium & Italic
    —Bold & Italic
    Medieval & Italic

DETTERER, ERNST FREDERICK
(1888-1947)
Designer, instructor, calligrapher.
    Nicolas Jenson (Eusebius)

DIETZ, AUGUST SR.
Letterer; Intertype director of
typography.
    Dietz Text

DOMBREZIAN, PETER (PETE DOM)
(1899-   )
    Dom Casual & Diagonal
    —Bold

DUENSING, PAUL HAYDEN
(1929-   )*
Operator, private press & typefoundry.
    Chancery Italic
    Quadrata II
    Rustica
    Sixteenth Century Roman
    Unciala
    Additions to other faces, recuttings

DWIGGINS, WILLIAM ADDISON
(1880-1956)
Illustrator, calligrapher, typographer,
book designer, author.
    Arcadia & Italic
    Caledonia & Italic
    —Bold & Italic
    Caravan
    Charter
    Eldorado & Italic
    Electra & Italic & Cursive
    —Bold & Italic & Cursive
    Falcon & Italic
    Hingham & Italic
    Metrothin & Italic
    Metrolite & Italic
    Metromedium & Italic
    Metroblack & Italic
    Stuyvesant & Italic
    Tippecanoe & Italic
    Winchester Roman & Italic
    Winchester Uncial & Italic

EIDENBENZ, HERMANN
(1902-   )
Swiss type designer.
    Clarendon

ERBAR, JAKOB (1878-1935)
German type designer.
    Erbar series

FARRAR, GILBERT POWDERLY
(1886-1957)
Intertype typographic director.
    Bert Black

FINK, WILLIAM E. (1905-   )
Designer, art director.
    Greenwich

FISCHER, EDMUND C.
    Artcraft series

FLINSCH, HEINRICH (fl. 1859)
Nineteenth-century German
typefounder.
    Aldine Condensed

FORMAN, JACK
    Roys Gothic No. 2

FOSTER, ROBERT (1895-   )
Designer, sculptor, typographer.
    Foster Abstract
    Pericles

FOURNIER, PIERRE SIMON
(1712-1768)
French typefounder.
    Fournier
    Fournier le Jeune

FREUND, HERMAN R. (1886-1956)
Intertype vice president for
engineering.
    Ideal News & Italic
    Regal & Italic
    Regal Bold

GARAMOND, CLAUDE (1480-1561)
French typefounder.
    Garamond
    Garamont

GAUNT, SIDNEY CLYDE
(c1874-1932)
Artist; BB&S type designer.
    Adstyle & Italic
    —Condensed
    —Extra Condensed & Headletter
    —Wide
    —Lightface
    —Black
    —Black Outline
    —Shaded
    Authors Oldstyle & Italic
    —Oldstyle Bold
    Authors Roman & Italic
    —Condensed
    —Wide
    —Bold
    —Bold Condensed
    Barnhart Oldstyle & Italic
    —No. 2

Barnhart Lightface
Cardstyle
Chester Text
Engravers Old Black
Engravers Roman Shaded
French Plate Script
Mission
Old Roman Condensed
—Bold
—Bold Condensed
—Black & Italic
—Semitone
Parsons Swash Initials
Pencraft Oldstyle & Italic
—Bold
—Shaded
Pencraft Text
Publicity Gothic
Stationers Semiscript
Talisman & Italic
Wedding Plate Script

GILLIES, WILLIAM S. (1911-   )
Letterer, illustrator.
    Gillies Gothic Light
    —Bold

GOODHUE, BERTRAM
GROSVENOR (1869-1924)
New York architect, artist, designer.
    Cheltenham Oldstyle & Italic
    Merrymount

GOUDY, FREDERIC WILLIAM
(1865-1947)*
Independent type designer & founder;
printer; author; Monotype art director.
    Aries
    Bertham
    Booklet Old Style
    Californian & Italic
    Camelot
    Caxton Initials
    Collier Old Style
    Companion Old Style & Italic
    Copperplate Gothic Heavy
    Cushing Italic
    Deepdene & Italic
    —Medium
    —Bold & Italic
    —Open Text
    —Text
    DeVinne Roman
    Forum
    Franciscan
    Friar
    Garamont & Italic
    Globe Gothic Bold
    Goethe & Italic
    Goudy Antique
    —Cursive
    —Heavyface & Italic
    —Lanston
    —Light Old Style & Italic
    —Modern & Italic
    —Newstyle
    —Old Style & Italic
    —Open & Italic
    —Ornate
    —Sans Serif Light & Italic
    —Sans Serif Heavy
    —Stout

GOUDY, FREDERIC W. *(continued)*
  Goudy Text
  —Thirty
  Goudytype
  Hadriano
  —Stone-Cut
  Hearst
  Italian Old Style & Italic
  Kaatskill
  Kennerley Old Style & Italic
  —Bold & Italic
  Klaxon
  Lombardic Capitals
  Marlborough
  Mediaeval
  Nabisco
  National Old Style
  Norman Capitals
  Pabst Old Style & Italic
  Powell
  Record Title
  Remington Typewriter
  Saks Goudy & Italic
  —Bold
  Scripps College Old Style & Italic
  Sherman
  Spencer Old Style
  Tory Text
  Trajan Title
  Truesdell & Italic
  University of California Old Style &
    Italic
  Venezia Italic
  Village
  —No. 2 & Italic
  Village Text

GRANJON, ROBERT (fl. 1545-1589)
French punch-cutter.
  Civilité
  Granjon & Italic
  Plantin & Italic

GRASSET, EUGENE (1841-1917)
French decorative artist.
  Grasset & Italic

GRIFFITH, CHAUNCEY HAWLEY
(1879-1956)
Linotype vice president in charge of
typographic development.
  Baskerville Bold & Italic
  Bell Gothic & Bold
  Bookman & Italic
  Corona & Italic
  Excelsior & Italic
  Granjon Bold
  Ionic No. 5 & Italic
  Ionic Condensed
  Janson & Italic
  Memphis Extra Bold & Italic
  —Extra Bold Condensed
  Monticello & Italic
  Opticon & Italic
  Pabst Extra Bold & Italic
  —Condensed & Italic
  Paragon & Italic
  Poster Bodoni & Italic
  Ryerson Condensed
  Textype & Italic
  Directed cutting of many other faces

GRIFFO, FRANCESCO
(fl. 1499-1518)
  Bembo

HAIGHT, A. V.
Poughkeepsie designer.
  Haight
  Rogers

HAMMER, VICTOR (1882-1967)
Printer, designer, type engraver,
teacher.
  American Uncial
  Andromaque
  Hammer Samson Uncial
  Several faces in Germany & Italy

HARVEY, MICHAEL (1931-   )
  Zephyr

HAUSER, GEORGE (1893-   )
New York letterer & artist.
  Hauser Script

HESS, SOL (1886-1953)
Monotype typographic manager & art
director.
  Alternate Gothic Modernized
  —Italic
  Artscript
  Baskerville Bold
  Bodoni Bold Condensed
  —Bold Paneled
  Bookman Old Style Condensed
  Broadway & Engraved
  Bruce Old Style & Italic
  Caslon Old Style No. 437 & Italic
  English Caslon No. 37 & Italic
  Century Bold Condensed Italic
  Cheltenham Wide Italic
  Cochin & Italic
  —Bold & Italic
  —Open
  —Bold Tooled
  Cooper Tooled
  Goudy Bible
  Goudy Bold Swash
  —Handtooled Swash
  —Heavyface Condensed
  —Heavyface Open
  Hadriano Stone-Cut
  Hess Bold & Italic
  Hess Monoblack
  Hess Neobold
  Hess New Bookbold & Italic
  Hess Old Style & Italic
  Hess Title & Italic
  Italian Old Style Wide
  Janson & Italic
  Jefferson Gothic
  Kennerley Open Caps
  Laurentian
  Martin & Italic
  New Bookman
  Onyx Italic
  Pendrawn
  Postblack Italic
  Post-Stout Italic
  Poster
  Sans Serif Light Condensed
  —Medium
  —Medium Condensed

  Sans Serif Extrabold & Italic
  —Extrabold Condensed
  Sans Serif Lined
  Scotch Roman Italic Swash
  —Open Shaded Italic
  Slimline
  Spire
  Squareface
  Stationers Gothic Light
  —Medium
  —Bold
  Stylescript
  Stymie Light Condensed
  —Medium Condensed
  —Extrabold & Italic
  —Extrabold Condensed
  Tourist Gothic & Italic
  20th Century Medium Condensed
    Italic
  —Bold Italic
  —Extrabold Italic
  —Extrabold Condensed Italic
  —Ultrabold & Italic
  —Ultrabold Condensed
  Ward & Italic
  Adapted many faces to Monotype
    unit system

HEYER, CHARLES E. (1841-1897)
Chicago punch-cutter.
  Greeting Card
  —Light
  Many 19th-century faces

HILL, JOSEPH E.
  Benedictine & Italic
  —Book & Italic
  —Bold & Italic

HIRT, EMIL
  Parkway Script

HOFFMAN, EDWARD
Swiss typefounder.
  Helvetica

HORNE, HERBERT PERCY
(1864-1916)
  Montallegro

HORNUNG, CLARENCE PEARSON
(1899-   )
  Lexington

HUGHES, CHARLES E.
Milwaukee graphic artist.
  Century Nova & Italic

HUNTER, DARD (1883-1966)
HUNTER, DARD JR. (1917-1989)
Private press printers.
  Mountain House Press Types

HUPIE or **HOOPER, CARL**
  Airport Black
  —Black Condensed Title
  —Broad

HUXLEY, WALTER (1890-1955)
Typographer.
  Huxley Vertical

IHLENBURG, HERMAN (1843-1905)
Punch-cutter.
American Italic
Bradley & Italic
—Extended
—Outline
Columbus
Post Oldstyle Italic
Roundhand
Schoeffer Oldstyle
Many 19th-century faces

IPSEN, LUDVIG S.
Florentine

IRVIN, REA (1881-1972)
New Yorker magazine art director.
Irvin

ISBELL, RICHARD
Detroit designer, illustrator, lettering
artist.
Americana & Italic
—Bold
—Extra Bold

JACOBS, SAMUEL A.
Designer & printer, Golden Eagle
Press.
Anacreon
Charter

JANNON, JEAN (1580-1658)
French printer & typefounder.
Garamond & Italic

JANSON, ANTON (1620-1687)
17th-century Dutch typefounder.
Janson

JENSON, NICOLAS (1420-1480)
Venetian typefounder.
Centaur
Cloister Oldstyle
Eusebius series
Hess Old Style
Jenson Oldstyle
Montaigne

JOHNSON, WILLIAM MARTIN
Curtis Publishing Co. lettering artist.
Bulfinch Oldstyle
Meriontype

JONES, GEORGE W. (1860-1942)
English printer & typographer.
Baskerville & Italic
Estienne & Italic
Granjon & Italic
Venezia
Several English faces

JOST, HEINRICH (1899-1948)
German designer.
Beton series

JUNGE, CARL STEPHEN
(1880-1972)
Chicago designer, artist, author.
Caslon Italic Specials
Swagger Capitals

KAUFMANN, MAX RICHARD
(1904-   )
Letterer, typographer, *McCalls*
magazine art director.
Balloon Light & Bold
—Extrabold
Kaufmann Script
—Bold

KIMBALL, INGALLS (1874-1933)
New York printer.
Cheltenham Old Style & Italic

KIS, NICHOLAS (1680-1702)
Hungarian punch-cutter & printer.
Janson

KITSON, E. J.
Saturday Evening Post artist.
Post Oldstyle Roman No. 1
—No. 2

KLUMPP, EMIL (1912-   )*
Lettering artist; ATF sales manager &
director of typeface design.
Murray Hill & Bold
Many photolettering faces

KOCH, RUDOLF (1876-1934)
German type designer & engraver.
Czarin
Eve & Italic
Kabel & Bold
Neuland & Inline
Many types in Germany

LAUSCHKE, ERNST
19th-century type engraver.
Handcraft Title
—Wide Title
Pekin

MacFARLAND, J. HORACE*
(1853-1948)
Pennsylvania printer.
French Round Face & Italic

MANUTIUS, ALDUS (1450-1515)
Venetian printer & publisher.
Bembo
Cloister Italic

MARDER, CLARENCE C.
Typefounder.
Copperplate Gothic Light
—Light Condensed
—Light Extended
—Italic
—Heavy Condensed
—Heavy Extended
—Bold

MARTIN, WILLIAM (fl. 1786-1815)
English punch-cutter, typefounder.
Bulmer & Italic

MASON, GIBBS
Vanden Houten

MAYEUR, GUSTAVE*
French typefounder.
Wedding Plate Script

McARTHUR, RICHARD N.
(1882-1956)*
Typographer, designer, printer; BB&S
advertising manager.
Old Dutch
Ratdolt Italic

McKAY, WALTER H. (1901-1956)
New York designer.
Columbia & Italic
—Bold & Italic
Heritage

McMURTRIE, DOUGLAS
CRAWFORD (1888-1944)
Typographer, designer, printing
historian.
McMurtrie Title
Ultra-Modern & Italic
—Bold
Vanity Fair Capitals

MENHART, OLDRÎCH (1897-1962)
Unciala

MIDDLETON, ROBERT HUNTER
(1898-1985)*
Ludlow director of typeface design.
Admiral Script
Andromaque
Artcraft Italic
Bodoni Black & Italic
—Black Condensed
—Campanile & Italic
—Modern & Italic
Cameo & Italic
Cheltenham Cursive
Coronet & Bold
Delphian Open Title
Eden & Bold
Eusebius & Italic
—Bold & Italic
—Open
Flair
Florentine Cursive
Formal Script
Garamond & Italic
—Bold & Italic
Karnak Light
—Intermediate & Italic
—Medium & Italic
—Black & Italic
—Black Condensed & Italic
—Obelisk
Lafayette Extra Condensed
Ludlow Black & Italic
Mandate
Mayfair Cursive
Radiant Medium & Italic
—Bold
—Bold Condensed & Italic
—Bold Extra Condensed
—Heavy
Record Gothic Condensed Italic
—Extended & Italic
—Bold & Italic
—Bold Condensed
—Bold Extended & Italic
—Bold Extended Reverse
—Thinline Condensed
—Heavy Condensed
—Light Medium-Extended

MIDDLETON, R. H. *(continued)*
  Record Gothic Medium-Extended &
    Italic
  —Bold Medium-Extended
  —Heavy Medium-Extended
  Samson
  Stellar & Bold
  Stencil
  Tempo Light & Italic
  —Medium & Italic
  —Medium Condensed
  —Bold & Italic
  —Bold Condensed & Italic
  —Bold Extended
  —Heavy & Italic
  —Heavy Condensed & Italic
  —Black & Italic
  —Black Condensed & Italic
  —Black Extended & Italic
  —Heavy Inline
  —Alternate Medium
  —Alternate Bold & Italic
  —Alternate Heavy
  Umbra
  Wave

MIEDINGER, MAX (1910-1980)
Swiss type designer.
  Helvetica

MOORE, GUERNSEY (-1925)
Saturday Evening Post artist.
  Post Old Style No. 1 & Italic
  —No.2

MORISON, STANLEY ARTHUR
(1889-1967)
Designer, author; English Monotype
typographic consultant.
  Baskerville & Italic
  Bell & Italic
  Bembo & Italic
  Times New Roman & Italic
  Many English faces

MORRIS, WILLIAM (1834-1896)
English printer, writer.
  Chaucer
  Collier Old Style
  Golden Type
  Jenson Oldstyle & Italic
  Morris Romanized Black
  Troy

MULLEN, JERRY
  Repro Script

NADALL, BERNE (1869-   )
  Caslon Antique & Italic

NELSON, STANLEY
Maryland avocational typefounder.
  Robin

ORCUTT, WILLIAM DANA
(1870-1953)
Book designer, typographer, author.
  French Round Face & Italic
  Humanistic
  Laurentian
  Suburban French & Italic
  Verona

OTTLEY, GEORGE OSWALD
  Mission

PARKER, WADSWORTH A.
(1864-1938)
Printer, typefounder; head, ATF
specimen department.
  Bookman & Italic
  Gallia
  Goudy Handtooled & Italic
  Graybar Book
  Lexington
  Modernistic
  Stymie Compressed
  —Inline Title

PECHEY, ELISHA
English designer.
  Cambridge
  Windsor series

PEIGNOT, GEORGES (1872-1914)
French designer & typefounder.
  Nicolas Cochin & Italic

PHEMISTER, ALEXANDER C.
(1829-1894)
Punch-cutter.
  Bookman & Italic
  Franklin Old Style & Italic

PHINNEY, JOSEPH W. (1848-1934)*
Typefounder; ATF director and vice
president.
  Abbott Oldstyle
  Bradley
  Camelot
  Cheltenham Old Style & Italic
  Cloister Black
  Engravers Old English
  Flemish Black
  Globe Gothic
  Jenson Oldstyle & Italic
  —Heavyface
  Satanick
  Taylor Gothic
  Vertical Writing
  Many 19th-century faces

PLANTIN, CHRISTOPHE
(1520-1589)
Dutch printer.
  Plantin

POWELL, GERRY (1899-   )
Typographer, industrial designer.
  Daily News Gothic
  Onyx
  Spartan series
  Stencil
  Stymie Light Title
  —Medium Title
  —Bold Condensed

RAND, PAUL (1914-   )
Graphics design consultant.
  Westinghouse Gothic
  —Light

RANSOM, WILL (1878-1955)*
Designer, letterer, typographer,
author.
  Clearcut Shaded Capitals
  Parsons & Italic
  —Bold

REINER, IMRE (1900-1987)
German architect & designer.
  Glamour series

RENNER, FRANZ (-1494)
German printer.
  Renner

RENNER, PAUL (1878-1956)
German architect & designer.
  Futura series

RENSHAW, BUD (JOHN L.)
(1924-   )
ATF staff designer.
  Franklin Gothic Wide
  News Gothic Bold
  Spartan series

RILEY, FRANK H. (1894-   )
Chicago artist, designer, typographer.
  Contact Bold Condensed & Italic
  Grayda

RIMMER, JAMES (1934-   )
Vancouver designer & illustrator;
avocational punch-cutter &
typefounder.
  Fellowship
  Juliana Oldstyle
  Nephi Mediaeval

ROBINSON, T. C.
  Adstyle Borders

ROGERS, BRUCE (1870-1957)*
Designer, printer, author.
  Centaur
  Goudy Bible
  Janson & Italic
  Montaigne

ROGERS, JOHN KIMBALL
(1821-1888)
  Menu Roman
  Skinner
  Other 19th-century faces

RONALDSON, JAMES (1768-1842)
Early American typefounder.
  Ronaldson

ROSART, JACQUES FRANÇOIS
(1714-1777)
Dutch typefounder.
  McMurtrie Title
  Vanity Fair Capitals

ROTHSTEIN, ROY
Cleveland typographer.
  Layout Gothic No. 1, 2, 3
  Roys Gothic No. 2, 3
  Photolettering faces

RUZICKA, RUDOLPH (1883-1978)
Wood-engraver, designer,
typographer.
  Fairfield & Italic
  —Medium & Italic
  Primer & Italic

ST. JOHN, JAMES A. (1841-1901)
Boston & St. Louis typefounder.
  DeVinne series
  Many 19th-century faces

SALTER, GEORGE (1897-1967)
  Flex

SCHAEFER, WILLY
German designer.
  Neon

SCHRAUBSTÄDTER, WILLIAM A.
(1864-1957)*
St. Louis punch-cutter & typefounder.
  Adcraft Medium
  DeVinne Recut
  —Outline
  Foster & Condensed
  French Script
  Webb
  Winchell Condensed
  Woodward series
  Many 19th-century faces

SCHROEDER, GUSTAV F.
(1861-   )
Punch-cutter.
  DeVinne series
  Pastel series
  Many 19th-century faces

SEYMOUR, RALPH FLETCHER
(1876-1966)
Designer, artist, publisher.
  Alderbrink or Seymour

SHAAR, EDWIN W. (1915-   )
Designer, writer; Monotype assistant
art director; Intertype art director.
  Czarin (lowercase)
  Flash & Bold
  Futura Book Oblique
  —Book Condensed
  —Demibold Oblique
  —Demibold Condensed
  —Extrabold & Oblique
  —Extrabold Condensed & Oblique
  Imperial & Italic
  Satellite & Italic
  —Bold
  Valiant
  Vogue Extra Condensed
  Several phototype faces

SHANKS, EDWARD
  Ivanhoe

SMITH, CHARLES WILLIAM
  John Hancock
  Lowell

SMITH, ROBERT E. (1910-   )
New York artist, art director.
  Brush
  Park Avenue

SMITH, THOMAS WHITE
(1835-1907)
English typefounder.
  Old Roman & Italic

SNIFFIN, WILLARD T.
  Adonis
  Hollywood
  Keynote
  Liberty
  Newport
  Nubian
  Piranesi
  Raleigh Cursive
  —Initials
  Rivoli & Italic
  Rosetti

SPRUNGER, LESLIE
  Ultra-Modern

STILLSON, R. L.
  Stillson

STREMIC, WILLIAM
  Airport Black

TAGLIENTE, GIOVANNANTONIO
(c1465/70-c1528)
16th-century typefounder.
  Bembo Italic

TALLONE, ALBERTO (1898-1968)
Italian designer & printer.
  Tallone & Italic

THOMPSON, SAMUEL WINFIELD
(TOMMY) (1905-   )
New York letterer, commercial artist.
  Baltimore Script
  Collier Heading
  Futura
  Mademoiselle
  Post Headletter
  Thompson Quillscript

THOMS, HELMITH
Phoenix designer.
  Lariat

TIEMANN, WALTER (1876-1951)
  Narciss

TRAFTON, HOWARD ALLEN
(1897-   )
New York artist, teacher, designer.
  Cartoon & Bold
  Trafton Script

TRENHOLM, GEORGE F.
(1886-1958)
Designer, printer, artist; Intertype
typeface design counsellor.
  Cornell & Italic
  Egmont Decorative Initials
  Georgian Cursive
  Nova Script

Trenholm Old Style & Cursive
  —Bold
  —Shaded Capitals
  Waverly & Italic

TUDOR, CHARLES WILLIAM (1903-
1970)
Life magazine art director.
  Tudor Medium & Italic

UPDIKE, DANIEL BERKELEY
(1860-1941)*
Typographer, printer, historian,
author.
  Montallegro

WARDE, FREDERIC (1894-1939)
New York printer, calligrapher,
typographer, author.
  Arrighi

WEATHERLY, S. M.
  Washington Text

WEISS, EMIL RUDOLF (1895-1942)
German designer.
  Cairo series
  Memphis series
  Weiss & Italic

WERNER, NICHOLAS J. (1858-1940)
Artist, editor, printer, typefounder,
writer.
  Bizarre Bold
  Brandon
  Bruce Title
  Corbitt
  Courts
  DeVinne & Italic
  —Condensed
  —Recut Italic
  Inland
  Menu Roman
  Mid-Gothic
  Pastel series
  Quentell
  Skinner
  Many 19th-century faces

WEST, JAMES (1830-   )
Punch-cutter, designer.
  Bank Script No. 1, 2, 3
  Many 19th-century faces

WIEBKING, ROBERT (1870-1927)*
Matrix engraver for several American
and English founders and for Ludlow;
designer; cut many of Goudy's types.
  Advertisers Gothic
  —Condensed
  —Outline
  —Condensed Outline
  Artcraft & Italic
  —Bold
  Bodoni Light & Italic
  —Bold & Italic
  Caslon Catalog
  Caslon Light Italic
  Clearface Caslon & Italic
  Engravers Roman & Bold
  Engravers Litho Bold
  —Condensed

WIEBKING, ROBERT *(continued)*
Invitation Text
Modern Text
Munder Venezian & Italic
—Bold & Italic
Square Gothic
True-Cut Bodoni & Italic
World Gothic & Italic
—Condensed

WINCHELL, EDWARD EVERETT
Art director.
Winchell

WORRELL, DR. WILLIAM HOYT
(1879-1952)
Calligrapher, author.
Worrell Uncial

ZAPF, HERMANN (1918-   )
German book designer, calligrapher,
type designer.
Hunt Roman
Melior & Italic
—Bold
Optima Medium & Italic
—Black

Palatino & Italic
—Semi-bold
Zapf Civilité
Many German types & phototype
faces

ZIMMERMANN, JOHN
BB&S head of matrix engraving.
Cubist Bold

Index of Names, Other Than Type Designers

THE PERSONS listed in this section are mentioned in connection with the typefaces listed. See text.
Names indicated with an asterisk (*) are also shown in the preceding appendix as designers.

ABBE, DOROTHY
Private press printer, Püterschein-
Hingham Press.
  Winchester

BARTH, HENRY
Typefounder, inventor.
  (Preface)

BATTEE, GEORGE*
Baltimore Type engraving dept. head.
  Baltimore Script
  Elegante

BENTON, LINN BOYD (1844-1932)*
Inventor of punch-cutting machine;
ATF director; head, engineering dept.
  Antique Shaded
  Clearface series
  Lithograph Shaded
  (Preface)

BROAD, CHARLES (-1965)
Typefounder.
  Many antique faces revived.

BULLEN, HENRY LEWIS
(1857-1938)
Head, ATF typographic library &
museum; author.
  Bodoni series
  Caslon Oldstyle & Italic
  Garamond series

CARROLL, JOHN S. (-1982)*
Typefounder.
  Early faces recreated

COCHIN, CHARLES NICOLAS
(1715-1790)
French artist & engraver.
  Nicolas Cochin

COMSTOCK, A. H.
Omaha printer.
  Comstock

COOPER, OSWALD BRUCE
(1879-1940)*
Chicago lettering artist, designer.
  Boul Mich

CUMMING, JOHN F. (1852-   )
Massachusetts punch-cutter.
  Jenson Old Style
  Montaigne
  Satanick
  Viking
  Many 19th-century faces

CUSHING, JOSIAH STEARNS
(1854-1913)
Noted New England printer.
  Cushing series
  Norwood Roman

DAVIS, WHEDON (1933-   )*
ATF sales manager & director of
typeface design.
  Americana series

DeVINNE, THEODORE LOW
(1828-1914)
Printer, typographer, publisher,
author.
  Century Roman & Italic
  DeVinne series
  Renner

DIDOT, FIRMIN (1764-1836)
French typefounder.
  French Round Face

DUENSING, PAUL HAYDEN
(1929-   )*
Operator, private press & typefoundry.
  Andromaque
  Dartmouth
  Zapf Civilité

FRY, DR. EDMUND (1754-1835)
18th-century English typefounder.
  Baskerville

GILLISS, WALTER (1855-1925)
New York book printer.
  Caslon Oldstyle & Italic

GOUDY, BERTHA M.
Wife & assistant to Frederic Goudy.
  Bertham
  Deepdene Italic

GOUDY, FREDERIC WILLIAM
(1865-1947)*
Independent type designer & founder;
printer; author; Monotype art director.
  Foster Abstract
  Cut many of his own typefaces

GRABHORN, EDWIN E. (1889-1968)
San Francisco printer.
  Franciscan

HOELL, LOUIS (1860-1935)
  Emerson

HUBBARD, ELBERT GREEN
(1856-1915)
Writer, printer, publisher.
  Roycroft

JOHNSON, LAURENCE (1801-1860)
American typefounder.
  Caslon Oldstyle & Italic

KENNERLEY, MITCHELL
(1878-1950)
New York printer, publisher.
  Cosmopolitan & Italic
  Kennerley & Italic

KLUMPP, EMIL (1912-   )*
Lettering artist; ATF sales manager &
director of typeface design.
  Americana

KOCH, PAUL
German punch-cutter (son of Rudolf
Koch).
  Hammer Samson Uncial

LANSTON, TOLBERT (1844-1913)
Monotype inventor.
  (Preface)

LIEBERMAN, DR. J. BEN
(1914-1984)
Printer, writer, publisher.
  (Preface)

MacFARLAND, J. HORACE*
Pennsylvania printer.
  MacFarland
  Suburban French & Italic

MAYEUR, GUSTAVE*
French typefounder.
  Elzevir
  French Plate Script

McARTHUR, RICHARD N.
(1882-1956)*
Typographer, designer, printer; BB&S
advertising manager.
  Boul Mich
  Cooper

McCLURE, SAMUEL SYDNEY
(1857-1949)
Magazine publisher.
  McClure

MERGENTHALER, OTTMAR
(1854-1899)
Linotype inventor.
  (Preface)

MIDDLETON, ROBERT HUNTER
(1898-1985)*
Ludlow director of typeface design.
  Hammer Samson Uncial

MOORE, ISAAC
English punchcutter.
  Baskerville

MUNDER, NORMAN THOMPSON
AEISLER (1867-1953)
Prominent Baltimore printer.
  Munder Venezian
  Norman Capitals

PHINNEY, JOSEPH W. (1848-1934)*
Typefounder; ATF director and vice
president.
  Oxford & Italic

PRINCE, EDWARD PHILIP
(1847-1923)
English punch-cutter.
  Montallegro

QUENTELL, WILLIAM S.
  Quentell

RANSOM, WILL (1878-1955)*
Designer, letterer, typographer,
author.
  Village

REHAK, THEO
Howell, N.J., typefounder.
  Village

ROGERS, BRUCE (1870-1957)*
Designer, printer, author.
  Bell & Italic
  Italian Old Style & Italic

SCHNOOR, HERMAN
Punch-cutter, matrix engraver.
  Airport Broad
  Mademoiselle
  Wide Line Gothic

SCHRAUBSTÄDTER, WILLIAM A.
(1864-1957)*
St. Louis punch-cutter & typefounder.
  Condensed Comstock
  Litho Antique
  Many 19th-century faces

SHERMAN, FREDERICK
FAIRCHILD (1874-1940)
Publisher and fine printer.
  Sherman
  Village

SPECKTER, MARTIN K. (1915-1988)
Advertising executive; printing
hobbyist.
  Americana

TAYLOR, CHARLES H.
  Globe Gothic

UPDIKE, DANIEL BERKELEY
(1860-1941)*
Typographer, printer, historian,
author.
  Bell & Italic
  Merrymount
  Oxford & Italic

VOLK, KURT H.
New York typographer.
  (Introduction)

WARDE, BEATRICE BECKER
(1900-1969)
Historian, writer, typographer;
English Monotype publicist.
  Garamond & Italic

WATTS, STEVENS L. (1895-1966)
ATF sales promotion manager.
  Dom Casual
  Light Oldstyle
  Oxford & Italic

WIEBKING, ROBERT (1870-1927)*
Matrix engraver for several American
and English founders and for Ludlow;
designer; cut many of Goudy's types.
  Centaur
  Collier Old Style
  Goudy Modern & Italic
  —Open & Italic
  Klaxon
  Marlborough
  Nabisco
  Norman Capitals
  Pabst Old Style & Italic
  Steelplate Gothic Light
  —Heavy & Italic
  —Light Condensed
  —Heavy Condensed
  —Light Extended
  —Heavy Extended
  —Outline
  —Extra Heavy
  —Shaded
  Tiffany Script

WOERNER, AUGUST E. (1844-1896)
Punch-cutter.
  Merrymount

Lanston Monotype Series Numbers, Numerical Index

SERIES NUMBERS provided the identification needed for every matrix produced for the Monotype machine, along with point size and sometimes other markings. In composition (keyboard) sizes, a letter was always added to the series number to indicate the class of face, as follows:

A Modern Roman
B Small Caps
C Modern Italic
D Italic Small Caps
E Old Style Roman
F Old Style Small Caps
G Old Style Italic
H Italic Small Caps
J Gothic or Bold Roman
K Gothic or Bold Italic
L Typewriter
M Foreign Faces
S Swash Characters

In display sizes, only the M and S suffixes were used, but in almost all cases italics had a figure 1 annexed to the number of the corresponding roman. In the data included with details of each face in the main section of this book, only the display numbers are listed except for faces made only in composition sizes. In the list below, the superior [1] following the number of a roman face indicates that the italic face has the same number with 1 annexed. Names of reassigned numbers are indicated by a virgule or slash (/). Names in parentheses are alternate names of the same design. Some typewriter, foreign, and nineteenth century faces are not included in the main text.

1	Modern Condensed	64[1]	Cheltenham OS	121	Chamfer Condensed
3	News	65	Craw Clarendon	123	Contour #6
4	Cosmopolitan	66	Lining Gothic #545	124	Gothic, Draftsman
5	Post Text (Easyread)	68[1]	MacFarland	125	Lanston (Melior)
6	Agate	69	Schoeffer	126	Initials, Massey
8	Modern	70	Typewriter Remington	127	Initials, Ben Franklin
9	Newspaper Modern	71	French Old Style #552	128	Title #28 (Side-Hole)
11	DeVinne [Italic: 1111]	72	Typewriter Reproducing	129	Lining Gothic Med #544
12	Cheltenham Bold Outline	73	Contour #5	132	Inclined Gothic Bold Italic
13	Modern	74	Typewriter Mailing List		(Modern Gothic Italic)
14	Modern Medium Cond	75	Bradley	134	Cushing Monotone
15	Farmer's Old Style	76	Antique, Modern Cond	137	Caslon Old Style, Inland
16	Ronaldson Old Style	77[1]	Alternate Gothic (#2)	138	Process
17	Typwr Remington Ribbon	78[1]	Caslon Old Roman	139	Howland
19	Modern Medium Extended	79[1]	Caslon Bold	140[1]	Modern Gothic Condensed
20[1]	Century Expanded	80	Modern		(Tourist Gothic)
21	Binny Old Style [It: 2111]	81	Clarendon	141	Cheltenham Bold Ex Cond
22	French Cadmus	82	Stationers Gothic Medium	142	John Hancock
23	Law Italic	83	Greek Vertical	143	Strathmore Old Style
25[1]	Cushing Oldstyle	84	Stationers Gothic Light	144	Antique, Bold
26	Antique, Modern	85	Stationers Gothic Bold	145	Antique, Bold Condensed
27	Antique, Old Style	86[1]	Cheltenham Bold	146	Condensed #54 (BB&S)
28	Title	88[1]	Cheltenham Bold Cond	149	Inland Gothic #6
31	Bruce Old Style #20	89[1]	Clearface	150[1]	French Round Face
32[1]	Tallone Max Factor	92	Manila	152	Wilson Series
33	Aldine	93	News Gothic Bold	153	Antique (Miller & Richard)
34	Modern #4	94	Latin Condensed	155	Greek Porson
35	Atlantic	95	Cloister Black	156	Ionic, Round (Inland)
36[1]	Scotch Roman	96	Howland Open	157	Century Old Style
37[1]	Caslon Old Style, English	97[1]	Powell	158	Masterman
38[1]	Goudy Old Style Light	98[1]	Bookman Old Style	159[1]	Hess Bold (Goudy Bold Face)
39	Winchell	99	German #32	160	Greek Title
40	Contour #1	100	German Heintzemann	161[1]	Hess Title (Hess Boldface)
41	DeVinne Outline Italic	101	German Schwabacher	162	Litho Roman Light or
42	DeVinne Outline	102	Washington Text		Litho Antique
43	Gothic Condensed Title	103	Title #104, Condensed	163	Adtype
44	Ben Franklin Outline	104	Runic Condensed #122	164[1]	Cheltenham Wide
45	Pabst Old Style	105	Title, Half	165	Lining Gothic #7 (Inland)
47	Gothic, Light	106	Lining Gothic (Light)	166	Copperplate Gothic Hvy Ext
48	Gothic Caps Condensed	107	Franklin Gothic	168	Copperplate Gothic Heavy
49	Gothic, Condensed	108	Compressed #30	169	Copperplate Gothic Hvy Cond
50	Gothic, Light Condensed	109	Gothic, Wide	170	Typewriter Smith Premier
51	Alternate Goth (#1)	110	Gothic Condensed #124	171	Typewriter New Royal
52	Lining Gothic, Philadelphia	111	DeVinne Condensed	172	Suburban French
56	Ionic / Gothic, Lining #525	112	Lining Gothic	173	Renner
57	Times New Roman Bold	113	Caslon Condensed	174	Renner Underscore
58	Jenson Old Style	114	Gothic, Tiffany	175[1]	Bodoni
59	Contour #4	115	Law Italic	176	Lining Gothic, Mid #2
60[1]	Plymouth	117	Grasset	177	Alternate Gothic Cond (#3)
61[1]	Cochin	118[1]	Century Bold	178	German Light
62	Ionic	119	Winchell Condensed	179	German Bold
63	Latin Antique	120	Modified #20	180	Lanston (Melior) Bold

489	Westinghouse Gothic Lt	
490	Stymie Extra Bold Cond	
495	German, Cloister Black	
496	Gothic (Helvetica)	
500	Granjon Bold	
503	Ward Extended	
505	Ward('s Memphis) or	
	Montgomery-Ward Lt	
507	Franklin Gothic Ex Cond	
508	Gothic (Helvetica Medium)	
515	Gothic, Condensed	
517	Speidotype Bold	
518	Century Bold Extended	
520	Century Mono-Photo (?)	
537[1]	Caslon, New	
543	Gothic Condensed, New	
548[1]	Garamond Bold	
551	Caps in Circle	
565	Caps in Circle	
566	Gothic, Octic #2	
571	Typwr Remington New	
	Elite Underscored	
572	Typewriter Reproducing	
	Bold Broadface	
575	Bodoni Bold Panelled	
582	Cooper Tooled	
590	Stymie Medium Cond	
600	Hess New Bookbold	
601	Plymouth Italic	
603[1]	20th Century Extra Bold	
604[1]	20th Century Bold	
605[1]	20th Century Medium	
606[1]	20th Century Light	
607[1]	20th Century Ex Bold Cond	
608[1]	20th Century Medium Cond	
609[1]	20th Century Ultra Bold	
610[1]	20th Century Ultra B Cond	
611	Cochin Italic	
612	20th Cent Bold Condensed	
613	20th Century Semi-Medium	
614	20th Century Ultra Bold Ext	
616[1]	Cochin Bold	
617	Speidotype Light	
618	Century Text (?)	
620	Century Schoolbook Bold	
630	Collier Heading	
637[1]	Caslon, American	
641	Cheltenham Old Style Ital	
648	Garamond, American	
650	Craw Clarendon Book	
665	Clarendon (Bold) Extended	
670	Typewriter Redesigned	
	Underwood	
671	Typwr New Royal Underscd	
675[1]	Bodoni, Ultra	
681	MacFarland Italic	
690	Stymie Light Condensed	
700	Poster	
701	Typwr Remington Goudy It	
707	Franklin Gothic Cond	
771	Alternate Gothic Italic	
775	Bodoni Bold Condensed	
781	Caslon Old Roman Italic	
790	Stymie Bold [Italic: 1891]	
791	Caslon Bold Italic	
861	Cheltenham Bold Italic	
875[1]	Bodoni Book	
881	Cheltenham Bold Cond It	
890	Squareface	
891	Clearface Italic	
901	Piece accents, roman	
902	Piece accents, bold	
903	Piece accents, gothic	
904	Piece accents, open	
905	Title, Half	
971	Powell Italic	
975	Bodoni Bold, Recut	
981	Bookman Old Style Italic	
1041	Runic Condensed Title	
1111	DeVinne Italic	
1181	Century Bold Italic	
1401	Tourist Gothic Italic	
1501	French Round Face Italic	
1591	Hess Bold Italic	
1611	Hess Title Italic	
1641	Cheltenham Wide Italic	
1751	Bodoni Italic	
1891	Stymie Bold Italic	
1901	Stymie Light Italic	
2111	Binny Old Style Italic	
2421	Hess Old Style Italic	
2431	Italian Old Style Italic	
2481	Garamont Italic	
2541	Gothic, Inclined	
2681	Kennerley Old Style Italic	
2691	Kennerley Bold Italic	
2751	Bodoni Bold Italic	
2901	Stymie Medium Italic	
2911	Goudy Open Italic	
2931	Goudy Modern Italic	
2941	Goudy Bold Italic	
2941S	Goudy Bold Italic Swash	
2951	Cloister Bold Italic	
3001	Californian Italic (?)	
3151	Deepdene Italic	
3171	Deepdene Bold Italic	
3291	Sans Serif Light Italic	
3301	Sans Serif Bold Italic	
3321	Sans Serif Ex Bold Ital	
3371	Caslon Old Style Italic	
3461	Copperplate Gothic [Bold] It	
3531	Baskerville Italic	
3591	Companion Italic	
3751	Bodoni Italic	
3801	Goudy Heavyface Italic	
3831	Goudy Handtooled Italic	
3831S	Goudy Handtooled It Swash	
3841	Goudy Sans Serif Light It	
3901	Stymie Extrabold Italic	
3941	Goudy Old Style Italic	
3951	Cloister Old Style Italic	
4011	Janson Italic	
4021	Bell Italic	
4031	Fournier Italic	
4041	Onyx Italic	
4051	Bembo Italic	
4102	Washington Text, German	
4181	Century Bold Cond Italic	
4201	Century Schoolbook Italic	
4371	Caslon Old Style Italic	
4491	Script Caps	
4611	Cochin, Nicolas, Italic	
4621	Bulmer Italic	
4821	Cooper Italic	
5371	Caslon, New, Italic	
5481	Garamond Bold Italic	
6031	20th Century Extrabold It	
6041	20th Century Bold Italic	
6051	20th Century Medium Ital	
6061	20th Century Light Italic	
6071	20th Century Exbold Cond It	
6081	20th Century Med Cond It	
6091	20th Century Ultrabold It	
6101	20th Century Ubold Cond It	
6161	Cochin Bold Italic	
6371	Caslon, American, Italic	
6751	Bodoni, Ultra, Italic	
8751	Bodoni Book Italic	

American Type Founders Series Numbers, Numerical Index

ABOUT 1930, ATF devised a series of numbers for more positive identification of its typefaces, using an alphabetical list of faces in production at that time. This basic list started with Abbott Oldstyle as No. 1, and ended with Winchell as No. 416. Faces acquired from Inland Type Foundry were grouped under "Inland," whether or not that was included in the name of the face.

Faces from Keystone Type Foundry were in a separate list, and were assigned numbers in the 800 and 900 series. Matrices from Barnhart Brothers & Spindler were given numbers from 1500 up to 1942.

Faces produced after the basic list was compiled were generally added consecutively in the 400 to 700 series, although a number of older faces, which presumably had not been in production when the original list was compiled, are also included. Unexplainedly, Piranesi Italic Plain Caps tag along at the end as number 1974.

Finally, ATF assigned numbers from 1000 to 1019 to the Univers series, which was cast by Deberny & Peignot in France to American standards, and numbers from 5001 to 5181 to a variety of faces similarly cast by Typefoundry Amsterdam, for sale by ATF. Since none of these faces were designed or cast in the United States, they are included in this book only under Foreign Types in the Appendix.

Many ATF fonts have the series number cast on the shoulder of the cap *H* and the lowercase *m,* where space permits. This serves as a simple method of positive identification.

These series numbers are not the same as the numbers which sometimes are part of the name of a typeface, such as Caslon Oldstyle No. 471, which is series 50. Such name-numbers starting with 4 indicate faces acquired from MacKellar, Smiths & Jordan, a predecessor of ATF, while those starting with 5 indicate faces which were recut or repositioned on the body to fit the system of standard alignment. Incidentally, in 1912 specimens ATF said: "To prevent confusion of identical numbers heretofore used by both this and other type foundries to identify body type faces, the numbers 570 have been added to the old numbers used by Inland Type Foundry. Thus, former No. 10 of Inland is now No. 580; 2 is 572; 9 is 579," etc.

The following list has been compiled from a number of ATF sources, and is as complete as possible, including a number of nineteenth-century, foreign, and typewriter faces which are not included in the text. Missing numbers may have been assigned to faces which were never completed, to private faces, or to fonts which were discontinued soon after their introduction and have not been found. If the necessary contractions are not clear, please consult the main text.

1	Abbott Oldstyle	43	Card Bodoni	84	Cheltenham Medium Italic
2	Adscript	44	Card Litho	85	Cheltenham Medium Condensed
3	Adtype	45	Card Light Litho		
5	Adver Condensed	46	Card Mercantile	86	Cheltenham Medium Expanded
6	Alternate Gothic #1	50	Caslon Oldstyle #471		
7	Alternate Gothic #2	51	Caslon Old Style Italic #471	87	Cheltenham Oldstyle
8	Alternate Gothic #3	52	Caslon Shaded	88	Cheltenham Oldstyle Condensed
9	American Extra Condensed	54	Cathedral Text		
11	American Typewriter	55	Century Bold	89	Cheltenham Wide
12	Antique Shaded	56	Century Bold Condensed	90	Church Text
13	Auriol	57	Century Bold Extended	91	Clearface
15	Baskerville Roman	58	Century Bold Italic	92	Clearface Bold
16	Baskerville Italic	59	Century Expanded	93	Clearface Bold Italic
18	Bewick Roman	60	Century Expanded Italic	94	Clearface Gothic
19	Blair	61	Century Oldstyle	95	Clearface Heavy
21	Blanchard Italic	62	Century Oldstyle Italic	96	Clearface Heavy Italic
22	Bodoni	63	Century Oldstyle Bold	97	Clearface Italic
23	Bodoni Italic	64	Century Oldstyle Bold Italic	98	Cloister Black
24	Bodoni Bold	65	Century Oldstyle Bold Cond	99	Cloister Bold
25	Bodoni Bold Italic	66	Chaucer Text	100	Cloister Bold Italic
26	Bodoni Bold Shaded	67	Cheltenham Bold	101	Cloister Bold Title
27	Bodoni Book	68	Cheltenham Bold Condensed	102	Cloister Oldstyle
28	Bodoni Book Italic	69	Cheltenham Bold Cond Italic	103	Cloister Italic
29	Bold Antique / Whitin Black	70	Cheltenham Bold Extra Cond	104	Cloister Title
30	Bold Antique Condensed / Whitin Black Condensed	71	Cheltenham Bold Ex Cond Title	105	Combination Gothic #501-510
				107	Commercial Script
31	Bold Litho	72	Cheltenham Bold Extended	108	Compact
32	Bond Script	73	Cheltenham Bold Italic	109	Compressed Litho (Title)
33	Bookman Italic	74	Cheltenham Bold Italic Shaded	110	Comstock
34	Bookman Oldstyle			111	Condensed Blair
35	Boston Breton	75	Cheltenham Bold Outline	112	Condensed Blanchard
36	Boston Breton Condensed	76	Cheltenham Bold Shaded	113	Condensed Caslon
37	Boston Breton Extra Condensed	77	Cheltenham Extrabold	114	Condensed Comstock
		78	Cheltenham Extrabold Shaded	115	Condensed Corbitt
38	Boxhead Gothics	79	Cheltenham Inline	116	Condensed Dorsey
39	Brandon	80	Cheltenham Inline Extended	117	Condensed Foster
40	Brandon Gothic	81	Cheltenham Inline Extra Cond	118	Condensed Litho
41	Bulfinch Oldstyle	82	Cheltenham Italic	119	Condensed MacFarland
42	Camelot Oldstyle	83	Cheltenham Medium	120	Condensed Matthews

121	Condensed Studley	200	Inland Condensed Gothic #10	297	Remington #2 Typewr
122	Condensed Title Gothic #3	201	Inland Cond Title Herald Gothic	298	Ronaldson #551
123	Condensed Title Gothic #11			304	Royal Script
124	Condensed Title Litho	202	Inland Copperplate	305	Shaeffer (sic) Old Style #2
125	Condensed Title Star Gothic	205	Elite Underwood Typewriter	306	Smith Premier Typewriter
126	Condensed Webb	206	Inland Extra Cond Gothic #1	307	Steelplate Script
127	Condensed Winchell	207	Gothic #6	308	Title #524
128	Copperplate Gothic Light	208	Gothic #578	309	Title #551
129	Copperplate Gothic Heavy Condensed	210	Inland Old Style It #20 or 590*	310	Tudor Black #2
		211	Inland Old Style #9 or 579	311	Victoria Italic
130	Copperplate Gothic Heavy	212	Inland Old Style Italic #9	312	Litho Antique/Rockwell Antique
131	Copperplate Gothic Light Condensed	213	Inland Roman #20 or 590	313	Litho Gothic
		216	Underwood Typewriter Inland	314	Litho Roman
132	Copperplate Gothic Bold	217	Invitation Shaded	315	Lithograph Shaded
133	Copperplate Gothic Italic	218	Jensen Bold Condensed	316	MacFarland
134	Copperplate Gothic Light Extended	219	Jensen Condensed	317	MacFarland Italic
		220	Light Dorsey	319	Matthews
135	Copperplate Gothic Heavy Extended	221	Light Dorsey Italic	321	Mercantile
		222	Lightline Gothic	323	Mercantile Gothic
136	Copperplate Gothic Shaded	223	Light Hobo	325	McClure
138	Cromwell	224	Light Litho Gothic	326	Miehle Extra Condensed
139	Curtis Post	225	Light Oldstyle	327	Miehle Extra Condensed Title
140	Cushing Antique	227	Antique #525	328	Mitchell
141	Della Robbia	228	Antique #524	329	Monotone Gothic
144	Dorsey	230	Boldface #520	330	Monotone [Gothic] Title
145	Drew	233	Caslon #540	331	New Caslon
146	Elite Oliver Typewriter	234	Caslon Italic #540	332	New Caslon Italic
147	Engravers Bold	239	Condensed Title #523	333	New Model Remington Typewr
148	Engravers Old English	240	Condensed Title #524	334	New Model Remington #3
149	Engravers Old English Bold	241	Condensed Title #525	335	New Model Smith Premier
150	Engravers Old English Open	242	Copperplate Roman	336	New Model Smith Premier #3
151	Engravers Shaded	243	Cushing #2	337	New Model Underwood Typewr
152	Studley Extended	244	Cushing Italic #2	338	News Gothic
153	Caslon Extra Condensed	248	DeVinne #2	339	News Gothic Condensed
154	Dorsey Extra Condensed	249	DeVinne Condensed #2	340	News Gothic Extra Condensed
155	Studley Extra Condensed	250	DeVinne Extended #2	341	News Gothic Extra Cond Title
156	Extra Cond Title Gothic #12	251	DeVinne Extra Condensed #2	342	Offset Light Litho Gothic
157	Flemish Black	252	DeVinne Italic #2	343	Oliver Printype
161	Foster	253	DeVinne Italic Outline #2	344	Oliver Typewriter
162	Franklin Gothic	254	DeVinne Open	345	Oldstyle #583
163	Franklin Gothic Condensed	255	Doric #520	346	Pabst Italic
164	Franklin Gothic Cond Shaded	258	French Oldstyle #552	347	Pabst Oldstyle
165	Franklin Gothic Extra Cond	259	French Old Style Italic #552	348	Packard
166	Franklin Gothic Italic	260	Gothic #519	349	Peignot
167	German #571	261	Gothic #510 to 526	350	Pen Print
168	German Fullface #150	262	Gothic #527-528-529	351	Pen Print Bold
169	German Text #10	263	Gothic #544	352	Pontiac
170	German Title Condensed #150	264	Gothic #545	353	Porson Greek
172	Globe Gothic	265	Gothic Condensed #521	354	Post Condensed
173	Globe Gothic Bold	266	Gothic Condensed #523	355	Post Monotone
174	Globe Gothic Bold Italic	267	Gothic Condensed #524	356	Post Monotone #2
175	Globe Gothic Condensed	268	Gothic Condensed #529	357	Post Oldstyle Italic
176	Globe Gothic Extended	269	Gothic Italic #512	358	Post Oldstyle Roman #1
177	Globe Gothic Extra Condensed	272	Ionic #522	359	Post Oldstyle Roman #2
178	Goudy Oldstyle	275	Jensen Italic #2	360	Pynson Oldstyle Italic
179	Goudy Italic	276	Jensen Oldstyle #2	361	Quick-Set Roman
180	Goudy Title	278	Latin Antique #520	362	Quick-Set Italic
183	Greek #2	279	Latin Condensed #550	363	Quick-Set Bold
185	Hearst	280	Law Italic #520	364	Railroad Gothic
186	Hearst Italic	281	Law Italic #522	365	Recut Caslon
187	Heavy Caslon	282	Lightface #558	366	Recut Caslon Italic
188	Heavy Face Greek	283	Livermore #2	367	Reproducing Typewriter
189	Hebrew	285	Mid-Gothic #2	368	Ribbonface Typewriter
190	Hebrew Typewriter	288	Oldstyle #523	369	Rimmed Litho
192	Herald Extra Condensed	289	Oldstyle Italic #523	370	Roundhand
193	Hobo	290	Oldstyle Antique #560	371	Roycroft
195	Ihlenburg Extended	291	Oldstyle Condensed #520	372	Roycroft Open
196	Inland Caslon Oldstyle #584	292	Oldstyle Condensed #522	373	Roycroft Tinted
197	Inland Caslon Oldstyle Italic #584	295	Quentell #2	374	Rugged Bold
				375	Rugged Roman
198	Inland Condensed Gothic #1			376	Saint John
199	Condensed Gothic #574			377	Schwabacher

*See note in introduction of this section about renumbering of Inland faces.

378	Schwabacher #2	458	American Caslon	531	Raleigh Cursive
379	Scotch Roman	459	Garamond	532	Bank Gothic Light
380	Scotch Roman Italic	460	Garamond Italic	533	Bank Gothic Medium
381	Self-Spacing Old Style Bold	461	Sterling	534	Bank Gothic Bold
382	Shaw Text	462	Colwell Handletter	535	Dynamic Medium
383	Silk Remington Typewriter	463	Colwell Handletter Italic	536	Paramount
384	Standard Typewriter	464	Goudy Bold Italic	537	Bernhard Gothic Medium Italic
385	Stenograf	465	Century Schoolbook Italic	538	Piranesi
386	Strathmore Oldstyle	466	Pen Print Open	539	Rosetti
387	Studley	467	Goudy Catalogue	540	Graybar Book
389	Times Gothic	468	Century Catalogue Italic	541	Engravers Text
390	Times Gothic Italic	469	Freehand	542	Monotone Cursive
391	Title Gothic #71-74	470	Goudy Catalogue Italic	543	Adonis
392	Title Gothic #9	471	American Caslon Italic	544	Bodoni Open
393	Title Light Litho	472	National Oldstyle	545	Bernhard Gothic Light Italic
394	Title Light Litho Gothic	473	Sterling Cursive	546	Bernhard Gothic Extra Heavy
395	Title Litho Roman	474	Garamond Bold	547	Piranesi Italic
396	Title Shaded Litho	475	Goudy Handtooled	548	Thermo 100
398	Typo Gothic	476	Goudy Handtooled Italic	549	Thermo 200
399	Typo Script	477	Goudy Cursive	550	Thermo 300
400	Typo Script Extended	478	Cloister Cursive	551	Stymie Bold
401	Typo Shaded	479	Century Schoolbook Bold	552	Stymie Medium
402	Typo Slope	480	Lightline Title Gothic	553	Stymie Light
403	Typo Text	481	Typo Roman Shaded	554	Stymie Light Italic
404	Typo Upright	482	Civilité	555	Stymie Medium Italic
405	Typo Upright Bold	483	Nicolas Cochin	556	Stymie Inline Title
406	Typotabular Gothic	484	Schoolbook Oldstyle	557	Garamond Open
407	University Script	485	Fournier	558	Caslon Oldstyle #472
408	Venetian	486	Cloister Lightface	559	Bernhard Booklet
409	Venetian Italic	487	Nicolas Cochin Italic	560	Newport
410	Victoria Underwood Typewriter	488	Card Roman	561	Stymie Bold Italic
412	Webb	489	Garamond Bold Italic	562	Ultra Bodoni Condensed
413	Wedding Gothic	490	Cloister Lightface Italic	563	Bernhard Booklet Italic
414	Wedding Text	491	Bulletin Typewriter	564	Raleigh Gothic Condensed
415	Wedding Text Shaded	492	Cochin	565	Colonial
416	Winchell	493	Cloister Cursive Handtooled	566	Benton / Whitehall
418	Armenian	494	Goudy Extrabold	567	American Text
419	Oldstyle #550	495	Cochin Italic	568	Hollywood
420	Roman #510	496	Goudy Extrabold Italic	569	Piranesi Bold
421	Roman Italic #510	497	Bulmer Roman	570	Piranesi Bold Italic
426	Roman Italic #524	498	Bulmer Italic	571	Lexington
427	Roman #524	500	Goudytype	572	Piranesi Bold Italic Plain
428	Roman #527	501	Engravers Bodoni	573	Ultra Bodoni Extra Condensed
429	Roman Italic #527	502	Gallia	574	Bank Gothic Condensed Light
430	Ronaldson Italic #551	503	French Script	575	Bank Gothic Condensed Medium
431	Norwood Roman	504	Greeting Monotone	576	Bank Gothic Condensed Bold
432	Oldstyle #11 or 581	505	Gravure	577	Park Avenue
433	Oldstyle Italic #11 or 581	506	Broadway	578	Agency Gothic
434	Oldstyle #12 or 592	507	Modernistic	579	Keynote
435	Roman #596 or 26	508	Canterbury	580	Agency Gothic Open
436	Roman Italic #596 or 26	509	Typo Roman	581	Eagle Bold
437	Roman #599 or 29	510	Nubian	582	Bernhard Tango
438	Roman Italic #599 or 29	511	Liberty	583	Pericles
439	Russian	512	Novel Gothic	585	Romany
440	Time Saving Mailing List	513	Parisian	586	American Backslant
441	Wayside Roman	514	Chic	587	Tower
442	Wayside Roman Italic	515	Rivoli	588	Gold Rush
443	Card Bodoni Bold	516	Ultra Bodoni Italic	589	Shadow
444	Century Catalogue	517	Modernique	590	Jumbo Typewriter
445	Della Robbia Light	518	Ultra Bodoni	591	Stymie Open
446	Goudy Bold	519	Louvaine Light	592	Poster Gothic
447	Motto	520	Louvaine Light Italic	593	Bernhard Tango Swash
448	Light Hobo	521	Louvaine Medium	594	Othello
449	Souvenir	522	Louvaine Medium Italic	595	Offset Title Light Litho Gothic
450	Venetian Bold	523	Louvaine Bold	596	Huxley Vertical
451	Cloister Bold Condensed	524	Louvaine Bold Italic	597	Empire
452	Anouncement Italic	525	Bernhard Gothic Medium	598	Stymie Black
453	Packard Bold	526	Rivoli Italic	599	Stymie Black Italic
454	Century Schoolbook	527	Bernhard Fashion	601	Oldstyle #10
455	Silk Rem Undrscrd Typewriter	528	Bernhard Gothic Light	602	Oldstyle Italic #10
456	Announcement Roman	529	Broadway Condensed	603	Oldstyle Italic #12
457	Invitation	530	Bernhard Gothic Heavy	604	Roman #593

605	Roman Italic #593	715	News Gothic Bold	1507	Adstyle Extra Condensed
609	Roman #598	716	Craw Modern Bold	1508	Adstyle Headletter
610	Roman Italic #598	717	Craw Clarendon Condensed	1509	Adstyle Italic
611	Roman #600	718	Ad Lib	1510	Adstyle Shaded
612	Roman Italic #600	719	Century Nova	1511	Adstyle Wide
615	Remington Standard Typewriter	720	Craw Modern Italic	1512	Advertisers Gothic
620	Self-Spacing Oldstyle	721	Century Nova Italic	1513	Advertisers Gothic Condensed
621	Self-Spacing Old Style Italic	722	Whedons Gothic Outline	1514	Advertisers Gothic Cond Outline
622	Smith Premier Typewriter	723	Caslon 641	1515	Advertisers Gothic Outline
623	Silk Remington Russian	724	News Gothic Condensed Bold	1516	Advertisers Upright Script
650	Headline Gothic	725	Americana	1517	Antique
651	Phenix	726	Franklin Gothic Cond Italic	1518	Antique Bold
652	Kaufmann Script	727	Americana Bold	1519	Antique Condensed
653	Stymie Light Title	728	Americana Italic	1527	Artcraft
654	Stymie Medium Title	729	Americana Extra Bold	1528	Artcraft Bold
655	Bernhard Gothic Light Title			1529	Artcraft Italic
656	Bernhard Gothic Medium Title	**(Keystone Type Foundry)**		1530	Authors Italic
657	Kaufmann Bold	807	Ben Franklin	1531	Authors Oldstyle
658	Stymie Bold Condensed	808	Ben Franklin Condensed	1532	Authors Oldstyle Bold
661	Onyx	809	Ben Franklin Open	1533	Authors Oldstyle Italic
662	Stencil	811	Bulletin	1534	Authors Roman
663	Caslon Oldstyle Ital #471 Swash	814	Caslon Adbold	1535	Authors Roman Bold
664	Caslon Italic #540 Swash	815	Caslon Adbold Extended	1536	Authors Roman Bold Condensed
666	Lydian	816	Caslon Adbold Extra Condensed	1537	Authors Roman Condensed
667	Lydian Italic	817	Caslon Bold	1538	Authors Roman Wide
668	Bernhard Modern Roman	818	Caslon Bold Condensed	1540	Bank Script
669	Bernhard Modern Italic	819	Caslon Bold Extended	1544	Barnhart Oldstyle
670	Bernhard Modern Bold	820	Caslon Bold Italic	1545	Barnhart Oldstyle #2
671	Bernhard Modern Bold Italic	821	Caslon Lightface	1546	Barnhart Oldstyle Italic
672	Bernhard Gothic Medium Cond	822	Caslon Lightface Condensed	1548	Bizarre Bold
673	Lydian Bold	823	Caslon Lightface Italic	1549	Bookman Bold
674	Lydian Bold Italic	826	Caslon Title Extended	1550	Bookman Bold Condensed
675	Balloon Light	828	Charcoal	1551	Bookman Lightface
676	Balloon Bold	829	Charter Oak	1552	Bookman Old Style (BB&S)
677	Balloon Extra Bold	830	Compressed Gothic	1553	Boul Mich
678	Grayda	832	Condensed Lining Gothic	1558	Cardstyle
679	Grayda Swash	834	Crayonette	1559	Caslon Antique
680	Spartan Medium	854	Harris Roman	1560	Caslon Antique Italic
681	Spartan Medium Italic	855	Harris Italic	1561	Caslon Black
682	Lydian Cursive	857	Herculean Gothic	1562	Caslon Black Condensed
683	Spartan Black	861	John Hancock	1563	Caslon Black Italic
684	Spartan Black Italic	862	John Hancock Condensed	1564	Caslon Catalog
685	Spartan Heavy	863	John Hancock Extended	1565	Caslon Clearface
686	Spartan Heavy Italic	864	John Hancock Outline	1566	Caslon Clearface Italic
687	Spartan Black Condensed	866	Keystone Gothic	1567	Caslon Medium
688	Spartan Black Condensed Italic	872	Lining Antique	1568	Caslon Medium Italic
689	Brush	879	Gothic #114	1569	Caslon Oldstyle
690	Contact Bold Condensed	880	Gothic Condensed #3	1570	Caslon Oldstyle Italic
691	Contact Bold Condensed Italic	882	Gothic #102	1571	Caslon Openface
692	Lydian Bold Condensed	898	Outline	1572	Caslon Open Title
693	Lydian Bold Condensed Italic	899	Outline Condensed	1574	Catalog Oldstyle
694	Spartan Extra Black	913	Skeleton Lining Gothic	1575	Century Italic
695	Verona	914	Skeleton Lining Gothic #19	1576	Century Roman
696	Dom Casual	918	Title Gothic	1577	Chester Text
697	DeRoos Roman	924	Elite Typewriter	1578	Clarendon
698	DeRoos Italic	925	New Model Remington Typewr	1579	Clarendon Bold
699	Dom Diagonal	927	Remington	1580	Clarendon Extra Condensed #5
700	Thompson Quillscript	928	Smith Premier	1581	Clarendon Medium
701	Franklin Gothic Wide	929	Remington Typewriter	1582	Clearcut Oldstyle
702	Heritage	935	Washington Text	1583	Clearcut Old Style Cond #52
703	Dom Bold	936	Washington Text Shaded	1584	Clearcut Oldstyle Italic
704	Brody	943	Old Bowery	1585	Clearcut Shaded Caps
705	Repro Script	944	P. T. Barnum	1589	Cooper
706	Spartan Medium Condensed			1590	Cooper Black
707	Spartan Book	**(BB&S Type Foundry)**		1591	Cooper Black Condensed
708	Oxford	1500	Adcraft Black	1592	Cooper Black Italic
709	Oxford Italic	1501	Adcraft Lightface	1593	Cooper Fullface
710	Craw Clarendon	1502	Adcraft Medium	1594	Cooper Hilite
711	Murray Hill	1503	Adstyle	1595	Cooper Italic
712	Craw Clarendon Book	1504	Adstyle Black	1596	Cooper Tooled Italic
713	Murray Hill Bold	1505	Adstyle Black Outline	1597	Copperplate Text
714	Craw Modern	1506	Adstyle Condensed	1598	Cosmos

370

1599	Cubist Bold	1686	Handcraft	1815	Oldstyle Title #59
1600	Degree Gothic #1	1687	Handcraft Title	1816	Pantagraph Script
1601	Demeter	1688	Handcraft Wide Title	1817	Paragon Plate
1602	Dennison Script	1689	Headletter Condensed	1818	Paragon Plate Italic
1604	DeVinne	1693	Invitation Text	1819	Parsons
1605	DeVinne Bold	1694	Japanet	1820	Parsons Bold
1606	DeVinne Compressed	1695	Kenilworth Italic	1821	Parsons Italic
1607	DeVinne Extra Compressed	1697	Latin Antique	1822	Pastel
1608	DeVinne Recut	1698	Latin Condensed	1823	Pastel Bold
1609	DeVinne Recut Outline	1699	Latin Expanded	1824	Pastel Condensed
1611	Dresden	1700	Latin Lightface	1825	Pastel Lightface
1615	Election Gothic #117	1701	Latin Modern	1826	Pastel Open
1618	Embossing Text	1703	Latin Oldstyle Bold	1827	Pekin
1619	Engravers Bold (BB&S)	1712	Bank Script #2	1828	Pencraft Italic
1620	Engravers Bold Condensed	1713	Bank Script #3	1829	Pencraft Oldstyle
1621	Engravers English	1724	Facade Condensed	1830	Pencraft Oldstyle Bold
1622	Engravers Gothic	1725	Facade Condensed #1	1831	Pencraft Oldstyle Bold Cond
1623	Engravers Litho Bold	1729	French Clarendon	1832	Pencraft Shaded
1624	Engravers Litho Bold Cond	1730	Gothic #47	1833	Pencraft Text
1627	Engravers Roman	1731	Gothic #53	1834	Pencraft Title
1628	Engravers Roman Condensed	1732	Gothic #54	1835	Pen Text #5
1629	Engravers Roman Shaded	1733	Gothic #55	1836	Plate Gothic
1630	Engravers Title	1734	Gothic #57	1837	Plate Gothic Bold
1631	Engravers Upright Script	1735	Gothic #67	1838	Plate Gothic Condensed
1633	French Elzevir	1736	Gothic #71	1839	Plate Gothic Light
1637	French Elzevir Italic #5	1737	Gothic #83 and 84	1840	Plate Gothic Light Condensed
1639	French Oldstyle #3	1738	Gothic #111	1841	Plate Script
1640	French Oldstyle #56	1743	Ionic	1847	Priory Black Text
1641	French Plate Script	1745	Light Modern	1848	Program Italic
1643	Gothic Chamfer	1751	Norman Condensed	1849	Publicity Gothic
1644	Gothic Clearcut Title	1752	Plate Script #2	1856	Scotch Roman (BB&S)
1645	Gothic Compressed	1753	Plate Script #3	1859	Sketch Circular
1646	Gothic Compressed #5	1764	Utility Gothic	1860	Sketch Title
1647	Gothic Compressed #7	1766	Vulcan	1861	Spire #5
1648	Gothic Compressed Title #7	1768	Yost Typewriter	1862	Stationers Plate
1649	Gothic Compressed Title #8	1771	Mazarin #5	1863	Stationers Semi-Script
1650	Gothic Condensed #2	1773	Menu Roman	1865	Steelplate Gothic Light Ext
1651	Gothic Condensed #117	1775	Menu Title	1866	Steelplate Gothic Heavy Ext
1652	Gothic Condensed Title #117	1777	Missal Text	1867	Steelplate Gothic Light
1653	Gothic Extra Compressed #8	1778	Mission	1868	Steelplate Gothic Heavy
1654	Gothic Extra Compressed #6	1779	Mode	1869	Steelplate Gothic Light Cond
1655	Gothic Ex Compressed Title #6	1780	Modern Roman Bold Condensed	1870	Steelplate Gothic Heavy Cond
1656	Gothic Inclined	1781	Modern Roman Bold Extra Cond	1871	Steelplate Gothic Italic
1657	Gothic Inclined Light	1782	Modern Roman Condensed	1872	Steelplate Gothic Shaded
1658	Gothic Italic	1783	Modern Roman Extra Cond	1873	Steelplate Gothic Bold
1659	Gothic Italic Light	1784	Modern Roman Italic	1874	Steelplate Gothic Extra Light
1660	Gothic Lightface #44	1785	Modern Roman Lightface	1875	Steelplate Text
1661	Gothic Lightface Title	1786	Modern Roman Medium	1876	Stillson
1662	Gothic Modern	1787	Modern Roman Wide	1879	Title #9
1663	Gothic Modern Condensed	1788	Modern Text	1880	Title #10
1664	Gothic Modern Condensed Title	1790	Morris Jensonian	1881	Title #11
1665	Gothic Modern Italic	1791	Morris Romanized Black	1884	Trenholm Bold
1666	Gothic Modern Title	1792	Munder Bold	1885	Trenholm Cursive
1667	Gothic #3	1793	Munder Bold Italic	1886	Trenholm Oldstyle
1668	Gothic #60	1794	Munder Italic	1887	Trenholm Shaded Caps
1669	Gothic #82	1795	Munder Venezian	1892	Two Line #56
1670	Gothic #90	1797	Offset Gothic Clearcut Title	1894	Typewriter Barnhart Utility
1671	Gothic Novelty	1798	Offset Engravers Roman	1895	Typewriter Elite Improved
1672	Gothic Novelty Condensed	1799	Offset Engravers Title	1896	Typewriter Elite Silk
1673	Gothic Novelty Title	1800	Offset Gothic Title #60	1897	Typewriter Oliver Printype
1674	Gothic #1	1801	Offset Pastel Condensed	1898	Typewriter Oliver Standard Silk
1675	Gothic #1 Condensed	1802	Offset Lining Gothic #47	1899	Typewriter Remington #2
1676	Gothic Outline Title #61	1803	Old Dutch	1900	Typewriter Remington Silk
1677	Gothic Title #3	1804	Old Roman	1901	Typewriter Remington Standard
1678	Gothic Title #60	1805	Old Roman Black	1902	Typewriter Reproduction
1679	Gothic Title #82	1806	Old Roman Black Italic	1903	Typewriter Smith-Premier Silk
1680	Gothic Title #90	1807	Old Roman Bold	1904	Typewriter Underwood New
1681	Gothic Utility Title	1808	Old Roman Bold Condensed		Model Silk
1682	Gothic Wide Title	1809	Old Roman Condensed	1905	Waldorf Text
1683	Greeting Card	1810	Old Roman Italic	1908	Wedding Plate Script
1684	Greeting Card Light	1811	Old Roman Semitone	1914	Modern Roman #64 Italic
1685	Grotesque Gothic #43	1813	Oldstyle Italic #59	1915	Modern Roman #80 Italic

1916	Modern Roman #64	1925	Oldstyle Italic #58	1939	Title #10 Italic
1918	Modern Roman #80	1929	Roman #60	1940	Hebrew Modern
1919	Oldstyle #58	1930	Roman #63	1941	Hebrew Condensed
1922	Oldstyle #100	1931	Roman #66	1942	Cooper Modern
1923	Oldstyle #300	1932	Roman #74		
1924	Oldstyle Italic #1	1937	Uniform Mailing Type	1974	Piranesi Italic Plain Caps (ATF)

OTHER SERIES NUMBERS are not used for identification as often as the foregoing, but Ludlow numbers are shown on the following pages to complete our list.

Linotype and Intertype assign numbers to fonts rather than to typefaces, and do not use the same numbers as each other even for duplicate faces. A face made in ten sizes of roman with italic and ten sizes of roman with bold will have twenty numbers for the series from each source, and it is not practical to list them all in this book.

Ludlow Series Numbers, Numerical Index

43-BI	Radiant Bold Italic	45-B	Lining Litho Bold	54-LI	Times New Roman Italic
43-BC	Radiant Bold Condensed	46-MEC	Greenwich	54-B	Times New Roman Bold
43-BCI	Radiant Bold Cond Italic	47-H	Samson	54-BI	Times New Roman Bold Ital
43-BEC	Radiant Bold Extra Cond	48-MIC	Flair	54-H	Times New Roman Heavy
43-H	Radiant Heavy	49-BIC	Admiral Script	55-HN	Zephyr
44-L	Commerce Gothic Light	50	Society Text	57-MIC	Parkway Script
44-M	Commerce Gothic Medium	51-MIC	Formal Script	58-M	Clarendon Medium
44-LC	Commerce Gothic Lt Cond	52-LIC	Florentine Cursive	58-B	Clarendon Bold
44-MC	Commerce Gothic Med Cond	53-BIC	Wave	58-H	Clarendon Heavy
45-L	Lining Litho Light	54-L	Times New Roman		

Common Typeface Synonyms

FOR THE PURPOSES of this book, typeface names from any *major* source are considered authentic, and are listed or cross-indexed in the main text. Major sources are defined as those which originate a substantial number of the typeface designs they offer. But secondary sources, including smaller founders (early twentieth century), certain dealers, and those that cast type fonts from Monotype or other such mats—as well as individual printers—do not always use "authentic" names; use of such names may vary from one such source to another. The following list is intended to help readers find such typefaces in the main text. Obviously this list cannot be entirely comprehensive, and there may be other uses of some of these same names.

Some faces listed here are copies by smaller founders, and may have some characters modified. Some of the secondary sources cast type from English Monotype matrices, and some make their own mats to cast duplicates of other English or European foundry faces. Some such faces are listed here and some under Popular Imports in the Appendix.

The Kelsey Company, which extensively supplied hobby printers, offered many faces (indicated by an asterisk) which were cast by American Type Founders but renamed and sometimes repackaged in smaller fonts by Kelsey; other Kelsey fonts were cast from Monotype or Intertype mats, and also often renamed.

Recently, types from Asian foundries have appeared on the American market. Many of these are copies of American or European types, sometimes under other names. Some of those are listed here with the notation (Univ) for Universal Type Foundry, Hong Kong.

Synonym = Authentic Name
Acme Cursive (Acme) = Bernhard Cursive
Acme Deluxe Gothic (Acme) = Medium Condensed Gothic (Ludlow)
Acme Light Script (Acme) = Light Script (EMono)
Ad-News Condensed (Kelsey*) = Cheltenham Bold Extra Condensed, ATF
Alpine = Helvetica
Alter Gothic = Alternate Gothic
Announcement Script (Kelsey*) = Typo Upright, ATF
Artistic Text (Damon) = Wedding Text
Bankers Medium (various) = Bank Gothic Medium
Beacon Hill (Kelsey) = Park Avenue, Inter
Big Top (Kelsey*) = P. T. Barnum, ATF
Bold Roman (Damon) = Engravers Bold
Bond Gothic (Kelsey*) = Bank Gothic Medium, ATF
Bridal Script (Neon) = Liberty, ATF, or Lotus, Inter
Byline Open = Agency Gothic Open
Calligraphia = Artscript
Carlton (Western) = Bookman Lightface (see main text)
Caslon (Kelsey*) = Caslon No. 540, ATF
Cathedral Bold = Glamour Bold
Centenary & Italic (Kelsey) = Century Expanded & Italic, Mono
Century Roman & Italic (Kelsey* & others) = Century Expanded & Italic, ATF
Century Roman & Italic (Univ) = Century Catalogue & Italic, ATF
Chelten series (Kelsey & others) = Cheltenham series
Clarendon (Kelsey*) = Craw Clarendon, ATF
Colonial (Kelsey*) = Goudy Oldstyle (since c1927) or Munder Venezian (earlier)
Comique = Cartoon Bold

Condensed Gothic [No. 056] (Kelsey*) = Gothic Condensed No. 529, ATF
Continental (Kelsey*) = Cheltenham Bold, ATF
Continental Script (Detroit) = Admiral Script
Craftsman series (Neon) = Goudy series
Craftsman series (various) = Cheltenham series
Duchess (LATF) = Bernhard Modern Roman
Egyptian Light & Bold (Kelsey) = Stymie Light & Bold, Mono
Embassy [Vertical] (Kelsey*) = Huxley Vertical, ATF
English Text (Kelsey*) = Wedding Text, ATF
Engravers Text (Damon) = Typo Text, ATF
Eric Gill Shadow (various) = Gill Sans Shadow, Eng Mono
Eros series (Detroit) = Venus series
Fairfield (Kelsey*) = Murray Hill Bold, ATF
Fashion (Kelsey*) = Bernhard Fashion, ATF
Franklin Card Gothic (Damon) = Typo Gothic, ATF
Franklin Gothic Condensed & Italic (various) = Tourist Gothic & Italic, Mono
Franklin Gothic Italic (Neon) = Bold Inclined Gothic, Mono
Frascati (Kelsey) = Hadriano Stone Cut, Mono
Girard Old Style (Damon) = Post Oldstyle Roman No. 2, ATF
Goudy Heavyface (Balto 6-12pt) = Cooper Black, Mono
Goudy Old Colony & Bold (Kelsey*) = Goudy Oldstyle & Bold (earlier, Munder Venezian), ATF
Grecian Bold = Greco
Groto series (Detroit) = Grotesque series, Eng Mono
Gutenberg series (Damon) = Goudy series, ATF
Hand Letter (Kelsey*) = Dom Casual, ATF
Heavy Old English (Kelsey*) = Engravers Old English, ATF
Highspot (Kelsey) = Flash, Mono
Invitation Text (Kelsey*) = Engravers Text, ATF
Kelsey Spacesaver Script (Kelsey*) = Typo Script, ATF
Kelsey Script (Kelsey*) = Typo Script Extended, ATF
Keystone = Keynote, ATF
Light Old English (Kelsey) = Wedding Text, Mono
Lincoln (Damon) = John Hancock, ATF
Lithographers Roman (Damon) = Litho Roman
Margery (Kelsey) = Greeting Monotone, Inter
Mayfair Initials (Kelsey*) = Bernhard Tango Swash Caps, ATF
Minuet (Kelsey*) = Liberty, ATF
Modern Bodoni (Kelsey) = Ultra Bodoni, Mono
Modern Gothic (Kelsey) = Franklin Gothic, Mono
Modern Script (Kelsey*) = Kaufmann Bold, ATF
Modern Script (Damon) = Typo Upright, ATF
Moderne (Kelsey) = Broadway, Mono
Modernistic (Kelsey*) = Broadway, ATF
Neon Cursive (Neon) = Bernhard Cursive
New Yorker (Kelsey) = Parisian, Inter
Newton (various) = Neuland
Norway = Neuland
N.R.A. Black (Sterling) = Basuto, SB
Novelty Gothic series (Univ) = Bernhard Gothic series, ATF
Novelty Gothic Cameo & Shadow (Univ) = Granby Cameo & Shadow, SB
Old Colony & Bold (Kelsey*) = Goudy Oldstyle & Bold (earlier, Munder Venezian), ATF
Outline Gothic (various) = Contour (in some cases)
Paramount series (Damon) = Garamond series, ATF
Park Lane Initials (Kelsey) = Artscript, Mono
Penn Gothic No. 10 (Damon) = Mercantile Gothic

Penn Old English (Damon) = Engravers Old English
Penn Old Style (Damon) = Ronaldson Old Style
Pittsburgh Black (Neon) = Cooper Black
Plaza [Initials] (Kelsey) = Slimline, Mono
Poster Black (Kelsey*) = Cooper Black, ATF
Printers' Black (Damon) = Cooper Black
Punch (Acme) = Signal Black (see Imports in Appendix)
Punch (Kelsey*) = Brush, ATF
Regent (Kelsey) = Onyx, Mono
Sans Condensed (Kelsey) = Twentieth Century Medium
    Condensed, Mono
Sans Medium (Kelsey) = Sans Serif Medium, Mono
Saybrook Script (Kelsey) = Swing (Kaufmann) Bold, Mono

Schoolbook (Kelsey*) = Century Schoolbook, ATF
Shaded Old English (Kelsey*) = Typo Text, ATF
Shaded Text = Typo Text
Skyline (various) = Corvinus Skyline, Bauer
Society Roman (Kelsey*) = Announcement Roman, ATF
Steelplate [Shaded] (Kelsey*) = Engravers Shaded, ATF
Tudor Place (Kelsey*) = Raleigh Cursive, ATF
Universal Old Style & Italic (Damon) = Century Oldstyle
    & Italic, ATF
Universal Schoolbook (various) = Century Schoolbook,
    ATF
Vogue Gothic (Kelsey*) = Franklin Gothic, ATF
Westminster Text (Kelsey) = Goudy Text, Mono

Colophon

Although this book has been set by contemporary electronic methods, it attempts to duplicate as closely as possible the typefaces, style and traditions of the era of American metal typesetting of the twentieth century. The principal typefaces are *Century Schoolbook and Italic, Century Schoolbook Bold,* and *News Gothic,* with *Caledonia Bold* on the title page and *Craw Clarendon* on the outside. Point and pica measurements have been used where applicable.

It was typed by the author into an IBM Personal Computer, using WordPerfect 5.1, coded for typesetting by the publisher, and output on a Linotron 202 by Chronicle Type & Design, Washington, D.C., who also did all the paste-up work. PMTs of the type specimens were made by Modern Reproductions, Inc., Pittsburgh, Pennsylvania. The book was printed and bound by Braun-Brumfield, Inc., Ann Arbor, Michigan.

Layout was done by the author, and the type on the cover is assembled from his collection, photographed by Hardman Eastman Studios, Inc., Pittsburgh.